AI and Data Analytics Applications in Organizational Management

Tereza Raquel Merlo
University of North Texas, USA & Merlo Management Consulting, USA

IGI Global
PUBLISHER of TIMELY KNOWLEDGE

A volume in the Advances in Business Information
Systems and Analytics (ABISA) Book Series

Published in the United States of America by
IGI Global
Business Science Reference (an imprint of IGI Global)
701 E. Chocolate Avenue
Hershey PA, USA 17033
Tel: 717-533-8845
Fax: 717-533-8661
E-mail: cust@igi-global.com
Web site: http://www.igi-global.com

Library of Congress Cataloging-in-Publication Data

Names: Merlo, Tereza Raquel, 1972- editor.
Title: AI and data analytics applications in organizational management / edited by Tereza Merlo.
Description: Hershey, PA : Business Science Reference, 2024. | Includes bibliographical references and index. | Summary: "The focus of this book on AI and data analytics is justified due to the rapidly evolving nature of the field, its increasing importance in various industries, its interdisciplinary nature, the need for practical guidance and real-world examples, the ethical and social implications, and the role it plays in knowledge sharing and education"-- Provided by publisher.
Identifiers: LCCN 2023049135 (print) | LCCN 2023049136 (ebook) | ISBN 9798369310588 (hardcover) | ISBN 9798369310595 (ebook)
Subjects: LCSH: Management--Statistical methods. | Management--Data processing. | Artificial intelligence.
Classification: LCC HD30.215 .A319 2024 (print) | LCC HD30.215 (ebook) | DDC 658.4/033--dc23/eng/20231027
LC record available at https://lccn.loc.gov/2023049135
LC ebook record available at https://lccn.loc.gov/2023049136

This book is published in the IGI Global book series Advances in Business Information Systems and Analytics (ABISA) (ISSN: 2327-3275; eISSN: 2327-3283)

British Cataloguing in Publication Data
A Cataloguing in Publication record for this book is available from the British Library.

Advances in Business Information Systems and Analytics (ABISA) Book Series

Madjid Tavana
La Salle University, USA

ISSN:2327-3275
EISSN:2327-3283

Mission

The successful development and management of information systems and business analytics is crucial to the success of an organization. New technological developments and methods for data analysis have allowed organizations to not only improve their processes and allow for greater productivity, but have also provided businesses with a venue through which to cut costs, plan for the future, and maintain competitive advantage in the information age.

The **Advances in Business Information Systems and Analytics (ABISA) Book Series** aims to present diverse and timely research in the development, deployment, and management of business information systems and business analytics for continued organizational development and improved business value.

Coverage

- Data Analytics
- Business Systems Engineering
- Business Intelligence
- Big Data
- Strategic Information Systems
- Data Strategy
- Business Decision Making
- Decision Support Systems
- Performance Metrics
- Data Governance

IGI Global is currently accepting manuscripts for publication within this series. To submit a proposal for a volume in this series, please contact our Acquisition Editors at Acquisitions@igi-global.com or visit: http://www.igi-global.com/publish/.

The Advances in Business Information Systems and Analytics (ABISA) Book Series (ISSN 2327-3275) is published by IGI Global, 701 E. Chocolate Avenue, Hershey, PA 17033-1240, USA, www.igi-global.com. This series is composed of titles available for purchase individually; each title is edited to be contextually exclusive from any other title within the series. For pricing and ordering information please visit http://www.igi-global.com/book-series/advances-business-information-systems-analytics/37155. Postmaster: Send all address changes to above address.

Titles in this Series

For a list of additional titles in this series, please visit: www.igi-global.com/book-series/advances-business-information-systems-analytics/37155

Data Envelopment Analysis (DEA) Methods for Maximizing Efficiency
Adeyemi Abel Ajibesin (American University of Nigeria, Nigeria) and Narasimha Rao Vajjhala (University of New York Tirana, Albania)
Business Science Reference • copyright 2024 • 389pp • H/C (ISBN: 9798369302552) • US $250.00 (our price)

Intersecting Environmental Social Governance and AI for Business Sustainability
Cristina Raluca Gh. Popescu (University of Bucharest, Romania & The Bucharest University of Economic Studies, Romania & The National Institute for Research and Development in Environmental Protection, Romania & INCDPM, Bucharest, Romania & National Research and Development Institute for Gas Turbines (COMOTI), Bucharest, Romania) and Poshan Yu (Soochow University, China & European Business Institute, Luxembourg & Australian Studies Centre of Shanghai University, China)
Business Science Reference • copyright 2024 • 371pp • H/C (ISBN: 9798369311516) • US $275.00 (our price)

Human-Centered Approaches in Industry 5.0 Human-Machine Interaction, Virtual Reality Training, and Customer Sentiment Analysis
Ahdi Hassan (Global Institute for Research Education and Scholarship, The Netherlands) Pushan Kumar Dutta (Amity University Kolkata, India) Subir Gupta (Swami Vivekanand University, India) Ebrahim Mattar (College of Engineering, University of Bahrain, Bahrain) and Satya Singh (Sharda University, Uzbekistan)
Business Science Reference • copyright 2024 • 369pp • H/C (ISBN: 9798369326473) • US $275.00 (our price)

Educational Perspectives on Digital Technologies in Modeling and Management
G. S. Prakasha (Christ University, India) Maria Lapina (North-Caucasus Federal University, Russia) Deepanraj Balakrishnan (Prince Mohammad Bin Fahd University, Saudi Arabia) and Mohammad Sajid (Aligarh Muslim University, India)
Engineering Science Reference • copyright 2024 • 348pp • H/C (ISBN: 9798369323144) • US $360.00 (our price)

Big Data Analytics Techniques for Market Intelligence
Dina Darwish (Ahram Canadian University, Egypt)
Engineering Science Reference • copyright 2024 • 512pp • H/C (ISBN: 9798369304136) • US $355.00 (our price)

Digital Twin Technology and AI Implementations in Future-Focused Businesses
Sivaram Ponnusamy (Sandip University, Nashik, India) Mansour Assaf (University of the South Pacific, Fiji) Jilali Antari (Ibn Zohr Agadir University, Morocco) Satyanand Singh (Fiji National University, Nasinu, Fiji) and Swaminathan Kalyanaraman (University College of Engineering, Pattukkottai, India)
Business Science Reference • copyright 2024 • 331pp • H/C (ISBN: 9798369318188) • US $285.00 (our price)

IGI Global
PUBLISHER of TIMELY KNOWLEDGE

701 East Chocolate Avenue, Hershey, PA 17033, USA
Tel: 717-533-8845 x100 • Fax: 717-533-8661
E-Mail: cust@igi-global.com • www.igi-global.com

"With the recent surge in interest in AI over the past several years, we see that soon 'AI-powered' or 'AI-enhanced' will be prevalent in most products and/or services. Whether GenAI, AI Ethics, or the coming Metaverse, AI seems to be omnipresent in society. Professor Merlo's book captures some of the key trends and research in AI and Analytics and provides a multinational perspective of interest to both educators and practitioners. I believe AI is here to stay, and this book is a great read towards being more informed in this field."

– Dr. Jay Liebowitz, *Touro University, USA*

This book is dedicated to my cherished husband, Jason Merlo, whose steadfast encouragement in my academic journey has been a pillar of strength, offering support not only during the development of this book but consistently throughout my professional journey. I also want to express special appreciation to my former mentors, professors, students, colleagues, and managers, as well as to the dedicated professionals, practitioners, and researchers, and professors committed to enhancing studies and organizational performance through the efficient utilization of information technologies. Additionally, recognition is extended to those advancing neural systems and complex machines integral to the field of AI. Through their diverse influence, they have all played a role in shaping the concept behind this book. Ultimately, this dedication is extended to the realm of science, illuminating the countless opportunities it unveils for enhancing information utilization and decision-making prowess within business landscapes.

Editorial Review Board

Table of Contents

Section 4
Artificial Intelligence Prompting Digital Transformation: Ethics, Robotics, Machine Learning, and New Trends

Detailed Table of Contents

This chapter provides an introduction to the foundations of Artificial Intelligence (AI). The history and concepts of Artificial Intelligence are outlined, highlighting the fact that AI is not a new area of knowledge or system, unlike the recent popular belief suggests. It discusses the dynamic context of the business world being impacted by AI, covering some core concepts for business, the strategic integration of AI, the critical role of data analytics and future perspectives within the field. This chapter emphasizes the adaptability and scalability of business in the face of AI-driven changes. The literature review encompasses a wide range of sources, including academic research publications, case studies, and industry reports, providing a well-rounded perspective on the subject matter. Key themes emerging from the literature, such as AI-driven productivity enhancements, the challenges and opportunities of AI in organizations, trends, and new professional roles, are examined. In conclusion, this chapter aims to equip readers with a solid foundation for understanding how AI was created and is reshaping business operations processes and outcomes. By elucidating the key principles, applications, and impacts of AI, it serves as a valuable resource that helps highlight the transformative influence of generative AI on decision-making processes, automation, data analytics, and organizational strategies, serving academics, business professionals, and anyone seeking to navigate the intricate landscape of AI in the corporate world.

The integration of many technologies has led to the emergence of a rapidly evolving discipline known as 'AI-driven data analytics.' This enables both information scientists and organisational managers to effectively derive practical insights from intricate datasets by using machine learning algorithms, natural language processing, and data mining techniques. This encompasses an examination of machine learning algorithms and their function in revealing patterns and associations in data, along with the importance of natural language processing in extracting insights from unstructured textual data. AI-powered data analysis and visualisation and facilitates predictive analytics—all while augmenting the transmission of intricate data via interactive visual representations—are analysied. This chapter presents a thorough examination of the transformational potential of artificial intelligence (AI) in the field of data analytics. It highlights the dynamic characteristics of AI and emphasises the boundless opportunities it presents in the contemporary digital era.

This chapter discusses the convergence of knowledge engineering and artificial intelligence in the context of knowledge management, highlighting the synergy between these disciplines to optimize organizational processes. Both have promising potential to improve knowledge management by automating tasks such as collecting, filtering, analyzing, and organizing data, information, and knowledge while identifying relevant patterns for strategic organizational development. It explores how knowledge engineering contributes to its representation and application, while artificial intelligence enhances hyper-automation and predictive analysis through advanced algorithms. The methodology adopted is an exploratory analysis that provides a comprehensive understanding of the dynamics involved in this disciplinary convergence and its implications for knowledge management. As a result, it highlights not only the unique contribution of knowledge engineering to representation and its efficient application, but also the amplifying role of artificial intelligence in organizational processes.

The learning curve has proven to be a useful tool for monitoring the performance of both new and experienced employees. For an analysis of the relationship between knowledge management and the reduction of the learning curve, this article presents a study conducted within an IT company in the city of Florianópolis. A questionnaire was administered to 70% of the employees, and their responses were analyzed. The study concluded that the research identified the key knowledge management tools that can impact the improvement of the learning curve. For questions that did not receive more than 50% positive responses, the application of knowledge management methods and techniques was carried out. As the techniques are implemented and refined by the company, the reduction of the learning curve is

be executed for validation purposes. Hence, prior to implementation, organizational practice cannot be expressed and experienced by concerned stakeholders as part of human-centered transformation processes.

This chapter outlines a case study of the development and sustainability process of an information governance (IG) program at a college in Texas. It employs an action research methodological approach to lay out the critical factors in executing and IG program. It discusses the key components in designing and implementing strategies, policies, practices, and compliance in IG. Findings emphasize the importance of aligning the IG program with strategic objectives and organizational culture. The participatory nature of action research enhances program sustainability and buy-in. Effective communication, training, and change management are highlighted as crucial for successful IG adoption, in addition to the importance of eDiscovery within the process. The study aims to provide a tailored governance framework within the context of a college program offering potential applicability to various industries.

AI and data analytics have revolutionized the field of market research and competitive intelligence. This chapter explores the multifaceted applications of AI and data analytics in gathering, analyzing, and deriving actionable insights from data sources to gain a competitive edge in the business landscape. It delves into various techniques, such as natural language processing, machine learning, and predictive analytics, showcasing how they empower organizations to make informed decisions, anticipate market trends, and outperform competitors. Furthermore, this chapter highlights the ethical considerations and challenges associated with AI-driven market research and competitive intelligence. In an era driven by data, AI emerges as an indispensable tool, enabling businesses to thrive in a dynamic and competitive marketplace.

This chapter presents the results of a study for improving the performance of the quiescence phase

Foreword

Artificial intelligence is literally transforming the way we work, live, and engage with each other. We are still in the early stages of the changes AI can bring to us. Organizations in the competitive landscape are not only enthusiastic about the opportunities AI can bring but also wary of the challenges it can create if not adopted faster. Being an AI-driven organization is no longer a choice but a necessity for survival. One of the key elements that is becoming prominent is how well an organization has prepared itself to manage AI. A case in point is the importance of leveraging data. Since AI heavily depends on data, it is crucial that the organization transforms itself into a system that generates enough and more data to be used for gaining insights through the application of AI.

"AI and Data Analytics Applications in Organizational Management," edited by Dr. Tereza Raquel Merlo, compiles a collection of insightful works that will prove immensely helpful for both practitioners and researchers seeking to understand approaches for leveraging AI in organizations. This edited collection addresses key aspects of AI and data analytics that are crucial for navigating the rapidly changing business landscape.

The book touches upon many key aspects, including ethical considerations, which is becoming a key area of concern, having impacts in different ways. While we are aware of the transformative power of these innovations, we should also focus on responsible innovation that keeps in mind the emerging requirements of the new world, including sustainability and inclusiveness. The book offers an interesting collection of work that focuses on practical applications of these technologies.

Chapter 1 provides a foundation for the readers to understand and appreciate the transformative approach of AI and analytics within the realm of organizations. It delves into the role of AI in organizations and the role of Generative AI which is destined to bring in a revolutionary impact on organizations. Chapter 2 blends very well with the foundation laid in Chapter 1, by taking the reader into aspects of AI driven data analytics and how to leverage the same for organizational management. It helps understand the transformative power of AI and exposes the reader to the many opportunities that can be leveraged by organizations.

One of the most important impacts that AI and analytics has on organizations is their ability to help mine the exhaustive knowledge they have and bring that knowledge to users in a contextualized manner. Chapter 3 focuses on this aspect. Knowledge Management (KM) as a field is seeing a huge impact through AI, especially generative AI, and this chapter gives the reader a good level of understanding on how this is happening. Chapter 4 builds on the topic of KM and focuses on the role of KM tools to reduce the learning curve. The reader will be able to appreciate the relevance of AI in this scenario. As AI becomes all pervasive, its role in managing knowledge and getting the most out of what we know becomes a competitive differentiator. This is true for small and large organizations. Chapter 5, a case study, deals with KM and Co-production deals in one such scenario.

Chapter 6 delves into creating business process intelligence through Value Network Analysis (VNA). They suggest a tagging mechanism to guide the transformation of value exchanges into communication and operational tasks, integrating a holomaps structure and semantic process design. Value-driven management, exemplified by VNA and holomaps, gains additional potency when integrated with AI. Chapter 7 is a case study a on the development and sustainability of an Information Governance (IG) Program at a Texas college, utilizing an action research approach. It outlines critical factors in IG program execution, emphasizing alignment with strategic objectives and organizational culture. The case study gives the reader an understanding of how to about define an information governance program with an aim of implementing artificial intelligence, predictive analytics and prescriptive analytics.

AI and Data Analytics have transformed Market Research and Competitive Intelligence, offering multifaceted applications. Chapter 8 explores their use in gathering, analyzing, and deriving actionable insights for a competitive advantage. It also addresses ethical considerations and challenges in AI-driven market research. In the data-centric era, AI becomes indispensable for businesses to thrive in a dynamic marketplace. Chapter 9 builds on Chapter 8 and presents a study on enhancing the quiescence phase of the Alpha-Beta (α-β) search in the Minimax algorithm. The research, relevant to organizational management, demonstrates how strategic algorithmic enhancements can efficiently manage and optimize decision-making processes, providing insights applicable to algorithmic decision support systems in various organizational contexts. The chapter on Smart Tourism gives a very good understanding of how AI-driven technologies are changing an industry. The chapter studies the impact of technology on travel pattern, personalized experiences, and improvement of efficiency overall.

Chapters 11 and 12 give an apt closure to the book, with an in-depth study on ethical and social consequences of data analytics on organizational management. The roles of AI and RPA in Intelligent Industry 4.0 is also addressed. Chapter 11 looks at the use of AI in accounting, addressing management changes, societal impact, bias, privacy concerns, transparency, and accountability, considering automation's effects on jobs and the accounting sector. Chapter 12 focuses on Intelligent industry 4.0. It explores RPA and AI in various industries, aiming to enhance functionality with ML, DL, and NLP algorithms. It discusses uses, trends, and applications of RPA and AI in management, supporting the theoretical implications of computational intelligence.

"AI and Data Analytics Applications in Organizational Management" offers a nuanced and comprehensive exploration of AI's disruptive influence on various organizational functions. This insightful collection, curated by Dr. Merlo, delves into practical applications, ethical considerations, and the future of Intelligent Industry 4.0. With its diverse perspectives and actionable insights, it caters to both seasoned professionals and curious newcomers, offering a nuanced understanding of AI's transformative potential. This is your key to unlocking the future of organizational success.

Randhir Reghunath Pushpa
Acies Innovations, Singapore

Preface

Open AI is a term that has been trending around the globe for the last couple of years, coinciding with the increased accessibility of Artificial Intelligence (AI) applications by the general public, such as ChatGPT, launched in November 2022 (Heaven, 2023). Throughout this period organizational leaders worldwide have intensified the conversation about automation and its impact on the workforce, seamlessly intertwining with the echoes of the Industrial Revolution in the late 18th and early 19th century (1760–1840). In the compelling narrative of our technological evolution, the advent of AI emerges as a pivotal chapter. Contemporary visionaries like Sam Altman, Elon Musk, Greg Brockman, and a few others are names behind the collaborative initiative of Open AI. Those names are also often associated with the creation of AI and the current state of revolution reshaping the production and processes in the business landscape. Musk, Altman, and other Silicon Valley developers and entrepreneurs cofounded OpenAI in 2015 with the vision of using Artificial Intelligence in a way that would benefit humanity (Kay, 2023). This romantic and visionary outlook on the phenomenon of AI has been met with skepticism by many, including British theoretical physicist Stephen Hawking, who warned that artificial intelligence could end mankind in an interview given to BBC news, claiming that: "The development of full artificial intelligence could spell the end of the human race" (Cellan-Jones, 2014, para. 2).

While AI is currently a widely discussed term, it is essential to note that the concept is not new, and that predecessors, prominent mathematicians, and researchers have collectively contributed to shaping the field of AI through their mathematical insights and theoretical frameworks. These scientists include Alan Turing, Norbert Wiener, Charles Babbage and many others whose contributions have played a critical role in the development of computer programming languages, LISP, and the development of deep neural networks and algorithms responsible for the development of Machine Learning (ML) and AI.

The term Artificial Intelligence was introduced at the Dartmouth Conference in 1956 by John McCarthy, Marvin Minsky, Nathaniel Rochester, and Claude Shannon (McCarthy, et al., 1955). These pioneers established the groundwork for the field, with McCarthy proposing a commonsense reasoning program during the conference, maintaining that: "to proceed on the basis of the conjecture that every aspect of learning or any other feature of intelligence can in principle be so precisely described that a machine can be made to simulate it." (Moor, 2006, p. 87). In 1833, mathematicians Ada Lovelace and Charles Babbage began a work relationship that would lead to the creation of an advanced machine, Analytical Engine, designed to perform automatic computations and non-numeric data programming, laying the foundation for the development of modern computers and artificial intelligence. Their successors have since made numerous advancements and contributions to the discipline.

This fusion of advanced algorithms, machine learning, and data analytics transforming the traditional paradigms, optimizing production processes, and propelling innovation to unprecedented heights is defined by Kshetri (2023) as the Fourth Revolution. In this context, the convergence of AI and the industrial landscape promises not only to increase productivity but also redefine roles and responsibilities, sparking a dialogue on the future of work and the dynamic interplay between man and machine. Khalil (1993) advocates that the goal of AI is to reduce "the real world's complexity into simple calculations that can be easily implemented" (p. 313). Improvement in AI, with its capacity for learning, problem-solving, and automation, becomes the contemporary driving force restructuring industries. Similar to the mechanization that characterized the Industrial Revolution, AI introduces a new era of efficiency and transformation.

The impact of AI on organizational management is profound and continues to evolve, affecting organizations' ability to remain competitive and survive. Some critical areas being impacted include automation in many areas of society, workforce augmentation and how employees remain productive and in synergy with machinery, the ethical considerations in the adoption of AI, customer services and data analytics, and the learning process itself, now being impacted by virtual and hybrid environments with adaptive platforms and systems. In a dynamic landscape of organizational management, the integration of AI and data analytics has emerged as a transformative force, reshaping the way businesses operate, strategize, and adapt in an increasingly data-driven world. According to Merlo (2022):

"Amidst the phenomenon of Big Data and analytics, businesses are facing a challenge to remain competitive and effectively use knowledge and technologies in such a way that knowledge workers will be attracted, valued, engaged, and have their knowledge assets incorporated as part of an organizational culture that will foster constant learning and innovation through a neural network system that utilizes AI and its subsets of machine and deep learning." (p. xx)

As AI continues to impact various spheres of society, some in unforeseeable ways and exploited for malicious purposes, prioritizing cybersecurity becomes imperative. This emphasis becomes especially critical as technology advances and the scalability of information access expands. Critics with a pessimistic perspective contend that the ascent of AI will lead to drastic employment reductions and pose a potential threat to human existence. Conversely, proponents of AI maintain that although automation may replace roles in the workplace, it will also give rise to new job opportunities, fostering learning, innovation, complex problem-solving, and progress. In the vast expanse of human knowledge and innovation, the realm of AI stands as a beacon of continuous exploration and transformative potential.

During this period, the future holds immense promise for those who embrace technological apparatuses to propel societies and organizations toward unparalleled performance. Join me in exploring the unfolding landscape where the marriage of artificial intelligence and data analytics not only becomes a driving force for change but a beacon of opportunity for those committed to utilizing these tools for the collective benefit of society and organizational excellence.

While organizations worldwide are challenged by an overwhelming influx of data, opportunities have also arisen to harness the power of AI and data analytics. It remains noteworthy that there is still a limited number of publications addressing the impact of artificial intelligence in organizational management. Despite the increasing integration of AI technologies into various businesses processes, the existing gap in scholarly literature poses a challenge to organizations and decision-makers seeking to effectively navigate the evolving landscape shaped by the most current transformative technologies. This book delves into the intricate fusion of AI and data analytics and explores their profound impact on modern organizations, seeking to contribute to addressing the existing gap. It begins by elucidating the foundational concepts behind AI and historical developments that have paved the way for AI's integration into organizational management. By offering an examination of the conceptualization, evolution, and application of these technologies, it aims to serve as a resource for business leaders, professionals, and researchers seeking to navigate the rapidly changing terrain of management. The heart of this book lies in its exploration of AI applications across various facets of business, ranging from data analytics applications to business intelligence, market analysis, knowledge engineering and management, ethics implications, to future trends illustrated in some case studies and investigative work in the relevant literature. These real-world case studies showcase the diverse ways in which AI is revolutionizing industry practices, enhancing efficiency, and opening new avenues for growth and innovation.

This book contains a multifaceted reading experience that caters to two distinct audiences. First, researchers in data analytics, computer systems, knowledge engineering and management, organizational management, systems management, artificial intelligence, as well as technologists and mathematicians will find the content of this book particularly relevant. Second, it serves as a valuable reference for professionals in these fields, including leaders and managers across various business sectors such as CEOs, CFOs, CIOs, and startup entrepreneurs.

Furthermore, this book was inspired by my experience working for multiple technology businesses, where I had the opportunity to lead teams, projects, and complex data and knowledge management programs, and business operations focusing on process improvement, sales and deal management, business intelligence, data analytics, and business strategies. As a professional actively engaged in practice, consulting, and academia, the impetus behind writing this book emerged from a fervent commitment to enhancing business processes and addressing the essential aspects of organizational management. I am relentless in my desire to constantly learn and, through an inquisitive mind, stay abreast of new technologies impacting organizational performance, outcomes, profitability, and individuals. Throughout the years, I have observed, written, discussed, and presented work aiming at enabling productivity, innovation, and effective decision-making processes. This book is intended to serve as a catalyst for additional research in the field, thereby broadening both the scope of knowledge and practices to enhance business effectiveness, and studies and practices in AI.

The organization of this book was designed to facilitate readers' seamless navigation through its pages and chapters, offering a clear and direct exploration of the topics. It delivers a thorough examination of AI, from fundamental concepts to practical applications in various sectors of business. The content encompasses case studies that look at AI applications, data analytics, ethical considerations, and emerging trends in the field.

ORGANIZATION OF THE BOOK

In order to shape the contributions from the authors, the book was organized in a coherent scheme presented in four sections with a structure that flows, discussing the foundations of artificial intelligence and data analytics applications in information sciences to the analysis of engineering of knowledge and co-creation. It then moves into the complexity of AI applications in different domains in society and layers of organizational management, and concludes with provocative chapters regarding trends and innovation imposed by AI as well as some ethical considerations in accounting, as follows:

Section 1: Foundations of Artificial Intelligence and Data Analytics – A Data-Driven Approach

Chapter 1: Foundations of Artificial Intelligence and the ever-evolving technological landscape in business

The book provides an introduction to the fundamental concepts of AI and underscores its pivotal role in societal development, particularly in the context of organizational management. It analyzes into how societal transformations reshape data and information processing and consumption, fostering innovation, and emphasizes how AI plays a crucial role in this paradigm shift. The author elaborates on the foundations and the application of AI, asserting AI's indispensability for organizational survival and competitiveness. The narrative contends that technological progress, catalyzed by AI, has sparked a quest for knowledge and a calculated use of data. Individuals adept at handling information, big data, and the digital knowledge discovery process have redefined the need for data analytics tools and applications for connectivity, specifically in the realm of organizational management. This chapter explores the intricate nature of knowledge production and organizational competitiveness, elucidates the correlation between data and information, and underscores the significant impact of AI in current and future societies within the context of organizational management.

Chapter 2: AI-Driven Data Analytics in Information Sciences and Organizational Management

This chapter explores the powerful alliance between AI and data analytics, a fusion that has dramatically reshaped academic and business landscapes. In the realms of information sciences and organizational management, this integration has ushered in a new era known as "AI-Driven Data Analytics." Here, we witness a vibrant relationship between cutting-edge computational intelligence and the vast wealth of digital information, presenting a methodology that goes beyond traditional data analytics.

At its heart, AI-Driven Data Analytics leverages machine learning, natural language processing, and data mining to empower information scientists and organizational managers. This synergistic approach not only extracts insights from historical and current data but also enables organizations to predict and shape future outcomes. The chapter dives into the multifaceted impact of AI-Driven Data Analytics, exploring its diverse applications, challenges, and ethical considerations.

Throughout this exploration, we uncover how this innovative amalgamation is not just redefining how we use information but is also propelling businesses towards a new era of data-driven excellence. By the end of this scholarly journey, readers gain a profound understanding of the transformative shift brought about by AI-Driven Data Analytics, a shift that not only alters the way we extract knowledge but fundamentally transforms the essence of contemporary organizational management.

Chapter 3: Artificial Intelligence, Knowledge Engineering and Management

This chapter probes the interconnected realms of AI, knowledge engineering, and knowledge management, emphasizing their collective goal of effectively utilizing knowledge to develop intelligent systems capable of addressing complex problems. Knowledge engineering focuses on representing, organizing, and applying expert knowledge to solve specific issues, while AI employs computational resources to automate tasks requiring human intelligence through codified algorithms.

The authors defend that Knowledge-based systems (KBS) serve as a common ground, with knowledge engineering often involving the creation of AI systems utilizing knowledge bases for decision-making. Machine learning, closely related to both fields, can benefit from knowledge engineering as it provides initial knowledge to train models. The chapter underscores the symbiotic relationship where knowledge engineering offers methods for representing knowledge, and AI implements these methods to create autonomous systems capable of learning and decision-making.

Furthermore, the chapter explores the integration of these concepts with knowledge management, a discipline focused on efficiently discovering, capturing, organizing, storing, distributing, and implementing knowledge in organizational settings. The collaborative efforts of AI, knowledge engineering, and knowledge management aim to optimize knowledge management processes, fostering innovation, efficiency, and continuous adaptation within organizations.

The concept of hyperautomation is introduced, highlighting its role in optimizing organizational processes by integrating various automation technologies, including AI and machine learning. Hyperautomation, considered a tactical approach to digital transformation, offers benefits such as operational efficiency and improved work quality but presents challenges related to technology management, data security, and the need for new skills.

While not discussing the technical specifics of hyperautomation, the chapter acknowledges its organization into three categories, providing an overview of its interaction with knowledge engineering and AI.

Section 2: Artificial Intelligence in Knowledge Engineering and Management – (Re)shaping the Knowledge Landscape and Fostering Innovation

Chapter 4: Knowledge Management Tools for Reducing the Learning Curve, a case study

This chapter delves into the significance of the learning curve in organizational settings, particularly in the context of adapting to new products or services. Organizations, aiming to minimize disruptions to their productive systems, seek effective models and techniques to reduce the learning curve for new employees. In today's fiercely competitive technological landscape, the deployment of quality tools has become pivotal for enhancing productivity, a trend increasingly prevalent in modern organizations.

The learning curve is presented as a mathematical and graphical representation of the levels achieved during a learning process. It assesses the relationship between acquired knowledge and the time required, providing insights into the effectiveness of educational actions at different stages. In the context of manual tasks, learning curves serve as mathematical representations of a worker's performance. As tasks are repeated, the worker becomes more proficient, reducing the time required for completion due to familiarity with production means, adaptation to organizational tools, or the discovery of efficiencies.

The study involves interviews with the head of the human resources department and company leaders in a technology-based firm in Florianópolis, the second most entrepreneurial city in Brazil. The case study provides valuable insights into the learning curve within the company, offering practices and techniques that accelerate employee adaptation and boost productivity. The presented results are thoroughly discussed to offer actionable strategies for organizations seeking to enhance their onboarding processes.

Chapter 5: Driving Innovation Ecosystem Transformation via Digital Platforms and Knowledge Co-Creation

In Chapter 5 the authors explore the pivotal role of co-production in public administration, focusing on the transformative journey and impact of the New Research and Innovation Arrangements Program (NAPI) in Paraná, Brazil. NAPI, an innovative initiative grounded in the commons principle, aims to enhance societal participation in shaping impactful public policies. Central to NAPI is the iAraucária digital platform, leveraging artificial intelligence to facilitate resource coordination among stakeholders in regional innovation systems. This fosters the co-production of knowledge and innovation, aligning projects with specific regional needs.

Since its inception, NAPI has catalyzed the establishment of more than 60 arrangements, involving over 4,000 participants in collaborative networks. The chapter highlights significant outcomes, including enhanced precision in research and innovation funding, strengthened connections among ecosystem actors, and the mitigation of risks in public policy co-production. These achievements contribute significantly to Paraná's sustainable development, showcasing the effectiveness of co-production in fostering impactful and regionally relevant public policies.

Chapter 6: Creating Business Process Intelligence through Value Network Analysis: A Tagging-based Approach

This chapter explores the established approach of value-driven management in networked business operations, emphasizing the efficacy of Value Networks in representing exchanges of value between stakeholders and the ensuing business transactions. At the core of the organizational development and transformation technique known as Value Network Analysis (VNA) are Holomaps — simple yet expressive representations of Value Networks.

The knowledge generated through the application of VNA serves as the foundation for specifying business process models. However, the transformation of value exchanges among stakeholders into communication and operational tasks lacks a structured and effective guidance system. To address this gap, the chapter proposes the implementation of a tagging mechanism. This mechanism takes into consideration both the structure of holomaps and semantic process design.

The authors defend that by employing a behavior specification technique to represent processes meaningfully, the resulting process models become executable for validation purposes. This approach allows organizational practices to be expressed and experienced by concerned stakeholders prior to implementation, contributing to human-centered transformation processes in digitalization projects. Importantly, this groundwork supports the automated generation of process models, potentially leveraging AI, in a transparent and explainable manner.

Section 3: Intersection of Business Intelligence and Artificial Intelligence on Multiple Domains

Chapter 7: Creating an Information Governance Program at a College to Ultimately Implement Artificial Intelligence, Predictive Analytics, and Prescriptive Analytics

A comprehensive analysis detailing the establishment and sustainability of an Information Governance (IG) Program at a college in Texas is presented in this chapter. The authors detail the employment of an action research methodology to approach a research problem and elucidate critical factors for the successful execution of an IG program in a college program. It explores key components in the design and implementation of strategies, policies, practices, and compliance within the IG framework. Emphasizing the alignment of the IG program with intentional objectives and organizational culture, the findings underscore the participatory nature of action research, contributing to sustained program buy-in. The chapter highlights the pivotal roles of effective communication, training, and change management for successful IG adoption, along with the significance of eDiscovery in the process. Beyond the college context, the study aims to present a tailored governance framework with potential applicability across industries. Additionally, it underscores the impact of Artificial Intelligence (AI) applications and systems in optimizing information governance practices and mitigating risks and threats in data and information management.

Chapter 8: AI and Data Analytics for Market Research and Competitive Intelligence

This chapter brings another analysis discussing the impact of AI in different organizational domains. The authors explore the revolutionary impact of integrating AI and Data Analytics on Market Research and Competitive Intelligence, providing organizations with unprecedented insights and strategic advantages. AI-driven technologies efficiently extract actionable intelligence from vast datasets, streamlining traditional market research methodologies and allowing organizations to anticipate market shifts and competitors' strategies with precision.

It is defended that the synergy of AI and Data Analytics examines unstructured data, offering nuanced insights into consumer preferences. Predictive analytics, powered by advanced algorithms, enables forecasting of market performance, enhancing the decision-making process. In Competitive Intelligence, AI-driven tools empower real-time competitor monitoring and extraction of valuable insights from digital touchpoints.

Chapter 9: Artificial Intelligence in Chess-Playing Automata: A Paradigm for the Quiescence Phase of a-ß Search

This book chapter explores the transformative contributions of key figures in the development of game theory and its profound impact on various disciplines, highlighting the collaborative work of John von Neumann and economist Oskar Morgenstern which resulted in the publication of "Theory of Games and Economic Behavior," (1944), laying the foundation for a groundbreaking mathematical theory that revolutionized economic and social organization. The chapter explores the consequential application of these principles by Claude E. Shannon in his 1950 paper, "Programming a Computer for Playing Chess," where game theory principles were applied to chess, becoming a cornerstone in the early stages of artificial intelligence research. The chapter further examines John Nash's introduction of Nash equilibrium in the 1950s, a pivotal concept in game theory with far-reaching implications across economics, computer science, political science, sociology, and biology. Nash's significant contributions earned him the Nobel Prize in 1994, solidifying the lasting impact of game theory on multiple fields.

Chapter 10: Smart Tourism Narratives: Maturity Matrix and Digital Transformation

The tourist sector is undergoing a profound transformation in the modern digital era. This systematic literature assessment provides an in-depth analysis of the shifting paradigms arising at the intersection of technology and tourism. The chapter investigates the crucial impact of cutting-edge technologies such as the Internet of Things (IoT), Metaverse, Artificial Intelligence (AI), Data Analytics, Virtual Reality, Augmented Reality (AR), and Blockchain on changing travel patterns. The combination of these technologies empowers destination stakeholders to manage resources more effectively, personalize and streamline traveler experiences, and equips policymakers with tools for data-driven decision-making. This research contributes to the ongoing discourse about how the tourist industry is evolving in the digital era by shedding light on the changing paradigms, possibilities, and challenges in the realm of smart tourism.

Section 4: Artificial Intelligence Prompting Digital Transformation – Ethics, Robotics, Machine Learning, and New Trends

Chapter 11: Understanding the Ethical and Social Consequences of Data Analytics for Organizational Management in the Age of AI - Accounting Ethics Perspective

In this chapter the authors examine the social and ethical implications arising from the integration of AI and data analytics in accounting operations. The focus is on the ethical and problem-solving dimensions of corporate governance. The chapter underscores the critical importance of addressing these issues and offers suggestions for making moral judgments within the context of AI-driven accounting.

The chapter aims to shed light on the complexities of AI-driven accounting by providing insights, principles, and recommendations. It encourages businesses to make ethical decisions while leveraging the benefits of this advanced technology. The focus is on ethical obligations that accompany technological progress, laying the foundation for a comprehensive evaluation of data, machine learning, and analytics in accounting.

Ultimately, the chapter concludes by stressing the importance of using new technology responsibly and ethically. It emphasizes the role of technology as a tool to enhance corporate governance and ethical decision-making rather than posing a threat. The subsequent section will explore the ever-evolving field of organizational management, particularly its adaptation to the dynamic realm of digital transformation.

Chapter 12: Intelligent Industry 4.0: Artificial Intelligence and Robotic Process Automation as Trendsetters

Our journey concludes with this last chapter looking at into the contemporary interpretation of the Industrial Revolution, shifting the focus to Industry 4.0—a transformative paradigm in manufacturing and industrial processes driven by advanced technologies. The chapter explores key components, including the Internet of Things (IoT), robotic process automation (RPA), cognitive computing, and cloud computing, which collectively contribute to the creation of smart industries and factories.

A fundamental aspect of Industry 4.0 is the interconnectedness facilitated by IoT, allowing for real-time communication among industrial components. RPA plays a pivotal role in automating routine tasks, enhancing precision and consistency in manufacturing. Cognitive computing harnesses artificial intelligence and machine learning to simulate human thought processes, making industrial systems more adaptable. Cloud computing serves as the infrastructure for managing vast data generated by smart industries, offering scalability and accessibility.

While Industry 4.0 promises real-time decision-making capabilities, its adoption varies across industries. Challenges such as outdated infrastructure, workforce skill gaps, and data security concerns need deliberate planning, technology investments, and collaborative efforts to overcome. The chapter concludes by highlighting the transformative features of Industry Revolution 4.0, emphasizing automation and smart factories' role in efficient commodity production, particularly in the manufacturing and service industry, where robotic process automation explores innovative approaches.

This anthology seeks to provide a panoramic view of AI's multidimensional impact on diverse segments of business, paying homage to the pioneers and visionaries who have shaped the way to a complex trajectory exploring technology and neural systems. As we navigate through the chapters, we invite you to join us on this intellectual exploration, where the fusion of artificial intelligence and human ingenuity reshapes the contours of the future and the way businesses strategically and operationally make decisions and apply critical analyses of the trends, challenges, and opportunities that AI presents in the realm of organizational management.

"I never am really satisfied that I understand anything; because understand it well as I may, my comprehension can only be an infinitesimal fraction of all I want to understand about the many connections and relations which occur to me." - Ada Lovelace, letter to Augustus de Morgan (1841)

Tereza Raquel Merlo
University of North Texas, USA & Merlo Management Consulting, USA

REFERENCES

Cellan-Jones, R. (2014, December, 2). Stephen Hawking warns artificial intelligence could end mankind. BBC. Retrieved on January 9, 2024, from: https://www.bbc.com/news/technology-30290540

Heaven, W. D. (2023). Artificial Intelligence: The inside story of how ChatGPT was built from the people who made it. MIT Technology Review. Retrieved on January 9, 2024 from: https://www.technologyreview.com/2023/03/03/1069311/inside-story-oral-history-how-chatgpt-built-openai/

Kay, G. (2023). The history of ChatGPT creator OpenAI, which Elon Musk helped found before parting ways and criticizing. Business Insider. Retrieved from: https://www.businessinsider.com/history-of-openai-company-chatgpt-elon-musk-founded-2022-12 on January, 9, 2024.

Khalil, O. E. M. (1993). Artificial decision-making and artificial ethics: a management concern. Journal of Business Ethics, 12(4). Springer. https://www.jstor.org/stable/25072403

Kshetri, N. (2023). Artificial Intelligence. Fourth Revolution and the Bottom Four Billion Subtitle: Making Technologies Work for the Poor. University of Michigan Press. https://www.jstor.org/stable/10.3998/mpub.12205632.9

McCarthy, J., Minsky, M. L., & Rochester, N. S. Claude E. (1955). A Proposal for the Dartmouth Summer Research Project on Artificial Intelligence Retrieved on January, 9, 2024 from: https://onlinelibrary.wiley.com/doi/epdf/10.1609/aimag.v27i4.1904

Merlo, T. R. (2022). *Understanding implementing and evaluating knowledge management in business settings*. IGI Global., doi:10.4018/978-1-6684-4431-3

Moor, J. (2006). The Dartmouth College Artificial Intelligence Conference: The Next Fifty Years. AI Magazine, 27, 87–91.

Acknowledgment

The editor extends gratitude for the diligent efforts and constructive feedback from the editorial board reviewers, whose input played a crucial role in the compilation of this book. Furthermore, heartfelt thanks are extended to all authors who generously shared their experiences and studies across various fields of knowledge management in business, enriching the content of this book.

Tereza Raquel Merlo
University of North Texas, USA & Merlo Management Consulting, USA

Section 1

Foundations of Artificial Intelligence and Data Analytics: A Data-Driven Approach

Chapter 1
Foundations of Artificial Intelligence and the Ever-Evolving Technological Landscape in Business

Tereza Raquel Merlo
https://orcid.org/0000-0002-2042-5415
University of North Texas, USA & Merlo Management Consulting, USA

ABSTRACT

This chapter provides an introduction to the foundations of Artificial Intelligence (AI). The history and concepts of Artificial Intelligence are outlined, highlighting the fact that AI is not a new area of knowledge or system, unlike the recent popular belief suggests. It discusses the dynamic context of the business world being impacted by AI, covering some core concepts for business, the strategic integration of AI, the critical role of data analytics and future perspectives within the field. This chapter emphasizes the adaptability and scalability of business in the face of AI-driven changes. The literature review encompasses a wide range of sources, including academic research publications, case studies, and industry reports, providing a well-rounded perspective on the subject matter. Key themes emerging from the literature, such as AI-driven productivity enhancements, the challenges and opportunities of AI in organizations, trends, and new professional roles, are examined. In conclusion, this chapter aims to equip readers with a solid foundation for understanding how AI was created and is reshaping business operations processes and outcomes. By elucidating the key principles, applications, and impacts of AI, it serves as a valuable resource that helps highlight the transformative influence of generative AI on decision-making processes, automation, data analytics, and organizational strategies, serving academics, business professionals, and anyone seeking to navigate the intricate landscape of AI in the corporate world.

DOI: 10.4018/979-8-3693-1058-8.ch001

I propose to consider the question, "Can machines think?"

—Alan Turing, 1950

INTRODUCTION

The business landscape, like society in general, is witnessing a sweeping period driven by the integration of AI in many aspects of human activity. The automatization of many segments of society is linked to the recent massive layoffs by some Fortune 500 companies and the decimation of many small businesses. OpenAI, created in 2015 and released through ChatGPT in 2020 by entrepreneurs and co-founders Elon Musk, Sam Altman, Greg Brockman, Ilya Sutskever, John Schulman, and Wojciech Zaremba, among others (Widder, West, & Whittaker, 2023), propelled an extraordinary level of public curiosity and engagement with AI systems, making it the buzzword that many believe disrupted the conversation about business productivity and the future of workforce. Questions also arose regarding the origin of AI and its impact on human interactions and survival.

Whilst organizations equipped with proper technological apparatuses and the vision to embrace the new challenges imposed by AI are thriving and new roles are emerging from this transformative moment, it is also true that many jobs are being reevaluated and ended as result of the phenomenon. Organizations and individuals leveraging the power of AI are quick to accept, adapt, adopt, and use automated systems in routine tasks as well as, and most importantly, in technical and professional actions; from entertainment to professional endeavors, individuals are seeking to innovate and use technology and access to information as means of production. As in classical Marxist theory, individuals are exploring new forms of labor and ways of fitting into an economic system where production and redistribution of wealth means a new way of using technology as a power dynamic within society. The evolution of Web 4.0 and its approach to a more decentralized use of technology by individuals in society is a perfect example of how AI is enabling users to interact with the web in an engaging, real-time manner. In discussing the new organizational management paradigm based on data, information, and knowledge management, Şen, Yilmaz, & Mert, (2020) defend that:

Web 4.0 applications are capable of processing knowledge in the big metadata at any time and place with the help of various carriers (not only PC, mobile phone). WebOS, Intellectual Agents, and intellectual web enable a personalized interaction according to the needs and expectations of the individual. Web 4.0 applications facilitate both mentally and intellectually true symbiosis life experience at the center of the virtual and real-life collaboration. (p. 520)

Semantic Web 4.0 and 5G Technology networks apply integrated and complex AI services and an enhanced algorithm that drive the data and analytics defining and enhancing the customer experience and leading to innovations. The use of technologies in shared data naturally invites collaboration and communication, bridging gaps in knowledge production and co-creation that are the cornerstone of AI. Nikiforova, Alor, and Lytras. (2023) assert that: "The openness of data is considered one of the crucial drivers for the sustainable economy and the knowledge-based economy in particular" (p. 220).

AI has surpassed mere imitation; it has become a catalyst for innovation, efficiency, and strategic advantage. This chapter delves into the bedrock principles that underpin AI, exploring its origins, key concepts, and the myriad techniques that constitute its diverse landscape. From machine learning and neural networks to natural language processing and computer vision, the building blocks of AI are assembled to create intelligent systems that can analyze, learn, and adapt. The power of AI is not confined to its technical prowess alone; it resides in its symbiotic relationship with the ever-evolving technological landscape. The interconnected web of technologies, such as cloud computing, big data analytics, and the Internet of Things (IoT) intertwines with AI, amplifying its capabilities and expanding its potential applications. In this chapter, some of the intricate connections between AI and these complementary technologies are discussed, illustrating how their synergy shapes the future of business.

WHAT IS ARTIFICIAL INTELLIGENCE?

AI is a multidisciplinary field of knowledge with many nuanced definitions contingent on the context and perspective in which it is being applied and investigated. The general consensus defining AI focuses on the development and use of specific applications like machine learning, natural language, and complex computer systems designed with the purpose of imitating human intelligence.

The Bayesian network concepts, rooted in the 18th-century work of Thomas Bayes, play a crucial role in AI and ML. These concepts are integral to constructing network parameters for graphical representation, probabilistic inferences, and modeling causal relationships. Employing a multifaceted statistical approach, Bayesian networks facilitate the processing of probabilities, hypotheses, and information, thereby enhancing decision-making abilities and transparency.

The term Artificial Intelligence (AI) itself was officially coined by John McCarthy and Marvin Minsky, both computer scientists, during the Dartmouth Summer Conference in 1956. The original proposal for the seminal Dartmouth College Summer Project argued that:

Every aspect of learning or any other feature of intelligence can in principle be so precisely described that a machine can be made to simulate it. An attempt will be made to find how to make machines that use language, form abstractions. and concepts, solve kinds of problems now reserved for humans, and improve themselves." (De Spiegeleire, Maas, & Sweijs, 2017, p. 28)

McCarthy, a prominent figure in the field who made significant contributions to various concepts in his seminal work, advocated that AI programs have human-like cognitive skills that include reasoning, problem solving, learning, perception, and self-correction, as conveyed below:

1. **Reasoning:** AI program focuses on choosing appropriate algorithm to achieve the expected results. This process is used to make judgments, decisions, and predictions. In reasoning process two categories will ensure the appropriateness of outcomes: the deductive and inductive reasoning approach to problem solving.
2. **Learning:** Its main objective is to acquire and process data towards driving actions, so there is a clear understanding about the subjects under investigation. This process of learning is prompted by algorithms and its neural systems are responsible for sequential data control.
3. **Problem-solving:** The act of selecting the best solution to problems, typically involving steps in identifying a problem, analyzing situations, evaluating possible complex solutions, and applying logic to address problems with clarity about outcomes.

4. **Perception:** Involves the interpretation and analysis of information either via sensory organs (humans) or mechanical systems (AI data sensors). In terms of AI, key components include sensory input, data processing, feature data extraction, and knowledge system integration to interpret data.
5. **Self-correction:** McCarthy elaborated on the relevance of systems self-improvement and the creation of adaptive and autonomous AI systems. This context accepts learning from mistakes and the ability of machines to develop and adapt.

From the viewpoints of business and computing systems, here are some concepts of AI:

In its strictest definition, AI stands for the imitation by computers of the intelligence inherent in humans. Purists point out that many current applications are still relatively simple and therefore not true AI. That makes this definition inappropriate for our report, too; to use it would be to imply that AI does not exist at present. We would effectively be defining the phenomenon out of existence. (Sheikh, Prins, & Schrijvers, 2023, p. 15)

AI can be described as intelligent systems created to use data, analysis, and observations to perform certain tasks without needing to be programmed to do so. The potential is thus derived from opportunities to automate decision making processes through human-like reasoning - which has created a hype among many industries and firms. AI can be categorized as a capital–labor hybrid with the ability to self-learn, continuously improve and quickly scale-up. As described by O'Leary (Antonescu, 2018; Plastino, 2018; O'Leary, 2013). AI often create the foundation for decision support through valuable insights and results, collected from large and complex data sets and compressed into a manageable scale. (Reim, Åström, & Eriksson, 2020, p. 180)

"The ability of a machine to perform cognitive functions that we associate with human minds, such as perceiving, reasoning, learning, interacting with the environment, problem solving, decision-making, and even demonstrating creativity" (Brendel, Mirbabaie, et. al., 2021, p. 1).

Artificial intelligence (AI) systems are software (and possibly also hardware) systems designed by humans that, given a complex goal, act in the physical or digital dimension by perceiving their environment through data acquisition, interpreting the collected structured or unstructured data, reasoning on the knowledge, or processing the information, derived from this data and deciding the best action(s) to take to achieve the given goal. AI systems can either use symbolic rules or learn a numeric model, and they can also adapt their behavior by analysing how the environment is affected by their previous actions. (European Commission High-Level Expert Group on Artificial Intelligence, 2018, p. 1)

"Artificial intelligence (AI) refers to a collection of techniques that are being developed to address a wide variety of practical problems" (Mayo, 2023, p. 121).

Artificial intelligence refers to systems that use technologies such as: text mining, computer vision, speech recognition, natural language generation, machine learning, deep learning to gather and/or use data to predict, recommend or decide, with varying levels of autonomy, the best action to achieve specific goals. (Samoili et al., 2020, p. 9)

AI refers to a category of algorithms known as machine learning – including deep learning (Hao, 2018). The current wave of AI are self-learning algorithms that rely on vast amounts of data, driving AI innovation across multiple sectors (Holdren and Smith, 2016). The promises brought by this process of datafication and algorithmization has lured both the public and private sectors with applications that show great potential to transform our society (Bean, 2018; Sousa, Melo, Bernejo et al., 2019; Ballester, 2021, p. 67)

Artificial Intelligence encompasses computer science applications and the development of machines capable of performing tasks intended to imitate human intelligence and offer the best possible decision-making process. The field of Artificial Intelligence intends to train machines to think and act like humans using reasoning and predictive analysis employing mathematical functions. Contemporary authors argue that AI is as perversive as it is critical for the development of society. It is undoubtedly a phenomenon affecting all aspects of human existence and launching difficult questions along the way; one recurring question tries to define intelligence itself and whether machines will ever be able to learn, re-learn, self-correct, and think critically. Philosophers and scientists alike comprise the group of curious individuals trying to discern its definitive meaning. Russell and Norvig (2009) articulate several definitions of artificial intelligence described in four categories: acting humanely, thinking humanely, thinking rationally, and acting rationally. Whatever skeptical, pessimistic, or overly optimistic individuals might feel about the current and future of AI, it is certainly a phenomenon that is currently in its most transformative stage ever. It permeates the core of societal solutions, and its advancement should be expected to occur at a much faster pace than it has up to this point in history because machines have proven to be intelligent enough to learn and produce complex information, replacing humans in many areas of production.

In determining the complexity and multilayered core of AI, Samoili, López, et al., (2020) propose a taxonomy of AI domains and subdomains that characterizes the field and serve as cornerstone in clas-

Table 1. AI domains and subdomains constituting one part of the operational definition of AI

	AI taxonomy	
	AI domain	**AI subdomain**
Core	**Reasoning**	Knowledge representation
		Automated reasoning
		Common sense reasoning
	Planning	Planning and Scheduling
		Searching
		Optimisation
	Learning	Machine learning
	Communication	Natural language processing
	Perception	Computer vision
		Audio processing
Transversal	**Integration and Interaction**	Multi-agent systems
		Robotics and Automation
		Connected and Automated vehicles
	Services	AI Services
	Ethics and Philosophy	AI Ethics
		Philosophy of AI

Source: Samoili, López, et al., 2020, p. 11

sifying aspects and the fundamental goals of AI, as detailed in **Table 1**- AI domains and subdomains constituting one part of the operational definition of AI, below. The authors highlight that those suggested classifications of domains and subdomains described in the AI Watch Taxonomy are subsets of AI. The presented classification is designed to serve as a comprehensive list of areas from a perspective of policy, research and industry, aspects targeted in the work for the report to the European Commission.

THE HISTORY OF ARTIFICIAL INTELLIGENCE: MILESTONES

Predecessors and Seminal Work in AI

The fascinating journey that spans several centuries is marked by significant milestones and the groundbreaking work of multiple researchers. It is undoubtedly important to mention the work of Ada Lovelace and Charles Babbage in the development of sequential mathematics operations that resulted in the creation of the calculating machine called the Difference Engine and inspired the conception of the Analytical Engine (1833).

In 1842 Luigi Menabrea, a mathematician and politician, published a book titled: *Notions sur la machine analytique de M. Charles Babbage*. It described the mathematical operations, tables, charts, and algebraic equations designed to conceive Babbage's Analytical Engine. This publication was later translated from French to English and improved upon by Ada Lovelace, whose contributions were valued by Babbage.

Lovelace is considered the world's first computer programmer, making her a significant figure in the history of computing, and therefore, the origins of AI. Her passion for mathematics is well documented and the ideas that inspired her work foreshadowed diverse applications in AI and extended to the fields of natural language processing, image recognition, symbolic reasoning, and the concept of algorithmic processing.

The roots of conceptual AI can be traced back to the mid-20th century (see timeline in **Figure 1** below) when pioneers like Alan Turing envisioned machines capable of mimicking human intelligence. Turing's work was heavily influenced by his predecessors, mathematicians that had worked on the foundations of computing and neural systems.

In "Computing Machinery and Intelligence", Alan Turing (1950) proposed the Turing Test, a method for defining if a computing machine can display behaviors that could be described as intelligent or identical equivalent to those of humans. The Turing Test, resulting from Turing's work on the application of mathematical and computing codes to mimic intelligence, is still employed today to identify intelligence in artificial systems.

During the 1950s and 1960s in the early conceptualization of AI, researchers made developments in computing and AI with the first AI Program, UNIVAC I, commercially produced in 1951, and many mathematical logic theorists, like Allen Newell and Herbert Simon, contributed to the solidification of symbolic AI problem solving through logical reasoning. Newell and Simon also contributed considerably to the General Problem Solver (GPS), designed to solve a wide range of problems. The work of Warren McCulloch and Water Pitts (1990) built upon these previous studies, establishing connections between neural networks and AI. The studies of McCulloch and Pitts were published in "A Logical Calculus of the ideas Immanent in Nervous Activity" in 1943, introducing mathematical models of artificial neurons.

Figure 1. Artificial intelligence milestone: Foundations
Note: *This figure demonstrates the timeline of the evolution of AI, from the preliminary mathematical work to the birth of AI with the Dartmouth Conference in 1956.*

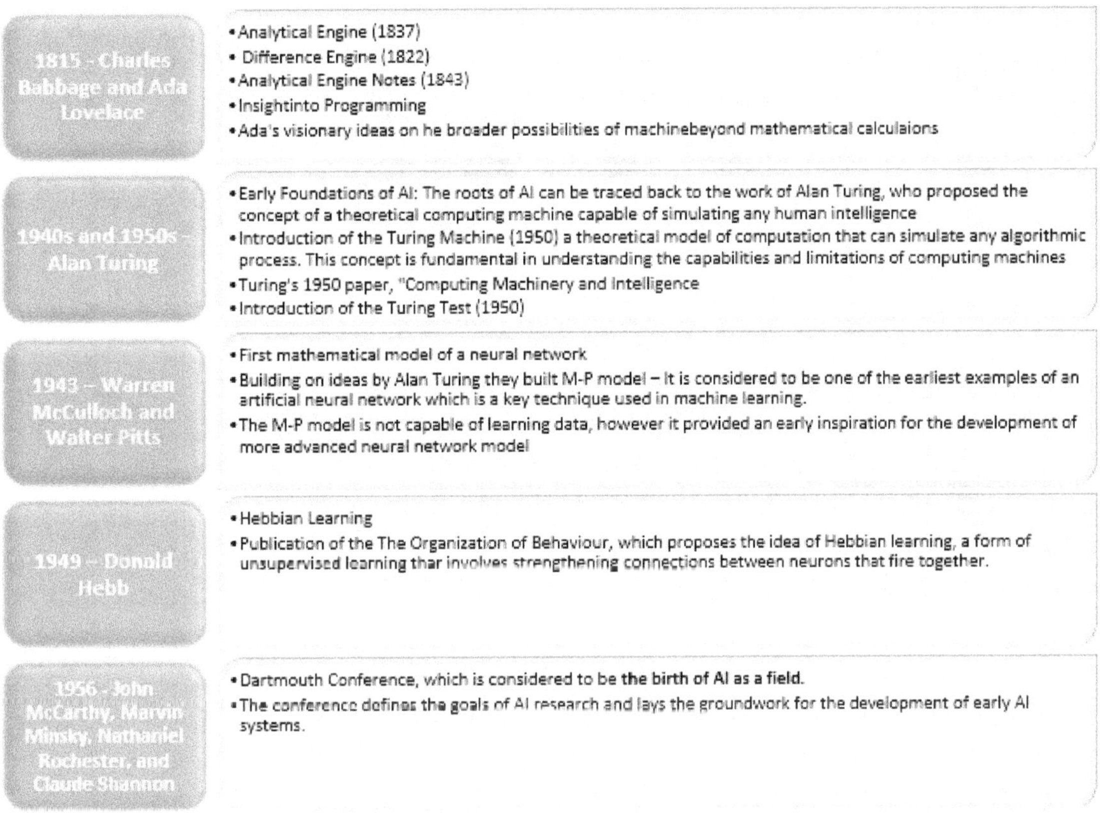

This work has had a significant impact on the development of computational neuroscience, contributing to advances in the study of brain functions.

Expanding on previous studies in neuroscience, Donald Hebb published his findings in the publication "The organization of behavior; a neuropsychological theory" in 1949 (Hebb, 1949), creating what was known as Hebbian Learning theory, which has become one of the most influential books in psychology and neuroscience. Hebb's work continues to inspire research in areas of learning and memory (Brown, 2020).

The early stages of AI are described in **Figure 2** below. In the consolidation of AI as a discipline, Machine Learning (ML) becomes prominent and AI applications expand. In 2010, Deep Learning flourishes as a leading tool for processing images, speech recognition, and natural language.

Those advances in AI applications became widespread as a formal science thanks to the Dartmouth Conference proposed by John McCarthy, Marvin Minsky, Rochester, and Claude Shannon, held at Dartmouth College in Hanover, New Hampshire in 1956. The purpose of the conference was to demonstrate how machines can simulate human intelligence in an attempt to "[…] find how to make machines use language, form abstractions and concepts, solve kinds of problems now reserved for humans, and improve themselves" (McCarthy, Minsky et al., 1955, p. 2).

Figure 2. Artificial intelligence milestone: The birth and consolidation of AI as discipline
Note: *This figure illustrates the timeline of AI as a discipline: major researchers and concepts.*

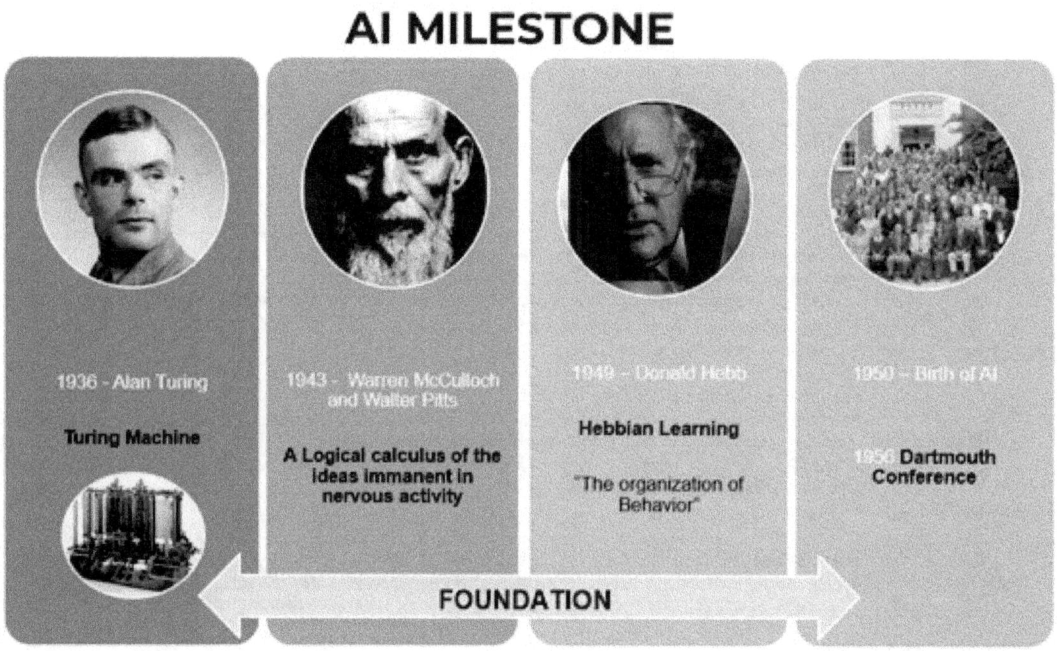

The authors sought to address problematic aspects of AI, listed below:

1) Automatic Computers

If a machine can do a job. then an automatic calculator can be programmed to simulate the machine. The speeds and memory capacities of present computers may be insufficient to simulate many of the higher functions of the human brain, but the major obstacle is not lack of machine capacity, but our inability to write programs taking full advantage of what we have.

2) How can a Computer be Programmed to Use a Language

It may be speculated that a large part of human thought consists of manipulating words according to rules of reasoning and rules of conjecture. From this point of view, forming a generalization consists of admitting a new word and some rules whereby sentences containing it imply and are implied by others. This idea has never been very precisely formulated nor have examples been worked out.

3). Neuron Nets

How can a set of (hypothetical) neurons be arranged to form concepts. Considerable theoretical and experimental work has been done on this problem by Uttley, Rashevsky and his group, Farley and Clark, Pitts and McCulloch, Minsky, Rochester and Holland, and others. Partial results have been obtained but the problem needs more theoretical work.

4). Theory of the Size of a Calculation

If we are given a well-defined problem (one for which it is possible to test mechanically whether a proposed answer is a valid answer) one way of solving it is to try all possible answers in order. This method is inefficient and to exclude it one I must have some criterion for efficiency of calculation. Some consideration will show that to get a measure of the efficiency of a calculation it is necessary to have on hand a method of measuring the complexity of a calculating device which in turn can be done if one has a theory of the complexity of functions. Some partial results on this problem have been obtained by Shannon and McCarthy.

5) Self-Improvement

Probably a truly intelligent machine will carry out activities which may best be described as self-improvement. Some schemes for doing this have been proposed and are worth further study. It seems likely that this question can be studied abstractly as well.

6) Abstractions

A number of types of "abstraction" can be distinctly defined and several others less distinctly. A direct attempt to classify these and to describe machine methods of forming abstractions from sensory and other data would seem worthwhile.

7) Randomness and Creativity

A fairly attractive and yet clearly incomplete conjecture is that the difference between creative thinking and unimaginative competent thinking lies in the injection of some randomness. The randomness must be guided by intuition to be efficient. In other words, the educated guess on the hunch includes controlled randomness in otherwise orderly thinking. (McCarthy, Minsky et al., 1955, pp. 2-4).

AI and Expert Systems Advances

In 1960s the Expert Systems emerged as a computer program designed to mimic the decision-making abilities of human experts in specific domains. Buchanan and Smith (1988) claim that expert systems is an exciting application program that: "allow a computer program to use expertise to assist in a variety of problems, such as diagnosing equipment failures and designing new equipment" (p. 23).

El-Najdawi and Stylianou (1993) states that:

Expert systems are computer programs that incorporate the knowledge of one or more human experts in a narrow problem domain and can solve problems that the expert(s) ordinarily solve. The major reasons a company may want to use an ES include:

- *Ability to capture critical expertise,*
- *Faster application development,*

- *Ability to distribute knowledge,*
- *Desire to gain competitive advantage,*
- *Flexibility to free experts from making repetitive decisions,*
- *Ability to combine knowledge from several experts. (p. 56).*

The originator of the Expert Systems, Edward Feigenbaum, is referred to as the "father of expert systems", having played a crucial role in the development and popularization of ES. Along with other experts, Feigenbaum created the Dendral (1960), an ES chemical analysis that focused on mass spectrometry data for organic chemistry. (Lindsay, Buchanan et al., 1993).

With the rise of ML, the historic evolution of AI in the 2000s intensified after years of advancement, as illustrated in **Figure 3**: Artificial Intelligence Evolution, from Symbiotic AI to Expert Systems and Deep Learning, below. From the Artificial Neural Network (ANN), composed of multiple layers of interconnected nodes or neurons, to the rise of data-driven AI in 2000s and the Open AI in 2015, relying on multifaceted Deep Learning applications used today.

The study of AI reveals a history of dedication, determination, innovation, and the reluctant pursuit of intelligence in machines in an attempt to replicate human intelligence. The milestones showed above summarize the most noteworthy moments in the evolutionary process of AI, from its conceptualization to its implementation in diverse areas of society, shaping aspects of our lives and industries. The promise is that AI technologies will continue to advance, bringing faster and critical changes. A crucial aspect of comprehending AI and the changes lying ahead lies in gaining clarity on the concepts of Machine Learning (ML), Deep Learning (DL), and Neural Networks, see **Figure 4:** AI Framework, below:

Figure 3. Artificial intelligence evolution, from symbiotic AI to expert systems and deep learning: An evolving process

Note*: This figure shows the noteworthy evolution of AI systems from 1960 to 2010, culminating with the application of advances expert systems, big data, and Machine and Deep Learning.*

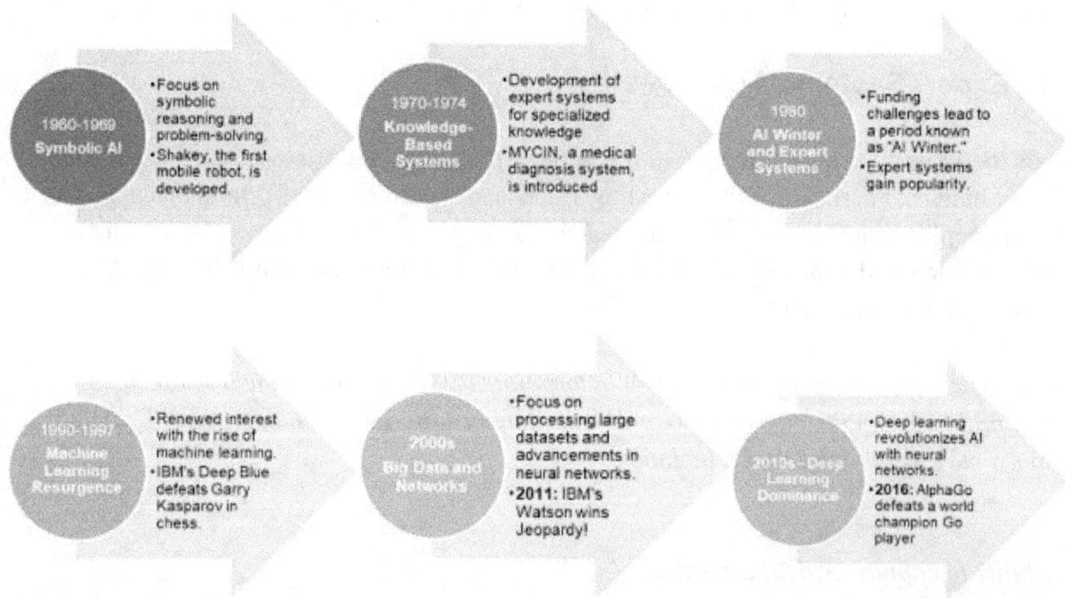

Figure 4. AI framework
Note: *This figure depicts hierarchical structure of AI framework, illustrating the distinctive layers of Machine Earning (ML) and Deep Learning (DL).*

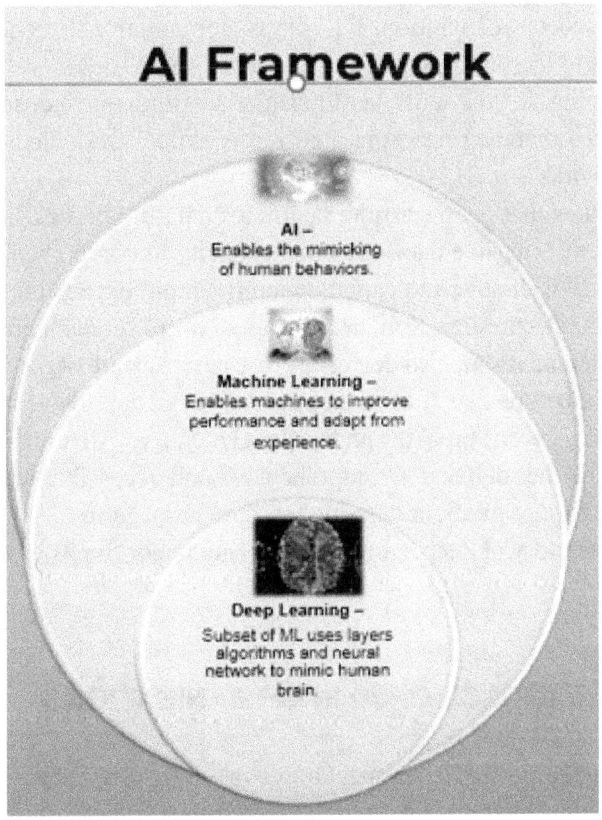

Machine Learning

The process of machine learning involves constructing a workflow and employing highly efficient techniques. It entails instructing a computer system to make precise predictions based on provided data. Following is a concise exploration of prevalent techniques and applications within the field, enabling insight into the different machine learning models for business problems. Mayo (2023) defines that: "Machine learning (ML) is the backbone of artificial intelligence (AI), comprising a suite of algorithms and techniques designed to solve the issues of categorization, clustering, and prediction." (p. 121).

According to the European Commission High-Level Expert Group on Artificial Intelligence (2018), in Machine Learning there are different types of neural networks and machine learning approaches. Deep learning is the most successful, seconded by what is called reinforcement learning and robotics, defined as "AI action in the physical world" (p. 5). In this work the commission stated:

Some machine learning approaches adopt algorithms that are based on the concept of neural networks, which is inspired by the human brain in that it has a network of small processing units (analogously to our neurons) with lots of weighted connections among them. A neural network has as input the data coming from the sensors (in our example, the picture of the floor) and as output the interpretation of the picture (in our example, whether the floor is clean or not). (p. 4)

Deep Learning

Deep learning, particularly deep neural networks, is an AI technology that enables considerable improvement in image and speech recognition. DL allows computational models that are composed of multiple processing layers to learn representations of data with multiple levels of abstraction. Kelleher (2019) defines Deep Learning as: "the subfield of machine learning that focuses on deep neural network models. In fact, the patterns that deep learning algorithms extract from datasets are functions that are represented as neural networks" (p. 8).

Kelleher (2019) illustrates that deep learning facilitates data-driven decision-making by discerning and extracting patterns from extensive datasets. In its capacity to comprehend intricate data positions, deep learning is particularly well-suited to capitalize on the rapid expansion of big data and increased computational power. In his discussion, Kelleher not only covers fundamental deep learning concepts and traces historical advancements but also delves into the current state of the field. The author explores crucial deep learning architectures, such as autoencoders, recurrent neural networks, and long short-term networks, and includes recent breakthroughs like Generative Adversarial Networks and capsule networks. Additionally, Kelleher delivers a comprehensive and accessible introduction to the two pivotal algorithms in deep learning: gradient descent and backpropagation. As a culmination, the author contemplates the future trajectory of deep learning, exploring major trends, potential developments, and significant challenges.

REFLECTING ON THE IMPACT OF AI IN ORGANIZATIONS

Advancements in AI permeate every single aspect of business, industry, segment, and market. It unveils a transformative organizational landscape with multilayered effects. From the perspective of innovation, AI introduces new levels of automation that relieve employees from having to perform mundane tasks, fostering an environment where human ingenuity and creativity can flourish. This automatization process prompts efficiency gains through streamlined processes and data-driven decision-making, propelling organizations toward higher productivity and possibilities for innovation. Conversely, AI automation also induces job displacement, ethical concerns surrounding biased algorithms (Khalil, 1993), regulatory compliance issues, and data security/threat risks. In the study investigating the impact of robotics and AI in business and economics, Dirican (2015) claims that "business and economics will face serious dangers, hits, change, exposures as well as opportunities and gains with the improvements in Artificial Intelligence and Robotics." (p. 564). The author suggests a calculation for depreciation/amortization of rotos in the company, suggesting a new perspective on the human-machine management in organizations and the future of artificial and human intelligence.

Authors Adam, Wessel, and Benlian (2021) investigated the impact of AI in customer service, concluding that: "chatbots continue to displace human service agents, the question arises whether compliance and persuasion techniques, which are intended to influence users to comply with or adapt to a specific request, are equally applicable in these new technology-based self-service settings (p. 428).

The increase in the adoption and integration of AI applications in organizations imposes the urgent need to discuss and implement measures aiming at addressing aspects of workforce transitions and regulatory compliance. Institutions are increasingly adopting machine and deep learning in a variety of operations. The acceptance of AI and all the changes it brings helps mitigate risks in organizational management and leverage the new dynamic landscape ensuring a future where AI contributes positively to both operations and the human experience.

Benefits of AI in organizational data management include:

- **Data and Knowledge Sharing** – It creates an environment that enables broader sharing of data/information across the organization promoting a more effective and faster data and information exchange and, therefore, ways for knowledge sharing and production.
- **Data Management** – More effective way to clean, extract, integrate, catalog, organize, use and store data, providing sophisticated retrieval capabilities.
- **Data Quality** – Superior data quality through the reduction of errors and better management of complex datasets; reduction of errors.
- **Data Integration** – Facilitates the integration of systems that enable more effective data management and governance by utilizing complex integrated and multifaceted information technologies to better respond to the demands of a digital society.
- **Data Security** – Facilitates the safeguard data from threats: internal and external. Generates mechanisms to protect the system from cyber threats and mishandling of data.

Overall, AI will allow data/information systems that are conducive to higher productivity and, therefore, ROI as well user and customer satisfaction. It enables systems integration that enables productivity and innovation through channels of communication and a data flow facilitating the exchange/production of knowledge, illustrated in **Figure 5:** Management of Information Systems, Data Flow, and the outcomes in effective data management though AI in **Figure 6:** Application of AI in Organizations predictive outcomes to improve decision-making, illustrated below:

The data-driven business landscape intertwined with complex expert learning systems support and integrated AI technologies enhance the flow of information, providing a foundation for collaboration and knowledge sharing systems that accelerates the organizational decision-making process. The decision maker now has an intelligent system that uses multiple interfaces of neural language and computing applications to improve data management capabilities and better respond to demands from the external environment and the needs of individuals in the organization.

The core purpose of AI is to help humans with problem solving and reasoning, as well stated by its founders in their studies during decades of work advancing the field and laying the groundwork that is critical to all and everything we do in AI today. Agrawal, Gans, and Goldfarb (2019) claim that: "artificial intelligence can improve decision-making by humans and consequently the productivity of labor, specifically by allowing workers to make state-contingent decisions that reduce errors, enhancing payoffs. (p. 39).

Organizations and leaders have unprecedented access to data to benefit business in efficiency, accuracy, personalized experiences to customers, data monitoring and transparency, and the improvement of business operations and strategies. It is undeniable that challenges in reshaping business involve the reduction of the workforce and a new vision for roles that better suit the needs of the market, the needs of professionals to handle technological advances, and the goal of increasing profitability and remaining competitive. This evolving process is still a blur to many scientists and practitioners because we are only in the beginning stage of this new revolution in generative AI. The future is unclear in terms of what can be accomplished, limited, and challenged. Professions are being extinguished and others created to better respond to the digital environment. Professionals that are anticipated to thrive in the new AI landscape

Figure 5. Management of information systems, data flow

Note*: Figures 5 shows the systematic and dynamic flow of data and information enabled by complex and intertwined AI management systems, leading to advanced predictive analytics that supports decision-making and enhanced business outcomes: stages of progression shown in Figure 6.*

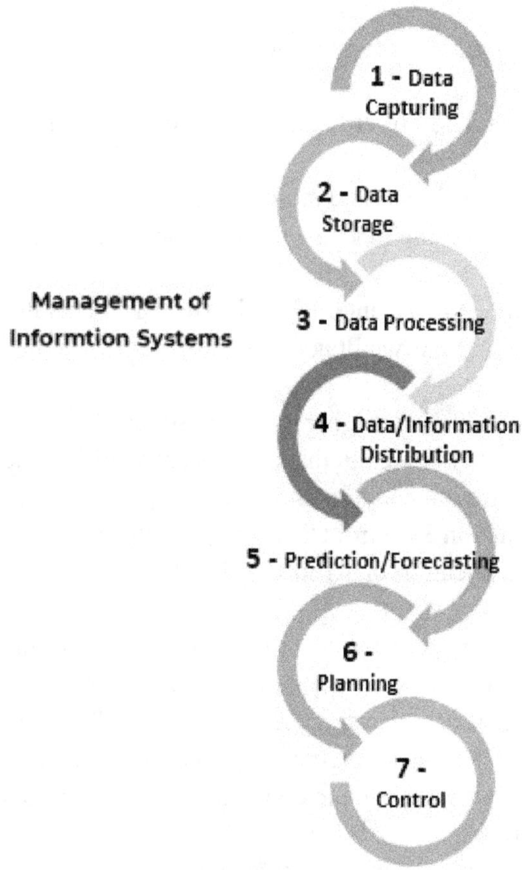

Figure 6. Application of AI in organizations, predictive outcomes to improve decision-making

will have a specific set of skills that combine technical talents and the ability to think critically and apply reasoning to decision making in a fast paced and ever-changing business environment and society. Research has shown that some of these positions include Generative AI Engineer, AI Data Engineer, AI Ethicist, AI Strategists, AI Product Manager, AI Data Governance Manager, among others.

CONCLUSION

A literature review on the inclusion, adoption, and challenges of AI in organizations has pointed out a lack of clarity concerning the possibilities and challenges ahead. The lack of consensus regarding the definition of AI is also evident. The widespread consensus that has resulted from this investigation is that organizations are navigating a series of complexities in a digitally transformative era marked by the implementation of powerful technological innovations transforming society and business processes. This major change is described by Herweijer and Waughray (2018) as the Fourth Industrial Revolution, an era that favors the precise use of data as a cornerstone for success. The importance of AI in organizations cannot be overstated. It plays a transformative role in various segments of society. Organizational aspects being strongly impacted by AI include automation, data analysis and decision-making, customer experience, marketing, predictive analysis, supply chain, cybersecurity, law, and healthcare, to mention a few.

This study focused on the foundation and evolution of AI and its impact in business today. It was based on a literature review, particularly in the studies of seminal researchers and academics in the field of AI. It highlighted the importance in comprehending and adopting new technologies and systems for effectively managing and utilizing data. Throughout this study it was evident that advances in AI are in their most prolific era with a high level of interconnected, complex systems that are intermingling in an unimaginably fast pace. This process is impacting society as a whole and the corporate world, in particular. Organizations must carefully and strategically craft and implement AI business strategies that will ensure preparedness for current and future challenges (Baker-Brunnbauer, 2020), some of which consist of ethics and the responsible use of AI, issues with human collaboration, legal aspects of regulation and data governance, AI dealing with a highly computerized and personalized environment, data forecasting and analytics, regulatory frameworks, ethical considerations, and legal implications.

As evidenced, AI is not a new term or application in business. It has been applied to many facets of business, research, and operations for many decades and in a variety of settings and formats. Organizations are using different AI system with the main objective of adding value to the business and optimize operations (Jarrahi, 2018). These transformations come with social impacts, but also with unmeasurable opportunities. This evolving context is already reshaping the workspace with processes being altered, positions eliminated, and new roles emerging. The future looks promising for organizations leveraging the power of AI and its limitless capabilities through the implementation of complex neural systems and deep learning in automatization and reasoning.

REFERENCES

Adam, M., Wessel, M., & Benlian, A. (2021). AI-based chatbots in customer service and their effects on user compliance. *Electronic Markets*, *31*(2), 427–445. doi:10.1007/s12525-020-00414-7

Agrawal, A., Gans, J. S., & Goldfarb, A. (2019). Artificial Intelligence: The Ambiguous Labor Market Impact of Automating Prediction. *The Journal of Economic Perspectives*, *33*(2), 31–50. https://www.jstor.org/stable/26621238. doi:10.1257/jep.33.2.31

Almeida, F. (2017). Concept and Dimensions of Web 4.0. *International Journal of Computers and Technology*, *16*(7), 7040–7046. doi:10.24297/ijct.v16i7.6446

Antonescu, D. (2018). Are business leaders prepared to handle the upcoming revolution in business artificial intelligence? *Quality - Access to Success*, *19*, 166.

Baker-Brunnbauer, J. (2020). Management perspective of ethics in artificial intelligence. *AI and Ethics*, *1*(2), 173–181. doi:10.1007/s43681-020-00022-3

Ballester, O. (2021). An Artificial Intelligence Definition and Classification Framework for Public Sector Applications. *The 22nd Annual International Conference on Digital Government Research (DG.O'21)*. ACM. 10.1145/3463677.3463709

Bean, R. (2018). How Big Data and AI are driving business innovation in 2018. *MIT Sloan Management Review*.

Brendel, A., Mirbabaie, M., Lembcke, T.-B., & Hofeditz, L. (2021). Ethical Management of Artificial Intelligence. *Sustainability (Basel)*, *13*(4), 1974. doi:10.3390/su13041974

Brown, R. E., & Donald, O. (2020). Hebb and the Organization of Behavior: 17 years in the writing. *Molecular Brain*, *13*(1), 55. doi:10.1186/s13041-020-00567-8 PMID:32252813

Buchanan, B. G., & Smith, R. G. (1988). Fundamentals of expert systems. *Annual Review of Computer Science*, *3*(1), 23–58. doi:10.1146/annurev.cs.03.060188.000323

De Spiegeleire, S., Maas, M., & Sweijs, T. (2017). What is Artificial Intelligence? In: Artificial Intelligence and the Future of Defence Strategic Implications or Small and Medium Sized Force Providers (pp. 25–42). Hague Centre for Strategic Studies. http://www.jstor.org/stable/resrep12564.7

Dirican, C. (2015). The Impacts of Robotics, Artificial Intelligence On Business and Economics. *Procedia - Social and Behavioral Sciences, 195,* 564-573. doi:10.1016/j.sbspro.2015.06.134

El-Najdawi, M. K., & Stylianou, A. C. (1993). Expert support systems: Integrating AI technologies. [-ff.]. *Communications of the ACM*, *36*(12), 55. doi:10.1145/163298.163306

European Commission High-Level Expert Group on Artificial Intelligence. (2018). Definition of AI: Main Capabilities and Scientific Disciplines. Europea. https://ec.europa.eu/futurium/en/system/files/ged/ai_hleg_definition_of_ai_18_december_1.pdf

Hao, K. (2018). What is AI? We drew you a flowchart to work it out. *City (London, England)*.

Hebb, D. O. (1949). The organization of behavior; a neuropsychological theory. NY: Wiley.

Herweijer, C., & Waughray, D. (2018). *Fourth industrial revolution for the Earth harnessing artificial intelligence for the Earth, PWC*. World Economic Forum.

Holdren, J. P. & Smith, M. (2016). *Preparing for the future of artificial intelligence*. Executive Office of the President National Science *a*nd Technology Council Committee on Technology.

Jarrahi, M. H. (2018). Artificial intelligence and the future of work: Human-AI symbiosis in organizational decision making. *Business Horizons*, *61*(4), 577–586. doi:10.1016/j.bushor.2018.03.007

Kelleher, J. (2019). *Deep Learning*. MIT Press. doi:10.7551/mitpress/11171.001.0001

Khalil, O. E. M. (1993). Artificial Decision-Making and Artificial Ethics: A Management Concern. *Journal of Business Ethics*, *12*(4), 313–321. https://www.jstor.org/stable/25072403. doi:10.1007/BF01666535

Lindsay, R., Buchanan, B., Feigenbaum, E., Lederberg, J. (1993). DENDRAL: a case study of the hypothesis formation. *Artificial Intelligence, 61*. Elsevier.

Mayo, S. M. (2023). Restrictions, Challenges and Opportunities for AI and ML. *International Journal of Innovations in Science & Technology*, *5*(2), 121–132.

McCarthy, J., Minsky, M., Rochester, N., & Shannon, C. (1955). A proposal for the Dartmouth Summer Research Project on Artificial Intelligence; 1955. *Computer History*. https://archive.computerhistory.org/resources/access/text/2023/06/102720392-05-01-acc.pdf

McCulloch, Warren. S., & Pitts, W. (1990). A logical calculus of the ideas immanent in nervous activity, Bulletin of Mathematical Biology, 52(1–2). 1990, pp. 99-115. ISSN 0092-8240, doi:10.1016/S0092-8240(05)80006-0

Menabrea, L. F. (1842). Notions sur la machine analytique de M. Charles Babbage. In: Bibliothèque Universelle de Genève. Nouvelle Série, 41, 352-376.

Minsky, M. L. (1966). Artificial Intelligence. *Scientific American*, *215*(3), 246–263. https://www.jstor.org/stable/24931058. doi:10.1038/scientificamerican0966-246

Nikiforova, A., Alor Flores, M. A., & Lytras, M. D. (2023). The Role Of Open Data In The Transformation To Society 5.0: A Resource Or A Tool For SDG-Compliant Smart Living? In Smart Cities and Digital Transformation Empowering Communities, Limitless Innovation, Sustainable Development and the Next Generation (pp. 219-252). Emerald Publishing Limited.

O'Leary, D. E. (2013). Artificial Intelligence and Big Data. *IEEE Intelligent Systems*, *28*(2), 96–99. doi:10.1109/MIS.2013.39

Peeters, M. M., van Diggelen, J., van den Bosch, K., Bronkhorst, A. W., Neerincx, M. A., Schraagen, J. M., & Raaijmakers, S. (2020). Hybrid collective intelligence in a human–AI society. *AI & Society*, *36*(1), 217–238. doi:10.1007/s00146-020-01005-y

Plastino, E., & Purdy, M. (2018). Game changing value from Artificial Intelligence: Eight strategies. *Strategy and Leadership*, *46*(1), 16–22. doi:10.1108/SL-11-2017-0106

Reim, W., Åström, J., & Eriksson, O. (2020). Implementation of Artificial Intelligence (AI): A Roadmap for Business Model Innovation. *AI*, *1*(2), 180–191. MDPI AG. doi:10.3390/ai1020011

Russel, S., & Norvig, P. (2009). *Artificial Intelligence: A Modern Approach. Prentice Hall PressOne*. NJ ISBN.

Samoili, S., López Cobo, M., Gómez, E., De Prato, G., Martínez-Plumed, F., & Delipetrev, B. (2020). Defining Artificial Intelligence. Towards an operational definition and taxonomy of artificial intelligence. EUR 30117 EN. Publications Office of the European Union, Luxembourg. doi:10.2760/382730

Sen, E., Yilmaz, O., & Mert, G. (2020). *Data, Information and Knowledge Management*. Nobel Bilimsel Eserler.

Sousa, W. G. d., Melo, E. R. P. d., Bermejo, P. H. D. S., Farias, R. A. S. & Gomes, A. O. How and where is artificial intelligence in the public sector going? A literature review and research agenda. *Government Information Quarterly, 36*(4).

Turing, A. M. (1950). Computing Machinery and Intelligence. *Mind*, *LIX*(236), 433–460. doi:10.1093/mind/LIX.236.433

Widder, D. G., West, S., & Whittaker, M. (2023). Open (For Business): Big Tech, Concentrated Power, and the Political Economy of Open AI. SSRN *Electronic Journal*. doi:10.2139/ssrn.4543807

Chapter 2
AI-Driven Data Analytics in Information Sciences and Organizational Management

Ayse Asli Yilmaz
https://orcid.org/0000-0003-1784-7307
Atilim University, Turkey

ABSTRACT

The integration of many technologies has led to the emergence of a rapidly evolving discipline known as 'AI-driven data analytics.' This enables both information scientists and organisational managers to effectively derive practical insights from intricate datasets by using machine learning algorithms, natural language processing, and data mining techniques. This encompasses an examination of machine learning algorithms and their function in revealing patterns and associations in data, along with the importance of natural language processing in extracting insights from unstructured textual data. AI-powered data analysis and visualisation and facilitates predictive analytics—all while augmenting the transmission of intricate data via interactive visual representations—are analysied. This chapter presents a thorough examination of the transformational potential of artificial intelligence (AI) in the field of data analytics. It highlights the dynamic characteristics of AI and emphasises the boundless opportunities it presents in the contemporary digital era.

INTRODUCTION

The integration of artificial intelligence with data analytics has brought about a significant transformation in several academic fields and enterprises in recent times. The disciplines of information sciences and organisational management have seen developments, with far-reaching impacts across several sectors. The current shift in paradigm is distinguished by the integration of artificial intelligence and data analytics (Batra, 2020). This integration has brought forth a new era of exceptional opportunities and capabilities, providing organisations with the ability to extract highly valuable insights, optimise operations, and make informed decisions based on data in the context of digital transformation. The

DOI: 10.4018/979-8-3693-1058-8.ch002

convergence of artificial intelligence and data analytics has led to the emergence of a rapidly developing discipline known as “AI-Driven Data Analytics.” This field is characterised by its dynamic nature and continuous evolution. The fundamental essence of AI-Driven Data Analytics is in its distinctive capacity to enable information scientists and organisational managers to use the tremendous potential of AI in order to extract actionable insights from extensive and complex datasets (Kar & Kushwaha, 2021). At its essence, this phenomenon is a symbiotic relationship between sophisticated computational intelligence and the continuously growing abundance of digital information, including both organised and unorganised forms. AI-Driven Data Analytics presents a comprehensive methodology for data analysis by integrating machine learning algorithms, natural language processing, and data mining methods. This approach enables organisations to get insights into historical and current data, while also helping them to forecast and influence future outcomes (Dwivedi et al, 2023). The recently acquired ability described here represents a significant and impactful influence, beyond conventional data analytics and reshaping the limits of what can be accomplished in the fields of information sciences and organisational management (Vernadat et al., 2018). This covers a thorough examination of the significant impact of AI-Driven Data Analytics on the current landscape of information sciences and organisational management. In this analysis, it is thoroughly explored the diverse range of applications associated with the subject, examined the obstacles it poses, and scrutinized the ethical principles that constitute the foundation of its potential for transformation. As the investigation is embarked on, it is discovered how this novel amalgamation is redefining the fundamental nature of information utilisation, and how it is driving enterprises towards achieving data-driven excellence and enduring success. Upon the conclusion of this scholarly expedition, a deep comprehension of the transformative change in thinking instigated by AI-Driven Data Analytics is acquired. This shift has not only redefined the parameters of extracting knowledge but has also fundamentally altered the essence of contemporary organisational management.

THE SYMBIOTIC RELATIONSHIP OF AI AND DATA ANALYTICS

The convergence of Artificial intelligence with data analytics signifies a dynamic and swiftly progressing domain that stands at the forefront of technological advancement. The integration of these two revolutionary realms has the potential to redefine sectors, reshape corporate strategies, and improve decision-making processes (Vernadat et al., 2018). It aims to reveal the many ways in which they cooperate to facilitate the emergence of a new age characterised by the pursuit of excellence via data-driven approache (Gupta et al.,2023).

The incorporation of artificial intelligence into data analytics is fundamentally indicative of the inherent progression of these two domains. The use of data analytics has historically played a crucial role in extracting valuable insights from data. However, the integration of artificial intelligence technology has significantly enhanced this process, pushing it to unprecedented levels of effectiveness and efficiency. It begins by examining the first use of AI in statistical analysis and then explores its progression towards modern applications such as machine learning, natural language processing, and computer vision Jöhnk et al., 2021) The historical analysis provides insight into the gradual integration of artificial intelligence into the field of data analytics, enabling organisations to effectively manage the intricate nature of contemporary data environments.Machine learning, an influential subfield of artificial intelligence, assumes a crucial role in facilitating the collaboration between AI and data analytics. This discussion explores a range of machine learning approaches and algorithms often used in the field of data analytics, including supervised learning, unsupervised learning, and reinforcement learning (Weber et al,2023). These algorithms enable organisations to autonomously detect patterns, anomalies, and correlations within data, providing a data-centric framework for decision-making that is characterised by efficiency and adaptability in response to dynamic conditions (Yablosky,2020). Natural language processing (NLP) is an essential component of the convergence between artificial intelligence and data analytics. This technological advancement facilitates the retrieval of useful insights from unstructured textual data, hence providing opportunities for sentiment analysis, topic modelling, and language translation. This delves into the use of natural language processing (NLP) algorithms in extracting valuable insights from various textual data sources, including but not limited to social media material, consumer reviews, and scientific publications. In the current epoch characterised by the abundance of multimedia data, computer vision serves as a compelling example of the profound impact of artificial intelligence in the realm of data analytics. In this discussion, it is explored the use of computer vision algorithms for the purpose of analysing and interpreting visual data (Böhmer&Schinnenburg,2023). This technological capability has facilitated the development of many applications across a wide range of sectors, including health-care (specifically, medical image analysis), retail (in the context of visual product identification), and autonomous vehicles (primarily in the domain of image-based navigation) (Jöhnk et al., 2021).

The incorporation of artificial intelligence technology into the field of data analytics not only serves to improve the efficiency of data processing, but also has significant consequences for the decision-making processes involved. The use of AI-Driven Data Analytics enables organisations to enhance their decision-making processes by using data-driven insights, resulting in improved operational efficiency and the attainment of strategic benefits. In this discourse, it is examined the forthcoming patterns, specifically elucidating AI and ethical deliberations, that are poised to influence the progression of this ever-evolving domain. In addition, the obstacles and constraints that organisations need to confront in their efforts to fully use the capabilities of AI-Driven Data Analytics are diiscussed. It establishes the context which will further investigate the methodology, applications, and real-world instances within this dynamic domain (Boire, 2017). Upon the culmination of this scholarly expedition, individuals will have acquired an all-encompassing comprehension of the integration of artificial intelligence technologies into the realm of data analytics. This integration seamlessly intertwines with the very essence of data analytics, providing enterprises with the necessary instruments to unveil the concealed value inherent in their data. Consequently, these organisations are empowered to achieve triumph in a world that is progressively centred around data (Batra, 2020).

AI-DRIVEN DATA COLLECTION AND PREPROCESSING

The integration of artificial intelligence has had a significant impact on the collection, cleaning, and preparation of data in the dynamic field of data analytics. The use of AI approaches in data collecting and preprocessing signifies a significant transformation, as it enables the automation and enhancement of procedures that were previously reliant on human efforts and consumed substantial amounts of time (Ghosh, 2016). It has the significant role of artificial intelligence in the foundational phases of data analytics. It emphasises the transformative impact of AI on data gathering methods, the reduction of human involvement, and the improvement of data preparation activities in terms of quality and efficiency. The collecting of data has historically been a fundamental aspect of data analytics, and artificial intelligence has recently emerged as a transformative force within this domain (Böhmer &Schinnenburg,2023). This analysis explores the ways in which artificial intelligence technologies facilitate the acquisition of data from many sources, including structured databases, unstructured text, and multimedia content. The use of AI-driven data collecting techniques has expanded beyond the constraints of conventional data gathering approaches, encompassing web scraping, sensor data capture, and real-time data streaming. This advancement enables organisations to efficiently amass extensive quantities of data, surpassing previous boundaries. One of the most notable characteristics of data collecting powered by artificial intelligence is its ability to engage in data mining and pattern detection. The use of machine learning algorithms in the analysis of extensive datasets, with the objective of discerning significant patterns, trends, and anomalies has effection on this advencement. (Cetindamar et al.,2022). With this approach, organisations are able to get more profound understandings of their data, hence revealing concealed information that can be used to guide strategic decision-making processes. The process of data collection often results in the presence of noise and imperfections within the gathered data. The use of artificial intelligence in data preparation expands its functionalities to include tasks such as data cleansing and quality improvement. This explicates the way artificial intelligence algorithms have the capability to autonomously identify and correct mistakes, missing values, and inconsistencies present inside datasets (Trocin et al.,2021). This leads to the generation of data that is not only characterised by increased reliability but also facilitates the use of sophisticated analytics methodologies. The process of data transformation is a crucial component in the preparation of data for analysis. The process of data preparation is automated and optimised via the use of AI-driven methodologies, such as feature engineering. In this discussion, it is explored the capacity of artificial intelligence to generate novel attributes and convert data into forms that are more suitable for targeted analytical endeavours: (Zhang et al., 2023) This capability serves to augment the comprehensiveness and intricacy of the information accessible for analysis. In the realm of data preparation, the use of Natural Language Processing (NLP) emerges as a potent instrument. This paper examines the use of natural language processing (NLP) methods for the purpose of processing unstructured textual data (AI-based Natural Language Processing (NLP) Systems, 2020). It focuses on the extraction of structured information from textual sources, as well as the facilitation of sentiment analysis, text categorization, and entity identification. The rise of AI-driven data collecting and preprocessing has led to a growing emphasis on ethical issues and legal compliance. Within this area, the ethical dilemmas and contemplations that need the attention of organisations while using artificial intelligence for the purposes of data gathering and preprocessing are discussed. This study investigates current developments in the field, specifically focusing on federated learning and data privacy. It also explores the potential obstacles that organisations may face as they strive to push the limits of what can be accomplished in data preparation (Tono & Okumura, 2020)..The efficacy of data analytics heavily relies on the efficient gathering and preparation of data. This investigation aims to provide readers with a thorough comprehension of how artificial intelligence is transforming these essential procedures, empowering organisations to get more value from their data and advancing the capabilities of data analytics in the era of digitalization (Haney, 2020).

AI-POWERED DATA ANALYSIS AND VISUALIZATION

In the contemporary age of data analytics, the use of artificial intelligence to drive data analysis and visualisation stands as a notable achievement in technical progress. The profound influence of artificial intelligence on the complete procedures of analysing complex facts and creating informative visual representations provide great assistance on the field of data analysis. It has been significantly transformed by the advent of AI technology (Prasertsuk & Busayarat, 2022). These advancements have not only enabled the identification of concealed patterns and trends but have also provided a mechanism to effectively present these findings in a visually appealing and easily understandable format. The use of artificial intelligence in data analysis facilitates the automation of processes, allowing organisations to efficiently navigate intricate information. This analysis explores the way artificial intelligence algorithms, including machine learning and deep learning methodologies, effectively handle extensive quantities of data with unparalleled velocity and accuracy. These algorithms have the capability to execute many tasks like classification, clustering, regression, and anomaly detection, hence revealing significant insights that may otherwise stay concealed inside the dataset (Slomiany et al., 2018).

One notable characteristic of data analysis driven by artificial intelligence is its ability to recognise patterns and conduct predictive analytics. This study investigates the ability of AI systems to autonomously detect recurring patterns and trends within datasets, hence enabling the use of both descriptive and predictive analytics. Organisations have the ability to use these insights in order to make well-informed choices, predict future trends, and proactively adapt to changing situations (Haney, 2020). The proper communication of data is essential for its transformation from inert information to valuable insights. AI-driven data visualisation surpasses conventional techniques by presenting information in a visually captivating and easily understandable way. This section focuses on the art of creating data visualisations that effectively enlighten and captivate the audience. This discourse pertains to the use of artificial intelligence in the development of interactive dashboards, infographics, and data-driven storytelling. These applications are recognised as potent instruments for effectively communicating intricate information (Zhang et al., 2023).Furthermore, the use of artificial intelligence in data analysis encompasses not just visual data but also unstructured textual data. This study examines the use of Natural Language Processing (NLP) methods in the analysis and extraction of significant insights from textual sources. These insights provide a substantial amount of information that can be utilised to influence decision-making and strategic planning.

The need for real-time data analysis has seen a significant increase due to the emergence of artificial intelligence. This section delves into the ways in which AI technologies enable real-time data processing, enabling organisations to make immediate choices based on live data streams. This paper examines the many uses of real-time data analysis in domains like financial trading, healthcare monitoring, and internet of things (IoT) systems. The increasing sophistication and widespread use of AI-powered data analysis need a heightened focus on ethical problems. (Cofre-Martel et al., 2021) This paper explores the ethical dilemmas and considerations that arise from the use of artificial intelligence in the realm of data analysis. It encompasses an examination of concerns pertaining to bias, transparency, and privacy. The last section of this examines the prospective advancements in data analysis and visualisation facilitated by artificial intelligence. This study examines upcoming developments in the field of artificial intelligence, specifically focusing on explainable AI and augmented analytics (Boire,2017). Additionally, it delves into the potential problems that both organisations and researchers may encounter as they strive to expand the scope of AI's involvement in data analysis. The use of AI-powered techniques for data analysis and visualisation plays a crucial role in facilitating organisations to fully leverage the value of their data. This provides a thorough comprehension of how artificial intelligence enhances the process of data analysis, including many stages such as data exploration and visualisation. This augmentation enables individuals to make better informed decisions and effectively communicate the insights derived from the study. This statement highlights the transformative impact of AI technology on data analysis, emphasising its dynamic nature and ability to reimagine the possibilities inside the digital era (Prasad Agrawal, 2023).

AI-ENABLED PREDICTIVE ANALYTICS: ANTICIPATING THE FUTURE

AI-enabled predictive analytics is a groundbreaking advancement in the field of veri science and decision-making. It enables the utilisation of past data to anticipate future results with an unprecedented level of accuracy, a capability that was previously inconceivable. This explores the capabilities of artificial intelligence in analysing past data and generating data-driven predictions on future events, trends, and behaviours. Through the use of sophisticated machine learning algorithms, robust data processing skills, and specialised knowledge in a particular field, organisations have the potential to extract important insights, transform their decision-making procedures, and acquire a competitive advantage within a dynamic and constantly changing environment (Cetindamar et al.,2022).The field of predictive analytics, which has traditionally relied on statistical models, has seen a significant transformation with the integration of artificial intelligence. This paper examines the historical development of predictive analytics and the ways in which advancements in artificial intelligence technology have significantly enhanced its capabilities. The field of AI-powered predictive analytics has evolved from using basic regression models to employing intricate neural networks, enabling a multidimensional approach capable of effectively processing extensive and heterogeneous information (Trocin et al., 2021).Machine learning serves as the fundamental framework for predictive analytics provided by artificial intelligence. This section explores a range of machine learning approaches used in the construction of predictive models, such as regression analysis, decision trees, support vector machines, and deep learning. This study emphasises the process by which these models acquire knowledge from past data and provide well-informed predictions, ranging from sales projections to healthcare results. The scope of predictive analytics goes beyond numerical predictions, including the ability to foresee trends and get insights into client behaviours (Giernindl et al.,2022). In this discourse, the capacity of AI-driven prediction models to forecast market trends, discern client preferences, and identify emerging patterns is scrutinized. Thus, this enables organisations to proactively make choices and customise their plans in order to successfully fulfil the demands of their customers. Resource allocation and optimisation is considered a crucial use of predictive analytics. AI-driven prediction models assist organisations in optimising resource allocation, including budgetary, personnel, and inventory management, to achieve maximum efficiency and cost-effectiveness (Maleh et al.,2023). This study investigates the potential impact of optimisation on organisational performance enhancement and waste reduction. The effectiveness of AI-enabled predictive analytics is not just dependent on algorithms, but also on the incorporation of domain knowledge Grover et al.,2018). The significance of domain knowledge is underscored throughout the process of refining prediction models, analysing outcomes, and formulating actionable recommendations. The optimal predictive analytics outcomes are achieved by the collaborative integration of artificial intelligence and human knowledge. In order to demonstrate the tangible effects of predictive analytics facilitated by artificial intelligence, concrete examples and empirical analyses of its implementation in diverse sectors are given. The aforementioned instances exemplify the transformative impact of AI-driven predictive models across several industries, ranging from predictive maintenance in manufacturing to fraud detection in finance. The use of AI-driven predictive analytics gives rise to ethical and transparency considerations. This study explores the ethical dilemmas linked to predictive analytics, including issues such as bias present in both data and algorithms, with the need of openness and comprehensibility (Chen et al.,2015).This finishes by examining the prospective developments and implications of AI-enabled predictive analytics. This study investigates the growing patterns in augmented analytics, whereby artificial intelligence not only forecasts future outcomes but also provides explanations for the underlying variables contributing to such predictions. Furthermore, an examination is conducted on the potential difficulties that organisations may face when attempting to adopt and use the capabilities of predictive analytics within a context that heavily relies on data.AI-enabled predictive analytics plays a crucial role in facilitating data-driven decision-making and serves as a powerful instrument for organisations aiming to forecast future outcomes with certainty (Ghosh,2016). This provides a thorough examination of the ways in which artificial intelligence, when used in conjunction with historical data, may empower organisations to make predictions and enhance their plans, hence leading to enhanced performance and competitiveness within a rapidly evolving and data-driven landscape (Schildt,2017).

AI FOR OPERATIONAL EFFICIENCY AND PROCESS OPTIMIZATION

In the current era characterised by digital transformation and the reliance on data-driven decision-making, the convergence of artificial intelligence and operational efficiency has emerged as a significant and transformational phenomenon. This delves into the significant influence of artificial intelligence on improving company operations and procedures, facilitating the smooth flow of tasks, and promoting optimisation across several sectors (Sun et al.,2018). Using artificial intelligence, organisations are granted the ability to automate various jobs, enhance decision-making processes, and optimise operational procedures. Consequently, this enables them to attain heightened levels of efficiency, productivity, and cost-effectiveness. The use of artificial intelligence in enhancing operational efficiency signifies the progression of optimising corporate processes Dwivedi ety al., 2023). This paper examines the historical progression of artificial intelligence's (AI) involvement in optimising operational processes, beginning with early automation systems and culminating in the present-day use of cognitive technologies. The inclusion of this historical viewpoint offers a contextual framework for comprehending the contemporary impact of artificial intelligence on operational efficiency. The use of artificial intelligence in process automation has become a fundamental aspect of enhancing operational efficiency (Maleh et al.,2023). This study investigates the use of robotic process automation (RPA) and AI-based automation technologies in the execution of repetitive and rule-based operations, achieving unparalleled levels of accuracy and speed (Ghosh, 2018). This not only enables the allocation of human resources to more important activities, but also serves to reduce mistakes and enhance operational consistency. The supply chain plays a crucial role in the efficient functioning of corporate operations, and artificial intelligence has emerged as a pivotal tool for enhancing its optimisation. In this discourse, the use of artificial intelligence technologies, such as predictive analytics and demand forecasting, to augment the management of supply chains are insighted. So,it encompasses several aspects, ranging from inventory control to the optimisation of logistics. (Singh, 2022). The use of AI-driven solutions plays a crucial role in attaining cost reductions and enhancing customer satisfaction. Efficient operational performance relies heavily on the implementation of effective inventory management strategies and accurate demand forecasting techniques (Singh, 2022). This section explores the capabilities of AI models in the analysis of historical data, prediction of future demand, and optimisation of inventory levels. Organisations may achieve cost reduction and improve customer experience by using strategies to avoid excess inventory and stockouts.

The function of artificial intelligence in enhancing operational efficiency include workforce planning and resource allocation. This discussion focuses on the use of AI-driven models to enhance personnel levels, allocate tasks effectively, and optimise resource allocation (Kedziora, 2022). This enables organisations to optimise productivity and efficiently allocate resources. This provides a comprehensive overview of real-world applications and case studies across diverse sectors, serving to exemplify the ways in which artificial intelligence contributes to the optimisation of operational efficiency. Illustrative instances include the use of artificial intelligence within the healthcare sector to enhance the efficiency of patient flow, in the manufacturing industry to facilitate predictive maintenance, and in the retail domain to enable dynamic pricing strategies (Slomiany et al., 2018). These instances provide valuable insights into the tangible advantages of artificial intelligence in optimising operational processes. The incorporation of artificial intelligence into the enhancement of operational efficiency gives rise to ethical concerns that need attention and resolution by organisations. The subjects such as bias in AI algorithms, transparency, and the effect of AI on the workforce are studied. The incorporation of ethical issues is of utmost importance to guarantee that the enhancement of operational efficiency via AI is equitable, accountable, and in accordance with the values upheld by society (Robotic Process Automation (RPA) Implementation Drivers: Evidence of Selected Nordic Companies," 2021). This finishes by examining the evolving landscape of AI for operational efficiency, including new trends such as AI-powered decision support systems. Additionally, So, this addresses the potential problems that organisations may have when implementing AI-driven solutions for operational efficiency (Prasertsuk & Busayarat, 2022). This analysis provides valuable perspectives on the potential implications of artificial intelligence in enhancing and streamlining corporate operations.AI for operational efficiency and process optimization is a crucial driver of competitiveness and innovation in contemporary enterprises (Slomiany et al., 2018). This offers a comprehensive analysis of the potential of AI to enable organisations to enhance their operations, enhance decision-making processes, and ultimately attain greater levels of efficiency, productivity, and cost-effectiveness within a dynamic business environment.

AI AND CUSTOMER RELATIONS: ELEVATING THE CUSTOMER EXPERIENCE

The incorporation of artificial intelligence into consumer interactions is enabling the emergence of a new age typified by an emphasis on customer-centricity. This examines the transformative influence of artificial intelligence on the way enterprises engage with their customers. The primary emphasis is placed on the delivery of tailored experiences, the enhancement of customer interactions, and the simplification of support operations (Indah Febriyanti & Tuti, 2023) Artificial intelligence has emerged as a formidable weapon for boosting consumer interactions, helping not just the development of client loyalty but also the stimulation of business growth. The integration of artificial intelligence into the realm of consumer interactions is a departure from traditional customer service models. Within the confines of this specific setting, an analysis of the evolutionary path of artificial intelligence, starting with the emergence of basic chatbots and concluding in the contemporary sophisticated customer experience platforms is gone onto. This extensive historical research provides valuable insights into the revolutionary effects of artificial intelligence on the dynamics of customer-business contact (Indah Febriyanti & Tuti, 2023). The incorporation of personalisation has become a crucial element in modern consumer engagements, whereby artificial intelligence plays a major role in facilitating this transforming procedure. This research examines the methodology through which artificial intelligence algorithms assess large datasets to provide personalised consumer experiences based on individual preferences. The use of personalization techniques is of utmost importance in cultivating customer engagement and loyalty (Customer Experience and Satisfaction: Importance of Customer Reviews and Customer Value on Buying Preference," 2023). This encompasses a variety of methods, including the provision of tailored product recommendations and the utilisation of personalised marketing communications. The use of sentiment analysis by artificial intelligence has introduced innovative prospects for understanding and managing customer emotions. This study investigates the use of artificial intelligence technology in the examination of customer feedback, reviews, and social media interactions to evaluate sentiment. This process enables enterprises to get vital information on customer satisfaction, so allowing them to proactively implement steps aimed at improving the customer experience (Eketu, 2016). The customer journey has considerable significance in the management of customer contacts, with artificial intelligence playing a crucial part in the mapping and enhancement of this experience. This discourse aims to examine the potential of artificial intelligence in analysing consumer interactions across several touchpoints, hence creating comprehensive customer journey maps. These maps provide valuable insights into areas that have the potential for improvement, allowing firms to optimise the client experience at every stage (Rachmawati & Utami, 2021). The use of artificial intelligence-driven chatbots and virtual assistants has significantly altered the customer service domain. This research examines the potential of artificial intelligence-powered systems in efficiently responding to customer inquiries, automating repetitive tasks, and offering continuous support. This strategy enhances customer satisfaction and enables the allocation of human agents to address more complex issues. The presents factual facts and case studies to illustrate the concrete benefits of using artificial intelligence in consumer interactions. The examples offered include several industries, such as e-commerce and healthcare, demonstrating the way artificial intelligence enhances customer engagement and cultivates loyalty. The ethical dilemmas associated with the growing incorporation of artificial intelligence in consumer interactions are becoming more prominent (Ningsih & Hurnis, 2023). The present research investigates the ethical quandaries linked to artificial intelligence, with a particular emphasis on concerns related to the safeguarding of data privacy, the presence of prejudice, and the level of openness. Moreover, this study examines alternative ways that enterprises may use to successfully address these challenges, hence maintaining confidence and promoting ethical utilisation of artificial intelligence. The last portion of it explores the potential developments of artificial intelligence in the realm of client interactions (Sabrina et al., 2023). This research investigates emerging patterns, such as voice interfaces powered by artificial intelligence, and the possible challenges that businesses may have as they continue to incorporate and enhance the utilisation of AI technology within their customer-centric approach. The use of artificial intelligence into consumer interactions has become a fundamental component of the modern business landscape. This provides a comprehensive examination of the potential impact of artificial intelligence on improving consumer experiences, fostering customer loyalty, and driving businesses towards new levels of success. In the contemporary digital landscape, enterprises are confronted with the mounting demands of consumers, hence necessitating the use of artificial intelligence as an imperative rather than a mere option (Tulcanaza-Prieto et al., 2023.)

ETHICAL CONSIDERATIONS IN AI-DRIVEN DATA ANALYTICS

The incorporation of artificial intelligence into the field of data analytics has presented several opportunities, allowing organisations to extract useful insights from data on an unprecedented level. Nevertheless, the possession of significant authority necessitates the assumption of considerable obligations. The ethical issues surrounding AI-driven data analytics are of utmost importance in order to guarantee that the use of AI technology in data analysis is carried out in a way that preserves individual rights, prevents damage, and maintains social values (Rachmawati & Utami, 2021). The increasing prevalence of AI-driven data analytics necessitates that organisations prioritise the resolution of ethical challenges in order to establish trust, mitigate the risk of abuse, and foster responsible practises. The integration of artificial intelligence technology into the field of data analytics calls for the establishment of a robust ethical framework (Ningsih & Hurnis, 2023). This study examines the fundamental principles that need to serve as the foundation for the use of artificial intelligence, including the concepts of justice, transparency, accountability, and the safeguarding of individual rights. By embracing and abiding by this ethical framework, organisations can guarantee that their data analytics projects powered by artificial intelligence are executed with a strong sense of integrity Sabrina et al., 2023. The ethical issues of data privacy and security are fundamental in the context of AI-driven data analytics. This paper examines the need for organisations to effectively protect sensitive data, including both personal and private information. Ensuring the preservation of people' privacy necessitates the use of ethical data handling practises, encryption techniques, and safe data storage mechanisms. The presence of bias in AI algorithms is a matter of great ethical significance since it has the potential to perpetuate discriminatory practises and exacerbate existing inequities. This study investigates the methods by which organisations may effectively address prejudice via the implementation of several techniques, including the use of varied and representative training data, the adoption of fairness-aware algorithms, and the establishment of ongoing monitoring mechanisms (Tulcanaza-Prieto et al., 2023). The mitigation of bias is a crucial first measure in guaranteeing the ethicality and impartiality of AI-powered data analytics. transparency is an additional crucial ethical aspect. This study explores the significance of comprehending the decision-making process of AI algorithms, particularly in domains where these judgements might have substantial consequences, such as healthcare or lending. Explainable AI (XAI) and model interpretability are methodologies that facilitate the enhancement of transparency and accountability (Katirai, 2023). This provides real-world applications and case studies to demonstrate the practical ramifications of ethical issues in AI-driven data analytics. The examples exemplify the effective resolution of ethical considerations in AI endeavours by organisations, hence highlighting exemplary methodologies that may be used across diverse sectors (Sivill, 2019). The legal and regulatory framework pertaining to the ethical considerations of artificial intelligence is undergoing fast development. This study focuses on the analysis of prevailing and developing ethical compliance standards and regulatory frameworks that are essential for organisations to conform to Burr & Leslie, 2022. Ethics committees, impact evaluations, and data protection rules play a crucial role in facilitating the ethical adoption of artificial intelligence. The ethical issues associated with AI-driven data analytics transcend technological aspects and include broader organisational culture and values Rice, 2021. This paper examines the significance of including many stakeholders, like as consumers, workers, and the wider society, in the process of ethical decision-making. The establishment of a culture centred on ethics and accountability is crucial in ensuring the sustained and ethical integration of artificial intelligence in many domains (Davis et al., 2022) This finishes by providing an analysis of the future implications of ethical que stions in the context of AI-driven data analytics. This study examines the increasing phenomenon of AI ethics certification and the persistent issues that organisations may have while navigating the intricate ethical terrain of artificial intelligence. Ethical issues are an essential component of AI-driven data analytics since they provide the basis for ethical and sustainable deployment of this technology. Thus, this provides a thorough examination of the strategies organisations may use to effectively navigate ethical considerations while using AI technology in data analytics Baird & Schuller, 2020. The primary objective is to guarantee that these organisations maintain people' rights, mitigate potential damage, and adhere to society norms. By cultivating a milieu that prioritises ethical conduct and accountability, organisations may effectively use the whole capabilities of artificial intelligence in the realm of data analytics, all the while ensuring adherence to the fundamental tenets of fairness, transparency, and accountability (Burr & Leslie, 2022).

CHALLENGES AND PROSPECTS IN ARTIFICIAL INTELLIGENCE-ENABLED DATA ANALYTICS

When organisations commence their efforts to deploy data analytics projects led by artificial intelligence, they encounter several hurdles and uncertainties. This delves into the intricate array of obstacles that organisations may face while navigating the dynamic realm of AI-powered data analytics (Future of Software Testing Using Artificial Intelligence, 2022). This illuminates the promising prospects that await us in this domain (Khan et al., 2023). The incorporation of artificial intelligence into the field of data analytics is not devoid of challenges. This paper explores the potential issues that organisations may have while using AI-driven data analytics, encompassing: The need for data of high quality, which is often dispersed across several sources, poses a notable obstacle in terms of data quality and integration (Khan et al., 2023).The ethical considerations pertaining to AI algorithms include a multifaceted and continuous endeavour, including the examination of ethical dilemmas, bias mitigation, transparency enhancement, and privacy preservation (Loebbecke, 2019). The phenomenon of talent shortage arises when the demand for specialists specialising in artificial intelligence and data analytics surpasses the supply of qualified individuals, hence creating difficulties in the recruiting process (Praful Bharadiya, 2023). The use of AI technology requires significant financial investment and resource allocation, hence presenting financial constraints. The process of effectively managing organisational change and successfully adapting to AI-driven processes may encounter obstacles in the form of opposition and cultural complexities. The future trajectory of AI-driven data analytics is characterised by a multitude of compelling patterns, which encompass, Explainable AI (XAI) refers to the field of research and development focused on creating artificial intelligence systems that can provide understandable and transparent explanations for their decision-making processes and outcomes (Hulsen, 2023). There is a growing emphasis on the development of artificial intelligence models that possess the capability to provide comprehensible explanations for their decision-making processes. This emphasis aims to improve transparency and foster confidence in AI systems.

The integration of artificial intelligence technology will persist in enhancing human decision-making processes via the provision of actionable insights, automation of insights creation, and facilitation of data exploration. The use of artificial intelligence for the purpose of delivering personalised customer experiences is an emerging trend that is expected to expand further (Nahm, 2023). This development is anticipated to yield enhanced marketing strategies and improved customer relations. The use of artificial intelligence in the context of sustainability is expected to gain increased prominence. This involves using AI techniques to tackle environmental and sustainability issues, including but not limited to energy optimisation and climate modelling.

The core focus of this discussion will revolve on the ethical issues and responsible use of artificial intelligence. This will be accompanied by the implementation of enhanced regulatory frameworks and certifications. The prospective ramifications of artificial intelligence on the fields of information sciences and organisational administration are significant (Rachmawati & Utami, 2021). In this discourse, the transformative impact of AI-powered data analytics on many disciplines, encompassing bythe use of artificial intelligence is revolutionising the decision-making process inside organisations, as it facilitates the integration of data-driven insights into strategic planning.Additionally,the allocation of resources is being redefined by the optimisation and automation of artificial intelligence, which encompasses the efficient distribution of money and human capital to achieve optimum outcomes.The deployment of AI needs a culture transformation that emphasises the importance of data-centric thinking and ethical responsibilities inside organisations (Asbaş & Tuzlukaya 2023).

Organisations that successfully harness the potential of artificial intelligence are able to attain a substantial competitive edge within their respective sectors. As this draw to a close, it is imperative to underscore the significance of establishing a comprehensive framework to facilitate the responsible deployment of artificial intelligence. This framework incorporates several aspects including ethical concerns, regulatory compliance, talent development, and an organisational culture that places importance on openness and responsibility in artificial intelligence activities (Loebbecke, 2019). This provides readers with a thorough comprehension of the obstacles that organisations can encounter in their data analytics initiatives powered by artificial intelligence (Nahm, 2023). Additionally, it offers an intriguing preview of the potential future of artificial intelligence in the fields of information sciences and organisational management. The extensive capacity of artificial intelligence to stimulate innovation and revolutionise many sectors is considerable; yet its full potential can only be achieved via the conscientious and ethical execution of its deployment. This functions as a foundational resource for both organisations and academics to effectively traverse the intricate realm of AI-powered data analytics within a swiftly changing global context.

CONCLUSION

In the contemporary era characterised by the prevalence of data, the integration of artificial intelligence and data analytics has emerged as a potent combination, revolutionising the practises, strategies, and success of organisations. In the course of this literary work, the complex terrain of data analytics propelled by artificial intelligence are traversed, delving into its diverse range of applications, ethical implications, and the obstacles it presents, all the while picturing its auspicious prospects. As the culmination of the scholarly journey is appreciated, it is essential to summarise the principal discoveries and underscore the significant contribution that AI-powered data analytics offers to the data-centric society.

The integration of artificial intelligence and data analytics has transitioned from being a new concept to being an essential need. This technology enables organisations to harness the whole potential of their data, converting it from raw information into actionable insights that facilitate achievement. As seen, artificial intelligence enhances the processes of data gathering, preprocessing, analysis, and visualisation, hence automating arduous activities and providing unmatched levels of accuracy and efficiency. The technology introduces a new phase of predictive analytics, so allowing organisations to proactively forecast forthcoming trends and client behaviours.

Consequently, this facilitates the optimisation of processes and resource allocation. The advancement revolutionises the dynamics of client connections by facilitating personalised experiences, augmenting support services, and cultivating customer loyalty. The significance of data analytics powered by artificial intelligence cannot be exaggerated. The statement highlights the crucial role played by this entity in guiding decision-making processes, uncovering concealed possibilities, and upholding ethical principles, fairness, and appropriate utilisation of data. In a highly competitive global landscape characterised by intense rivalry, continuous innovation, and the increasing value of data, the use of AI-powered data analytics emerges as a crucial factor in maintaining relevance and achieving a competitive edge.

However, the implementation of AI-driven data analytics presents some problems. Organisations are faced with the challenge of effectively managing data privacy, bias, and transparency, while simultaneously meeting the requirements for talent acquisition, resource allocation, and cultural adaption. Despite their intimidating nature, these difficulties may be overcome via the use of appropriate strategies and a steadfast dedication to the ethical and responsible deployment of artificial intelligence.

As contemplated the next years, it is anticipated a scenario in which artificial intelligence persists in redefining the limits of attainability. Explainable artificial intelligence, augmented analytics, and responsible AI adoption are anticipated to emerge as prominent trends in the field. The potential ramifications of artificial intelligence on the field of information sciences and organisational management are extensive, presenting organisations with the opportunity to adopt a more data-driven approach, enhance operational efficiency, and gain a competitive edge.

In conclusion, the exploration of AI-driven data analytics has shown a vast array of potential opportunities. The significance of artificial intelligence in the realm of data analytics extends beyond its efficiency, including the essential aspects of survival and achievement in contemporary data-centric society. The decision is unequivocal: adopt AI-powered data analytics or face the potential consequences of lagging behind in a society were data reigns supreme. Organisational development and success in the future will be determined by the ability of individuals to effectively use artificial intelligence to fully exploit the potential of data.

REFERENCES

AI-based Natural Language Processing (NLP) Systems. (2020). AI-based Natural Language Processing (NLP) Systems. *Journal of Algebraic Statistics*. doi:10.52783/jas.v11i1.1431

Asbaş, C., & Erdem Tuzlukaya, Ş. (2023). Siber Uzay Alanını Keşfetmek: Grup İçi ve Gruplar Arası İlişkiler Üzerinde Siber Tehditlerin Etkileri. In M. Kızrak (Ed.), *Örgütlerde Grup İçi ve Gruplar Arası İlişkiler* (pp. 97–109). Siyasal Kitabevi.

Automation, R. P. (RPA) Implementation Drivers: Evidence of Selected Nordic Companies. (2021). *Issues in Information Systems*. doi:10.48009/2_iis_2021_21-40

Baird, A., & Schuller, B. (2020, September 2). Considerations for a More Ethical Approach to Data in AI: On Data Representation and Infrastructure. *Frontiers in Big Data*, *3*, 25. Advance online publication. doi:10.3389/fdata.2020.00025 PMID:33693398

Batra, D. (2020). The impact of the COVID-19 on organizational and information systems agility. *Information Systems Management*, *37*(4), 361–365. doi:10.1080/10580530.2020.1821843

Böhmer, N., & Schinnenburg, H. (2023). Critical exploration of AI-driven HRM to build up organizational capabilities. *Employee Relations: The International Journal.*

Boire, R. (2017). Understanding AI in a world of big data. *Big Data & Information Analytics*, *2*(5), 23–43. doi:10.3934/bdia.2018001

Burr, C., & Leslie, D. (2022, June 22). Ethical assurance: A practical approach to the responsible design, development, and deployment of data-driven technologies. *AI and Ethics*, *3*(1), 73–98. doi:10.1007/s43681-022-00178-0

Cetindamar, D., Shdifat, B., & Erfani, E. (2022). Understanding big data analytics capability and sustainable supply chains. *Information Systems Management*, *39*(1), 19–33. doi:10.1080/10580530.2021.1900464

Chen, D. Q., Preston, D. S., & Swink, M. (2015). How the use of big data analytics affects value creation in supply chain management. *Journal of Management Information Systems*, *32*(4), 4–39. doi:10.1080/07421222.2015.1138364

Cofre-Martel, S., Lopez Droguett, E., & Modarres, M. (2021, October 14). Big Machinery Data Preprocessing Methodology for Data-Driven Models in Prognostics and Health Management. *Sensors (Basel)*, *21*(20), 6841. doi:10.3390/s21206841 PMID:34696058

Davis, J., Purves, D., Gilbert, J., & Sturm, S. (2022, January 31). Five ethical challenges facing data-driven policing. *AI and Ethics*, *2*(1), 185–198. doi:10.1007/s43681-021-00105-9

Dwivedi, R., Nerur, S., & Balijepally, V. (2023). Exploring artificial intelligence and big data scholarship in information systems: A citation, bibliographic coupling, and co-word analysis. *International Journal of Information Management Data Insights*, *3*(2), 100185. doi:10.1016/j.jjimei.2023.100185

Eketu, C. A. (2016). Customer Personality Taxonomy: A Theoretical Analysis of Customer Diversity Management in the Hospitality Industry. *International Journal on Customer Relations*, *4*(1). Advance online publication. doi:10.21863/ijcr/2016.4.1.012

Febriyanti, I. (2023, July 10). Assuring Customer Value, Customer Experience, and Trust to Improve Customer Loyalty. *Jurnal Dinamika Manajemen Dan Bisnis*, *6*(2), 37–51. doi:10.21009/JDMB.06.2.3

Future of Software Testing Using Artificial Intelligence. (2022, December 1). Future of Software Testing Using Artificial Intelligence. *Data Analytics and Artificial Intelligence*, *2*(6), 17–22. doi:10.46632/daai/2/6/4

Ghosh, G. (2018, August 31). Automation with RPA (Robotic Process Automation). *International Journal on Computer Science and Engineering*, *6*(8), 475–477. doi:10.26438/ijcse/v6i8.475477

Ghosh, J. (2016). Big data analytics: A field of opportunities for information systems and technology researchers. *Journal of Global Information Technology Management*, *19*(4), 217–222. doi:10.1080/1097198X.2016.1249667

Giermindl, L. M., Strich, F., Christ, O., Leicht-Deobald, U., & Redzepi, A. (2022). The dark sides of people analytics: Reviewing the perils for organisations and employees. *European Journal of Information Systems*, *31*(3), 410–435. doi:10.1080/0960085X.2021.1927213

Gotterbarn, D., & Kreps, D. (2020, November 18). Being a data professional: Give voice to value in a data driven society. *AI and Ethics*, *1*(2), 195–203. doi:10.1007/s43681-020-00027-y

Grover, V., Chiang, R. H., Liang, T. P., & Zhang, D. (2018). Creating strategic business value from big data analytics: A research framework. *Journal of Management Information Systems, 35*(2), 388–423. doi:10.1080/07421222.2018.1451951

Gupta, S., Modgil, S., Lee, C. K., & Sivarajah, U. (2023). The future is yesterday: Use of AI-driven facial recognition to enhance value in the travel and tourism industry. *Information Systems Frontiers, 25*(3), 1179–1195. doi:10.1007/s10796-022-10271-8 PMID:35529102

Haney, B. S. (2020). AI Patents: A Data Driven Approach. SSRN *Electronic Journal*. doi:10.2139/ssrn.3527154

Hulsen, T. (2023, August 10). Explainable Artificial Intelligence (XAI): Concepts and Challenges in Healthcare. *AI, 4*(3), 652–666. doi:10.3390/ai4030034

Jöhnk, J., Weißert, M., & Wyrtki, K. (2021). Ready or not, AI comes—An interview study of organizational AI readiness factors. *Business & Information Systems Engineering, 63*(1), 5–20. doi:10.1007/s12599-020-00676-7

Kar, A. K., & Kushwaha, A. K. (2021). Facilitators and barriers of artificial intelligence adoption in business–insights from opinions using big data analytics. *Information Systems Frontiers*, 1–24.

Katirai, A. (2023, June 20). Ethical considerations in emotion recognition technologies: A review of the literature. *AI and Ethics*. doi:10.1007/s43681-023-00307-3

Kedziora, D. (2022, October 3). Botsourcing, Roboshoring or Virtual Backoffice? Perspectives on Implementing Robotic Process Automation (RPA) and Artificial intelligence. *Human Technology, 18*(2), 92–97. doi:10.14254/1795-6889.2022.18-2.1

Khan, M. A., Saleh, A. M., Waseem, M., & Sajjad, I. A. (2023). Artificial Intelligence Enabled Demand Response: Prospects and Challenges in Smart Grid Environment. *IEEE Access : Practical Innovations, Open Solutions, 11*, 1477–1505. doi:10.1109/ACCESS.2022.3231444

Shaoyu Liu, S. L. (2022, December). Robotic Process Automation (RPA) in Auditing: A Commentary. *International Journal of Computer Auditing, 4*(1), 022–027. doi:10.53106/256299802022120401003

Loebbecke, C. (2019, December 30). Digitization, Big Data Analytics, and Artificial Intelligence Transforming Business, Society, and Research. *Moscow University Economics Bulletin, 2019*(6), 9–11. doi:10.38050/01300105201962

Lyytinen, K., & Damsgaard, J. (2011). Inter-organizational information systems adoption–a configuration analysis approach. *European Journal of Information Systems, 20*(5), 496–509. doi:10.1057/ejis.2010.71

Maleh, Y., Abd El-Latif, A. A., & Zhang, J. (2023). Guest Editorial AI-Driven Decision-Making: Managerial and Organizational Promise and Potential. *IEEE Engineering Management Review, 51*(1), 11–15. doi:10.1109/EMR.2023.3243071

Nahm, E. S. (2023, February 28). A Study on Modeling of Activated Sludge Process in Wastewater Treatment System Utilizing XAI(eXplainable AI). *The Transactions of the Korean Institute of Electrical Engineers, 72*(2), 263–269. doi:10.5370/KIEE.2023.72.2.263

Ningsih, A., & Hurnis, D. (2023, June 1). Pengaruh Customer Experience, Customer Expectation Terhadap Customer Satisfaction Dan Customer Loyalty D′ Besto Chicken & Burger. *Jesya*, *6*(2), 2219–2229. doi:10.36778/jesya.v6i2.1240

Prasad Agrawal, K. (2023). Towards adoption of Generative AI in organizational settings. *Journal of Computer Information Systems*, 1–16. doi:10.1080/08874417.2023.2240744

Prasertsuk, S., & Busayarat, C. (2022, November 22). 3D Data Visualization and Analysis Tools for AI Ready City: Space Syntax and Social Media Data. *Nakhara : Journal of Environmental Design and Planning*, *21*(2), 214. doi:10.54028/NJ202221214

Rachmawati, D. G., & Utami, C. W. (2021, March 31). Customer Experience Terhadap Customer Loyalty Dengan Mediasi Customer Engagement Dan Customer Trust Cv. Wahyu Pratama. *Performa*, *5*(5), 440–448. doi:10.37715/jp.v5i5.1821

Rice, S. (2021, March 23). Ethical Considerations: Applying Natural Systems to AI for Better Situational Understanding. *A Common Place*. doi:10.21428/6ffd8432.d47f1790

Sabrina, N. N., Ginting, P., & Silalahi, A. S. (2023, May 4). The Effect Of Customer Value, Customer Experience And Customer Trust On Customer Satisfaction (Ace Hardware Medan Customer). *Warta Dharmawangsa*, *17*(2), 718–732. doi:10.46576/wdw.v17i2.3183

Schildt, H. (2017). Big data and organizational design–the brave new world of algorithmic management and computer augmented transparency. *Innovation (North Sydney, N.S.W.)*, *19*(1), 23–30. doi:10.1080/14479338.2016.1252043

Singh, V. (2022, July 31). Automation of Business Process Using RPA (Robotic Process Automation). *International Journal for Research in Applied Science and Engineering Technology*, *10*(7), 68–71. doi:10.22214/ijraset.2022.45111

Sivill, T. (2019, August 16). Ethical and Statistical Considerations in Models of Moral Judgments. *Frontiers in Robotics and AI*, *6*, 39. doi:10.3389/frobt.2019.00039 PMID:33501055

Slomiany, M., Galli, J., Harris, B., & Kuehn, M. (2018, October). Prm140 - Utilizing Advanced Data Analysis And Visualization, Powered By Artificial Intelligence, To Analyze Price Migration Data For Oncology Products. *Value in Health*, *21*, S380. doi:10.1016/j.jval.2018.09.2260

Sun, Z., Sun, L., & Strang, K. (2018). Big data analytics services for enhancing business intelligence. *Journal of Computer Information Systems*, *58*(2), 162–169. doi:10.1080/08874417.2016.1220239

Trocin, C., Mikalef, P., Papamitsiou, Z., & Conboy, K. (2021). Responsible AI for digital health: A synthesis and a research agenda. *Information Systems Frontiers*, 1–19.

Tulcanaza-Prieto, A. B., Cortez-Ordoñez, A., & Lee, C. W. (2023, August 16). Influence of Customer Perception Factors on AI-Enabled Customer Experience in the Ecuadorian Banking Environment. *Sustainability (Basel)*, *15*(16), 12441. doi:10.3390/su151612441

Weber, M., Engert, M., Schaffer, N., Weking, J., & Krcmar, H. (2023). Organizational capabilities for ai implementation—Coping with inscrutability and data dependency in ai. *Information Systems Frontiers*, *25*(4), 1549–1569. doi:10.1007/s10796-022-10297-y

Yablonsky, S. A. (2020). AI-driven digital platform innovation. *Technology Innovation Management Review*, *10*(10), 4–15. doi:10.22215/timreview/1392

Zhang, B., Lin, J., Du, L., & Zhang, L. (2023, May 8). Harnessing Data Augmentation and Normalization Preprocessing to Improve the Performance of Chemical Reaction Predictions of Data-Driven Model. *Polymers*, *15*(9), 2224. doi:10.3390/polym15092224 PMID:37177370

Section 2

Artificial Intelligence in Knowledge Engineering and Management: (Re)shaping the Knowledge Landscape and Fostering Innovation

Chapter 3
Artificial Intelligence, Knowledge Engineering, and Management

Lillian Maria Araujo de Rezende Alvares
https://orcid.org/0000-0002-8920-0150
University of Brasília, Brazil

Marta Lígia Pomim Valentim
https://orcid.org/0000-0003-4248-5934
São Paulo State University, Brazil

ABSTRACT

This chapter discusses the convergence of knowledge engineering and artificial intelligence in the context of knowledge management, highlighting the synergy between these disciplines to optimize organizational processes. Both have promising potential to improve knowledge management by automating tasks such as collecting, filtering, analyzing, and organizing data, information, and knowledge while identifying relevant patterns for strategic organizational development. It explores how knowledge engineering contributes to its representation and application, while artificial intelligence enhances hyper-automation and predictive analysis through advanced algorithms. The methodology adopted is an exploratory analysis that provides a comprehensive understanding of the dynamics involved in this disciplinary convergence and its implications for knowledge management. As a result, it highlights not only the unique contribution of knowledge engineering to representation and its efficient application, but also the amplifying role of artificial intelligence in organizational processes.

INTRODUCTION

Artificial intelligence and knowledge engineering are interrelated fields that aim to manage and apply knowledge to solve complex problems. They both seek the conditions to be able to perform tasks that normally require human intelligence. Knowledge engineering involves representing, organizing, and

DOI: 10.4018/979-8-3693-1058-8.ch003

applying expert knowledge to address specific problems while artificial intelligence employs computational resources to automate tasks requiring human intelligence, often through codified algorithms.

Knowledge-based systems (KBS) underpin both: knowledge engineering often involves the creation of artificial intelligence systems that use knowledge bases to make decisions or solve problems. Machine learning is also related to both, and knowledge engineering can provide the initial knowledge to train machine learning models. With regard to automated decision-making, knowledge engineering provides methods for representing expert knowledge, while artificial intelligence, using algorithms, processes these representations to make decisions. In short, it is possible to present knowledge engineering as the area that provides methods for representing knowledge, while artificial intelligence implements these methods to create systems that learn and make decisions autonomously. Both are therefore intertwined by the aim of using and managing knowledge to develop intelligent systems that can perform complex tasks.

Both artificial intelligence and knowledge engineering have strong connections with knowledge management, which can be defined as a discipline that concentrates on discovering, capturing, arranging, storing, distributing, and implementing knowledge efficiently in organizational settings. The three domains are interconnected in terms of discovering, collecting, and organizing knowledge in terms of: knowledge base and expert systems construction; data analysis; hyper-automation, adaptation, and evolution of knowledge management processes; systems integration; and knowledge sharing. Working together, artificial intelligence, knowledge engineering and knowledge management have the potential to create a robust system for optimizing the management and application of knowledge within organizations, thereby fostering innovation, efficiency, and continuous adaptation.

It is worth noting the concept of hyperautomation, which describes the convergence and integration of various automation technologies to further optimize and extend organizational processes. This method surpasses traditional automation that concentrates on repetitive and simple tasks, as it aims to automate a wide range of activities in a comprehensive and intelligent way. The goal is to integrate various technologies such as artificial intelligence, machine learning, workflow automation, and data analysis to develop an environment that enables machines to perform both simple and complex organizational tasks. Often considered a strategic approach to the digital transformation of organizations, hyperautomation enables organizations to achieve greater operational efficiency, reduce errors, improve the quality of work, and free up employees for more value-added tasks. As new technologies and approaches emerge, hyperautomation continues to evolve in response to the ongoing incorporation of digital technology into business operations across a wide range of sectors and processes. Hyperautomation provides various advantages, but it also brings difficulties, which consist of managing and preserving a multifaceted technology environment, concerns about data security, and the need for organizations to develop new skills and competencies in order to fully operate in this environment.

The intention of this chapter is not to delve into the technological ecosystem of hyperautomation, but it is worth mentioning how it is organized into three categories, according to the compilation by Madakam, Holmukhe, and Revulagadda (2022), in order to understand its interaction with knowledge engineering and artificial intelligence. There are three categories: (i) technologies to identify and prioritize automation processes, i.e., primary technologies necessary in the initial stage of discovering automation opportunities, (ii) technologies aimed at reducing the effort and cost of automation at different levels of companies, and (iii) technologies that extend the capacity of automation. Figure 1 will provide some detail on these levels.

Figure 1. Ecosystem of hyperautomation technologies
(Madakam, Holmukhe, and Revulagadda, 2022)

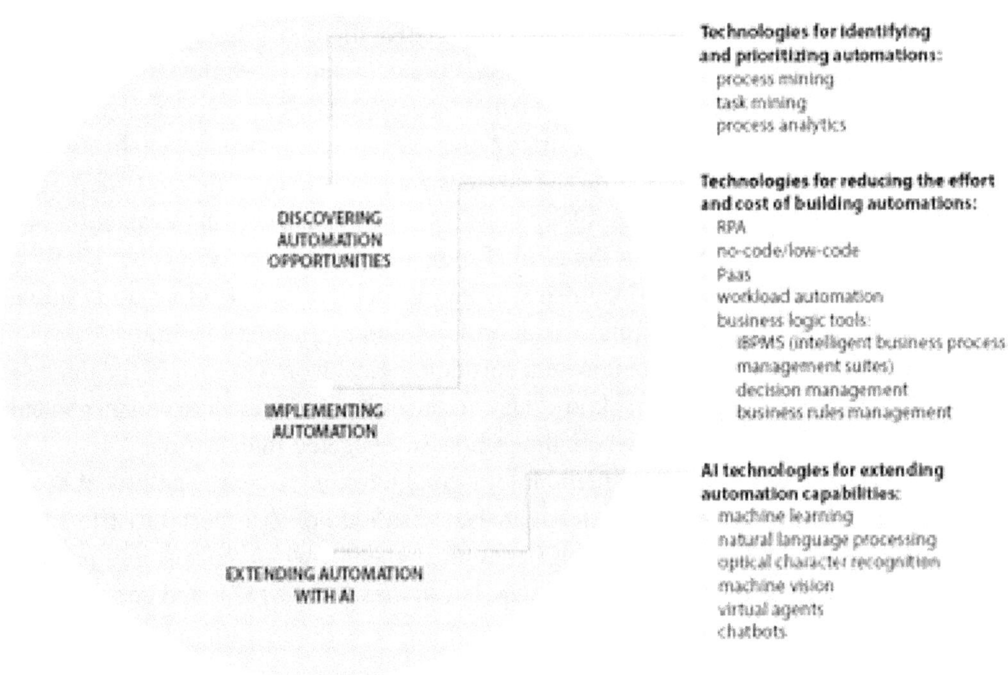

In this Chapter, the objective is to understand knowledge management from the perspective of artificial intelligence and knowledge engineering, given the ability of these disciplines to improve the efficiency and effectiveness of the knowledge lifecycle within an organization. It explores how knowledge engineering contributes to the representation and application of knowledge, while artificial intelligence, through advanced algorithms, enhances hyperautomation and predictive analysis. It also highlights the significance of integrating artificial intelligence and knowledge engineering for improving operational efficiency, innovation, and decision-making in organizations. The proposed approach not only integrates technologies, but also emphasizes the strategic synergy between artificial intelligence and knowledge engineering in improving the ability of organizations to effectively manage and apply knowledge in the dynamic business environment.

As a result, the article highlights not only the unique contribution of knowledge engineering in the representation and efficient application of knowledge, but also the amplifying role of artificial intelligence. As final considerations, it concludes that the synergy between them emerges as a strategic differentiator, enabling organizations to manage and apply their knowledge in an agile and effective way in a constantly evolving environment.

Method

Research approach of a qualitative nature, suitable for investigations that focus on the understanding and interpretation of the analyzed phenomena in order to explore and comprehend experiences, meanings, perspectives, and contexts through descriptive and interpretative methods. It employed an unstructured data collection method for the identification and analysis of documents, with the aim of understanding the context in which the phenomena occur, recognizing the complexity of organizational interactions.

In this regard, the adopted methodological strategy was organized in two stages. In the first stage, there is a narrative literature review based on the consensus and critique of the authors regarding the available scientific production. This methodology considers the experience and evaluation of experts familiar with the evidence accumulated in the field. The result of the procedure is a critical literature review, based on intentionally selected documents, which gathered a set of information initially and descriptively, aiming to reveal patterns, trends, relationships, and preliminary insights.

The selected studies are essentially fundamental epistemological works in each of the three thematic cores of the research (artificial intelligence, knowledge engineering, and knowledge management), with the purpose of building a preliminary understanding of the investigated intersection.

In the second stage of the research, the methodology conducted an in-depth analysis of the selected works, using the qualitative and inductive content analysis methodology proposed by Elo and Kyngäs (2008), highly suitable for the analysis of multifaceted phenomena, "when there are no previous studies dealing with the phenomenon or when knowledge is fragmented" (p.113), and content analysis by Bardin (1977).

RESULTS

Knowledge Engineering and Knowledge Management

Knowledge engineering has become a vital discipline in enhancing knowledge management in today's organizations. Its function involves representing, structuring, and systematically applying specialized knowledge, ultimately transforming it into accessible and applicable resources. By developing models and systems that capture the expertise of specialists and transforming tacit knowledge into explicit knowledge, knowledge engineering contributes to knowledge management.

The formal representation of knowledge is a distinctive addition from knowledge engineering to knowledge management. Utilizing precise languages and structures, knowledge engineering simplifies the complexity of knowledge into formats that can be understood by computer systems, thereby facilitating the efficient organization and dissemination of knowledge within the organizations.

Another key role of knowledge engineering in knowledge management is to facilitate the automation of knowledge-related processes, such as knowledge-based systems that can automate complex decisions and tasks, enabling the rapid application of knowledge to real-world scenarios. This not only increases operational efficiency, but also reduces sole reliance on manual processes, minimizes errors, and optimizes workflows.

Feigenbaum (1977) proposed the term knowledge engineering, at a time when the focus was on "[...] practices the art of bringing the principles and tools of AI research to bear on difficult applications problems requiring experts' knowledge for their solution." (p. 1). The author was specifically referring to

Table 1. Knowledge engineering concepts

Feigenbaum & Mccorduck (1983)[1]	An engineering discipline that involves integrating knowledge into computer systems in order to solve complex problems that normally require a high level of human expertise.
Abramson & Ng (1993)[2]	Knowledge engineering has been called an art, a process, a technology, a technique, a conception step, etc., but it has rarely if ever been described as a science. The importance of this distinction is not merely semantic; there are real differences between artistic and scientific activities
Schreiber, Akkermans, & Van de Velde, (1994)[3]	The artificial intelligence community exhibited minimal interest in the development of methodologies. The prevailing paradigm for constructing knowledge-based systems relied heavily on rapid prototyping techniques, with little emphasis on methodology.
Schreiber *et al.* (2002)[4]	Structured approaches to developing knowledge architectures gained prominence among many developers and managers during the 1980s and 1990s. They have become increasingly complex in terms of how they are implemented and integrated into their application contexts.
Ribeiro Júnior (2010)	This field emerged from a set of techniques applied to the development of systems in the field of artificial intelligence, evolving into an area of knowledge that addresses concerns related to the processes of modeling, validation, repetition and reuse of models and methods, considering knowledge no longer as an element to be transposed, but as something inherent in the dynamics of knowledge-intensive activities.

Source: Adapted from Ribeiro Júnior (2010).

Figure 2. Evolution of knowledge systems
(Ribeiro Júnior, 2010, p. 96)

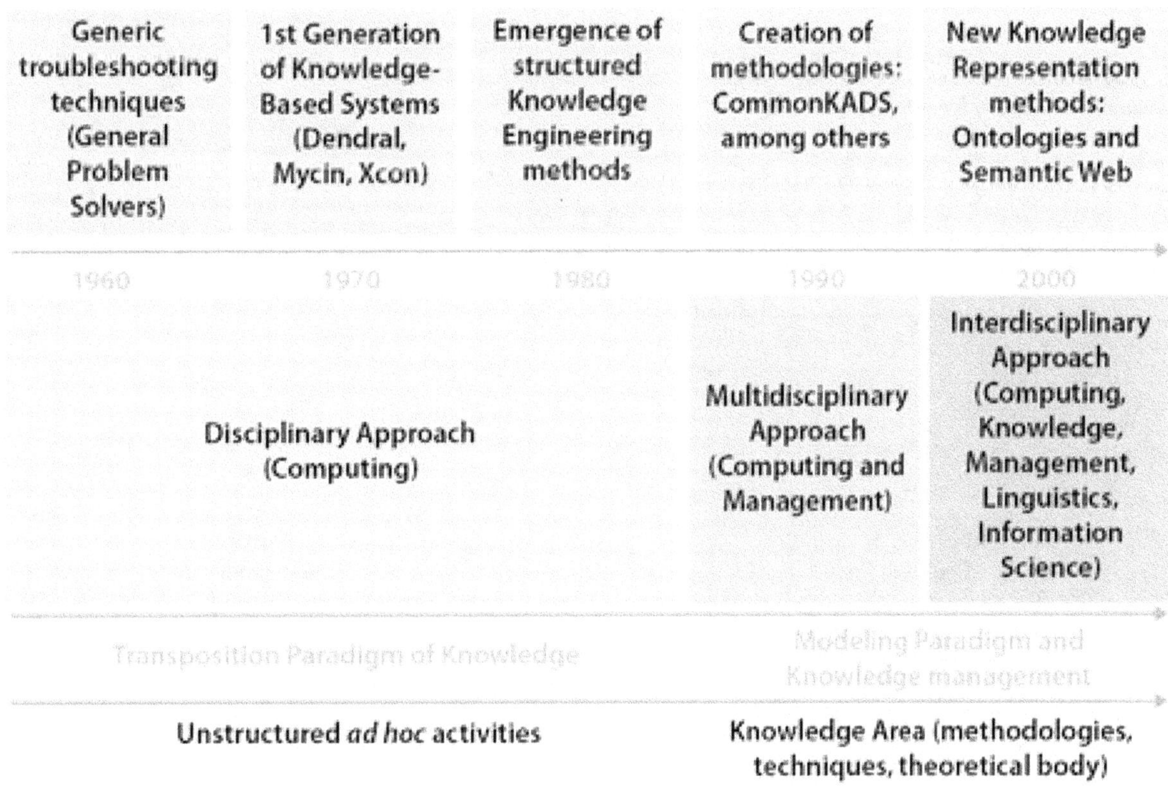

how to deal with knowledge, as "[...] representing it and using it appropriately to construct and explain lines-of-reasoning, are important problems in the design of knowledge-based systems." (p. 1). Ribeiro Júnior (2010) presents the concepts that have evolved with the term knowledge engineering (Table 1 and Figure 2).

Four decades later, knowledge engineering has significantly advanced, strengthening its unique original identity. The current scenario involves processing non-canonical knowledge, which is defined as untreated and characterized by confusion, inaccuracy, inconsistency, noisiness, dependence on an open and massive context, and constantly changing (see Figure 2).

According to Gaines and Shaw (1993), knowledge engineering meets the need for knowledge acquisition for the development of expert systems, following Hayes-Roth, Waterman, and Lenat's (1983[5], apud Gaines & Shaw, 1993) vision of the knowledge engineer as mediating between the expert and the knowledge base, extracting knowledge from the expert, encoding it for the knowledge base, and refining it in collaboration with the expert to achieve an acceptable performance.

Knowledge acquisition is a bottleneck in building expert systems. The knowledge engineer's job is to act as a mediator to help the expert build a system. The knowledge engineer has less knowledge regarding the expert's domain, however, and communication problems hinder the process of transferring knowledge to a program. The vocabulary initially used by the expert to talk about their domain to a knowledge engineer can be difficult for problem-solving, meaning that the knowledge engineer and the expert must work together to expand and refine it. One of the most difficult aspects of the knowl-

Figure 3. Basic knowledge engineering
(Gaines & Shaw, 1993, p. 4)

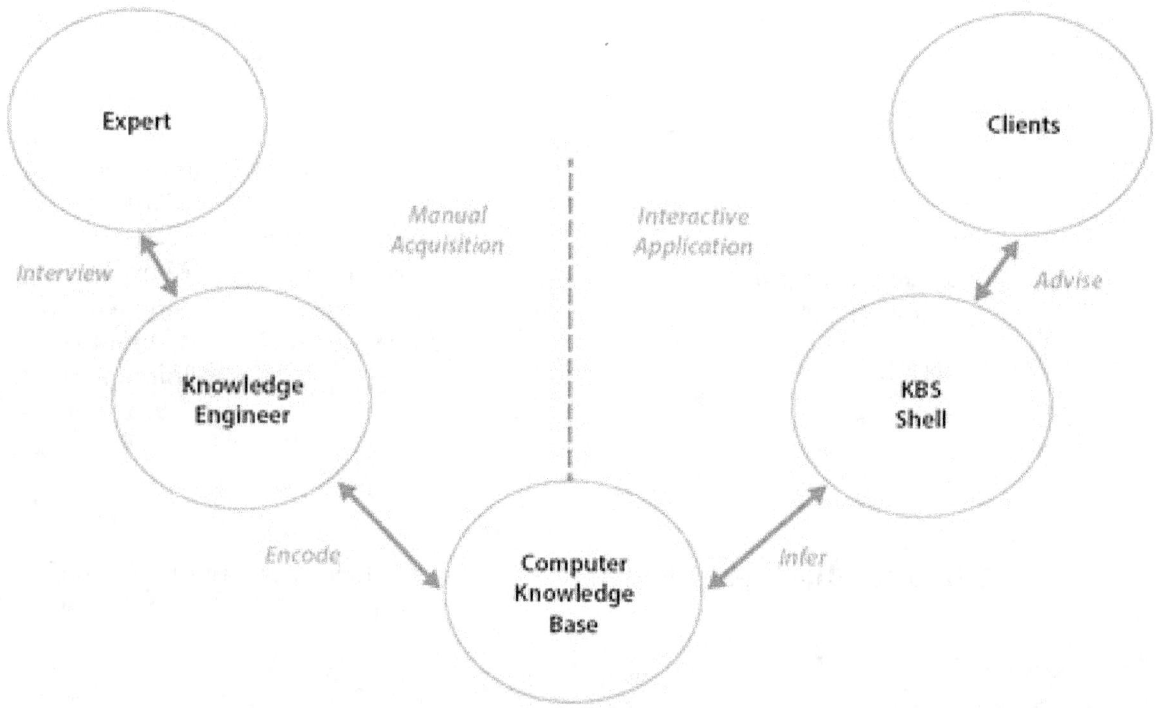

edge engineer's task is to help the expert in structuring the domain knowledge, in order to identify and formalize the domain concepts.

From this perspective, the proposed model can be represented as the knowledge acquired from an expert being inserted into a knowledge base. The knowledge base is then utilized by a knowledge-based system for a specific application.

In Gaines and Shaw's (1993) initial model, the knowledge engineer conducts an interview with the expert to extract their knowledge. Then, the knowledge obtained is encoded into the knowledge base and used to make inferences about particular cases specified by the clients, and the clients use the KBS shell inferences to obtain advice about particular cases. If the model takes into consideration knowledge elicitation with interactive tools (such as computer-based knowledge acquisition tools), then it is represented as in Figure 4.

Figure 4. Knowledge engineering with interactive tools
(Gaines & Shaw, 1993, p. 5)

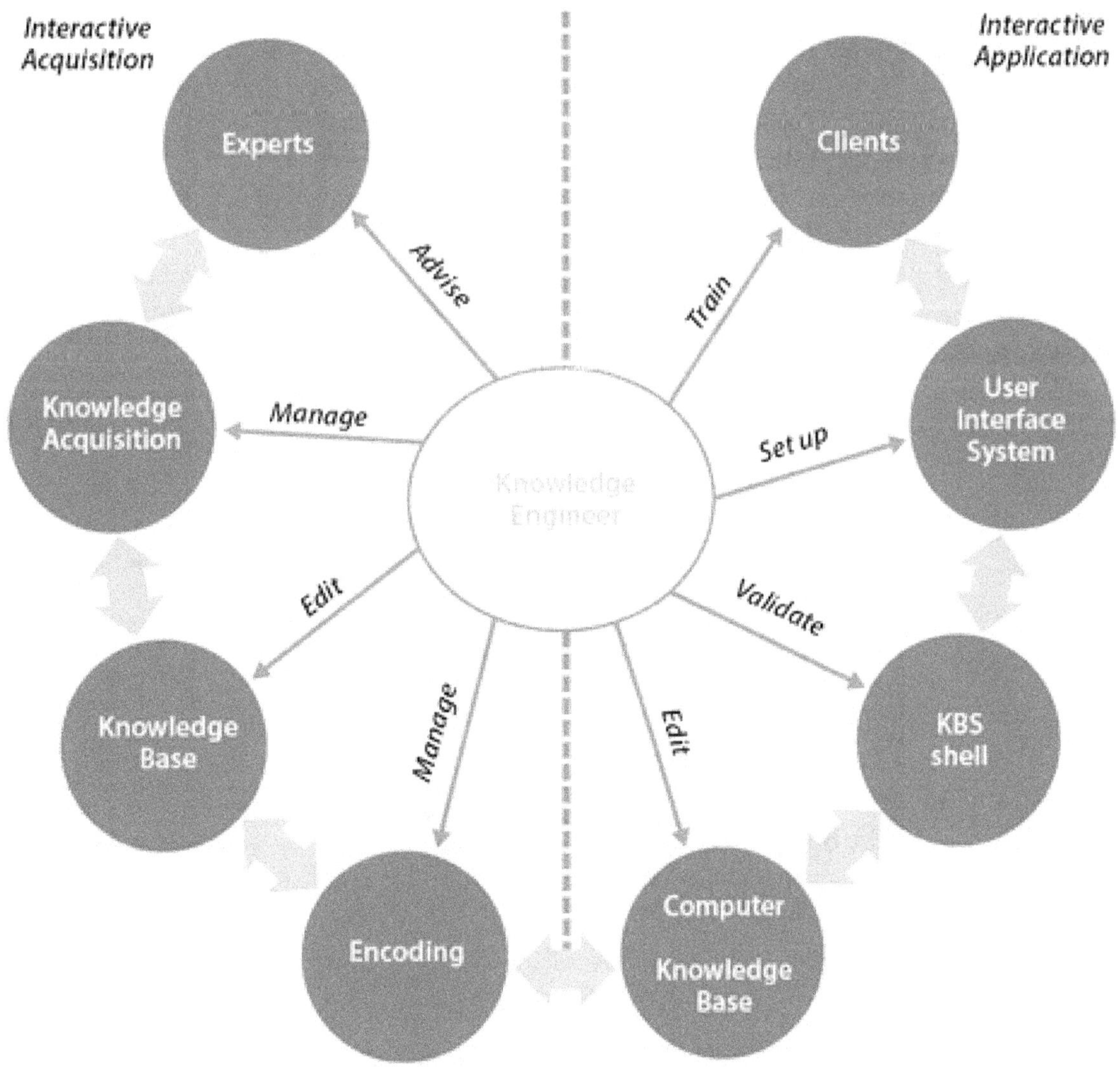

Gaines and Shaw (1993, p. 5) improve the model and define that the knowledge engineer is responsible for

advising the experts on the process of interactive knowledge elicitation; managing the interactive knowledge acquisition tools, setting them up appropriately; editing the unencoded knowledge base in collaboration with the experts; managing the knowledge encoding tools, setting them up appropriately; editing the encoded knowledge base in collaboration with the experts; validating the application of the knowledge base in collaboration with the experts; setting up the user interface in collaboration with the experts and clients; training the clients in the effective use of the knowledge base in collaboration with the expert by developing operational and training procedures.

In the case of Knowledge Based Systems (KBS), they focus on solving a single task, attempt to automate reasoning processes (or parts of them), and require formalized knowledge developed specifically for a given purpose. Brachman and Levesque (2004) state that "[…] what makes a system knowledge-based […] it is the presence of a knowledge base, a collection of symbolic structures representing what it believes and reasons with during the operation of the system." In addition, there must be an inference mechanism, an algorithm for the management of the knowledge in the knowledge base.

Rezende (2005, p. 15) defines a KBS as "[...] computer programs that use explicitly represented knowledge to solve problems" and that must have the following attributes: (i) everything that is known about the problem must be explicitly represented in the system's knowledge base; (ii) the knowledge base must be interpreted by an inference mechanism; (iii) the problems solved by a KBS are those for which no deterministic procedure is known (Figure 5).

Figure 5. Basic elements of knowledge-based systems
(Adapted from Rezende, 2005)

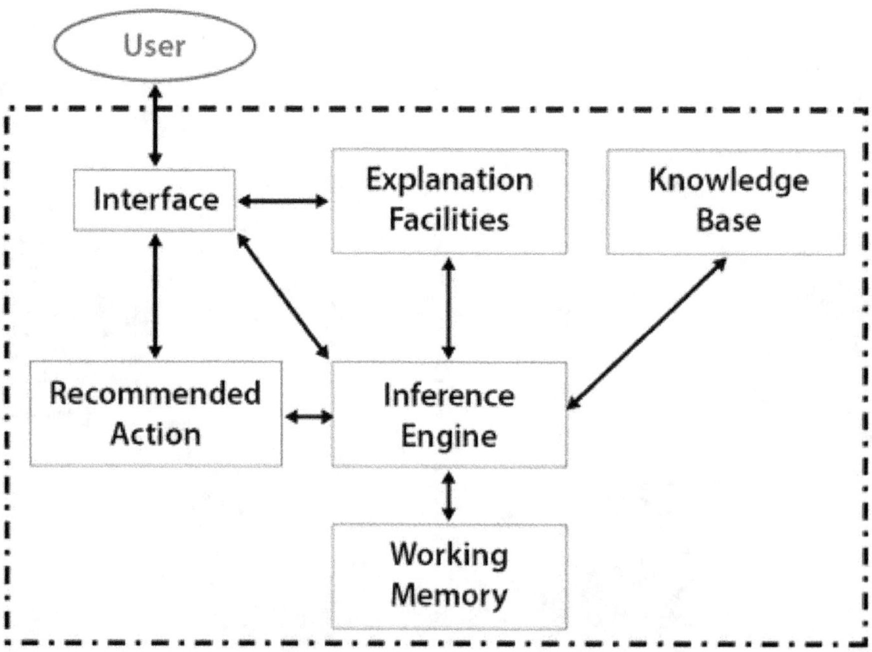

In Figure 6, Rezende (2005) explains that the Working Memory refers to a system that stores initial conditions, intermediate hypotheses, decisions, and final solutions. The Explanation Facilities module explains the behavior of the KBS as the system asks specific questions, which enables the system to arrive at the correct conclusion by rejecting certain alternatives. In other words, the system refers to the logic of the operation to arrive at the conclusion, among other possibilities. Knowledge refinement involves monitoring, analyzing, learning, and enhancing the system's performance to improve the knowledge base.

Figure 6. Complementary elements of knowledge-based systems
(Adapted from Rezende, (2005))

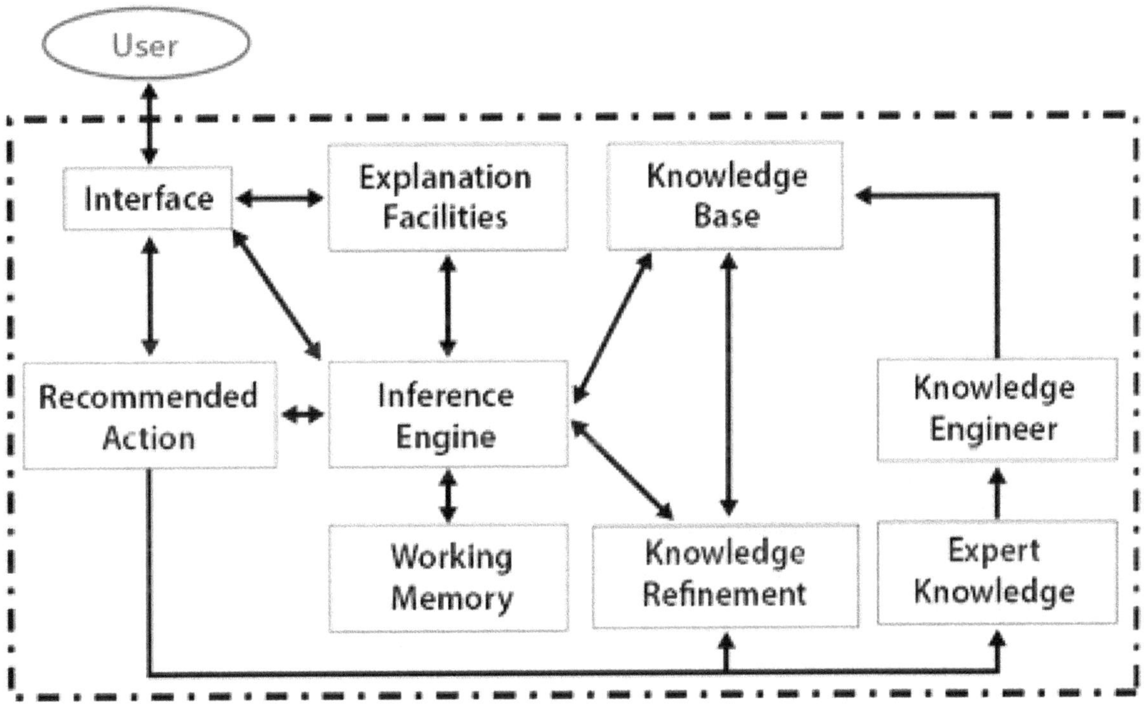

The distinction between Knowledge-Based System and Expert System (ES) is emphasized. The Expert Systems is a sub-area of the field known as artificial intelligence, defined as "[...] the part of computer science that comprises the design of computer systems that exhibit characteristics associated, when present in human behavior, with intelligence" (Mariano & Rebelatto, 2010, p. 7), which, in turn, is structured into three domains: (i) the development of programs that read, speak or understand human language, (ii) the development of intelligent robots, and (iii) the development of programs that simulate the behavior of human experts (Expert Systems). Mariano and Rebelatto (2010, p .7) define an ES as

a type of knowledge-based system specially designed to emulate human expertise in a specific domain. [...] they were developed from the need to process non-numerical information [...]. The basic idea of an expert system is to develop programs that enable the storage and sequencing of information, as well as self-learning, and they warn that "[...] one of the most important points when designing an expert system is the choice of knowledge representation system".

Knowledge-based systems can be classified as expert systems when their development is aimed at applications in which the knowledge to be managed is limited to a specific domain and has a high degree of specialization. According to Rezende (2005), KBS and ES are anchored in data structures, deterministic algorithms, the knowledge embedded in the program code, and the difficulty in explaining the reasoning behind its construction. Additionally, knowledge-based systems are based on knowledge representation, heuristic search, and knowledge represented explicitly and separated from the code that manages and interprets it and whose explanation can (and should) be explained.

Figure 7. The process of knowledge engineering
(Sharda, Delen, & Turban, 2015, p. 489)

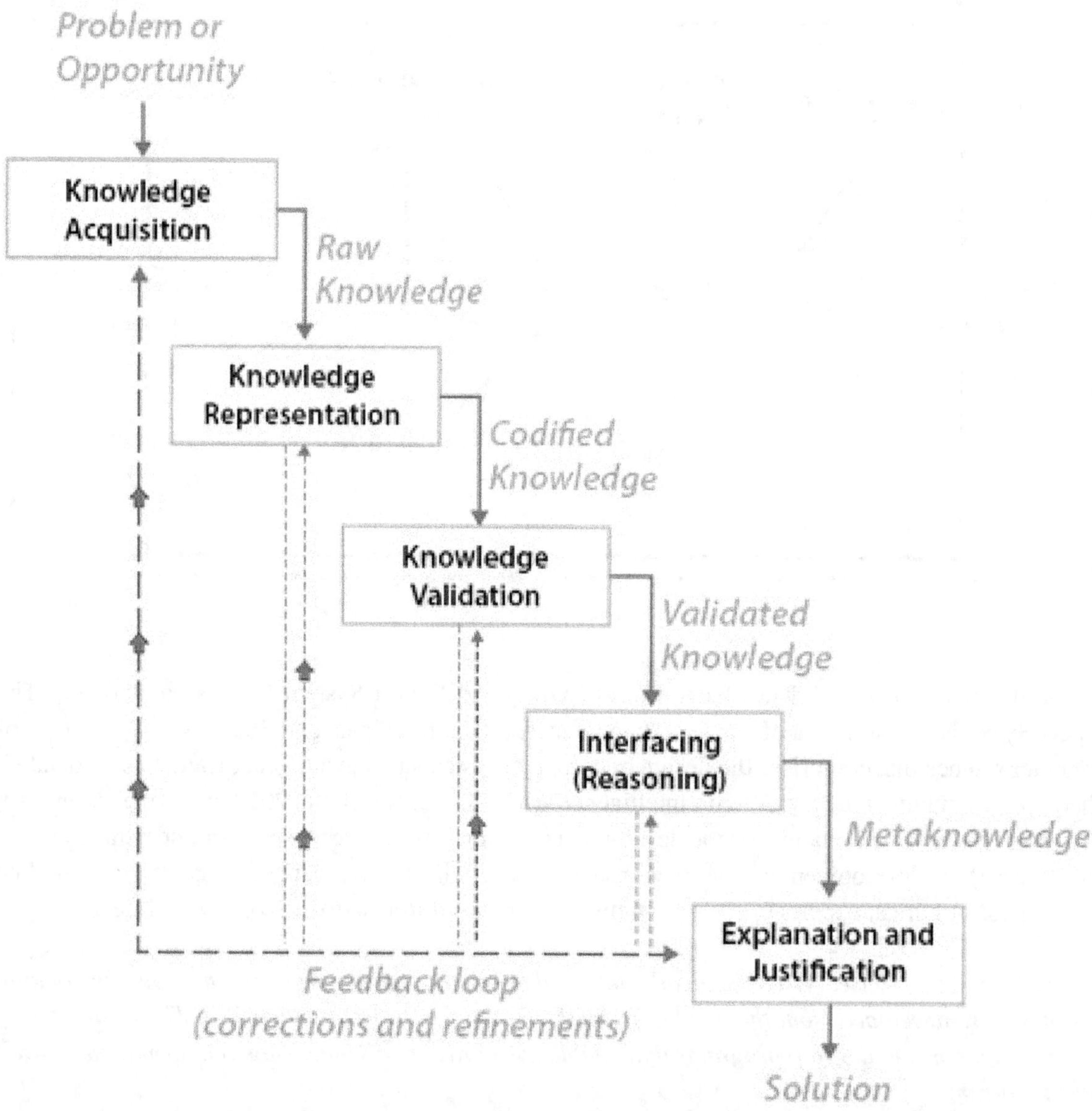

Returning to the knowledge acquisition process, it should be noted that this is merely the first of several steps. Sharda, Delen, and Turban (2015) outline five activities and their interrelationships within the knowledge engineering process (see Figure 7). The first stage is the process of acquiring knowledge about a particular domain, which involves eliciting knowledge from humans and non-humans. The second stage involves validation, which requires checking that the acquired knowledge satisfies quality requirements. The third stage encompasses the representation process that involves organizing and codifying the knowledge in the knowledge base. The fourth process involves inference, which allows the computer to make statements (deductions) based on what is already known and then it advises the user on specific issues. Finally, in the fifth stage, the computer explains why it selected a particular path instead of another. The authors posit that knowledge engineering is an effective approach to managing organizational knowledge, encompassing its creation, sharing, and maintenance.

The knowledge engineering process proposed by Sharda, Delen, and Turban (2015) begins with identifying a problem and/or opportunity. The process involves interrelated activities, including knowledge acquisition (obtaining raw data), knowledge representation (codification), knowledge validation (ensuring veracity), interface (reasoning), and the construction of meta-knowledge for explanation and justification. The process is continuous and allows for ongoing corrections and refinements.

Ouali, Mhiri, and Gargouri (2017) detail the knowledge base building process that includes the acquisition, representation, validation, inferencing, explanation, justification, and maintenance of knowledge (Figure 8). This process is very similar to the one proposed by Sharda, Delen, and Turban (2015).

Figure 8. Principe of the construction a business knowledge base
(Ouali, Mhiri, & Gargouri (2017, p. 83)

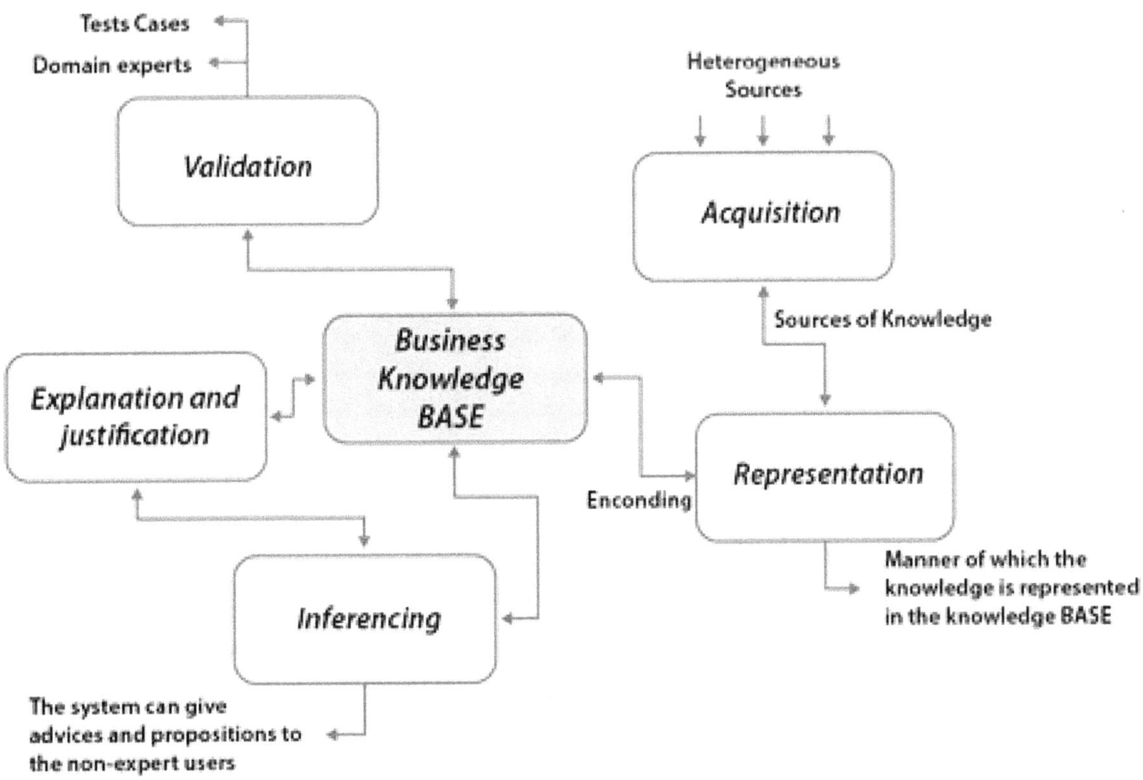

Figure 9. Knowledge engineering process, in the interpretation of Joram, Harrison e Joseph
(Joram, Harrison, & Joseph, 2017, p. 41)

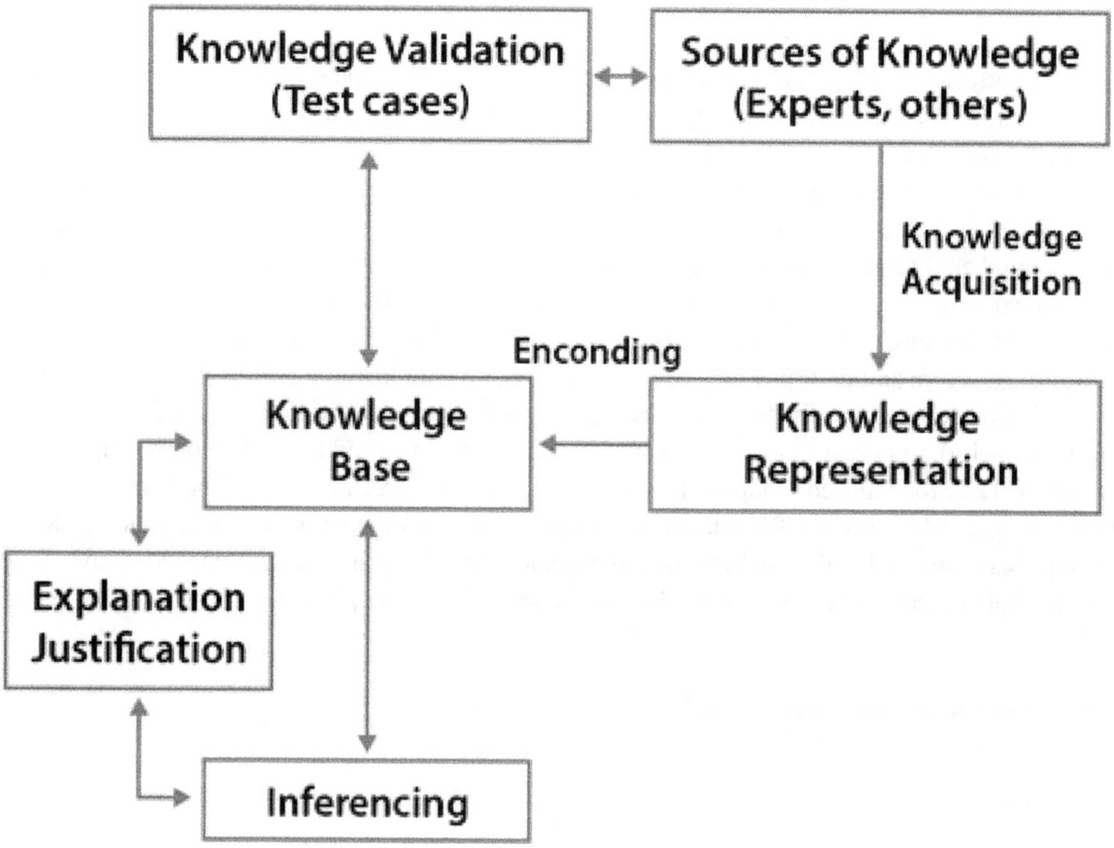

Figure 10. Knowledge engineering process, in the interpretation of Hanum and Salamah
(Hanum & Salamah, 2011, p. 13)

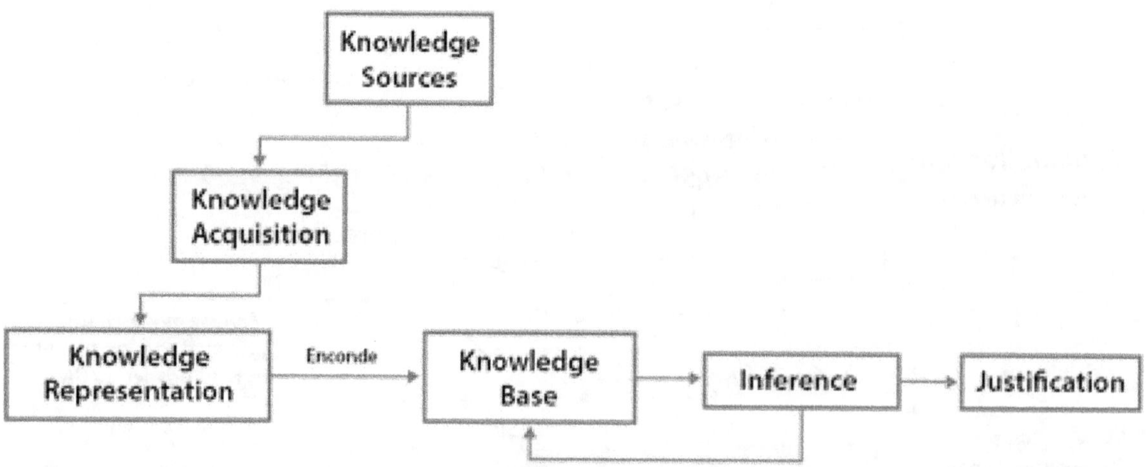

Joram, Harrison and Joseph's (2017) process has slightly different stages, These authors define knowledge engineering as the process of building a KBS containing six main stages: (i) problem assessment; (ii) data and knowledge acquisition; (iii) prototype development; (iv) complete system development; (v) system evaluation and revision; and (vi) system integration and maintenance (Figure 9).

Hanum and Salamah (2011) identify four stages of knowledge engineering: knowledge acquisition, knowledge representation, knowledge inferencing, and knowledge transfer. Knowledge transfer encompasses transferring conclusions to the user and providing an explanation, as illustrated in Figure 10.

In summary, it is possible to state that the main processes associated with knowledge engineering are acquisition (extraction of tacit and explicit knowledge); representation (organization and codification of knowledge in the organization's knowledge base, effectively resulting in a map of the organization's knowledge); validation (verification of conformity with reality); inference (using stored knowledge to enable the system to give guidance to different types of users); explanation and maintenance (making knowledge available to be used to clarify doubts). Among the methodologies applied to knowledge engineering, this research highlights Common KADS as a reference for future analysis.

Lai (2007) proposes an approach to knowledge engineering specifically focused on knowledge management, based on the view that many researchers conceive of knowledge management from different perspectives, such as the management perspective (which examines critical factors and challenges in knowledge management in an organizational context), or the projects perspective (which focuses on the creation and evolution of knowledge), and even ontology (which seeks to develop common concepts to facilitate knowledge sharing), as well as the technological view (which discusses how information and communication technologies and knowledge management are related). This author proposes a knowledge engineering approach, called the Knowledge Engineering Approach to Knowledge Management (KMKE), to mitigate usual knowledge management issues. These include the difficulty in integrating knowledge management activities due to the lack of a systematic approach, the challenge of identifying relevant information in a scenario of increasing information overload, the possible means of sharing and interoperating knowledge, and the need to ensure that knowledge management effectively supports the creation and use of knowledge.

In the KMKE approach, the activities are integrated into a synergistic structure consisting of: (i) knowledge modeling; (ii) knowledge verification; (iii) knowledge storage; and (iv) knowledge querying. In the first stage, knowledge models are used to organize and express the typology of knowledge present in the organization in a unified and consolidated representation which, in turn, helps to capture the semantics of organizational knowledge, including the elicitation of tacit knowledge and the ability to deal with the meaning of specific knowledge in different domains. The verification mechanism of the second stage is concerned with the validation and evolution of the models from the first stage and its main objective is to ensure model consistency. The third stage, related to storage, considers that the representations and knowledge itself can be classified and stored in a hierarchical ontology, used for the common understanding of knowledge. And finally, the fourth stage, which deals with the use of knowledge in a query interface (with special attention paid to language) and which can promote the dissemination of knowledge, including its reuse by combining, retrieving, and inferring from knowledge models.

In addition, Lai (2007) points out that in order to unveil knowledge management through knowledge engineering, it is desirable to take a systematic approach to the different types of knowledge (tacit and explicit), the application of knowledge (general, from common sense or specific, from the domain expert), the formalization of knowledge (declarative knowledge and procedural knowledge), and the use and reuse of knowledge (Figure 11).

Figure 11. An overview of the KMKE approach
(Lai, 2007, p. 4075)

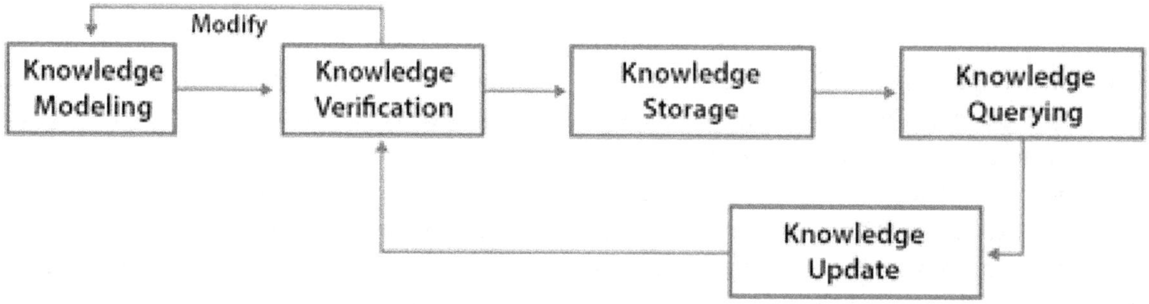

With regard to declarative knowledge[6] and procedural knowledge addressed by Anderson (1981)[7], "both types of knowledge try to describe the process of how human beings learn. Solti (2016, p. 8) presents both in a didactic way: the first (declarative knowledge) refers to "knowing about something", it is

information stored in factual memory and is static in nature and does not 'operate' on other forms of knowledge. It is the part of knowledge that describes processes, events, and the way things are [...] it is characterized by verbalized language, dependent on memory and analysis, and is represented by propositions that represent ideas. It is the gateway to information that will later be 'matured' and possibly transformed into procedural knowledge.

An important aspect of declarative knowledge is that it does not involve psychomotor skills, unlike procedural knowledge, which requires constant practice. Solti (2016) defines procedural knowledge as "knowing how to do something", or rather "how to carry out a cognitive activity". Based on the understanding of different authors, Solti (2016, p. 10) also explains that procedural knowledge goes through three stages of development:

in the first stage, called the cognitive stage, the individual uses declarative encoding to perform the skill [...]. The second stage, the associative stage, is when errors are eliminated through numerous trial and error actions, where the connections between the elements that make up the production or skill are strengthened. At this stage, procedural knowledge, alone or in combination with declarative knowledge, begins to rule the performance of the skill in question, and constant practice is an inherent characteristic. The third stage, the autonomous stage, is characterized by the automaticity of production or skill. Precision and speed are also innate characteristics of this stage, where verbal mediation disappears.

At this point, it is worth mentioning, albeit briefly, some efforts not yet cited here, whose absence creates a significant gap in the chapter—specifically, initiatives related to knowledge sharing, particularly those occurring within communities of practice. Indeed, the true convergence between knowledge engineering and knowledge management will occur through the paths of knowledge sharing among organizational groups. Dalkir (2011) discusses the importance of communities of practice as an effective means of sharing knowledge and promoting organizational learning. She defines communities of practice as groups of people who share a common interest and are committed to continuously learning about that interest. She emphasizes that these communities are natural forms of social organization that emerge in work environments and play a crucial role in the creation and dissemination of knowledge. The author underscores that communities of practice provide a conducive environment for the exchange of experiences, problem-solving, and innovation. She points out that these groups help overcome organizational barriers by promoting collaboration among members from different departments and hierarchies. Furthermore, Dalkir argues that communities of practice are fundamental to knowledge management as they contribute to creating an environment that facilitates the capture, organization, and dissemination of tacit knowledge—the knowledge that resides in people's minds and is often not formalized.

Beyond communities of practice, it is important to emphasize the essential role of the knowledge-sharing process in the acquisition of knowledge by algorithms, such as the training of artificial intelligence models. For instance, AI algorithms (like machine learning and deep learning) rely on robust datasets to learn patterns and perform specific tasks, and knowledge transfer, as knowledge engineering involves encoding specialized knowledge into computational systems.

Knowledge engineering and artificial intelligence effectively benefit from the sharing of knowledge through the creation of a broad and diverse information base. This allows algorithms to learn from varied experiences and adapt effectively to different contexts and challenges.

Artificial Intelligence Applied to Organizational Knowledge Management

The integration of artificial intelligence into organizational knowledge management represents a significant advancement in the way organizations approach operational efficiency and strategically use internal knowledge. By automating processes that can range from prospecting, collecting, and filtering information, to complex tasks such as predictive analysis powered by advanced algorithms, artificial intelligence provides a deeper understanding of organizational dynamics, enabling leaders to anticipate trends and make more informed decisions.

A critical aspect in this scenario is the ability of artificial intelligence to personalize individuals, directing users to relevant content based on their profiles and backgrounds. This condition optimizes knowledge discovery and access, contributing to a more collaborative and effective environment. In addition, Natural Language Processing (NLP) enables artificial intelligence to extract meaning from unstructured information, facilitating the management of knowledge bases (explicit and implicit) in an intelligent and efficient manner.

According to Smuts and Van der Merwe (2022, p. 2),

Society 5.0, [...] represents a vision where humans, nature, economic advancement, and technology create a sustainable balance for social good through a system that integrates cyberspace and physical space. This cyber-physical system is based on the proposition that significant amounts of data from the physical space are accumulated in cyberspace. These data are then analysed with super-smart AI systems, which exceed human capabilities.

Artificial intelligence in knowledge management facilitates collaboration between teams and drives innovation by facilitating the discovery and efficient use of existing knowledge and promoting the rapid identification and use of new ideas or existing solutions, leading to a more innovative environment. At the same time, it plays an essential role in information security by detecting anomalies and protecting against potential threats. This synergy between artificial intelligence and knowledge management is emerging as an essential strategy for meeting the challenges of a constantly evolving business environment.

In particular, machine learning and data analytics are valuable applications for knowledge management, especially when dealing with large data sets, as they lead to the identification of patterns and trends, the extraction of insights, and the uncovering of organizational knowledge. Specifically, as organizations deal with large amounts of data, artificial intelligence can help manage this information effectively, facilitating the identification, organization, and retrieval of relevant knowledge at scale. From this perspective, artificial intelligence can provide predictive analysis to guide short, medium, and long-term decision-making strategies. Another prominent application of artificial intelligence is to facilitate the efficient sharing of knowledge in the organizational environment, by recommending relevant content based on individual user needs and fostering collaboration.

From a hyperautomation perspective, artificial intelligence can be used to automate and integrate some knowledge management processes, such as automatically categorizing documents, identifying experts in specific areas, and recommending relevant content based on preferences and history. When it comes to integration, it is worth noting that organizations often deal with information from different environments, both internal and external, different sources of knowledge, in different formats. Artificial intelligence helps with integration, and the result is more comprehensive solutions that improve the search for information in knowledge bases, automatically identify knowledge gaps, and suggest improvements. Also in knowledge management systems, artificial intelligence plays a fundamental role in their adaptation and evolution, helping the systems to continuously adapt and evolve, allowing the incorporation of new information, updating knowledge models, and improving knowledge management practices. It should also be noted that systems based on artificial intelligence can personalize the knowledge management experience, providing customized recommendations to users based on their preferences, history and specific needs.

The integration of artificial intelligence into knowledge management represents a strategic alliance for modern organizations. By using advanced technologies, organizations can not only optimize the acquisition, organization, sharing, and application of knowledge, but also improve aspects that are crucial to business success. Operational efficiency is improved by automating tasks and quickly analyzing large data sets. In addition, artificial intelligence catalyzes innovation by providing valuable insights and identifying opportunities that may not be easily identified using traditional methods. This improvement in knowledge management not only promotes a more agile and adaptive environment, but also increases the competitiveness of organizations in a dynamic and challenging business environment.

It is worth highlighting some tools that can be applied within the scope of KM: 'IBM Watson' used to process large volumes of unstructured data from different documents types, thus contributing to effective knowledge management; 'Salesforce Einstein' analyzes customer data, interaction histories and purchasing patterns, helping organizations to customize products and services, as well as their marketing and sales strategies; some natural language processing tools such as 'Google Cloud' help organize large sets of textual data, assist in the context of knowledge management by categorizing and extracting relevant information; Google's 'DeepMind' project that features deep learning capabilities, whose applications include improving search algorithms and optimizing data management for more efficient results; AI-based 'chatbots' provide customer support and automated interactions; AI-based 'Predictive Analytics' platforms can be used to identify patterns in large data sets, within the scope of KM they contribute to predicting future trends and guiding strategic decisions.

However, the digital transformation brought about by artificial intelligence may not be well received by knowledge workers, who are not always prepared to operate in this new context. It is worth highlighting the importance of developing new skills and capabilities in organizational subjects so that in this new scenario they can act appropriately and with confidence.

The changes brought about by information and communication technologies are not new; on the contrary, over time technologies have been constantly evolving and changing people's way of life, and especially in the organizational context, workers need to constantly update themselves in order to respond effectively to new ways of working.

According to Manuti and Monachino (2020), knowledge management aims to collect and manage knowledge, connect people, and reduce redundancies and cognitive gaps, and in this context artificial intelligence stands out as a relevant resource, since it facilitates the replication of organizational processes adopted by the organizational collective.

Figure 12. Framework for the symbiosis of artificial intelligence and knowledge management (Bencsik, 2021, p. 86)

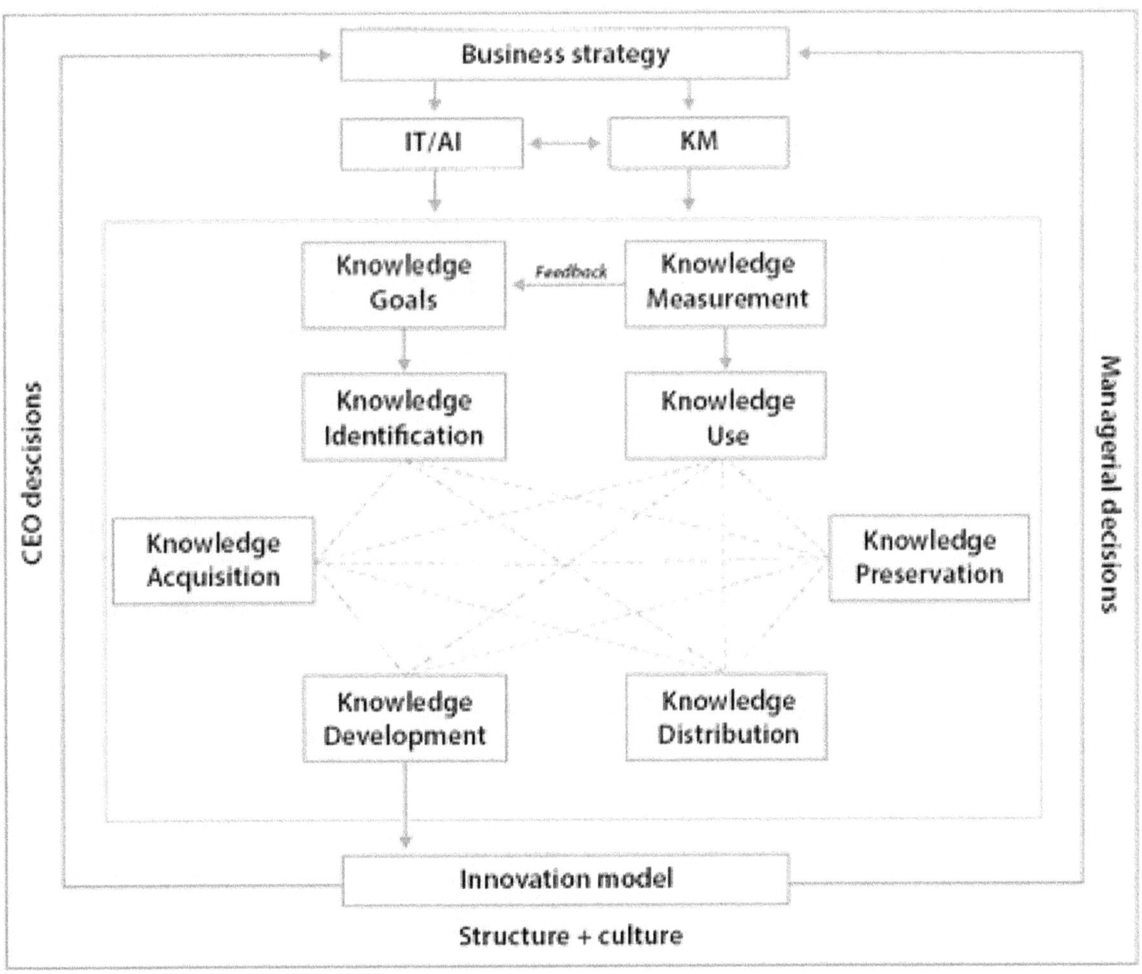

Table 2. Possible artificial intelligence support for knowledge management steps

Digitization Areas			**Artificial intelligence solutions**
Building blocks of KM	**Processes**	**Methodological background, management toolbox**	
Strategic knowledge goals	Setting normative, strategic, and operative goals – knowledge organisation, preparation, qualification of directions of innovation, creation of access opportunities	Network building Decision models Brainstorming	OCR (optical character recognition), text generation from data, deep learning, identity management, Digital Boardroom, probabilistic networks etc.
Knowledge identification	Comparison of existing knowledge and knowledge required to implement a strategy	Benchmarking, Knowledge map, Competence map, databases, data storages, document management systems	Machine learning (self-teaching system), content-based semantic search, smart response suggestion system, keyword recognition and self-reflection, Big Data solutions, cloud-based service
Knowledge acquisition	Acquisition of missing knowledge from external and/or internal resources	Company records, learning, competitor monitoring, market information, Peer Assist, Lessons learned, After Action Review, etc.	OCR, text analysis, biometrics, chatbot, content-based semantic search, text mining, competitor intelligence (CI), language translators, speech recognition (hidden Markov models), Attract, Onboard
Knowledge development/ Knowledge creation	Combining, supplementing, updating, and refreshing existing and acquired knowledge	Learning, e-learning, follow-up, brainstorming, talent programs, training and career plan, development programs, language teaching, building professional communities, lifelong learning, blended learning	Follow-up systems, complex learning-teaching systems, chatbot, multi-agent intelligent tutoring system, virtualization, MOOC (Massive Open Online Courses), thinking, consulting artificial intelligences
Knowledge distribution	Dissemination of the necessary knowledge to all stakeholders, information distribution	Knowledge relay, on-the–job, video sharing, videoconference, wikis, World Café, Storytelling, blogs, documentation systems, discussions, forums, brainstorming, ROCK (Retention of Critical Knowledge), etc.	Virtualization, speech recognition systems, text analysis, Google Docs, SharePoint, Social Learning, MyNet, GrapeVINE, search tools supported by artificial intelligence, company intelligent escalation system, Deep Coder, case-based reasoning, artificial neural network, genetic algorithm, agent approach, language translators, speech recognition (hidden Markov models)
Knowledge preservation / recording	Cases that have occurred, typical problems solutions, recording, necessary retrieval and application of all past information and knowledge	Records, work instructions, data storages, catalogues, paper- based and electronic forms, archive training and educational materials, etc.	Expert systems, Deep Coder, knowledge-based system, case-based reasoning, meaning-based search programs, personal knowledge management and content development software
Use of knowledge	Acquired, up-to-date knowledge application and integration into work processes	AAR (After Action Review), Retrospect, lessons learned, informal discussions, teamwork, Big Data, etc.	IoT (Internet of Things), content management software, speech recognition software, smart response suggestion system, robots, virtualization, speech recognition (hidden Markov models)
Knowledge evaluation / measuring	Comparison of the achieved results and the strategic goals	Analytical systems, measurement and management model, measurement breakdown structures, etc.	IoT (Internet of Things), content management software, neural networks

Source: Bencsik (2021, p. 91).

Knowledge management has made use of information and communication technologies, and various methods and techniques of knowledge management include the application of different types of ICT tools and systems. These include: yellow pages and talent banks; storytelling; communities of practice; collaborative and cooperative networks; concept maps and knowledge maps; data mining; big data analytics; machine learning; expert systems; the Internet of Things (IoT); cyber-archaeology; neural networks, among others. Knowledge management can use artificial intelligence in different applications aimed at decision-making, problem-solving, strategic planning of future scenarios, and innovation generation (Figure 12).

Bencsik (2021) points out that it is necessary to develop competencies, skills, and aptitudes in organizational subjects with regard to the use and/or application of artificial intelligence to generate strategic knowledge aimed at innovation, but stresses the importance of the ethical use of artificial intelligence. She also points out that it is essential to properly manage the possibilities offered by artificial intelligence in a way that enhances organizational practices involving knowledge management.

According to Bencsik, "this means that each step of a KM process can be assigned solutions supported by artificial intelligence that help you take the necessary intervention or solve the task arising in the actual phase faster, more efficiently and more successfully" (Alani et al., 2019 apud Bencsik, 2021, p. 88).

Artificial intelligence can contribute and make knowledge management processes more efficient (Table 2). Taherdoost and Madanchian (2023) note that various methods such as deep learning, neural networks, and supervised machine learning are used by artificial intelligence to replicate human intelligence. According to these authors, "many see AI as the next major source of economic value, as a key technology at the forefront of a new technological revolution and industrial change" (Taherdoost & Madanchian, 2023, p. 2).

From the perspective of Society 5.0, both knowledge management and artificial intelligence have an impact on the organization; therefore, it is crucial to share methods and techniques in order to achieve common goals, with a view to planning sustainable organizational activities, since they can simultaneously produce social, economic, and environmental benefits, and this means that they can provide differentials for obtaining a competitive advantage in the market in which the organization operates (Smuts & Van der Merwe, 2022).

Figure 13. Artificial intelligence advantages for knowledge management
(Taherdoost & Madanchian, 2023, p. 4)

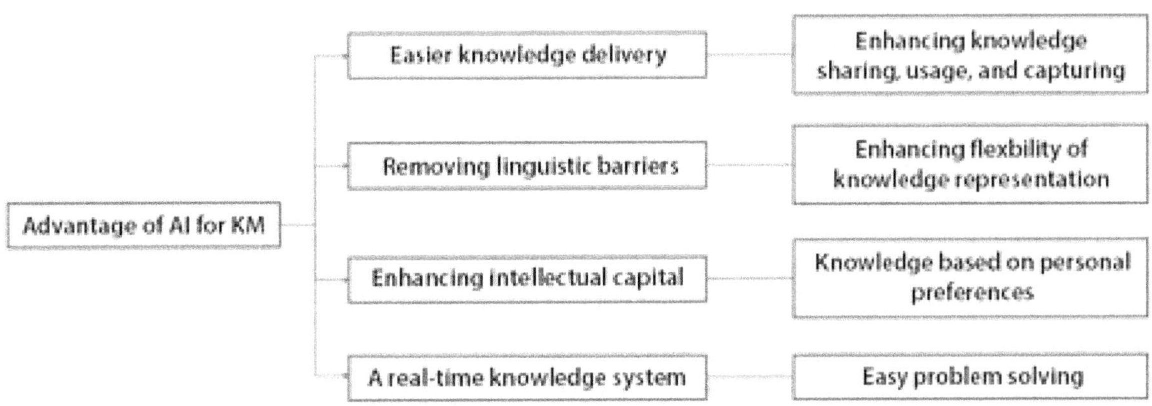

Figure 14. Symbiotic relationship between humans and AI in managing knowledge
(Jarrahi, Askay, Eshraghi & Smith, 2023, p. 92)

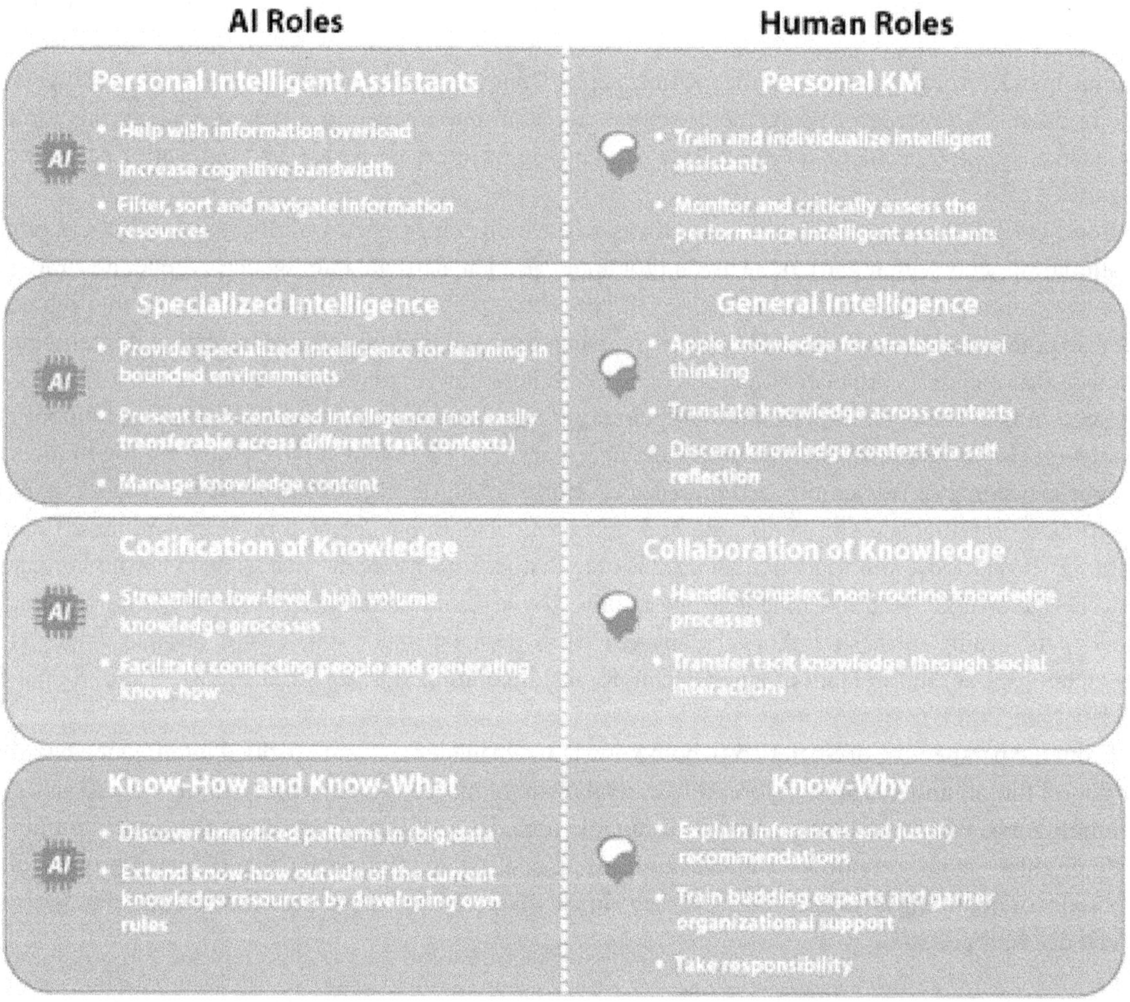

The potential of artificial intelligence in terms of deep learning for generating knowledge lies in its predictive power in situations such as, for example, probability-based forecasting, i.e., "[...] the ability to take information you have and generate information you didn't previously have" (Agrawal et al., 2017, p. 23 apud Jarrahi, Askay, Eshraghi, & Smith, 2023, p. 88).

With the automation of processes and activities via artificial intelligence, organizations must develop specific skills to interact with intelligent systems. Information competency should prioritize the enhancement of critical and analytical abilities to support strategic decision-making (Jarrahi, Askay, Eshraghi, & Smith, 2023, p. 95).

Some knowledge management processes are being replaced by artificial intelligence and, therefore, there are some functions performed by organizational subjects that could be replaced by this technology. Figure 15 shows a matrix divided into two axes, where the horizontal axis refers to the level of complexity of the activities and tasks carried out (from repetitive to complex). It is clear that complex

Figure 15. Job matrix format fourth industrial revolution
(Anshari, Syafrudin, & Fitriyani, 2022, p. 6)

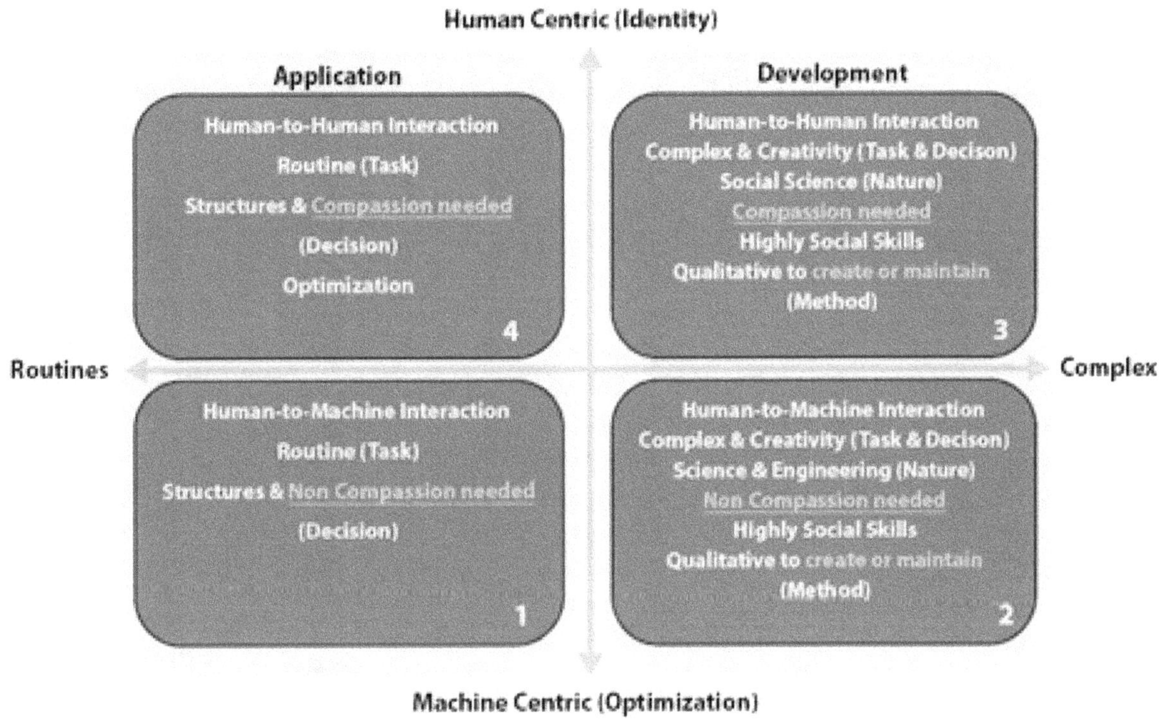

activities require consistent decision-making on the part of the organizational subjects, who must have a high level of experience. On the other hand, repetitive tasks can be performed without the need for specialized knowledge and complex decision-making processes. The vertical axis has two components, one centered on the organizational subject and the other centered on the machine. Activities centered on the organizational subject are those that require interactions between peers, and, on the other hand, machine-centered tasks require a high level of technological interaction (Anshari, Syafrudin, & Fitriyani, 2022, p. 6).

Organizations need to debate the ethical issues related to this technological evolution, since as automation takes place and replaces human labor in the labor market, it can become increasingly paradoxical, and generate low-skilled low-paid segments and high-skilled high-paid segments, which can lead to increased social tensions (Anshari, Syafrudin, & Fitriyani, 2022, p. 8).

Santana and Díaz-Fernández (2023, p. 1975) state that

the changes caused by digital technologies and innovations, such as big data, autonomous robots, IoT, clouds, virtual reality, and virtual intelligence, necessarily imply training and adapting the workforce. However, some of the traditional competencies such as emotional intelligence, creativity, flexibility and managing others cannot be performed by machines.

Figure 16. Evolution map of the competencies and skills for AI application themes for the periods 1992–2010, 2011–2015, and 2016–2020
(Santana & Díaz-Fernández, 2023, p. 1987)

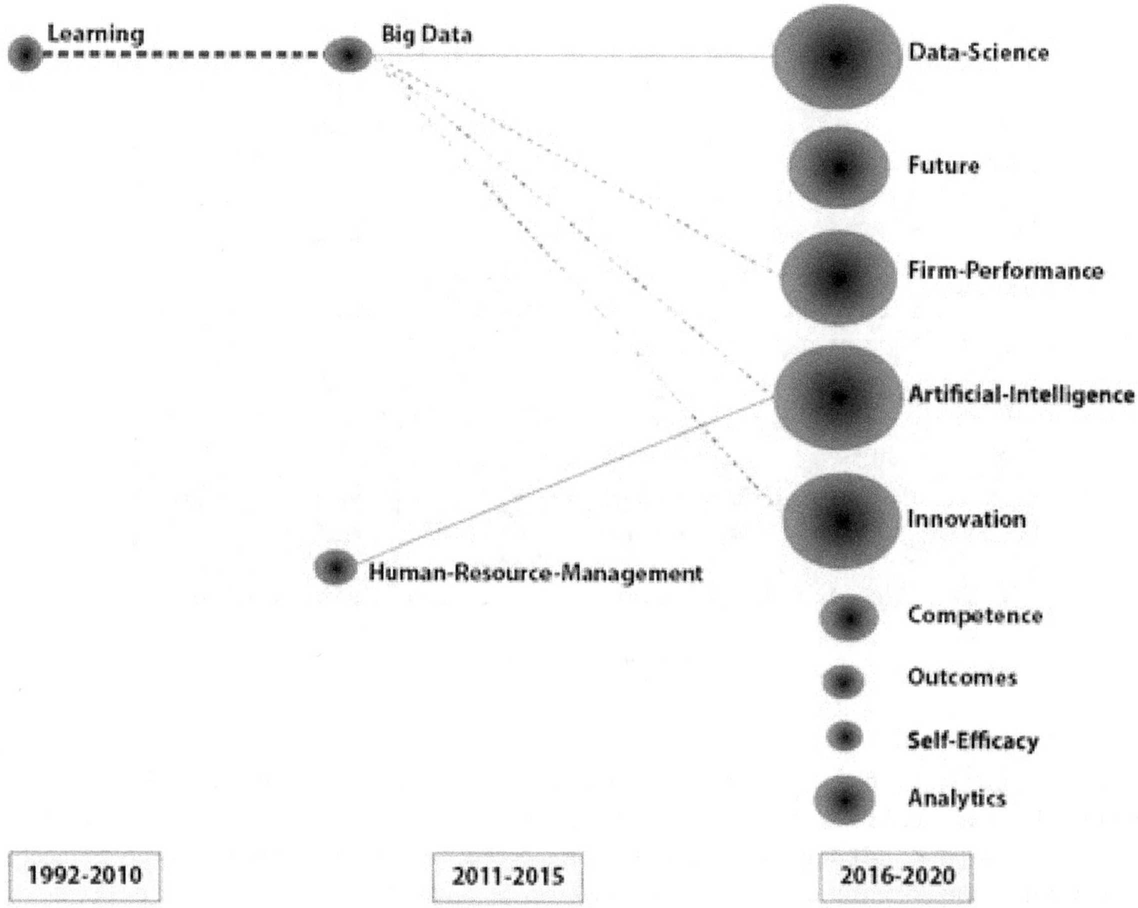

In the organizational context, managers' trend towards technology-intensive practices poses risks. Data lose their meaning and value when taken out of context. Moreover, when large data sets are transformed into mathematical models, the data are decontextualized and reduced to only what fits these models.

On the other hand, collecting, analyzing, and organizing data in a personalized manner would take a human being days, weeks, or even months. Gathering data and making decisions about past incidents is not effective. Efficiently stopping negative incidents, swiftly concluding investigations, and quarantining unreliable sources are imperative from this perspective. In addition, providing managers with safe conditions for assertive decision-making is crucial.

Knowledge workers mediate between raw data and relevant information for organizational subjects to construct meaningful knowledge. To accomplish this, individuals must develop skills and abilities to handle information within the realm of big data, including proficiency in mapping and identifying valuable data, interpreting trends, and share with managers what is relevant in the organizational context. As the information and communication technologies and the languages and methods utilized continue to evolve, they are certainly reshaping the informational future of people, organizations, and society.

In the context of KM, the ethical challenges associated with the implementation of AI are extremely relevant, as it involves issues interrelated to the privacy and security of individuals and organizations. Another aspect that must be observed refers to algorithmic bias, that is, distortions in the results obtained due to the incorporation of prejudices existing in the training data or in the algorithm rules themselves, generating discriminatory or unfair results, especially when it comes to machine learning algorithms, when they are trained on data sets that reflect existing inequalities in society. Furthermore, aspects relating to responsibility within the scope of AI are a crucial issue, given the growing influence of this technology in the most diverse sectors. Therefore, developers, platforms, users, governments, entrepreneurs, etc. they must respect specific policies, legislation and regulations providing transparency, respect and continuous improvement aimed at the good of society.

DISCUSSION

The convergence of knowledge engineering, knowledge management, and artificial intelligence is a proven reality. These interrelated fields of research and action aim to optimize the creation, sharing, and utilization of knowledge within organizations.

Knowledge engineering is the discipline dedicated to capturing, representing, and implementing expert knowledge in computer systems. This encompasses the creation of expert systems, ontologies, and inference rules, and enables the structured codification of human knowledge. Knowledge management involves developing strategies for acquiring, storing, sharing, applying, and utilizing knowledge in organizational contexts. Processes, technologies, and organizational culture promote collaboration and innovation based on existing knowledge. On the other hand, artificial intelligence involves systems capable of learning and making decisions by analyzing data and utilizing techniques such as machine learning and natural language processing.

Artificial intelligence can be used to automate knowledge management processes and activities, such as document identification and classification, extraction of relevant information, and databases organization. Machine learning techniques extract data from large volumes of unstructured data and transform them into usable knowledge. Artificial intelligence systems can assist organizations in decision-making, data analysis, trend identification, and action recommendations based on the data analyzed.

The integration of artificial intelligence and knowledge engineering can lead to more advanced knowledge repositories, so that systems not only store information, but also interpret it and make it accessible in a more customized way. Artificial intelligence can personalize the access to information, providing relevant evidence according to the profile and needs of each organizational subject, which is an activity developed in the context of knowledge management.

As artificial intelligence gains more autonomy, ethical questions arise about the autonomy of machines and who would be accountable for their actions. The resolution of these moral dilemmas demands cooperation between the government, organizations, civil society, and experts. Establishing rules that clearly define the appropriate boundaries of artificial intelligence is an essential action to ensure the responsible and beneficial use of knowledge engineering, knowledge management, and artificial intelligence for contemporary society.

Integrating ethical considerations not only protects the organization from risks of different kinds, but also fosters a healthier and more sustainable working environment, a factor that helps to build relationships of trust between organizational subjects and stakeholders in order to boost competitive differentials for the generation of innovation.

The convergence of knowledge engineering, knowledge management, and artificial intelligence presents organizations with chances to enhance their knowledge management efficiency, boost innovation, and improve decision-making, thereby achieving effective results. Nevertheless, it also poses challenges pertaining to ethics, privacy, algorithmic bias, and data security, which need to be carefully considered and evaluated when implementing artificial intelligence solutions in organizational environments.

CONCLUSION

Artificial Intelligence (AI), Knowledge Engineering (KE), and Knowledge Management (KM) are intricately connected, with profound implications for managers and researchers. This synergy presents significant opportunities to advance how organizations handle and leverage knowledge, ultimately promoting innovation and efficiency.

In brief, within the realm of KE, AI plays a pivotal role in automating the creation of expert systems—computer programs designed to solve problems in specific domains by applying existing knowledge. When interfacing with KM, AI is instrumental in extracting insights from extensive datasets, streamlining the identification, capture, and organization of knowledge.

In the context of AI, KE is essential for developing knowledge-based systems and other models used in decision-making or problem-solving within specific domains. As for KM, KE contributes to the effective capture of organizational knowledge and the creation of knowledge bases that can be shared and utilized more efficiently.

In the AI domain, KM benefits from automation in identifying pertinent knowledge, classifying information, and enhancing decision-making efficiency. Collaboratively with KE, KM endeavors to establish systems and practices facilitating the streamlined use of organizational knowledge.

For managers, a crucial understanding of how AI can enhance decision-making processes and streamline operations is paramount. Implementing KM practices ensures valuable knowledge is captured, shared, and effectively utilized within the organization. KE can be leveraged to create expert systems supporting day-to-day operations.

Researchers have the opportunity to explore the integration of AI into KE for the development of advanced and adaptable systems. Investigating how KM processes can be optimized through AI techniques is another avenue. Research can also delve into creating sophisticated models of knowledge representation easily comprehensible and utilizable by AI systems.

Potential research directions include the integration of AI in KE—developing methods for effectively incorporating AI techniques into knowledge modeling and representation. Exploring how machine learning algorithms can automatically update and expand knowledge bases is a promising avenue.

In the realm of AI in KM, researchers can investigate the application of AI algorithms for automatically identifying and categorizing organizational knowledge. Additionally, developing AI-based recommendation systems can facilitate effective knowledge sharing and utilization.

Research on KE and KM in decision-making explores the integration of knowledge-based models (KE) and KM practices to enhance decision-making processes. This line of inquiry can further investigate how AI can improve the quality and speed of decisions based on available knowledge.

REFERENCES

Anshari, M., Syafrudin, M., & Fitriyani, N. L. (2022). Fourth industrial revolution between knowledge management and digital humanities. *Information (Basel), 13*(6), 292. doi:10.3390/info13060292

Bardin, L. (1977). *Análise de conteúdo.* 1. ed. Lisboa, Portugal: Edições 70.

Bencsik, A. (2021). The sixth generation of knowledge management: The headway of artificial intelligence. *Journal of International Students, 14*(2), 84–101. doi:10.14254/2071-8330.2021/14-2/6

Brachman, R. J., & Levesque, H. J. (2004). *Knowledge representation and reasoning*. Elsevier. doi:10.1016/B978-1-55860-932-7.X5083-3

Dalkir, K. (2011). *Knowledge management in theory and practice* (2nd ed.). The MIT Press.

Elo, S., & Kyngäs, H. (2008). The qualitative content analysis process. *Journal of Advanced Nursing, 62*(1), 107–115. doi:10.1111/j.1365-2648.2007.04569.x PMID:18352969

Feigenbaum, E. A. (1977). *The art of artificial intelligence.* Stanford University Press.

Gaines, B. R., & Shaw, M. L. G. (1993). Eliciting knowledge and transferring it effectively to a knowledge-based system. *IEEE Transactions on Knowledge and Data Engineering, 5*(1), 4-14. doi:10.1109/69.204087

Hanum, S., & Salamah, U. (2011). Expert system to predict product lifecycle. *International Conference on Informatics for Development*. Research Gate. https://www.researchgate.net/publication/331829748

Jarrahi, M. H., Askay, D., Eshraghi, A., & Smith, P. (2023). Artificial intelligence and knowledge management: A partnership between human and AI. *Business Horizons, 66*(1), 87-99. doi:10.1016/j.bushor.2022.03.002

Joram, M. K., Harrison, B. K., & Joseph, K. N. (2017). A knowledge-based system for life insurance underwriting. *International Journal of Information Technology and Computer Science, 9*(3), 40–49. doi:10.5815/ijitcs.2017.03.05

Lai, L. F. (2007). A knowledge engineering approach to knowledge management. *Information Sciences, 177*(19), 4072–4094. doi:10.1016/j.ins.2007.02.028

Madakam, S., Holmukhe, R. M., & Revulagadda, R. K. (2022). The next generation intelligent automation: Hyperautomation. *Journal of Information Systems and Technology Management, 19*, e202219009. doi:10.4301/S1807-1775202219009

Manuti, A., & Monachino, D. (2020). Managing knowledge at the time of artificial intelligence: An explorative study with knowledge workers. *East European Journal of Psycholinguistics, 7*(2), 179–190. doi:10.29038/eejpl.2020.7.2.man

Mariano, E. B., & Rebelatto, D. A. do N. (2010). Sistematização do processo de escolha dos modelos e perspectivas da análise envoltória de dados por meio de um sistema especialista. *XXX Encontro Nacional de Engenharia de Produção: Competitividade das Empresas, Condições de Trabalho, Meio Ambiente.* doi:10.13140/2.1.1236.0645

Ouali, S., Mhiri, M., & Gargouri, F. (2017). Knowledge engineering for business process modeling. *12th International Conference on Evaluation of Novel Approaches to Software Engineering (ENASE 2017)*, (pp. 81-90). ScitePress. 10.5220/0006323200810090

Rezende, S. O. (2005). *Sistemas inteligentes: fundamentos e aplicações*. Manole.

Ribeiro Júnior, D. I. (2010). *Modelo de sistema baseado em conhecimento para apoiar processos de tomada de decisão em ciência e tecnologia.* [Tese]. Programa de Pós-graduação em Engenharia e Gestão do Conhecimento, Universidade Federal de Santa Catarina (UFSC), Florianópolis. https://repositorio.ufsc.br/bitstream/handle/123456789/94123/297613.pdf?sequence=1&isAllowed=y

Santana, M., & Díaz-Fernández, M. (2023). Competencies for the artificial intelligence age: Visualisation of the state of the art and future perspectives. *Review of Managerial Science, 17*(6), 1971–2004. doi:10.1007/s11846-022-00613-w

Sharda, R., Delen, D., & Turban, E. (2015). *Decision support and expert system: Business intelligence and analytics systems for decision support. 10*. Pearson.

Smuts, H., & Van der Merwe, A. (2022). A knowledge management in Society 5.0: Sustainability perspective. *Sustainability (Basel), 14*(11), 6878. doi:10.3390/su14116878

Solti, E. (2016). Os conhecimentos declarativo e processual de John Anderson no ensino a distância de guitarra elétrica e violão popular. *Simpósio Internacional de Educação a Distância (SIED) e Encontro de Pesquisadores em Educação a Distância (EnPED)*. UniCamp. www.bibliotecadigital.unicamp.br/document/?code=000951159

Taherdoost, H., & Madanchian, M. (2023). Artificial intelligence and knowledge management: Impacts, benefits, and implementation. *Computers, 12*(4), 1-18.

ENDNOTES

1. Feigenbaum, Edward Albert & Mccorduck, Pamela (1983). *The fifth generation*: Artificial intelligence and Japan's computer challenge to the world. Boston: Addison-Wesley. 275p.
2. Abramson, Bruce & Ng, Keung-Chi (1993). Toward an art and science of knowledge engineering: A case for belief networks. *Knowledge and Data Engineering, IEEE Transactions on*, v. 5, n. 4, p. 705-712.
3. Schreiber, Gus, Akkermans, Hans, & Van de Velde, Walter (1994). CommonKADS: A comprehensive methodology for KBS development. *IEEE Expert*, v. 9, n. 6, p. 28-37, Dec.
4. Schreiber, Gus *et al.* (2002). *Knowledge engineering and management*: The commonKADS methodology. Cambridge, Massachusetts (MA): MIT Press. 401p.
5. Hayes-Roth, F., Waterman, D. A., & Lenat, D. B. (Org.) (1983). *Building expert systems*. Reading (MA): Addison-Wesley.
6. Also knowledge as descriptive or propositional knowledge.
7. Anderson, J. R. (1981). *As competências cognitivas e sua aquisição*. Hillsdale (NJ): Lawrence Erlbaum.

Chapter 4
Knowledge Management Tools for Reducing the Learning Curve:
A Case Study

Patricia De Sá Freire
Federal University of Santa Catarina, Brazil

Fillipe Calza
Federal University of Santa Catarina, Brazil

Talita Caetano Silva
Federal University of Santa Catarina, Brazil

Ana Claudia Donner Abreu
https://orcid.org/0009-0004-3918-6292
Federal University of Santa Catarina, Brazil

Yuqing Yao
Federal University of Santa Catarina, Brazil

ABSTRACT

The learning curve has proven to be a useful tool for monitoring the performance of both new and experienced employees. For an analysis of the relationship between knowledge management and the reduction of the learning curve, this article presents a study conducted within an IT company in the city of Florianópolis. A questionnaire was administered to 70% of the employees, and their responses were analyzed. The study concluded that the research identified the key knowledge management tools that can impact the improvement of the learning curve. For questions that did not receive more than 50% positive responses, the application of knowledge management methods and techniques was carried out. As the techniques are implemented and refined by the company, the reduction of the learning curve is likely to happen in a natural and progressive manner.

DOI: 10.4018/979-8-3693-1058-8.ch004

INTRODUCTION

Since the process of adapting to a new product or service can impact a reduction in the productive system, organizations seek models and techniques that can decrease the learning curve for their new employees. In the highly competitive technological market, quality tools are capable of enhancing productivity and are increasingly widespread in modern organizations. In this context, the learning curve emerges as a valuable tool for monitoring the performance of workers undergoing new operations (ANZANELLO, 2005).

For an understanding related to learning, Freire et al. (2021) define the Learning Curve as a mathematical and graphical representation of the levels achieved during a learning process, conducted through the relationship between the acquired knowledge and the time required for it, aimed at measuring the effectiveness of different stages of educational actions.

The employee is evaluated as progress is made, and with each repetition, it acts as an assessment system. Learning curves are mathematical representations of a worker's performance when engaged in repetitive manual tasks (WRIGHT, 1936). As tasks and processes are executed, the worker reduces the time required for completion. This happens due to familiarity with the means of production, adaptation to the tools used by the organization, or the discovery of "shortcuts." According to Wright (1936), research involving learning curves aims to enhance production quality by optimizing process performance, resource utilization, and processing cost reduction, among other factors.

More recently, in the glossary titled "GLOSSARY: Multilevel Governance of Knowledge and Learning and its mechanisms of Networked Corporate University and Dialogic Communication" published in 2021 (FREIRE et al., 2021), the term Knowledge Management is defined as a macroprocess of managing knowledge through the combination of human and non-human sources, for the purpose of multilevel decision-making, utilizing various subprocesses, from auditing to the application of knowledge in such a way that significant understanding generates organizational learning.

Based on this information, Knowledge Management was used in this study as a tool to assist in reducing the learning curve for incoming employees. An interview was conducted with the head of the human resources department to map the new employee integration process in a technology-based company in the city of Florianópolis. According to the 2020 Entrepreneurial Cities Index developed by Endeavor and ENAP, Florianópolis is the second most entrepreneurial city in the country, right after São Paulo. The city stands out particularly in innovation, technology, and human capital indicators. Subsequently, company leaders were also interviewed to understand, from a leadership perspective, the learning curve of new employees in the studied company. The case study aims to gather data that complements the understanding of the learning curve in the analyzed company. Finally, the presented results are discussed to provide companies with practices and techniques that accelerate the employee's adaptation and productivity process.

THEORETICAL FRAMEWORK

This chapter addresses the fundamentals and concepts of knowledge management, technology companies, and the learning curve. It presents studies and various theoretical perspectives that have been developed on the subject.

Knowledge Development

According to the Brazilian Association of Software Companies (ABES), the Brazilian Information Technology market, which includes hardware, software, services, and IT exports, generated approximately R$ 506.5 billion in 2020. This represents about 6.8% of the Brazilian GDP, with a growth of 2.4% compared to the year 2019. Technological advancement and high competitiveness force both large and small companies to be increasingly innovative to remain in the market. Knowledge becomes one of the most valuable resources organizations possess. According to Crawford (1994), information and knowledge replace physical and financial capital, becoming one of the most significant competitive advantages in business.

Knowledge requires continuous development and must be protected and nurtured continually. The less effort is put into applying and renewing knowledge, the easier it is for it to become outdated and depreciated (TERRA, 2000). Active knowledge must be constantly transformed and updated.

Before constructing and elaborating on knowledge, data acquisition and structuring into information are necessary. Sometimes there's the idea that to exist and reach the act of knowledge, one must initially have the main element known as data, whether it's an axiom, a logical principle, or a sensory impression (FERREIRA et al., 1999). Stair and Reynolds (2002) present categorization as processes involving the acquisition of data and their organization into information. The first stage consists of the data, and the second stage involves their consolidation into information, as observed in the continuum of understanding explained by Sherdroff (2000).

After collecting, identifying, and obtaining data, there's the possibility of organizing it in the form of information. It is up to the individual who processes the data into information to establish their objectives and interests so that the generated information is as useful as possible. Knowledge is a skill pertinent to individuals and a human, dynamic process of justification according to the beliefs, goals, and personal obligations of the knowledge holder (NONAKA; TAKEUCHI, 2008).

Development of Knowledge Management

The term knowledge management can be understood as a set of activities focused on promoting organizational knowledge. Organizations have integrated generating value during their processes and in the internal knowledge of the organizational structure into their business strategies. Thus, to achieve and fulfill organizational objectives, knowledge management emerges as a set of processes that guide the creation, dissemination, and utilization of knowledge that is of common interest among stakeholders (DAVENPORT and PRUSAK, 1998).

The culture of knowledge management involves practices of creation, storage, sharing, utilization, and ongoing updating of information and processes that are mapped over time. The objectives of knowledge management can generally be divided into four stages for a better execution of the process: knowledge acquisition, development, dissemination, and memorization (FLEURY and FLEURY, 2001). Models serve as representations of a process, describing the characteristics of a particular structure, event, or simulation of everyday elements. There are several ways to present knowledge management in the form of models, some of which include:

- The organizational knowledge creation model: developed by Nonaka and Takeuchi (1997), applied in large companies and among managers in Japan, aims to understand and improve organizational behavior. It considers two dimensions of knowledge creation: ontological and epistemological.
- The generic knowledge management model: unifies common aspects of other models in applying processes within organizations (Stollenwerk, 2001). It encompasses identification, capture, selection and validation, organization and storage, sharing, application, and creation of knowledge.
- The strategic knowledge management model: this model consists of four fundamental layers for the knowledge management process. The elements should be overlapped and interconnected, emphasizing the need for successful completion of the previous layer to enable the implementation of the next layer (ROSSATO, 2003).

In addition, knowledge management systems have a constant need for feedback. Communication can be stimulated by a change in intelligence matters or by a specific organizational transformation. Comments and opinions can be exchanged in person, through social networks, emails, or specific online/offline documents. Information Technology (IT) can be used to mediate this person-to-person communication more rapidly, effectively, and efficiently. The perpetual concern of organizations lies in the storage and retention of their intellectual property or specialized knowledge. Albuquerque (2011, p.104) emphasizes that Information Technology (IT) continues to play a fundamental role as a tool for capturing and disseminating information, while knowledge management seeks to understand and develop techniques and methodologies that can expand the experiences, skills, and competencies of employees, organizations, and society. "It is through the information produced, with the help of a system of signs, that man seeks to relate his lived experience to other people; to spread to others his experience, which was experienced only by him." Current information and communication systems allow for real-time information gathering, platform integration, and reliability.

The Job Market and Turnover in Technology Companies

The Brazilian Association of Information Technology and Communication Companies (BRASSCOM) estimates that by 2025, the demand for professionals in the technology field will reach 800,000 individuals. Presently, Brazil produces around 50,000 professionals annually. Therefore, to meet this goal, more than 70,000 professionals per year need to enter the job market. In terms of revenue, the Brazilian technology sector generated R$ 426.9 billion in 2020, representing approximately 5.6% of the GDP. This revenue distribution is region-specific, with São Paulo accounting for 48.4%, approximately R$ 206 billion. Regarding the state of Santa Catarina, it was considered the sixth-largest technology hub in Brazil in terms of the number of companies, representing 4.4% in 2021 (ACATE, 2021).

Turnover, or employee turnover rate, is an index that incurs costs for companies. Besides the expenses related to an employee's departure, it's important to consider that onboarding a new employee can cost up to 30% (GEEKHUNTER, 2022). In terms of tenure, IT employees, on average, remain with a company for about 2.6 years. This turnover is considered high, as compared to other sectors with an average tenure of 3.8 years.

Figure 1. Reduction of time with the learning process
(Adapted from Peinado and Graeml, 2007)

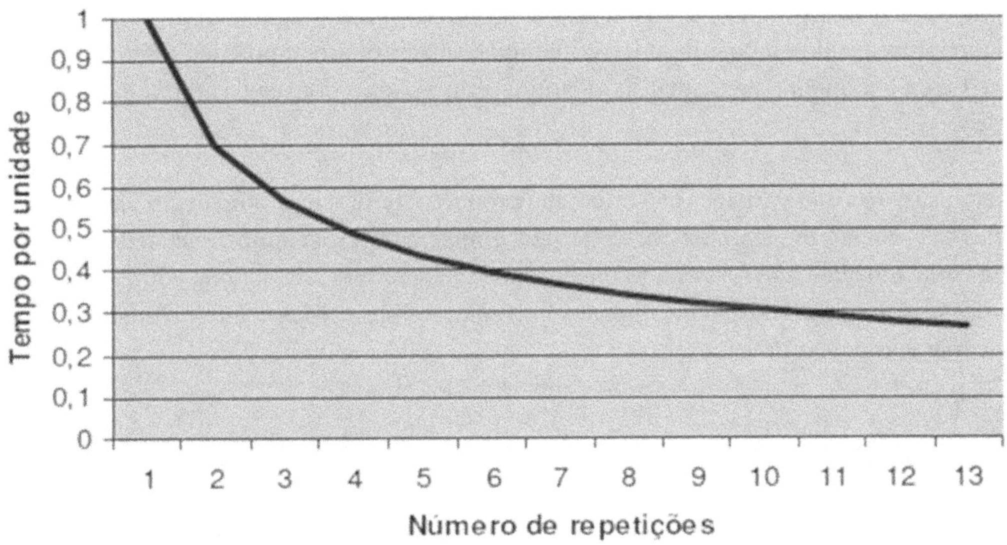

The Learning Curve in Technology Companies

The learning curve is literally described as a graphical record of cost reduction as employees gain experience and increase total production within the same time period. The higher the repeatability, the greater the employee's refinement, expediting task execution until perfection is achieved.

WRIGHT's study (1936) demonstrates how the time required for a task decreases as learning through repetition occurs, as shown in Figure 1. In the figure, it can be understood that the vertical axis, also known as the value axis (y), represents time per unit. In turn, the horizontal axis, known as the categories axis (x), represents the quantity of repetitions.

The learning curve serves as a tool capable of monitoring employee performance. Through these curves, it's possible to analyze and plan productive tasks, reducing losses resulting from the employee's lack of skill, typically observed in the initial production cycles (ARGOTE, 1999; DAR-EL, 2000). Productivity can be influenced by various aspects, often divided into categories such as labor; design and work content aspects; environmental conditions; management control practices; execution methods; and project organizational structure.

There are various learning curve models, applicable to specific product types or classes of activities, including:

- Linear Model: Applied in analyzing construction activities, represented by a straight line when plotted on a logarithmic scale. This assumes a constant learning curve throughout the activity duration (THOMAS et al., 1986).
- Stanford B Model: A more sophisticated and realistic approach than the linear model. It assumes the learning curve consists of three distinct phases: cognitive, associative, and autonomous. This

model modifies the linear model, considering the experience gain leading to increased productivity (THOMAS et al., 1986).

- Cubic Model: An even more sophisticated approach than linear and Stanford B models. It's based on a mathematical equation describing the relationship between practice time and performance over time. The model states that the learning rate is not a constant variable (THOMAS et al., 1986).

Numerous aspects and variables can affect the productivity of a new employee. Sharing knowledge contributes to reducing the learning curve for new employees, but caution is needed to ensure the information is documented and resistant to the constant changes and adaptations within companies. The use of process-related methods and techniques is crucial for knowledge management and reducing the learning curve within organizations.

STUDY DEVELOPMENT

This study developed a methodology for evaluating the learning curve of companies, through the application of a questionnaire in a company within the IT sector, engaged in activities related to developing solutions for businesses operating in the consigned credit market. Data collection took place from October to November 2022. The aim was to assess how the company understands the learning curve and what actions are taken to enhance its performance.

The questionnaire was designed and conducted in electronic format, distributed to respondents via email with access permission through a link, using Google Forms. The questionnaire development procedure was divided into two categories: the first for characterizing the interviewees, and the second for understanding the processes and activities undertaken by the company.

Sample and Population

The population used was determined according to the analyzed company, encompassing 70% of the company's workforce, as the total staff comprises 49 employees. The questionnaire was administered throughout the company, including positions in management, supervision, development, less experienced employees, and/or those in training. This approach facilitated the identification of personal characteristics of employees, as well as their understanding of company procedures and information dissemination.

The questionnaire comprised 26 multiple-choice questions. This format was chosen to ensure respondent anonymity. Data storage occurred after the established period ended. Employees were allowed to respond only once, without the option to modify or update their answers, preventing bias.

The questionnaire was divided into two sections: the first pertained to personal characteristics of the employees to define their profile, and the second group focused on measuring the processes utilized by the company. The responses aimed to assess the methodology of educational processes and information dissemination employed by the company and their impact on the learning curve. The complete questionnaire description is provided in Calza (2023).

Figure 2. Employees' time of service in the company

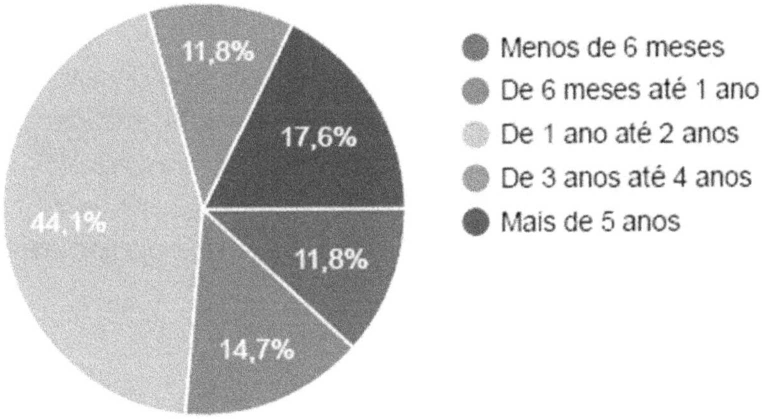

RESULTS

For the results of this article, responses were statistically analyzed and related to the sample space of the analyzed company. The total sample was composed of responses from 34 employees.

In terms of characterizing the employees by age, the responses were as follows: 38.2% were between 21 and 25 years old; 29.4% were between 26 and 30 years old; 23.5% were between 31 and 35 years old, and 8.8% were above 35 years old. None of the interviewed employees were under 20 years old. The duration of employment was also evaluated as one of the main factors influencing the learning curve, and it's presented in Figure 2.

More than 40% of the employees have been with the company for 1 to 2 years, which adds a high level of reliability to the responses. This response also aligns with turnover rates in the technology sector. The employees' level of education was also verified and presented in Figure 3.

The diverse educational backgrounds can also be considered a positive aspect for the company, as it values employees and their opportunities. The educational advancement of employees since the start of their careers in the company was not evaluated in this study. However, considering the duration of employment, an association can be made if the average time for completing each phase is considered. Therefore, it can also be inferred that the company acts as an encouraging platform for employees to pursue further education and development.

Analyses About the Company

The identification of departments, process management, and methods of information dissemination are tools that enhance knowledge transmission and directly impact the learning curve. It was identified that the company's teams are relatively small, consisting of up to 10 people. A concerning question arose about the internal communication between teams within the company (Figure 4). Employee responses indicate that 73.5% believe that internal communication occurs partially, and another 20.6% state that there is no such communication. These high percentages are detrimental from the perspective of a technology company dealing with a high volume of information daily, subject to constant updates. Thus,

Figure 3. Employees' educational background in the company

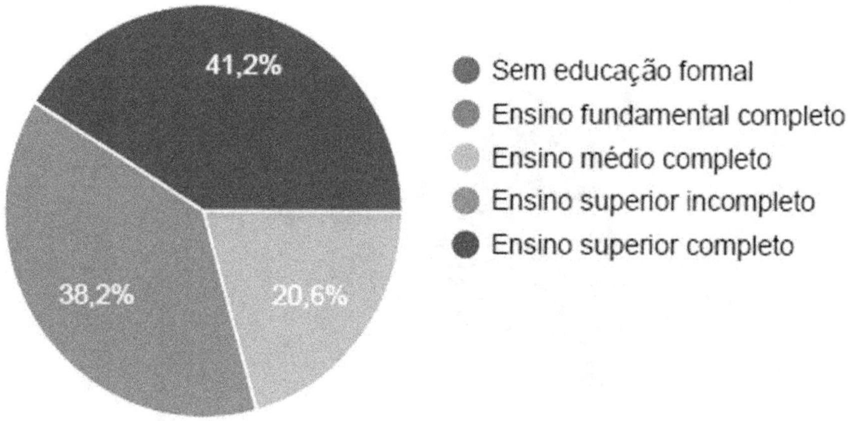

this is undoubtedly an aspect deserving the attention of the management to immediately minimize productivity impacts.

The second point regarding information dissemination within the company also aimed to address the encouragement received from leadership positions. Positively, responses from employees, with over 60.0%, highlight the presence of such encouragement. Approximately 30.0% of employees responded that leadership positions offer partial incentives.

Regarding the impacts of knowledge dissemination, the knowledge base provided and made available by the company is of great importance. Figure 5 presents the relationship of employees with the availability of the knowledge base.

Over 40% of employees confirm the extensive availability of stored knowledge in the company. A significant portion of employees, however, responded that such sharing occurs partially (38.2%). It is noteworthy that the percentage of responses indicating no availability of knowledge for all employees remained consistent with those who consider the storage unreliable, at around 21%.

Figure 4. Internal communication of processes among employees in the company

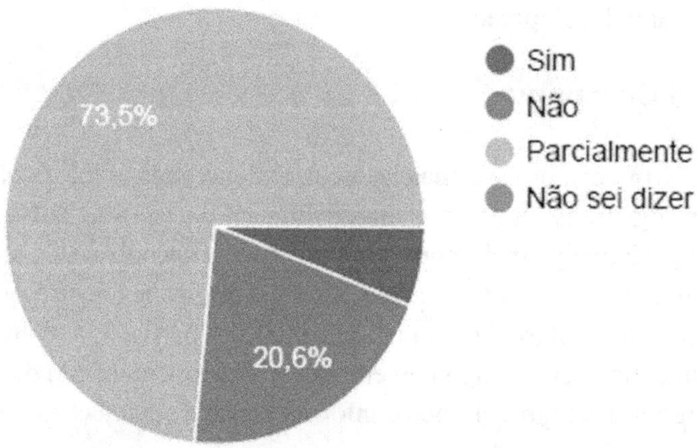

Figure 5. Availability of the knowledge base in the company

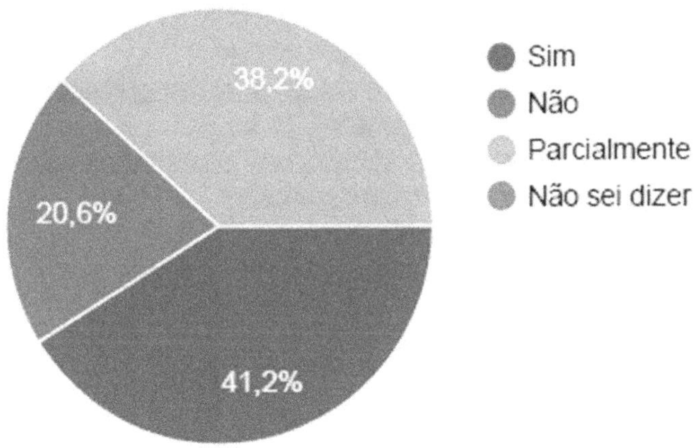

Other significant aspects regarding methods of accessing company knowledge and its dissemination among teams were analyzed more broadly. Regarding information retrieval from the database, over 64.7% of surveyed employees responded that they know where to search for such information to some extent, indicating a partial familiarity. Thus, processes for improvement or specific training could easily alter these percentages. The vast majority of employees acknowledged the importance of information and knowledge storage, at 91.2%. The remaining 8.8% responded that there is only partial importance in such storage.

Analyses on Information and Knowledge Storage

The second analysis regarding the methods used by the company pertains to the sharing of knowledge among employees and leadership. This dissemination of content is one of the key actions that should be encouraged within companies to reduce the learning curve. Therefore, the initial question on this topic addressed the existence of processes and methods to disseminate acquired knowledge among members. The primary platforms for accessing and sharing information are presented in Figure 6.

Given that it's a technology company, it was expected that information exchange would predominantly occur digitally. While this modernized communication can be beneficial, without a proper storage system, knowledge can easily be lost. The company's culture of incentives, particularly concerning knowledge sharing, was also examined and is presented in Figure 7.

The results gathered from employees align with the notion that the company follows good practices when it comes to incentivizing knowledge sharing. Approximately 41.20% of employees confirmed this attitude, and an additional 47.10% responded that it exists to some extent. In general, the results indicate that the company adopts positive practices regarding disseminating knowledge to employees.

Concluding this stage of the analysis on information processes employed by the company and disseminated among employees, respondents were asked about the importance of this data. Nearly 80% of employees answered that the information and knowledge stored by the company are useful. This implies that even if there isn't a complete understanding of the storage or dissemination processes, employees recognize the significance of this data. Thus, it underscores the need for the company to focus on methods of information sharing with its employees.

Figure 6. Platforms for knowledge sharing among company members

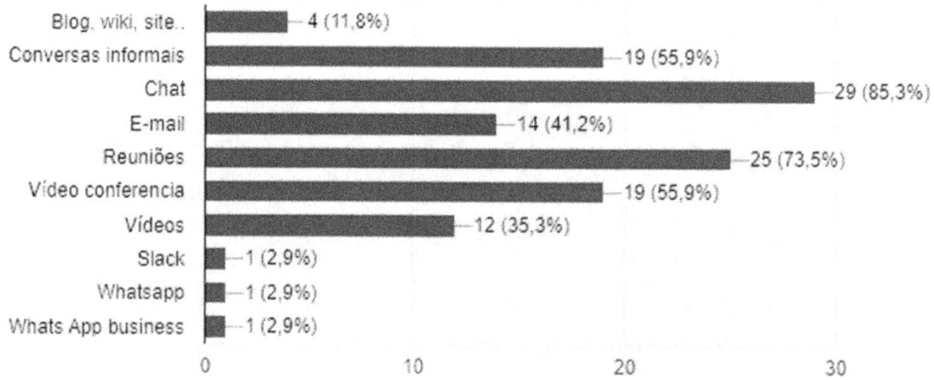

Figure 7. Company culture and incentives for knowledge sharing among everyone

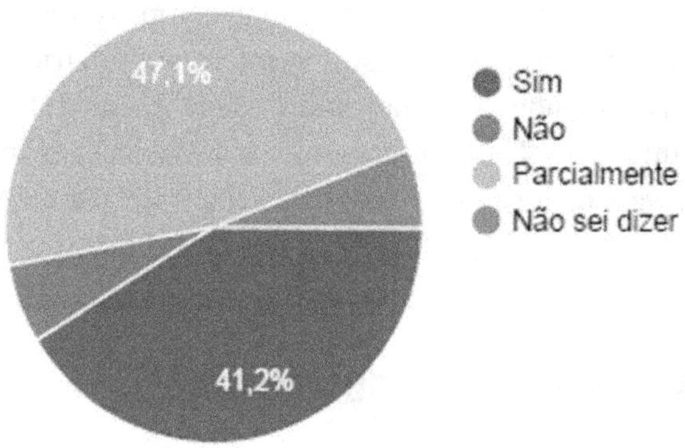

Company-Provided Training

Throughout the development of this article, it has been observed that at times, more crucial than the learning itself is how it is shared by leadership roles with other employees. Therefore, with a focus on employee training, they were queried about when these activities began. The goal was to understand the actions initiated shortly after an employee's hiring and the level of information provided. Satisfactorily, over 55% of employees responded that they received training and guidance immediately after joining the company, as shown in Figure 8.

Around 26.50% of employees indicated that training is received partially, a percentage that requires careful evaluation for improvement. Lastly, 17.60% of employees answered that they did not receive this information, with 2.90% stating that such procedures are absent. To delve deeper into training, employees were also asked about its importance in engaging with the team and the company. Impressively, over 85.0% of employees valued this activity and recognized its significance.

There is evident interest among employees in participating in and receiving these training sessions and orientations. Therefore, this process should be thoroughly developed and implemented by the company to enhance its actions (WIIG, 2004; RAO, 2005; SERVIN, 2005 cited in OROFINO, 2011). The need for the company's commitment to training and orientation was further emphasized by another survey.

Figure 8. Reception of training, orientation, or onboarding process

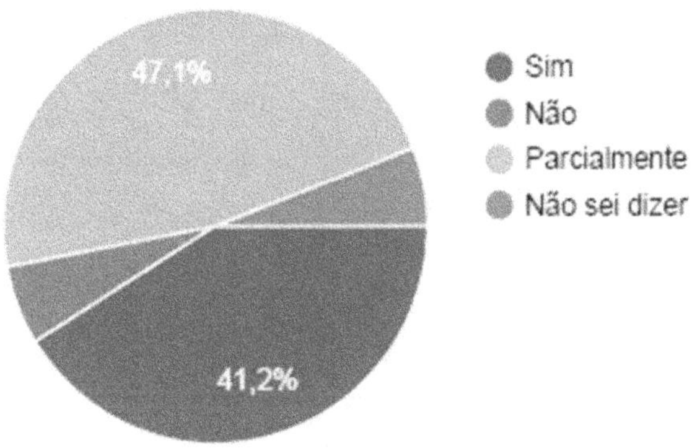

Figure 9. Adequacy of training and orientation for engagement with the company/team

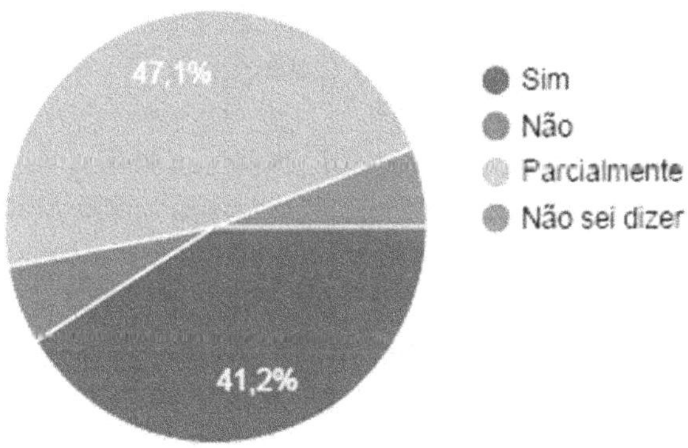

Employees were asked about the adequacy of the training and orientation received for understanding processes, information, and the functioning of the company/team. With a wide range of responses, this question raises a new concern about the procedures executed by the company, as only 26.5% of employees responded affirmatively (Figure 9). Over 67% of employees indicated that the methods used are partially satisfactory or even unsatisfactory.

The dissemination of knowledge among employees can be an excellent way to improve training programs. Employees understand the challenges within departments and can point out flaws that might not be apparent to management. Involving employees in these introductory actions has shown that improving them can positively and rapidly impact the team (WIIG, 2004; RAO, 2005; SERVIN, 2005 cited in OROFINO, 2011). This prediction is based on the active participation of a significant portion of employees. Concluding this training section, employees were asked about the means through which this information exchange occurs. As expected, being a technology company, over 90% of responses referred to rapid information exchange via the internet.

From the perspective of the impacts generated by the learning curve on company processes, small affirmative actions can lead to significant advantages. Results indicated employee collaboration in actions, facilitating the dissemination of knowledge and training. Thus, a refinement process emerges as essential.

Figure 10. Training plans for development in the department and team

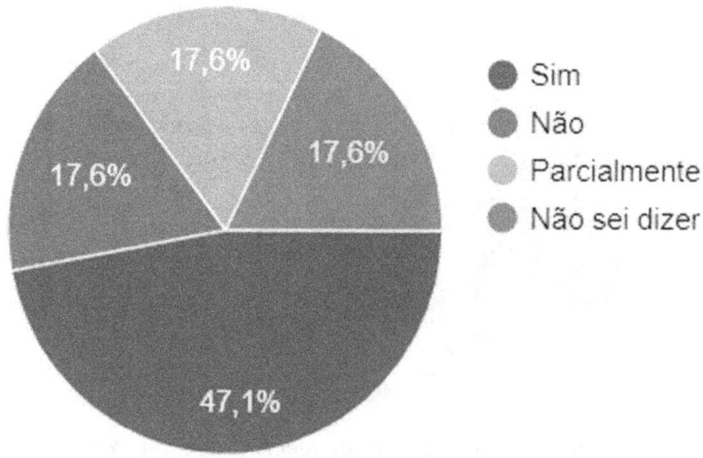

Availability of Employee Training by the Company

The process of employee training becomes a means of constant updating on technologies, which evolve concurrently in this field. This type of process can be carried out in various ways, commonly disseminated through external materials such as online and in-person courses, as well as participation in lectures and events. Technologically speaking, there are countless ways to provide the team with access to the best and most current techniques for process development (GEEKHUNTER, 2022).

To assess this condition within the company, employees were queried about training plans as part of their development in their respective departments and teams. The responses obtained exhibited variability among employees' opinions, with only 47.1% responding affirmatively (Figure 10). Several employees indicated a negative response, whether partially or even stating that they do not know how to identify these plans.

The lack of training plans is an issue that requires immediate intervention by the company. Another realization emerged when employees were asked about sharing the knowledge gained in these events

Figure 11. Sharing of information obtained in training plans

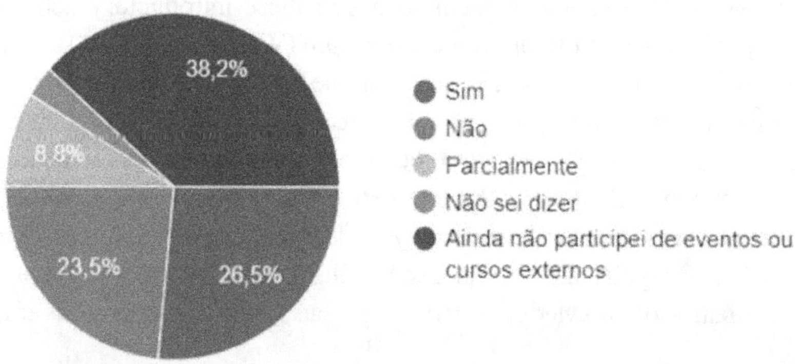

and/or courses. As depicted in Figure 11, around 38% of employees responded that they did not participate in these activities. Among the employees who did participate in such actions, they indicated that the acquired knowledge was shared partially, or sometimes not shared at all. This limited participation, about 26.5%, highlights the need to revisit the company's goals and activities.

It's understood that employees who have not received training might be those who recently joined the company. However, the promotion and existence of these training plans should be transparent and well-known to all. Activities related to information dissemination can require time and a trained team. However, once established, the process becomes automated and can be carried out by trained employees. The concept of a chain execution comes into play, directly impacting the clarity of the information being disseminated (SILVA, 2019).

IMPROVEMENTS IN THE COMPANY THROUGH ADOPTED PRACTICES

Based on the questions posed to the employees of the technology company located in Florianópolis, the responses were carefully analyzed and cross-referenced with the technical practices and knowledge management tools identified in the literature. This process identified the most effective practices, techniques, and tools to drive organizational learning and promote better performance and productivity outcomes for a specific context. This analysis contributes to refining existing practices and developing more effective knowledge management strategies.

The goal was to identify opportunities for enhancement and development, aiming to optimize learning processes and maximize individual and collective performance. The following practices that can be adopted were identified:

- **Employee Communication Process:** Tools that facilitate access and sharing of relevant information, promoting collaboration among employees (APO, 2010; BERGERON, 2003; RAO, 2005).
- **Information Storage Methods:** Tools to facilitate access and sharing of relevant information, promoting collaboration among employees (APO, 2010).
- **Information Retrieval Process:** Tools that enable employees to conduct more accurate and efficient searches (WELCHEN, MUKERNDI, FACHINELLI, and PEDRO, 2022 apud OROFINO, 2011).
- **Dissemination and Sharing of Knowledge:** Transforming individual knowledge into organizational assets (WIIG, 2004; RAO, 2005; SERVIN, 2005 apud OROFINO, 2011).
- **Culture and Knowledge Incentives:** Sharing knowledge, experiences, and ideas in a relaxed and collaborative environment (GEEKHUNTER, 2022).
- **Conducted Trainings:** Assisting new employees in understanding the technical and cultural aspects of the organization (WIIG, 2004; RAO, 2005; SERVIN, 2005 apud OROFINO, 2011).

By implementing these practices, the company can foster a culture of continuous learning, effective knowledge sharing, and improved performance. The specific needs and context of the company should be considered while tailoring and integrating these practices into its operations.

FINAL REMARKS

To understand the impacts of the learning curve in a technology company based in Florianópolis, Santa Catarina, a questionnaire was administered to employees. This survey included responses from 34 employees in various roles within the company. After analyzing the results, categories of questions were created to understand both the employees' and the company's characteristics. The employees' level of training within the company was also assessed through the questionnaire. The results obtained from the questionnaire analysis led to the conclusion that the research objectives were met.

Regarding the company-related questions, its characterization, and the provision of information to employees, it was noted that internal communication and knowledge sharing did not occur simultaneously, as indicated by over 73% of the respondents. The lack of clear and effective information exchange between departments and management emerged as a significant challenge. The effectiveness of knowledge storage was recognized by only 20.6% of the employees, and the availability of the knowledge base was acknowledged by 41%.

The employees were also asked about the encouragement from leadership roles to document and record knowledge. This time, over 60% of the responses were affirmative, suggesting that the company should improve its techniques and materials for knowledge dissemination. The dissemination of acquired knowledge among company members is currently done through more than eight methods, with online methods being prominent. However, this dissemination occurs only partially for 61.8% of the employees, indicating a need for improvement.

The final analysis of the company was related to the provision of training and information to employees. Satisfactorily, over 55% of the employees responded that they received training and guidance immediately after being hired by the company. It is concluded that the company needs to urgently improve its information sharing. Regarding the sharing of information about training plans, only 26.5% responded affirmatively, a relatively low percentage. These results reflect flaws in the company's information sharing and training actions for its employees. Consequently, these aspects require special attention and decision-making for improvement, as they have a direct impact on employees' daily work.

By relating the obtained results to the literature on the learning curve, several processes need improvement to reduce it. The lack of training plans, knowledge dissemination, and free access to the company's database hinders various processes. These difficulties decrease team productivity and constrain operations. When changes occur in teams, productivity dips are expected until the new employee gains a full understanding of activities and performs at the level of their predecessor. This thesis fulfills its objectives of identifying and categorizing company actions that can contribute to reducing the learning curve and optimizing processes. It presents knowledge management practices, techniques, and tools that can aid in reducing the learning curve for new employees

FUTURE WORKS

We have demonstrated how the strategic adoption of knowledge management practices can mitigate identified challenges and improve the learning curve. Identifying these challenges suggests implementing improvements to not only facilitate communication and information sharing but also strengthen organizational culture and overall efficiency.

In conclusion, it is suggested that new researchers explore how knowledge management models and approaches can enrich communication, storage, and sharing of information to decrease the learning curve for new employees. As seen, academic studies have indicated that the implementation of effective knowledge management systems facilitates the exchange of information and experiences, which are crucial for reducing the learning curve. By integrating these contemporary theories with new case studies, GC models can be validated for different realities and complex knowledge management challenges, and identified gaps can be overcome.

The gaps exist, considering organizational culture, communication structure, and training methods. Often, the lack of clear communication and inefficient knowledge storage are the results of outdated systems or a culture that does not value knowledge sharing. This chapter points to discussion paths of specific solutions for these gaps, which could be: Implementing collaborative platforms that encourage interaction and information sharing, such as corporate social networks; adopting knowledge management systems that categorize and facilitate access to previous documents and records; integrating advanced search tools that allow for efficient and precise queries; promoting workshops and knowledge-sharing meetings to transform individual knowledge into organizational assets; cultivating a culture that values and rewards knowledge sharing; and finally, developing continuous and focused training programs for new employees.

We conclude by emphasizing the importance of a holistic and adaptive approach to knowledge management to promote a continuous and collaborative learning environment.

REFERENCES

ABES. (2017). *Mercado Brasileiro de Software - Panorama e Tendências*. ABES. https://www.abessoftware.com.br/dados-do-setor/estudo-2017--dados-2016

ACATE. (2021). *Tech Report*. Panorama do setor de tecnologia catarinense.

Adler, P. S., & Clark, K. B. (1991). Behind the learning curve: A sketch of the learning process. *Management Science*, *37*(3), 267–281. doi:10.1287/mnsc.37.3.267

Albuquerque, J. C. M. (2011). *Sistemas de informação e comunicação no setor público*. Departamento de Ciências da Administração/UFSC.

Anzanello, M. J., & Fogliatto, F. S. (2005). Alocação de modelos de produtos a equipes de trabalhadores baseada em modelos de curvas de aprendizagem. *Production*, *15*(2), 221–234. doi:10.1590/S0103-65132005000200007

Anzanello, M. J., & Fogliatto, F. S. (2007). Curvas de aprendizado: Estado da arte e perspectivas de pesquisa. *Gestão & Produção*, *14*(1), 109–123. doi:10.1590/S0104-530X2007000100010

Bergeron, B. (2003). Essentials of Knowledge Management. *Studies in Health Technology and Informatics*, *160*, 1–208.

BRASSCOM - Associação das Empresas de Tecnologia da Informação e Comunicação (TIC) e de Tecnologias Digitais. (2021). *Demanda de Talentos em TIC e Estratégia Σ TCEM*. Brasscom. https://brasscom.org.br/pdfs/demanda-de-talentos-em-tic-e-estrategia-tcem/

Calza, F. (2023). *Impacto do uso da gestão do conhecimento para a gestão da curva de aprendizagem de uma empresa do setor de TI, da cidade de Florianópolis/SC*. Trabalho de Conclusão de Curso, Universidade Federal de Santa Catarina.

Crawford, R. (1994). *Na era do capital humano*. Editora Atlas.

Davenport, T. H., & Prusak, L. (1998). *Conhecimento empresarial: como as organizações gerenciam seu capital intelectual*.

Endeavor & ENAP. (2021). *Índice de Cidades Empreendedoras*. Brasil. https://repositorio.enap.gov.br/bitstream/1/6097/1/relatorio_ICE_2020.pdf

Ferreira, A. B. H., Anjos, M., & Ferreira, M. B. (1999). *Novo Aurélio, Século XXI: o dicionário da língua portuguesa* (3rd ed.). Nova Fronteira.

Fleury, A., & Fleury, M. T. L. (2007). *Internacionalização e os países emergentes*. Atlas.

Freire, P. de S., Alvares, L. M. A. de R., Rizzatti, G., Bresolin, G. G., Martins, G. J. T., Kempner-Moreira, F., & Silva, T. C. (2021). *Glossário: Governança Multinível do Conhecimento e da Aprendizagem e seus mecanismos de Universidade Corporativa em Rede e de Comunicação Dialógica*. CRV.

Geekhunter. (2022). Turnover em TI: como reduzir a rotatividade de desenvolvedores da sua empresa. https://rhtech.geekhunter.com.br/turnover-em-ti-2/#Por_que_ficar_de_olho_no_turnover_em_TI

Gil, A. C. (2002). *Como elaborar projetos de pesquisa* (4th ed.). Atlas.

Nonaka, I., & Takeuchi, H. (1997). *Criação de conhecimento na empresa. Empresas japonesas geram a dinâmica da inovação* (20th ed.). Elsevier.

Nonaka, I., & Takeuchi, H. (2008). Teoria da criação do conhecimento organizacional. In H. Takeuchi & I. Nonaka (Eds.), *Gestão do conhecimento*. Bookman.

Orofino, M. A. R. (2011). *Técnicas de criação do conhecimento no desenvolvimento de modelos de negócio. Dissertação, Programa de Pós-graduação em Engenharia e Gestão do Conhecimento*, Universidade Federal de Santa Catarina.

Rossatto, M. A. (2003). *Gestão do Conhecimento: a busca da humanização, transparência, socialização e valorização do intangível*. Interciência.

Shedroff, N. (2000). 11 Information Interaction Design: A Unified Field Theory of Design. *Information design, 267*.

Silva, T. C. (2019). *Framework Ponte TAP: Gestão da curva de aprendizagem para a efetivação da transferência de aprendizagem para a prática do trabalho* [Dissertação, Universidade Federal de Santa Catarina].

Stair, R. M., & Reynolds, G. W. (2002). *Princípios de Sistemas de Informação: uma abordagem gerencial*. Livros Técnicos e Científicos.

Stollenwerk, M. F. (2001). *Gestão do Conhecimento, inteligência competitiva e estratégia empresarial: em busca de uma abordagem integrada*. Anais do Workshop Brasileiro de Inteligência Competitiva.

Terra, J. C. C. (2000). *Gestão do conhecimento: o grande desafio empresarial*. Editora.

Thomas, H. R., Mathews, C. T., & Ward, J. G. (1986). Learning curve models of construction productivity. *Journal of Construction Engineering and Management*, *112*(2), 245–258. doi:10.1061/(ASCE)0733-9364(1986)112:2(245)

Wright, T. P. (1936). Factors Affecting the Cost of Airplanes. *Journal of the Aeronautical Sciences*, *3*(4), 122–128. doi:10.2514/8.155

Chapter 5
Driving Innovation Ecosystem Transformation via Digital Platforms and Knowledge Co-Creation

Denilson Sell
Universidade do Estado de Santa Catarina, Brazil

Luiz Márcio Spinosa
Fundação Araucária, Brazil

Ramiro Wahrhaftig
Fundação Araucária, Brazil

Gérson Luiz Koch
Fundação Araucária, Brazil

Maria Angélica Jung Marques
https://orcid.org/0000-0002-9710-2518
Universidade Federal de Santa Catarina, Brazil

Alfredo Cesar dos Anjos
Universidade Federal de Santa Catarina, Brazil

Neri dos Santos
Universidade Federal de Santa Catarina, Brazil

Roberto Carlos dos Santos Pacheco
Universidade Federal de Santa Catarina, Brazil

ABSTRACT

Co-production in public administration is essential for increasing societal participation in shaping impactful public policies. This chapter delves into the evolution and impact of the new research and innovation arrangements program (NAPI) in Paraná, Brazil. NAPI, an innovative approach, fosters networks for co-producing knowledge and innovation to address state challenges, rooted in the common principle. At the core of NAPI lies the iAraucária digital platform, harnessing artificial intelligence to streamline resource coordination among stakeholders in regional innovation systems, thereby nurturing research and innovation projects aligned with regional needs. Since its inception, NAPI has spurred the formation of over 60 arrangements, involving more than 4,000 participants in collaborative networks. Noteworthy outcomes include increased precision in research and innovation funding, the cultivation of stronger ties among ecosystem actors, and risk mitigation in public policy co-production, all making substantial contributions to Paraná's sustainable development.

DOI: 10.4018/979-8-3693-1058-8.ch005

INTRODUCTION

The socioeconomic advancement of nations and regions is deeply anchored in Science, Technology, and Innovation (ST&I). The 1988 Brazilian Constitution marked a significant step in this direction by advocating for the decentralization of research management and funding. This strategic shift aimed to empower each Brazilian state to foster and manage research and innovation within its territories, leading to the establishment of various State Research Support Foundations (FAPs). These FAPs have emerged as decentralized catalysts for support in ST&I, becoming essential instruments for scientific and technological progress across Brazil.

Present in each of Brazil's 27 federal units, the FAPs are instrumental in local evolution, aligning with the national ST&I system to induce structural transformations in regional economies. Their role extends beyond merely training researchers; it encompasses the promotion and dissemination of research and innovation. This effort is fundamental in promoting a balance between innovation, economic growth, and the valorization of cultural and resource peculiarities in different regions. As noted by Da Silva, Howells, and Meyer (2018), and Shearmur, Carrincazeaux, and Doloreux (2016), regional innovation policies are crucial at both local and national levels, balancing innovation, economic growth, and the recognition of each region's cultural and resource peculiarities. In this context, FAPs play a critical role in regional development by planning and implementing research funding mechanisms and fostering the development of relational capital. The FAPs' initiatives, thus, not only contribute to the advancement of scientific and technological capabilities but also strengthen the relational networks essential for sustainable regional development.

In the State of Paraná, Brazil, the Araucária Foundation has taken on the critical role of stimulating the development of the ST&I system. Traditionally, the foundation operated on a conventional model, relying on public calls for research and innovation project funding. Although efficient, this process faced substantial challenges in understanding and addressing the specific needs of the territory for effective development through ST&I. This complexity becomes apparent when considering the large number of Ph.D. holders (over 20,000 residing in the territory) and other key players in the innovation ecosystem, including the infrastructure available in university laboratories and innovation centers.

The Araucária Foundation recognized the need to restructure its operational model to tackle three main challenges. The first was understanding the territorial needs and identifying the state's science and technology potential. The second challenge, in line with the findings of Audretsch and Link (2019) and Hoffecker (2019), involved the complexity of regional innovation ecosystems, requiring better integration among various actors to effectively co-produce research and innovation. The third challenge lay in the governance of collaborative research and innovation arrangements, primarily due to the distance between actors in research and innovation initiatives.

To address these challenges, the Araucária Foundation in Paraná, Brazil, implemented a new model called the New Research and Innovation Arrangements (NAPIs). Inspired by Hess and Ostrom's (2005) model of co-production of common goods (or *commons*), NAPIs aim to facilitate collective actions of innovation and modernization within the state. A NAPI is perceived as a collective of agents with aligned goals and visions, dedicated to developing innovative solutions through co-production. This model marks a significant step forward in promoting regional development based on ST&I, fostering the co-production of knowledge and innovation among researchers and other actors in Paraná's innovation system.

In this context, the role of digital platforms and artificial intelligence is paramount. Digital platforms serve as arenas where diverse actors can converge, collaborate, and share resources and ideas (Ansell and Torfing, 2021). They not only facilitate interaction among participants but also provide infrastructure for data, project, and resource management (De Reuver; Sørensen; Basole, 2017; Parker; Alstyne; Choudary, 2016). Artificial intelligence adds an additional layer of analysis and pattern recognition, aiding in decision-making and identifying innovation opportunities. This leads to a more efficient and targeted approach to research and innovation, in line with the state's actual needs.

The NAPIs model represents a revolutionary approach in the field of ST&I. It is grounded in data-driven public calls and focuses on creating collaborative networks. These networks are crucial for effectively integrating the multiple actors and resources that make up the quadruple helix – academia, industry, government, and civil society (Leydesdorff; Smith, 2022). At the heart of this model is the concept of arenas, which refers to collaborative spaces where these diverse actors meet and interact to co-create knowledge and innovation (Ansell and Torfing, 2021; Pereira et al., 2018).

In these arenas, co-production is not just a methodology but a philosophy that infuses all aspects of the NAPI model. The co-production of knowledge and innovation in a networked environment occurs when diverse actors, each bringing their unique knowledge and experience, collaborate to develop innovative solutions that meet local and regional needs. This process is facilitated and enhanced by a sophisticated digital platform, which supports every operational phase of the NAPI model. This digital platform acts as an enabler of co-production, providing essential tools for communication, data management, information sharing, and effective collaboration among participants.

The digital platform serves as a catalyst for co-production, bridging ideas, people, and resources, thereby expanding the potential for innovation achievable through multidisciplinary collaboration. It functions as a connecting bridge that enhances the flow of ideas and resources, significantly amplifying the innovation potential.

This chapter unveils the NAPI strategy in Paraná, Brazil, a pioneering initiative using AI to revolutionize regional innovation. NAPI, aided by the AI-powered iAraucária platform, has not only fostered over 60 collaborative arrangements involving more than 4000 participants but has also streamlined connections between actors and supported their projects efficiently. The intelligent allocation of funds has allowed us to extend our reach, supporting more researchers with the same amount of funding, thereby amplifying the program's impact.

The upcoming section of the document will delve into the key elements that make up this innovative model, highlighting how Co-production Arenas and co-production itself are vital for the success and effectiveness of the NAPIs in driving innovation and regional development.

THEORETICAL BACKGROUND

Funding Agenda and Regional Challenges in the ST&I Systems

Brazilian public research support organizations aim to drive transformations in the productive structure through an agenda encompassing policy definition, grant allocation, financing of events, and research, extension, and innovation projects, among other interventions (McManus; Neves, 2021). These interventions can be achieved through systemic actions that alter the competitive environments where business strategies are formed. According to Howells (2005), governmental action should seek alignment with regional realities, recognizing existing structures and the possibilities for change within its jurisdiction.

In this context, national ST&I policies have shifted from top-down approaches to favoring more place-based approaches (Okamuro et al., 2019).

The international literature highlights initiatives that transcend traditional top-down policies to facilitate bottom-up movements, aiming to create conditions for setting priorities aligned with local and regional development needs. The smart specialization strategy, guiding two major European Union funds (the Multi-annual Research and Innovation Framework Program and the European Structural and Investment Funds), is cited by Corpakis (2020) as an example of practices involving national and regional authorities, along with other stakeholders like universities and industries, to align investment priorities with local and regional competencies and needs. Guimón (2019) discusses similar examples in Sweden, Germany, and the United States. Similarly, OECD (2014) refers to South Korea's Leading Industry Program as a good practice, and OECD (2017) highlights the interplay between national and regional levels in Finland.

The interaction between different government levels regarding innovation support requires deeper understanding. Okamuro et al. (2019) highlight a gap in existing literature about the interplay between local R&D and innovation programs and various governance levels, and the extent to which national governance systems align with specific local needs. In terms of both national and regional policies, resource allocation is guided by prioritizing sectors, areas of knowledge, and strategic options. ST&I and industrial policies in Brazil, like in many developing countries, have historically been managed in this manner. However, as Jin and Mc Kelvey (2019) note, there is limited research on strategic priorities in developing countries.

The specific dynamics of companies and the productive structure associated with the innovation process should guide intervention policies. According to Howells (2005), regional innovation policies are crucial at both local and national levels as they stimulate alignment between innovation, growth, and value production, recognizing disparities in resources, culture, and innovative activities across different regions (Doloreux and Parto, 2005). In this context, while their primary mission is financial contribution through a wide range of contracting mechanisms and instruments, the State Research Support Foundations (FAPs) also play a significant role in planning and promoting relational capital in the ST&I system. The Araucária Foundation, part of the state science and technology system in Paraná, Brazil, bases its projects on three main strategic axes (Fundação Araucária, 2023): promotion of scientific and technological research; verticalization of higher education and researcher training; and dissemination of scientific and technological research.

The Araucária Foundation's actions are operationalized through public calls for projects and the process of public call inapplicability involving peer-reviewed scientific merit evaluations. These processes are conducted in close partnership with federal, state, municipal, and private non-profit higher education institutions, along with other research institutes. The general funding flow of a ST&I system comprises processes designed to define, organize, prioritize, monitor, and invest in human capital, infrastructure, companies, and other means to promote tangible socioeconomic development. Each stage of promotion involves the responsible organization applying specific factors and criteria for various decision-making and operational tasks, as outlined by Pacheco, Steil, and Sell (2016). These stages include programmatization, public calls, evaluation, contracting and monitoring, and dissemination of results.

The funding flow of the Araucária Foundation is anchored in identifying the demands of society and the government of the State of Paraná. Once a demand is identified, the Foundation issues a public call where candidates, often working individually, submit their project proposals for research or innovation development funding. However, the Foundation has recognized limiting issues in its current model:

a) difficulty in understanding the needs for territorial development through ST&I and identifying the potential for science and technology production in the state; b) isolation of actors and a lack of culture for conducting research and innovation through co-production and limited sharing of infrastructure and knowledge among local actors; and c) the complexity and heterogeneity of local innovation ecosystems.

Turnhout et al. (2020) found numerous instances where attempts to innovate the relationship between science, politics, and co-production were hindered due to a political context favoring traditional roles of science. To circumvent this, co-production processes can be organized as part of a broader political agenda (Turnhout et al., 2020). In this light, the Araucária Foundation, as a state agency, is implementing a new model for funding research and innovation, based on the process of co-production, the theory of commons, and new public services, associated with digital platforms. These elements will be explored in the following sections.

Co-production as a Strategy for Creating Sustainable Common Goods

Co-production, a concept initially developed in the 1970s and 80s by the political economist Elinor Ostrom, describes processes where inputs to provide a good or service are contributed by individuals from different organizations (Ostrom, 1996). According to Parks and colleagues, co-production occurs when public service agents and citizens collaborate in providing public services, merging professionalism with voluntary efforts to enhance the quality and quantity of these services (Parks et al., 1980; Brandsen; Honingh, 2015; Marques, 2020; Ostrom, 1990; Pestoff, 2006).

Ostrom highlighted the need for legal frameworks to facilitate co-production, underlining the importance of reliable commitments among co-producers (Ostrom, 1996). Her work elevated public administration to the level of market theories, advocating its application in business organizations and service development (Miller; Wyborn, 2018). Nabatchi et al. (2017) expanded the concept of co-production, viewing it as an umbrella term that encompasses various collaborative activities in the public service cycle (Nesti, 2018).

Knowledge co-production is acknowledged as an effective means of generating applicable scientific knowledge and promoting commons through collaboration between scientists and decision-makers (Djenontin; Meadow, 2018). Berkes (2010) emphasized knowledge co-production in environmental sciences as an iterative process of learning and adaptive governance, leading to new patterns of governance and power redistribution (Miller; Wyborn, 2018). Mauser et al. (2013) described the co-creation of science in three phases: co-design, co-production, and co-dissemination of research (Bremer et al., 2019), underlining the dynamic nature of collaborative scientific endeavors.

Elinor Ostrom's work on common goods and governance is essential for understanding co-production, with recent research delving into governance in socio-ecological systems (Wyborn, 2015; Van Kerkhoff; Lebbel, 2015). Co-productive governance, as proposed by Wyborn (2015), provides a conceptual framework addressing context, knowledge, process, and governance vision, highlighting the need for more critical and contextualized approaches. A key contribution of Ostrom's theory was identifying principles to govern the community management of common resources and their users. According to Ostrom (1990 – pp. 90-102) and expanded upon by Pacheco (2016), the eight essential principles for effective management of common resources are:

1) Delimitation: Clear definition of the boundaries of common goods, as well as who has access rights and usage rights.

2) Contextual Appropriateness: Usage rules should be tailored to local needs and conditions, such as time, space, available technologies, and resource quantities.
3) Participation and Co-production: Affected members can participate in defining/adapting their own rules – collective agreements.
4) Monitoring and Evaluation: Usage rules, the status of the common good, and member behavior are monitored.
5) Proportional Sanctions and Rewards: A graduated system of sanctions, with penalties for transgressors.
6) Resolvability: Easy access to low-cost conflict resolution methods is ensured, and the benefits from common management are proportional to the usage costs.
7) Autonomy: The right of community members to review their own rules should be respected by external authorities.
8) Adhocracy: Governance (appropriation, provision, monitoring, sanctions) and conflict resolution, following a multi-layered responsibility structure

Drawing inspiration from Zittrain's (2006) insights on the generative power of the Internet to produce spontaneous change by large, diverse, and uncoordinated audiences, Ansell and Torfing (2021) delve into the concept of generative governance, defined as 'governance that facilitates and enables productive interactions among distributed actors'. The authors posit that generative governance aims to create opportunities for the co-creation of solutions to complex challenges by assembling tools, processes, and infrastructure that enable distributed actors to collaboratively generate knowledge, products, and more. In this framework, platforms emerge as supportive infrastructures for co-production and the governance of arrangements involving multiple engaged actors. This concept is further explored in the next section.

Platforms as Alternatives for Co-Production of Research and Innovation

The term 'platform' has evolved to hold a broad and multi-dimensional meaning, especially in the realm of technology and innovation. Originally denoting a physical or structural base, such as collaborative workspaces and community centers, the concept has expanded to represent digital systems or infrastructures like social networks and marketplaces, which facilitate interaction and collaboration among various user groups (Ansell and Torfing, 2021; Parker; Alstyne; Choudary, 2016). More recently, it has been used to describe contemporary business models based on enabling value-creating interactions between external producers and consumers. These platforms aim to consummate matches among users and facilitate the exchange of goods, services, or social currency, thus enabling value creation for all participants (Parker; Alstyne; Choudary, 2016).

With advancements in digital technologies, new models of value production have emerged, recently culminating in the perspective of business models based on platforms. This approach promotes the feasibility of new flows of value production by bringing actors together in multilateral arrangements, enhancing value through their interactions (O´Reilly, 2011). In the realm of innovation, digital platforms play a crucial role in enabling collaboration among diverse stakeholders. These platforms offer a virtual space where ideas can be shared and collectively developed, transcending the geographical limitations of participants (Ansell and Torfing, 2021; Harmaala, 2015).

The discussion of platform-based models gained further attention with analyses on the economic perspective of platforms, exemplified by Jean Tirole, who was awarded the Nobel Memorial Prize in Economic Sciences in 2014 for his work on platformization (Rochet; Tirole, 2003). In public management, digital platforms are seen as enablers of open and participatory governance models. The shift towards citizen inclusion in public administration signifies a move from party politics to representative governance and from centralized management to public and democratic engagement, with the goal of encouraging community participation in the development of their own cities (Gil-Garcia et al., 2016; Pereira et al., 2018). Consequently, digital platforms foster new ways of community interaction and mediated co-creation (De Reuver; Sørensen; Basole, 2017; Harmaala, 2015).

In the challenging and ever-changing environment where FAPs operate, knowledge management becomes crucial to assist in creating, sharing, structuring, and disseminating the intangible resources necessary to fulfill the mission, vision, and strategic objectives of organizations (APQC, 2015; Young, 2020). In this context, Expertise Locator Systems (ELS) can provide essential resources to digital platforms, enabling access to knowledge stored in the minds of individuals, documents, processes, systems, and services (Becerra-Fernandez & Sabherwal, 2014). ELS has been highlighted in the literature for its role in identifying and locating experts who possess the knowledge and experience needed by others or in locating knowledge sources for various demands (APQC, 2015; Balog et al., 2012; Young, 2020).

Ehrlich and Shami (2008) outline that ELS support the location of expertise for: (i) individuals to perform specific organizational functions; (b) acting as information sources for simple knowledge transfer; (c) sharing knowledge; (d) developing knowledge on a specific subject; (e) informing individuals about valuable information.

Balog et al. (2012) state that the construction of ELS began in the 1960s, motivated by the difficulty in finding expertise to solve a problem that had been previously resolved. In this setting, ELS involves tools that allow sharing existing knowledge, connecting people who need certain knowledge with those who possess it (Young, 2020). ELS also aids in the process of forming new project teams, aggregating the necessary knowledge. This tool can be materialized in electronic yellow pages or systems to support the location and connection of people (Balog et al., 2012; Young, 2020).

Artificial Intelligence plays a pivotal role in the development of ELS and digital platforms, offering sophisticated solutions for identifying and recommending qualified professionals. Through advanced algorithms in machine learning and natural language processing, AI can analyze large volumes of data, including publications, social media profiles, and professional histories, to accurately identify individuals' competencies and areas of expertise, enhancing efficiency and accuracy in locating knowledge sources (Becerra-Fernandez; 2000, Lin et al.; 2017). Additionally, AI contributes to the continuous maintenance and updating of these systems, adapting to changes in experts' skills and market demands (Balog et al., 2012).

Despite the importance of ELS, literature highlights various challenges in their implementation. This research seeks to identify such challenges to guide the creation of a solution that supports the development of a digital platform to aid in the instrumentalization of the New Research and Innovation Arrangements (NAPIs) in the State of Paraná, Brazil.

METHODOLOGY

To identify key challenges for the Expertise Locator System (ELS) project and establish design principles guiding the development of a digital platform to enable a new vision for research and innovation at the Araucária Foundation, the Design Science Research Methodology (DSRM) was employed in this research. DSRM is an approach focused on creating artifacts or practical solutions for real-world issues within specific contexts (Peffers et al., 2007). This methodology was selected for its structured process that guides researchers through the initiation, development, and evaluation of the impact of an artifact aimed at solving a particular problem. The produced artifact must undergo rigorous assessment to ascertain its applicability as a novel research contribution, intended to enhance the efficacy, efficiency, quality, or utility of an existing system, process, or service, or to innovate something entirely new. The meticulousness of the research is paramount in DSRM, which encompasses a systematic process and a comprehensive supporting knowledge base.

The research was conducted following the stages of Design Science Research (DSR) as outlined by Peffers et al. (2007), which includes:

1) Problem Identification and Motivation: This phase involves recognizing the practical issue that needs addressing and establishing the rationale for its resolution.
2) Solution Objective Definition: Here, specific goals are set to steer the artifact's creation process. These objectives must be succinct, quantifiable, and pertinent to the problem at hand.
3) Design and Development: In this stage, the artifact is crafted and built, guided by a conceptual framework delineating its functionalities and attributes, and illustrating how it addresses the identified issue.
4) Artifact Demonstration: The artifact is showcased in a simulated setting to assess its efficacy and user-friendliness.
5) Artifact Evaluation: This phase evaluates the artifact's performance, efficiency, quality, and utility against the established objectives, using methods like experiments, simulations, or other evaluative approaches.
6) Results Dissemination: Findings from the research are shared with relevant audiences, including potential users of the artifact, those involved in its creation, and the broader research community that could benefit from the insights.

Following the DSRM steps, stages 1 and 2 focus on identifying needs and defining solution objectives. Initially, an integrative literature review was conducted as described in Dos Anjos et al. (2023). According to Whittemore and Knafl (2005), integrative reviews synthesize theoretical and empirical literature on a phenomenon or problem, showcasing the state of the art on a specific topic, and supporting the development of theories and knowledge applications. Thus, the integrative literature review in this study was based on the method proposed by Botelho et al. (2011), and its six stages were developed as follows in this research (Dos Anjos et al.; 2023):

1) Topic Identification and Research Question Selection: The established research strategy is detailed in Table 1.
2) Setting Inclusion and Exclusion Criteria: The following inclusion (IC) and exclusion (EC) criteria were applied:
    a. IC1: Must address characteristics of ELS;
    b. IC2: Must discuss approaches in developing ELS;
    c. IC3: Must explore models for developing ELS.
    d. EC1: Must not focus on technical or specific issues that are not generalizable or address the research theme only peripherally.

Table 1. Systematic review strategy

Planning	Execution
Research Topic	Identify the main problems in the development of individual location systems in an organizational context.
Research Question	What are the main problems in developing expert location systems, and in what context do they occur?
Keywords	("EXPERT* LOCATO*" OR "EXPERT* SEEK" OR "EXPERT* FINDER" OR "EXPERT* LOCATOR SYSTEM" OR "EXPERT* RECOMMENDER" OR "EXPERT* SEARCH*" OR "EXPERTISE SOFTWARE").
Databases	Scopus accessed through the Capes periodicals portal.
Search Strategy	(a) Keywords applied to the title, abstract, and keywords of each publication in the target database; (b) Time period from 2013 to 2022; (c) Languages Portuguese, English, or Spanish; (d) The title, abstract, and keywords of each returned publication will be read; (e) Available for download.
Search Date	August 1, 2022.

Source: Adapted from Dos Anjos et al. (2023)

3) Pre-selection and Selection of Studies: A total of 122 publications were initially found, with 21 pre-selected and, after thorough review, 14 publications were ultimately selected. The pre-selected publications were assessed using the established inclusion and exclusion criteria, and the results are shown in Table 2.
4) Categorization of Selected Studies: The outcomes of the categorization are presented in Table 3.
5) Analysis and Interpretation of Results and Presentation of Review or Synthesis of Knowledge: The outcomes of these stages are presented in the following section.

The outcomes of the integrative review served as foundational inputs in identifying the needs and objectives of the platform. This was done in conjunction with the application of organizational context modeling techniques following the CommonKADS methodology (Schreiber et al., 2002). Organizational context modeling included surveying needs and opportunities for implementing a network-oriented fostering system, involving the identification and engagement of actors in the territory around strategic themes for the development of the State of Paraná, according to the government plan. Managers from the Araucária Foundation, along with representatives from universities, companies, and government agencies, participated in the research. This collaboration gathered information for designing the initial research and innovation arrangements and shaping the priority themes for expertise location. As a result, the objectives of the NAPI model and the digital platform that instrumentalizes expertise location, named iAraucária Platform, and its design principles were established.

The third stage encompassed various research paths. Regarding the construction of the ontology (Fan; Wang; Zheng, 2016) used to organize the platform's information, the steps of Ontology Development 101 (Noy; McGuinness, 2001) were followed. The resulting ontology was represented through a SKOS model (Milles; Wyborn, 2009). The functionalities of the iAraucária Platform were designed to allow the integration of data on experts, research groups, research and innovation institutions, and scientific and technological production from different data sources. Modules were developed for data supplementation, the formation of collaborative groups, searches for actors and assets, and the creation of indicators to support fostering actions. Various analytical outputs were established by the structure systems to demonstrate and evaluate the structure, according to steps 4 and 5 of the DSRM.

Table 2. Pre-selected publications for review in relation to the criteria

#	Title, Authors and Year of Publication	IC1	IC2	IC3	EC1
P1	Comparison of the results of an authorship-based expert recommender against data from a directory of experts. Kraß e Försterling (2013).		X		
P2	CSSeer: an Expert Recommendation System based on CiteSeerX. CHEN et al. (2013).				X
P3	FINDING AN EXPERT: A MODEL RECOMMENDATION SYSTEM. Sun et al. (2013).	X			
P4	I Need Someone to Help! A Taxonomy of Helper-Finding Activities in the Enterprise. Yarosh et al. (2013).			X	
P5	Mining Expertise and Interests from Social Media. Guy et al. (2013).	X			
P6	Defining dimensions in expertise recommender systems for enhancing open collaborative innovation. Nguyen et al. (2014).	X			
P7	Project team selection based on social networks. Fitsilis et al. (2014).		X	X	
P8	Shaping an Experts Locator System: Recommending the Right Expert. Alhosan et al. (2014).	X			
P9	Breaking the Recursivity: Towards a Model to Analyse Expert Finders. Vergne e Susi (2015).	X			
P10	Expertise Search System: Profile Extraction and Analysis of Doctor's Community. Kaveri et el. (2015).				X
P11	InsERT: the Inspirational Expert Recommender Tool. Nguyen et al. (2015).		X		
P12	Software Project Team Selection Based on Enterprise Social Networks. Fitsilis et al. (2015).	X		X	
P13	Expertise in Social Networks: How Do Experts Differ From Other Users? Horne et al. (2016).				X
P14	How do Users Handle Inconsistent Information? The Effect of Search Expertise. Umemoto et al. (2016).				X
P15	Expert Location Tool for Global Software Development Environments based on Knowledge Profile Management. Córdova-Moras et al. (2017).			X	
P16	An Expertise Recommender System Based on Data from an Institutional Repository (DiVA). Angelova et al. (2018).		X		
P17	Supporting Expertise Location in Coding Phase of Software Development Process. Martínez et al. (2018).				X
P18	Characteristics of Expertise Locator System in Academia: A Systematic Literature Review. Rampisela et al. (2020a).	X			
P19	Expert Locator System for Finding Co-authors Using Snowball Network Method: A Case Study of Fasilkom UI Lecturers. Rampisela et al. (2020b)		X		
P20	Ontology for knowledge condensation to support expertise location in the code phase during software development process. Martínez-García et al. (2020).				X
P21	Web Application Development for Expertise Search and Research Collaboration of Chiang Mai University's Researchers Using Text Mining. Paphawasit et al. (2020).				X

Source: Adapted from Dos Anjos et al. (2023)

Finally, stage 6 addresses the bibliographic production and knowledge transfer actions to the organizations involved in the project. The following sections describe the results of the integrative review, the modules of the iAraucária Platform, and the outcomes of the platform's application.

Model for the Creation and Management of New Research and Innovation Arrangements

The Araucária Foundation operates through public calls for research and innovation projects, traditionally following a model led by government agendas to support individual or group research projects. Recognizing the STI system as a common good, the Foundation is shifting towards a model that encourages the formation of extensive networks, integrating various actors from the quadruple helix (Leydesdorff; Smith, 2022) to foster wealth creation and well-being in the region.

Research at the Foundation has highlighted three main challenges in transitioning from individual to collaborative research within the innovation ecosystem. The first is understanding the development needs of the region through STI and recognizing the potential for scientific and technological production, especially considering the over 20,000 PhDs and other key actors in the territory. The second challenge is overcoming the isolation of these actors and the lack of a co-production culture. Lastly, the complexity and diversity of the ecosystems present unique governance challenges for collaborative research and innovation arrangements.

Therefore, the following strategic requirements were established to guide the structuring process of the new funding model to be implemented by the Araucária Foundation:

- Establish a model that allows for better identification of the potential and demands of the territory, ensuring greater assertiveness in funding research and innovation and better return on R&D investments.
- Promote wealth creation and well-being through the mobilization of Paraná's science, technology, and innovation system in research and innovation projects guided by co-production.

Acknowledging these objectives and the challenges identified in collaboration with various stakeholders in the research, a novel model for promoting research and innovation called New Arrangements for Research and Innovation (NAPIs) was established. These NAPIs incorporate elements of the commons-based co-production model (Hess; Ostrom, 2005) to support collective actions promoting innovation and modernization in Paraná. A NAPI is envisioned as a collaborative framework of agents with defined goals and a shared vision, aimed at developing innovative collective solutions through co-production. This model represents a regional development strategy grounded in STI, designed to stimulate the co-production of knowledge among researchers and other actors in Paraná's innovation system, driven by priority development needs in strategic sectors for the State.

The NAPI model is anchored in a set of public calls driven by data and focused on establishing networks that integrate actors and assets from the quadruple helix. It is based on a model of networked knowledge and innovation co-production, with its instrumentation detailed in the following section.

The establishment and development of each NAPI follow a process flow aligning the lifecycle of a state sponsored project with elements characterizing the model as a common good. As depicted in Figure 1, the process starts with demand identification, guided by government plan directives, identification of latent demands and opportunities based on territorial mapping, or demands identified by emerging quadruple helix arrangements. This stage is supported by the comprehensive mapping of territorial intellectual capital conducted by the iAraucária platform. Fundamentally, a NAPI involves multi-actor arrangements and is not confined to addressing internal management issues of a single organization.

Figure 1. Stages of the NAPI creation and management flow
(Aráucaria Foundation)

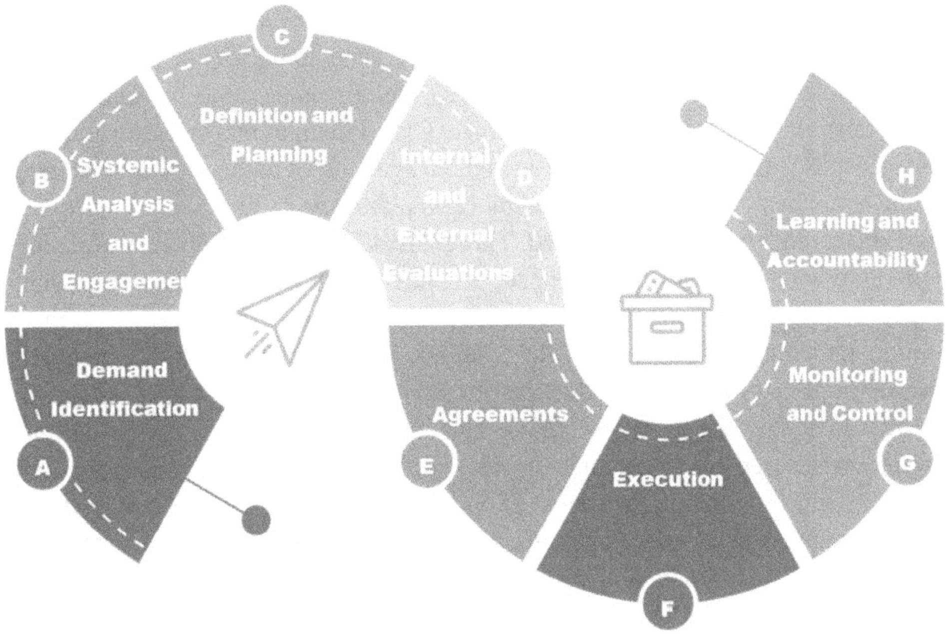

Table 3. Elements of the canvas for defining NAPIs

Item	Description
Value to Society	What is the mission and vision of the NAPI? What are the objectives and goals of the NAPI?
Contribution to Public Policies	What justifications underlie the creation of the NAPI? What public policies can be established or favored by the achievement of the NAPI?
Identity	What defines the NAPI? What differentiates the NAPI from other initiatives?
Target Ecosystem	What is the scope of the NAPI? Who are the actors that will act as agents of professional and scientific value co-production? Who are the key agents to be mobilized in knowledge co-production activities and in value co-creation by the NAPI? Who will be the beneficiaries of the NAPI?
Value Proposition	Deliverables, innovation, and knowledge to be co-produced. What will the NAPI offer to the beneficiary public and the co-producers? What services, products, or gains in convenience and access/reach can the NAPI provide to the ecosystem actors?
Channels and Context	What types of relationships and transactions should be established or improved to ensure the success of the NAPI? What channels will be used to promote the mobilization of agents in the co-production and dissemination of knowledge and innovation?
Promotion	What promotion mechanisms should be established for the achievement of the NAPI?
Key Activities	What activities are critical for value delivery and for the sustainability of the NAPI?
Key Infrastructure and Resources	What physical and digital assets, tangible and intangible components (physical, intellectual, financial) are critical for the NAPI?
Stakeholders	What actors can impact or be impacted by the NAPI, who have an interest in the success or failure of the NAPI and therefore demand attention in the management plan?

Moreover, it involves applying Araucária Foundation's fostering mechanisms (using public funds or otherwise), adhering to the principles of New Public Services (Denhardt & Denhardt, 2003).

The second stage of the flow, named Systemic Analysis, delves deeper into demand analysis, incorporating broad discussions on the key factors and movements impacting or potentially affecting the ecosystem related to the future NAPI. This stage may include conducting knowledge co-production workshops with quadruple helix actors, utilizing World Café dynamics and brainstorming sessions. The ecosystem analysis, as well as the identification and engagement of actors in this stage, are facilitated by the actor and asset location features of the iAraucária platform.

In the third stage, the NAPI is characterized. This characterization may involve workshops mobilizing ecosystem representatives who will lead or support the NAPI's development. Given that innovation ecosystems rely on knowledge flows that drive collaboration and co-creation to convert this knowledge into added value, the commons theory provides a foundation for establishing the identification of actors and their relationships for the co-production of knowledge and innovation. This approach aims to manage resources in a fairer and more sustainable manner (Marques, 2020). The definition of NAPI is supported by a Canvas based on the commons theory, encompassing the elements described in Table 3.

During stage C and progressing into stage D, management and governance plans for a NAPI are established. This stage addresses the commons principles that can promote the sustainability of the knowledge and innovation co-production arrangement. This includes defining mechanisms to promote: i) participation and co-production of knowledge; ii) conflict resolution; iii) application of sanctions and recognition of actors in the arrangement; iv) assessing the reasonableness and proportionality of the initiative; and v) promoting the governance of the initiative, including defining responsibilities, risk management, and strategies for monitoring and evaluating the arrangement's actions.

Subsequently, in stages E, F, and G, cooperation agreements are defined, fostering mechanisms are implemented, action plans for management and governance are executed, and monitoring and evaluation of the results are conducted. Finally, in the last stage, lessons learned are evaluated, best practices identified, and the dissemination of knowledge is promoted.

The flow of establishing and developing NAPIs is supported by the iAraucária digital platform. The iAraucária platform was established to facilitate the mapping of intellectual capital in the territory and to enable the mobilization and engagement of actors in the innovation system within research and innovation co-production arrangements. The iAraucária platform is designed to incorporate the principles of sustainable commons and address the primary challenges of ELS, which are presented in the next section.

iAraucária PLATFORM

Qualification of the Basic Characteristics of ELS for Platform Design

The literature review on ELS aimed to identify key challenges in their development to guide intellectual capital mapping and stakeholder engagement in co-production arrangements. This review, summarized in Table 4, reveals significant challenges in ELS development.

Yarosh et al. (2013) highlight a lack of studies on ELS in large organizations and propose a broader concept of "helper-finder" to facilitate collaboration, addressing sociotechnical challenges like location criteria selection. This concept influenced the iAraucária platform, enhancing intellectual capital mapping around sustainable development opportunities in Paraná. Sun et al. (2013) and Cordova-Moras

Table 4. Main challenges for the expertise locator systems project

Demands	Challenges	Publications
Construction, Maintenance, and Updating of Profiles	Facilitate the construction and updating of experts' profiles, on which consultations and recommendations are made for various purposes.	P1; P5; P11; P16
Knowledge Representation	The need for means to represent the main concepts of the field, for example, how to measure expertise, competence, knowledge, and other concepts, based on information.	P3; P4; P7; P12; P15; P18
Evaluation of Expert Locator Systems	The need for means of evaluating expert locator systems that provide an assertive view of the coverage and quality of data and services.	P3; P9; P19
Accreditation Mechanisms	The need to consider elements from sources, context, and others that demonstrate that the individual is an expert.	P5; P6; P8; P9; P11
Intelligent Support	Enable support for mapping, selecting, and recommending experts according to the challenges.	P2; P3; P6; P8; P11; P18; P19

Source: Adapted from Dos Anjos et al. (2022)

et al. (2017) suggest using ontologies for improving search experiences in ELS, a concept applied in iAraucária for organizing content from various data sources.

Kraß and Försterling (2013) and Nguyen et al. (2014) focus on expert recommendation in organizational contexts, considering challenges like legal issues and user engagement. This aspect was incorporated into iAraucária's recommendation mechanisms. Guy et al. (2013) note that social media introduces new opportunities for ELS, albeit with challenges like maintaining expert profiles and inferring information from multiple sources. Angelova et al. (2018) discuss methodologies for ELS development, including unstructured data mining and network data, approaches utilized in iAraucária for data collection and treatment.

Alhosan et al. (2014) and Vergne and Susi (2015) discuss ELS from a knowledge management perspective, emphasizing characteristics like purpose, accessibility, and self-assessment. These principles are reflected in iAraucária's information quality maintenance and diverse data source handling.

Rampisela et al. (2020a; 2020b) focus on ELS application in academia, identifying key characteristics and the importance of scientific collaboration. Their findings informed iAraucária's data treatment routines and intelligent recommendation mechanisms.

The next section details how iAraucária addresses these ELS challenges and incorporates principles of sustainable commons.

iAraucária PLATFORM RESOURCES

The iAraucária platform is a digital infrastructure that provides data, information, knowledge systems, and collaborative resources to identify and mobilize technical-scientific competencies supporting the mission of Araucária Foundation and the promotion of NAPIs.

Designed to assist actors in Paraná's innovation system, iAraucária aids in mapping, accessing, analyzing, and disseminating data and information about individual and institutional competencies and the production of STI in the state. Aimed at fostering value creation and wealth through innovation, the platform identifies and connects local expertise and intangible assets, using technology engineered and developed by Instituto Stela to facilitate and promote co-production of innovation.

Figure 2. iAraucaria platform modules

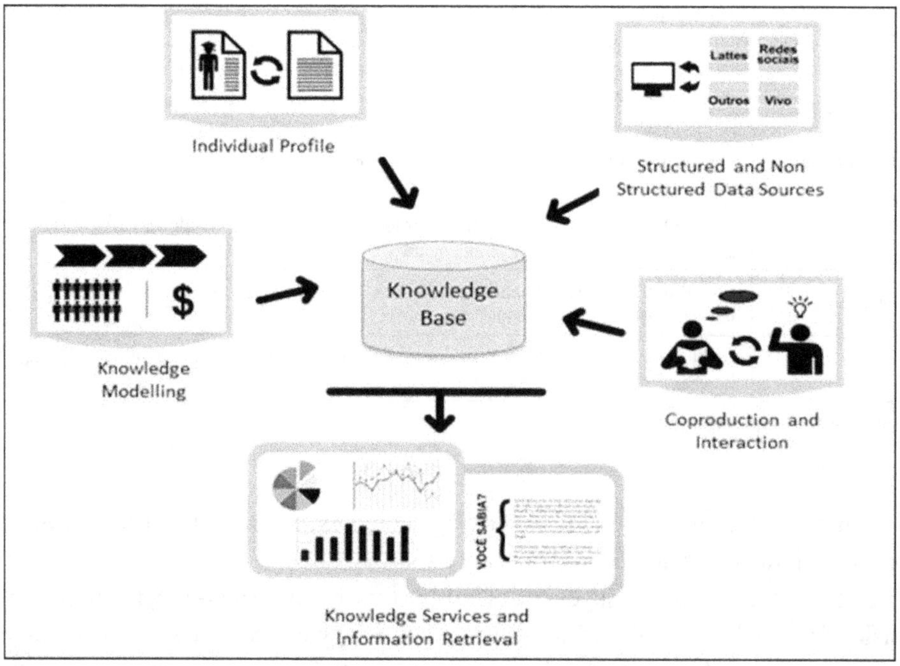

iAraucária supports the engagement of STI actors by offering territorial intelligence services, enabling the mapping of intellectual capital in the territory through big data and artificial intelligence. The platform aims to support the location and analysis of competencies in STI, scientific and technological production, research groups, and research and innovation institutions aligned with the strategic themes of Araucária Foundation and Paraná's governmental bodies.

Established to operationalize the NAPIs, iAraucária helps actors in Paraná's regional innovation system to map, access, analyze, and disseminate data and information about individual and institutional competencies and STI production. Its core element is an ELS that supports the identification and connection of local expertise and other territorial assets in co-production of innovation actions. The platform also includes tools to support the instrumentation of knowledge and innovation co-production networks.

iAraucária supports all stages of the creation and management flow of NAPIs, with its main modules highlighted in Figure 2. The platform provides services for expert registration, allowing users to complement information integrated into their curriculum, along with resources to support co-production and the location and analysis of knowledge, research groups, and scientific and technological production. To achieve this purpose, iAraucária was designed using knowledge engineering methodologies (Schreiber et al., 2002) and ontology engineering techniques (Gómez-Pérez, 2004), such as ontologies (i.e., shared representations of knowledge). Knowledge engineering offers design forms for iAraucária to model knowledge systems, while ontology engineering provides methods and tools to represent this knowledge, both in the domain and at the application level.

One of the key challenges for knowledge generation within the iAraucária platform is understanding the structure and behavior of complex networks of interactions among processes, humans, and systems. Given the size and complexity of the data, derived from various sources in heterogeneous formats, digital platform and ELS designers require differentiated approaches (Fortino, 2014). In the iAraucária platform, data on the profile of human, relational, and structural capital in the territory is automatically fed from national databases, such as Plataforma Lattes curricula and research groups, LinkedIn, and documents produced by researchers (such as their bibliographic production), among other sources. For this purpose, data extraction, transformation, and loading routines (Chen, Mao & Liu, 2014) were established to enable three stages: staging, slicing, and dimensional.

iAraucária's data bus consists of data from national STI databases, including Lattes Platform curricula and research groups, gathering information on over 8 million academics and professionals related to STI Institutions, their more than 90 million items of scientific and technological production, and about 46,000 active research groups in Brazil. Additionally, various data from national and international sources are collected to characterize the available tangible and intangible competencies and assets in Brazil. The information consulted in the staging phase is subsequently annotated based on the platform's ontology during the slicing stage, with the final index of the dimensional stage maintained through an unstructured data repository.

Based on the data bus, it is possible to analyze the demands and opportunities of the territory (as per stages 1 and 2 of the NAPIs creation flow) and identify actors and assets to compose the NAPIs and develop co-production actions in research and innovation, supporting stages 2, 3, and 5 of the flow.

Figure 3. Illustration of navigation support through ontology

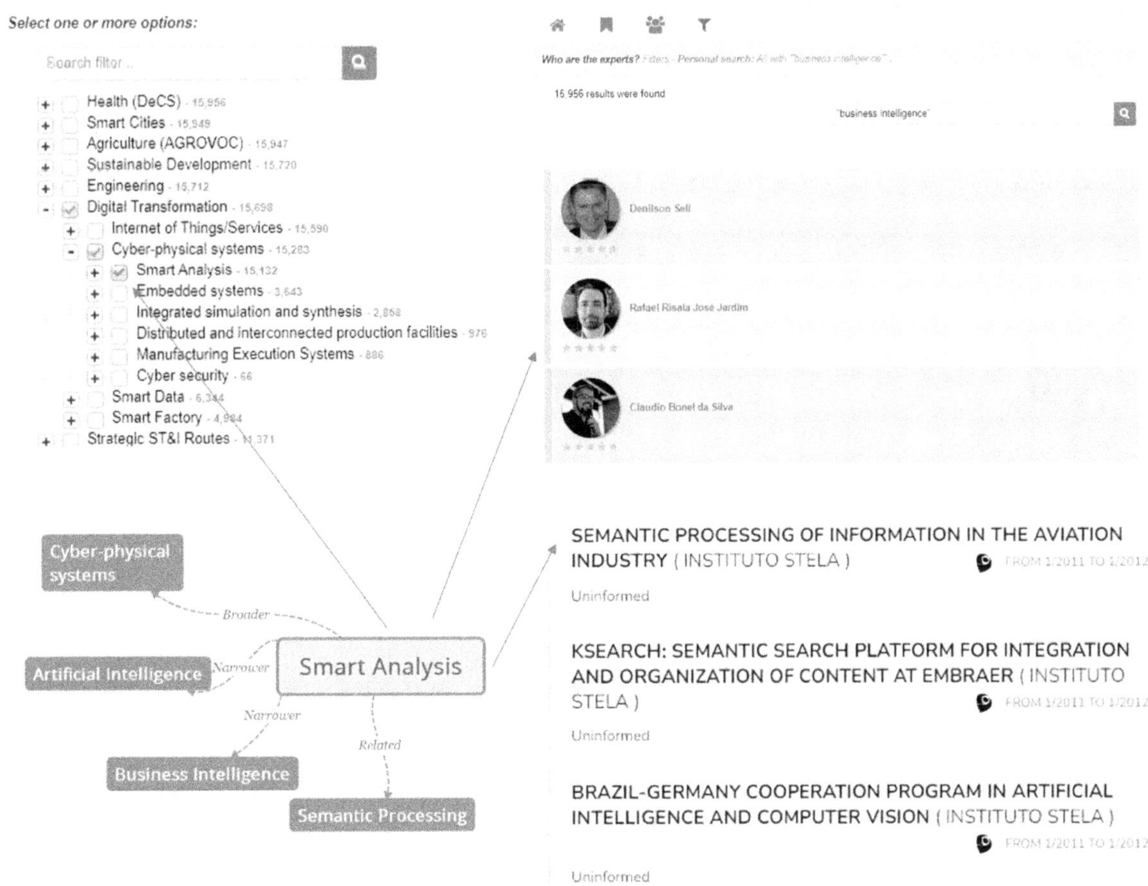

The iAraucária Platform features a domain ontology structured according to the SKOS standard (Milles; Wyborn, 2009) to describe prioritized themes in territorial development, involving topics such as digital transformation, sustainable development, energy, health, among others. The ontology aims to meet the needs for slicing and semantic indexing of the data bus, in addition to supporting knowledge extraction and analytical processing within iAraucária. All platform components are supported by the ontology, which enables the annotation of content inserted in the platform modules, allowing indexing and information retrieval, and recommending contents according to the users' profiles or co-production missions launched on the platform.

Figure 3 schematically illustrates the application of the ontology. In the example, data incorporated from LinkedIn and CV Lattes about project involvement are associated with concepts in the ontology. In the example, the user has a project whose description includes the term "semantic processing". This term is covered in the ontology and is linked through the property "skos:related" to the concept "Smart Analysis". In the platform's yellow pages, when searching for people with experience in "Business Intelligence" projects, the same expert is presented among the search results due to the prior annotation of their data and the association between concepts "Business Intelligence" and "Smart Analysis" in the ontology.

Each NAPI implemented features a space for collaborative development of research and innovation projects. Utilizing the capabilities for locating and recommending actors and assets, and for engagement in co-production, iAraucária fosters collaborative work with intelligent assistance. The platform's yellow pages and location and analysis resources enable quick identification of expertise and contents, facilitating the mapping of opportunities and demands in the territory and supporting co-production of knowledge within NAPIs.

Figure 4. Examples of NAPIs registered in iAraucária

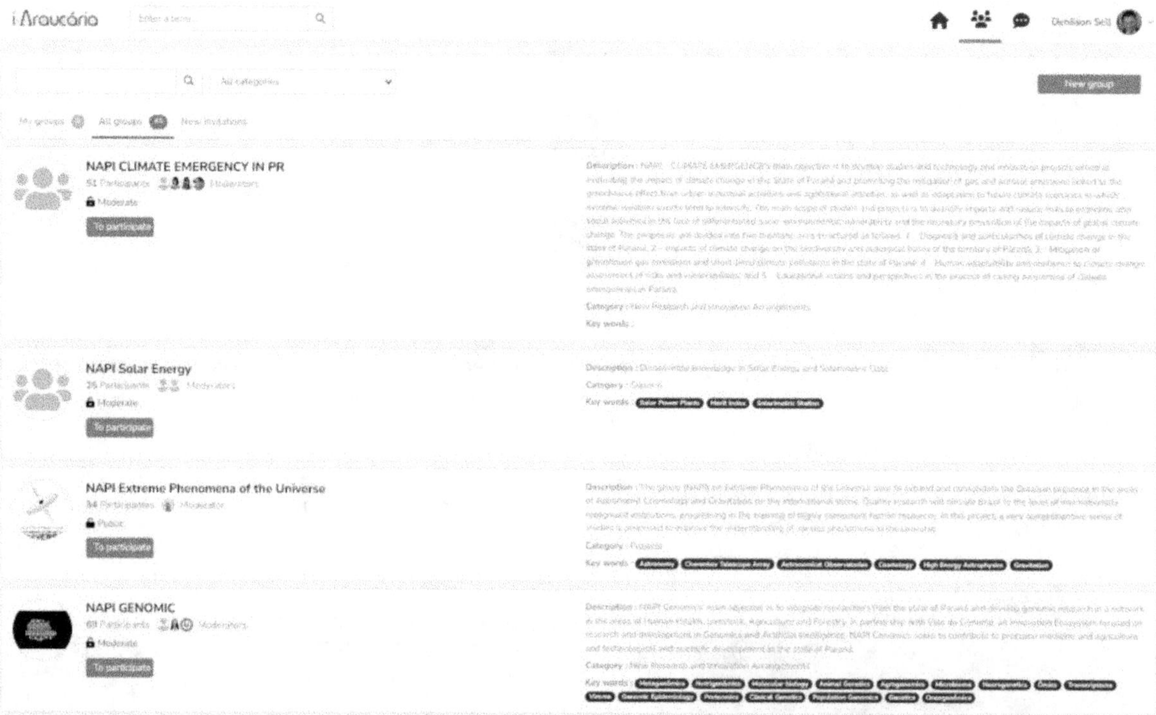

Figure 5. Illustration of recommendations to support the knowledge co-production

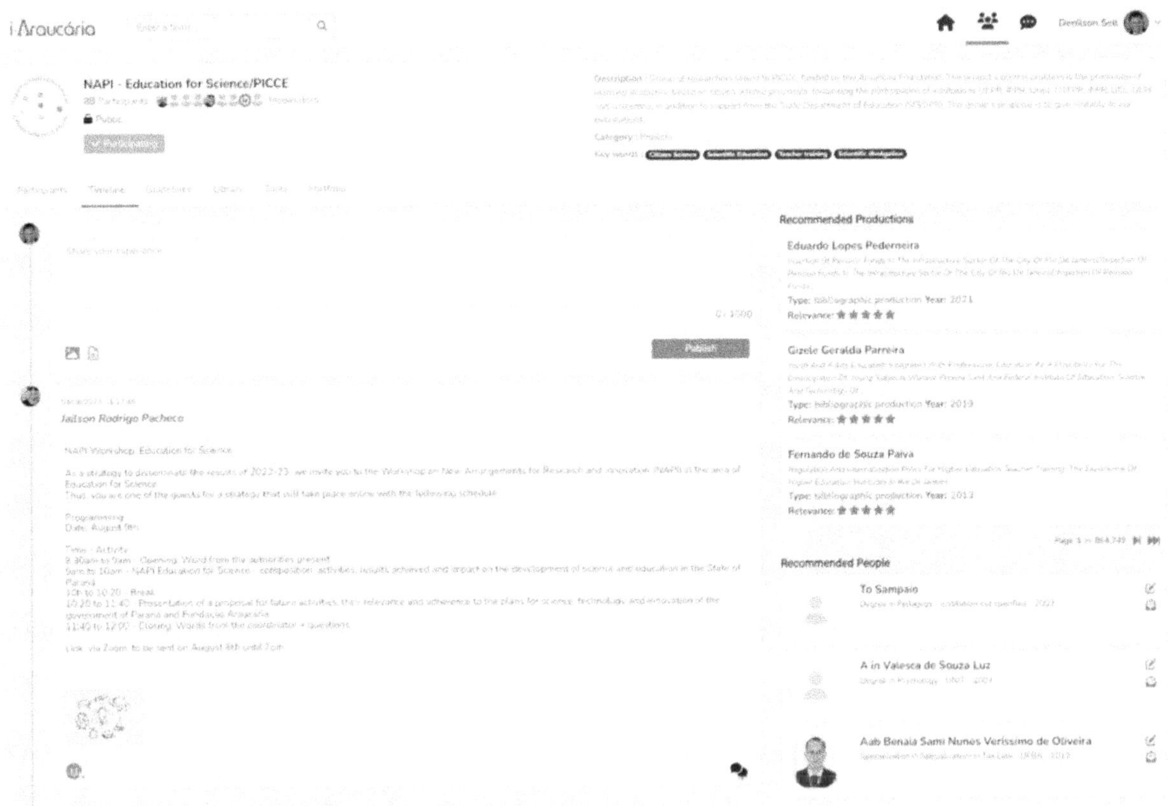

In the collaborative environment of NAPIs, as illustrated in Figures 4 and 5, resources are provided for locating NAPIs and supporting discussion, organization, and distribution of activities within them. These resources also allow for the organization of inputs, the repository of co-production tools, and the content produced in research. Throughout, with the support of artificial intelligence resources, the platform recommends people and content according to the context of the NAPIs' collaborative actions (Figure 5).

Finally, as depicted in Figure 6, the iAraucária platform supports the management and governance of initiatives by providing various indicators related to engagement, collaboration, and the achievement of program outcomes. This comprehensive support helps ensure the effectiveness and sustainability of the initiatives, fostering a robust framework for monitoring and guiding the progress and impact of the research and innovation projects under the NAPI program.

Table 5 summarizes the design principles applied in developing the expert location system of the iAraucária platform. These principles are grounded in DSRM and were identified through an extensive literature review. The table effectively consolidates the key design elements and methodologies, showcasing how they align with DSRM and the insights gathered from the literature to create a robust and efficient expert location system within the platform.

In addition to addressing the challenges of Expertise Locator Systems (ELS), the iAraucária platform project was guided by design principles rooted in concepts like digital commons and co-production. Thus, the iAraucária platform embodies several elements characterizing or operationalizing the New Research and Innovation Arrangements (NAPIs), considering the sustainable commons principles proposed by

Figure 6. Example of analytical resources to support knowledge management and governance

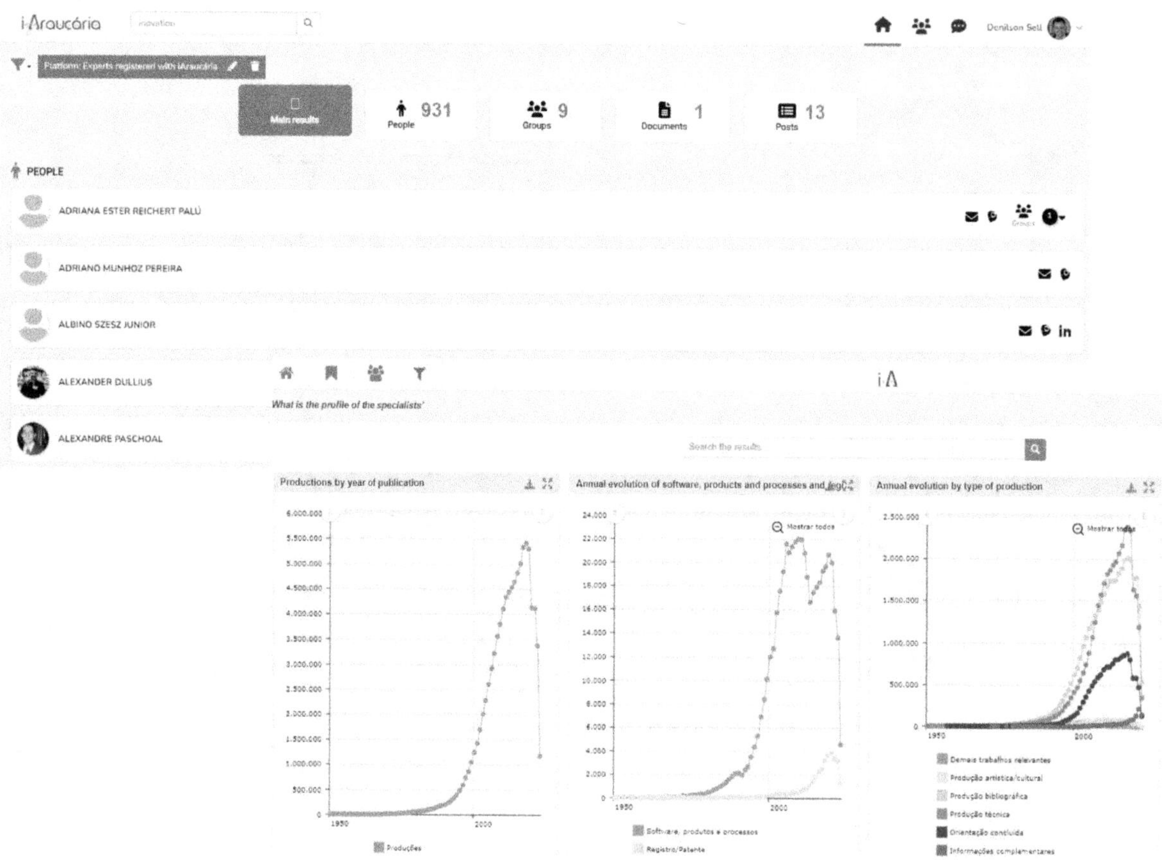

Table 5. Design principles of the iAraucária platform

Demands	Challenges
Profile Construction, Maintenance, and Updating	Data from sources like Lattes Platform and LinkedIn are automatically integrated. Users can supplement their information through the platform's curriculum system.
Knowledge Representation	A domain ontology organizes information around priority themes for the development of the Paraná innovation ecosystem.
Evaluation of Expert Locator Systems	Experts involved in each NAPI analyze the profiles of experts found and recommended by the platform. Feedback mechanisms based on search results and selection of recommendations are being studied to enhance the experience.
Accreditation Mechanisms	High visibility is given to integrated data from public sources and entered by users, to encourage social control. Discussion rounds on the effectiveness of the platform and the quality of information are being developed with representatives from the Araucária Foundation and NAPIs.
Intelligent Support	Artificial intelligence resources and semantic searches are used to support the recommendation of experts and assets according to the profiles of the users or the challenges being developed by NAPIs in collaborative groups.

Table 6. Application of commons principles in the iAraucária platform

Principle	iAraucária Platform Design Principle	iAraucária Components and Resources
Delimitation	The iAraucária Platform aims to meet the specific development demands of the digital commons oriented to the Government Plan of the State of Paraná.	Co-production groups can be established describing the delimitation of each collaborative group.
Contextual Appropriateness	Address various contexts of demands (Health, Agriculture, Sustainable Development, etc.) with customized service in the initial phase of demand identification.	An Ontology is being applied to describe strategic themes and guide research, analysis, and recommendations. The collaborative group creation feature allows each arrangement to establish specific adherence policies.
Participation	The project involves the participation of multiple potentially interested actors, limited to presentations and representation in specification meetings.	Working groups enable STI actors to co-produce innovation and decide on the future of their groups.
Autonomy	The Platform is still in the process of forming a user community and its own rules.	Working groups operate according to specific rules established by each specific co-production group, following the general policies being established by the NAPI initiative.
Monitoring	A user collective with identification of profiles and usage behaviors.	The platform offers specific analyses to show how users are engaged in working groups and to examine their profiles.
Sanctions	Standard NAPI governance policies are being established to support each specific agreement.	Each working group on the platform can establish its specific sanctions in the collaborative group policies.
Affordable Cost	NAPI governance policies are being developed to provide practical guidance for each specific initiative, considering affordable costs.	iAraucária working groups can define specific governance rules considering local characteristics.
Multi-level Governance	NAPI governance policies are being designed to offer flexibility in the distribution of roles and definition of specific privileges.	iAraucária working groups can define specific governance rules considering local characteristics.

Ostrom (1990, pp. 90-102) and further elaborated by Pacheco (2016). Table 5 provides a concise analysis of how the current solution of the iAraucária Platform aligns with these sustainable commons principles.

CONCLUSION

This chapter aimed to present the foundations of the New Research and Innovation Arrangements (NAPI) model and the guiding principles of the iAraucária platform. Both artifacts were established to enable a new paradigm for funding research and promoting sustainable development in the State of Paraná, Brazil, through the co-production of knowledge and innovation.

NAPI's implementation in Paraná showcases a significant leap in public policy and innovation, driven by AI integration. Our approach has efficiently utilized funding, stretching its impact to support a greater number of researchers. This effective use of resources, coupled with the creation of robust knowledge-sharing networks, presents a compelling model for sustainable development and innovation in other regions. The success of NAPI illustrates the potential of AI in enhancing collaboration and optimizing funding in research ecosystems worldwide.

The NAPI model offers an innovative approach to engaging actors from the quadruple helix in the co-production of knowledge and innovation and in fostering the common good. To date, there are 62

NAPIs established or being created, covering themes such as sustainable agriculture, renewable energies, biotechnology, education, health, among others. These have mobilized over 4,000 actors in NAPIs, integrating participants from the innovation ecosystem who traditionally did not collaborate.

To gauge the perceived contribution of the NAPI program, a survey was conducted in October 2022 among actors in the innovation ecosystem. The survey received 1,916 responses, and among the contributions and results recognized by respondents, the following stand out:

- Development and national and international recognition of the state's STI environment.
- Increased recognition, protagonism, and greater integration of actors and assets within the ecosystem.
- Enhanced competitiveness of Paraná through a focus on STI.
- Effective implementation of actions aimed at promoting wealth and well-being in Paraná.
- Valuing regional governance and identities, contributing to a more cohesive innovation ecosystem.
- Quantitative and qualitative enhancement of STI within Paraná's innovation ecosystem.
- Significant contribution to the United Nations Sustainable Development Goals 2030, particularly those related to education, industry, innovation and infrastructure, health and well-being, economic growth, and sustainable cities and communities.

Finally, it's noteworthy that the initiative has garnered three highly prestigious national awards in the Science, Technology, and Innovation (STI) sector, acknowledging the innovative nature and significant value generated by the NAPI model in Brazil. Additionally, it has been recognized as the best knowledge management project at the 10th Knowledge Management and Intellectual Capital Excellence Awards at ECKM, a traditional and renowned annual international event.

Among the primary challenges faced during the development of this initiative, several key issues were particularly prominent:

- The traditional culture of conducting research and innovation individually and in isolation, without coordination among academic actors and a low culture of sharing knowledge and tangible assets within the innovation ecosystem, has been transformed. The networking-based financing strategy, supported by a platform for identifying complementary actors and assets, has encouraged the development of a collaborative work culture in the territory.
- The absence of networking-oriented research and innovation financing models that could serve as a reference for the initiative has been addressed. The NAPI model drew support from the theory of Commons and underwent several revisions throughout its implementation cycle, incorporating lessons learned from the initial financing cycles.
- The lack of integrated information on competencies, assets, demands, and opportunities within the territory was overcome by integrating national and international databases. This strategy provided a comprehensive view of the territory, enhancing the planning of financing and the articulation of networks.
- The inherent difficulty in coordination and communication when involving groups from diverse academic and professional backgrounds was mitigated. The recommendation system and collaboration resources integrated in the digital platform promoted closer interaction and exchange of experiences among the various actors mobilized in the NAPIs.

A notable contribution of this work is the identification of a new application field for ELS in public policy planning, specifically in fostering research, innovation, and the development of innovation ecosystems. The iAraucária platform project addresses the main challenges highlighted in the literature, providing assertive support for the development of the Paraná innovation ecosystem. The resources compiled in this environment continuously and dynamically support regional innovation systems and organizations in mapping, accessing, analyzing, and disseminating data and information about individual and institutional competencies, as well as about R&D production in Paraná. Key results of this strategy include more targeted support, enhanced connections among innovation ecosystem actors, and ease in locating key competencies in strategic areas for ecosystem development. Through the established ELS, a clear view of the latent potential and existing gaps in the territory was obtained, guiding the allocation of public resources for research funding. The network-oriented approach, supported by the platform, facilitated the formation of multiple connections among actors, potentially forming competence clusters that enable participants to continue collaborative actions and develop new competencies.

Among the key learning outcomes, the following aspects are noteworthy:

- The application of commons principles in designing and operating the New Research and Innovation Arrangements (NAPIs) has been a critical element in achieving results in heterogeneous arrangements of actors in the co-production of knowledge and innovation. Notably, these principles significantly support the engagement of diverse stakeholders, aiding in understanding their needs and perspectives, and in coordinating their efforts towards a common goal for promoting wealth and well-being.
- The ability to map, manage, and engage different actors in co-production arrangements for innovation is an essential skill introduced by the digital platforma for the program's success.
- The digital platform and its features play a crucial role in processing data about actors and assets in the territory, supporting collaborative activities, enhancing actor engagement and proximity, and mapping the state's demands and potential.
- Elements of commons and knowledge governance have proven fundamental in constructing and effectively managing collaborative innovation networks, including establishing bases for coordination among different types of actors in the innovation ecosystem.

Among future endeavors, a more in-depth assessment of the long-term impact of the NAPI program is envisioned to comprehend the various contributing elements and whether the observed benefits thus far are sustainable over time. Additionally, there is an intention to explore the handling of new data sources and promote integration with other platforms to expand information coverage of the innovation ecosystem. This includes exploring resources based on blockchain and AI to enhance support for co-production of knowledge initiatives. Finally, there is a recognized need to expand the governance and knowledge management strategy to foster greater alignment and knowledge sharing among NAPIs, along with enhancing the performance evaluation and risk management strategy for networked actions.

REFERENCES

Alhosan, N., & Fayyoumi, A., FARIS, H. (2014). Shaping an Experts Locator System: Recommending the Right Expert. *Journal of Theoretical and Applied Information Technology*, *66*(2).

Angelova, M., Vishnu Manasa, D., Boeva, V., Linde, P., & Lavesson, N. (2018). *An Expertise Recommender SystemBased on Data from an Institutional Repository (DiVA).* In 22nd edition of the International Conference on ELectronic PUBlishing-Connecting the Knowledge Commons: From Projects to Sustainable Infrastructure, Toronto.

Ansell, C., & Trofing, J. (2021). Co-creation: The new kid on the block in public governance. *Policy and Politics*, *49*(2), 211–230. doi:10.1332/030557321X16115951196045

APQC - American Productivity & Quality Center. (2015). *Knowledge Management Priorities.* APQC. https://www.apqc.org/knowledge-base/download/340305/K05834_2015_KM_Priorities_ExecSum.pdf

Araucária, F. (2023 12 30). *A Fundação Araucária.* FAPPR. https://www.fappr.pr.gov.br/Pagina/Fundacao-Araucaria

Audretsch, D. B. & Link, A. N. (2019). Embracing an entrepreneurial ecosystem: an analysis of the governance of research joint ventures. *Small Business Economics*, *52*(2), 429–436.

Balog, K. (2012). Expertise Retrieval. Foundations and Trends in Information Retrieval. doi:10.1561/9781601985675

Becerra-Fernandez, I. (2000). The role of artificial intelligence technologies in the implementation of People-Finder knowledge management systems. *Knowledge-Based Systems*, *13*(5), 315–320. doi:10.1016/S0950-7051(00)00091-5

Becerra-Fernandez, I., & Sabherwal, R. (2014). Knowledge Management: Systems and Process (2. Ed). Routeledge.

Berkes, F. (2010). Adaptive Co-Management and Complexity: Exploring the Many Faces of Co-Management. *Adaptive Co-Management: Collaboration, Learning, and Multi-Level Governance*, 19.

Botelho, L. L. R., Cunha, C. C. A., & Macedo, M. (2011). O método da revisão integrativa nos estudos organizacionais. *Gestão e Sociedade, Belo Horizonte*, *5*(11), 121–136. doi:10.21171/ges.v5i11.1220

Brandsen, T., Honingh, M. (2015). Distinguishing Different Types of Coproduction: A Conceptual Analysis Based on the Classical Definitions. *Public Administration Review*, *76*(3), 427–435.

Bremer, S. (2019). *Toward a multi-faceted conception of co-production of climate services* (Vol. 13). Climate Services. [s. l.], doi:10.1016/j.cliser.2019.01.003

Chen, M., Mao, S., & Liu, Y. (2014). Big Data: A Survey. *Mobile Networks and Applications*, 19.

Cordova-Moras, L. G., Rodriguez-Elias, O. M., & Serna-Encinas, M. T. (2017). Expert Location Tool for Global Software Development Environments Based on Knowledge Profile Management: A Mobile Application Approach. In *2017 5th International Conference in Software Engineering Research and Innovation* (CONISOFT) (pp. 89-96). IEEE. 10.1109/CONISOFT.2017.00018

Corpakis, D. (2020). Powering Synergies Between Innovation Policy and Regional Development Frameworks: The Case of Smart Specialisation. In: A. Abu-Tair et al. (Eds.*), Proceedings of the II International Triple Helix Summit, Lecture Notes in Civil Engineering*. Springer. 10.1007/978-3-030-23898-8_8

Da Silva, C. L., Ieis, F., & Farah, M. F. Jr. (2015). As interfaces da Política de Ciência, Tecnologia e Inovação com a Política Industrial: Dilemas na trajetória recente do Brasil. *Desenvolvimento em Questão, 13*(30), 60–100. doi:10.21527/2237-6453.2015.30.60-100

De Reuver, M., Sørensen, C., & Basole, R. C. (2017). The digital platform: A research agenda. *Journal of Information Technology, 33*(2), 124–135. doi:10.1057/s41265-016-0033-3

De Silva, M., Howells, J., & Meyer, M. (2018). Innovation intermediaries and collaboration: Knowledge-based practices and internal value creation. *Research Policy, 47*(1), 70–87. doi:10.1016/j.respol.2017.09.011

Denhardt, R. B., & Denhardt, J. V. (2003). *The New Public Service: Serving, not Steering*. M. E. Sharpe.

Di Vaio, A., Palladino, R., Hassan, R., & Escobar, O. (2020). Artificial intelligence and business models in the sustainable development goals perspective: A systematic literature review. *Journal of Business Research, 121*, 283–314. doi:10.1016/j.jbusres.2020.08.019

Djenontin, I. N. S., Meadow, A. M. (2018). The art of co-production of knowledge in environmental sciences and management: lessons from international practice. *Environmental Management*. doi:10.1007/s00267-018-1028-3

Doloreux, D., & Parto, S. (2005). Regional innovation systems: Current discourse and unresolved issues. *Technology in Society, 27*(2), 133–153. doi:10.1016/j.techsoc.2005.01.002

Dos Anjos, A. C., Sell, D., Spinosa, L. M., Wahrhaftig, R., Koch, G. L., dos Santos, N., & dos Santos Pacheco, R. C. (2023). Sistemas para Localização de Especialistas: Desafios e oportunidades para o desenvolvimento de ecossistemas de inovação. *Revista Ibérica de Sistemas e Tecnologias de Informação*, (E55), 311–326.

Ehrlich, K., & Shami, N. S. (2008). Searching for Expertise. CHI 2008, 2008, Florence. *Proceedings of the SIGCHI Conference on Human Factors in Computing Systems*. New York: ACM. 10.1145/1357054.1357224

Fan, H., Wang, F., & Zheng, M. (2016). Research on knowledge fusion connotation and process model. In: China Conference On Knowledge Graph And Semantic Computing (CCKS 2016). Springer. doi:10.1007/978-981-10-3168-7_18

Fitsilis, P., Gerogiannis, V., & Anthopoulos, L. (2014). Project team selection based on social networks. *2014 IEEE International Technology Management Conference*. IEEE. 10.1109/ITMC.2014.6918598

Fitsilis, P., Gerogiannis, V., & Anthopoulos, L. (2015). Software Project Team Selection Based on Enterprise Social Networks. In *Gen, M., Kim, K., Huang, X., Hiroshi, Y. (eds.). Industrial Engineering, Management Science and Applications 2015, Lecture Notes in Electrical Engineering*. Springer. doi:10.1007/978-3-662-47200-2_40

Fortino, G., Rovella, A., Russo, W., & Savaglio, C. (2014). On the Classification of Cyberphysical Smart Objects in the Internet of Things. In Ubicitec (pp. 86-94). Springer.

Gil-Garcia, J. R., Zhang, J., & Puron-Cid, G. (2016). Conceptualizing smartness in government: An integrative and multi-dimensional view. *Government Information Quarterly, 33*(3), 524–534. doi:10.1016/j.giq.2016.03.002

Gómez-Pérez, A., Fernandez-Lopez, M., & Corcho, O. (2004). *Ontological engineering with examples from the areas of knowledge management, e-commerce and the semantic web*. Springer-Verlag.

Guimón, J. (2019). *Policy initiatives to enhance the impact of public research: Promoting excellence, transfer and co-creation, OECD Science, Technology and Industry Policy Papers, No. 81*. OECD Publishing., doi:10.1787/a4c9197a-

Guy, I. (2013). Mining Expertise and Interests from Social Media. *International World Wide Web Conference Committee* (IW3C2). ACM. 10.1145/2488388.2488434

Harmaala, M. M. (2015). The sharing city as a platform for a more sustainable city environment? *International Journal of Environment and Health, 7*(4), 309–328. doi:10.1504/IJENVH.2015.077116

Herling, R. W. (2000). Operational definitions of Expertise and Competence. *Advances in Developing Human Resources, 2*(1), 8–21. doi:10.1177/152342230000200103

Hess, C., & Ostrom, E. (2005). A Framework for Analyzing the Knowledge Commons: A chapter from Understanding Knowledge as a Commons. *Theory into Practice*.

Hoffecker, E. (2019). *Understanding Innovation Ecosystems: A Framework For Joint Analysis And Action*.

Hoffmann, M. G., Sell, D., & da Cunha Lemos, D. (2020). Convergence analysis between federal and state agendas for the promotion of science, technology and innovation (STI): A study focused on ICT sector priorities in the State of Santa Catarina–Brazil. *Base Revista de Administração e Contabilidade da UNISINOS, 17*(4), 545–572.

Howells, J. (2005). Innovation and regional economic development: A matter of perspective? *Research Policy, 34*(8), 1220–1234. doi:10.1016/j.respol.2005.03.014

Jin, J., & McKelvey, M. (2019). Building a sectoral innovation system for new energy vehicles in Hangzhou, China: Insights from evolutionary economics and strategic niche management. *Journal of Cleaner Production, 224*, 1–9. doi:10.1016/j.jclepro.2019.03.118

Kendal, S., & Creen, M. (2006). *An Introduction to Knowledge Engineering*. Springer.

Kitsios, F., & Kamariotou, M. (2021). Artificial Intelligence and Business Strategy towards Digital Transformation: A Research Agenda. *Sustainability (Basel), 13*(4), 2021. doi:10.3390/su13042025

Kraß, W., & Försterling, U. (2013). Comparison of the results of an authorship-based expert recommender against data from a directory of experts. i-Know '13, Graz, Austria.

Leydesdorff, L., & Smith, H. L. (2022). Triple, quadruple, and higher-order helices: Historical phenomena and (neo-) evolutionary models. *Triple Helix (Heidelberg), 9*(1), 6–31. doi:10.1163/21971927-bja10022

Lin, S., Hong, W., Wang, D., & Li, T. (2017). A survey on expert finding techniques. *Journal of Intelligent Information Systems, 49*(2), 255–279. doi:10.1007/s10844-016-0440-5

López-Arellano, J. Romero-Rubio, S., Morales-Ávila, M. (2022). La cooperación interacadémica como factor determinante para la productividad académica de la Universidad Autónoma de Sinaloa. *Revista lbérica de Sistemas e Tecnologias de Informação, 47*, 09/2022.

Marques, M. A. J. (2020). *Framework conceitual do potencial de coprodução de inovação em ecossistemas de inovação* [Thesis, Universidade Federal de Santa Catarina].

Mauser, W. (2013). Transdisciplinary global change research: The co-creation of knowledge for sustainability. Current Opinion in Environmental Sustainability, 5(4), 420–431. doi:10.1016/j.cosust.2013.07.001

McManus, C., & Baeta Neves, A. A. (2021). Funding research in Brazil. *Scientometrics*, *126*(1), 801–823. doi:10.1007/s11192-020-03762-5

Miles, A.; Bechhofer, S. (2009). *SKOS simple knowledge organization system reference.* W3C recommendation.

Miller, C. A., & Wyborn, C. (2018). Co-production in global sustainability: Histories and theories. *Environmental Science and Policy*. Elsevier. https://linkinghub.elsevier.com/retrieve/pii/S1462901117306366

Nabatchi, T.; Sancino, A.; Sicilia, M. (2017). Varieties of Participation in Public Services: The Who, When, and What of Coproduction. *Public Administration Review*, *77*(5), 766–776.

Nesti, G. (2018). *Co-production for innovation: the urban living lab experience experience* (Vol. 4035). Policy and Society. [s. l.], doi:10.1080/14494035.2017.1374692

Nguyen J. et al. (2014). Defining dimensions in expertise recommender systems for enhancing open collaborative innovation. *Frontiers in Artificial Intelligence and Applications.*

Nguyen, J. (2015). InsERT: the Inspirational Expert Recommender Tool. *2015 IEEE International Conference on Fuzzy Systems* (FUZZ-IEEE), IEEE. 10.1109/FUZZ-IEEE.2015.7337984

Noy, N. F. & McGuiness, D. L. (2001). *Ontology Development 101: A Guide to Creating your First Ontology.* Stanford. https://protege.stanford.edu/publications/ontology_development/ontology101.pdf

O'Reilly, T. (2011). Government as a Platform. *Innovations: Technology, Governance, Globalization*, *6*(1), 13–40. doi:10.1162/INOV_a_00056

OECD. (2014). *Industry and Technology Policies in Korea, OECD Reviews of Innovation Policy.* OECD Publishing. doi:10.1787/9789264213227-

OECD. (2017). *OECD Reviews of Innovation Policy: Finland 2017, OECD Reviews of Innovation Policy.* OECD Publishing. doi:10.1787/9789264276369-

Okamuro, H., Nishimura, J., & Kitagawa, F. (2019). Multilevel policy governance and territorial adaptability: Evidence from Japanese SME innovation programmes. *Regional Studies*, *53*(6), 803–814. doi: 10.1080/00343404.2018.1500687

Ostrom, E. (1990). *Governing the Commons: The Evolution of Institutions for Collective Action* [s.l.]. Cambridge University Press. Cambridge. http://www.cambridge.org doi:10.1017/CBO9780511807763

Pacheco, C. S. R. (2016). Coprodução em Ciência, Tecnologia e Inovação: fundamentos e visões. *Interdisciplinaridade: Universidade e Inovação Social e Tecnológica*, CRV Editora. https://encurtador.com.br/evERV

Pacheco, R. C. S., Steil, A. V., & Sell, D. (2016). A multi e a interdisciplinaridade na visão de áreas de avaliação da Capes. In: A. Philippi Jr; V. Fernandes, & R. C. S. Pacheco. (eds.). Ensino, Pesquisa e Inovação. Desenvolvendo a Interdisciplinaridade.

Parker, G. G., Van Alstyne, M. W., & Choudary, S. P. (2016). *Platform revolution: How networked markets are transforming the economy and how to make them work for you.* WW Norton & Company.

Parks, R. B. (1980). *Consumers as coproducers of public services: Some economic and institutional considerations.* Research Gate.

Peffers, K., Tuunanen, T., Rothenberger, M. A., & Chatterjee, S. (2007). A design science research methodology for information systems research. *Journal of Management Information Systems*, *24*(3), 45–77. doi:10.2753/MIS0742-1222240302

Pereira, G. V., Parycek, P., Falco, E., & Kleinhans, R. (2018). Smart governance in the context of smart cities: A literature review. *Information Polity*, *23*(2), 143–162. doi:10.3233/IP-170067

Pestoff, V. (2006). Citizens and co-production of welfare services. *Public Management Review*, [s. l.], v. 8, n. 4, p. 503–519.

Rampisela, T. V. (2020a). Characteristics of Expertise Locator System in Academia: A Systematic Literature Review. *2020 International Seminar on Intelligent Technology and Its Applications* (ISITIA). Springer.

Rampisela, T. V. (2020b). *Expert Locator System for Finding Co-authors Using Snowball Network Method: A Case Study of Fasilkom UI Lecturers. ICEMT.* ACM.

Rochet, J. C., & Tirole, J. (2003). Platform competition in two-sided markets. *Journal of the European Economic Association*, *1*(4), 990–1029. doi:10.1162/154247603322493212

Schreiber, G., Akkermans, H., Anjewierden, A., Hoog, R., Shadbolt, N., Velde, W., & Wielinga, B. (2002). *Knowledge engineering and management: the commonKADS methodology.* MIT Press.

Shearmur, R., Carrincazeaux, C., & Doloreux, D. (Eds.). (2016). *Handbook on the Geographies of Innovation.* Edward Elgar Publishing. doi:10.4337/9781784710774

Sun, J., Ma, J., Cheng, X., Liu, Z., & Cao, X. (2013). *Finding an expert: A model recommendation system.* Research Gate.

Turnhout, E., Metze, T., Wyborn, C., Klenk, N., & Louder, E. (2020). The politics of co-production: Participation, power, and transformation. *Current Opinion in Environmental Sustainability*, *42*, 15–21. doi:10.1016/j.cosust.2019.11.009

Van Kerkhoff, L. E.; Lebel, L. (2015). Coproductive capacities: Rethinking science-governance relations in a diverse world. *Ecology and Society*, *20*(1).

Vergne, M., & Susi, A. (2015). Breaking the Recursivity: Towards a Model to Analyse Expert Finders. *Lecture Notes in Computer Science*, *9381*, 539–547. doi:10.1007/978-3-319-25264-3_40

Wang, X. (2020). KM 3.0: Knowledge Management Computing Under Digital Economy. In *Matos, F. (ed.) Knowledge, People, and Digital Transformation. Contributions to Management Science*. Springer. doi:10.1007/978-3-030-40390-4_13

Whittemore, R., & Knafl, K. (2005). The integrative review: Updated methodology. *Journal of Advanced Nursing*, *52*(5), 546–553. doi:10.1111/j.1365-2648.2005.03621.x PMID:16268861

Wyborn, C. (2015). Co-productive governance: A relational framework for adaptive governance. *Global Environmental Change*, *30*, 56–67. doi:10.1016/j.gloenvcha.2014.10.009

Yarosh. (2013). I Need Someone to Help! A Taxonomy of Helper-Finding Activities in the Enterprise. CSCW, 13, San Antonio.

Young, R. (2020). *Asian Productivity Organization (org.). APO Knowledge Management: tools and techniques manual*. Omega Communications. doi:10.61145/COEE1851

Zittrain, J. L. (2006). The generative internet. *Harvard Law Review*, *119*(7), 1975–2040.

KEY TERMS AND DEFINITIONS

Commons: Shared resources or assets, often held collectively by a community or group, where access, usage, and management are governed by agreed-upon rules to ensure sustainability and equitable distribution (Hess and Ostrom, 2005; Ostrom, 1996; Marques, 2020).

Co-Production: Co-production is a collaborative process in which multiple individuals or entities work together to create or produce something, typically involving the active participation and contributions of all involved parties (Parks et al., 1980; Brandsen; Honingh, 2015; Marques, 2020; Ostrom, 1990; Pestoff, 2006)

Co-Productive Governance: A collaborative approach to decision-making and public administration in which government authorities work closely with different stakeholders to jointly design and deliver public services and policies, fostering active participation and shared responsibility in governance processes (Wyborn, 2015; Van Kerkhoff; Lebbel, 2015)

Digital Plataforms: Online infrastructures that facilitate interactions, transactions, and the exchange of information between users or entities in a digital environment. (De Reuver; Sørensen; Basole, 2017; Parker; Alstyne; Choudary, 2016; Ansell and Torfing, 2021).

Expertise Locator Systems: Digital tools designed to identify and connect individuals or experts with specific knowledge or skills within a specific context (APQC, 2015; Balog et al., 2012; Ehrlich and Shami, 2008; Young, 2020).

New Research and Innovation Arrangements: A collective of agents with aligned goals and visions, dedicated to developing innovative solutions through co-production (Dos Anjos, 2023).

Quadruple Helix: Collaborative innovation model involving government, academia, industry, and civil society working together to drive socioeconomic development and innovation in a region or ecosystem (Leydesdorff; Smith, 2022)

Section 3

Intersection of Business Intelligence and Artificial Intelligence on Multiple Domains

Chapter 6
Creating Business Process Intelligence Through Value Network Analysis:
A Tagging-Based Approach

Iniga Antonia Baum
https://orcid.org/0009-0009-2792-0409
Johannes Kepler University, Linz, Austria

Christian Stary
https://orcid.org/0000-0001-9764-5021
Johannes Kepler University, Linz, Austria

ABSTRACT

Value-driven (process) management is an established means of networked business operation. Value networks effectively represent value exchanges between stakeholders and the resulting business transactions. Holomaps as simple, but expressive value network representations form the core of the organizational development and transformation technique value network analysis (VNA). Knowledge generated throughout a VNA application is the baseline to specify business process models. Value exchanges among concerned stakeholders need to be transformed to communication and operational tasks. So far, this transformation has not been guided in a structured and thus effective way. The authors propose a respective tagging mechanism. It takes into account the structure of holomaps and semantic process design. By using a behavior specification technique for semantic process design, process models can be executed for validation purposes. Hence, prior to implementation, organizational practice cannot be expressed and experienced by concerned stakeholders as part of human-centered transformation processes.

DOI: 10.4018/979-8-3693-1058-8.ch006

INTRODUCTION

In networks of business operation, stakeholders with different assets and competencies collaborate in organizational structures. These structures allow to create jointly value for target groups, including customers and business partners (Normann et al., 1993; Parolini, 1999; Normann, 2001; Clegg et al., 2002; Pallotti et al., 2015; Agostini et al., 2017). For instance, the cross-disciplinary domain of digital healthcare involves experts from different disciplines, including medical, logistics, and technology specialists, when clients need to be provided with integrated home monitoring devices and health services. In order to create value for customers and business partners, value management considers relations between customers and marketing (Payne et al., 2001L Mazurek, 2014), customers and construction industry (Kelly, 2014), among project partners (Fleming et al., 2016), and between stakeholders in new public management (Alford et al., 2008, Bryson et al. 2014). These relations need to be manageable for organizational structuring and development, in particular when designing business processes (Allee, 2003, 2008).

Value management denotes an organizational design process that involves business-relevant stakeholders in their functional roles. For instance, healthcare service procedures are redesigned due to feedback from the clients indicating which features were valued in a different way by customers as intended by service development. Value-led development proposals depend on the creativity of involved stakeholders and their motivation to contribute to process design and change management (cf. Keeney, 2009). The more context can be acquired, the larger becomes the design space for structuring operational procedures (Song et al., 2018), e.g., for re-arranging services for healthcare customers in emergency situations. However, for successful operation, business processes models need to be constructed and understood by the stakeholders performing work tasks (Hammer, 2015).

Recent approaches to Business Process Management have recognized this need (Laguna et al., 2018). Business operation should be modelled in a stakeholder-oriented way, and simulated to probe business processes and understand their contribution to value generation (ibid.). For instance, service processes in healthcare should be analyzed from the perspective of each involved stakeholder group to check process semantics ('Are we doing the right things?' and 'Are we doing them right?') on an individual and collective level. It is the semantic quality of process designs that lays ground for effective organizational transformation processes by digital means (cf. Baiyere et al., 2020).

It means that the model representation contains the work procedure the way humans actually accomplish the expected and specified tasks. Still, disruptive technology shifts lead to gaps between value generation and semantic process design (Vial, 2021). Business process design needs to match business capabilities and demands when adopting Business Process Management technologies for business operation (Bosilj Vukšić et al., 2018). In the addressed digital healthcare provision case, 24/7-service demand could be a need to be met. It concerns a transactional value between service provider and clients whose health conditions need to be continuously monitored.

Value Network Analysis (Allee, 1997, 2003, 2008, 2015) (VNA) has been established as organizational transformation technique. It recognizes business dynamics in terms of complex adaptive systems like other approaches to knowledge management and organizational learning (cf. McElroy, 2003) which impacts the development of business processes (Cagnin et al., 2021). VNA primarily captures value transactions from a stakeholder perspective in business-relevant roles, features individual reflection for semantic process design. Although preparing value exchanges for mapping them to semantic process designs, there is still a lack of facilitating guidelines and methodological or instrumental support for transformation value exchanges to semantic process models. Value network applications, such as in Zhang et al. (2019), or by Tsoukas et al., (2023), focus on elicitation rather on direct processing of acquired process information. Once an organizational value network representation has been developed, stakeholders are not supported so far with dedicated inputs to map the value network to process models for operational use. Hence, our objective of the presented research is to facilitate this mapping by an easy-to-use and effective instrument. The resulting method input It should guide concerned stakeholders to develop workflows for business operations based on a collaboratively adjusted and aligned value network representation (i.e. holomap).

Consequently, value-driven business, such as a healthcare provider, should be able to follow a set of well-defined steps when having developed value transactions and consequently, putting them to operation. A major challenge thereby is the mapping of declarative knowledge, as expressed by values and exchanged values in a holomap, to a semantically correct operational knowledge. In particular, business processes representing this type of knowledge, relate roles ('who') to activities ('doing') that are arranged in some sequence ('how') with input and output data ('object') to achieve specific business objectives.

The paper starts with related work and some background on mapping value relations to business processes. It proceeds with a methodology and terminology briefing to clarify the meaning of concepts and terms for the rest of the paper. We subsequently detail holomapping as baseline activity to value-driven alignment of organizational transformation proposals targeting the specification and implementation of business processes. Subsequently, we detail and exemplify the tagging mechanism on sales development. Tagging facilitates (i) the identification of basic process elements as utilized in holomaps, and (ii) detailing and mutual aligning the behavior of stakeholders in process models based on the generated VNA knowledge. As such it enables organizational transformation based on value exchanges in a structured and transparent way for the involved stakeholders.

The paper concludes with summarizing the achievements and providing topics for further research.

BACKGROUND AND RELATED WORK

In this section we first provide some methodological and terminological background. We then relate value-based business operation to organizational transformation enabled by Value Network Analysis, before reviewing related work on eliciting value exchanges and modelling value networks.

Methodology

As detailed in Baum et al. (2020) we follow the Design Science operationalization as proposed by Peffers et al. (2007). Value Network Analysis (VNA) allows making explicit drivers and hindrances of PjBL development while stepwise investigating PjBL-roles and their interactions. The procedure captures the development stages described in the following: The identification of concerned objects and motivation - in our case the improvement of deriving process specifications from qualitative network data. The definition of objectives for a solution includes a mechanism to identify the relevant information for process design.

The core of Design-Science-based research is the design and development of an artefact: An artefact can be a model, a concept, a method, an object, an application, or a combination of those. For this research the aforementioned mechanism corresponds to the intended artefact. Together with a demonstrator and its evaluation, design cycles have been instantiated. Each Design Science cycle uses the current version of the artefact to exemplify whether and how the addressed problem is solved in practice. In our case, a tagging variant is exemplified in an initial design cycle.

In each of the Design Science cycles the current solution is evaluated, based on the objectives and the requirements developed so far. It is checked whether the results from the use of the artefact in the demonstration case meet the specified requirements. As there are backward links from evaluation to further design and definition of objectives, either the artefact requires further refinement/adjustment, or the objectives need to be reconsidered by revisiting the conceptual foundation of the approach, before a new design cycle can be started. The described design cycle in this research targets the identification of roles and detailing their interactions according to the data and control flow that are relevant for process design.

The communication of all collected information and achievements includes the problem, the artefact, and its utility and effectiveness to other researchers and practitioners. The described case and mechanisms of this paper corresponds to the communication step of the Design-Science-based research methodology.

Key Terms

In this sub section we explain essential terms as used in the following sections:

- Value Network: A set of interacting roles, exchanging values in terms of formal or contracted, and informal or voluntary relations.
- Holomap: Visual representation of a Value Network in an easy-to-grasp and easy-to-handle way.
- Value Network Analysis (VNA): A set of three analyses based on a holomap. Exchange Analysis aims at finding patterns of value exchanges, Impact Analysis details the effects of received values, and Value Creation Analysis details the outputs of accomplished tasks and their potential to further impact organizational behavior.
- Digital Transformation: In the context of VNA-based organizational development, the mapping of a holomap and knowledge gained through the three VNA analyses to executable business process models by a respective software system, such as a workflow management system, process engine, or BPM suite.
- Tagging: An annotation mechanism developed for Digital Transformation.
- Semantic Process Design: Networked procedures as perceived by involved stakeholder groups when achieving business objectives.
- Business Process Model: Procedural specification of task accomplishment according to stakeholder roles.
- Executable Process Model: Procedural model that can be run by software to validate task accomplishment procedures from a stakeholder and organization perspective.
- Subject-orientation: Communication and interaction-oriented approach to Business Process Management.

Value-Based Business Operation and Transformation

Value-based business has its origin in management activities targeting cost relations to market-relevant product qualities and customer relations (Miles, 1961, Martin et al 2001). It finally concerns underlying processes, so that organizational networks and related design may support or hinder the achievement of business objectives (cf. Bosilj Vukšić et al., 2018, Val, 2021). Going beyond value as a "customer's perceived preference for, and evaluation of, those product attributes, attribute performances, and consequences that arise from use and that facilitate, or block, the customers in achieving their goals and purposes in use" (Woodruff, 1997, p. 142) value analysis and design thus are part of managing operational structures and their impact upon performance (cf. Knight, 2002). It affects both, the local level, and the network level, particularly what is considered the "whole" of a network (cf. Provan et al., 2007). The local perspective corresponds to the business operation from an individual stakeholder perspective, according to individual qualification, task profile, or organizational role, such as client support in digital healthcare operation. The organizational perspective corresponds to the "whole" of a network, as it captures all business cases or parts of a value chain an organization is part of.

When focusing on network aspects, empirical performance data, e.g., from a hospital operation in a regional community (Pallotti et al., 2015), indicates the need to understand the direct relations among stakeholders, as they are main drivers of network performance (see also Acosta et al., 2018; Asamoah et al. 2020). Those relations concern formal and informal contacts of a stakeholder network. However, Ihm et al. (2015) could show how different actors of a network can perceive the network structure in different ways, by studying the interaction between service providers and clients. According to this study, organizational relations served either as means of navigation in a functional role, or as a means to receive benefits. Once stakeholder interactions in a network are perceived in a variety of ways, they need to be studied in collaborative task settings for the sake of aligning transformation processes.

Interestingly, even in case of collaborative governance and well-documented organizational networks, e.g., by means of process specifications, the relationship between business-relevant stakeholders, such as sales specialists and customer service experts, is not always clear (Scott et al., 2015). In those cases, taking into account formal and relational governance in network relationships helps explaining relational outcome (Gurcaylilar-Yenidogan et al., 2015). An outcome perspective differs from an output perspective as it considers the effect of an activity or interaction among stakeholders. The outcome perspective enables to consider and ensure value congruence in business operation in and across organizations (Massingham, 2015; Yates-Mercer et al., 2002). Value Network Analysis (VNA) (Allee, 2008) has been introduced to that respect, in particular addressing the formal or contracted, and informal relations between stakeholders. VNA facilitates eliciting knowledge on business transactions and their collaborative consolidation for value congruence in diagrammatic form, so-called holomaps. This adapted form of concept maps (Novak, 1998, Novak et al., 2006, 2008) can be generated and manipulated by stakeholders with minimal prior practice. They represent business transactions as exchanges of tangible and intangible deliverables (i.e. formal or contracted, and informal ties) that need to be aligned across individual value systems. Holomaps, together with three types of analyses represent the knowledge base to align value exchanges and to derive operational business processes. The specification of stakeholder behavior in process models finally has an impact accomplishing organizational objectives when being implemented.

The three types of analyses of VNA enable each network actor for successful task completion and process accomplishment to reflect on the value alignment through mutual interactions with other actors, i.e. in how far his/her role-specific organizational transactions is coherent with his/her individual value system. Although in business-to-customer relationships governing value (co-)creation is well established (cf. Payne et al., 2008; Vargo et al., 2008), alignment with subjective intentions and capabilities are not common, and essential informal ties might be overlooked or un-recognized (cf. Jankowicz, 2001; Agostini et al., 2017). The strength of the VNA technique lies (i) in allowing to capture formal ties (so-called tangible transactions) and informal ties (so-called intangible transactions) and their structural dynamics, and (ii) in capturing individual perspectives on both types of ties, thus reflecting on a possible integration or redesign of formal and informal ties.

The VNA finally should lead to a shared understanding of business operation, i.e. a congruence between individual and collective value exchanges among stakeholders (cf. Treem et al., 2017). This understanding needs to be transformed to a proper representation of business processes. As the VNA like other value-led development approaches does not directly provide means for deriving process specifications from value networks (cf. Augl et al., 2015; Stary, 2014), we suggest to develop effective transformation support. Support provision should not only facilitate the identification of basic process elements as captured by holomapping, but rather help to improve business process models with the knowledge acquired in the course of the analyses of the VNA. This knowledge refers to activities and effects of inputs and outputs (i.e. the outcome) of networked operations.

Modelling Value Exchanges

In this section we review existing work on value-based modelling and the context of representing value exchanges, since the VNA is based on value exchanges between concerned stakeholders. In value-based modelling, information and information flows are represented as fundamental 'resource whose value is fundamentally multidimensional' (Kranti, 1997, p. 93). Most important, 'it is meaningless to model the value of information in isolation away from the context and the specific parties between which this information is exchanged' (ibid). For instance, value exchanges in digital healthcare require domain context, such as remote monitoring in digital home healthcare settings targeting patient autonomy. Modelling information flows rather than information itself brings transactions involving information flows and their fundamental properties in multiparty transactions to the center of representation. For instance, customer records are less informative than the flow of information between the customer service department and the customer. The latter allows tracking the origin of information and enriches the transformation space due to structural context.

Stakeholder Roles Matter for Value Exchange

According to Hyvarinen (1970) as cited in Kranti (1997, p. 97) the pragmatic level of interaction is the one where 'we are concerned with the 'value' or 'utility' of information, which is necessarily even more a function of the receiver than was the case in semantics. It also depends on time.' On the semantic layer, meaning or practical significance plays a significant role as the receiving stakeholder needs to understand information that is delivered. For organizations, the pragmatic quality means the capability of its members to act upon receiving information rather than having to ensure proper understanding information before acting. Hence, each value exchange is related to intelligible inputs or outputs of work tasks informing stakeholders how to proceed, e.g., customer service's knowing when to contact a customer accurately recognizing a state of emergency.

A major bridge of value-based modelling to digital system design has been proposed by the software engineer Boehm. He recognized value-neutral software development methods as insufficient, as they can lead to misuse of (organizational) resources. The value-based software engineering agenda (Boehm, 2003) ranges from requirements engineering to fundamental developing principles and practices. Starting with identifying a system's success-critical stakeholders, it requires eliciting their value propositions with respect to the system (cf. Murfaza et al., 2010, Geissdoerfer et al., 2016). For instance, for digital home

Figure 1. Value elicitation framework
(Murfaza et al., 2010)

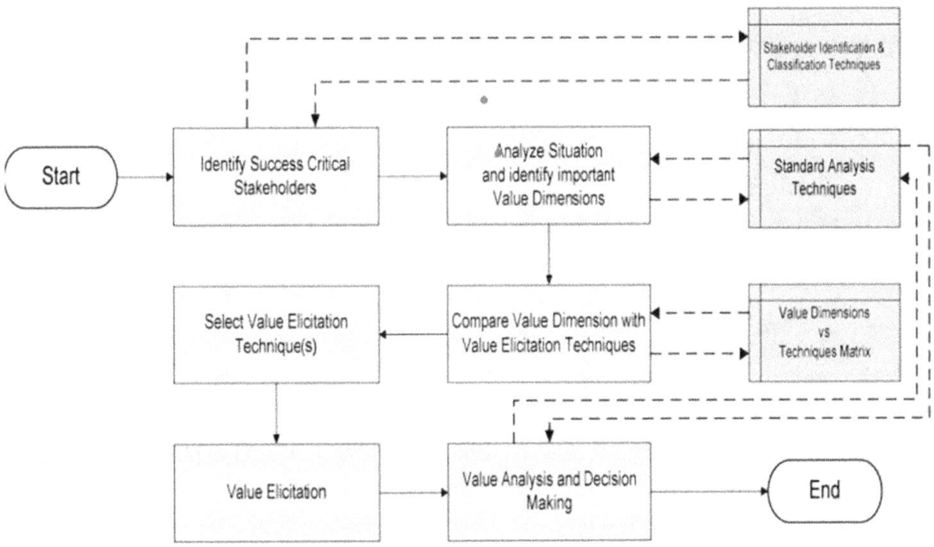

healthcare, success-critical stakeholders are patients, caretakers, medical experts, Internet-of-Things specialists, cyberphysical system developers, and service agents. The acquired value propositions are then reconciled into a 'mutually satisfactory set of objectives for the system' (Boehm, 2003, p.1), such as continuous monitoring, and 24/7 service availability for emergency cases. The subsequent development steps include architecting, design and implementation, verification, and validation. They ensure that 'a software solution satisfies its value objectives' (ibid, p.2). The software development activities are accompanied by project management tasks taking into account the elicited system values in planning and controlling quality and risks. Hence, system values and stakeholder roles need to guide transformation processes and finally, need to be mapped on to behavior specifications.

Knowledge Elicitation Matters to Understand Organizational Value Generation

Murfaza et al.'s (2010) framework for eliciting values from system stakeholder – see Figure 1 – includes various categories of values.

- The *Business Value* goes beyond economic value considerations and includes short term and long-term business objectives, whereas the Economic Value concerns the value related to an asset's ability to generate (financial) income.
- The *Technical Value* denotes information system properties and technologies capabilities, including the integration with other domains.
- The *Epistemic Value* refers to building a shared knowledge base and the value that a software development project and the resulting software system could add to existing resources, in particular literature, technology, literacy and awareness of society.

Figure 2. Value-based modeling for service design
(Weigand et al., 2006)

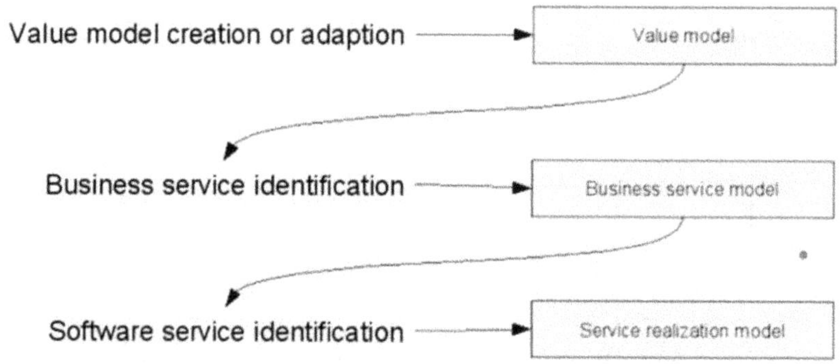

- The *Personal Value* subsumes emotional, psychological, and ethical aspects of values aside others and bring individual value systems and instantiations into play.
- The *Social Value* sets the stage for value dimensions that are considered relevant for society beyond individual value considerations.

The framework does not refer explicitly to value modeling or value-exchange documentations between stakeholders. Nevertheless, driven by the experiences in value-based software engineering, value considerations propagated to service-oriented development, in particular to service-oriented architecting through the need for analysis and design methods. The proposed approaches also went beyond the functional development of digital systems, as service-oriented system development aligns business and IT through a service perspective on the functionality of a system to be provided. The recognized need for a unified view on services and a corresponding service layer architecture finally has led to service models based on elicited stakeholder value (systems). Weigand et al. (2006) proposed the refinement of values along a three-step procedure, leading to business service definitions and software service specification for implementation (see Figure 2).

Representation Matters for Conveying Value Exchanges

According to the authors value models are generated when analyzing resources (i.e. material and immaterial value object or asset under control of an organization) that are either modified or exchanged in processes. Conversion processes require input resources to produce or modify assets, whereas exchange processes denote the exchange of external resources between two actors. Processes are composed of so-called economic events that are triggered by an actor and affects an asset involved in some business case. In Wiegand et al.'s proposed value-based approach models are based on a graphical notation including actors, resources, value ports, value interfaces, value activities and value transfers. Actors denote economically independent entities, and resources (also termed value objects) are assets of economic value for at least one actor. Value ports are interaction points of actors to exchange resources with other actors. They are subsumed by their in- and output functions through the value interface. The value ports enable value exchanges referring to value activities. The latter denote operations 'that can be carried out in an economically profitable way for at least one actor' (Wiegand et al., 2006, p. 413). Hence, besides the stakeholder interactions, in this approach, the values capture the motivation of stakeholders to accomplish the tasks involved when interacting with others.

Recent service-based development in the health domain, consider value-based modelling as a means to identify 'what is being offered [termed value objects] and what is being requested in return [termed value propositions]' (Lipscomb et al., 2022, p.2). The state of the actors in relation to these value propositions are described in the course of value-based modelling. The authors compare value-based modelling to process-based modelling by assigning the latter focus on tasks to be accomplished when being driven by value objects. As such, process- and value-based modelling are considered mutually complementary. Case study results, such as provided by Alharti et al. (2022), reveal essential benefits for users and customers when getting insight toward the desired final value along each development step. In particular, users and domain specialists can gain value in the early steps because they have access to needed services. Particularly effective is questioning mutual dependencies between stakeholders affecting the transfer of information. Rather than asking for the sequence of tasks to be accomplished (as it is the focus in process-based modelling) the value-based modeler needs to ask: "Was it worth it?" This question refers to the interaction with other stakeholders and their (re-)actions in a networked business context. The quest for perceived value of a transaction is in with other value-based approaches, such as the Value Network Analysis detailed in the subsequent section of this paper.

Value Transformation to Process Models Matters for Organizational Management

A different approach to process- and value-based modelling has been taken by Snoek et al. (2022). Stemming from model-based engineering, process and information models form the basis for dealing with value-based development – see Figure 3. Both models serve as baseline or point or reference along agile development cycles, as user stories and system versions are judged by involved stakeholders according to the perceived and economical value of the current development. Hence, values are encoded either in development objectives (cf. Neiger, et al., 2009 also for process-based development) or in requirements to be implemented along agile development cycles.

Resilience Matters for Developing Process-Based Organizations

Agile development, can be facilitated through using executable models and simulation support engines, both in terms of organizing the development process and utilizing technology. From an organizational perspective business processes based on executable models can be experienced in terms of activity sequences before roll-out in an organization. By providing operational data the behavior in operation can be experienced in an even more realistic way. For instance, Traoré et al. (2022) recently provide a simulation approach in the context of value-based healthcare, equating the objectives of healthcare development with low costs + high quality + wide accessibility, arguing with the high complexity in this domain. When measuring value, some concrete formulation of increase in quality, while reducing cost, and increasing access can be of benefit for earned or economic value. The focus on the economic value type has been accompanied by representing work processes in a business process model using BPMN (www.bpmn.org), both facilitating the case when "understanding the behavior of the overall system is becoming a major concern among healthcare managers and decision-makers intent on increasing value for their systems" (ibid., p. 481). However, even recent studies addressing the complimentary nature of value and process model reveal different notations for each of them. For instance, Hotie et al. (2019)

Figure 3. Meta-model in UML for model- and value-based modeling in service-oriented development
(www.uml.org), (Snoek et al., 2022)

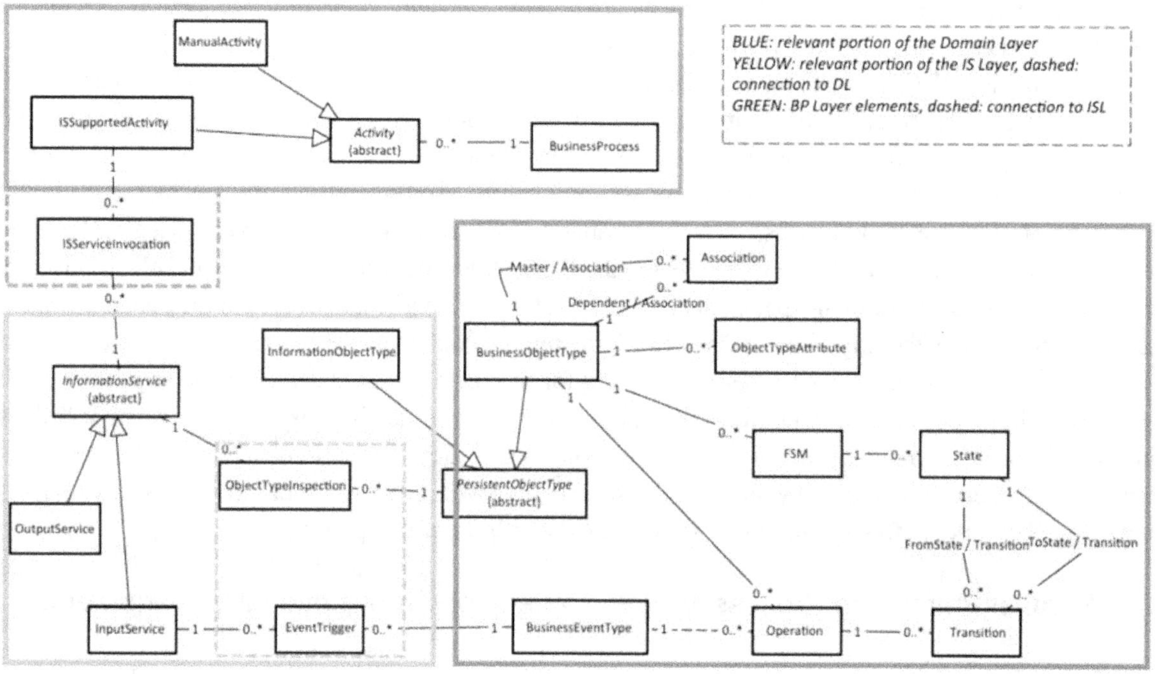

Figure 4. Diagrammatic value model
(Hotie et al., 2019)

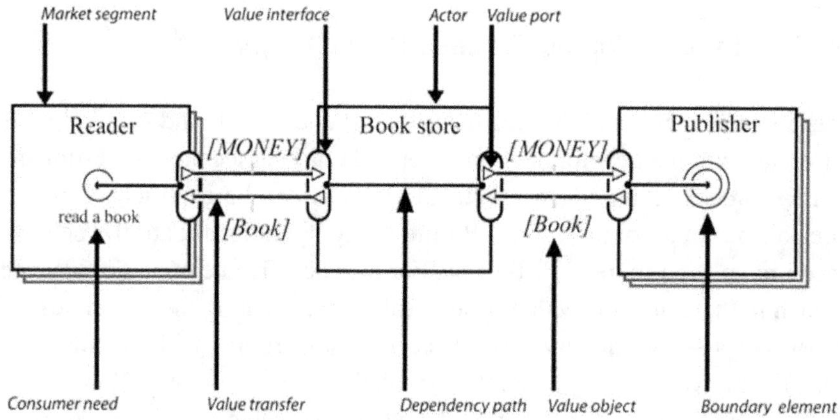

rely on implicit mapping of values represented in a value model and BPMN-based process models – see Figure 4.

According to the concept of Hotie et al. (2019) organizations as well as stakeholders are actors or market segments in the value model. Value objects, as offers from actors, have an economic value for at least one actor. Since value models abstract through value ports requesting and offering value objects, business process design is required to specific how value objects are delivered. Each value port of an actor is a means of value transfers for exchanging value objects with other actors. Dependency paths sketch how the demand of a stakeholder, e.g., customer, can be met through exchanging value objects via actors' value interfaces. Although the model is of declarative nature, the sequence of transfers indicates the business logic that needs to be represented from a business process perspective.

Conclusive Summary

From the findings detailed above we can conclude that

(i) value-based thinking is well established in networked business and the respective organizational and socio-technical development settings,
(ii) value-based modelling has been developed to a stage where semantic representations can be delivered to stakeholders, and
(iii) the complementary nature of value-based modelling to business process modelling has been recognized in networked settings.

Given the finding that value-based modelling and process modeling have not been aligned by defining and unifying notation or providing a transformation or mapping scheme, an effective instrument to that respect could facilitate the transparent and traceable transformation of value models to operational digital structures.

GROUNDING TRANSFORMATION FOR SEMANTIC PROCESS DESIGN

In this section we introduce the VNA as value-based process development technique based on elicited formal and informal value exchanges between concerned stakeholders. We exemplify the use of holomaps as point of reference reflecting on perceived stakeholder interactions and developing offerings for change by involved stakeholders.

Holomaps as Networks of Transactions

The VNA as introduced by Allee (2008) aims at developing organizations or network of organizations beyond the value chain, since traditional value-chain models represent a linear, if not mechanistic view of business and its operation. Complex constellations of values, however, require analysing business relationships taking into account the role of knowledge and intangible (i.e. so far not explicated) value exchange as a foundation for value creation. Value exchange needs to be analyzed before changing business transactions in practice. In particular, complex relationships require pre-processing from a value-based perspective, as they influence effectiveness and efficiency, and possible friction in operational processes (*ibid.*).

VNA is meant to be a development instrument to understand organizational dynamics, and thus to govern structural knowledge from a value seeking perspective, for individuals and for the organization as a whole. It is based on several fundamental principles and assumptions (Allee, 1997, 2003, 2008, Allee et al., 2015):

- Participants of an organization and organizationally relevant network actors participate in a value network by converting what they know, both individually and collectively, into so-called tangible (already explicated) and intangible value that they contribute to the network, and thus to the organization.
- Participants accrue value from their participation by converting value inputs into positive increases of their tangible and intangible assets, in ways that will allow them to continue producing value outputs in the future.
- In such a network, each participant contributes and receives value in ways that sustain both own success and the success of the value network as a whole. This mutual dependency is a condition sine qua non. Once active participants either withdraw or are expelled, the overall system becomes unstable and may collapse, and need to reconfigure.
- Value networks require trusting relationships and a high level of integrity and transparency on the part of all participants. Then, insights can be gained into interactions by identifying and analyzing not only the patterns of exchange, but rather the impact of value transactions, exchanges, and flows, and thus, the dynamics of creating and leveraging value.
- A single transaction is only meaningful in relation to the system as a whole. It is set by role carriers who utilize incoming deliverables from other role carriers (inputs) and can asses their value, and they realize value which is manifest by generating output.

The VNA considers as fundamental activity the act of exchange. Exchange includes goods, services, and revenue, but considers the transaction between network actors also as representation of organizational intelligence, thus as cognitive interaction process. Transactions ensure successful task accomplishment and business through cognitively reflected exchanges of information and knowledge sharing, opening pathways for informed decision making. Thereby,

- Tangible exchanges include goods, services, and revenue, in particular physical objects, contracts, invoices, return receipts of orders, requests for proposals, confirmations, and payments. They also include knowledge, products or services that directly generate revenue, or that are expected (contractual) and paid for as a part of a service or good.
- Intangible exchanges comprise knowledge and benefits. Intangible knowledge and information exchanges occur supporting the core product and service value chain, but are not contractual. Intangibles are extras network actors in a certain role provide to others to help keep the business operation running. For instance, a service organization asks sales experts to volunteer time and knowledge on organizational development, in exchange for an intangible benefit of prestige by affiliation.

Network actors involved in intangible transactions help building relationships by exchanging strategic information, planning knowledge, process knowledge, technical know-how, and in this way sharing collaborative design work, performing joint planning activities, and contributing to policy development. Intangibles, like other assets, are increased and leveraged through deliberate actions. They affect business relationships, human competence, internal structure, and social culture. VNA considers intangibles as assets and negotiables that can actually be delivered by network actors engaged in a knowledge exchange. They can be held accountable for the effective execution of that exchange, as they are able to articulate them accordingly when following the VNA's structured procedure.

Value networks represent organizations or network of organizations as a web of relationships that generates tangible and intangible value through transactions between two or more roles. These roles stem from any public or private organization or sector and stand for individuals, groups, entire organizations or networks. The network, instead of representing hierarchical positions, structures the dynamics of processing and delivering tangibles and intangibles. Although the roles related to the organization at hand, suppliers, partners, and consumers regardless of their physical location, need to become part of the network once they generate value or receive transactional deliverables.

Value exchanges are modelled in a special type of concept map (Novak et al., 2006), termed holomap – see Figure 5. The VNA mapping from the observed reality to a holomap is based on the following elements:

- Nodes (Ovals) represent functional roles of network actors, termed Participants of the value network, i.e. the nodes of the network.
- Participants send or extend deliverables to other Participants. One-directional edges (labeled links) represent the direction the Deliverables are moving during a specific Transaction.

In VNA an exchange only occurs when a Transaction results in a particular Deliverable coming back. A gap is considered the case when something is provided without anything being received in return. Hence, not only information sources or sinks in networked business settings, but also the flow of information is of interest in VNA-based developments. For successul value exchange, a deliverable sent to another network node should result either directly or indirectly, i.e. involving further network nodes, to an input deliverable to the sender.

In the following we exemplify a VNA case in Sales and Presales from different organizations of a networked service company providing innovative instruments (methods and technologies) for knowledge acquisition and sharing. Due to a merger with another company Presales should complement the service chain of the company providing all other services, including Sales. In order to understand the overall patterns of exchange, and determining the impact of tangible and intangible inputs for each Participant, the merging companies decided to perform a VNA. It should not only help analyzing the state of affairs, but also leverage potential changes for each Participant. Sales and Pre-Sales aim to improve their ability to utilize operation and customer feedback in further developing their services, although stemming from different organizations.

The first step Participants need to consider in the modeling process are all the roles, organizational units or work groups, both internally and externally, that are considered of relevance in the activities of the Sales and Pre-Sales group. In this case, three network actors (Participannts) inside the organization, namely Sales, Product Development, and Customer Service, and two network actors, Presales and free-

Figure 5. Sample holomap for Pre/Sales Development – Intangible value exchanges are non-contractual transaction, marked by a dotted line, the others are tangible ones, contracted as deliverable from a network actor (node) to another

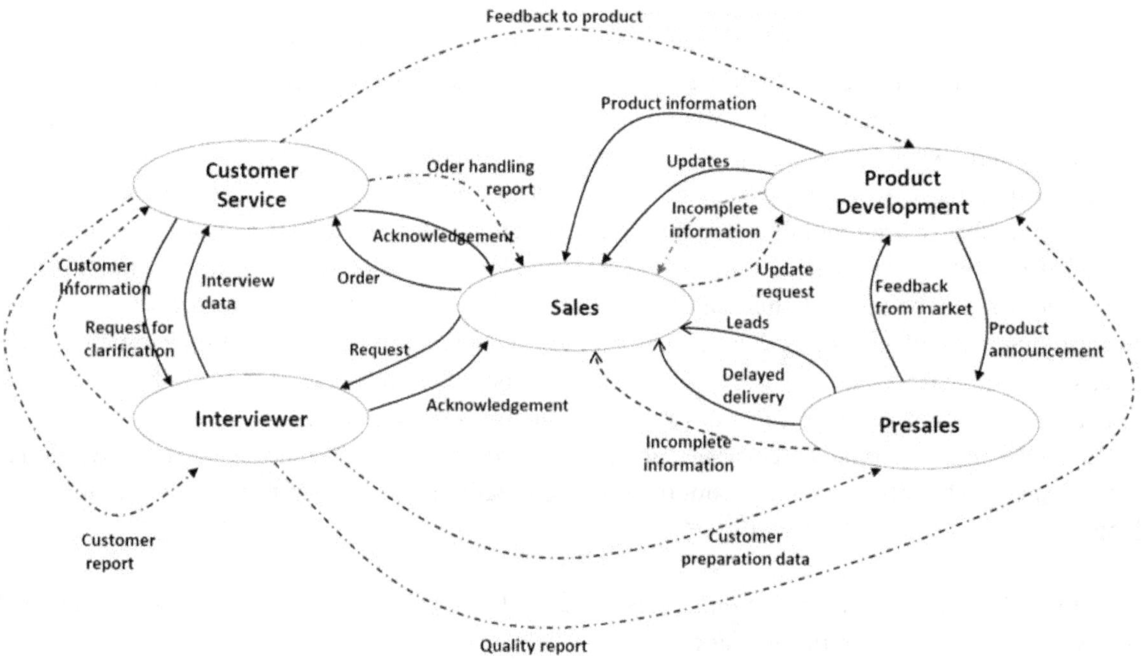

lanced Interviewers of different organizations are identified. They represent the nodes in the holomap in Figure 5.

Figure 5 shows tangible Deliverables such as product information, feedback from market, requests, updates. For these cases, the transaction and communication channel is considered a tangible Deliverable because it either comprises core data relevant for operating the business, or affects essential relations to organizational units for product and (customer) knowledge management. Intangible transactions or exchanges are modeled the same way. In order to distinguish the intangible Deliverables from the tangible Deliverables modelers use a different line style (dotted line in Figure 5). For the original service provider, intangibles are incomplete information, order handling report, customer report, customer preparation data etc., which various network actors make available through reporting and active sharing of knoiwledge (see Figure 5). They are considered intangible because the is no direct monetary income related to them. They are neither contracted by the provider nor expected by the recipients. They are extra offerings to Participants to keep the operation running, and product development informed, mainly based on informal learnings and experiential knowledge.

As shown in Figure 5, several tangible exchanges occur, e.g., Product Development provides product announcements to Presales in exchange for feedback from the market, Sales provides requests to Interviewers who acknowledge them. In addition, several intangible exchanges occur, such as Interviewers provide customer information to Customer Service in exchange to customer reports. The latter complements the formal, role-specific exchange specified through the pair 'request for clarification – interview data'. It documents the intention to provide a comprehensive picture of customers in order to build trustful relationships to customers (representing the benefits of the exchange). However, several one-sided transactions with respect to tangibles and intangbles become evident, as also shown in the holomap in Figure 5: For instance, concerning intangibles, the Interviewers provide customer preparation data and quality reports to Presales and Product Development, respectively, without any intangible return. Concerning tangibles, e.g., Product Development provides both, product information and updates to Sales without any return.

It needs to be noted, that the holomap represents declarative knowledge, abstracting from actual workflows. Moreover, Participants specify the nodes and value exchanges in the sequence they externalize their mental model.

Holomaps as Points of Reference for Analysis

According to Verna Allee, analyzing the capabilities of a value network and developing opportunities for constructive change requires three different types of analysis. The first one is about assessing the structure and dynamics of the represented inter-organizatioal network as a whole. The second and third analysis focus on each Participant's role he or she plays in the interactions of the value network: (i) Exchange Analysis: What is the overall pattern of exchanges in the represented system?, (ii) Impact Analysis: What impact does each value input have on the Participants?, and (iii) Value Creation Analysis: How can a (networked) organization create, extend, and leverage value, either through adding value by Participants, extending value to other Participants, or converting one type of value to another?

The **Exchange Analysis** investigates the overall patterns of exchanges addressing a variety of structural issues. When starting with identiyfing missing relations for operating the business or links requiring a rationale, potential breakdowns in flow that can be critical for the business can be determined. In that context, the coherence of relations and resulting flows how value is generated in the network can be evaluated. By checking the amount of tangibles and intangibles, a possible dominance of a particular type of exchange can be determined. The overall pattern of reciprocity reveals involvement data of the Participants (as perceived by the respective modeler). Exentensive sources and sinks of interactions should be noted as potential for optimizing the network, avoiding specific Participants benefiting at the expense of others.

In the holomap in Figure 5, several patterns can be noticed. Sales and Presales gain knowledge about the product from Product Development, but that knowledge "dead ends" with them and is not passed on explicitly to Customer Service and Interviewers. In fact, there is no significant product knowledge exchange between Sales, Presales, Customer Service, and Interviewers. Another pattern that shows up is that knowledge from Customer Service to Product Development only flows one way. Customer Service delivers feedback to product as intangible, but does not have any channel for a two-way communication about product-related data with Product Development.

The **Impact Analysis** has the focus on received inputs that trigger some response by the receiver. The analysis considers activities and effort for handling the input and for leveraging the value received. The concerned network actors need to estimate the tangible and intangible costs (or risks) and gains for each input. They need to describe how a certain activity is generated in response to a certain (tangible/intangible) input. Then, they are asked to describe the estimated increase or decrease of tangible assets in terms of overall cost/risk-benefit analysis – see Table 1.

Table 1 shows part of the value inputs for Sales. Each of the received inputs is explored according to the various activities to be set, costs and benefits it brings. In this way, each Sales Participant can address the value impact for the whole organization. Each input presented in the holomap (see Figure 5) is

Table 1. Part of sample impact analysis of sales participant

Transactions			Impact Analysis							
Deliverable	**From**	**To**	**Activities that are generated**	**Impact on financial resources (positive/ negative)**	**Impact on intangible assets (positive/negative)**			**Overall cost/risk for this input**	**Overall benefit of this input**	**Perceived value in view of recipient**
					Human Compe-tence	Internal Structure	Business Relationships	H = High M = Medium L = Low	H = High M=Medium L = Low	+2, +1 Neutral -1, -2
Order handling report (Intangible)	Customer service	Sales	Evaluation of report	Extra time and effort to be calculated	Knowledge on calculation schema	Contact to presales and accounting	Knowledge on competition and market	H: 2 hours/ M: re-calculation required	M: Docu-mentation of order handling	Neutral
Incomplete information (Intangible)	Product development	Sales	Additional information from product development to be collected	Effort to be spent for information collection	Knowledge on product	Expert interviews	Technical skills and knowledge	H: 3 hours/ H: Availability of experts required	M: Comple-teness of product information	Neutral
Delayed delivery (Tangible)	Presales	Sales	Delay in customer service to be communicated	Loss of service time	-	Presales contact	Presales reminder	H: Extension of loss of service time / H: Loss of loyality	L	-2

described in a single line as it may affect essential tangible and intangible inputs to Sales and Presales. For instance, the fourth-line item shows incomplete delivery of information from Presales to Sales. It results in low value since required knowledge on sales transcations is not available in time. Presales needs to be contacted for availability to overcome shortcomings in customer relationship management.

The **Value Creation Analysis** does not only reflect the situation as-it-is but supports proposing changes in a way a Participant is committed to deliver. The structure of this analysis is similar to the Impact Analysis, however, it focuses on a Participant's capabilty how to extend value to other Participants represented in the holomap. It analyzes the tangible and intangible costs (or risks) and gains for each value output. Each value output could add new tangible or intangible value and thus, extend value to other Participants represented in the holomap. By assessing each value output, a Participant needs to determine activities, resources, and processes required, as well as the costs and anticipated benefit of each value-creating activity.

In Table 2 a sample analysis is given for Sales. An important value creation for Sales is to add value to product features received from Product Development by provding timely information for Interviewers and Customer Service (in terms of what is actually ordered). Their role in contributing to timely information in cooperation with Product Development is actually very small, being of both low cost for them and also low benefit in case of not actively requesting updates. Hence, they could be an active agent to extend value through targeted requests and other efforts to reach Product Development. They would need to engaged in a value conversion process where they convert one relevant type of value to another with respect to a working product life cycle. Engaging to increase value creation actually explores new strategic possibilities and changes in costs and benefits for the organization. It is the moment where a member of the networked organizations develops an offer to others by individual behavior change instead of elaborating expectation to behavior of others.

Looking at the value outputs that go to Product Development, Sales can open a tangible communication channel to support the product development process, and an intangible transaction of feeding back product-relevant information. In this way, Sales can leverage their intangible value outputs (information about product use) into more advanced product development that could be turned into a revenue stream.

Table 2. Sample value creation analysis

Transactions			Perceived Value	Value Creation Analysis		
Deliverables	From	To	**Recipient highly values this deliverable.** Strongly agree(+2) Agree(+1) Neutral(0) Disagree(-1) Strongly disagree(-2)	**Tangible asset utilization** is: H = high M = medium L = low	**What are the tangible** costs? (financial and physical resources)	**How high is the risk factor in providing this output?** H = high M = medium L = low
Update request (Intangible)	Sales	Product development	-1	L	Processing time by request	L
Request (Tangible)	Sales	Interviewer	+2	H	Interview	M
Order (Tangible)	Sales	Customer service	+2	H	Processing time per order	M

Value Creation Analysis (continued)								
Intangible asset utilization is: H = high M = medium L = low (Human competence Internal structures Business relationships)			**What are other intangible** costs or benefits? (Industry, society, environment)			**How do we add** to, enhance, or extend value?	**What is the overall combined cost/risk** for this input?	**What is the overall benefit** for us in providing this input?
HC	IS	BR	Industry	Society	Env			
M	M	M	Benefit-timely information	-	-	Formal procedure	Formulating request/--	Trigger to product development
H	H	H	Customer care	-	-	-	-	High customer satisfaction
H	H	H	Order management	-	-	CRM-Database update	Delivery of update/complete ness of data	Enriched CRM-Database

In the example, the communication channels were mostly one way, conveying product knowledge from Product Development to Sales. With a focus on converting that expected communication channel to another type of value gain, Sales enables communication after gaining feedback for product development. Both, converting an intangible value to gain a tangible value, and establishing an intangible deliverable with product feedback, supports the strategic intent of rapid response to changing needs of customers.

Although Value Creation Analysis can become very rich due to anticipated governance and thus, changes in the flow of deliverables, the Participants need to understands what impact a particular output has on the Participant who receives it. From an organizational management perspective it could happen, that a Particpant could maximize the effeciveness and efficiency of a certain business operation when following the created value. The overall cost benefit analysis could result in excellent data. However, a closer analysis of the proposed value creation could lead to inconveniences of the involved Participants, in particular networked business partners and customers (cf. Augl et al., 2015, 2017). For instance, collecting context data from Interviewers when applying the product in the field could easily lead to rejecting the proposed value creation once they consider a request for preparing such a report as a negative value input.

Before proposed value creations can become effective in business operation they need to be acknowledged by the involved Participants. In order to allow constructive elaboration of value creations affecting the collective, the holomap serves as point of reference of accepted changes that will be further implemented in operational business. Each proposed value creation could beome part of the original holomap. It may either be a new actore (i.e. actors like Customer – see Figure 7), a new relation leading to a value exchange, e.g., Request in Figure 7, or reinforce existing transactions, i.e. when intangible ones become tangible. In either case, the holomap is adapted (see Figure 7). When an intangible transaction is proposed to become tangible, formal ties are strengthened. When a tangible transaction is removed or becomes intangible, formal ties in a network get lost or are loosened. Any proposed modifications of transactions can be integrated to the initially constructed holomap, in order to document novel organizational behavior.

TRANSFORMATION TOWARDS SEMANTIC PROCESS MODELS

In this section we detail the proposed tagging mechanisms and the related methodological steps to construct process models based on VNA holomaps.

The Tagging Scheme

We take into account experiences from concept map-based knowledge transformation (cf. Novak, 1998; Pailai et al., 2016; Xie et al., 2018). Semantic concept tags are metadata that help constructing process models through classifying information represented in the VNA's holomap and analyses' tables. Figure 6 puts the tagging mechanisms in context of the VNA described in the previous section. It shows on the left side the fundamental VNA steps. VNA starts with holomapping when network actors describe from a specific role perspective their knowledge on tangible and intangible transactions. The subsequent Exchange Analysis aims to recognize sources and sinks of transactions, leading to patterns of (inter-) organizational behavior, and checking direct and indirect value exchanges, as indicated on top of the right side in Figure 6. The Impact Analysis reveals the activities resulting from receiving a deliverable as experienced by a network actor, including perceived benefits, overheads, and risk assessment. This input-oriented perspective is indicated graphically on the right side of Figure 6 for the Impact Analysis for a selected actor. Finally, the Value Creation Analysis provides insight into the current delivery of transactions to others from an individual network actor's perspective, and all suggestions to enrich transactional behavior, either in terms of tangible or intangible transactions. This perspective is also outlined graphically on the right side (bottom) in Figure 6.

In Figure 6, the black dot indicates that VNA is performed along a specific role perspective. It refers to a fundamental process element, namely functional or organzational roles performing a set of tasks, and is part of the tagging scheme (see circled R in a black circle in Figure 7). The directed arcs represent transactions, those depicted with dotted lines represent intangible transactions. They also represent fundamental process elements when being implemented in buinsess operation. Both, tangibles and intangibles can be part of process models. When tagging transactions of the holomap, they can either refer to activities leading to the deliverable denoted by the transaction (see A in a black circle in Figure 7), or data that is part of the transaction or the respective deliverable (see D in a black circle in Figure 7).

Although various definitions have been provided in the literature to capture business processes and corresponding models (cf. Ubuaid et al., 2020), most of them include a temporal dimension, i.e. processes have a start and end state, and comprise a set of activities or logically related tasks performed by a hu-

Figure 6. VNA constellation in the context of tagging the holomap and entries of the VNA-analyses' tables. The black nodes represent the the role of the Participant creating a holomap and filling in the VNA-analyses' tables.

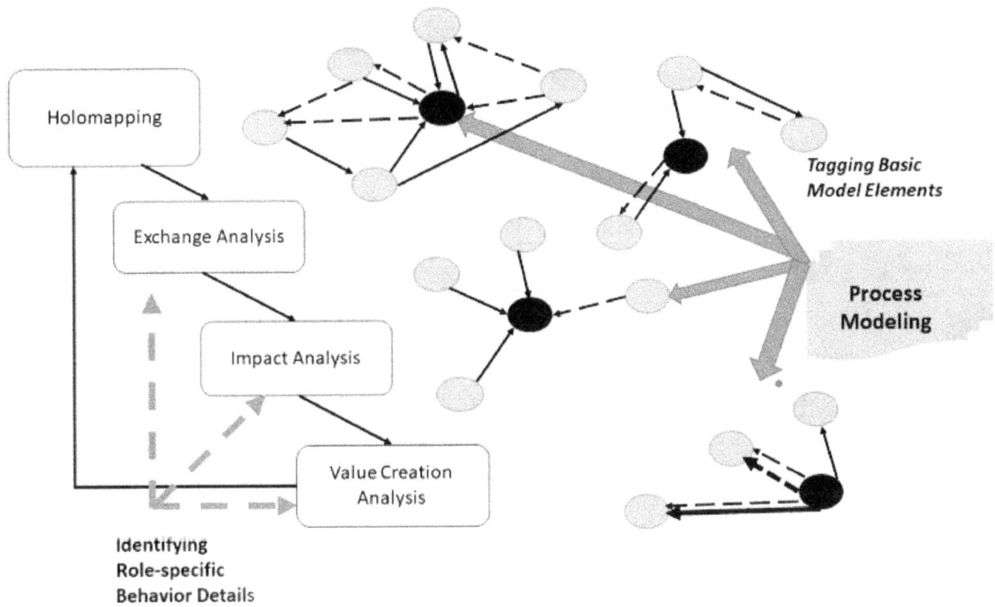

man role carrier, machine or digital system, manipulating input data and producing some output of value for customers or network partners. Hence, tagging for business process mapping has to comprise roles, activities, input/output of activitics, and the sequence of activities to produce some output. Consequently, the tagging scheme for basic model elements targets the following elements of holomaps, namely by inspecting each element without requiring any specific sequence of specification:

- Roles in terms of holomap nodes (tag R in a black circle in Figure 7)
- Activities as indicated by holomap transactions (tag A in a black circle in Figure 7)
- Data as input or output of activities in terms of holomap deliverables (incoming and outgoing) (tag D in a black circle in Figure 7)
- Causal/Temporal relations sequencing activities, in terms of a holomap's directed links (tags are numbers along transactions – each transaction can be part of more than a single sequence)

Beside tagging holomaps with basic process meta data like roles and data, in Figure 6 the second type of tagging is shown, namely identifying role-specific behavior details. This types of tagging is required for contextual process modeling (cf. Helbin et al., 2021), in particular referring to the culture related to process management (cf. Schmiedel et al., 2020), the way organizational change is managed (cf. Binci et al., 2020) and the way organizations are approached as socio-technical interaction systems (cf. Fleischmann et al., 2015, Neubauer et al., 2017). In Figure 7 the adapted holomap from the case presented in section 3 is shown, inluding Customer as new role, and its incoming and outgoing transactions to Presales, Sales, and Interviewer. The latter provides contextual sales development information as it

Figure 7. Tagged Holomap for roles (R), activities (A), and data (D) – each tag is set in the sequence determined by the participant

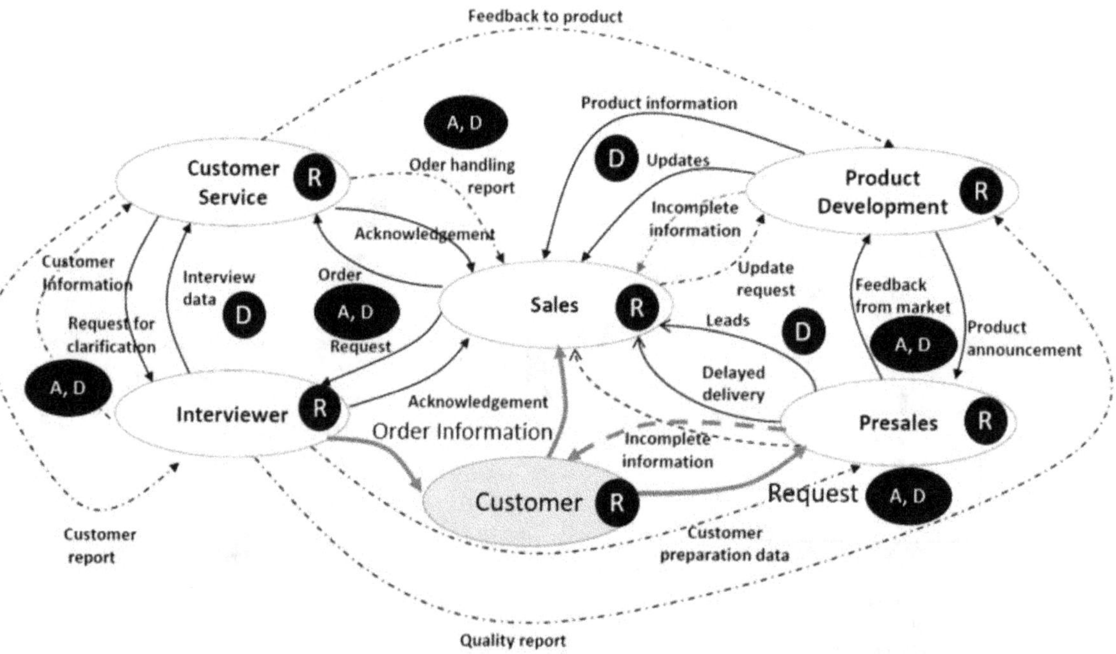

refers to additional value creation and its expected benefits. The respective entries in the Value Creation Analys tables are tagged as process context (PC) through circling the respective cell.

Subject-Oriented Process Specification and Validation

The tagged nodes and relations allow for straightforward specification of role-based process models. Roles as functional bundles of tasks correspond to pools or lanes in BPMN (www.bpmn.org) or subjects in S-BPM (Fleischmann et al., 2012). S-BPM follows a choreographic approach facilitating the representation of networks with inherently parallel operating actors, in contrast to orchestrating a concurrent behavior structure in terms of linearizing behavior. As such the mapping of holomaps to operational process structures lays ground to further refinements in a straightforward way (cf. Stary, 2020). Like in holomapping, an organization is a value stream network that is modelled by identifying patterns of interactions targeting for value exchanges. These interactions are relations between behavior-encapsulating entities representing the nodes of the network. Each of them corresponds to a set of tasks or certain organizational role that produces and delivers products or services that are part of transactions between the network actors. Consequently, the process definition follows a small set of simple rules:

- Each node or actor of the process represents a behavior entity, i.e. a role of a network actor that is relevant for the business at hand.
- Behavior entities send or extend deliverables to other behavior entities.
- Directed links indicate which network behavior entity (actor) is the sender and which is the receiver of a deliverable.

Figure 8. Sample subject-oriented business process specification: Subject interaction diagram (upper part) and subject behavior diagrams (lower part)

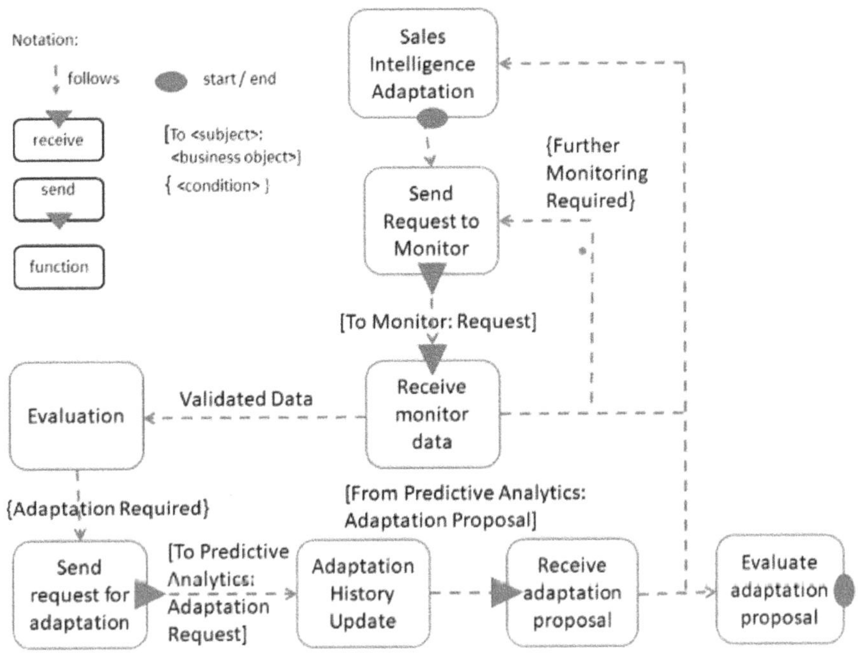

- Deliverables are entities that move from one behavior entity (network actor) to another. A deliverable can be a material or immaterial asset: It also can either be contracted (i.e. tangible in VNA terms), or not (being intangible in VNA terms).
- Deliverables carry business objects, data or information, when moving in the course of a specific transaction, originating from one behavior entity to another.
- Transactions are carriers of exchanged deliverables along a bi-directional value stream to meet a business objective.
- A value exchange occurs when a transaction results in a deliverable coming back to the originator either directly or indirectly. Hence, the deliverable may pass several behavior entities before being part of an incoming transaction of an actor.
- Value exchanges should be triggered by any outgoing deliverable to reveal 'roundtrip' patterns typical of organizational relationships.

Figure 8 shows an example of a behavior-centered process model using the S-BPM notation, as it has a small set of diagrammatic elements, and provides two different layers of abstraction that support the mapping of VNA-results and their refinement to executable process models. The upper part of Figure 8 shows part of a Subject-Interaction Diagram (i.e. high level of abstraction) that enables direct mapping of VNA-nodes and transactions to subjects as behavior encapsulations, e.g., Customer, and message exchanges, e.g., order, between them. The lower part zooms into the Customer and Order Handling (representing Sales from the VNA) subject and shows part of a Subject Behavior Diagrams for each subject involved (lower level of abstraction). In S-BPM not only activities, like Prepare Order, but also

Figure 9. Sample subject behavior diagram for dynamic adaptation

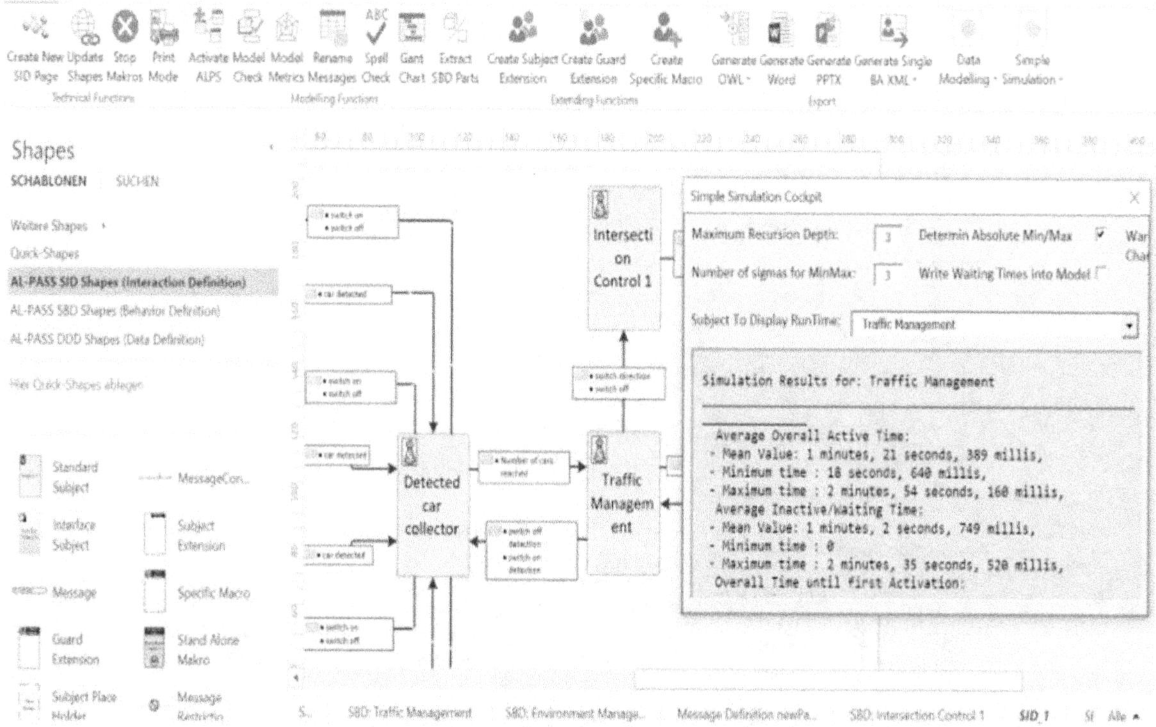

communication in terms of Send and Receive patterns, like Send Order and Check delivery, are modelled. In this way, the transactional nature of value creation can be represented explicitly.

Of particular importance for the mapping are value exchanges, i.e. each output of a node (i.e. an actor) leading to an immediate or intermediate input to that actor, as the VNA strives for balanced interaction between networked actors. Using S-BPM facilitates those checks due to explicit send-receive patterns that can be controlled pairwise for each actor (i.e. subject) involved.

These diagrams can be enhanced with digital intelligence. Figure 9 shows an enrichment for dynamic adaptation based on monitored behavior for prediction.

For validation of behavior models using the S-BPM notation several tools can be utilized, among them commercial ones, such as the compunity suite (www.compunity.eu), and research platforms, such as UeberFlow or Sisi (which can be downloaded from the Institute of Innovative Process Management i2pm.net). These tools allow to run subject-oriented process models showing graphical interaction elements for each state while navigating through Subject Behavior Diagrams. Figure 9 shows a screenshot of Sisi, taken from a recent S-BPM application (Stary et al., 2022). It shows in the left part elements of the modeling language for process specification, the model in the center, and runtime information on the right side.

Both tagging mechanims have been tested in educational settings in two types of academic courses in Business Informatics master programs. On one hand, they were courses on Knowledge Management at a German university's School of Management and Technology, on the other hand they were courses on Business Engineering and Management at an Austrian university's Business School. In both courses,

Figure 10. Sample screenshot of a subject-oriented process validation session using Sisi Left side: subject-oriented modeling notation, center: part of Subject Behavior Diagram, right side: data set provided for simulation
(Stary et al., 2022)

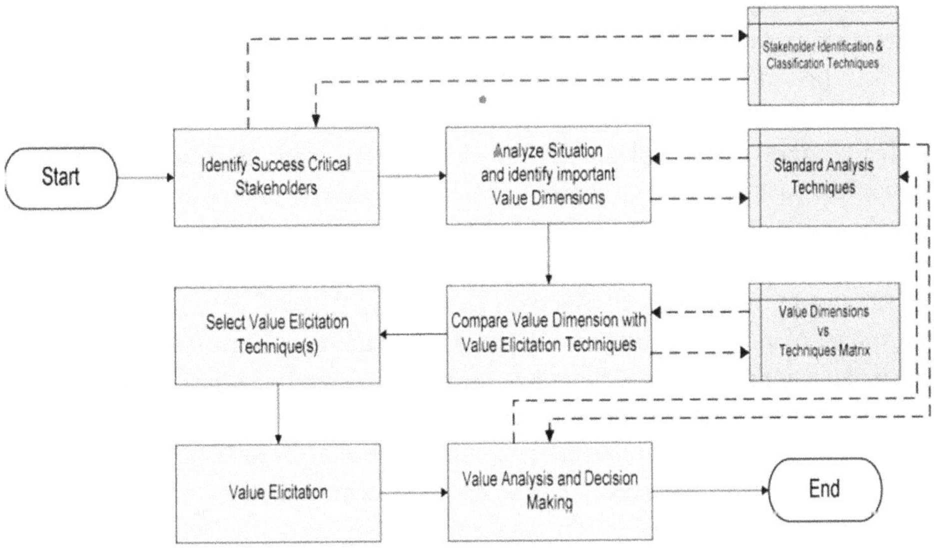

15-30 students were asked to come up with an executable process model derived from a holomap as a result of holomapping and performing VNA analyses. In both settings they received the tagging guidelines for identifying basic elements of process models, and identifying role-specific behavior details. Subsequently, the students could use any diagrammatic modeling and execution tool for choreographic behavior modeling and messaging like S-BPM. The provided tagging information signifcantly helped improving their development performance, when the empirical data of tagging holomaps and VNA tables has been compared to control groups without tagging support.

From applying the propoed tagging scheme we could learn that the provision of a minimal set of W-questions could facilitate the identification of information to be tagged:

- Who, in terms of a functional role descriptor, is in charge of handling a particular task in the addressed business unit or organization?
- Which activities are set to accomplish a task by an identified role?
- Which sequence of activities needs to be followed to accomplish a task by an identified actor in a specific role?
- What data are required to accomplish a task by an identified role?
- Which data are produced and need to be delivered to other stakeholders in a specific role?

CONCLUSION

Although value-based operation and respective process development are established in networked business settings, our review of findings revealed various implementation strategies of different granularity and structure. A major cornerstone is value-based thinking of stakeholders that underlies networked business operation and its socio-technical development. It concerns stakeholders handling their business. Building on value thinking a first milestone is to structure value networking in terms of business-relevant value modeling. It leads to semantic representations of value-led activities and the related flow of information and resources between networked stakeholders. Such an achievement facilitates reflecting on network values and value streams and in further consequence, network development and re-organization.

However, as long as value-based modelling and business process modelling rely on complimentary but disintegrated methodological and notational approaches, some manual mapping of exchanged values and value streams to business processes on a case-to-case basis is required. In case of remaining implicit, the mapping of values on and the refinement of value flows to networked business processes is neither part of value nor process modeling. Moreover, the declarative type of knowledge represented by value exchanges and in value networks requires an explicit mapping mechanism to the procedural type of knowledge that characterizes business operation and can serve as blueprint for implementation.

Our analysis of recent value-based development approaches revealed that value and process modeling can be handled effectively by established notations or modeling schemes. Hence, an effective mapping instrument from diagrammatic value network representations to business process models of the same kind is likely to facilitate the transparent and traceable transformation of value models to operational digital structures. In this contribution we have shown how holomaps as particular type of value networks can be enriched by element tagging when being used as part of the value-based development and organizational transformation technique Value Network Analysis (VNA). The concepts being encoded are stakeholder roles involved in business transactions, and value exchanges of these stakeholders. Holomaps form the core representation for the subsequent VNA analyses focusing on the interaction between stakeholders and their perceived values, either for outgoing or received deliverables.

Since the VNA technique has been designed to lay empirical ground for process specifications to improve business operation based on the shared understanding of value creation by its stakeholders, guidance to map the knowledge created in each step of the VNA to process models could facilitate the transformation process. The proposed tagging scheme to that respect works twofold. It supports marking the roles, activities, transactions and their sequences as basic elements of process models. Furthermore, it supports the identification of behavior details from VNA tables as they provide valuable context for refining transactions in terms of operational models. The tagging mechanism has been complemented with a modeling notation enabling straightforward transformation to executable models. Both turned out to be effective in educational settings when students performed VNAs and accomplished valid process models after completing the tagging of holomap elements and entries of VNA tables.

Our current research has its focus on developing digital support of both tagging mechanisms. Given a holomap, proposals will be generated automatically for process roles, activities, and data exchange. The sequencing could profit from AI (leaning) support or require manual intervention albeit being supported by graph-based algorithms checking for value exchanges. Both should lead to more efficient process design based on organizational value creation proposals.

REFERENCES

Acosta, A. S., Crespo, Á. H., & Agudo, J. C. (2018). Effect of market orientation, network capability and entrepreneurial orientation on international performance of small and medium enterprises (SMEs). *International Business Review*, *27*(6), 1128–1140. doi:10.1016/j.ibusrev.2018.04.004

Agostini, L., & Nosella, A. (2017). Interorganizational relationships in marketing: A critical review and research agenda. *International Journal of Management Reviews*, *19*(2), 131–150. doi:10.1111/ijmr.12084

Agostini, L., Nosella, A., & Filippini, R. (2016). Towards an Integrated View of the Ambidextrous Organization: A Second-Order Factor Model. *Creativity and Innovation Management*, *25*(1), 129–141. doi:10.1111/caim.12167

Alford, J., & Hughes, O. (2008). Public value pragmatism as the next phase of public management. *American Review of Public Administration*, *38*(2), 130–148. doi:10.1177/0275074008314203

Alharthi, A., Alhefdi, M., Lipscomb, M. M., & Jololian, L. (2022). Value-Based Modeling of an Addiction Recovery Healthcare System. In *Proceedings SoutheastCon 2022*, IEEE. 10.1109/SoutheastCon48659.2022.9764037

Allee, V. (1997). The Knowledge Evolution. Expanding Organizational Intelligence. Amsterdam: Butterworth-Heinemann.

Allee, V. (2003). The future of Knowledge. Increasing Prosperity Through Value Networks. Amsterdam: Butterworth-Heinemann.

Allee, V. (2008). Value network analysis and value conversion of tangible and intangible assets. *Journal of Intellectual Capital*, *9*(1), 5–24. doi:10.1108/14691930810845777

Allee, V., Schwabe, O., & Babb, M. K. (2015). *Value Networks and the true nature of collaboration*. Meghan-Kiffer Press.

Asamoah, D., Agyei-Owusu, B., & Ashun, E. (2020). Social network relationship, supply chain resilience and customer-oriented performance of small and medium enterprises in a developing economy. *Benchmarking*, *27*(5), 1793–1813. doi:10.1108/BIJ-08-2019-0374

Augl, M., & Stary, C. (2015). Communication-and Value-Based Organizational Development at the University Clinic for Radiotherapy-Radiation Oncology. In *S-BPM in the Wild* (pp. 35–53). Springer International. doi:10.1007/978-3-319-17542-3_3

Augl, M., & Stary, C. (2017). Adjusting Capabilities Rather Than Needs in Computer-Supported Daily Workforce Planning. In *Designing Healthcare that Works* (pp. 175–188). Academic Press/Elsevier.

Baiyere, A., Salmela, H., & Tapanainen, T. (2020). Digital transformation and the new logics of business process management. *European Journal of Information Systems*, *29*(3), 238–259. doi:10.1080/0960085X.2020.1718007

Baum, I. A., & Stary, C. (2022). Value exchange exploration supporting project-based learning. In: *Proceedings 17th International Conference on Knowledge Management 'Knowledge. Uncertainty and Risks: From individual to global scale.* ICKM. https://digital.library.unt.edu/ark:/67531/metadc2047067/?q=ickm%202022%20stary

Binci, D., Belisari, S., & Appolloni, A. (2020). BPM and change management: An ambidextrous perspective. *Business Process Management Journal, 26*(1), 1–23. doi:10.1108/BPMJ-06-2018-0158

Boehm, B. (2003). Value-based software engineering: Reinventing. *Software Engineering Notes, 28*(2), 1–11.

Boehm, B., & Huang, L. G. (2003). Value-based software engineering: A case study. *Computer, 36*(3), 33–41. doi:10.1109/MC.2003.1185215

Bosilj Vukšić, V., Brkić, L., & Tomičić-Pupek, K. (2018). Understanding the success factors in adopting business process management software: Case studies. *Interdisciplinary Description of Complex Systems: INDECS, 16*(2), 194–215. doi:10.7906/indecs.16.2.1

Brandenburger, A. M., & Nalebuff, B. J. (1996). *Co-opetition.* Currency/Doubleday.

Bryson, J. M., Crosby, B. C., & Bloomberg, L. (2014). Public value governance: Moving beyond traditional public administration and the new public management. *Public Administration Review, 74*(4), 445–456. doi:10.1111/puar.12238

Cagnin, M. I., & Nakagawa, E. Y. (2021). Towards dynamic processes-of-business processes: A new understanding. *Business Process Management Journal, 27*(5), 1545–1568. doi:10.1108/BPMJ-08-2020-0349

Clegg, S. R., Pitsis, T. S., Rura-Polley, T., & Marosszeky, M. (2002). Governmentality matters: Designing an alliance culture of inter-organizational collaboration for managing projects. *Organization Studies, 23*(3), 317–337. doi:10.1177/0170840602233001

Fleischmann, A., Schmidt, W., & Stary, C. (2015). *S-BPM in the wild: Practical value creation.* Springer. doi:10.1007/978-3-319-17542-3

Fleischmann, A., Schmidt, W., Stary, C., Obermeier, S., & Börger, E. (2012). *Subject-oriented business process management.* Springer Nature. doi:10.1007/978-3-642-32392-8

Fleming, Q. W., & Koppelman, J. M. (2016). *Earned value project management.* Project Management Institute. www.pmi.org

Geissdoerfer, M., Bocken, N. M., & Hultink, E. J. (2016). Design thinking to enhance the sustainable business modelling process–A workshop based on a value mapping process. *Journal of Cleaner Production, 135*, 1218–1232. doi:10.1016/j.jclepro.2016.07.020

Gurcaylilar-Yenidogan, T., & Windsperger, J. (2015). Complementarity between formal and relational governance mechanisms in inter-organizational networks: combining resource-based and relational governance perspectives. In *Interfirm Networks* (pp. 229–248). Springer. doi:10.1007/978-3-319-10184-2_12

Hammer, M. (2015). What is business process management? In *Handbook on business process management 1* (pp. 3–16). Springer. doi:10.1007/978-3-642-45100-3_1

Helbin, T., & Van Looy, A. (2021). Is business process management (BPM) ready for ambidexterity? Conceptualization, implementation guidelines and research agenda. *Sustainability (Basel), 13*(4), 1906. doi:10.3390/su13041906

Hotie, F., & Gordijn, J. (2019). Value-based process model design. *Business & Information Systems Engineering, 61*(2), 163–180. doi:10.1007/s12599-017-0496-y

Hyvarinen, L. P. (1970). *Information theory for systems engineers*. Springer.

Ihm, J., Shumate, M., Bello-Bravo, J., Atouba, Y., Ba, N. M., Dabire-Binso, C. L., & Pittendrigh, B. R. (2015). How do Service Providers and Clients Perceive Interorganizational Networks? *Voluntas, 26*(5), 1769–1785. doi:10.1007/s11266-014-9515-5

Jankowicz, D. (2001). Why does subjectivity make us nervous? Making the tacit explicit. *Journal of Intellectual Capital, 2*(1), 61–73. doi:10.1108/14691930110380509

Keeney, R. L. (2009). *Value-focused thinking: a path to creative decision making*. Harvard University Press.

Kelly, J., Male, S., & Graham, D. (2014). *Value management of construction projects*. John Wiley & Sons. doi:10.1002/9781119007258

Knight, L. (2002). Network learning: Exploring learning by interorganizational networks. *Human Relations, 55*(4), 427–454. doi:10.1177/0018726702554003

Kraatz, M. S. (1998). Learning by association? Interorganizational networks and adaptation to environmental change. *Academy of Management Journal, 41*(6), 621–643. doi:10.2307/256961

Kranti, N. K. M. M. N. (1997). An approach to value-based modeling of information flows. *The Information Society, 13*(1), 93–105. doi:10.1080/019722497129304

Laguna, M., & Marklund, J. (2018). *Business process modeling, simulation and design*. Chapman and Hall/CRC. doi:10.1201/9781315162119

Lipscomb, M. M., Mohammad, A., Abdulrahman, A., & Jololian, L. (2022). Value-based modeling for mobile health application development. *mHealth, 8*, 16. doi:10.21037/mhealth-21-32 PMID:35449507

Martin, J. D., & Petty, J. W. (2001). Value based management. *Baylor business review, 19*(1), 2.

Massingham, P. (2014). An evaluation of knowledge management tools: Part 1–managing knowledge resources. *Journal of Knowledge Management, 18*(6), 10. doi:10.1108/JKM-11-2013-0449

Mazurek, G. (2014). Network value creation through marketing. Management and Business Administration. *Central Europe, 22*(4), 70–77.

McElroy, M. W. (2003). *The new knowledge management: Complexity, learning, and sustainable innovation*. Routledge.

Miles, L. D. (1961). *Techniques of value analysis and engineering*. McGraw-Hill.

Murtaza, G., Basit, A., & Ikram, N. (2010). Value elicitation in value based software engineering. In *Proceedings of the 9th WSEAS international conference on Software engineering, parallel and distributed systems,* (pp. 184-189). IEEE.

Neiger, D., Rotaru, K., & Churilov, L. (2009). Supply chain risk identification with value-focused process engineering. *Journal of Operations Management, 27*(2), 154–168. doi:10.1016/j.jom.2007.11.003

Neubauer, M., & Stary, C. (2017). *S-BPM in the Production Industry. A stakeholder approach.* Springer. doi:10.1007/978-3-319-48466-2

Normann, R. (2001). *Reframing business: when the map changes the landscape.* John Wiley & Sons: Chicester.

Normann, R., & Ramírez, R. (1993). From value chain to value network: designing interactive strategy. *Harvard Business Review, 71*(4), 65-77.

Novak, J. D. (1998). *Learning, creating, and using knowledge: Concept Maps as Facilitative Tools in Schools and Corporations.* Lawrence Erlbaum Associates. doi:10.4324/9781410601629

Novak, J. D., & Cañas, A. J. (2006). The origins of the concept mapping tool and the continuing evolution of the tool. *Information Visualization, 5*(3), 175–184. doi:10.1057/palgrave.ivs.9500126

Novak, J. D., & Cañas, A. J. (2008). The theory underlying concept maps and how to construct and use them. *Technical Report IHMC CmapTools 2006-01 Rev 01-2008.* Florida Institute for Human and Machine Cognition. https://cmap.ihmc.us/Publications/ResearchPapers/TheoryUnderlyingConceptMaps.pdf

Pailai, J., Wunnasri, W., Hayashi, Y., & Hirashima, T. (2018). Correctness-and confidence-based adaptive feedback of kit-build concept map with confidence tagging. In *Int. Conf. on AI in Education.* 395-408, Springer, Cham. 10.1007/978-3-319-93843-1_29

Pallotti, F., Tubaro, P., & Lomi, A. (2015). How far do network effects spill over? Evidence from an empirical study of performance differentials in interorganizational networks. *European Management Review, 12*(3), 189–208. doi:10.1111/emre.12052

Parolini, C. (1999). *The value net: A tool for competitive strategy.* John Wiley.

Payne, A., & Holt, S. (2001). Diagnosing customer value: Integrating the value process and relationship marketing. *British Journal of Management, 12*(2), 159–182. doi:10.1111/1467-8551.00192

Payne, A. F., Storbacka, K., & Frow, P. (2008). Managing the co-creation of value. *Journal of the Academy of Marketing Science, 36*(1), 83–96. doi:10.1007/s11747-007-0070-0

Peffers, K., Tuunanen, T., Rothenberger, M. A., & Chatterjee, S. (2007). A design science research methodology for information systems research. *Journal of Management Information Systems, 24*(3), 45–77. doi:10.2753/MIS0742-1222240302

Provan, K. G., Fish, A., & Sydow, J. (2007). Interorganizational networks at the network level: A review of the empirical literature on whole networks. *Journal of Management, 33*(3), 479–516. doi:10.1177/0149206307302554

Schmiedel, T., Recker, J., & vom Brocke, J. (2020). The relation between BPM culture, BPM methods, and process performance: Evidence from quantitative field studies. *Information & Management*, *57*(2), 103175. doi:10.1016/j.im.2019.103175

Scott, T., & Thomas, C. (2015). Do collaborative groups enhance interorganizational networks? *Public Performance & Management Review*, *38*(4), 654–683. doi:10.1080/15309576.2015.1031008

Snoeck, M., & Wautelet, Y. (2022). Agile MERODE: A model-driven software engineering method for user-centric and value-based development. *Software & Systems Modeling*, *21*(4), 1–26. doi:10.1007/s10270-022-01015-y

Song, R., Vanthienen, J., Cui, W., Wang, Y., & Huang, L. (2019). Towards a comprehensive understanding of the context concepts in context-aware business processes. In *Proceedings of the 11th International Conference on Subject-Oriented Business Process Management* (pp. 1-10). ACM. 10.1145/3329007.3329020

Stary, C. (2014). Non-disruptive knowledge and business processing in knowledge life cycles–aligning value network analysis to process management. *Journal of Knowledge Management*, *18*(4), 651–686. doi:10.1108/JKM-10-2013-0377

Stary, C. (2020). The Internet-of-Behavior as organizational transformation space with choreographic intelligence. In *International Conference on Subject-Oriented Business Process Management*. Springer, Cham. 10.1007/978-3-030-64351-5_8

Stary, C., Elstermann, M., Fleischmann, A., & Schmidt, W. (2022). Behavior-Centered Digital-Twin Design for Dynamic Cyber-Physical System Development. *Complex Systems Informatics and Modeling Quarterly*, (30), 31–52. doi:10.7250/csimq.2022-30.02

Traoré, M. K., Zacharewicz, G., Duboz, R., & Zeigler, B. (2019). Modeling and simulation framework for value-based healthcare systems. *Simulation*, *95*(6), 481–497. doi:10.1177/0037549718776765

Treem, J. W., & Leonardi, P. M. (2017). Recognizing Expertise: Factors Promoting Congruity Between Individuals' Perceptions of Their Own Expertise and the Perceptions of Their Coworkers. *Communication Research*, *44*(2), 198–224. doi:10.1177/0093650215605154

Tsolkas, D., Giannopoulou, K. (2023). *Technoeconomic Analysis and Stakeholders Engaging (Intermediate Report), Horizon 2020.* European Union, Deliverable 6.2, evolved5G-Project.

Ubaid, A. M., & Dweiri, F. T. (2020). Business process management (BPM): Terminologies and Methodologies Unified. *International Journal of System Assurance Engineering and Management*, *11*(6), 1046–1064. doi:10.1007/s13198-020-00959-y

Vargo, S. L., Maglio, P. P., & Akaka, M. A. (2008). On value and value co-creation: A service systems and service logic perspective. *European Management Journal*, *26*(3), 145–152. doi:10.1016/j.emj.2008.04.003

Vial, G. (2021). Understanding digital transformation: A review and a research agenda. *Managing Digital Transformation*, 13-66.

Weigand, H., Johannesson, P., Andersson, B., & Bergholtz, M. (2009, June). Value-based service modeling and design: Toward a unified view of services. In *International Conference on Advanced Information Systems Engineering* (pp. 410-424). Springer, Berlin, Heidelberg. 10.1007/978-3-642-02144-2_33

Woodruff, R. B. (1997). Customer value: The next source for competitive advantage. *Journal of the Academy of Marketing Science*, *25*(2), 139–153. doi:10.1007/BF02894350

Xie, Y., & Lin, S. Y. (2016). Tagclouds and group cognition: Effect of tagging support on students' reflective learning in team blogs. *British Journal of Educational Technology*, *47*(6), 1135–1150. doi:10.1111/bjet.12293

Yates-Mercer, P., & Bawden, D. (2002). Managing the paradox: The valuation of knowledge and knowledge management. *Journal of Information Science*, *28*(1), 19–29. doi:10.1177/016555150202800103

Zhang, K., Wang, J., Feng, L., & Cheng, Y. (2019). The evolution mechanism of latecomer firms value network in disruptive innovation context: A case study of Haier Group. *Technology Analysis and Strategic Management*, *31*(12), 1488–1500. doi:10.1080/09537325.2019.1628939

Chapter 7
Creating an Information Governance Program at a College to Ultimately Implement Artificial Intelligence, Predictive Analytics, and Prescriptive Analytics

Kris Swen Helge
Rutgers University, USA

Tereza Raquel Merlo
https://orcid.org/0000-0002-2042-5415
University of North Texas, USA & Merlo Management Consulting, USA

ABSTRACT

This chapter outlines a case study of the development and sustainability process of an information governance (IG) program at a college in Texas. It employs an action research methodological approach to lay out the critical factors in executing and IG program. It discusses the key components in designing and implementing strategies, policies, practices, and compliance in IG. Findings emphasize the importance of aligning the IG program with strategic objectives and organizational culture. The participatory nature of action research enhances program sustainability and buy-in. Effective communication, training, and change management are highlighted as crucial for successful IG adoption, in addition to the importance of eDiscovery within the process. The study aims to provide a tailored governance framework within the context of a college program offering potential applicability to various industries.

DOI: 10.4018/979-8-3693-1058-8.ch007

INTRODUCTION

In the rapidly evolving digital age, the exponential growth of data has become an unmistakable hallmark of the modern world. Organizations and academic institutions alike find themselves at the epicenter of this data deluge, grappling with the challenges posed by its management, utilization, and protection. With the staggering volume, velocity, and variety of information, the need for a robust and comprehensive framework to govern this treasure trove has never been more apparent. This chapter seeks to explore the relevance of information governance in both organizational and academic contexts, shedding light on its pivotal role in ensuring efficiency, compliance, and innovation. It discusses case study findings completed at a college in Texas, United States.

An Information Governance (IG) program helps an organization establish standards and policy that dictate how information and data are organized to increase efficiency in locating and sharing data and information (Smallwood, 2014). It also allows for future implementation of business intelligence. A successful IG Program offers records retention, proper security and compliance policy, data governance initiatives, and a solid knowledge management program. These endeavors can equate to the ultimate IG goals which are to reduce costs and potential legal liability, improve security for an organization's data and information, and optimize efficient access to, storage, sharing and retention of data and information.

Information governance refers to the strategic management and control of an organization's information assets to ensure they are effectively utilized, protected, and compliant with legal and regulatory requirements. It involves the establishment of policies, procedures, and processes for collecting, storing, accessing, and disposing of information in a way that maximizes its value while minimizing risks. (Moynihan, 2016). In this chapter, the authors discuss the concept of information governance and its relevance in both achieving compliance with regulations and gaining a competitive edge for organizations. They explore the challenges and benefits of effective information governance implementation.

THEORETICAL FRAMEWORK

Data management is the rising driving force behind any successful organization, regardless of its size, segment, or industry. Data and information governance are organizational approaches to build and effectively use tacit and explicit knowledge towards building business intelligence and competitiveness. Kooper, Maes & Lindgreen (2010) investigates the governance of information, technology and management support defending that:

Governance is generally interpreted as a hierarchical framework for guidelines, policies, responsibilities, and procedures to ensure a certain level of control within an organization. But the definition of information governance does not necessarily restrict its use to one specific framework. Information governance may vary from a set of policies, a way of working, or the creation of a space within a predefined settlement (such as an online community). (p. 197).

The proliferation of digital technologies, coupled with the advent of the Internet of Things (IoT), has led to an unprecedented surge in data generation. Organizations and academic institutions are now inundated with vast amounts of structured and unstructured information streaming from a plethora of sources. Embracing the potential of this data holds the promise of informed decision-making, transformative research, and enriched learning experiences. However, without a well-defined information governance program, the influx of data can quickly transform from a blessing to a burden, hampering productivity, and exposing vulnerabilities. Information governance serves as the backbone of prudent data management strategies. At its core, it involves the systematic alignment of policies, processes, and technologies to facilitate the seamless handling of data throughout its lifecycle. By ensuring data integrity, security, and accessibility, information governance empowers organizations and academic institutions to harness the full potential of their data while minimizing risks and enhancing compliance (Davoudi et al., 2020).

The challenges surrounding information governance are multifaceted and require a nuanced understanding to effectively address. In organizations, compliance with data protection regulations, such as the General Data Protection Regulation (GDPR) and the Health Insurance Portability and Accountability Act (HIPAA), poses significant hurdles (Krol, 2018). Moreover, ensuring data quality, interoperability, and data sharing among diverse departments demand a coherent governance framework. In academia, the need to preserve the integrity and confidentiality of research data while promoting open access presents a unique set of challenges (Moulaison, 2018). Balancing the desire for data-driven innovation with ethical considerations regarding data privacy calls for a delicate yet effective information governance approach.

This study engages stakeholders, including faculty, administrators, and Information Technology, Human Resources, Student Admissions, Finance, and other College business units fostering a participatory and inclusive approach. It aims to delve into the fundamental aspects of information governance, examining its relevance in both organizational and academic settings. Studies have shown that IT structure is an important factor in the adoption and use of IG, either enabling or challenging the holistic management of information; however, a successful IG goes beyond data protection as one of the critical aspects of the program, it involves information artifacts that includes leadership, organizational culture, IT governance, and strategic processes that will boost the organizational performance (Tallon, Ramirez, Shirt, 2013).

The action plan described below reflects an existing program currently in implementation in a college in Texas. It serves as evidence in the emphasis on successfully data management within the context of a college program shedding light on the best practices and strategies employed to confront the challenges posed by the ever-expanding data landscape. By elucidating the symbiotic relationship between information governance and successful organizational performance and academic advancements, this study seeks to underscore the indispensability of a robust information governance program.

Planning for Research: Identifying the Critical Factors in the Data Governance Program Implementation and Data Collection

Executive Level Support

A vital key to success in developing an Information Governance Program is obtaining executive level administrative support in an organization. Trying to implement any program that relies on culture and behavior change is very difficult, if not impossible, without an executive level sponsor. This sponsor may be a Chief Information Officer, Chancellor, Chief Executive Officer, or some other C-suite level individual. Without appropriate muscle to help advocate the importance of and the need for an IG Program, this is a monumental task (Saldanha, 2019). This C-suite level individual provides consistent, high-level support, creative advocacy, and necessary tools and staffing to ensure the success of a new IG program (Milton & Lambe, 2020).

Enforcement Policies

One of the main reasons new IG programs fail is because they have no enforcement mechanisms. Often, a mid-level employee is told to create IG initiative such as email retention, eDiscovery, or data governance projects/programs. The new employee spends countless months or years developing a potentially successful program and then attempts to implement the program. Any IG sub-program such as email retention, eDiscovery, or data governance, requires a lot of training and culture change to obtain broad acceptance and implementation. However, mid-level employees often do not have the political clout to enforce participation by all employees at an institution and to endure the painful change required to implement the new IG program. Thus, the program never reaches full implementation. However, having a C-suite sponsor with appropriate political clout can ensure full adoption of IG programs (Hilger & Wahl, 2022). Therefore, one of the first steps to having a successful and sustainable IG program is to obtain and maintain a high-level executive sponsor.

Appropriate Staffing

After obtaining executive level support, it is vital to ensure adequate staffing to establish and sustain an IG program. Often, by default, a Chief Information Officer may appoint one person to create an IG program. That person is then responsible for data governance, knowledge management, accessibility issues, privacy and compliance, and other related IG tasks. One person cannot create and maintain an entire IG program. This person will simply have too many responsibilities and never accomplish any task. Instead, a multitude of people in various roles is needed for such an endeavor. For example, a plethora of writing is involved in creating, editing, reviewing, retiring, and amending processes and procedures, thus technical writers are vital for an IG program. A Director and Associate Director are also usually needed so that high level issues can be divided and conquered by two high level employees who have substantial knowledge of IG issues. One or two Knowledge Management Specialists are required to supervise knowledge bases; organize, preserve, delete, and provide adequate access to organizational information. A data scientist or two are further needed to manage the data governance issues. It is additionally important to employee a records manager to deal with records and data retention issues. Also, it is helpful to employee multiple project managers, and other flexible business analysts who can assist with accessibility, privacy, knowledge management, compliance, legal, and records management issues (Blummauer & Nagy, 2020).

The Discovery Phase

After obtaining appropriate levels of staffing, it is also important to complete a thorough discovery phase prior to attempting to develop a data governance, knowledge management, information retention program, or any other information governance endeavor. The discovery phase manifests what organizations already have in place, what works, what is broken, what improves employee efficiency and saves money, and what contributes to high legal risk (Blumauer & Nagy, 2020). For example, if creating a knowledge management program, a properly implemented discovery phase reveals where people store digital information, how they access and share it, whether such access and sharing is efficient, is an information retention program in place, and other key issues. In essence, the discovery phase is a gap analysis and a learning process in that it highlights potential areas of improvement and what is working well. (Garfield, 2022).

To discover where the gaps are and what processes and technology are already operating efficiently, various triangulation research methodologies are utilized. Focus groups, one-on-one interviews, questionnaires, surveys, and observations are effective discovery data collection tools. A discovery phase should touch as many departments of an organization with as many research tools as possible. A sample size of about 30 individuals total from many different departments offers a rich data pool. Since, most IG discovery phases are qualitative approaches, tools such as Nvivo, Delve, or Dovetail are helpful to quickly garner gaps and effective processes and technologies. For example, thematic analysis of the qualitative data gathers can manifest technologies that are causing knowledge workers to spend 20% of their day searching for stored information. Whereas the thematic approach can also highlight in-place efficient software that allows employees to seamlessly share information. When these gaps and efficiencies are discovered, this gives the IG team a starting place to determine which gaps to address first, and how to efficiently make use of existing tools.

Key Findings From the Discovery Phase-Data Collection and Analysis

The discovery phase should ultimately discover where all an organizations data is located, it should apply data classifications to that discovered data (e.g., open to public, sensitive – PII, PHI…, confidential – patents, governmental contracts…), it should map all data and systems, and using file analysis should create automated guises to continue to discover, classify and map data. The discovery phase is also an opportunity to apply retention to redundant, outdated, and trivial (ROT) data. Usually, 65-75% of data stored by an organization is ROT (Smallwood, 2014). Applying retention during a discovery phase lays the groundwork for future business intelligence and artificial intelligence tools, discussed later in the chapter.

Communication: Email and Chat Retention Programs

After completing a fruitful discovery period and garnering the needs of an organization, the IG team can begin to implement pieces of the IG program. One of the key programs often built into the overarching information governance program is an email retention program. Email retention programs define how long organizational emails will be retained and when they must be deleted. Some emails are saved longer due to legal holds. For example, an email retention program may mandate that all emails 4 years old or older will be automatically deleted by an information technology department. Having a consistent process to discard emails can greatly reduce legal risk for organization (ING, 2013). Legal risk is reduced because organizational personnel can reference that they have common business practice in effect to delete all company emails unless a legal hold exists. It also reduces the number of emails that must be discovered and culled when a request for information is presented (Smallwood, 2014).

Similarly, organizations can implement chat and text messaging retention programs. These programs primarily discourage company personnel from using personal devices to send business related chat or text messages. They also mandate a standardized process of deleting chat or text messages such as 90 days, one year, or two years. Generally, chat and text messaging retention programs mandate smaller time periods for retaining data compared to email retention programs. Usually, text and chat messaging data contain more transitory information compared to email (Ragbeer, 2021).

Chat and text messaging programs also direct correct etiquette and behavior. For example, an effective chat and text messaging retention program instructs personnel not to use profane language, make derogatory statements, and basically to not chat or text anything someone would not want posted on the front page of a paper or digital newspaper (Ragbeer, 2021). Maintaining a chat and text retention program can also save organizations money and reduce legal risk (Smallwood, 2014).

eDiscovery and Compliance

Another important facet of a successful IG program is the implementation of eDiscovery. eDiscovery is the process of locating, collecting, preserving, culling, and delivering data and information to appropriate authorities during a request for information or litigation (Broucek, 2020). When faced with requests for information or lawsuits, many organizations today manually search through email and other electronic communication platforms to locate pertinent data. Such a process can take 80-85% of legal, human resources, or other departments time for weeks or months. However, implementing an automated eDiscovery program can save time and reduce legal liability. Such software as Lexbe can reduce time spent on locating data. An automated eDiscovery tool such as Lexbe can allow an organization to thematically locate and gather pertinent data and information within a 12-24 hour period (Lexbe, 2023). Once gathered in-house counsel, paralegals, or contracted consultants can cull the data, place specific data into legal hold systems, and organize in preparation for delivery of relevant data. Coupling an eDiscovery automated program with proper email and text retention tools, an organization can reduce legal risk and cost by a large percentage (Smallwood, 2014). Additionally, utilizing technology assisted review (TAR) tools can improve efficiency during eDiscovery. TAR applies predictive coding and is utilized to review large data sets for responsive determinations within the discovery phase of litigation (Broucek, 2020).

Data Governance Program Implementation in a Texas College: Methodological Approach

Aiming at verifying the relevance and impact, as well as the factors impacting the data governance process, the authors conducted action research (AR) approach during the data governance program implementation in a college in Texas, USA. The methodology AR for this paper shares the experience of a three-year process of implementing and maintaining an IG program at a college, the process involved, best practices, critical factors, the challenges, and the opportunities identified, which can, hopefully, be utilized as roadmap by other organizations seeking to implement an IG Program.

The first phase of this study consisted of a college-wide discovery phase to learn the IG needs of the College (6-8 months). The next phase included hiring new IG staff to ensure proper person-power to create an IG Program (6- 8 months). The last two years involved the creation, implementation, and sustainment of an IG Program.

The action research process commenced with an initial assessment of the college's existing information management practices, followed by the formulation of a comprehensive governance framework encompassing policies, procedures, and technological solutions. Through cycles of planning, action, observation, and reflection, the research team engaged with stakeholders to address emerging challenges, fine-tune the program, and ensure seamless integration within the college's operations. This iterative approach facilitated continuous feedback and adaptation, fostering an information governance culture that transcended silos and promoted data stewardship among all stakeholders. The current IG program implementation within the studied college involves six (6) major phases, from the discovery to compliance, as described below:

Phase One: Discovery Phase and Establishing an IG Program

The first phase of this case study consisted of a discovery phase that lasted six to eight months. This discovery phase helped locate data systems implemented at the college, learned where data and information were stored, and how it was shared and accessed. This discovery phase also explored what worked well for knowledge workers and what problems manifested. The discovery phase also probed the College's record lifecycle, and current eDiscovery, risk management, compliance, and data management processes and workflows.

Findings of the Discovery Phase

The discovery phase manifested that information and data were being stored in unsafe locations such as flash drives, on personal devices, via paper, and in other insecure locations. It also became apparent that knowledge workers spent hours and sometimes days trying to locate stored information. This is common in organizations that do not have an IG Program in place (Smallwood, 2014). Additionally, the discovery phase indicated knowledge workers were storing and disseminating personally identifiable information (PII) and personal health information (PHI) via email and chat. Also, despite having a records retention program in place, no email retention or electronic communications retention policy was in place. Thus, numerous PII and PHI was being stored and transmitted via email and other electronic communications.

The discovery phase further manifested that the College administration was open to an IG program that could provide better security, more efficient access to and sharing of information, and a reduction of ROT (redundant, outdated, and trivial information). It also revealed that the College was lacking in IG policy that could help improve data and information and reduce potential legal liability.

Phase Two: Challenges and Opportunities

Many immediate challenges manifested via the discovery phase. Some of these included needing to obtain buy-in from administration, developing training and communications to support the IG program, craft and gain acceptance of IG policies such as email retention and data governance, create a knowledge management sub-program, partner with the legal department to streamline eDiscovery processes, and improve compliance issues for the College.

Obtain Administrative Buy-In

Any successful and sustainable IG Program must have a strong executive sponsor (Seiner, 2014). Therefore, after the discovery phase was completed, a meeting with the Chancellor, Campus Presidents, and other upper administration was organized to explain the importance of the IG Program and the necessity of their muscle to enforce the IG Program. Fortunately, these stakeholders comprehended these necessities of an IG Program and offered perpetual encouragement, support, and enforcement. However, there were issues preventing the successful implementation of the IG Program due to lack of staff.

Phase Three: Hiring Staff and Establishing a Tiered Steering Committee

After the discovery phase, it was evident a need existed to hire staff to complete the necessary tasks that were discovered during the discovery phase (the need to create trainings, effective communications, policies…). Thus, in the budget cycle a request for five new positions was submitted - to help establish the IG Program. Due to first obtaining administrative support, College administration understood the need for these requested positions, and although obtaining the positions took time, the five new positions were created and included in the next budget cycle.

Nevertheless, there was still the need of help outside of the staff to roll out an IG program with an organization that employes about 5,000 knowledge workers and serves approximately 46,000 students. Therefore, once the new employees were hired, we established a tiered, steering committee that had representation across all 6 campuses at the College. This committee was created to develop and offer new training and to disseminate IG communications across the College.

Phase Four: Developing and Implementing IG Policy

Communication: Email Retention Policy

During the discovery phase it was apparent that the College lacked IG policy that could improve the security of stakeholder data and reduce legal liability. Thorough and effective IG policy can reduce security and legal risk for an organization (Franks, 2018). For example, many College employees transmitted and stored PII and PHI via electronic communications and retained unnecessary data for 10 + years. Thus, the IG department crafted, obtained approval from General Counsel, and implemented an email retention policy and a data classification policy. Before the adoption of these policies, the College allowed employees to save PII and other information in email in perpetuity. Also, data floated in and out of the College at the will of the employees.

The new email retention policy mandated emails four years old or older were automatically deleted. Training and communications were developed by the tiered steering committee to teach people how to save College records, remove them from email, and store them in an appropriate place. Training and communications were also developed and conveyed that explained the why and the benefit (reducing legal liability, reduction of storing redundant, outdated, and trivial information) (Smallwood, 2014) of applying an email retention program. We also developed a data classification policy for the College.

Phase Five: Data Governance Policy

While crafting the email retention policy we discovered that the College had no data classification standards either. Thus, highly sensitive data was stored with public data. There was no direction for people in the College as to where to store data, and which types of data should be stored in what repositories. Having no direction as to where to store data can lead to confusion, legal risk, client risk, and lost information and data (Eisen, 2020). Therefore, a data governance classification was crafted -upon received approval from General Counsel-, and a new policy implemented observing the following standards – Public Confidential, Restricted, Prohibited. These categories are depicted in Table 1.

These data classification standards are just now being implemented as data was transfer from legacy systems to the new systems during the ERP implementation. Ultimately, the objective was to apply data

Table 1. Data governance classifications

Data Classification Level	**Data Governance Practice**
Public	Information the College is obligated to make public, e.g., certain annual reports, salary surveys…
Confidential	Information typically exempted from the Public Information Act.
Restricted	Information and associated information systems used in the conduct of college business in which data is not legally regulated, but which an expectation of privacy exists, e.g., Information protected via contractual obligation.
Prohibited	Information and associated information systems that are legally regulated with a requirement to self-report to the government and or provide notice to the individual if such information is inappropriately accessed, e.g., PII, PHI, PCI…

Source: The Authors, 2024.

loss prevention and identity access management to data as existing data governance program became more mature. Both DLP and IAM were implemented to provide further security for the College.

Electronic Communications Retention Policy

Through the process of crafting the email retention and data governance policies, it was evident that many people utilize MS TEAMs chat and other electronic chat to store data. Moreover, this chat feature had no retention applied. Thus, data stored in these electronic chat tools potentially expose the College to legal liability. Additionally, data stored in chats would be difficult to retrieve later, whereas if it were stored in an appropriate knowledge repository such as OneDrive or Laserfiche, it could be more efficiently retrieved and shared later. Therefore, the evolving process prompted the development of an electronic chat retention schedule that will be presented to the General Counsel for approval.

Phase Six: Working with Legal and Compliance

The eDiscovery Process

Through developing the IG Program at the College, the team working on this project have become close partners with the Legal department. While forming this partnership, it was clear that the Legal team would need help with the initial stages of the data collection process during the FOIA requests, lawsuits, and other requests for information. For most organizations today, the volume, variety, and velocity of information requested via a FOIA request, discovery request in a lawsuit, or other request for information can be very time consuming and burdensome. Having help with eDiscovery systems is vital (Broucek, 2020). After learning about this need, the Information Management Office interviewed the Legal Department to discover their specific needs. Subsequently the project lead worked with the procurement office and posted a Request for Proposals from vendors who could help with this process. Through this process, vendors were selected and contracted to help with the initial collection for a FOIA request, lawsuit, or other request for information. The stakeholders in the Office of Information helped with subsequent culling of information post-gathering of the initial data. Thus, forming a helpful eDiscovery partnership with the Legal Department. Providing eDiscovery services for an organization can increase response time to general requests for information.

Identifying Compliance Issues

During the discovery process, the Office of Information also learned that documentation of process and procedure information lacked when implementing new software, executing new data systems, or procuring new systems. Not collecting and preserving documentation can lead to subsequent compliance and legal risk issues (Stamper, Phillips, Goodman, & Bonney, 2022). For example, two years after implementation for a new data system, auditors may ask who created certain processes, who made specific decisions, who managed the system rollouts. By not having documentation to show these process implementations, who was responsible, this can lead to legal risk, fines, and other regulatory violations. Thus, the Information Governance Program created a new Compliance Program in partnership with Information Security and Legal to begin documenting important data system implementation, software rollouts, decision making, project management, employee responsibility. These actions, responsibilities, and decisions are documented and preserved in a Knowledge Base in TeamDynamix (Team Dynamix, 2023).

Developing and Implementing Knowledge Management

The discovery phase also revealed that knowledge workers stored word documents, slide decks, videos, pedagogical material, transcripts, contracts in many unsafe locations. These locations included personal devices, flash drives, email, Google form, as examples. Storing information in such insecure locations can open individuals up to personal liability and can increase compliance, security, and legal risk for an organization (Milton & Lambe, 2020).

Therefore, throughout the identification of five repositories in which to -safely - store such unstructured data, direct knowledge workers were identified to work with the storage of formalized documents such as contracts, memorandums of understanding, transcripts, and other formalized documents with potential PII and PHI in Laserfiche. Those direct knowledge workers were instructed to store and share working documents such as slide decks, videos, word documents still work in progress in either MS TEAMS or OneDrive. They were also directed to store processes and procedures in the Knowledge Base inside TeamDynamix, the Information Technology Management System. Additionally, clarity was provided on the work with faulty to help the team members better understand how to ephemerally store

Table 2. Knowledge management storage chart

Document Type	Laserfiche	MS TEAMS	MS OneDrive	ITSM	LMS
Formalized Documents	Yes	No	No	No	No
Student Records	Yes	No	No	No	No
PII, PHI	Yes	No	N	No	No
Processes and Procedures, KAs	No	No	No	Yes	No
Working Documents	No	Yes	Yes	No	No
Pedagogical Material	No	No	No	No	Yes

Source: The Authors, 2024.

pedagogical material in Canvas and on the Learning Management System, while ultimately transferring any formalized documents to Laserfiche.

A chart we use to help direct knowledge worker information storing and sharing behavior is depicted in Table 2.

The need to help knowledge workers learn to store and share unstructured data in secure locations was part of the impetus for the creation of a Knowledge Management Program as a subset of the IG Program. The KM Program has evolved to include teaching knowledge workers how to transition from paper to digital, reduce printing, rely more on digital technologies, and offer safer more efficient ways to share and store information.

Next Steps: Locate, Map, and Classify Data and Data Systems

Since laying a good foundation with important Information Governance foundations, e.g., retention policies, obtaining executive sponsorship, creating data classification standards, establishing a knowledge management program, and an eDiscovery program, next this College and any organization needs to complete data discovery endeavors. All organizations establishing IG programs need to locate all their data and data systems, classify their data, and map their data and their systems. Such data/system discovery, and data classification and mapping can be complete with file analysis tools. The benefit of using file analysis tools is that these processes can be completed via automation and can be automated in perpetuity. One of the worst outcomes is an organization discovers, maps, classifies its data, and then in a couple of months the data is ROT, or the maps are incorrect (Smallwood, 2014). Thus, applying file analysis can allow an organization to initially locate, classify, map… its data and data systems; and keep these classifications and maps up to date in perpetuity.

Apply Retention

Another important step while discovering data, classifying it, and mapping it, is to apply retention. Just as the College in this case study, all organizations should have a records retention program. The bare minimum for solid IG programs is a records retention program and a legal hold process (Smallwood, 2014). In this case study, the College developed a robust records retention program. Thus, while discovering, classifying, and mapping data, this College, and organizations following this model should apply retention to data while in the discovery process. By doing so, most if not all ROT can be removed. 65-70% of all data organizations maintain is ROT. Thus, by eliminating this ROT from the beginning this allows organizations to perpetuate a clean data lake.

Enhancing Data Governance and Management Opportunities via Artificial Intelligence

Initially ensuring that an organization's data lake is well organized as described above, allows that organization's knowledge workers to utilize business analytics tools to produce descriptive and diagnostic analytics. Unfortunately, most organizations process data from unorganized data lakes or via only one-third of the data they own because they never complete a discovery phase mentioned above and do not even realize they have another 60- 75% of data in their possession. Or organizations run statistical analysis on ROT and their reports are useless. Many companies' executives have little to no faith in the analytics reports their organization's knowledge workers produce because they know their organization has never completed a discovery phase to locate, organize, map, and classify their data (Smallwood, 2014). Fortunately, organizations that commit to and complete discovery phases and maintain their data in an organized guise can produce descriptive and diagnostic analytics.

Descriptive analytics allow an organization to examine what happened. For a college or University, descriptive analytics could reveal that a percentage of their business students had increased graduation rates over a five year period. These analytics can show past trends. Having an organized and well perpetually classified data lake also allows organizations to produce diagnostic analytics. Diagnostic analytics allow an organization to understand why certain events happened. At a college or University, diagnostic analytics could reveal that the increase in business student graduation rates over five years was caused by an increase in community partnerships with local businesses, great faculty service, access to business school digital information resources, or some other factors or combinations of factors. The point of emphasis is when an organization takes time to carefully locate, organize, map, and classify its data, the organization can begin to understand what is happening and why (Laney, 2018).

Leads to Artificial Intelligence

Descriptive and diagnostic statistical tools provide an abundance of value to organizations, however, today coupling these tools with predictive and prescriptive statistical tools can optimize and organizations housed data. Predictive analytics allow an organization to predict what will happen based on past trends, external factors, internal influences, and an organized data lake. At a college or University, a business school could predict an increase in even higher graduation rates for their students who take classes with specific faculty, obtain internships with certain companies, and who already have specific life experience. Thus, they can recruit students who will be successful in their program based on certain known factors. Prescriptive analytics allow organizations to make actions occur. At a College or University, prescriptive analytics may enable a business school to climb a certain percentage of points in a national ranking system (e.g., U.S. News and World Reports, 2023) by recruiting certain students to their program, helping those students obtain internships with specific companies, and recruiting specific faculty (Laney, 2018).

Brett (2023) investigated the IG processes and policies effectiveness through the deployment of AI in business highlighting the aspects of Large Language Models (LLMs) that the consolidation of frameworks and tailored AI policy and governance provides leadership resources for assurance of Information and data governance practices. The author elaborates on the study conducted in UK government indicating the 5(five) pillars to be considered to facilitate safety and innovation in the application of AI in certain industries, as follows: **1. Safety, security, and robustness** (risk management); **2. Transparency and communication** (clear communication regarding the deployment, use, and risks related to AI); **3.Fairness** (AI used in compliance with the law); **4.Accuntability and governance** ((clear measurements for appropriate use and clear accountability/outcomes); **5. Contestability and redress** (Clarity on the harmful outcomes of AI and decisions resulted by AI). (p. 5).

AI Tools Are a Key to Predictive and Prescriptive Analytics

When utilized with organized and well classified data lakes, AI tools can produce valid and reliable predictive and prescriptive analytics. AI tools such as ChatGPT (ChatGPT, 2023) or Microsoft's Copilot

AI (Microsoft, 2023) tool produce valuable predictive and prescriptive analytics when operated over a clean data lake. Also, tools like Microsoft's Power BI can offer predictive and prescriptive analytics when used with a clean data lake. The problem most organizations manifest is using these tools with unorganized data lakes. Using these tools with unclassified, unorganized data lakes lead to the AI tools giving you bizarre results. The tool is not self-conscious, it is not willingly trying to become human, or willing attempting to offer bizarre results. It may produce bizarre results because the user is asking it to produce answers, predictions, prescriptions… from unorganized data (Cantor, 2023).

FUTURE RESEARCH AND OPPORTUNITIES

A plethora of future research opportunities are available based on this past three-year endeavor. Research needs to be completed to see how the new data governance classifications can be applied as data is migrated into the new ERP systems. User testing then needs to be completed to see how effective the new data classification systems are as the team try to implement IAM and DLP. Other user testing also needs to occur to ensure the new process mapping and ERP documentation is properly housed within the Knowledge Base in TeamDynamix, and that said documentation can be easily accessed by those who should have access.

This process could be extrapolated and applied to other organizations, whether corporate, non-profit, government, or other. This paper further conveys the experience, benefits, and challenges in developing an IG Program, which include obtaining and maintaining executive approval and support; effectively communicating throughout an organization what Information Governance is, why it is important…; promoting culture change; creating and offering IG training and implementing the various pieces of IG. Some of these pieces include records management, knowledge management, eDiscovery, data governance, privacy, and compliance. Implementing these areas of IG ultimately prevent legal liability, save institutions time and money, and increase security.

While this study contributes valuable insights into the development and execution of an Information Governance (IG) Program within a college program in Texas, there remains intriguing avenues for future research in this domain. Several possibilities for further studies emerge from the findings and gaps identified in this investigation:

1. **Comparative Analysis:** A comparative analysis of information governance practices across different educational institutions in Texas or even on a national scale could provide a broader perspective on the effectiveness of various strategies and approach an International Comparative Studies.
2. **Long-Term Impact Assessment:** Conducting a longitudinal study to assess the long-term impact and sustainability of implemented IG programs would offer insights into how these initiatives evolve over time and adapt to changing circumstances.
3. **Cultural and Contextual Variations:** Exploring how information governance practices differ in various cultural and contextual settings, both within and outside of educational institutions, can deepen our understanding of the dynamics influencing their success.
4. **Technological Integration:** Investigating the role of emerging technologies, such as artificial intelligence, machine learning, and blockchain, in enhancing information governance processes and compliance mechanisms could be a promising area of research.

5. **Legal and Ethical Considerations**: Delving deeper into the legal and ethical dimensions of information governance, especially in the context of student data and privacy regulations, can offer valuable insights into compliance challenges and potential solutions.
6. **Cross-Industry Application:** Exploring how the lessons learned from IG implementation in academia can be extrapolated and applied to other sectors, such as healthcare, finance, or government, could provide valuable cross-industry insights.

By pursuing these avenues of research, scholars and practitioners can further enrich the field of information governance and contribute to the continuous improvement of strategies for managing and utilizing data in complex organizational environments.

CONCLUSION

In conclusion, the significance of information governance in organizations and academia cannot be overstated. As data continues to redefine the way we operate, understanding and implementing effective governance mechanisms will become a critical differentiator for success. This study sheds light on the intricate process of developing and sustaining an Information Governance (IG) Program within a Texas college program. By employing an action research methodology, the research has outlined some of the pivotal factors crucial for executing the IG program effectively. Through an in-depth examination of key components, encompassing the design and implementation of strategies, policies, and compliant practices, this paper has underscored the significance of aligning the IG program with strategic objectives and the organizational culture.

The participatory nature of the action research approach has proven instrumental in enhancing the longevity and acceptance of the IG program. Furthermore, this investigation has revealed that effective communication, comprehensive training, and adept change management stand as cornerstones for the successful adoption of information governance. This is bolstered by the acknowledged relevance of eDiscovery in the process, emphasizing the importance of managing electronic information for legal and compliance purposes.

By navigating through the intricacies of information governance, this paper, also, aspires to contribute to the broader discourse surrounding data management, enabling organizations and academic institutions to harness the full potential of their data assets while safeguarding against potential pitfalls. It aims at contributing to the growing body of literature on information governance, offering insights into the practical application of action research in a college context. By elucidating the process of developing and implementing an information governance program through collaboration and reflection, this study serves as a valuable guide for other educational institutions seeking to bolster their data management practices. The outcomes of this research demonstrate that an action research approach can foster the evolution of a robust and adaptive information governance program, positioning colleges to effectively navigate the data landscape and uphold data integrity, security, and compliance in the digital era.

As a result, the study's primary objective of providing a tailored governance framework for a college program context has been achieved. By addressing the unique needs inherent to the educational setting, this framework extends its potential utility to a wide array of industries beyond academia. Ultimately, this research advances our understanding of how to implement and sustain an information governance program effectively, underlining its pivotal role in managing data within diverse organizational contexts.

REFERENCES

Blumauer, A., & Nagy, H. (2020). *The knowledge graph cookbook: Recipes that work.* Monochrom.

BrettM. (2023). Issues to consider relating to Information Governance and Artificial Intelligence Background to AI and Context a practitioner's viewpoint. doi:10.13140/RG.2.2.11285.09442

Broucek, C. E. (2020). eDiscovery for the legal professional. Frederick, MD: Walters Kluwer.

Cantor, M. (Oct 12, 2023). Incredibly smart or incredibly stupid? What we learned from using ChatGPT for a year. *The Guardian.* https://www.theguardian.com/technology/2023/oct/12/chatgpt-uses-writing-recipes-one-year

ChatGPT. (2023). *ChatGPT.* Open AI. https://openai.com/blog/chatgpt-plus on November 1, 2023.

Davoudi, S. M. M., Ghiasi, A., & Kowsari, R. (2020). A systematic review of information governance in organizations. *International Journal of Information Management, 54,* 102146.

Eisen, L. S. (2020). *Rules: A guide to drafting respectful policies and directives.* Pixley Press.

Franks, P. C. (2018). *Records and information management* [2d ed.]. Neal-Schuman.

Garfield, S. (2022). *The five Cs of KM.* Lucidea.

Hilger, J., & Wahl, Z. (2022). *Making knowledge management clickable: Knowledge management systems strategy, design, and implementation.* Springer. doi:10.1007/978-3-030-92385-3

ING. (2013). *ING firms settle email retention case.* Compliance Reporter.

Kooper, M. N. R. (2011). On the governance of information: Introducing a new concept of governance to support the management of information. *International Journal of Information Management, 31*(3). doi:10.1016/j.ijinfomgt.2010.05.009

Krol, M. (2018). Information governance in a digital world: A general data protection regulation (GDPR) perspective. *Computer Law & Security Review, 34*(2), 193–204.

Laney, D. B. (2018). *Infonomics: How to monetize, manage, and measure information as an asset for competitive advantage.* Bibliomotion.

Lexbe. (2023). *eDiscovery platform.* Lexbe. https://lexbe.com/

Microsoft. (2023). *Microsoft Copilot.* https://www.microsoft.com/en-us/windows/copilot-ai-features?r=1

Milton, N., & Lambe, P. (2020). *The knowledge manager's handbook: A step-by-step guide to embedding effective knowledge management in your organization* [2d ed.]. Kogen Page.

Moulaison, S. H. (2018). Ethical information governance: Challenges and opportunities. *Journal of Librarianship and Information Science, 50*(1), 3–16.

Moynihan, D. P., & Kroll, A. (2016). Information Governance: Compliance, or Competitive Advantage? *Communications of the Association for Information Systems, 38*(1), 3.

Ragbeer, R. (2021). Texting: Your next big vulnerability. Law Practice Today, Dec (2021). https://www.lawpracticetoday.org/article/texting-your-next-big-vulnerability/

Saldanha, T. (2019). *Why digital transformations fail: The surprising disciplines of how to take off and stay ahead.* Barrett-Koehler Publishers, Inc.

Seiner, R. S. (2014). *Non-invasive data governance: The path of least resistance and greatest success.* Technics Publications.

Smallwood, R. F. (2014). *Information governance: Concepts, strategies, and best practices.* Wiley.

Stamper, M., Phillips, J., Goodman, D., & Bonney, B. (2022). *Data privacy program guide: How to build a privacy program that inspires trust.* CISO DRG Publishing.

Tallon, P., Ramirez, R., & Short, J. (2013). The Information Artifact in IT Governance: Toward a Theory of Information Governance. *Journal of Management Information Systems, 30*(3), 141–178. doi:10.2753/MIS0742-1222300306

Chapter 8
AI and Data Analytics for Market Research and Competitive Intelligence

Tarun Kumar Vashishth
https://orcid.org/0000-0001-9916-9575
IIMT University, India

Bhupendra Kumar
https://orcid.org/0000-0001-9281-3655
IIMT University, India

Vikas Sharma
https://orcid.org/0000-0001-8173-4548
IIMT University, India

Sachin Chaudhary
https://orcid.org/0000-0002-8415-0043
IIMT University, India

Kewal Krishan Sharma
https://orcid.org/0009-0001-2504-9607
IIMT University, India

Rajneesh Panwar
https://orcid.org/0009-0000-5974-191X
IIMT University, India

ABSTRACT

AI and data analytics have revolutionized the field of market research and competitive intelligence. This chapter explores the multifaceted applications of AI and data analytics in gathering, analyzing, and deriving actionable insights from data sources to gain a competitive edge in the business landscape. It delves into various techniques, such as natural language processing, machine learning, and predictive analytics, showcasing how they empower organizations to make informed decisions, anticipate market trends, and outperform competitors. Furthermore, this chapter highlights the ethical considerations and challenges associated with AI-driven market research and competitive intelligence. In an era driven by data, AI emerges as an indispensable tool, enabling businesses to thrive in a dynamic and competitive marketplace.

DOI: 10.4018/979-8-3693-1058-8.ch008

INTRODUCTION

The integration of Artificial Intelligence (AI) and Data Analytics has revolutionized the landscape of Market Research and Competitive Intelligence, ushering in an era of unprecedented insights and strategic advantages for businesses. In an age characterized by data abundance, AI-driven technologies play a pivotal role in extracting actionable intelligence from vast datasets. Machine learning algorithms enhance the efficiency and accuracy of data analysis, enabling businesses to glean meaningful patterns, consumer behaviors, and market trends. The marriage of AI and Data Analytics has not only streamlined traditional market research methodologies but has also opened new frontiers, allowing organizations to anticipate market shifts and competitors' moves with remarkable precision. This transformative synergy facilitates the exploration of unstructured data, such as social media sentiments, enabling a nuanced understanding of consumer preferences and opinions. Predictive analytics, powered by advanced algorithms, propels the capability to forecast market dynamics, enhancing strategic decision-making processes. In the realm of Competitive Intelligence, AI-driven tools empower organizations to monitor competitors in real-time, analyze their market strategies, and glean valuable insights from various digital touch points. Natural Language Processing (NLP) and sentiment analysis tools decipher textual information, offering a deeper understanding of market dynamics and consumer sentiments. Zohuri and Moghaddam's (2020) discussion on the transition from business intelligence to artificial intelligence, while informative, lacks a thorough examination of the potential challenges and complexities in implementing AI in diverse business environments and strategies.The utilization of AI and Data Analytics in Competitive Intelligence not only expedites the process of information gathering but also allows businesses to stay agile in responding to evolving market conditions. Ethical considerations and compliance with data privacy regulations are integral to this evolution, ensuring that the deployment of AI and Data Analytics in Market Research and Competitive Intelligence is conducted responsibly and with due regard for privacy. As we navigate the data-driven future, the synergistic power of AI and Data Analytics is poised to redefine how businesses perceive, interpret, and leverage information for a competitive edge in the ever-evolving global marketplace. Alghamdi and Al-Baity's (2022) study on augmented analytics driven by AI, while innovative, lacks a robust evaluation of the feasibility and potential trade-offs of their proposed solutions, particularly in terms of performance and cost.

The landscape of business and market dynamics is continuously evolving, driven by the rapid advancement of technology and the increasing availability of data. In this era of digital transformation, organizations are presented with both unprecedented challenges and opportunities in understanding their markets and competitors. Market research and competitive intelligence have emerged as critical functions for businesses seeking to thrive in this complex environment. The convergence of Artificial Intelligence (AI) and Data Analytics has revolutionized the way companies approach market research and competitive intelligence. This chapter serves as a gateway to the exploration of AI and Data Analytics in the context of these vital business functions. Al-Okaily, Teoh, and Al-Okaily's (2023) enterprise-level analysis of data analytics-oriented business intelligence technology effectiveness, while comprehensive, does not sufficiently address the potential limitations and challenges in implementing these technologies in smaller businesses with different resource constraints.

Overview of Market Research and Competitive Intelligence

Market Research is the systematic process of collecting, analyzing, and interpreting data related to markets, customers, and industry trends. It serves as the compass that guides organizations in understanding the demands and preferences of their target audiences. Market research enables businesses to make informed decisions regarding product development, pricing, marketing strategies, and expansion opportunities. It is the foundation upon which successful marketing campaigns and market entry strategies are built. Bharadiya's (2023) comparative study of business intelligence and artificial intelligence with big data analytics, while informative, lacks a thorough examination of the potential challenges and complexities in implementing these technologies in diverse business environments.

Competitive Intelligence, on the other hand, is the art of gathering, analyzing, and leveraging information about competitors and the competitive environment. It involves monitoring and dissecting the strategies, strengths, weaknesses, and movements of rivals in the market. Competitive intelligence equips organizations with the insights necessary to anticipate competitor actions, identify market gaps, and devise strategies to gain a competitive advantage.

Figure 1. AI and data analytics in market research

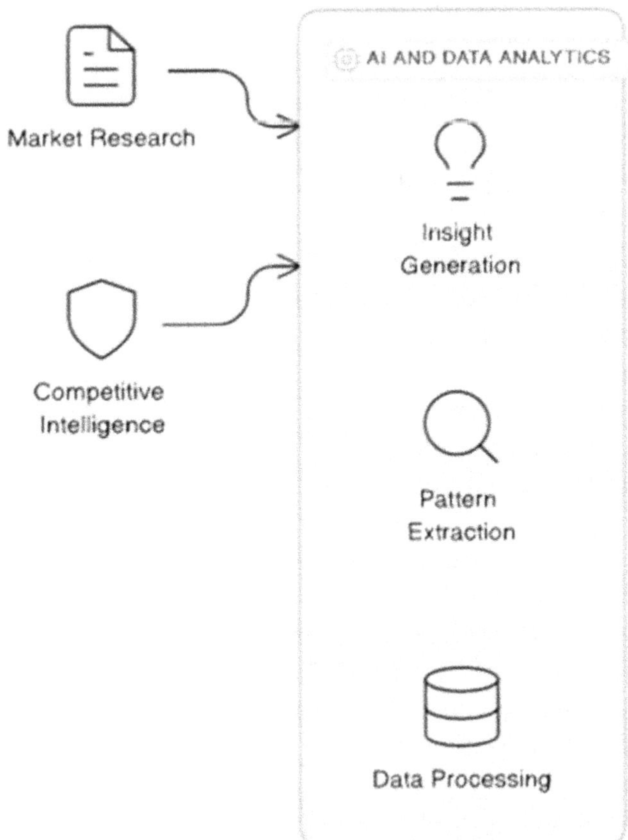

In today's digital age, where data is generated at an unprecedented pace, these two disciplines have been greatly influenced by technological advancements, particularly in the realms of Artificial Intelligence (AI) and Data Analytics. AI and Data Analytics have revolutionized how market research and competitive intelligence are conducted. These technologies enable the processing of vast datasets, the extraction of meaningful patterns, and the generation of actionable insights at speeds and scales that were previously unimaginable. . Chintalapati and Pandey's (2022) systematic literature review on artificial intelligence in marketing provides a broad overview, but it falls short in critically examining the potential negative impacts and limitations of AI applications in this field.

This chapter explores the evolving landscape of market research and competitive intelligence in the age of AI and Data Analytics. It delves into the significance of these disciplines in modern business, highlighting their pivotal role in shaping strategies, fostering innovation, and driving growth. Through this exploration, we aim to set the stage for a comprehensive journey into the world of AI and Data Analytics for market research and competitive intelligence, uncovering the tools and techniques that are transforming these fields and enabling organizations to stay ahead in a rapidly changing business environment.

Importance of AI and Data Analytics in Modern Business

In the digital era, data has become the lifeblood of businesses across industries. The ability to collect, process, and derive actionable insights from data is a fundamental determinant of success. This is where Artificial Intelligence (AI) and Data Analytics step in as indispensable tools for modern businesses. The importance of AI and Data Analytics can hardly be overstated, and their impact is felt in various critical aspects:

a. **Data-Driven Decision Making**: AI and Data Analytics enable organizations to make informed decisions based on evidence rather than intuition. By analyzing historical and real-time data, businesses gain a deeper understanding of customer behaviors, market trends, and operational efficiencies. This data-driven decision-making process enhances the chances of success and minimizes risks.
b. **Customer Understanding**: In the age of AI and Data Analytics, businesses can develop a 360-degree view of their customers. They can analyze customer interactions, preferences, and feedback to create highly personalized experiences. This not only improves customer satisfaction but also drives customer retention and loyalty.
c. **Competitive Advantage**: Competitive intelligence powered by AI allows businesses to monitor competitors in real time. They can track pricing strategies, product launches, and customer sentiment regarding rivals. This information is invaluable for staying ahead in the market and identifying opportunities for differentiation.
d. **Innovation and Product Development**: AI can sift through vast datasets to identify gaps in the market or areas where innovation is required. Data-driven insights guide the development of new products and services that align more closely with customer needs.
e. **Marketing and Sales Optimization**: AI-driven marketing automation and lead scoring help businesses target the right audience with personalized content. Sales teams benefit from predictive analytics that prioritize leads most likely to convert into customers.
f. **Risk Management**: AI and Data Analytics are powerful tools for identifying and mitigating risks. For instance, financial institutions use predictive analytics to detect fraudulent transactions, and healthcare organizations employ AI for early disease diagnosis.

Figure 2. Importance of AI and data analytics in modern business

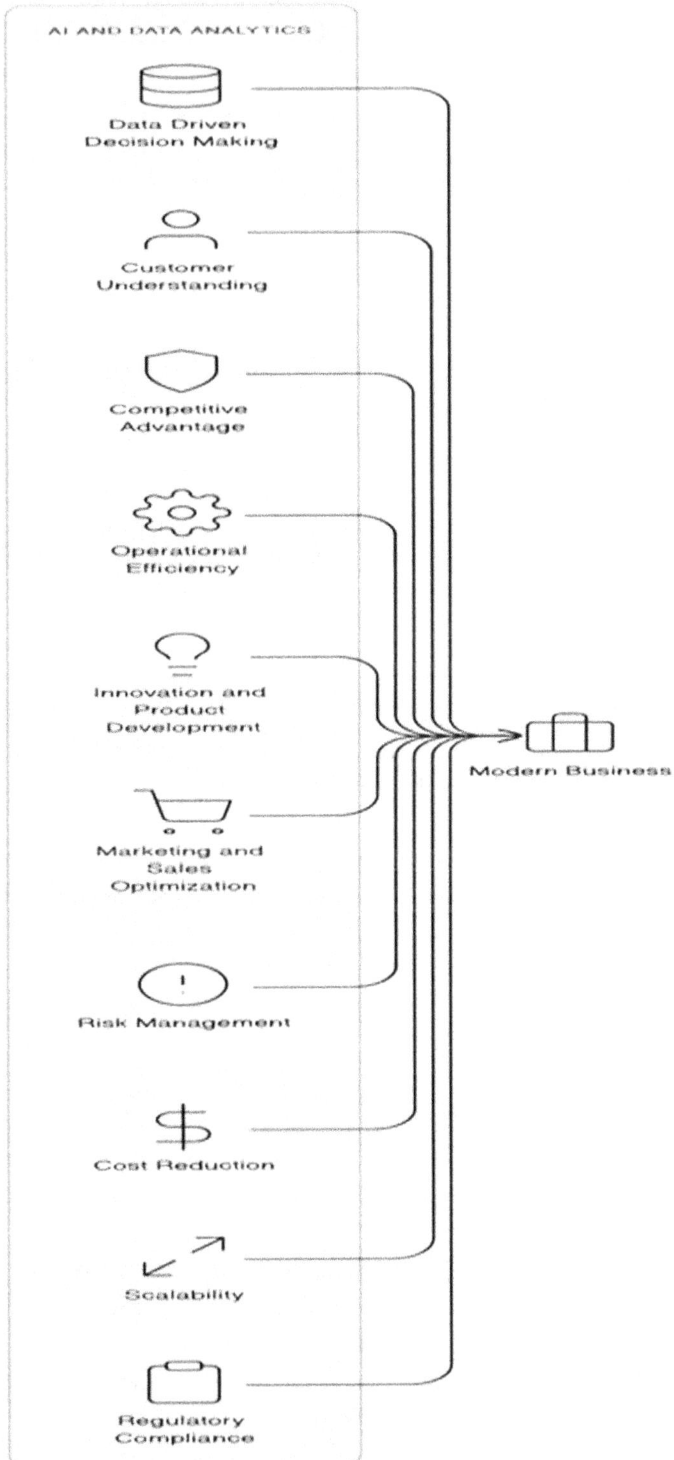

g. **Cost Reduction**: Efficiency gains achieved through AI can lead to substantial cost reductions. Automation of routine tasks, chatbots for customer support, and AI-driven predictive maintenance all contribute to lower operational expenses.
h. **Scalability**: AI and Data Analytics solutions can scale effortlessly with growing data volumes. This scalability ensures that businesses can continue to extract value from data as they expand.
i. **Regulatory Compliance**: In highly regulated industries such as finance and healthcare, AI and Data Analytics help ensure compliance by monitoring transactions and patient data, flagging any anomalies or violations.

Objectives and Scope of the Chapter

The primary objectives and scope of this chapter on "AI and Data Analytics for Market Research and Competitive Intelligence" are outlined below:

Objectives

- **Understanding AI and Data Analytics:** To provide a comprehensive understanding of AI and Data Analytics, their underlying principles, and their significance in the context of modern business practices.
- **Market Research Techniques:** To explore traditional and contemporary market research techniques and highlight how AI and Data Analytics have transformed these methods.
- **Applications in Market Research:** To discuss practical applications of AI and Data Analytics in market research, including consumer behavior analysis, sentiment analysis, and demand forecasting.
- **Case Studies:** To present real-world case studies and examples from various industries that demonstrates the successful implementation of AI and Data Analytics in market research and competitive intelligence.
- **Benefits and Challenges:** To evaluate the advantages and challenges associated with using AI and Data Analytics in these domains, including ethical considerations and data privacy concerns.

Scope

- **Fundamentals of AI and Data Analytics:** The chapter will begin with an overview of the fundamental concepts of AI and Data Analytics, including machine learning, data mining, and natural language processing.
- **Market Research Techniques:** It will delve into the traditional methods of market research, such as surveys and focus groups, and discuss how AI and Data Analytics have expanded the toolkit with advanced techniques like predictive analytics and social media analysis.
- **Competitive Intelligence Framework:** The chapter will outline a framework for conducting competitive intelligence, emphasizing the role of AI in collecting and analyzing data from both public and proprietary sources.
- **Practical Applications:** Practical use cases will be explored, covering how AI and Data Analytics are employed to gain insights into consumer preferences, market trends, and competitor strategies.

- **Future Trends:** The chapter will conclude by looking at emerging trends and technologies in AI and Data Analytics for market research and competitive intelligence, offering insights into what the future may hold in these domains.

By addressing these objectives and scope, this chapter aims to equip readers with a comprehensive understanding of the transformative role that AI and Data Analytics play in enhancing market research practices and sharpening competitive intelligence strategies in the dynamic landscape of contemporary business.

LITERATURE REVIEW

Asare et al.'s (2020) study on optimizing business performance through agile business intelligence and data analytics during COVID-19, while timely, lacks a thorough exploration of the potential long-term implications and sustainability of these strategies post-pandemic. Awan et al.'s (2021) work on the use of artificial intelligence for supply chain success in the era of data analytics, while forward-thinking, lacks a comprehensive exploration of the potential ethical implications and challenges associated with the use of AI in this context. Davenport et al.'s (2020) predictions on how artificial intelligence will change the future of marketing, while insightful, lack a thorough examination of the potential challenges and complexities in implementing AI in diverse marketing environments and strategies.

Jayawardena et al.'s (2022) study on AI-based market intelligence and customer insights, while innovative, lacks a robust evaluation of the feasibility and potential trade-offs of their proposed solutions, particularly in terms of performance and cost. Kumar et al.'s (2019) exploration of the role of artificial intelligence in personalized engagement marketing, while informative, lacks a thorough examination of the potential ethical implications and challenges associated with the use of AI in this context. Ranjan and Foropon's (2021) study on big data analytics in building the competitive intelligence of organizations, while insightful, lacks a thorough exploration of the potential security and privacy concerns that may arise in such a data-intensive setting. Vashishth et al.'s (2023) exploration of AI-enabled IoT applications in high-tech agriculture, while innovative, lacks a comprehensive exploration of the potential ethical implications and challenges associated with the use of AI and IoT in this context. Wu, Yan, and Umair's (2023) study on the role of competitive intelligence and practices of dynamic capabilities in business accommodation of SMEs, while insightful, lacks a thorough exploration of the potential challenges and complexities in implementing these practices in diverse SME environments.

FOUNDATIONS OF AI AND DATA ANALYTICS

In this section, we delve into the foundational concepts of Artificial Intelligence (AI) and Data Analytics, providing readers with the essential knowledge needed to understand their applications in market research and competitive intelligence.

Fundamental Concepts of Artificial Intelligence (AI)

Artificial Intelligence (AI) encompasses a broad and dynamic field dedicated to creating systems and machines that can perform tasks that typically require human intelligence. Several fundamental concepts underpin AI and shape its capabilities and applications.

Machine Learning: Machine learning is a subset of AI focused on the development of algorithms that enable computers to learn from data. Through training and exposure to vast datasets, machines can recognize patterns, make predictions, and improve their performance over time. Supervised learning, unsupervised learning, and reinforcement learning are common approaches within machine learning.

Neural Networks and Deep Learning: Neural networks are AI models inspired by the human brain's structure, consisting of interconnected layers of artificial neurons. Deep learning, a subfield of machine learning, uses deep neural networks to process complex data and solve intricate tasks, such as image recognition and natural language processing.

Natural Language Processing (NLP): NLP focuses on enabling machines to understand, interpret, and generate human language. It plays a vital role in applications like chatbots, language translation, and sentiment analysis.

Data and Big Data: Data is the lifeblood of AI. AI systems require vast amounts of data to train and operate effectively. Big data technologies handle the storage, processing, and analysis of immense datasets, enabling AI to extract meaningful insights.

Ethical and Responsible AI: With the rise of AI, ethical considerations have become paramount. Responsible AI encompasses the principles of fairness, transparency, accountability, and the avoidance of biases in AI systems. Ethical AI ensures that AI technologies are developed and used in ways that benefit society while respecting individual rights and values.

Figure 3. AI model with types and importance

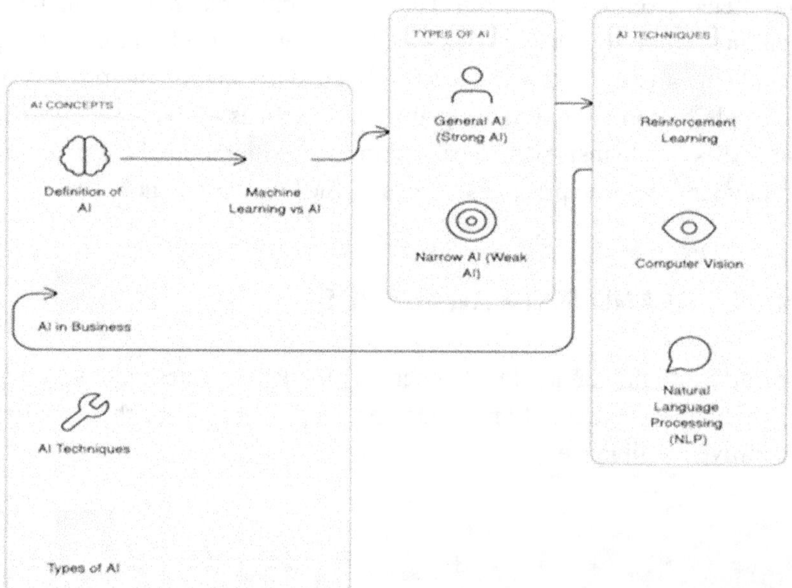

AI in Business and Industry: In the business world, AI aids in process automation, supply chain optimization, and customer service through chatbots. It's a valuable tool for data-driven decision-making and competitive advantage.

These fundamental concepts provide a foundation for understanding the breadth and depth of AI's capabilities. As AI continues to evolve, it will play an increasingly integral role in various aspects of our lives, from healthcare and business to education and entertainment, ushering in a new era of possibilities and challenges.

Basics of Data Analytics and Big Data

In the context of AI and Data Analytics for Market Research and Competitive Intelligence, the basics of data analytics and big data are fundamental. Data analytics involves the systematic exploration and analysis of data to reveal actionable insights, trends, and patterns that can inform strategic decisions. It encompasses techniques like machine learning, natural language processing, and statistical modeling. Big data refers to the vast and diverse data sources, including social media, customer reviews, and real-time market data, which need specialized tools and technologies to manage and analyze. When applied to Market Research and Competitive Intelligence, these concepts allow organizations to extract valuable insights from large and complex datasets, enabling a deeper understanding of market dynamics, consumer behavior, and competitor strategies. The synergy of AI and data analytics with big data empowers businesses to make data-driven decisions, track real-time market developments, and gain a competitive advantage by anticipating market trends and adapting their strategies accordingly. Sun et al. (2021) work on the integration innovation of competitive intelligence, AI, and big data analysis, while forward-thinking, lacks a comprehensive exploration of the potential ethical implications and challenges associated with the use of AI and big data in this context.

Role of Machine Learning and Deep Learning

In the realm of Market Research and Competitive Intelligence, the role of Machine Learning (ML) and Deep Learning stands as a transformative force, shaping the way businesses extracts insights from vast datasets. Machine Learning algorithms, a subset of AI, serve as the backbone for automating the analysis of diverse data sources, enabling organizations to discern patterns, consumer behaviors, and market trends with unparalleled efficiency. ML algorithms can adapt and learn from historical data, refining their predictive capabilities over time. This adaptability is particularly beneficial in predicting market shifts, consumer preferences, and competitive strategies, allowing businesses to make informed decisions. Deep Learning, a subset of ML inspired by the structure and function of the human brain's neural networks, excels in processing and understanding unstructured data, such as images, audio, and text. In Market Research, this translates to the ability to analyze vast amounts of textual data from social media, customer reviews, and forums, uncovering nuanced insights into consumer sentiments and preferences.

In Competitive Intelligence, Machine Learning and Deep Learning techniques enhance the monitoring and analysis of competitors' activities. ML algorithms can track and interpret competitors' online presence, product launches, and market positioning, providing real-time intelligence. Deep Learning models excel in extracting insights from multimedia content, allowing businesses to dissect visual elements and interpret complex patterns in competitors' marketing materials. Sentiment analysis powered by these technologies provides a deeper understanding of how consumers perceive competitors in the

Figure 4. Integration of machine learning and deep learning

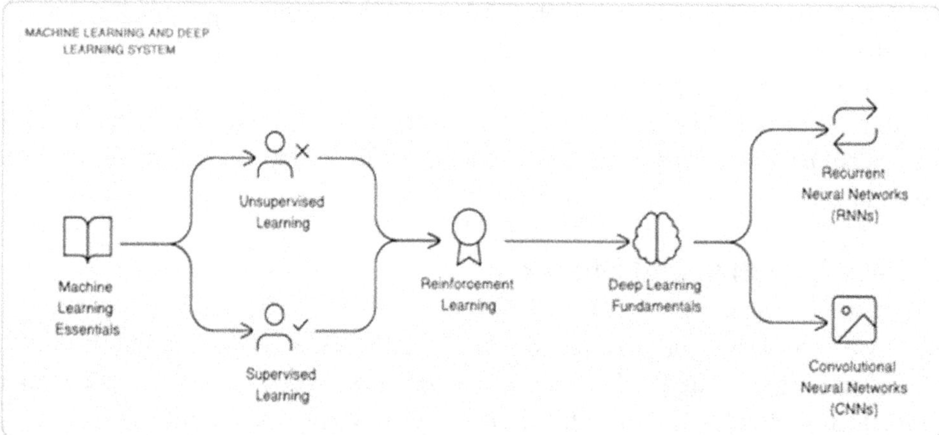

market. Furthermore, ML and Deep Learning facilitate anomaly detection, helping organizations identify irregularities or unexpected trends in the competitive landscape. As AI continues to advance, the symbiotic relationship between Machine Learning, Deep Learning, and Market Research and Competitive Intelligence will play a central role in fostering innovation, strategic decision-making, and maintaining a competitive edge in dynamic markets.

DATA COLLECTION AND MANAGEMENT

Data Sources for Market Research and Competitive Intelligence

Data sources for Market Research and Competitive Intelligence have expanded exponentially in the digital age, offering a rich tapestry of information that organizations can leverage for strategic insights. Traditional sources such as industry reports, government publications, and proprietary databases remain fundamental, providing foundational data on market trends, economic indicators, and regulatory landscapes. However, the advent of the internet and digital technologies has significantly diversified the data landscape. Social media platforms offer a treasure trove of unstructured data, providing real-time insights into consumer sentiments, preferences, and interactions. Web scraping tools extract valuable information from websites, forums, and online discussions, enabling organizations to monitor competitors, industry influencers, and emerging trends. Customer feedback, collected through surveys, reviews, and online forums, serves as a crucial source for understanding product perceptions and identifying areas for improvement. E-commerce platforms and sales data provide granular insights into product performance, pricing strategies, and consumer behavior.

Alternative data sources, such as satellite imagery, geospatial data, and sensor data, are becoming increasingly relevant for specific industries, offering unique perspectives on supply chains, logistics, and regional market dynamics. Collaborative partnerships and industry associations contribute to a collective intelligence pool, providing access to aggregated data, benchmarking metrics, and best practices. Subscription-based market intelligence platforms curate diverse datasets, offering comprehensive industry analyses and competitive landscapes. Importantly, advancements in Artificial Intelligence and Natural Language Processing enable the automated extraction of insights from textual data, facilitating efficient analysis of news articles, research papers, and industry blogs. The synthesis of data from these varied sources empowers organizations to construct a holistic understanding of market dynamics, consumer behavior, and competitive positioning, enabling informed decision-making in the ever-evolving business landscape.

Data Collection Techniques

Data collection techniques are methods used to gather information, facts, and observations for research, analysis, or decision-making purposes. The choice of data collection technique depends on the research objectives, the type of data needed, available resources, and ethical considerations. Here are some common data collection techniques:

Surveys and Questionnaires: Surveys involve structured sets of questions administered to a sample of respondents. Questionnaires can be conducted in person, over the phone, via mail, or online. They are useful for collecting quantitative data and opinions.

Interviews: Interviews involve face-to-face or remote conversations with participants. They can be structured (using a predetermined set of questions) or unstructured (open-ended discussions). Interviews are valuable for obtaining in-depth insights and qualitative data.

Observation: Observational techniques involve direct or participant observation of subjects or events. Researchers watch, record, or participate in the activities being studied. Observation is commonly used in ethnographic and behavioral research.

Focus Groups: Focus groups bring together a small, diverse group of participants to discuss a specific topic. They are particularly useful for exploring opinions, attitudes, and perceptions and generating qualitative data.

Document Analysis: Document analysis involves reviewing existing documents, records, reports, or archives. It is an essential technique for historical research, content analysis, and extracting data from pre-existing sources.

Experiments: Experiments involve manipulating one or more variables to observe their impact on a particular outcome. Controlled experiments allow researchers to establish causation and test hypotheses.

Sensor Data: With the proliferation of Internet of Things (IoT) devices, sensor data is increasingly used. Sensors can collect data on temperature, humidity, motion, and various environmental factors in real-time.

Social Media Listening: Social media listening tools capture data from social platforms to analyze public opinions, trends, and consumer sentiment.

Geospatial Data: Geospatial data collection techniques, such as Geographic Information Systems (GIS) and GPS, are used to gather location-based data, which is essential for applications like mapping and urban planning.

Telephone Surveys: Similar to traditional surveys, telephone surveys involve calling respondents to gather information. They are often used for market research and opinion polling.

Secondary Data: Secondary data refers to data collected by others for a different purpose. Researchers can access existing datasets, reports, and literature for their own analysis.

Biometric Data: Biometric data collection involves the use of physical or behavioral characteristics for identity verification, such as fingerprints, retinal scans, and voice recognition.

Figure 5. Data collection flow layout using AI and various techniques

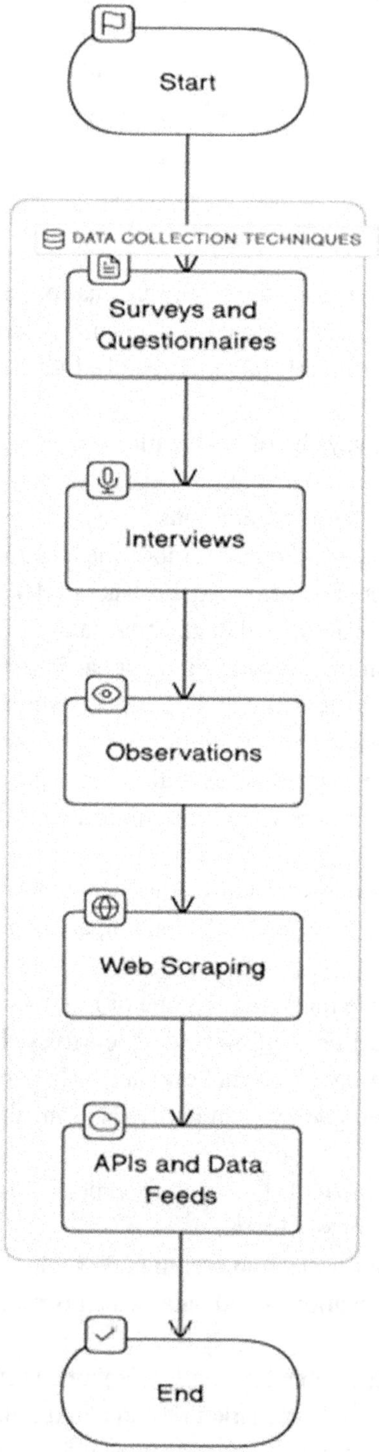

Each data collection technique has its advantages and limitations. Researchers must carefully select the appropriate method based on their research objectives, the type of data required, and the resources available. Ethical considerations, privacy concerns, and data quality should also be taken into account when designing data collection strategies.

Data Preprocessing and Cleaning

Data preprocessing and cleaning are essential steps in the data analysis process. They involve the transformation of raw data into a structured and reliable format for meaningful analysis and insights. This encompasses tasks such as handling missing values, detecting and addressing outliers, converting data types, and standardizing formats. Data cleaning ensures the removal of duplicates and the correction of data entry errors, resulting in consistent, high-quality data. Transformation techniques like normalization and encoding categorical data make the data suitable for modeling and analysis, while feature engineering can unveil hidden patterns. Proper data preprocessing and cleaning are crucial for improving the accuracy and effectiveness of machine learning models, enhancing the quality of research, and supporting informed decision-making across various domains.

Data Storage and Management Strategies

In the realm of Market Research and Competitive Intelligence, effective data storage and management strategies are critical components to harness the vast volumes of information generated through AI and Data Analytics. The sheer scale and diversity of data require scalable and flexible storage solutions. Cloud-based storage platforms have emerged as a cornerstone, providing businesses with the ability to scale their storage infrastructure dynamically while ensuring accessibility and collaboration across geographically dispersed teams. Additionally, edge computing plays a pivotal role, allowing organizations to process and store data closer to the source, reducing latency and facilitating real-time analytics. Data lakes, characterized by their ability to store raw, unstructured data at scale, offer a comprehensive repository for diverse data types, enabling more holistic analyses. The implementation of structured data warehouses optimized for querying and reporting ensures efficient storage and retrieval of organized datasets.

Effective data management encompasses not only storage but also the organization, quality assurance, and security of data. Metadata, tagging, and categorization systems are instrumental in organizing data for easy retrieval and analysis. Master data management (MDM) practices ensure consistency and accuracy across datasets, enhancing the reliability of insights derived from analytics. As data privacy and security become paramount concerns, organizations implement robust governance frameworks, ensuring compliance with regulations and safeguarding sensitive information. Encryption techniques, access controls, and regular audits contribute to a secure data environment. The adoption of DataOps principles, emphasizing collaboration and automation in data management workflows, streamlines processes and enhances the agility of organizations in adapting to evolving data needs. Ultimately, a well-crafted data storage and management strategy, considering scalability, organization, quality, and security, is foundational for unlocking the full potential of AI and Data Analytics in Market Research and Competitive Intelligence.

DISCUSSION

The utilization of Artificial Intelligence (AI) and Data Analytics in the realms of Market Research and Competitive Intelligence has brought about a transformative shift in how organizations gather, process, and leverage information for strategic decision-making. AI-driven data analytics enables businesses to extract valuable insights from vast and diverse data sources, offering a competitive edge in understanding market dynamics and the activities of competitors. Machine learning algorithms, natural language processing, and predictive analytics are just a few of the AI tools that empower organizations to discern market trends, consumer behavior, and competitive strategies with a granularity that was previously unattainable.

In Market Research, AI and data analytics can streamline the collection and analysis of consumer sentiment, preferences, and feedback, whether from social media, surveys, or customer reviews. This data can inform product development, marketing campaigns, and customer targeting strategies. AI can also identify emerging market trends and predict future consumer behavior, aiding in the development of more responsive and proactive business strategies. Furthermore, organizations can gain a competitive edge through AI-powered market segmentation, allowing them to target specific customer groups with personalized products and services. Huang and Rust's (2021) strategic framework for artificial intelligence in marketing, while comprehensive, does not sufficiently address the practical challenges and potential solutions for implementing AI in diverse marketing environments and strategies.

Competitive Intelligence, on the other hand, benefits immensely from AI and data analytics by automating the monitoring and analysis of competitors' activities. AI-driven web scraping and data mining can track competitor pricing, product launches, marketing initiatives, and customer reviews. This real-time intelligence enables organizations to adapt their strategies, stay ahead of the competition, and seize opportunities as they arise. Additionally, AI algorithms can forecast market movements and help businesses position themselves more strategically in the marketplace.

In summary, AI and data analytics have redefined the landscape of Market Research and Competitive Intelligence by offering a data-driven, real-time, and predictive approach to decision-making. Organizations that embrace these technologies gain a more profound understanding of market trends, consumer behavior, and competitive dynamics, ultimately enhancing their ability to make informed, agile, and strategic decisions in an increasingly dynamic business environment.

PREDICTIVE ANALYTICS

Predictive analytics is a powerful tool for market research and competitive intelligence, enabling businesses to anticipate future trends, forecast customer behavior, and optimize sales and demand strategies. Predictive analytics, bolstered by AI and Data Analytics, has become an indispensable tool for Market Research and Competitive Intelligence. This approach leverages historical data, statistical algorithms, and machine learning to uncover hidden patterns and make informed predictions about future market trends, consumer behavior, and competitive strategies. In Market Research, predictive analytics allows businesses to anticipate demand, optimize pricing strategies, and tailor marketing campaigns. By analyzing past data, including sales figures, customer reviews, and website traffic, organizations can forecast market trends and understand the factors influencing their products or services' success. Machine learning models can predict customer churn, helping businesses retain valuable clients and boost profitability.

Moreover, predictive analytics enables dynamic customer segmentation, providing personalized recommendations and content to enhance user experiences. In the realm of Competitive Intelligence, predictive analytics empowers organizations to anticipate and respond to their competitors' moves effectively. By monitoring competitors' historical data, such as pricing changes, product launches, or market positioning, businesses can build predictive models that reveal future competitor strategies. This insight allows companies to proactively adjust their own tactics and maintain a competitive edge. Sentiment analysis powered by AI reveals how competitors are perceived by the public, helping organizations identify potential vulnerabilities or strengths in the market. Tamang et al.'s (2021) study on improving business intelligence through machine learning algorithms, while technically sound, lacks a thorough discussion on the potential trade-offs between the complexity of machine learning algorithms and the interpretability of their results, which are crucial considerations in business intelligence.

The advantages of predictive analytics extend to data collection and interpretation, streamlining the data-driven decision-making process. AI algorithms can automatically collect and process data from various sources, including websites, social media, IoT devices, and sensor data. These algorithms accelerate data cleansing and integration, reducing the time and resources required for these critical tasks. Furthermore, AI-driven predictive analytics can uncover nuanced trends and outliers that might be challenging to detect through conventional methods, providing a more accurate and comprehensive view of the market landscape.

In summary, predictive analytics, supercharged by AI and Data Analytics, is a game-changer for Market Research and Competitive Intelligence. Its ability to forecast market trends, consumer behavior, and competitive moves empowers organizations to make data-driven decisions, stay ahead of the competition, and unlock new growth opportunities. As technology advances, the role of predictive analytics is set to become even more critical, reshaping the way businesses strategize and thrive in an increasingly competitive and data-driven landscape.

Case Studies in Predictive Analytics

Case Study 1 - Retail Sales: A retail chain employs predictive analytics to optimize inventory levels. By analyzing historical sales data and external factors (e.g., holidays, weather), the company predicts demand at each store location. This enables them to reduce excess inventory and stock products more efficiently, resulting in cost savings.

Case Study 2 - Customer Churn Prediction: A telecommunications provider uses predictive analytics to identify customers at risk of churning. By analyzing usage patterns, customer service interactions, and billing data, the company predicts which customers are likely to cancel their services. They can then proactively offer incentives to retain these customers.

Case Study 3 - Financial Market Forecasting: A financial institution employs predictive modeling to forecast stock market trends. By analyzing historical market data, news sentiment, and economic indicators, the institution develops models that predict market movements. Traders use these insights for investment decisions.

Case Study 4 - Demand Forecasting in Manufacturing: A manufacturing company uses predictive analytics to optimize production schedules. By considering historical production data, order volumes, and lead times, the company creates a demand forecasting model. This allows them to schedule production more efficiently, reduce costs, and minimize lead times.

Predictive analytics empowers businesses to make data-driven decisions, enhance customer experiences, and gain a competitive edge. By leveraging historical and real-time data, organizations can better understand their markets, customers, and operations, ultimately driving growth and profitability.

COMPETITIVE INTELLIGENCE AND AI

Competitive Intelligence (CI) refers to the process of collecting, analyzing, and leveraging information about competitors, market trends, and industry developments to gain a strategic advantage in business. It involves systematically gathering data from various sources, including competitors' activities, market research, public information, and more, to make informed decisions and stay ahead in a competitive landscape.

The Role of AI in Competitive Intelligence

Competitive Intelligence (CI) refers to the process of collecting, analyzing, and leveraging information about competitors, market trends, and industry developments to gain a strategic advantage in business. It involves systematically gathering data from various sources, including competitors' activities, market research, public information, and more, to make informed decisions and stay ahead in a competitive landscape.

Artificial Intelligence (AI), on the other hand, involves the development of computer systems that can perform tasks that typically require human intelligence, such as understanding natural language, recognizing patterns, making predictions, and learning from data.

The role of AI in Competitive Intelligence is transformative and impactful in several ways:

a. Automated Data Collection: AI-powered tools can automatically collect data from a wide range of sources, including websites, social media, news articles, and financial reports. This automation speeds up the data gathering process and ensures that organizations have access to the latest information.
b. Advanced Analytics: AI algorithms can analyze vast datasets much faster and more accurately than humans. They can identify patterns, trends, and anomalies in data that might be missed by human analysts. This leads to deeper insights into market dynamics and competitor behavior.
c. Predictive Analytics: AI enables predictive modeling, which helps organizations forecast market trends, customer preferences, and competitive strategies. By analyzing historical data, AI can provide valuable predictions about future developments.
d. Natural Language Processing (NLP): AI-driven NLP tools can parse and understand unstructured text data from sources like customer reviews, social media comments, and news articles. This helps organizations gauge public sentiment, track brand mentions, and assess competitor sentiment.
e. Competitor Monitoring: AI can continuously monitor competitors' digital footprints, identifying changes in pricing, product offerings, marketing strategies, and customer reviews in real-time. This proactive monitoring ensures that organizations can respond swiftly to competitive threats or opportunities.

Competitive Analysis With AI

Competitive analysis is a critical component of competitive intelligence (CI) that involves assessing and understanding the strengths, weaknesses, strategies, and market positioning of competitors. The integration of Artificial Intelligence (AI) into competitive analysis brings several advantages:

a. Data Aggregation and Processing: AI tools can automatically collect and process large volumes of data from diverse sources. This includes competitor websites, social media, financial reports, news articles, and customer reviews. AI can aggregate this information into a structured format for analysis.
b. Market Scanning: AI-driven algorithms can continuously scan the market to identify emerging competitors or new entrants. This proactive monitoring helps organizations stay ahead of potential threats.
c. Competitor Profiling: AI can create comprehensive profiles of competitors by analyzing historical data, financial performance, product catalogs, and customer sentiment. These profiles provide a holistic view of each competitor.
d. Pricing Analysis: AI can track competitors' pricing strategies in real-time, allowing organizations to adjust their own pricing strategies for competitiveness.
e. Product and Service Comparison: AI can compare the features, quality, and performance of competitors' products or services against those of the organization. This helps in identifying gaps and opportunities for improvement.

Tracking Competitor Strategies

Tracking competitor strategies is a fundamental aspect of competitive intelligence (CI) that has been greatly enhanced by the integration of Artificial Intelligence (AI). AI-driven tools and techniques offer several advantages in monitoring and understanding the strategies employed by competitors:

a. Data Collection at Scale: AI can automatically collect vast amounts of data from various sources, including competitors' websites, social media, press releases, and financial reports. This data is then processed and structured for analysis.
b. Real-time Monitoring: AI tools can provide real-time or near-real-time updates on competitor activities. This includes tracking changes to their websites, product launches, marketing campaigns, and social media engagement.
c. Pattern Recognition: AI algorithms can identify patterns in competitor behavior over time. This helps in recognizing recurring strategies, such as seasonal promotions or product release cycles.
d. Competitor Benchmarking: AI can assist in benchmarking a company's performance against that of its competitors. This involves comparing key performance indicators (KPIs) such as market share, revenue growth, and customer satisfaction.
e. Market Entry and Expansion Analysis: AI can detect when a competitor enters a new market or expands its operations. It can also assess the success of these endeavors by analyzing market-specific data.

Figure 6. Tracking competitor strategies using AI

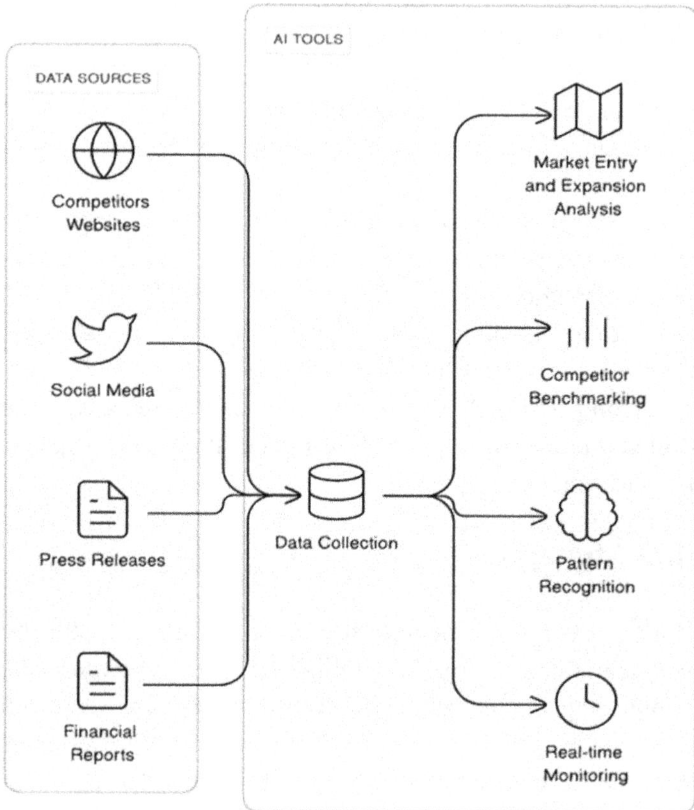

ETHICAL CONSIDERATIONS AND CHALLENGES

Ethical Considerations in AI and Data Analytics

Ethical considerations in AI and Data Analytics are paramount as these technologies wield substantial influence over individuals, societies, and businesses. The increasing use of AI and data analytics raises concerns related to privacy, bias, transparency, and accountability. The collection and processing of vast amounts of personal data for analytics purposes necessitate robust measures to safeguard individual privacy. Striking a balance between data utilization for insights and the protection of personal information becomes crucial to avoid breaches of confidentiality. Bias in algorithms is a pervasive ethical challenge, as machine learning models can inherit biases present in training data, potentially leading to discriminatory outcomes. Efforts to mitigate bias involve careful selection and preprocessing of training data, ongoing monitoring, and the incorporation of fairness metrics in model evaluation.

Transparency in AI and data analytics processes is vital for building trust. Understanding how algorithms make decisions is crucial for users and stakeholders. Explainable AI (XAI) techniques aim to demystify complex models, providing insights into their decision-making processes. Accountability is another key ethical consideration. As AI systems make increasingly impactful decisions, establishing clear lines of responsibility for their outcomes becomes essential. Ethical guidelines and frameworks, such as those developed by organizations like the IEEE or ACM, can provide a foundation for responsible AI development and deployment. Regular audits, assessments, and adherence to ethical standards contribute to maintaining accountability.

Additionally, the ethical use of AI and data analytics involves informed consent and transparency with individuals whose data is utilized. Clear communication regarding data usage, the purposes of analytics, and the potential impact on individuals is essential. Ongoing education and awareness programs for data professionals, AI developers, and decision-makers ensure a culture of ethical responsibility. As AI and data analytics continue to evolve, a commitment to ethical principles becomes instrumental in harnessing the transformative power of these technologies responsibly and for the benefit of society as a whole.

Bias and Fairness in Data Analysis

Bias and fairness in data analysis are critical considerations as they directly impact the integrity and ethicality of insights derived from datasets. Bias can manifest at various stages of the data analysis process, from data collection to model training and interpretation of results. It refers to systematic errors or prejudices in the data that may lead to skewed or inaccurate conclusions. Biases can emerge due to historical disparities, cultural influences, or unintentional sampling errors. One notable area where bias often arises is in the selection of training data for machine learning models, leading to biased algorithms that perpetuate and potentially exacerbate existing inequalities.

Addressing bias requires a comprehensive and conscious approach. During data collection, efforts should be made to ensure representative sampling, avoiding underrepresentation or exclusion of certain groups. In machine learning, techniques such as re-sampling, data augmentation, and fairness-aware algorithms can be employed to mitigate bias. Regular audits and evaluations of models for disparate impacts on different demographic groups are essential. It's crucial to consider not only the fairness of the model's predictions but also the interpretability of those predictions to ensure transparency.

Fairness in data analysis extends beyond eliminating bias and involves ensuring that the benefits and impacts of data-driven decisions are distributed equitably. Adopting fairness metrics and frameworks, such as demographic parity or equalized odds, facilitates the quantitative assessment of fairness in algorithmic outcomes. Ethical considerations demand that data analysts actively engage in ongoing dialogue about potential biases, their implications, and strategies for promoting fairness. Transparency in the data analysis process, open communication about limitations and potential biases, and involving diverse perspectives in decision-making are essential steps toward achieving fairness in data analysis and building trust in the outcomes of data-driven systems.

IMPLEMENTING AI AND DATA ANALYTICS IN BUSINESS

Building AI-Driven Teams

Implementing AI and Data Analytics in business necessitates the development of AI-driven teams that combine domain expertise with technical proficiency to maximize the potential of these transformative technologies. Building such teams involves assembling a diverse group of professionals, including data scientists, machine learning engineers, domain experts, and data engineers. Data scientists play a central role in extracting actionable insights from vast datasets, requiring expertise in statistical analysis, data modeling, and algorithm development. Machine learning engineers focus on deploying and optimizing machine learning models, ensuring they integrate seamlessly into business processes. Domain experts, possessing a deep understanding of the industry context, contribute crucial insights that guide the application of AI to real-world challenges. Data engineers are instrumental in managing and structuring data, ensuring its quality, and creating the necessary infrastructure for AI applications.

Fostering collaboration and communication between these team members is paramount. Cross-disciplinary teamwork facilitates the alignment of AI initiatives with organizational goals and enhances the contextual relevance of data-driven insights. Continuous learning and professional development are crucial for team members to stay abreast of evolving technologies and industry trends. Organizations should invest in training programs and create an environment that encourages experimentation and innovation. Establishing a culture that values diversity, both in terms of skill sets and perspectives, enriches problem-solving approaches and fosters creativity.

Effective leadership plays a pivotal role in steering AI-driven teams toward success. Leaders should possess a nuanced understanding of AI technologies, a strategic vision for their application, and the ability to articulate the business value of AI initiatives. By building collaborative, well-rounded, and adaptable teams, organizations can successfully integrate AI and Data Analytics into their business strategies, unlocking new opportunities for innovation, efficiency, and informed decision-making.

Tools and Platforms for Market Research

Market research relies on a variety of tools and platforms to gather, analyze, and interpret data efficiently. Here are some widely used tools and platforms for market research:

1. SurveyMonkey: SurveyMonkey is a versatile online survey tool that allows businesses to create and distribute surveys to collect valuable feedback and insights from their target audience. It offers a range of survey types and analytics features.
2. Google Analytics: Google Analytics is a web analytics service that provides in-depth information about website traffic, user behavior, and conversion data. It helps businesses understand how users interact with their online platforms.
3. Social Media Analytics Tools (e.g., Hootsuite, Sprout Social): Social media analytics tools help businesses monitor and analyze their social media presence. These tools provide metrics on engagement, reach, and audience demographics, offering valuable insights for market research.
4. SEMrush: SEMrush is a comprehensive marketing toolkit that includes features for SEO (Search Engine Optimization), content marketing, competitive analysis, and advertising research. It helps businesses understand their online visibility and performance.
5. Statista: Statista is a statistical data platform that offers a wide range of industry reports, statistics, and infographics. It's a valuable resource for gathering quantitative data and market trends.
6. Google Trends: Google Trends provides insights into the popularity of search queries over time. It helps businesses understand the relative interest in specific topics and identify emerging trends.
7. Qualtrics: Qualtrics is an experience management platform that offers solutions for survey research, customer feedback, and market segmentation. It provides advanced analytics and reporting features.
8. Ahrefs: Ahrefs is a powerful tool for SEO analysis, providing insights into competitors' search strategies, backlink profiles, and keyword rankings. It can be useful for understanding the online presence of competitors.

9. ZoomInfo: ZoomInfo is a B2B contact database that provides accurate and up-to-date information on businesses and professionals. It helps businesses identify and reach their target audience for marketing and sales purposes.
10. FocusVision: FocusVision offers market research solutions, including online survey tools and qualitative research platforms. It enables businesses to conduct online focus groups, interviews, and usability testing.

These tools and platforms cater to different aspects of market research, from collecting primary data through surveys to analyzing competitors and monitoring online presence. The selection of tools depends on the specific research objectives and the nature of the data needed.

Integrating AI Into Competitive Intelligence

Integrating Artificial Intelligence (AI) into Competitive Intelligence represents a revolutionary leap in the efficiency and depth of strategic analysis for businesses. AI augments traditional competitive intelligence methods by automating data collection, processing vast amounts of information, and uncovering patterns that might elude manual analysis. Machine learning algorithms excel at detecting anomalies and predicting market trends based on historical data, providing organizations with proactive insights. Natural Language Processing (NLP) capabilities enable AI to sift through a myriad of textual sources, including news articles, social media, and industry reports, distilling relevant information about competitors' activities and market dynamics. Sentiment analysis powered by AI discerns public perceptions, gauging the impact of competitors' strategies on consumer sentiments. Predictive analytics, a key facet of AI in competitive intelligence, forecasts potential future moves by competitors, facilitating strategic decision-making. Vashishth et al.'s (2023) comparative analysis of the evolution of AI and its transformative effects on computing, while comprehensive, does not sufficiently address the practical challenges and potential solutions for implementing these developments in diverse computing environments.

Furthermore, AI-driven competitive intelligence is not limited to structured data but extends to unstructured data sources such as multimedia content. Computer vision algorithms can analyze visual content, including competitor advertisements, product packaging, and even sentiments conveyed in images. The integration of AI not only enhances the speed and accuracy of information processing but also allows for continuous learning and adaptation, ensuring that competitive intelligence efforts remain agile in dynamic markets. As businesses navigate increasingly complex competitive landscapes, leveraging AI in competitive intelligence empowers organizations to stay ahead of the curve, anticipate market shifts, and make well-informed decisions to gain a competitive edge.

Measuring the Impact of AI

Key Performance Indicators (KPIs): Define KPIs to measure the impact of AI and data analytics initiatives. These might include improved customer satisfaction, increased revenue, or reduced operational costs.

A/B Testing: Conduct A/B tests to assess the effectiveness of AI-driven marketing campaigns, product recommendations, or pricing strategies.

Customer Feedback: Gather and analyze customer feedback to understand how AI-driven solutions are perceived and make necessary adjustments.

ROI Analysis: Calculate the return on investment (ROI) for AI projects by comparing the costs and benefits generated by AI implementations.

FUTURE TRENDS IN AI AND DATA ANALYTICS

Future Trends in AI and Data Analytics are shaping the landscape of Market Research and Competitive Intelligence. Here are some emerging trends and future directions:

Emerging Trends in AI and Data Analytics

Emerging trends in Artificial Intelligence (AI) and Data Analytics are reshaping the landscape of industries, offering unprecedented opportunities and challenges. One significant trend is the increasing integration of AI with edge computing, enabling real-time processing of data closer to the source, reducing latency, and enhancing efficiency. Federated learning has gained prominence, allowing AI models to be trained across decentralized devices without compromising data privacy. The fusion of AI and the Internet of Things (IoT) is creating intelligent, interconnected systems capable of autonomously collecting, analyzing, and acting upon vast amounts of data. Explainable AI (XAI) is becoming crucial for transparency and accountability, ensuring that AI models provide comprehensible insights and decisions. Quantum computing is on the horizon, promising exponential improvements in data processing speed and capability, revolutionizing complex problem-solving in AI and data analytics.

In data analytics, there is a growing emphasis on Augmented Analytics, leveraging machine learning to automate data preparation, insight discovery, and sharing within organizations. The rise of DataOps practices is streamlining data management, ensuring more agile and collaborative approaches to analytics. Automated machine learning (AutoML) is democratizing the use of AI models, allowing users with varying technical expertise to create and deploy machine learning models without extensive coding requirements. Ethical AI and Responsible AI frameworks are gaining traction, with a focus on mitigating biases, ensuring fairness, and fostering ethical considerations in the development and deployment of AI and analytics solutions.

The proliferation of Natural Language Processing (NLP) is enhancing the ability of systems to understand and generate human-like text, enabling applications such as sentiment analysis, language translation, and chatbots. Continuous advancements in AI explainability, quantum computing, data governance, and ethical considerations are at the forefront of shaping a future where AI and data analytics play increasingly pivotal roles across diverse sectors, influencing decision-making, innovation, and the overall evolution of technology.

Future Directions for Market Research and Competitive Intelligence

Future directions for Market Research and Competitive Intelligence are poised to undergo transformative shifts driven by technological advancements, evolving consumer behaviors, and the dynamic business landscape. Artificial Intelligence (AI) and machine learning will play a central role, automating data collection, analysis, and interpretation, enabling faster and more accurate insights. Predictive analytics will become more sophisticated, allowing organizations to anticipate market trends, consumer preferences, and competitive moves with higher precision. Augmented Reality (AR) and Virtual Reality (VR) might

Figure 7. Future trends in AI and data analytics are shaping the landscape of market research

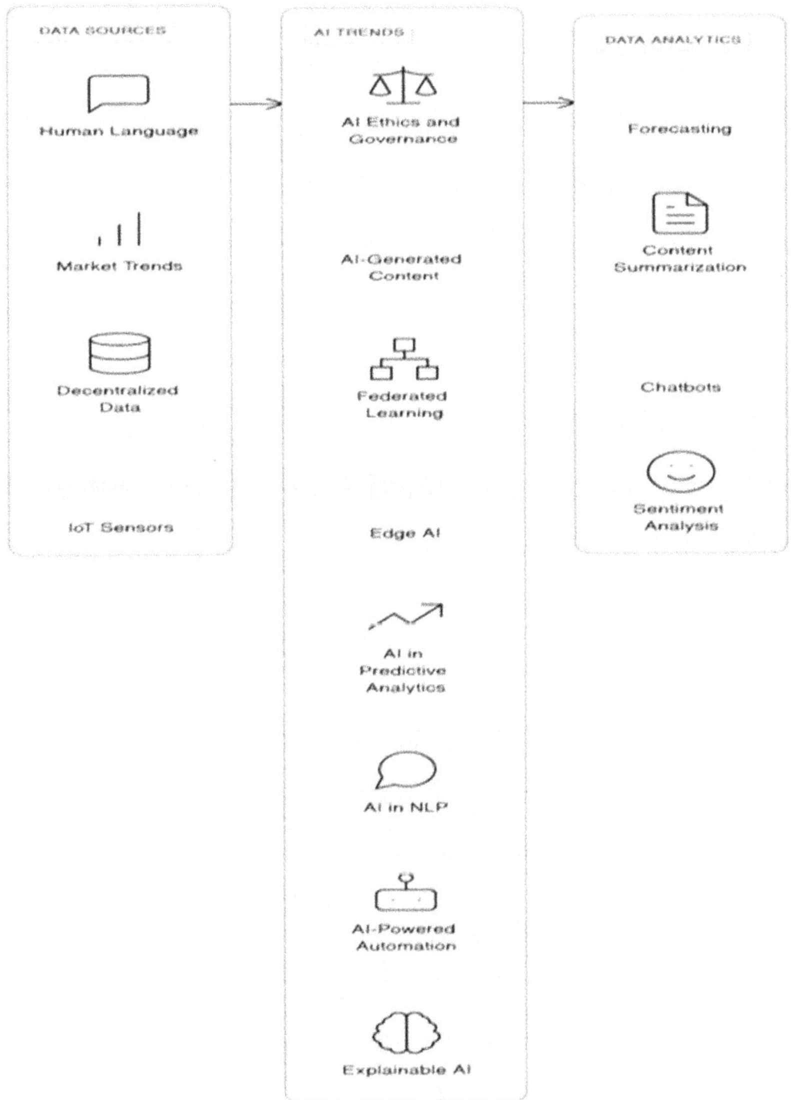

revolutionize how researchers gather consumer feedback and conduct immersive market studies. The integration of blockchain technology is anticipated to enhance data security and transparency in market research processes, ensuring the integrity of collected data. Advanced sentiment analysis powered by Natural Language Processing (NLP) will enable a deeper understanding of consumer sentiments expressed across various channels, including social media and online forums. Mobile-driven research methodologies will become increasingly prevalent, capturing real-time data and enabling location-based insights.

In terms of Competitive Intelligence, the focus will shift towards real-time monitoring of competitors' activities, leveraging AI-driven tools to track market moves, product launches, and strategic shifts. Social media and open-source intelligence will gain prominence as valuable sources for understanding competitors' strategies and customer interactions. Emphasis on ethical considerations and compliance with data privacy regulations will shape the future of competitive intelligence, ensuring responsible and lawful practices in information gathering. Collaborative platforms and knowledge-sharing networks will facilitate a more holistic understanding of competitive landscapes, fostering a collective intelligence approach.

The convergence of these trends will lead to a more agile, data-driven, and ethically grounded approach to market research and competitive intelligence. Organizations that embrace these future directions will be better equipped to navigate the complexities of rapidly changing markets, gain a competitive edge, and foster innovation in their respective industries.

CONCLUSION

In conclusion, AI and Data Analytics have ushered in a transformative era for Market Research and Competitive Intelligence. These technologies have empowered organizations to navigate the complexities of the modern business landscape with unprecedented precision, efficiency, and agility. As we reflect on the myriad ways in which AI and Data Analytics have reshaped these domains, several key takeaways emerge. First and foremost, the ability to harness and analyze vast volumes of data, both structured and unstructured, has opened up new frontiers in Market Research and Competitive Intelligence. AI-powered analytics has made it possible to collect, clean, and process data at an unprecedented scale, enabling organizations to derive actionable insights from data sources that were once too overwhelming to harness effectively. This has resulted in more informed decision-making, better-informed strategies, and a deeper understanding of market dynamics and consumer behavior.

AI-driven predictive analytics, in particular, has revolutionized the way businesses anticipate trends, forecast demand, and optimize pricing strategies. It has equipped organizations with the ability to adapt to changing market conditions proactively, thus gaining a competitive advantage. The real-time monitoring of competitors, made possible by AI, has elevated Competitive Intelligence to a new level, enabling businesses to react swiftly to rival strategies and market shifts. Moreover, the emergence of explainable AI and the focus on ethical considerations and bias mitigation underscore the importance of responsible AI applications in Market Research and Competitive Intelligence. These developments serve to enhance transparency and build trust, critical in an era where data privacy and fairness are paramount concerns. Looking forward, the future of AI and Data Analytics in Market Research and Competitive Intelligence holds even more promise. As technology advances, we can expect increased automation, greater integration of AI with everyday business operations, and a deeper reliance on AI for decision support. The utilization of AI in edge computing, quantum machine learning, and federated learning are all on the horizon, promising further innovation and efficiency in data analytics.

AI and Data Analytics have redefined the rules of engagement in Market Research and Competitive Intelligence. The ability to extract actionable insights from data has become a competitive advantage in its own right. The embrace of these technologies, along with ethical considerations and responsible practices, is crucial for organizations seeking not only to survive but to thrive in an ever-evolving and data-centric business landscape. The path forward in Market Research and Competitive Intelligence is clear: harness the power of AI and Data Analytics, maintain a commitment to responsible and ethical practices, and remain agile in adapting to the ongoing technological advancements that continue to shape these domains.

REFERENCES

Al-Okaily, A., Teoh, A. P., & Al-Okaily, M. (2023). Evaluation of data analytics-oriented business intelligence technology effectiveness: An enterprise-level analysis. *Business Process Management Journal, 29*(3), 777–800. doi:10.1108/BPMJ-10-2022-0546

Alghamdi, N. A., & Al-Baity, H. H. (2022). Augmented Analytics Driven by AI: A Digital Transformation beyond Business Intelligence. *Sensors (Basel), 22*(20), 8071. doi:10.3390/s22208071 PMID:36298421

Asare, A. O., Addo, P. C., Sarpong, E. O., & Kotei, D. (2020). COVID-19: Optimizing business performance through agile business intelligence and data analytics. *Open Journal of Business and Management, 8*(5), 2071–2080. doi:10.4236/ojbm.2020.85126

Awan, U., Kanwal, N., Alawi, S., Huiskonen, J., & Dahanayake, A. (2021). Artificial intelligence for supply chain success in the era of data analytics. *The fourth industrial revolution: Implementation of artificial intelligence for growing business success,* 3-21. doi:10.1007/978-3-030-62796-6_1

Bharadiya, J. P. (2023). A Comparative Study of Business Intelligence and Artificial Intelligence with Big Data Analytics. *American Journal of Artificial Intelligence, 7*(1), 24. doi:10.11648/j.ajai.20230701.14

Chintalapati, S., & Pandey, S. K. (2022). Artificial intelligence in marketing: A systematic literature review. *International Journal of Market Research, 64*(1), 38–68. doi:10.1177/14707853211018428

Davenport, T., Guha, A., Grewal, D., & Bressgott, T. (2020). How artificial intelligence will change the future of marketing. *Journal of the Academy of Marketing Science, 48*(1), 24–42. doi:10.1007/s11747-019-00696-0

Huang, M. H., & Rust, R. T. (2021). A strategic framework for artificial intelligence in marketing. *Journal of the Academy of Marketing Science, 49*(1), 30–50. doi:10.1007/s11747-020-00749-9

Jayawardena, N. S., Behl, A., Thaichon, P., & Quach, S. (2022). Artificial intelligence (AI)-based market intelligence and customer insights. *Artificial intelligence for marketing management*, 120-141.

Kumar, V., Rajan, B., Venkatesan, R., & Lecinski, J. (2019). Understanding the role of artificial intelligence in personalized engagement marketing. *California Management Review, 61*(4), 135–155. doi:10.1177/0008125619859317

Ranjan, J., & Foropon, C. (2021). Big data analytics in building the competitive intelligence of organizations. *International Journal of Information Management, 56*, 102231. doi:10.1016/j.ijinfomgt.2020.102231

Sun, W., Nan, Y., Yang, T. Z., Hu, X. Y., & Jiang, Y. (2021). Integration Innovation of Competitive Intelligence, AI and Big Data Analysis. In *Advances in Artificial Intelligence and Security: 7th International Conference, ICAIS 2021*, (pp. 347-357). Springer International Publishing. 10.1007/978-3-030-78621-2_28

Tamang, M. D., Shukla, V. K., Anwar, S., & Punhani, R. (2021, April). Improving business intelligence through machine learning algorithms. In *2021 2nd International Conference on Intelligent Engineering and Management (ICIEM)* (pp. 63-68). IEEE. 10.1109/ICIEM51511.2021.9445344

Vashishth, T. K., Kumar, B., Sharma, V., Chaudhary, S., Kumar, S., & Sharma, K. K. (2023). The Evolution of AI and Its Transformative Effects on Computing: A Comparative Analysis. In *Intelligent Engineering Applications and Applied Sciences for Sustainability* (pp. 425–442). IGI Global. doi:10.4018/979-8-3693-0044-2.ch022

Vashishth, T. K., Sharma, V., Chaudhary, S., Panwar, R., Sharma, S., & Kumar, P. (2023). Advanced Technologies and AI-Enabled IoT Applications in High-Tech Agriculture. In Handbook of Research on AI-Equipped IoT Applications in High-Tech Agriculture (pp. 155-166). IGI Global.

Wu, Q., Yan, D., & Umair, M. (2023). Assessing the role of competitive intelligence and practices of dynamic capabilities in business accommodation of SMEs. *Economic Analysis and Policy*, *77*, 1103–1114. doi:10.1016/j.eap.2022.11.024

Zohuri, B., & Moghaddam, M. (2020). *From business intelligence to artificial intelligence. Journal of Material Sciences & Manufacturing Research.* SRC/JMSMR.

KEY TERMS AND DEFINITIONS

Artificial Intelligence (AI): This refers to the development of computer systems that can perform tasks that typically require human intelligence, such as learning, problem-solving, decision-making, and natural language understanding.

Deep Learning: Deep learning is a subfield of machine learning that focuses on teaching computers to learn and make decisions in a way inspired by the human brain. It uses artificial neural networks, which are computational models composed of interconnected nodes called “neurons.” These neural networks are structured in multiple layers, hence the term “deep” learning.

Internet of Things (IoT): The Internet of Things (IoT) is a concept that refers to the connection of everyday objects to the internet, allowing them to send and receive data. These objects can include devices like smartphones, thermostats, wearables, home appliances, and even vehicles. The idea behind IoT is to create a network where these objects can communicate with each other, collect and share data, and perform tasks more efficiently.

Natural Language Processing (NLP): Natural Language Processing (NLP) is a branch of artificial intelligence that focuses on enabling computers to understand, interpret, and interact with human language in a natural and meaningful way. NLP involves the development of algorithms and models that allow computers to process, analyze, and generate human language.

Chapter 9
Artificial Intelligence in Chess-Playing Automata:
A Paradigm for the Quiescence Phase of a-ß Search

Stephen F. Wheeler
University of North Texas, USA

ABSTRACT

This chapter presents the results of a study for improving the performance of the quiescence phase of Alpha-Beta (α-β) search. The Minimax algorithm's α-β enhancement enhances depth-first search performance by optimizing solutions in near best-first order, thereby reducing the computational effort from $O(b^d)$ to $O(\sqrt{b^d})$ where b is the branching factor of the game-tree and d is the depth of the search. This research uses a full breath search to delay the asymptotic behavior of the combinatorial explosion to five levels of depth. A narrow width search involves expanding solutions involving material exchange, pawn promotion, or king-in-check until the position reaches quiescence without any material exchanges or promotions. When quiescence is reached, the evaluation function scores the leaf nodes of the game-tree. This chapter's research shows that α-β pruning is enhanced when a solution without material exchange or promotion is attempted first during the quiescence phase of α-β search which applies to chess playing programs as well.

INTRODUCTION

In 1944, mathematician, physicist, and computer scientist, John von Neumann in collaboration with an economist, Oskar Morgenstern, authored their seminal work, "Theory of Games and Economic Behavior" (Neumann & Morgenstern, 1947). Together they conceived a revolutionary mathematical theory of economic and social organization based on a theory of games of strategy. Not only would this theorem revolutionize economics, but it would give rise to an entirely new field of scientific inquiry known as Game Theory and the Minimax Theorem.

DOI: 10.4018/979-8-3693-1058-8.ch009

Claude E. Shannon, an MIT mathematician and Bell Labs researcher is regarded as the founder of information theory and the father of computer chess, applied this principle in a paper he published in 1950 titled "Programming a Computer for Playing Chess" (Shannon, 1950). By applying game theory to the chess problem he identified the principles that form the essence of today's chess playing programs. Since the publication of Shannon's paper, programming a computer for playing chess has moved from a conceptual framework to one of the early cornerstones of artificial intelligence research. Chess was then and is now the Drosophila Melanogaster (fruit fly) of Artificial Intelligence research.

John Nash introduced the idea of Nash equilibrium, a key concept in game theory in his paper in the 1950's. Economists predict the results of strategic interactions based on this theory. Nash Equilibrium is a set of actions, one for each decision maker, where each action is the best for that decision maker considering the actions of others. As no decision maker has any incentive to change his course of action, this list of actions forms equilibrium. The work of Nash has had a major impact on economics. In addition to revolutionizing economics, Nash's work had a major influence on various fields including computer science, political science, sociology and biology. He was awarded the Nobel Prize in 1994 for his work in game theory.

MODIFICATION OF GAME THEORY BY THE NASH EQUILIBRIUM

Prior to Nash's equilibrium, game theory was primarily focused on cooperative games in which players could communicate and form binding agreements. John Nash contributed to the field of non-cooperative games in which players cannot communicate and must make their decision only on what they anticipate other players will do. This highlights the fact that the outcome of a player's decision not only depends on their own actions but also on the actions of other players. This allowed researchers to analyze strategic interactions in the real world such as political campaigns, business deals and evolutionary biology and predict how rational players will behave in such situations.

Nash equilibrium modified many real-world situations in a way that made it possible to simulate realistic models. Not every interaction is zero-sum (purely competitive), where one player's gain is directly proportional to another player's loss. Cooperation and mutual gain are possible, and Nash equilibrium helps capture these situations accurately.

The book and movie "A Beautiful Mind," highlights John Nash's contributions to game theory, and helped to publicize his work. His idea of equilibrium became a pillar in the study of strategic interactions of decision makers, in a number of fields like economics, political science, sociology and biology.

THE PRISONER'S DILEMMA

The Prisoner's Dilemma is a well-known illustration of Nash Equilibrium in game theory in which two people are arrested for the commission of a crime and each one is given a choice by the prosecutor: confess to the crime that they both committed in exchange for more moderate sentence for both or betray the other by keeping quiet. The incentives are such that if either betrays the other, they will both face a severe punishment. If one betrays the other while the other keeps silent, the betrayer is let off while the silent person is given a harsh punishment. If neither speaks, they will each receive a moderate punishment.

The problem occurs because each prisoner must choose between putting their faith in the other to keep quiet (cooperate) or give up on the other (defect). Regardless of what the other does, from an individual perspective, betrayal is a powerful tactic. One prisoner will betray the other if they both assume the other will keep quiet (cooperate). Betrayal also lessens the penalty if one anticipates the other will do so. Because of this, it happens frequently that both convicts wind up betraying one another, which results in a less favorable outcome for both, than if they had both remained silent.

When both players decide on their optimal course of action given the other player's strategy in the Prisoner's Dilemma, the Nash Equilibrium develops. So, in this scenario both prisoners remaining silent results in the Nash Equilibrium as both receive moderate punishment.

MINIMAX SEARCH, THE ESSENCE OF APPLIED GAME THEORY

The Minimax Theorem is the algorithmic realization of Game Theory in two-player, zero-sum games of perfect information, such as chess. In the Minimax theorem, the two players are Min and Max. The algorithmic realization of Minimax requires a Minimizer and a Maximizer. The Minimizer returns the minimum of the values produced by the Maximizer and passes that value one level up the game-tree toward the root node of the game-tree, if that value is less than the value previously passed up one level of the game-tree. The Maximizer, on the other hand, returns the maximum of the values produced by the Minimizer and passes that value one level up the game-tree toward the root node of the game-tree if that value is greater than the value previously passed up the game-tree. This process continues until the best move, from the machine's perspective, has been backed up the game-tree to the root node of the game-tree. Minimax search discovers the Principal Continuation that is the best path through the game-tree from the root node to the leaf node of the game-tree with the best minimax value (Nilsson, 1971). A four ply illustration of a minimax game-tree is shown below (Fig 1) with its backed-up values shown in parentheses.

Figure 1. Minimax game tree above showing branches without pruning provided by α-β

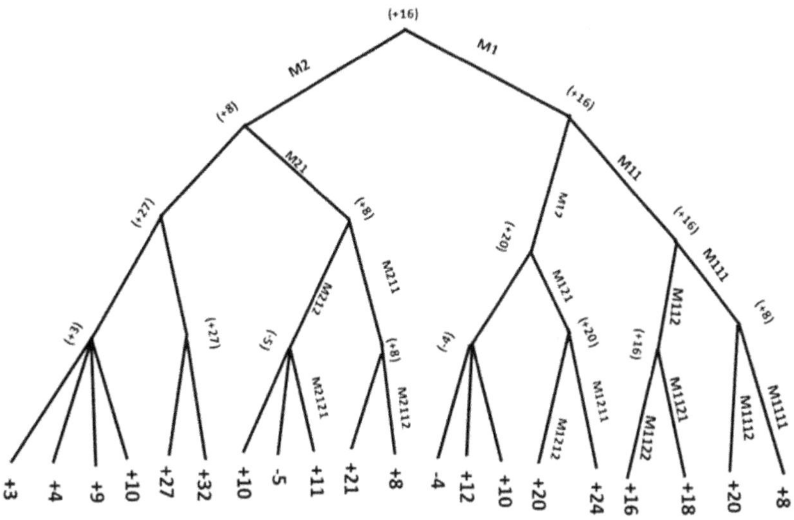

ALPHA-BETA (α-β) ENHANCEMENT TO MINIMAX

The discovery of the α-β extension of minimax search is not clear. Arguably, the most thorough and detailed description of the α-β extension to minimax was described by Donald E. Knuth and Ronald W. Moore of Stanford University who described the algorithm in a paper they published in 1975. Although Knuth and Moore were among the first to describe the algorithm, other researchers included some of the principles of the α-β extension of minimax in their experimental models, including Arthur Samuel of IBM in his checkers playing program (Samuel, 2000).

Without α-β pruning, the minimax game-tree grows exponentially, where b is the branching factor of the game tree and d is the depth of search, where the effort coefficient is described as $O(b^d)$. With α-β enhancement of minimax search, when the game-tree is arranged in near best-first order, the game-tree growth rate is reduced to $O(\sqrt{b^d})$ (Knuth & Moore, 1975). The odd levels of the α-β game-tree including the root node are Alpha (α) nodes. Even levels of the α-β game-tree consist of Beta (β) nodes. Alpha nodes of the game-tree maximize and Beta nodes minimize. During α-β search of the game-tree a node that has a returned value that is less than Alpha or that is greater than Beta will be pruned from the game-tree search as an Alpha or Beta cutoff. Alpha and Beta are dynamic values that when taken together form what is known as the Alpha-Beta window. The α-β window narrows as α-β search progresses and more nodes and branches of the game-tree are pruned whose values fall outside of the narrowing α-β window.

MCTS SEARCH VS. α-β MINIMAX SEARCH

Monte Carlo Tree Search (MCTS) forms the search component of Deep Mind's AlphaZero reinforcement deep machine learning algorithm that was trained to play chess, beating Stockfish 8 in a computer chess match. Independent research, however, has shown that in certain applications α-β search out-performs MCTS (Baier, 2016). The Komodo-MC (Komodo Monte Carlo) chess program, for example, has effectively replaced the α-β search algorithm with the MCTS search algorithm. Komodo-MC plays at Grandmaster level, but not quite as strongly as Komodo with α-β search presently. Komodo's FIDE rating is 3200. Komodo is the world's second highest rated linear symbolic chess-playing computer program. Stockfish 11 at the time of this writing is the highest rated chess program in terms of player strength.

Monte Carlo Tree Search (MCTS) is a probabilistic minimax search variant that expands only the nodes with the highest probability of yielding the greatest gains. It is generally combined with a policy network that proposes moves with a high probability of success. The MCTS paradigm is enhanced by UCT (Upper Confidence bounds applied to Trees) proposed by Levente Kocsis and Csaba Szepesvari in 2006 that accelerates Monte-Carlo Tree Search in games such as chess and go.

HAL (HEURISTIC ASSOCIATIVE LINEAR-ALGORITHM) CHESS-PLAYING AUTOMATA

HAL (Heuristic Associative Linear-algorithm), this author's chess-playing program, has never been officially rated in terms of its player strength. However, in a chess game played between HAL and Komodo on chess.com, Komodo required fifty moves to defeat HAL, and HAL was not playing at its highest level of play (Wheeler, Stephen F, 2010). HAL is a linear symbolic chess playing automata. At its core

Figure 2. Alpha-Beta game tree above showing branches pruned as α and β cutoffs

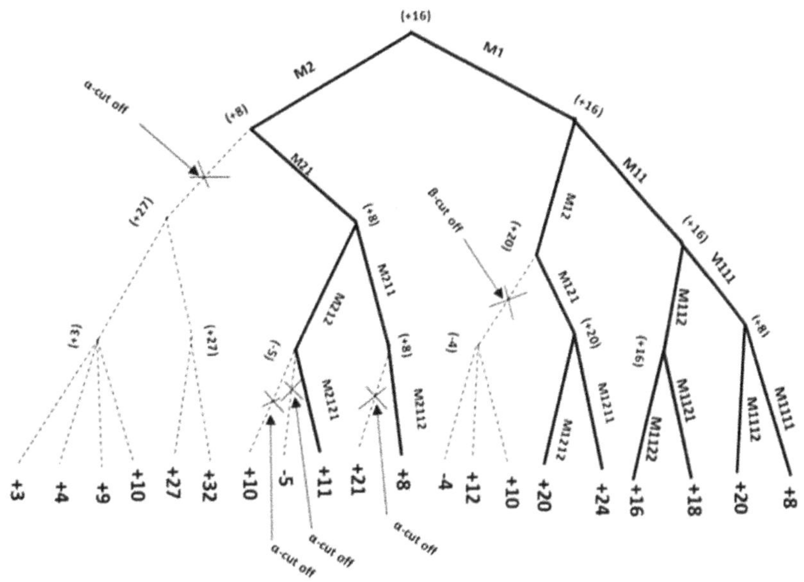

is an iterative-deepening α-β aspiration search variant known as Fail-Soft Negamax. To enhance the performance of α-β search, HAL contains a special enhancement of the quiescence phase of α-β search that optimizes game tree pruning during singular-extension that is the subject of the experimentation reported in this chapter. This enhancement will be discussed in greater detail later in this chapter.

HAL also contains the Killer heuristic consisting of a list of four killer moves at each level of the game tree. A killer move is a move that has caused an alpha-node cutoff or a beta-node cutoff during the pruning of the game tree. When a new node (move) is found in the list of legal moves that matches a move in the killer list it is tried before other moves. The idea is, if the move has caused a branch of the game tree to be pruned previously, it will probably cause game tree pruning to occur for the present level of the game tree in which the matching move occurs. This will cause α-β search to perform more efficient early pruning of irrelevant branches of the game tree allowing a deeper search to occur.

The forward pruning of α-β search cuts-off or prunes branches of a strongly ordered game-tree whose backed-up values fall outside the established α-β search window as illustrated in the graphic (Fig 2) below.

THE NEGAMAX IMPLEMENTATION OF ALPHA-BETA SEARCH

Negamax is a hybridization of the Alpha-Beta (α-β) algorithm. As mentioned earlier, the Alpha-Beta algorithm contains both a maximizer and a minimizer, while the Negamax algorithm contains only a Maximizer (Marsland, 1987). Negamax returns the maximum score for the side whose turn it is to play. The maximum returned score for the opponent player is then negated making the result behave as the value returned by the Minimizer in standard Alpha-Beta search. Hence the name Negamax, is the negative of the maximum returned score. Negamax pruning is identical to Alpha-Beta pruning, but is more easily implemented as a recursive function (Marsland & Campbell, 1982). The Pascal source code logic for the Negamax function of this author's chess program, HAL, follows below.

```
(*                          ALPHA-BETA                       *)
(* NegaMax Fail-Soft Alpha-Beta Function*)
(* Note: in Pascal, P^. is a pointer reference to a variable or data structure
in dynamic memory (the Heap) *)
FUNCTION NFAB(P: POINTER; Alpha, Beta, Depth: INTEGER): INTEGER;
   VAR
         I, Width: INTEGER;
         Score, Value: INTEGER;
         NewPly: POINTER;
   BEGIN
      IF (Depth <= 0) THEN
         BEGIN
       NFAB:= Eval(P)              (* If depth = 0 then score terminal node *)
         END
      ELSE
         BEGIN
            IF (P^.LX > 1) THEN          (* If Level > 1, not a terminal node *)
               BEGIN
                  Width:= Generate(P);   * Generate new branch of Game-Tree *)
                  IF (Width > 0) THEN
                     BEGIN
                        Locate_Refutations(P);
                                 (* Locate Refutations and Killer moves then *)
                        Order(P)
                                (* Sort this branch (level) of the Game-Tree *)
                     END
                  ELSE
                     BEGIN
                        NFAB:= Eval(P)             (* Otherwise call Evaluator *)
                     END
               END;
            Score:= -INF;                         (* set maximizer to low-score *)
            I:= 0;                                   (* initialize move index *)
            NewPly:= Create(P);        (* create a new level of the Game-Tree *)
            REPEAT
               I:= I + 1;                              (* Increment move index *)
               Make(P);              (* make move at P.I then call Alpha-Beta *)
               Value:= -NFAB(NewPly, -Beta, -Max(Alpha, Score),
               Decrement(P, Depth));
               Undo(P);          (* After Alpha-Beta scored move, unmake move *)
               IF (Value > Score) THEN
                          (* If Move is an Improvement, Save Better Score *)
                  BEGIN
                     Score:= Value;                     (* save better score *)
```

```
                  Save_Refutation(P)
                                  (* save better move in refutation table *)
               END;
            (*  Build Refutation Table from Triangular Work Array  *)
            IF (P^.LX = 1) THEN               (* IF first level of Game-Tree *)
               BEGIN
                  Build_Refutation_Table(P)
               END;
         (*  Test for end of Iteration Sequence at Level P^.LX  *)
         UNTIL ((Score >= Beta) OR (I = Width));
         IF ((Score >= Beta) AND (P^.LX > 1)) THEN
            BEGIN
               Save_Killer(P)              (*  Put KILLERS into Killer List  *)
            END;
          Drop(NewPly);                     (* drop new ply of the Game-Tree *)
         NFAB:=    Score                                (* Return best score *)
     END          (*  Back Score up to previous level of the Game-Tree *)
END;                                     (* End of NFAB Alpha-Beta Function *)
```

QUIESCENCE SEARCH EXTENSION OF ALPHA-BETA SEARCH

Quiescence search is a narrow-extended search after the full-width, fixed-depth α-β search reaches its fixed-depth limit. This is known as the search horizon (Figure 3).

Figure 3. Quiescence extension to alpha-beta search

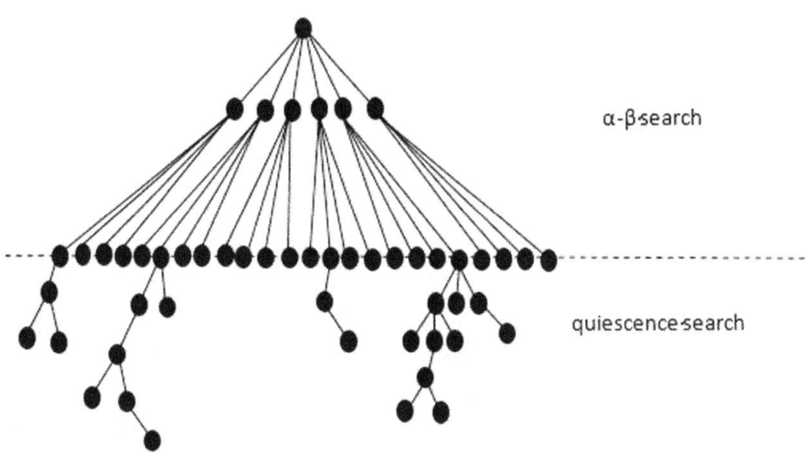

By extending α-β search with a narrow but deep quiescence search, the horizon effect can be addressed and eliminated. The horizon effect refers to a condition occurring when a fixed-depth, exhaustive α-β search ends on a terminal-node that contains an action that might be incomplete without knowing the consequence of that action if the next level of the game tree were known (Berliner, 1974). For example, if the fixed-depth search ends at a terminal-node on the search horizon that is a capture of an opponent's piece, the returned score of the exchange of material might appear to be a good action for the program, but had the search been extended another ply of depth we might discover that the opponent would capture the capturing piece. The net value of the exchange might be less than favorable for the machine. By extending the search with a narrow search until the position becomes quiet where no exchanges occur, the program can avoid the consequences of the horizon effect. This narrow-extended search is known as quiescence search (Marsland & Schaeffer, 1990). In addition to single-ply extensions for capture moves, many implementations of quiescence search also extend for king-in-check situations for one or two additional plys of depth. Some implementations of the quiescence phase of α-β search also extend additional plies of depth when a pawn promotion is present at a terminal-node (Frey, 2012). This author's chess program, HAL, will also extend an additional ply of depth for a capture, pawn promotion or a king-in-check situation.

In this author's chess-playing program, HAL, the quiescence phase of α-β search is managed by a Decrement function that is called as a parameter within the recursive call to the α-β search function, NFAB. In a recursive call to α-β search (NFAB) we must include a reference to a variable that contains a value initially indicating to what depth (number of plies) we wish the full-width fixed-depth α-β search to be performed. If, for example, we wish the program to generate a fixed-depth game-tree of five levels of depth, we would initialize the value of that variable to 5 and decrement it by 1 each time another recursive call to the α-β search function is performed. When the Depth variable is decremented to 0, five levels (or ply) of the game-tree have been generated. At that point the program has reached the terminal-node (leaf node) of that path through the game-tree. An Evaluation function is then called to score the value ascribed to that path through the game-tree.

In this author's chess-playing program, HAL, the depth-limit for recursive calls to the α-β search function is located in an integer variable named Depth. This variable is passed to the Decrement function as an imbedded parameter within the recursive call to the α-β search function NFAB thusly:

Value:= –NFAB(NewPly, –Beta, –Max(Alpha, Score), Decrement(P, Depth));

It should be noted that the initial call to the Alpha-Beta Function NFAB is as follows:

Value:= NFAB(P, Alpha, Beta, Depth);

Where:
NFAB(...) *is the α-β search function*
Value *is the value of the best move returned by α-β NFAB search function*
P is a pointer to the list of legal chess moves for the side whose turn it is to move;
NewPly is the pointer to the new list of legal chess moves for the side whose turn it is to move;
Score *is the value of the best move returned by α-β NFAB search on the previous iteration;*
Alpha is initialized to –maximum integer value (i.e. -infinity);
Beta is initialized to +maximum integer value (i.e. +infinity);

Depth is the desired size of the full-width search.

The Decrement Function

The Decrement function will then decide whether to decrement the Depth variable or not. If the Decrement function does not decrement the Depth variable, then it has found that the move at the terminal-node is a capture, a pawn promotion, or a King-in-check situation, and an additional level of the game-tree will be generated until Quiescence has been reached. When Quiescence is reached during the Quiescence phase of α-β search the terminal position is said to be a Dead position to which the Evaluation function (Eval) is invoked to compute the value of that path through the game-tree that ends on the terminal-node in question (Newell, Shaw, & Simon, 1958). The value returned by the Evaluation function will be backed-up the game-tree toward the root-node of the game-tree by the rules of Minimax. The value returned by the Evaluation function is known as the Provisional Backed-up Value (PBV) (Nilsson, 1971). The Pascal source code for the Decrement function of the HAL chess program follows in (Fig 5) below.

```
(*                    QUIESCENCE                    *)
(*  Decrement Function for Depth Value in Quiescent Phase of N FAB α-β Search
Function  *)
FUNCTION Decrement(P:POINTER; N:INTEGER): INTEGER;
   VAR
      D, I, L, S, X: INTEGER;
   BEGIN
   (* Note: in Pascal, P^. is a pointer reference to a variable or data struc-
ture in dynamic memory (the Heap) *)
      S:= P^.SX; (* S = Side whose turn it is to move, White = 1, Black = 2 *)
      I:= P^.IX;
     (* I = Index of move in Move-List that might be a capture or Promotion *)
      L:= P^.LX;        (* L = Level of depth of the Game-Tree being expanded *)
      D:= N - 1;
         (* D = Recursive α- β value of full-width levels yet to be expanded *)
      X:= S + ((S - 1) * -2) + 1;
                  (* X = Opponent; If S = 1 then X = 2, If S = 2 then X = 1 *)
   (* Test for Singular Extension for Quiescence Move Generation *)
      IF (N = 1) THEN       (* A Leaf-Node of the Game-Tree has been reached *)
         BEGIN
            IF ((L = Horizon) OR (L = Quiescence) OR
                 (P^.Move_List[P^.MLI[I]].Mode_Cell = 'M'))
            THEN
               (* Mated or Search Horizon Reached *)
               BEGIN
                  D:= 0
               END
            ELSE
               BEGIN
```

```
                IF (P^.Move_List[P^.MLI[I]].Mode_Cell IN ['C', 'P'])
                THEN
                   BEGIN                          (* Capture or Promotion *)
                      D:= N
                 (* IF a Capture or Pawn Promotion, don't decrement Depth *)
                   END             (* Allow one more level to be generated *)
                ELSE
                   BEGIN
                      D:= N - 1
                  (* Else, IF not a Capture or Promotion, decrement Depth *)
                   END
             END
         END
      ELSE
         BEGIN
            D:= N - 1            (* Else, IF None of above, decrement Depth *)
         END;
      Decrement:= D      (* Return Depth value to Alpha-Beta Recursive Call *)
   END;
```

OPTIMIZATION METHOD FOR QUIESCENCE IN ALPHA-BETA SEARCH

Quiescence search might extend the search many additional levels before reaching quiescence. If the program can cause a cutoff to occur before extending search to quiescence, a large amount of time and computational effort can be saved to achieve the same result. The way to achieve this is to try a move that is not a capture, a pawn promotion, or a king-in-check situation before expanding a capture or pawn promotion move or a king-in-check situation. During the quiescence phase of α-β search the move list is sorted bringing captures and pawn promotions to the top of the move-list. If after sorting there is a capture or promotion move at the top of the move-list, the algorithm will index up through the move-list until a move is found that is not a capture or pawn promotion. The move index for that move is then moved to a hold variable and all moves above the non-capture, non-promotion move are moved down in the move-list leaving a place at the top of the move-list for the move saved in the hold variable. The move in the hold variable is then moved to the top of the move list to be expanded first(Fig 6). If the move inserted at the top of the move-list does not cause a cutoff to occur, the next move in the move list is expanded that will cause quiescence search to occur.

```
(* Move Ordering and Quiescence Search Optimization Algorithm Called from NFAB
α-β *)
(* Note: Pascal, P^. is a pointer reference to a variable or data structure in
dynamic memory *)
   PROCEDURE Order(P: POINTER);
      VAR
```

```
    H, I: INTEGER;
BEGIN
   Sort(P, P^.WX);                    (* Sort Move-List at P for width WX *)
   IF ((P^.LX > 1) AND (Depth = 1) AND
                           (* Leaf Node if Depth=1, LX is Level Index *)
       (P^.Move_List[P^.MLI[1]].Mode_Cell IN ['C', 'P']))
                                     (* Test for Capture or Promotion *)
   THEN                                   (* at the top of Move-List *)
      BEGIN                                          (* IF True Then *)
         I:= 1;                                  (* Initialize Index I *)
         WHILE ((P^.Move_List[P^.MLI[I]].Mode_Cell IN ['C', 'P']) AND
                 (I < P^.WX)) DO
                              (* Loop down Move-List incrementing I *)
            BEGIN       (* until a move is found that is not a Capture *)
               I:= I + 1                      (* nor a Pawn promotion. *)
            END;
         IF (NOT(P^.Move_List[P^.MLI[I]].Mode_Cell IN ['C', 'P']) AND
               (I <= P^.WX))
         THEN             (* IF the move at index location in Move-List *)
            BEGIN               (* is not a Capture nor Promotion then *)
               H:= P^.MLI[ I ];
                           (* move the index of that move's location *)
               FOR I:= (I - 1) DOWNTO 1 DO
                           (* to the Move-List index hold variable H *)
                  BEGIN    (* and then Move all moves in the Move-List *)
                     P^.MLI[ I + 1 ]:= P^.MLI[ I ]
                        (* down by one until the Move-List index = 1 *)
                  END;
               P^.MLI[ I ]:= H
                        (* then insert H in the top of the Move-List *)
            END
      END
END;
```

THE EXPERIMENT

When the chess program, HAL, enters the quiescence phase of α-β search of the game-tree, the search is extended one additional ply (level) of depth if the last move considered was a capture move or a pawn promotion or king-in-check situation. This process continues until there are no captures or promotions produced and the search is said to have reached quiescence. At which point the static evaluator is called and the terminal position is scored, and the returned value is backed-up the game-tree toward the root node of the game-tree by the minimax α-β search algorithm.

This research expands on the author's earlier published research involving the behavior of α-β search on game-trees (Wheeler, S. F., 1987), and an optimization technique first introduced in theory by Dr. Monroe Newborn in his chess playing algorithm: Ostridge (Newborn, 1975). Dr. Newborn incorporated a one-move-generator to generate and try only the first move of a move-list before generating a complete list of all legal moves for the present board position. If the first move causes an Alpha or Beta cutoff, generating a complete move-list is unnecessary. If a cutoff does not occur on the first move, the full-move-list-generator is called, and a list of all legal moves is generated for the current board position.

THE EXPERIMENTAL MODEL

The experimental model that rendered the metrics reported in this chapter was created by its author, S. Wheeler (Wheeler, Stephen F, 2010). The source code of which is written in Turbo Pascal 6.0, consisting of 8,000+ lines of source code. The program has been set up to report the metrics that support this research. The Turbo Pascal 6.0 compiler produces only a 32-Bit DOS executable (.exe). To execute HAL on a 64-bit Windows Operating System, an emulator, such as DOSBOX must be used. HAL can be executed on a Linux or UNIX operating system with DOSEMU.

The chess program, HAL, utilizes the Iterative-Deepening, Fail-Soft Negamax (α-β) search algorithm (NFAB) with Quiescence search singular extensions, the Killer Heuristic that maintains four Killer moves in its Killer-Table and a larger Refutation-Table of previously discovered moves that caused pruning to occur (Gillogly, 1972). These methods collectively help ensure that moves with the highest probability of achieving maximum α-β pruning will be arranged at the top of the move-list after reordering of the move-list occurs. These processes are applied to each level (ply) of the game-tree as each new ply of legal chess moves is generated. The chess program, HAL, has full communications capability through natural language processing (NLP) such that it can be configured through a series of English directives given to the chess automaton, HAL, at start-up.

The hardware on which HAL was executed consisted of a Hewlett Packard, Elitebook 8530w laptop computer with 8 Gigabytes of DRAM memory and an Intel T9900 3.06 Gigahertz Core2 Duo CPU installed. The operating system (OS) was 32- Bit Windows Professional.

THE EXPERIMENTAL RUNS

To gather the metrics supporting the research reported in this chapter, the chess program, HAL, was run twice. Both runs of the program were given the identical set of 24 legal chess moves. HAL (the chess program) played the black pieces in both instances, although HAL can play with the white pieces as well if directed at startup. One execution of the chess program was set up to include the author's quiescence search extension optimization enhancement. The other execution of the chess program was set up to exclude the quiescence search extension optimization enhancement.

The setup for both runs of the program, HAL, only required setting a Boolean variable to True (quiescence optimization) or False (without quiescence optimization) through natural English typed commands. The two executions of the chess program were configured by commands given to HAL's initial NLP (Natural Language Processing) interface dialogue. To set the chess program up to run with quiescence optimization the following request was entered: "HAL, attempt quiescence optimization." To set the chess program up to run without quiescence optimization the following request was entered:

"HAL, do not attempt quiescence optimization." HAL must also be requested to report the metrics for both program setups by entering the following request when the chess program prompts for user input, "HAL, report game statistics." HAL was also requested to play with skill level 5, which generates a 5-ply full-width game-tree before extending with a narrow-width quiescence search. HAL "thinks" on the opponent's time, so this option must also be turned off for both runs. To deselect this feature, the following request was given: "HAL, don't speculate on the opponent's time."

THE METRICS PRODUCED BY THE EXPERIMENTAL MODEL, HAL

The metrics produced by the two separate runs of the chess program, HAL, are included in the Table (Fig 7) below. One run was without quiescence optimization and the other was run with quiescence

Table 1. Table produced from the two runs of the chess program, HAL, both with and without optimization

Human White-Moves	HAL Black-Moves	Time with Optimization Min:Sec.Hnd	Time Without Optimization Min:Sec.Hnd	Nodes Expanded with Optimization	Nodes Expanded Without Optimization	Branches Pruned: Alpha-Beta Cutoffs without Optimization	Branches Pruned: Alpha-Beta Cutoffs with Optimization
e2-e4	e7-e5	00:00.60	00:00.50	792	860	108	107
g1-f3	g8-f6	00:00.77	00:01.43	118,987	119,031	15,200	14,066
f1-b5	f8-d6	00:00.61	00:01.25	98,123	103,685	13,665	13,809
d2-d3	a7-a6	00:00.43	00:00.99	56,116	85,608	11,257	9,740
b5-c4	b7-b5	00:00.31	00:00.65	39,374	59,978	7,565	6,085
c4-b3	0-0	00:00.32	00:02.14	46,380	149,232	25,161	6,993
0-0	b8-c6	00:00.82	00:07.58	142,661	773,163	67,940	17,437
a2-a3	c6-d4	00:04.51	00:14.50	778,288	1,150,234	135,374	78,988
b3-a2	c8-b7	00:04.17	00:16.15	785,565	1,606,844	146,695	75,755
h2-h3	d4xf3	00:17.70	00:43.18	339,779	485,855	353,683	245,852
d1-f3	d6-c5	00:12.41	00:22.78	1,129,705	2,218,876	201,930	119,815
b1-c3	d7-d6	00:16.70	00:39.99	1,541,251	3,813,630	369,283	158,496
f3-g3	f6-h5	00:40.30	01:27.49	3,139,953	7,555,786	758,308	364,512
g3-h2	d8-h4	00:10.70	00:49.31	950,458	4,718,602	431,837	96,570
b2-b4	c5-d4	00:51.51	00:20.75	4,447,001	1,782,210	178,761	438,498
c1-b2	h5-f4	00:51.25	01:08.00	4,984,948	6,273,266	610,099	483,596
a1-e1	a6-a5	01:52.82	03:59.96	10,807,657	22,214,772	2,217,027	1,069,545
b4xa5	a8xa5	00:49.71	02:06.99	4,667,748	11,646,847	1,166,199	456,105
h2-h1	d4xc3	00:42.73	01:18.81	3,964,597	7,151,202	746,377	423,911
b2xc3	a5-a3	00:05.48	00:06.86	477,992	593,873	74,412	61,489
a2-b3	f4xd3	00:07.25	00:10.44	665,984	997,150	115,033	82,843
e1-e3	d3-f4	00:08.89	00:14.78	856,418	1,438,775	145,665	89,376
c3-b2	a3-a5	00:09.56	00:21.25	891,364	1,988,336	202,731	93,377
b2-c3	a5-a6	00:18.67	00:26.35	1,839,570	2,435,221	245,140	176,240

Figure 4. Line graph of the elapsed move times with optimization and without optimization

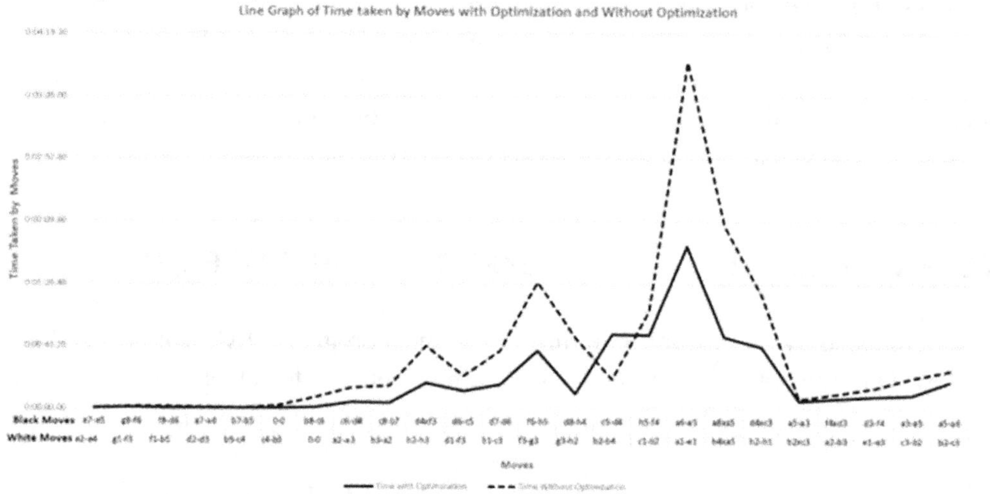

Figure 5. Line graph for the computational effort of moves with optimization and without optimization

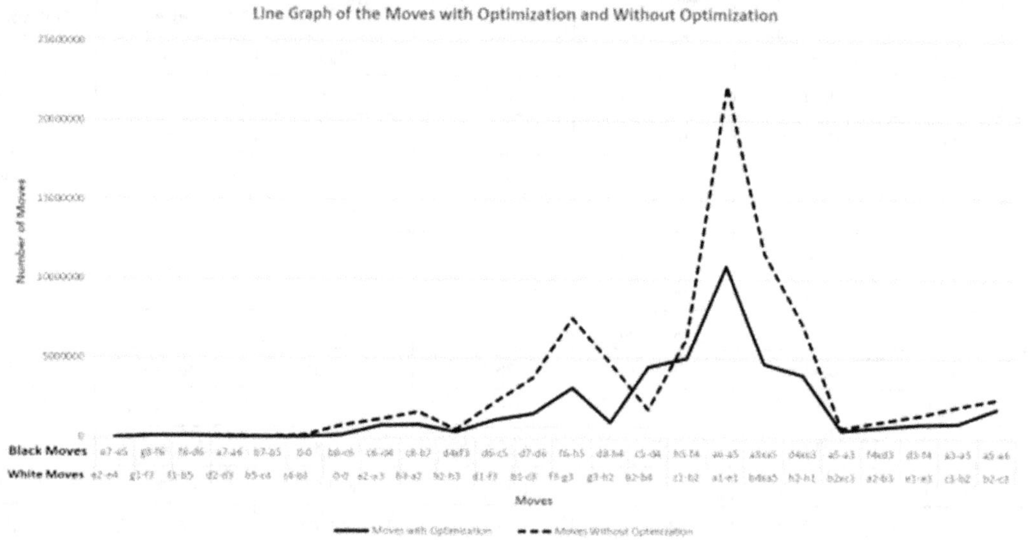

optimization. The following table (Table 1) shows the computation time and number of nodes (moves) processed for each of the twenty-four chess moves for both runs of the chess program, HAL.

A line graph illustrating a comparison of the performance metrics and variance produced by quiescence optimization as compared to the performance metrics without quiescence optimization is offered below.

In line graphs below (Figures 4,5), a solid line is with optimization and a dashed line is without optimization.

THE HYPOTHESES

The Null Hypothesis

H0: Trying a move that will not cause a singular extension of the game-tree before a move that will cause a singular extension will not demonstrate a statistically significant improvement in performance of the quiescence phase of α-β search.

The Alternative Hypothesis

Ha: Trying a move that will not cause a singular extension of the game-tree before a move that will cause a singular extension will demonstrate a statistically significant improvement in performance of the quiescence phase of α-β search.

The Hypothesis Test

The hypothesis test was performed by a standard T-Test as applied to the output metrics produced by the chess program for both the quiescence alpha-beta search with optimization and quiescence alpha-beta search without optimization.

T-Test Results

With a confidence interval of 95% and an α (alpha) of 0.05, for both a two-tailed and a one-tailed t-test of the standard distribution of the data points, the P value of the t-test was less than α rejecting the Null hypothesis in favor of the alternative hypothesis. Thus, this establishes the statistical significance of the quiescence phase of alpha-beta search with optimization over quiescence the quiescence phase of alpha-beta search without optimization. The T-Test results are below (Figure 9).

```
Paired t-test
------------------------------------------------
Sample size                                   24
Difference Mean                      1.52468e+06
t                                        2.63178
Df                                            23
P-value (one-tail)                    0.00745401
P-value (two-tail)                      0.014908
Lower 95.0%                               326237
Upper 95.0%                          2.72312e+06
α                                           0.05
```

The P value is less than α 0.05 in both one-tail and two-tail t-test, which means we can reject the null hypothesis in favor of the alternative hypothesis.

GAME THEORY

Central to Game theory is minimax search with alpha-beta (α-β) pruning, a concept that is primarily employed in the field of Artificial Intelligence and decision making in strategic competitive situations. The principle of game theory is a very insightful process in strategic decision making and corporate analytics in an organizational management context.

Applied game theory assists management in analyzing the strategic interactions between competitors in the market place. By understanding competitors' strategies and potential reactions, a company can make informed decisions regarding pricing, product development, and market entry. Principles from game theory are frequently used in negotiation tactics. Managers can predict the moves of the opposing parties and prepare appropriate answers and counter measures.

For example, within a given organization departments frequently compete for resources. Resource allocation can be modeled and optimized by employing game theory, ensuring that departments are motivated to work cooperatively rather than engaging in unhealthy internal competition.

Games of Strategy

Games of Strategy such as chess, Go, and real-time strategy games utilize minimax with α-β pruning to formulate planned action through the look-ahead property inherent in Minimax and Monte Carlo Tree Search (MCTS). These algorithms let the AI foresee potential moves and counter moves efficiently making the game play more challenging for the human opponent. By arranging potential moves in highest probability order first in the list of legal moves, it facilitates more efficient α-β pruning resulting in faster decision making by the AI algorithm. Improved search algorithms enable game and simulation designers to create adaptable AI systems that are a great training tool for professional players in competitive gaming.

ARTIFICIAL INTELLIGENCE AND MACHINE LEARNING

Machine Learning (ML) without search can only be trained to classify or cluster data environments. To solve problems, Machine Learning must be coupled with search as in Reinforcement Learning (RL) that contains a probabilistic version of Minimax known as Monte Carlo Tree Search (MCTS) to solve a broad spectrum of problems empirically through trial-and-error self-play. Therefore, organizational planning through AI applications employing minimax look-ahead, weighing consequences and rewards of future actions will assist in attaining desirable organizational management outcomes.

Chess has always been the experimental model for testing improvements to minimax search. To assess chess positions, perform calculations, and play at a superhuman level of play, KomodoMC and AlphaZero mainly rely on artificial intelligence methods, including deep neural networks and Monte Carlo Tree Search (MCTS), a probabilistic variant of minimax search. Decision making procedures, optimization tasks, data analytics and applications in AI and machine learning can all be significantly influenced by research on α-β pruning and quiescence enhancement to minimax game tree search.

Some variation of minimax is employed in simulation, automated trading systems, game creation, resource allocation, Natural Language Processing (NLP), and optimization problems. Enhanced minimax search algorithms can be applied to augmenting the efficiency and profitability of financial systems, and to optimize resource allocation in energy distribution and logistics. Additionally, minimax variations improve cybersecurity by predicting and discovering vulnerabilities and recommending actions to help mitigate security threats and safeguard computer systems and networks from attacks. In the problem domain of robotics, minimax with α-β pruning is key to optimizing shortest path and safest routes for movement.

MINIMAX WITH ALPHA-BETA PRUNING IN ORGANIZATIONAL STRATEGY

Minimax is a useful tool for predicting competitors' strategic behavior. With the applied minimax theorem of game theory, organizations are able to analyze competitors' strategies and develop plans to help ensure they are prepared for any competitive moves that their competitors might take.

For decision making in corporate organizations, decision trees, specifically game trees are searched by minimax with alpha-beta (α-β) pruning that will eliminate insignificant strategic options and concentrate on potential opportunities for positive outcomes. In minimax with α-β pruning, unnecessary branches of decision trees are pruned to save computational resources very effectively.

REAL WORLD APPLICATIONS OF GAME THEORY IN AI

The research reported in this chapter focuses on enhancing the performance of the quiescence phase of Minimax with Alpha-Beta (α-β) search, particularly in the field of chess playing automata. Although the application seems to be specialized to games of strategy, the principles and techniques researched in this chapter can have a wide range of real-world applications. A few potential applications in various fields are reported below.

DOD WAR GAMES

Chess is a game of war. The U.S. Department of Defense (DOD) has for many years realized the importance of modeling military strategic planning and response in simulations based on the artificial intelligence developed in chess-playing automata. The organizational management within the DOD relies largely upon such simulations as decision support systems and in risk assessment planning. In such systems the pawns, knights, bishops and rooks of chess-playing systems are replaced by military assets posed against opposing forces in war game simulations and the outcome of each response is weighed as a prediction in theater warfare.

The 1983 movie "War Games'' built a fictional scenario around a chess-playing and war-gaming supercomputer, WOPR, an acronym for War Operations Planned Response. Although the movie was fictional it was based on a DOD AI planning paradigm involving game theory.

BIOINFORMATICS

A key component of Bioinformatics is protein folding, which enables the search for new medicines and research of disease. Proteins are intricate, three-dimensional molecules with complex, correlated functions. The examination of the protein folding problem requires extensive computer work, therefore better search approaches can be effective. Reinforcement Learning methods have been used effectively in bioinformatics to study protein folding, reducing computational complexity and enhancing the investigation of protein folding methods. This can lead to drug discovery, disease research, and personalized pharmaceuticals. Scientists and bioengineers can create medications that perfectly address the active regions of proteins by mimicking protein folding, altering the functionalities of the protein pathogens to treat such diseases.

Even though the research described in this chapter focuses on chess-playing programs, these techniques and methodologies have a broad application across diverse fields requiring efficient search and decision making. For this reason, chess has often been described as the Drosophila Melanogaster (Fruit Fly) of Artificial Intelligence research.

RISK MITIGATION IN ORGANIZATIONAL MANAGEMENT

Minimax forms a core component for modeling a task for adaptive management of enterprise innovative processes (EIP) that are under certain organizational risks. To mitigate these dynamic risks requires the development of an algorithm for managing EIP that are under risks. It is necessary to formalize the process of optimizing the EIP adaptive management for its solution as an ensured result based on the application of minimax. By incorporating optimized minimax with alpha-beta (α-β) pruning and quiescence singular-extensions ensures a result that mitigates risks. In this case, risks in the system of EIP management are considered factors that negatively affect the results of the processes or actions considered.

For example, certain organizational decisions can give rise to risks in uncertain market conditions; the Minimax algorithm of game theory can be comparable to a risk management application. Managers assess potential losses and derive plans to reduce losses and increase gains by making decisions that are robust and profitable against the most unfavorable market conditions and downturns.

PROJECT RISK PLANNING

During project planning managers perform a risk assessment considering the current and future market and financial climate to develop contingency plans to help ensure the project is robust against potential challenges. The Minimax theorem of game theory provides organizational-management the capability of long-range planning and trend-line analytics to ensure the organization navigates a profitable path toward continued positive outcomes.

CYBER SECURITY ANALYTICS IN ORGANIZATIONAL MANAGEMENT

Central to the Cyber Security problem is the development of techniques to support human decision-making and algorithms that assist organizational management in enabling cyber security decision making. The proposed solution is a game theory paradigm in minimax search that is employed in concert with principles derived from the Nash Equilibria (NE) of game theory enhancements to minimax. In this proposed approach a simulation designed as a two player game of sorts in which known cyber security vulnerabilities are assaulted by attacks on those vulnerabilities. Remedies are applied to each attack and the best combinations are evaluated. The system then recommends the best solution found to each attack based on the minimax derived solution.

PRIVACY AND SECURITY IMPLICATIONS

Privacy is a major concern with AI advancement. As game theory is increasingly employed in data analytics and organizational management, the proliferation of proprietary data driving these processes becomes a security concern and a social stigma for the organizations in question. As organizational data is generated at an immense rate, many organizations rely increasingly on third-party agencies to maintain their data and data security. As cloud services become more prolific, giving algorithms designed around the game theory paradigm unrestricted access to third-party agencies such as DSAAS (Data Science AS A Service) and SAAS (Software AS A Service) the possibility of proprietary data leaks is of increasing security concern for organizational management. As a result, the algorithms' extensive data collection and disposition behavior will become inevitable. To help mitigate the security risk of organizational data leakage, the autonomy of AI tools must be closely monitored and managed when employed.

MINIMAX WITH ALPHA-BETA PRUNING IN ORGANIZATIONAL STRATEGY

Minimax is a useful tool for predicting competitors' strategic behavior. With the applied minimax theorem of game theory, organizations are able to analyze competitors' strategies and develop plans to help ensure they are prepared for any competitive moves that their competitors might take.

For decision making in corporate organizations, decision trees, specifically game trees are searched by minimax with alpha-beta (α-β) pruning that will eliminate insignificant strategic options and concentrate on potential opportunities for positive outcomes. In minimax with α-β pruning, unnecessary branches of decision trees are pruned to save computational resources very effectively.

MARKET RESOURCES

Minimax with Alpha-Beta (α-β) pruning can be compared to an efficient market research paradigm, where organizations analyze various market segments as branches of the game tree. This is achieved by focusing on the segments with the most promising profitability and pruning the branches with less favorable outcomes. Minimax with α-β pruning discovers the path through the game tree with minimum loss and maximum gain, hence its name Mini-Max. Employing this strategy helps ensure efficient resource allocation when applied to the organizations' marketing problem domain.

MITIGATING STRATEGIES

To help build trust among users concerning applied AI, the organization should invest in educational programs that focus on developing AI training for those using AI tools for strategic planning and organizational management. Developers should consider various skill levels while designing organizational AI tools to make applied AI more user-friendly. Implementing AI guidelines and policies should evolve within the organizational management structure as the AI tools evolve in utility and complexity. With technological advancements in AI, efforts must be taken that will address the ethical and social implications proactively. Developers and policy makers will experience the benefits of AI advancements while reducing the potential negative consequences on society.

CONCLUSION

The findings of the research reported in this chapter have been demonstrated by experimentation and empiricism. The modification to the quiescence extension of iterative-deepening alpha-beta aspiration search demonstrates a statistically significant performance improvement of deep game-tree search as established by this research for game-trees of the type and dimension described in this chapter.

For researchers who wish to verify the research results reported in this chapter, and for peer review of these findings, the author offers the Windows executable code (.exe) and the complete Pascal source code (.pas) for the chess program, HAL, with instructions for setting up the experiment to anyone requesting a copy. To request a copy of the experimental model, HAL, used in this research, send a request by email to swheeler@ai-scientist.com. The experimental model, HAL, will be returned to the requester, free of charge by Zipped file folder attachment in a reply email. Please place "Request for HAL" in the subject line of the requesting email.

REFERENCES

Berliner, H. J. (1974). *Chess as problem solving: the development of a tactics analyzer* [Doctoral dissertation, Carnegie-Mellon University].

Frey, P. W. (Ed.). (2012). *Chess skill in man and machine*. Springer Science & Business Media.

Knuth, D. E., & Moore, R. W. (1975). An analysis of alpha-beta pruning. *Artificial Intelligence*, *6*(4), 293–326. doi:10.1016/0004-3702(75)90019-3

Marsland, T. A. (1987). Computer chess methods. Encyclopedia of Artificial Intelligence, 1, 159-171.

Marsland, T. A., & Campbell, M. (1982). Parallel search of strongly ordered game trees. *ACM Computing Surveys*, *14*(4), 533–551. doi:10.1145/356893.356895

Marsland, T. A., & Schaeffer, J. (Eds.). (1990). *Computers, chess, and cognition.* Springer. doi:10.1007/978-1-4613-9080-0

Russell, S. J. (2010). *Artificial intelligence a modern approach.* Pearson Education, Inc.

Samuel, A. L. (2000). Some studies in machine learning using the game of checkers. *IBM Journal of research and development, 44*(1.2), 206-226.

Wheeler, S. F. (1987). A Performance Benchmark of the Alpha-Beta Procedure on Randomly Ordered Non-Uniform Depth-First Game-Trees Generated by a Chess Program. *ICGA Journal, 10*(1), 43–43. doi:10.3233/ICG-1987-10108

Wheeler, S. F. (2010). The HAL (Heuristic Associative Linear-algorithm) Chess Program. *Chess Programming Wiki.* https://www.chessprogramming.org/HAL

KEY TERMS AND DEFINITIONS

AI: This is an acronym for Artificial Intelligence.

Alpha-Beta (α-β) Pruning: An extension to the minimax search algorithm employed in game trees to cut down on the number of nodes considered and increase efficiency by removing branches that do not have an impact on the outcome.

Alpha-Beta Search: Alpha-Beta (α-β) search is an extension of minimax complemented by a heuristic technique used in game tree search that prunes branches at minimizing or maximizing nodes whose values fall outside of the α-β window, streamlining the search process to quickly identify the best option.

Alpha-Beta Window: In game playing algorithms employing minimax search with alpha-beta pruning, the alpha-beta window refers to the set of values (alpha and beta) that are used to prune game tree branches at nodes that are less than alpha or greater than beta to optimize the search, when the real score is outside of this range.

Combinatorial Explosion: Also 'Combinatorial effect,' refers to the increase in the number of possibilities as the depth of search (denoted as d) increases. In a combinatorial problem there are multiple options at each level of the game tree and the number of possible combinations grows exponentially with the increasing depth of the game tree which is given by the expression b^d.

Data Leakage: This term refers to the risk of giving full data autonomy to AI systems for data management and the risk of data loss by third-party data management agencies and cloud data repositories.

EIP: This is enterprise innovative processes in which minimax forms a core component for modeling a task for adaptive management of enterprise innovative processes that are under certain organizational risks.

Game Theory: Forms a theoretical framework for social situations among competing players as generally applied strategically to situations involving economic behavior, and all two-player games of strategy.

Game Tree: A graphical representation in game theory and artificial intelligence that shows every possible action and counteraction in a decision-making process that progresses sequentially as the game tree grows, allowing for algorithmic optimization and strategic analysis to occur.

HAL (Heuristic Associative Linear-Algorithm): A chess playing program designed and developed by Dr. Stephen F. Wheeler. It is named after the fictional HAL 9000 computer from the Space Odyssey series by Arthur C. Clarke.

Look-Ahead: This refers to the ability of minimax to search the consequences of proposed actions and counter actions into the future by simulating those proposed actions and counter actions and weighing the outcome to find and suggest the best course of action that results in the minimum loss and the maximum gain of a proposed action.

Minimax Search: A game theory decision rule that reduces the potential for loss and increases the potential for gain in two-player games of strategy. Minimax is commonly implemented in artificial intelligence for game-playing strategies in zero-sum games where a gain for one player is an equal loss for the other player, the sum of which is zero.

Nash Equilibrium (NE): In game theory John Nash contributed to the field of non-cooperative games in which players cannot communicate and must make their decision only on what they anticipate other players will do.

Negamax: An α-β variant of the Minimax algorithm that makes it easier to implement as a recursive algorithm. It evaluates both players' moves from the perspective of one player, always maximizing for the player whose turn it is to move.

NLP: This is an acronym for Natural Language Processing.

One Move Generator: An algorithm that generates only the first legal move and plays it to see if that move will cause the branch of the game tree to be pruned before calling the full-move generator to generate the full list of legal moves if pruning does not occur.

Ply: This is one level of depth of the game tree. If a game tree has 6 levels of depth it is known as a 6-ply game tree.

Provisional Backed up Value (PBV): A temporary evaluation of the game state assigned during the search process in a game playing algorithm with an assumption that the optimum value for the state is within the given range.

Quiescence Search: Also known as singular-extension will extend the full-width, fixed-depth search beyond its maximum search depth by one additional level of depth if the move on the search horizon is a capture, pawn promotion or king-in-check move. These narrow singular extensions will repeat until there are no more such moves to consider. At which point, the search is known to have reached quiescence.

The Horizon Effect: This refers to the limitation where the evaluation of a game position is influenced by moves or positions within a certain depth limit and fails to predict future actions that might lead to a better or worse outcome beyond that terminal depth.

Chapter 10
Smart Tourism Narratives:
Maturity Matrix and Digital Transformation

H. Sandhya
Christ University, India

Bindi Varghese
Christ University, India

ABSTRACT

The tourist sector is going through a transformational change in the modern digital era. An in-depth analysis of the shifting paradigms that have arisen at the nexus of technology and tourism is provided in this systematic assessment of the literature. The chapter examines the crucial impact that cutting-edge technologies like the internet of things (IoT), metaverse, artificial intelligence (AI), data analytics, virtual reality, augmented reality (AR), and blockchain have had on changing travel patterns. The combination of these technologies enables destination stakeholders to manage resources more effectively, personalizes and streamlines the traveler experience, and provides policymakers with tools for data-driven decision-making. This research adds to the current discussion on how the tourist business is changing in the digital era by shedding light on the shifting paradigms, possibilities, and problems in the field of smart tourism.

INTRODUCTION

A key component of the global economy and cross-cultural interchange is the dynamic and always changing tourism sector. As a result of technological improvements, the tourism industry has undergone a significant transition recently. This change, also referred to as "Smart Tourism," has altered how people organize, enjoy, and share their travels. In this article, the idea of "smart tourism" is examined, along with its essential elements, advantages, and difficulties, as well as how it affects different stakeholders in the travel industry. The idea of "smart tourism" refers to the incorporation of cutting-edge technologies and data-driven solutions into the travel and tourism sectors to improve the entire travel experience. It makes travel more convenient, customized, ecological, and immersive by utilizing digital advancements.

DOI: 10.4018/979-8-3693-1058-8.ch010

Numerous digital platforms and mobile applications have emerged as a result of the widespread use of smartphones and internet access, making it easier than ever for passengers to plan and handle their travels. These systems include services including lodging, travel, and activity booking, as well as real-time weather, traffic, and local event information. Businesses and locations involved in tourism are utilizing big data analytics to learn more about the preferences and actions of travelers. They may specifically design their solutions to match the demands of diverse client segments by evaluating data from numerous sources, such as social media, mobile applications, and IoT devices. Destinations worldwide are transforming from the traditional and conventional management style to a much evolved and dynamic technology driven system which enables better and efficient resource utilization. Smart Tourism entails the fundamental framework and approaches that tourist firms must employ if they are to succeed in an increasingly data- and technology-driven sector of the economy. It includes a variety of components, such as cutting-edge technology, environment friendly procedures, customer-focused methods, and efficient management techniques. Businesses that lay solid foundations are better prepared to react to changing customer demands, address socioeconomic and environmental issues, and maintain a competitive edge in the global tourist industry. This idea highlights the significance of incorporating modern technologies and environmentally friendly practices into every facet of tourism operations, from marketing and visitor interaction to resource management and intergenerational cooperation.

SMART TOURISM MINDSET

Smart foundations are ultimately the cornerstones around which robust and successful tourist companies are built. Perles-Ribes & Ivars-Baidal, (2018) developed the smart sustainable tourism business model that depicts all the elements of a sustainable business. Governance and Innovative approaches that are directed towards long term sustainability and effective utilization of the scarce resources form the strategic relational elements of the business model. A sophisticated information system with integration of big data and artificial intelligence to create a digital economy and smart infrastructural is instrumental in developing such a model. These systems are then applied into the destination infrastructure to create smart solutions regarding information dissemination to tourists and stakeholders, enriching the visitor experience and better management of the destinations thus creating a global image and visibility through intelligent destination management practices.

Literature substantiates the integration of smart technologies into every aspect of the existing infrastructure of the destination in order to create a unique travel experience for the visitors. A competency development program and a maturity matrix based on destination management scenario get closer to being an Intelligent and smart Tourism Destination (Joseph C and B. Varghese, 2023). To draw tourists and improve the overall visitor experience, a destination management organization (DMO) is an organization tasked with managing and promoting a particular destination, usually a city, region, or nation. Creating and implementing plans that support the destination's tourism industry's sustainability and economic growth is a DMO's main objective. This can only be done with the help of effective stakeholder collaboration by involving the DMOs, tourism and travel fraternity both private and public, technology and software developers, the local community and the tourists themselves. A cooperative and interconnected strategy for promoting sustainable and prosperous tourism throughout a particular geographic area is represented by a regionally integrated and connected system of tourism stakeholders. This system brings together a number of stakeholders, such as tourism boards, businesses, community organizations, and

Figure 1. Smart tourism ecosystem conceptual model
(Developed and compiled by authors)

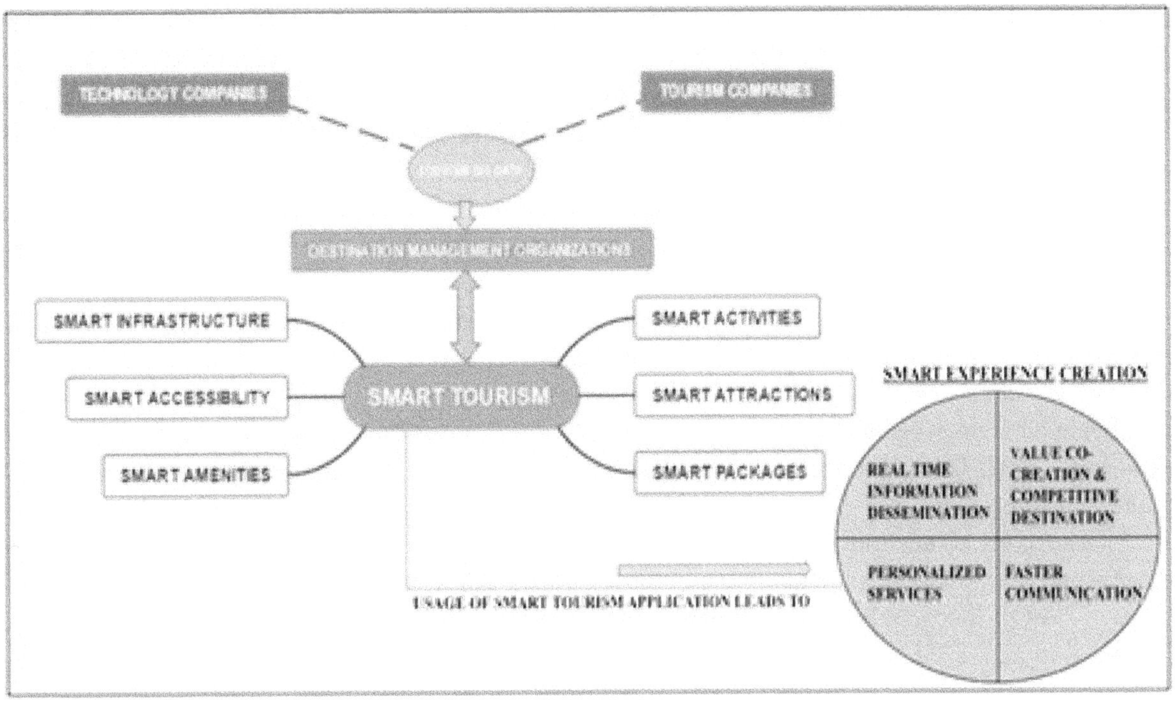

local governments, who collaborate to market the area's attractions and improve the overall experience for tourists. In order to create distinctive tourism products, improve infrastructure, and develop coordinated marketing strategies, these stakeholders must work together. In addition to optimizing the financial gains from tourism, this integrated strategy guarantees sustainable development that preserves the area's natural and cultural heritage. DMOs utilize the huge amount of data and information available to create smart infrastructure facilities, smart mobility systems, smart amenities and facilities, smart activities, attractions and packages to the potential tourists. The tourists will be benefited with this data as it provides real time information about the destinations, offer them personalized services, enables faster and easier communications and ensure value co creation at the destination. This ultimately results in a smart and enriched visitor experience thereby creating a global image for the transformed smart destination. DMOs are essential for promoting a destination, drawing tourists, and creating a happy, sustainable tourism environment. They frequently collaborate with different stakeholders to accomplish their goals and are supported by a mix of public and private sources. Fig 1.1 explains a conceptual model of smart destination management by integrating technology into the various aspects of a destination to enrich visitor experience and make the destination more attractive and resilient.

MATURITY MATRIX INDICATORS

Human beings are habituated to the usage of smart devices and ICT enabled systems for decision making (Kontogianni et al., 2022). This has been the trend in the tourism industry, with much of the services and facilities becoming automated and digitized since the past few decades. Technology has been successful in the revival of saturated destinations and creation of better marketing opportunities for such destinations (Nannelli et al., 2023). Usage of social media, internet and the world wide web has opened up a new window for service providers to connect and engage with tourists from all over the world (Kashem et al., 2022). Destination Management Organizations (DMOs) have shifted focus to the usage of smart applications that enable them to track and understand tourist behavior and motivations with the help of location-based search history and social media presence (Gretzel, 2022). The smart transformation of a destination requires the development of a regionally integrated and connected system of stakeholders working together in the tourism supply chain (Solazzo et al., 2022). The need to include academia such as universities and other research organizations is also important as these institutions are directly or indirectly involved in the tourism development process. Traditional businesses need further renewal and creation of value-added customized services to the tourists thus creating a more personalized experience (Mandić & Kennell, 2021).

Implementation of a smart and intelligent system to monitor and forecast the tourism demand is also equally essential. This is possible only through effective stakeholder engagement and collaboration and at the same time promoting social entrepreneurship in the tourism sector of the region (Fyall & Garrod, 2020). The role and functions of the regional DMOs have been redefined as they are not only limited to the creation of travel packages and upkeep of the tourist sites (Ma, & Lam, 2019). There is a shift in the focus of DMO's functionality to being an information and knowledge sharing center of innovative tourism products and services to the tourists in the most efficient and effective manner (Solazzo et al., 2022).

DIGITAL TRANSFORMATION AND COCREATION

Smart experience creation focuses on enhancing and enriching the experience of tourists through personalization and real-time monitoring (Sorokina et al., 2022). Tourists play a major role in participating and co-creation of such experiences by sharing them on social media or word-of-mouth publicity. An extensive review of literature of 126 articles was conducted by Dorcic et al., (2019) on the application of mobile technologies in smart tourism. This comprehensive study focussed on three major perspectives of smart technology ie., consumer perspective, technological perspective and provider perspective (Ma, & Lam, 2019). The study highlighted convenience, ease of usage, faster and simpler transactions and personalization as some of the reasons customers opt mobile technologies for their booking, reservation and travel plans. QR code scanners, Near -Field communication systems (NFC), Automated self-check-in kiosks are much popular in the hospitality and aviation industries as they enable faster and more efficient transactions and avoid long queues and delays for the passengers (Pasquinelli, & Trunfio, 2023).

Integrating smart technologies into the physical infrastructure of the destinations has been the key focus area of destination planners and policy makers (Gretzel, 2022). This was implemented through strategies such as the introduction of smart GPS-enabled bicycles at destinations which not only provides tourists with a means of sustainable transportation but also a healthy exercise and one of the best methods to explore the city on their own. There are also smart local tourist buses that are GPS enabled providing all the information regarding route, time, schedule, and destinations covered (Fyall & Garrod, 2020).

Recently most of the major tourist destinations have installed free wifi services with good internet connectivity and language translation assistance. Augmented Reality (AR) has gained much popularity in recent years and is often considered an effective method for marketing and branding destinations worldwide. Mobile applications like PokemonGo have led to a considerable increase in the usage of AR (Bulchand-Gidumal, 2022). Cultural heritage sites are the most unique attraction of many countries and these can be developed and restored digitally with the help of AR-based applications. The benefits of augmented reality technology makes it one of the most 'revolutionary inventions' in recent times (He et al., 2018). Digital restoration of heritage, artifacts, and recreation of historic events can further enhance the visibility and attractiveness of the sites (Bethune et al., 2022). Much research has been conducted on AR with specific reference to the usefulness, readiness of tourists to accept the applications, value creation, and learning experiences, etc (Hyunae et al., 2018; Samara et al., 2020; Hsu, 2018). Visual dimensions of AR are an area that has received much attention and has been explored to a large extent. Creating AR-enabled visual images at heritage sites and tourist destinations is contributing to enhancing and enriching tourist experiences. AR techniques have been adopted at many destinations by combining all the relevant technologies like high-speed processors, high-resolution rear-facing cameras, GPS-enabled systems, and many other features (Bulchand-Gidumal, 2022). Most of the tourists use smartphones to navigate and gather information about destinations and tourist attractions, but there are certain limitations like limited screen size, lesser visibility of the screen during bright and sunny days, and the inconvenience and danger associated with frequently checking mobile phones during driving and cycling through the destination (Sorokina et al., 2022). This has led to the creation of haptic and audio displays at tourism destinations to assist tourists in navigating through places of interest. Pocket Navigator App is an example of the audio display smart mobile app that helps navigate users by guiding them along a specific route or destination with the help of certain vibration patterns (Muniz et al., 2021).

Use of AR in the tourism industry is much more focused at present, as there is a considerable shift from the traditional services offered to a much sophisticated, personalized and value-added services (Hartman, & Heslinga, 2022). The customer expectations are high due to the complex supply system in the tourism industry and abundance of information available (Solazzo et al., 2022). Development of AR technology requires careful planning, investment and continuous updations to keep the service providers competitive and on track (Cranmer, & Jung, 2018). The augmented power of such applications helps to enrich travel experiences by taking the travelers to an entirely different artificial environment showing images of things that do not exist at present in the real world (Mariani et al, 2021). AR devices like interactive displays were installed in tourist sites like museums and places of historic importance, wearable technology like smart glasses, smart watches were gaining much popularity as they are easy to handle and carry around (Muniz et al., 2021).

When applied to tourism, "smart" refers to a sophisticated combination of all of the aforementioned. The realization of smart tourism is backed by strong institutional support and in certain cases, even pressure. There have been deliberate attempts to advance the agenda for smart tourism, particularly in Asia. Initiatives primarily aimed at developing the technology infrastructure necessary to enable smart tourism are being heavily funded by the governments of China and South Korea (Wang et al., 2013). As a result of the fact that many of the smart tourism initiatives in Europe originated from smart city projects, the number of smart tourism destinations in Europe is rising. But in Europe, the emphasis is more on innovation, competitiveness, and creating intelligent end-user applications that facilitate enhanced travel experiences by combining and processing data that already exists in novel ways (Lamsfus et al. 2015; Boes et al. 2015a, b). Open data, in particular, and smart governance are prioritized in Australia. Governments all agree that smart technologies have the ability to revolutionize not just the economic but also the social and experiential spheres.

BIG DATA IN SMART TOURISM: DATA PRIVACY CONCERNS AND CHALLENGES

Technology has become an integral and inevitable part of our daily lives due to the speed, ease, and simplicity of transactions. The field of data protection and privacy has undergone significant change as a result of the General Data Protection Regulation (GDPR), the California Consumer Privacy Act (CCPA), and other state-level privacy laws. The significance of individual rights and control over personal data is emphasized by these regulations (Das, 2018). Important guidelines include giving people adequate notice of data collection methods, giving them meaningful options, and getting their express consent before processing their data. The regulations also cover how data is used and retained, setting guidelines for how long data must be stored and restricting the uses for which data may be processed (Houser & Voss, 2018). One essential component is access rights, which allow people to ask questions and get copies of the personal data that organizations have about them. Furthermore, these laws control the sharing of data with third parties, demanding openness and frequently requiring express consent (Sharma, 2019). The main objective is to give people more control over their personal data while making organizations accountable for managing it in an equitable, safe, and open way. These laws have an international effect, affecting how companies handle data privacy to adhere to changing legal requirements (Rustad, & Koenig, (2019).

A method for improving privacy in recommendation systems is to use suitable algorithmic or cryptographic methods. For instance, as a structural component of their systems, the two illustrative works suggest using homomorphic encryption (Boes et al. 2015a, b). Another system has been proposed in that substitutes randomized perturbation for encryption. The authors suggest using differential privacy techniques to gather data about users' preferences for points of interest (POIs) in mobile recommender systems for tourism. Formal privacy is then enforced by querying these statistics to generate recommendations (Noh et al., 2020).

BLOCKCHAIN-EMPOWERED METAVERSE TOURISM

Tourism facilitated by metaverse technology and blockchain. The most revolutionary technologies that would change the present tourist and hospitality environment are thought to be blockchain and the metaverse. Despite the recent emergence of publications on the metaverse and blockchain, the majority are conceptual and theoretical, with little attention paid to how a location may adopt such cutting-edge technologies and foster blockchain-enabled metaverse tourism. A maturity matrix framework for empowering destinations may be seen in the use of blockchain and the metaverse framework for stakeholder involvement and alliance (V Jose et.al, 2023). The adoption of blockchain and metaverse technology by stakeholders, as well as the effects of these activities on the expansion of blockchain-enabled metaverse tourism among destinations are examined by a tech-enabled and empowered governance. Augmented Reality Smart Glasses (ARSG) helps to provide virtual information into the user's direct field of vision with the help of a glass like device (Noh et al., 2020). Many smartphones are equipped with inbuilt features like location sharing through GPS, Near Field Communication and sharing which provides the users with all the relevant information and data during their visit to the destination (Martins et al., 2021). AR enabled devices are also said to help tourists to explore unfamiliar places and surroundings and empower them with abundant data and information (Macrorie et al., 2021). From the supplier perspective, though setting up an AR system requires initial capital investment, it enables attractive returns, generates more revenue and reduces the risk of seasonality in travel patterns (Gelter et al., 2021). Integration of AR into the tourism system gives considerable opportunities to upsell and enhance the overall travel experience. In the hospitality industry, many accommodation providers are coming up with AR technology to assist the tourists during the pre booking process by providing real time digital and virtual information about the property and its facilities (Muniz et al., 2021; Bethune et al., 2022). This can further enhance the overall tourist experience and also establish an emotional connection between the user and the service provider. The mix of AR and VR technology contributes to value co-creation through active participation of tourists and service providers in the tourism industry (Femenia-Serra, & Ivars-Baidal, 2021). With the help of AR, the needs and expectations of the customers can be evaluated during the pre-booking stage itself, thus enabling the service provider to offer more personalized services to the customers (Ivars-Baidal et al., 2021). Another significant benefit of AR technology is value co-creation. As multiple stakeholders are involved in the tourism process, effective engagement and collaboration of stakeholders and customers helps joint creation of value by the customer and the service provider (Fyall & Garrod, 2020). This helps in creating a competitive advantage as well as an opportunity to innovate more and integrate technology into the tourism system (Estevao et al., 2020).

According to Samara et al. (2020), big data analytics and artificial intelligence are being quickly adopted by the tourism industry because of the advantages they provide, including cost savings, personalized experiences and services, analysis of customer behavior patterns, and opportunities to increase performance and revenue by destinations. Sorokina et al.,(2022) propagates artificial intelligence was quickly implemented in a number of sectors, including IT, telecommunications, marketing, education, and healthcare (Noh et al., 2020). As customers today are more focused on meaningful experiences than ever before, the travel and tourism sector, with its rapid expansion and ongoing evolution, necessitates flexibility to new and creative technology and solutions (Ruiz-Molina et al., 2018). Businesses' priorities have significantly shifted from being supplier-centric to becoming customer-centric (Mrsic et al., 2020). Tsaih and Hsu (2018) investigated particular marketing and destination management techniques in order to offer a framework for integrating big data applications in the tourism sector. Customers are allowed to pick a supplier's services solely based on user evaluations on websites like Tripadvisor and Airbnb, for instance (Solazzo et al., 2022). Although the initial investment in creating and integrating Big Data and Artificial Intelligence into the tourism system can be substantial, (Pillmayer et al., 2021) noted that the ongoing advantages brought about by these systems are enticing more destination planners to adopt and modify to these technologies for their long-term survival.

FUTURE OUTCOME AND IMPLICATIONS

Technology has become an integral and inevitable part of our daily lives due to the speed, ease, and simplicity of transactions. Use of AR in the tourism industry is much more focused at present, as there is a considerable shift from the traditional services offered to a much sophisticated, personalized and value added services (Hartman, & Heslinga, 2022). The customer expectations are high due to the complex supply system in the tourism industry and abundance of information available (Solazzo et al., 2022). Development of AR technology requires careful planning, investment and continuous updations to keep the service providers competitive and on track (Cranmer, & Jung, 2018). The augmented power of such applications helps to enrich travel experiences by taking the travelers to an entirely different artificial environment showing images of things that do not exist at present in the real world (Mariani et al, 2021). AR devices like interactive displays were installed in tourist sights like museums and places of historic importance, wearable technology like smart glasses, smart watches were gaining much popularity as they are easy to handle and carry around (Muniz et al., 2021). Augmented Reality Smart Glasses (ARSG) helps to provide virtual information into the user's direct field of vision with the help of a glass like device (Noh et al., 2020). Many smartphones are equipped with inbuilt features like location sharing through GPS, Near Field Communication and sharing which provides the users with all the relevant information and data during their visit to the destination (Martins et al., 2021). AR enabled devices are also said to help tourists to explore unfamiliar places and surroundings and empower them with abundant data and information (Macrorie et al., 2021). From the supplier perspective, though setting up an AR system requires initial capital investment, it enables attractive returns, generates more revenue and reduces the risk of seasonality in travel patterns (Gelter et al., 2021).

Integration of AR into the tourism system gives considerable opportunities to upsell and enhance the overall travel experience. In the hospitality industry, many accommodation providers are coming up with AR technology to assist the tourists during the pre-booking process by providing real time digital and virtual information about the property and its facilities (Muniz et al., 2021; Bethune et al., 2022). This can further enhance the overall tourist experience and also establish an emotional connection between the user and the service provider. The mix of AR and VR technology contributes to value co-creation through active participation of tourists and service providers in the tourism industry (Femenia-Serra, & Ivars-Baidal, 2021). With the help of AR, the needs and expectations of the customers can be evaluated during the pre-booking stage itself, thus enabling the service provider to offer more personalized services to the customers (Ivars-Baidal et al., 2021). Another significant benefit of AR technology is value co-creation. As multiple stakeholders are involved in the tourism process, effective engagement and collaboration of stakeholders and customers helps joint creation of value by the customer and the service provider (Fyall & Garrod, 2020). This helps in creating a competitive advantage as well as an opportunity to innovate more and integrate technology into the tourism system (Estevao et al., 2020). According to Samara et al. (2020), big data analytics and artificial intelligence are being quickly adopted by the tourism industry because of the advantages they provide, including cost savings, personalized experiences and services, analysis of customer behavior patterns, and opportunities to increase performance and revenue by destinations. Sorokina et al., (2022) propagates artificial intelligence was quickly implemented in a number of sectors, including IT, telecommunications, marketing, education, and healthcare.

CONCLUSION

As customers today are more focused on meaningful experiences than ever before, the travel and tourism sector, with its rapid expansion and ongoing evolution, necessitates flexibility to new and creative technology and solutions (Ruiz-Molina et al., 2018). Businesses' priorities have significantly shifted from being supplier-centric to becoming customer-centric (Mrsic et al., 2020). Tsaih and Hsu (2018) investigated particular marketing and destination management techniques in order to offer a framework for integrating big data applications in the tourism sector. Customers are allowed to pick a supplier's services solely based on user evaluations on websites like Tripadvisor and Airbnb, for instance (Solazzo et al., 2022). Although the initial investment in creating and integrating Big Data and Artificial Intelligence into the tourism system can be substantial, (Pillmayer et al., 2021) noted that the ongoing advantages brought about by these systems are enticing more destination planners to adopt and modify to these technologies for their long-term survival.

REFERENCES

Bethune, E., Buhalis, D., & Miles, L. (2022). Real time response (RTR): Conceptualizing a smart systems approach to destination resilience. *Journal of Destination Marketing & Management*, *23*, 100687. doi:10.1016/j.jdmm.2021.100687

Boes, K., Borde, L., & Egger, R. (2015a). The Acceptance of NFC Smart Posters in Tourism. In I. Tussyadiah & A. Inversini (Eds.), *Information and Communication Technologies in Tourism 2015* (pp. 435–448). Springer. doi:10.1007/978-3-319-14343-9_32

Boes, K., Buhalis, D., & Inversini, A. (2015b). Conceptualising Smart Tourism Destination Dimensions. In I. Tussyadiah & A. Inversini (Eds.), *Information and Communication Technologies in Tourism 2015* (pp. 391–403). Springer. doi:10.1007/978-3-319-14343-9_29

Brennan, B. S., Koo, C., & Bae, K. M. (2018). Smart Tourism: A Study of Mobile Application Use by Tourists Visiting South Korea. *Asia-pacific Journal of Multimedia Services Convergent with Art, Humanities, and Sociology*, *8*(10), 1–9. doi:10.21742/AJMAHS.2018.10.15

Buhalis, D., & Amaranggana, A. (2015). Smart tourism destinations enhancing tourism experience through personalisation of services. In *Information and communication technologies in tourism* (pp. 377–389). Springer.

Bulchand-Gidumal, J. (2022). Impact of artificial intelligence in travel, tourism, and hospitality. In *Handbook of e-Tourism* (pp. 1943–1962). Springer International Publishing. doi:10.1007/978-3-030-48652-5_110

Calle-Lamelas, J. V., García-Hernández, M., & García-Muiña, F. E. (2023). What is a Smart Destination in Practice? The Interpretation of DMO Managers from Spanish World Heritage Cities. *Tourism Planning & Development*, 1–23. doi:10.1080/21568316.2023.2214123

Choe, Y., & Fesenmaier, D. R. (2021). Designing an advanced system for destination management: A case study of Northern Indiana. *Industrial Management & Data Systems*, *121*(6), 1167–1190. doi:10.1108/IMDS-02-2020-0063

Cranmer, E. E., Dieck, M., & Jung, T. (2018). How can tourist attractions profit from augmented reality? In *Augmented reality and virtual reality* (pp. 21–32). Springer. doi:10.1007/978-3-319-64027-3_2

Das, A. K. (2018). European Union's General Data ProtectionRegulation, 2018: A brief overview. [ALIS]. *Annals of Library and Information Studies*, *65*(2), 139–140.

Doborjeh, Z., Hemmington, N., Doborjeh, M., & Kasabov, N. (2022). Artificial intelligence: A systematic review of methods and applications in hospitality and tourism. *International Journal of Contemporary Hospitality Management*, *34*(3), 1154–1176. doi:10.1108/IJCHM-06-2021-0767

Dorcic, J., Komsic, J., & Markovic, S. (2019). Mobile technologies and applications towards smart tourism–state of the art. *Tourism Review*, *74*(1), 82–103. doi:10.1108/TR-07-2017-0121

Estevao, J., Carneiro, M. J., & Teixeira, L. (2020). Destination management systems' adoption and management model: Proposal of a framework. *Journal of Organizational Computing and Electronic Commerce*, *30*(2), 89–110. doi:10.1080/10919392.2020.1724765

Femenia-Serra, F., & Ivars-Baidal, J. A. (2021). Do smart tourism destinations really work? The case of Benidorm. *Asia Pacific Journal of Tourism Research*, *26*(4), 365–384. doi:10.1080/10941665.2018.1561478

Fyall, A., & Garrod, B. (2020). Destination management: A perspective article. *Tourism Review*, *75*(1), 165–169. doi:10.1108/TR-07-2019-0311

Gelter, J., Lexhagen, M., & Fuchs, M. (2021). A meta-narrative analysis of smart tourism destinations: Implications for tourism destination management. *Current Issues in Tourism*, *24*(20), 2860–2874. doi:10.1080/13683500.2020.1849048

Gretzel, U. (2022). The Smart DMO: A new step in the digital transformation of destination management organizations. *European Journal of Tourism Research*, *30*, 3002–3002. doi:10.54055/ejtr.v30i.2589

Hartman, S., & Heslinga, J. H. (2022). The Doughnut Destination: applying Kate Raworth's Doughnut Economy perspective to rethink tourism destination management. *Journal of Tourism Futures*.

He, Z., Wu, L., & Li, X. R. (2018). When art meets tech: The role of augmented reality in enhancing museum experiences and purchase intentions. *Tourism Management*, *68*, 127–139. doi:10.1016/j.tourman.2018.03.003

Houser, K. A., & Voss, W. G. (2018). GDPR: The end of Google and Facebook or a new paradigm in data privacy. *SSRN*, *25*, 1. doi:10.2139/ssrn.3212210

Hsu, C. C. (2018). Artificial intelligence in smart tourism: A conceptual framework. In *Proceedings of The 18th International Conference on Electronic Business* (pp. 124- 133). ICEB, Guilin, China.

Ivars-Baidal, J. A., Celdrán-Bernabeu, M. A., Femenia-Serra, F., Perles-Ribes, J. F., & Giner-Sánchez, D. (2021). Measuring the progress of smart destinations: The use of indicators as a management tool. *Journal of Destination Marketing & Management*, *19*, 100531. doi:10.1016/j.jdmm.2020.100531

Joseph, C., & Varghese, B. (2023). *Community Resilience and Crisis Management*. Stakeholders Perspective of the Tourism Industry.

Kashem, M. A., Shamsuddoha, M., Nasir, T., & Chowdhury, A. A. (2022). The role of artificial intelligence and blockchain technologies in sustainable tourism in the Middle East. *Worldwide Hospitality and Tourism Themes*.

Kontogianni, A., Alepis, E., & Patsakis, C. (2022). Smart tourism and artificial intelligence: Paving the way to the post-covid-19 era. *Advances in Artificial Intelligence-based Technologies: Selected Papers in Honour of Professor Nikolaos G. Bourbakis*, *1*, 93–109.

Lamsfus, C., Martín, D., Alzua-Sorzabal, A., & Torres-Manzanera, E. (2015). Smart tourism destinations: An extended conception of smart cities focusing on human mobility. In I. Tussyadiah & A. Inversini (Eds.), *Information and Communication Technologies in Tourism* (pp. 363–375). Springer.

Lee, H., Chung, N., & Claudia tom Dieck, M. (2018). The effect of hedonic and utilitarian values on satisfaction and loyalty of Airbnb users. *International Journal of Contemporary Hospitality Management, 30*(3), 1621–1645. doi:10.1108/IJCHM-09-2016-0504

Ma, R., & Lam, P. T. (2019). Investigating the barriers faced by stakeholders in open data development: A study on Hong Kong as a "smart city". *Cities (London, England), 92*, 36–46. doi:10.1016/j.cities.2019.03.009

Macrorie, R., Marvin, S., & While, A. (2021). Robotics and automation in the city: A research agenda. *Urban Geography, 42*(2), 197–217. doi:10.1080/02723638.2019.1698868

Mandić, A., & Kennell, J. (2021). Smart governance for heritage tourism destinations: Contextual factors and destination management organization perspectives. *Tourism Management Perspectives, 39*, 100862. doi:10.1016/j.tmp.2021.100862

Mariani, M., Bresciani, S., & Dagnino, G. B. (2021). The competitive productivity (CP) of tourism destinations: An integrative conceptual framework and a reflection on big data and analytics. *International Journal of Contemporary Hospitality Management, 33*(9), 2970–3002. doi:10.1108/IJCHM-09-2020-1102

Martins, C. A., Carneiro, M. J. A., & Pacheco, O. R. (2021). Key factors for implementation and success of destination management systems. Empirical evidence from European countries. *Industrial Management & Data Systems, 121*(6), 1287–1324. doi:10.1108/IMDS-11-2019-0598

Mrsic, L., Surla, G., & Balkovic, M. (2020). Technology-driven smart support system for tourist destination management organizations. In *International Conference on Innovative Computing and Communications: Proceedings of ICICC 2019,* Volume 1 (pp. 65-76). Singapore: Springer Singapore. 10.1007/978-981-15-1286-5_7

Muniz, E. C. L., Dandolini, G. A., Biz, A. A., & Ribeiro, A. C. (2021). Customer knowledge management and smart tourism destinations: A framework for the smart management of the tourist experience–SMARTUR. *Journal of Knowledge Management, 25*(5), 1336–1361. doi:10.1108/JKM-07-2020-0529

Nannelli, M., Capone, F., & Lazzeretti, L. (2023). Artificial intelligence in hospitality and tourism. State of the art and future research avenues. *European Planning Studies, 31*(7), 1–20. doi:10.1080/09654313.2023.2180321

Ng, V., & Kim, H. M. (2021). Autonomous vehicles and smart cities: A case study of Singapore. In *Smart cities for technological and social innovation* (pp. 265–287). Academic Press. doi:10.1016/B978-0-12-818886-6.00014-9

Noh, S. M., Kang, H. S., & Jang, S. Y. (2020). The Effects of Smart Tolling for the Improvement of Traffic Flow on the Seoul Tollgate with ARENA. *Journal of Advanced Simulation in Science and Engineering, 7*(2), 279–290. doi:10.15748/jasse.7.279

Pasquinelli, C., & Trunfio, M. (2023). Smart and Sustainable Destination Management: An Analytical Framework. *Sustainability-oriented Innovation in Smart Tourism: Challenges and Pitfalls of Technology Deployment for Sustainable Destinations*, 63-110.

Pillmayer, M., Scherle, N., & Volchek, K. (2021). Destination Management in Times of Crisis-Potentials of Open Innovation Approach in the Context of COVID-19? In *Information and Communication Technologies in Tourism 2021: Proceedings of the ENTER 2021 eTourism Conference,* (pp. 517-529). Springer International Publishing. 10.1007/978-3-030-65785-7_49

Prasad, D., Alizadeh, T., & Dowling, R. (2021). Multiscalar smart city governance in India. *Geoforum, 121*, 173–180. doi:10.1016/j.geoforum.2021.03.001

Ramadoss, T. S., Alam, H., & Seeram, R. (2018). Artificial intelligence and Internet of Things enabled circular economy. *The International Journal of Engineering and Science*, *7*(9), 55–63.

Ramesh, R., Divya, G., Dorairangaswamy, M. A., Unnikrishnan, K. N., Joseph, A., Vijayakumar, A., & Mani, A. (2019, July). Real-time vehicular traffic analysis using big data processing and IoT based devices for future policy predictions in smart transportation. In *2019 International Conference on Communication and Electronics Systems (ICCES)* (pp. 1482-1488). IEEE. 10.1109/ICCES45898.2019.9002261

Ribes, J. & Baidal, J. (2019). Smart sustainability: A new perspective in the sustainable tourism debate. *Investigaciones Regionales., 42*, 151–170.

Rustad, M. L., & Koenig, T. H. (2019). Towards a global data privacy standard. *Florida Law Review, 71*, 365.

Sharma, S. (2019). *Data privacy and GDPR handbook.* John Wiley & Sons. doi:10.1002/9781119594307

Soares, J. C., Domareski Ruiz, T. C., & Ivars Baidal, J. A. (2022). Smart destinations: A new planning and management approach? *Current Issues in Tourism*, *25*(17), 2717–2732. doi:10.1080/13683500.2021.1991897

Solazzo, G., Maruccia, Y., Lorenzo, G., Ndou, V., Del Vecchio, P., & Elia, G. (2022). Extracting insights from big social data for smarter tourism destination management. *Measuring Business Excellence*, *26*(1), 122–140. doi:10.1108/MBE-11-2020-0156

Sorokina, E., Wang, Y., Fyall, A., Lugosi, P., Torres, E., & Jung, T. (2022). Constructing a smart destination framework: A destination marketing organization perspective. *Journal of Destination Marketing & Management, 23*, 100688. doi:10.1016/j.jdmm.2021.100688

Wang, D., Li, X. R., & Li, Y. (2013). China's "smart tourism destination" initiative: A taste of the service-dominant logic. *Journal of Destination Marketing & Management*, *2*(2), 59–61. doi:10.1016/j.jdmm.2013.05.004

Yigitcanlar, T., Kankanamge, N., & Vella, K. (2021). How are smart city concepts and technologies perceived and utilized? A systematic geo-Twitter analysis of smart cities in Australia. *Journal of Urban Technology*, *28*(1 2), 135 154. doi:10.1080/10630732.2020.1753483

Zainal-Abidin, H., Scarles, C., & Lundberg, C. (2023). The antecedents of digital collaboration through an enhanced digital platform for destination management: A micro-DMO perspective. *Tourism Management, 96*, 104691. doi:10.1016/j.tourman.2022.104691

Section 4

Artificial Intelligence Prompting Digital Transformation: Ethics, Robotics, Machine Learning, and New Trends

Chapter 11
Understanding the Ethical and Social Consequences of Data Analytics for Organizational Management in the Age of AI:
Accounting Ethics Perspective

Siriyama Kanthi Herath
Clark Atlanta University, USA

Laksitha Maheshi Herath
New York University, USA

ABSTRACT

This chapter addresses the ethical and social consequences of using AI and data analytics in accounting. It looks into the impact of contemporary innovations on corporate governance and emphasizes the value of moral judgment. Despite the fact that AI and data analytics have digitized and given insights into accounting, understanding their ethical and social effects is crucial. The chapter addresses the advantages and drawbacks of applying AI to accounting, including changes in management, societal repercussions, prejudice, privacy issues, openness, and accountability. It additionally takes into account how automation will affect jobs and the accounting sector. The chapter urges stakeholders to prioritize ethics and control possible risks by highlighting ethical awareness and responsible decision-making when integrating AI and data analytics.

INTRODUCTION

This chapter examines the social and ethical implications of artificial intelligence (AI) and data analytics in accounting operations. The ethical and problem-solving facets of corporate governance serve as the

DOI: 10.4018/979-8-3693-1058-8.ch011

focus. The chapter will highlight how crucial it is to deal with these issues and provide suggestions for moral judgments that ought to be made in the context of AI-driven accounting.

Recent developments in artificial intelligence (AI) and data analytics have had an important effect on several business-related industries, including accounting. Unexpectedly, these cutting-edge technologies can manage massive amounts of financial data, automate time-consuming company processes, and generate in-depth analytical findings that could affect corporate strategic decision-making. Businesses employing AI and data analytics to enhance their accounting procedures must be aware of the financial rewards and the social and ethical implications of this revolutionary journey.

Two benefits of integrating data analytics and artificial intelligence into accounting procedures are increased efficiency and improved decision-making. Businesses must, however, acknowledge and deal with the serious ethical challenges this transition raises. To shed light on the complicated subject of AI-driven accounting, this chapter makes an effort to provide insights, principles, and recommendations that will allow firms to make moral decisions while utilizing the benefits of this cutting-edge technology.

With an emphasis on the ethical obligations that come along with technological advancement, this chapter concludes by laying the groundwork for an in-depth evaluation of data, machine learning, and analytics in accounting. It is important to use new technology responsibly and ethically, making sure they become tools to improve corporate governance and ethical choice-making rather than trying to destroy them. In the section that follows, we will explore the dynamic and constantly evolving area of organizational management, particularly its adaptation to the dynamic world of digital transformation.

THE EVOLVING AREA OF ORGANIZATIONAL MANAGEMENT

The subject of organizational management is always moving and adapting to changes in society, new technological advancements, and emerging trends. Businesses always try to change and improve their work to meet new demands in a difficult world where things are changing all the time (Cushing & Osti, 2023; Deloitte, 2021; Al-Haddad & Kotnour, 2015; Burnes, 2011). The main driving force behind organizational changes is the desire to capture possibilities that would ultimately boost internal productivity (Hussain, 2023). The process of establishing new policies, structures, or practices within an organization is known as organizational change or transformation. According to Hussain (2023), organizational change refers to the process through which a company or organization adjusts its objectives or regular activities, for example, to address and react to various situations or markets. Sharma (2020) asserts that six different types of organizational changes are frequently used, depending on the situation: structural change, strategic transformational change, people-centric organizational change, technical change, remedial change, and unplanned change. Managing transformation is a complex and risky process, which often leads to companies struggling with changing organizational projects and falling short of expected outcomes (Errida & Lotfi, 2021; Jacobs et al., 2013). Businesses must invest significantly in making numerous changes to adapt to the changing environment (Errida & Lotfi, 2021). Companies must also have the necessary skills and resources to manage a successful transformation. They must also have a clear plan in place to make the necessary changes and monitor their progress. Finally, companies must be willing to embrace change and take risks in order to achieve their desired outcomes.

Numerous change management models have been developed by academics and consulting firms in an effort to increase the success rate of organizational change management projects. A change management model, according to Rothwell and Sullivan (2005), acts as a directing tool that approves and

Figure 1. The evolving area of organizational management

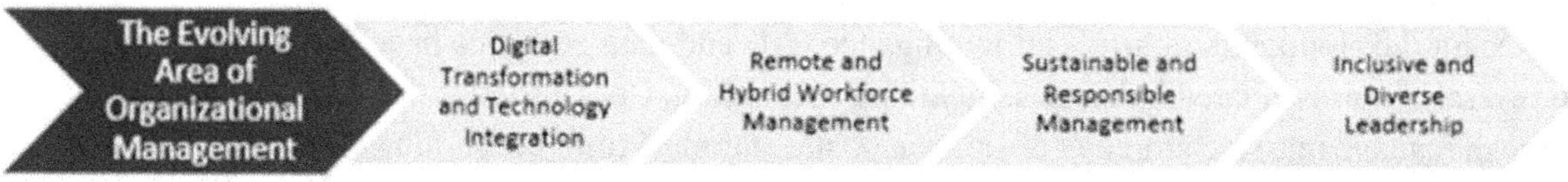

guides change projects. Procedural and descriptive models are the two categories of change management models that Parry et al. (2013) differentiate between. The steps necessary to plan and carry out change are explained by process models. These theories include Lewin's three-stage model of change (1947), Kotter's eight-step model (1995), and Kanter's change wheel model (2011). Conversely, a descriptive model pinpoints the critical components and factors that influence organizational performance and the success of programs aimed at organizational transformation. Errida & Lotfi (2021) examined 37 organizational change management models (2021) examined 37 organizational change management models to determine the variables influencing the efficacy of change management. Different kinds of organizational change models highlight unique characteristics and viewpoints to help identify the various factors affecting the results of organizational transformation activities (Errida & Lotfi, 2021).

The path that organizational management will take in the future is dictated by recent events such as changing technological, economic, and political settings, which are the outcome of various important concerns that have recently gotten more attention. This section examines how these crucial factors (Figure 1) influence enterprises and decision-makers.

Digital Transformation and Technology Integration

The use of artificial intelligence (AI) and data analytics in accounting operations is examined in this chapter regarding its social and ethical implications. The ethical and problem-solving facets of corporate governance serve as the focus. The chapter will highlight how crucial it is to deal with these issues and provide suggestions for moral judgments that ought to be made in the context of AI-driven accounting.

Because of the technology's rapid advancement, specifically in the areas of artificial intelligence, data analytics, automation, and cloud computing, organizations are going through a digital transformation (Jedynak et al., 2021). Businesses are now utilizing technology to increase productivity, improve customer experiences, and collect meaningful data from processes. Because digital tools and platforms are now so important in decision-making, resource allocation, and performance evaluation, organizations are transitioning into a more agile and data-driven era of management.

Remote and Hybrid Workforce Management

The COVID-19 epidemic made remote work and a mix of onsite and offsite jobs very popular. Because businesses are now open to these flexible ways of working more often, there has been a major shift in how teams at companies are managed (Jiang et al., 2023). To ensure the effectiveness and productivity of distributed teams, virtual collaboration technologies, remote communication techniques, and a focus on worker wellness have all become essential components. Effective change management, according to Carnall (2007), demands a combination of three managerial skill sets: managing transitions, addressing organizational culture, and developing the politics of organizational change. He also emphasized the need for competencies and abilities during times of change. New methods for group dynamics, leadership, and corporate culture need to be developed because of the shifting makeup of the workforce.

Sustainable and Responsible Management

Increasing awareness of environmental and social issues has placed sustainability and corporate social responsibility (CSR) at the forefront of organizational management. The practice of treating a company's or institution's stakeholders ethically or responsibly is known as corporate social responsibility. "Ethically or responsibly" refers to dealing with significant stakeholders in a way that is accepted by global standards (Hopkins, 2010). Stakeholders, including customers, investors, and employees, now demand that businesses demonstrate ethical and sustainable practices. Organizations are integrating sustainability initiatives into their strategies, supply chains, and reporting mechanisms to align with global sustainability goals and foster long-term success. Here is a practical example of how a company might use corporate social responsibility (CSR) programs to promote ethical and sustainable business practices:

For instance: The Sustainable Supply Chain Management of a Retail Company

Consider a retailer that has decided to run its operations more ethically and sustainably. The company aspires to meet the needs of its employees, investors, and clients while simultaneously upholding global environmental standards. It acknowledges that its supply chain has a substantial impact on society and the environment.

- **Supplier Selection and Ethical Practices:** First, the company not only looks at cost-effectiveness when picking suppliers but also thinks about their moral and environmental practices. We prefer suppliers who use nature-friendly materials, have fewer carbon emissions, and follow fair work rules.
- **Reducing Carbon Footprint:** Reducing the transportation sector's carbon footprint is the company's aim. The company wants to lower the carbon footprint of transport. Combining commodities, using more efficient vehicles, and investing in renewable energy sources are some of the strategies that will be used to achieve this goal. The company is also encouraging employees to use public transportation.
- **Waste Reduction:** To reduce waste, the company recycles things and uses less packaging. It also asks customers to return unwanted items for fixing up again.
- **Fair Employment and Ethical Labor Practices:** Every employee of the company is guaranteed fair compensation, secure working conditions, and opportunities for professional growth. They also promise to hire a diverse workforce and promote gender equality.
- **Community Engagement:** The business interacts socially with the communities in which it conducts business. This means giving money to local non-government organizations, environmental projects, and schools. They encourage workers to volunteer so they can help the community.
- **Transparent Reporting:** The firm publishes an annual report each year about its path to reach targets for the environment and community. In this research, the main ways to measure how well something is doing are reducing carbon emissions, adding funds to social activities, and lessening waste.

- **Product Innovation:** The business puts money into research and development to make eco-friendly goods. They think about using less energy in creation and employing resources that can be recycled or renewable.
- **Consumer Education:** The firm wants to teach its customers why sustainability is important. This will help them convince people of the need for environmentally good choices. We might give prizes to people who bring back used items and recycle them for future use.

The shop saves cash, grows customer loyalty, and decreases trash and power use. It shows the company's care for the community by using these steps. This picture shows how businesses can incorporate caring for the environment and doing good, or CSR, into their main jobs. This lets them reach worldwide standards to succeed in the long run.

Inclusive and Diverse Leadership

Organizations understand the importance of diversity and inclusion in leadership roles. Leadership that includes everyone helps with different ideas, makes new things happen, and builds a good place to work. Businesses are trying hard to make everyone feel welcome. They work against unfairness, give equal chances, and support different people in all parts of the company.

The changing areas of how we manage businesses show the huge influence of new technology, different work habits, being aware of society, and changes in doing business. To do well in today's fast-changing business world, companies need to use technology better. They must also get used to people working from home and care for the environment while leading everyone fairly. By keeping an eye on changing areas and making plans that match new trends, companies can build strength, compete well, and succeed in the always-changing world of managing businesses. The digital revolution and new business models have made customer needs and behaviors very different. This puts a lot of stress on current companies while also shaking up some markets (Verhoef et al., 2021). Now, we are going to examine what data analytics and artificial intelligence (AI) do in the field of accounting.

THE ROLE OF AI AND DATA ANALYTICS IN ACCOUNTING

Let us now look in more detail at how data analytics and AI have revolutionized the accounting industry. We also discovered that these high-tech technologies may significantly help the industry in numerous ways, such as better risk management, cutting-edge data analytical strength, enhanced performance of operations, and more conscious decision-making. We will also present issues and dilemmas related to the use of AI as well as data analytics in accounting. Artificial intelligence, AI, and data analytics have led to a considerable upheaval in the accounting industry over the past several years. This section highlights the many benefits that these advanced technologies bring to accounting procedures and the significant transformations they have brought. There are quite a few interesting new potentials for accountants provided by data analytics and AI, but there are also some ethical issues that need to be carefully discussed. We will now discuss the benefits and potential applications of data analytics and artificial intelligence in accounting.

Figure 2. Benefits and opportunities of AI and data analytics in accounting

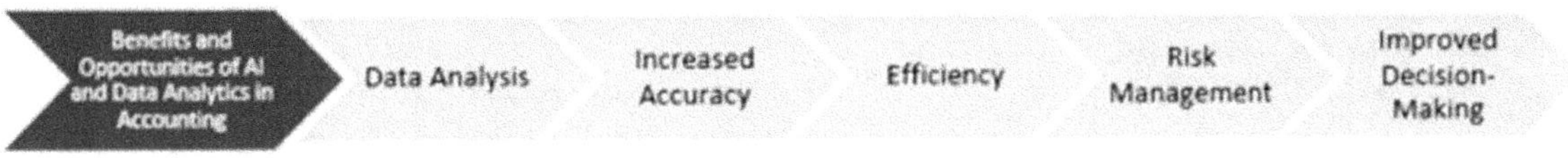

Benefits and Opportunities

The advantages and opportunities associated with integrating data analytics and artificial intelligence (AI) in the accounting sector are depicted in Figure 2. The next section discusses these. Businesses will be able to make well-informed decisions about incorporating artificial intelligence and data analytics into accounting procedures by looking at and clarifying these benefits and opportunities.

Data Analysis

Through AI and data analytics, accountants can process massive amounts of financial information quickly and accurately. Advanced algorithms enable information extraction from both structured and unstructured data, therefore improving the decision-making process. Similarly, AI integration with data analytics would open a world of predictive capabilities that could transform strategic planning and financial forecasts. By analyzing historical data patterns and identifying new trends, organizations will be able to predict market changes, anticipate risks for the organization beforehand, and formulate intelligently crafted strategies based on changing markets. In this constantly changing ecosystem, accounting specialists can keep up with innovations and maintain a competitive edge in the face of disruption by leveraging big data, analytics insights from data, and AI (Bose et al., 2023).

Increased Accuracy

Automation of routine tasks reduces the likelihood of human errors, enhancing the accuracy of financial reporting and analysis. AI-powered tools can perform complex calculations with precision, minimizing the risk of mistakes. With the use of AI and data analytics, the historically static accounting landscape is transformed into a dynamic environment of insights and efficiencies. Due to the accuracy and speed incorporated into AI-driven processes, accounting and financial specialists can navigate vast data sets with exceptional accuracy, enabling them to draw relevant insights in real time. A company can sustain a competitive advantage in a market that is always changing by encouraging proactive financial management and accelerating decision-making.

In this real-world example, the retail firm's accounting and financial management procedures have undergone a substantial transformation thanks to automation and AI-driven financial analysis tools. This gives the organization a competitive edge in the market by improving accuracy and speeding up decision-making.

Figure 3. Ethical issues and challenges

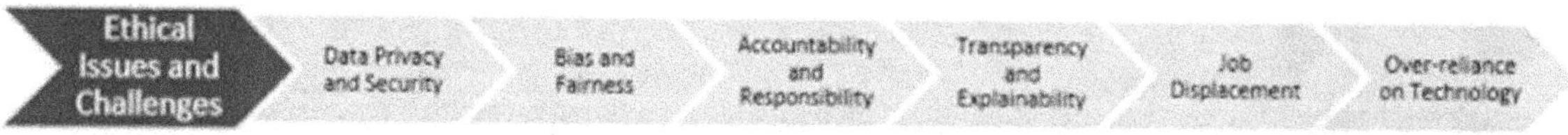

Efficiency

AI-powered automation simplifies accounting processes, allowing accountants to focus their time on more strategic and added-value roles. This greater efficiency could translate into cost savings and productivity. There are other advantages beyond the balance sheet. AI helps in decision-making processes, and they become faster as well as more informed, which provides businesses with an edge over the competition within a fast-paced corporate setting. Accounting professionals' satisfaction and morale increase as they move from mundane tasks to analytical or, in other terms, strategic posts whereby an increased engagement with the official staff is possible. In other words, incorporating AI into accounting practices transforms the specific dynamics of company success as well as how financial duties are handled in general.

Risk Management

Financial management is a field whose calculus alone has the power to reveal patterns and peculiarities under large amounts of financial information. AI and data analytics are used in this particular area. This skill is vital for enhancing the detection of fraud and, consequently, increasing the effectiveness of risk assessment procedures. Perhaps AI-powered analytics, playing the role of diligent guardian against any fraud or eccentricities, would not be spotted if they were incapable of sorting through large volumes of data and singling out variations deviating from standard rules.

Other than fighting fraud, though, this interaction between AI and data analytics spans a greater set of risk management actions. It can detect trends, facilitate the conduct of proactive risk assessment, and contain financial crime. Through the consideration of potential dangers and lessening them before they escalate, businesses can create a more favorable environment to sustain risk management principles. With the help of AI and data analytics, businesses could enhance their overall risk management methodology and strengthen their financial defenses against fraud. But it helps them to cross the dangerous terrain of financial security and risk management much faster.

Improved Decision-Making

To give managers a complete picture of financial performance and pinpoint potential improvement areas, data-driven insights are leveraged. Better corporate results are usually obtained using this style of informed decision-making. Data is made available to organizations so they can improve techniques and use it as a compass, encouraging a culture of ongoing improvement. In the next section, we will discuss the issues and challenges of data analytics and artificial intelligence in accounting.

Ethical Issues and Challenges

The numerous ethical issues and challenges resulting from the accounting industry's usage of data analytics and artificial intelligence (AI) (Figure 3) are covered in this section. The chapter makes an effort to shed light on the ethical issues that surface as these cutting-edge technologies transform conventional accounting methods.

Data Privacy and Security

Data security and privacy pose major concerns due to how heavily the areas of artificial intelligence (AI) and data analytics rely on massive data repositories. One of the most significant duties given to accountants is safeguarding private financial information from illegal access and potential breaches (Nakamura, 2023; Lee & Xiao, 2018). As technology-driven processes advance, it is necessary to preserve the confidentiality and integrity of financial data to meet moral standards and legal obligations. The compromise of critical financial data must be averted by developing an extensive cybersecurity protection strategy. Consumer opinions, anxieties, and reservations over the use and disclosure of their personal information are intimately tied to privacy issues (Malhotra et al., 2004). The identity of the disclosed data, the particular context of data exposure, and the individual perceptions of the entity in charge of data collection are just a few of the many variables that affect these worries, which are inextricably linked to the complex dynamics of data handling (Bansal et al., 2016). In turn, strong data security and privacy laws are the basis for artificial intelligence, data analytics, and financial data protection. Below are some tools and practical applications associated with these regulations:

Data Encryption:

Example: Financial data must be encrypted in transit and at rest.
Discussion: Data encryption provides the assurance that information cannot be read or used improperly, even if forbidden access is somehow gained. Personal financial information and privacy need to be protected.

Access Control:

Example: RBAC, which means role-based access control, is a technique that helps to secure data in such a way that it can be accessed by only the rightful people at any given time.
Discussion: RBAC will ensure only those with legitimate access to financial data are allowed, which will prevent the risk of data breaches.

Regular Audits and Monitoring:

Example: Use intrusion detection systems to monitor network activity and conduct regular security audits.
Discussion: Frequent monitoring and audits are conducted to allow for finding and addressing any alleged vulnerabilities or unauthorized access attempts promptly.

Employee Training:

Example: Educate employees on adequate privacy and data security protocols.

Discussion: Data breaches tend to be detected by employees first because they become suspicious that their security protective tools are not functioning as planned. This education enables them to understand their duty to safeguard information in the financial sector.

Data Minimization:

Example: For example, having only the needed company operational focus data to be gathered and stored is 'necessary information', meaning sensitive details are much less at risk.
Discussion: One way to offset the potential consequences of a security breach is by reducing both what data you collect and how much information you collect.

Privacy Policies and Consent:

Example: Ensure to inform and obtain the consent of customers before collecting or using their personal information.
Discussion: In addition to this, it is imperative that the consent of a consumer be sought and transparency maintained so that consumer confidence remains intact even as compliance with applicable privacy laws is adhered to.

Data Anonymization:

Example: You can apply data anonymization techniques in analytics datasets for extracting personally identifiable information (PII).
Discussion: Anonymization is one of the methods that can be used by commands to protect personal data objects during the process of their analysis.

Incident Response Plan:

Example: Install the latest security patches for all software and systems.
Discussion: Outdated software, also noted as the use of unsupported systems, is one of the most common aspects observed in a majority, if not all, of the compromises that occur. Frequent updates help to seal up every single possible security hole.

Regular Software Updates and Patch Management:

Example: Update all software and systems with the latest security patches.
Discussion: Outdated software is a common target for security risks. Regular updates help close any potential security gaps.

Third-Party Risk Management:

Example: Ensure that the data security practices of outside contractors who might have private access to your financial details are well-vetted and closely monitored.
Discussion: Third-party services are often a source of vulnerabilities for data breaches. To mitigate this danger, good investigation and effective monitoring are required.

Therefore, it can be said that ensuring financial information protection, analysis, and AI through data security and privacy considerations must always remain an integrated measure by also taking into account the following aspects, such as staff training, technological innovation, or progression—the balance between being innovative yet compliant with one's respective laws regarding anti-privacy. By implementing these security measures, enterprises will probably attract new customers as a result of the promises they can make that their financial data is secure and that the business complies with all laws necessary by law.

Bias and Fairness

Systematizing processes are becoming more and more automated, and it can be quite challenging to determine who is to blame for errors or questionable judgments. Accountants must therefore urgently develop transparent accountability frameworks that are compatible with AI-driven processes. These frameworks serve as essential road maps, outlining the roles of both human accountants and automated technologies to increase transparency, lower risks, and protect the integrity of financial processes. People who address ethical issues in the workplace are particularly concerned about what is now known as the responsibility gap, or the extent to which or likelihood that the adoption of technology will result in the abdication of ethical responsibility for the consequences of decisions made by real people, in this case, accountants and taxpayers. Gunz and Thorne (2020) claim that this is a major concern for these individuals.

Transparency and Comprehensibility

Transparency and interpretability often make AI and data analytics processes intricate complicated even obscure Thus, some findings appear to serve absolutely no clear justifiable reason. Stakeholder trust needs to be established by accountants with regard to explanationability and transparency. Moreover, accountants aid in a better perception of the financial landscape by imparting knowledge about how these technologies function and illuminating good concepts regarding decision-making. This pursuit of transparency aligns with modern accounting ethics codes and enhances trust among shareholders.

Job Displacement

One of the main risks is that accounting professionals may lose their jobs since AI and automation are getting better and better. Therefore, the impact of the workforce must be handled with care from now on in terms of moral considerations. With this in mind, it is desirable from a professional point of view to start addressing opportunities to up-skill and re-skill even beforehand, besides taking a proactive approach towards how layoffs could occur when labor market alterations are triggered. Organizations can strike a balance between technological advancement and the welfare of their human labor force by emphasizing some ethical considerations.

Over-Reliance on Technology

Despite the many advantages that AI provides, a word of caution should be kept in mind: relying too much on technology without human control might even lead to blind trust in algorithms. Confidence without proper reason only increases the probability of mistakenly failing to spot significant mistakes or risks that could easily evade analytic detection. That said, the need for a balance between AI strength and human supervision scrutiny becomes critical to making sure that full and accurate results can be achieved during complicated procedures throughout.

The main benefits of AI and data analytics for the accounting profession include better analysis of information, accuracy, workflow efficiency, risk management improvement, and successful decision-making practices. However, these technologies also raise ethical concerns and issues that need to be resolved for their responsible and sustainable application. Diakopoulos (2016) suggests that businesses such as Automated Insights and Narrative Science use automated writing algorithms to create news articles from structured data, which is an efficient way of accomplishing this task without incurring costs.

Accounting ethics help guide the ethical application of AI and data analytics in accounting practices. Accountants must be guided by the three principles of integrity, transparency, and accountability when deploying these technologies. By being proactive in identifying and addressing ethical issues, the accounting profession can fully harness AI capabilities and data analytics tools without jeopardizing its overall integrity. Floridi and Taddeo (2016) argue that the solutions data ethics will provide will only maximize the benefits of data science for our societies, for all of us, and for our ecosystems as a macro-ethics. The section below discusses the ethical frameworks that accountants may use to ensure the moral application of AI and data analytics in the accounting business.

ETHICAL FRAMEWORKS FOR AI AND DATA ANALYTICS IN ACCOUNTING

Moral and just action is based on ethical frameworks for AI as well as data analytics in accounting. When implementing AI and data analytics in accounting, the following frameworks and considerations should be considered.

- **Explainability and Transparency Framework:** Make sure that data analytics and AI processes are explainable and visible to stakeholders so they know why certain choices were made and what results were produced. Detail the methodology, data sources, and algorithms used in accounting analytics.
- **Data Privacy and Security Framework:** To protect sensitive financial and personal information, adhere to data protection regulations like GDPR (General Data Protection Regulation) or HIPAA (Health Insurance Portability and Accountability Act).
  Implement reliable cybersecurity practices to safeguard information from attacks and unwanted access.
- **Fairness and Bias Mitigation Framework:** Evaluate biases in data and algorithms regularly, and take the necessary steps to stop treating various individuals or groups unfairly.
  Strictly forbid the use of protected variables in activities requiring AI and data analytics, such as age, gender, or ethnicity.
- **Accountability and Responsibility Framework:** Describe the duties and roles for the data analytics and AI projects the accounting department is working on.
  Create a system of responsibility for AI-based judgments.
- **Making Decisions Using Information and Consent:** Before gathering and using someone's data for analytics, get their permission.
  It is important to thoroughly inform stakeholders about how and why their information will be used.

- **Compliance with Regulatory Requirements:** Keep up with accounting and data privacy requirements to maintain compliance.
  Create and adhere to reporting and issue-resolution procedures for compliance.
- **Constant observation and auditing:** Regularly evaluate the ethical framework and enhance it in light of the lessons learned.
  Continuously monitor and audit data analytics and AI systems to find and correct ethical issues.
- **Professional Code of Conduct Framework:** Accountants are required to abide by their professional code of conduct, which frequently includes moral and honest standards.
- **Ethics Education Framework:** Provide accounting professionals with programs and training on the moral application of AI and data analytics.
- **Ethics Committees and Oversight Framework:** Create ethics committees to monitor and provide ethical guidance for initiatives leveraging AI and data analytics.
- **Stakeholder Engagement Framework:** Involve relevant parties in discussions and decision-making about AI and data analytics, such as clients, staff members, and regulatory bodies.
- **Public Reporting and Accountability Framework:** Disseminate studies on the ethical uses of data analytics and artificial intelligence in accounting. This will demonstrate that you are forthright and truthful about your moral deeds.

In this section, we will also provide ethical standards that guide the use of AI and data analytics in the accounting industry. The moral principles and goals that influence a corporation's decisions and actions are known as business ethics. Maintaining credibility, goodwill, and long-term viability in business requires upholding ethical norms. 'Business ethics', according to Thomas (2005), consists of at least three components:

- **Corporate Values:** Integrity, honesty, and fairness are the cornerstones of a company's ethical foundation.
- **Codes of ethics**: A code of ethics is a set of rules that, beyond personal values, specify the specific actions that a firm will or will not take, such as prohibiting employees from accepting bribes.
- **Corporate governance:** Corporate governance, which includes non-executive members of the Board of Directors, is a catch-all word for the rules and procedures that regulate boards of directors. It is directly tied to corporate ethics because these policies are influenced by the Board moral standards.

The increasing adoption of AI and data analytics in accounting practices has raised moral concerns related to bias, responsibility, openness, and privacy in AI-driven processes. As the role of technology becomes more prominent in the accounting profession, it becomes essential to establish and implement accounting-related ethical standards to ensure the ethical and proper use of AI and data analytics.

Moral Concerns in AI-Driven Accounting Processes

In this section, we will explore the ethical considerations surrounding AI-driven accounting processes. The discussion will address moral concerns and their implications within this technological context. AI-generated technology has greatly improved the accuracy and effectiveness of accounting procedures.

It also creates significant ethical concerns regarding accountability, transparency, and potential biases associated with the automated nature of financial decision-making.

- **Bias**: As artificial intelligence systems become more complicated, decisions can be influenced by potential biases in the training data. This concern is particularly relevant when historical biases in statistics relate to ongoing discriminatory practices, such as gender-based reimbursement disparities. Accountants play a critical role in navigating this moral minefield, identifying prejudice, and ensuring that AI-driven procedures generate fair and equitable outcomes for all parties involved.
- **Responsibility:** More problems with accountability arise as tasks of accounting are automated by AI and data analytics. Hence, accountants play a key role in defining clear lines of power and ensuring that AI systems stay within corporate rules and morals when making decisions. Accountants ensure that the financial procedures are reliable and transparent within the company by establishing these limitations. This concerted effort combines the growth of technology with moral principles that support ethical financial management.
- **Openness:** AI and data analytics, when applied to accounting, are key building blocks of transparency as well as explainability. Accountants must ensure that the findings provided by AI systems can be comprehended and validated so that they gain the credibility and trust of stakeholders. By focusing on these principles, which not only support moral values but also ensure the reliability of financial processes, accountants enhance their connections with stakeholders.
- **Privacy**: Since AI and data analytics depend highly on huge databases, the security and privacy of such information need to be ensured. They are therefore essential to maintaining strict privacy rules and making sure that illegal access to sensitive financial information does not occur and that the data is safe. By vigilantly safeguarding this data, accountants maintain moral norms and create stakeholder trust that promotes the maintenance of a secure and stable financial environment. This commitment to data security is synchronous with the increase in digital responsibility and responsible financial management.

AI in accounting raises ethical issues related to bias, accountability, transparency, and data security on the one hand while enhancing accuracy on the other. Accountants are critical in resolving these issues by setting moral standards, facilitating transparency, and ensuring data security for AI-powered accounting processes.

Accounting-Related Ethical Standards

It is accepted that adherence to moral principles and the incorporation of accounting mandates as an original point for honest financial reporting are vital aspects of ensuring the integrity and reliability of proprietary data. These rules help accountants to secure ethics and law and order, maintain stability in their business partners, and ensure the truthfulness of financial reporting.

- **Professional Codes of Conduct:** This means that accounting agencies and organizations have a critical role to play in the process of guiding ethical integration into AI and data analytics by defining sound ethical standards of behavior. These standards should comprehensively address the ethical responsibilities that accountants have when using AI technology and data analytics. These entities can potentially help professionals address AI-driven systems' problematic ethical decisions by setting well-defined principles, promoting financial action accountability, and enhancing morals. The formation and maintenance of such ethical bases will contribute to the long-term reliability, as well as moral decency, of accounting and technology businesses.

- **Ethical Review Boards**: In the case of businesses incorporating AI into accounting functions, they must form ethical review committees. These committees are necessary to review AI systems, identify possible ethical issues, and ensure adherence to the library's pre-specified moral standards. By promoting a proactive ethical approach, organizations can lessen the risk of biases, data privacy violations, and unexpected outcomes, which will boost confidence in AI-driven accounting processes. Last but not least, ethical review committees serve as solid groundwork for promoting openness and honesty in the application of AI in the accounting sector.
- **Ethical Awareness**: In their efforts to discuss the ethical aspects of AI and data privacy, accountants should be engaged in programs aimed at training and awareness. Through this, we train accountants sufficiently so that they have skills and knowledge of how to use AI technology with ethics. Being experts and experienced professionals, accountants are more equipped to handle the difficult tasks that may accompany AI use as well as data analytics in line with their work, owing to the training they have on issues related to ethical awareness. Awareness about ethical matters is specified as a strong element of this norm for numerous professional and commercial standards. One of the most important goals is to motivate people and groups to conduct themselves morally and correctly towards society. Some examples of how ethical consideration is typically included in standards are as follows:
- **Code of Conduct and Ethics:** These codes of ethics and conduct describe the moral principles as well as standards that participants or members of a variety of professional organizations and industries are assumed to adhere to. These regulations set norms and patterns of conduct as well, imparting morals to the local setup.
- **Ethical Guidelines:** Moral Principles Standards are characteristically specific ethical principles that provide clearly defined instructions on how to handle moral dilemmas or difficult ethical situations. Such standards can be utilized when judging so-called conflicts of interest, privacy issues, and questions about fairness and honesty.
- **Protections for Reporters and Whistle-blowers:** Many standards also have clauses that protect individuals who report violations or unethical behavior to the authorities. This promotes ethical identification since people who witness unethical activities are not afraid to report them.
- **Legal and Regulatory Compliance:** It is usually the case that legal and regulatory compliance translates into ethical awareness. Standards, in this sense, may include the requirements being imposed by laws and regulations that are ethically relevant, stressing the importance of doing what is morally right.

  For standards to contain an ethical dimension, it is important and necessary since ethics awareness can facilitate responsible behavior that sees individuals and organizations approach the world 'morally' safely, starting with their conduct; they suggest moral decisions should be taken based on how one acts (which suits a particular occasion) morally, not rebuking personal failures of people; rather, social arrangements have failed in guiding morality by doing activities beneficial to both parties Standards can serve as a good strategy for raising ethical awareness and behavior by defining the targeted types of ethical requirements to be observed and advising on how they may be accomplished.

- **External Audits and Certifications**: In this respect, organizations can demonstrate their dedication to the standards of ethics in AI and data analytics across all domains by subjecting themselves to independent audits and obtaining necessary certifications. Such impartial appraisals not only increase the stakeholders' confidence but also provide solid proof that the organization is committed to ethical and transparent conduct in these advanced fields.

Maintaining ethical standards and accounting regulations is crucial to ensuring the dependability and integrity of financial information, especially as AI and data analytics grow more prevalent in the sector. Accountants are guided by a comprehensive framework that upholds accountability, openness, and stakeholder trust while protecting the long-term legitimacy of AI-driven accounting procedures. Professional conduct standards, ethical review panels, education efforts, and external audits make up this system.

Ethical and Proper Implementation

The adoption of new technologies, particularly AI, has led to significant changes in a variety of industries, and accounting is no exception. However, if accounting processes driven by AI are to be beneficial, mitigate risks, and preserve moral virtue, then they must succeed. The new technology, particularly AI, has led to significant changes in a range of industries, including accounting. For AI-driven accounting procedures to help eliminate risks and be aligned with ethical standards, they should be implemented properly.

The use of AI may be gaining steam in accounting operations; however, human oversight remains paramount. It cannot be overstated that the role of accountants is to preserve their right to make final selections while also ensuring the accuracy and ethical conduct of duties guided by AI under active supervision. Attention should always be focused on the possibility of including ethical themes in AI deployment within accounting. On the one hand, by upgrading AI systems and monitoring them regularly while assessing their functions, potential ethical twists can be identified immediately and resolved to maintain moral behavior that is also unbiased against all parties involved. It calls for collaboration to create accounting ethical best practices and form an altogether round comprehension of AI ethics. Collaboration among accounting industry stakeholders, regulatory bodies, and academic researchers to develop a framework that facilitates the ethical use of AI may make it easier for people to share ideas, information, and thoughts.

Finally, since artificial intelligence (AI) and data analytics are becoming a distinctly integrated part of accounting processes, they are currently addressing the ethical implications. Accountants can address moral issues associated with prejudice, accountability, transparency, and confidentiality to ensure AI-driven decisions comply with ethical guidelines. Additionally, the setting of ethical standards related to accounting and prudent practices in artificial intelligence will create a basis for using technology well and ethically when using it in accounting. In addition, trust will be formed among the stakeholders in a way that makes them believe in their decision-making process within the accounting profession, making ethical frameworks have a positive impact when it comes to reacting to AI. In the subsequent part, we will analyze the potential bias and equity in accounting algorithms.

ADDRESSING BIAS AND FAIRNESS IN ACCOUNTING ALGORITHMS

In this section, possible prejudices in the accounting algorithms and data sets used in AI and data analytics will be investigated. As it examines strategies and methods for identifying and eradicating prejudice, the importance of fairness and equity in accounting practices will be underlined. We will look at the potential functions that AI could play in assisting us in achieving these goals, with a focus on the need to address bias and guarantee fair outcomes in AI-driven accounting decision-making.

In this section, we delve into the critical issue of bias and fairness in accounting algorithms used in AI and data analytics. As AI-driven decision-making becomes more prevalent in the accounting profession, it is essential to investigate and mitigate possible prejudices present in the algorithms and data sets used. The overarching goal is to ensure fairness, equity, and ethical integrity in accounting practices.

Possible Biases in Accounting Algorithms

There is a risk of bias in the data sets used to train AI systems in the field of accounting, since previous financial data may have underlying biases. Accountants must carry out thorough data set audits to find any potential biases and stop biased historical data from influencing the AI's decision-making processes.

AI-driven accounting is more difficult because of algorithmic bias. Biases that form as a result of parameter selection and algorithm design may lead to skewed results. One must extensively look for and comprehend these biases to remedy them and finally establish an environment that is factual and impartial.

When applying AI to accounting, it's critical to take into account how it might reproduce human prejudices. Because AI learns from prior human decisions, accounting experts must carefully evaluate whether biases are upheld or challenged during the decision-making process. This highlights the necessity of proactive prejudice reduction strategies.

Accountants have to perform thorough data audits and employ proactive bias reduction evaluations to ensure fair and accurate decision-making due to the danger of biases in AI-driven accounting algorithms resulting from historical data and algorithm design. The importance of accounting professionals in promoting impartiality and transparency in AI-enhanced processes for accounting is highlighted by protections against the reproduction of human biases in AI systems.

Strategies for Identifying and Eradicating Bias

The crucial issue of bias in AI systems has received increased attention as AI continues to transform the accounting profession. Financial AI judgments that are biased could have a big influence on accuracy and ethical concerns. This study focuses on specific methods developed specifically for the subject of AI-driven accounting to handle the challenging issue of recognizing and eliminating bias in data sets, algorithmic frameworks, and human-technology interactions.

- **Data auditing:** Business growth and decision-making are expected to accelerate with the usage of technology (Gonzales & Hargreaves, 2022; Brit, 2021). When operating in the internet economy, however, AI runs into several prejudices (Varsha, 2023). Data auditing, which requires frequent evaluations to detect and remove biases inherent in datasets, is one of the most crucial elements of bias identification for AI-driven accounting. Accountants are in charge of making sure that the information used to train AI reflects diversity and inclusivity and is free from prejudice.

- **Algorithmic Testing:** An accounting AI bias identification method should involve comprehensive testing of algorithms. To make the system a bit more balanced, accountants have to go through these algorithms very thoroughly, using several test scenarios that show potential biases and how they influence decision-making.
- **Explainable AI:** Accounting professionals can understand how the algorithms operate through some explainable AI methodologies. This openness means that equipping the AI systems in accounting with the capability to spot biased results and take immediate action improves the accountability of those systems.

So, this section considered how to identify and eradicate bias in AI-based accounting because of the impact that it has on accounting. Addressing bias-related problems in AI accounting systems, the study suggests that data auditing must be used to eliminate existing biases; algorithm testing should ensure fairness and the use of explainable AI, promoting transparency and system accountability. This study outlines the approaches developed for this market.

The Importance of Fairness and Equity in Accounting Practices

To maintain the correctness of accounting systems, fairness and equality are crucial building blocks. By assuring accuracy in financial reporting, these principles help stakeholders have faith in financial information. The pursuit of justice and equity by accounting professionals strengthens the pillars of sound economic decision-making and organizational sustainability.

- **Trust and Reputation:** Fairness and equity serve as the cornerstones for establishing trust among stakeholders and promoting an environment of openness and dependability. A company's reputation and consumer and public trust are enhanced when unbiased and fair decision-making processes are maintained.
- **Regulatory Compliance:** Many nations have emphasized the importance of justice and non-discrimination in the decision-making processes in the rules and regulations that have been put in place. To avoid legal repercussions and sustain ethical standards in their professional responsibilities, accountants are responsible for ensuring rigorous adherence to these norms. Accounting experts contribute to a just and acceptable financial system by abiding by legal requirements.
- **Social Impact:** Algorithms used in biased accounting may worsen social inequality, which has negative effects on people and societies. Due to their proficiency in navigating the ethical and cultural consequences of AI-driven decision-making, accountants are vital in identifying and minimizing these effects. Accountants should actively promote ethical behavior and help create a more hospitable financial environment by taking into account the wider societal ramifications.

Fairness and equity are vital factors in trustworthy accounting processes if you want to maintain stakeholder confidence and regulatory compliance. Accountants are essential to attaining these objectives because they allow companies to protect their reputations, follow the law, and contribute to society.

AI's Role in Addressing Bias and Ensuring Fair Outcomes

In a time of widespread integration, the capacity of AI to both encourage and oppose bias has come into sharp focus. As AI systems have an increasing impact on critical decision-making processes across a range of disciplines, the need to eliminate bias and offer fair conclusions has grown increasingly important. The different ways that AI can aid in the fight against bias are examined in this study, including strategies that employ these technologies to encourage justice, diversity, and moral decision-making.

- **Fair AI Development:** Integrating fairness considerations into AI development from the outset can prevent the perpetuation of biases.
- **AI Decision Auditing:** AI algorithms can be programmed to flag potentially biased decisions for human review, providing an opportunity for corrective action.
- **Diversity in AI Development:** Diverse teams developing AI algorithms can lead to more comprehensive perspectives on fairness and bias, fostering inclusive decision-making.

Addressing bias and ensuring fairness in accounting algorithms is crucial for ethical and responsible AI-driven decision-making. Works by Wong (2020), Costanza-Chock (2020), and Grusky (2019) focus on algorithmic bias based on racial bias, disparities in gender, and class and economic inequality in social theory.

By investigating possible biases, implementing strategies for bias identification and eradication, and prioritizing fairness and equity in accounting practices, accountants can build trust, comply with regulations, and mitigate the adverse social impacts of biased AI decisions. AI has the potential to play a positive role in achieving these goals, but it requires proactive efforts and a commitment to ethical AI development and implementation in the accounting profession. Gaps between the design and operation of algorithms and our understanding of their ethical implications can have severe consequences, affecting individuals as well as groups and whole societies (Mittelstadt et al., 2016).

PRIVACY AND DATA PROTECTION IN ACCOUNTING ANALYTICS

Issues related to anonymity have been posed about the recent development and implementation of AI, as well as data analytics within accounting practices. Some of the topics that will be covered in this course include best practices for obtaining, storing, and preserving financial data that comply with privacy regulations. When talking about security measures and practices that have been put in place to make sure that personal financial information is secure, an emphasis will be laid on the aspect of ethics concerning how accounting systems empowered by AI are handling data.

Privacy and Data Protection in Accounting Analytics

Just like those with sociology degrees criticize social media issues, similar problems regarding privacy have surfaced on the heels of initiatives involving data analytics and AI in accounting. It becomes even more important as financial information is digitized and falls under the control of AI technologies that are capable of handling massive groups of classified data. In addition, ethical considerations must be integrated into the data practices in accounting systems based on AI algorithms to protect people's privacy rights and promote responsible treatment of private financial information.

- **Financial Data Sensitivity:** Financial information such as income statements and tax reference numbers should be well protected since they are not only highly sensitive but also require robust protection to prevent unauthorized access and misuse.
- **Third-Party Data Sharing:** Most of the time, accounting associations partner with third-party service providers and manufacturers. It is critically important to ensure data privacy and security when sharing financial information externally.
- **Data Breach Risks:** AI-driven systems require a large amount of data to process and are thus vulnerable targets for cyberattacks or information that ends up in the wrong hands. Strong security measures are needed by accountants to prevent such risks. This includes measures such as encryption of data, two-factor authentication, and secure networks. Additionally, accountants should review their security protocols regularly and update them as needed.

The adoption of AI and analytics-based technologies in accounting practices brings privacy concerns that have necessitated a highly assured look into the respective data protection processes. Given that AI-driven accounting is used to handle financial data through the digitization of records where sensitive information is processed, ethical and responsible accounting practices need to comply with privacy laws as well as protect the sensitivity of this piece of information while addressing risks associated with third-party sharing, among other forms of data breaches. As concerns expand in responsible AI, there is a need to ensure that aspects of justice, accountability, and transparency with safety in mind, coupled with privacy concerning governance, are included while thinking about societal well-being plus the environment (Mikalef et al., 2022).

Proper Data Collection, Handling, and Storage

To ensure the overall security of entire financial processes, accounting professionals must be engaged in several vital procedures that involve effective data collection, cautious processing, and support elements, as well as secure strategies to keep the output packed for further storage aspects. However, the benefit of advancing technology and increasing uses for AI also brings with it a greater risk if proper data management systems are not put in place to protectprocess against unauthorized access or breaches that may result in ethical issues. Also, this sensitive information is processed by AI systems.

- **Informed Consent**: For accountants, this means that they can only collect or financial data of individuals or businesses if explicitly consented to. It is very important to have transparent process thecommunication with the customers who are providing their data.
- **Minimizing Data Collection:** It also promotes data minimization, which means that accountants should only collect the relevant information for a specific accounting function and minimize the potential risk in case of a breach.
- **Data Anonymization**: Anonymizing or pseudonymizing financial data can help to preserve privacy by adding an extra layer of name and personally identifiable information removal when analyzing and sharing data for research purposes, as well as more general analysis.

Proper data collection, careful processing, and secure storage are essential for the desired confidentiality and integrity of financial reported information in accounting, especially with the future advances towards the integration of artificial intelligence. AI technologies shouldn't violate users' privacy, which means the responsibility of developers embraces a few key aspects.

Tactics for Data Protection and Securing Personal Financial Data

The confidentiality of individual financial information is more important than ever in the modern world as a result of innovations in technology. Applying the right information security processes is critical to ensuring the accuracy, usability, and privacy of personal financial data.

- **Encryption:** Encrypting financial data during both transmission and storage increases the safety of the information by only allowing authorized persons to access data that is incomprehensible.
- **Access Controls:** Proper implementation of strong access controls will restrict access to data only to authorized personnel and therefore prevent the risk of unauthorized data breaches.
- **Regular Data Audits:** Data audits are done periodically to help identify any vulnerabilities and weaknesses that may be present concerning data protection practices; hence, corrective measures can be taken as soon as possible.

Accounting systems need to incorporate measures such as encryption, secure access rules, and constant data audits in an attempt to protect sensitive financial information. In a world where technology continues to evolve, accountants can strengthen their data protection policies and reduce the risk inherent in them by encrypting all data relating to the accounting records of an organization in such a way that only those individuals authorized a priori will be able to have access, such as through a partial or full encryption system.

Ethical Data Handling Practices in AI-Driven Accounting Systems

In a world where AI-driven bookkeeping systems are quite ordinary, upholding the principles of moral data administration is important. At the same time, appropriate training has to be provided for stakeholders and accountants to increase awareness about the necessity of responsible data management; strong data governance frameworks must be created, which would help limit potential damage from privacy breaches or misuse of personal information; and ethical considerations must also become a part of AI development plans and strategies.

- **Data Governance:** Clearly defined data governance frameworks help ensure that ethical standards in the handling of data are embedded across AI–driven accounting processes.
- **Ethical AI Development:** The impacts of data should always be an important consideration in the design and development process for accountants as well as developers.
- **Training and Awareness:** To create a culture of data ethics, various stakeholders, such as accountants, needed in-depth training and instruction on proper ways to handle information ethically.

Encryption], access controls, and audits are all necessary techniques to protect financial information from unauthorized disclosure and ensure private financial information. Moreover, the presence of ethical procedures regarding data management and sharing is also highly important in accounting AI systems to ensure that private rights are safeguarded as well. For instance, big data has been used in social sciences and medical research, which are areas where collecting and analyzing very large sets of data leads to ethical issues (Mittelstad & Floridi, 2016). Accountants can increase trust in their customers and clients while ensuring that they do not let down on the tremendous opportunities that AI and data analytics give them by prioritizing the ethical use of data and safeguarding customer information. There, the argument was made in the classic book "The Right to Privacy" that there should be recognition of the common law right to privacy for people's protection from an increasing number of intrusions due to the establishment of modern society and progress in technical matters (Warren & Brandeis, 1890).

ACCOUNTABILITY AND TRANSPARENCY IN ACCOUNTING PRACTICES

The essential components of transparency and accountability in AI-driven accounting systems are addressed in this section. As AI plays a larger role in accounting decisions, it has become essential to ensure transparency and accountability. This depends on stakeholders' ability to comprehend and assess moral issues related to AI model explainability while also looking into audit procedures that support the accuracy and precision of AI-powered accounting solutions.

Ensuring Accountability in AI-Driven Accounting Systems

Another important issue in the stated context is ensuring accountability as a controller, since no system of AI can manage accounting without specific procedures to control and check balances. From this perspective, the study should consider how programmers and accountants realize their ethical roles in building accounting software and ensure that these programs are developed on a basis that corresponds with GAPs while also addressing major moral imperatives related to compliance with laws encapsulated through human control.

- **Ethical Responsibility:** This would mean that when a team comes up with an AI model design and implementation, ethical issues are taken into consideration. To elaborate, this could be achieved by ensuring that AI models are not prejudiced against by some sections of the public or by using data irresponsibly in a way that infringes on their right to privacy, and also by being accountable for how the model works.
- **Human Oversight:** Even though accounting processes can be automated to a high degree, AI decisions require human review for there to be accountability. But the final decision should be made by accountants, who will need to assess AI's impacts too.
- **Legal and Regulatory Compliance:** It is also required to verify that AI-augmented accounting systems fully address all the applicable legal and regulatory requirements. First, compliance means that AI does not violate moral and legal requirements controlling its decisions.

With the rise of AI-powered accounting, maintaining accountability that encompasses human monitoring, ethical concerns, and compliance with laws becomes more difficult. This means that program developers and even accountants must cooperate to achieve the requisite level of accountability. Building AI should be based on ethical principles; the decision-making process must involve human oversight and all legal norms, as well as any specific regulatory requirements. It will safeguard the integrity and validity of AI-augmented accounting systems.

The Importance of Transparency in AI Decision-Making

A major concern with a digital data-driven ecosystem involves openness and AI decision-making. Based on the findings of this study, transparency in AI-driven transactions is very significant, and more clarity about its role needs to be made. When people don't have clear lines of communication and there is no transparency in accounting practices or model development, it makes sense to say that management cannot expect success because these are all built on the foundation of confusion. These conditions collectively could mean that the accounting profession is an aware one in matters of decision-making, thereby internalizing it and using it to embrace a moral agency that leans towards application.

- **Explainability of AI Models:** Accountants should prioritize the creation of AI models that are understandable. Transparency as to how an AI makes some decisions is helpful for stakeholders in understanding the rationale behind them.
- **Comprehensibility for Stakeholders:** Accounting professionals need to explain the outcomes of decisions derived from AI in a manner that is easy for stakeholders to understand. It should be ensured that it facilitates the establishment of trust and confidence in AI-based systems.
- **Interpretable AI Algorithms:** When accountants and other users work with interpretable AI algorithms, traceability is created, allowing both stakeholders and the accountant to understand why a specific decision was taken; this ensures communication.

This section investigates the role of openness in AI decision-making by looking at transparent accounting systems, intelligible models, and open communication. Interpreting algorithms will be applied to enable stakeholders' understanding levels to increase and their trust development in artificial intelligence as a top priority of explicit explanations for AI models. Also, 'understanding' will increase confidence in the deployment of AI-based decision support, hence contributing towards enhancing stakeholder comprehension about machine learning as a helpful tool.

Auditing Practices for AI-Based Systems

The impact of using artificial intelligence AI is much further as it relates to many businesses, especially accounting, and the audit field has opened up a new dimension. This stage considers the basic function of accounting and auditing practices in providing fairness, algorithmic integrity, and data fidelity. It does this by looking at how the field of accounting auditing methods has evolved and discussing some popular AI-based systems that have emerged.

- **Ethical AI Audits:** An ethical audit should be an integral part of the accounting system to ensure that when these tools make such AI decisions, there is a code or some set moral standards they need to adhere to if one does not want these gadgets used as ways through which stereotypes or biases are perpetuated.
- **Algorithmic Fairness Audits:** Regular audits for algorithmic fairness can be a solution to catch those kinds of moves before they blow up as ugly public relations disasters.

- **Data Auditing:** To address the issues of data quality, thorough audits of the used data are conducted to ensure its accuracy and reliability within AI models.

AI-based accounting systems make auditing techniques complicated. To address those goals, implementation-oriented mechanisms like ethical AI audits can improve the fairness and non-discriminatory judgments made by artificial intelligence, up to moral standards. Data audits contribute to accuracy because the data might be of poor quality, while algorithmic fairness audits inspect and remove biases in an analysis. These measures also boost the confidence of stakeholders and, at the same time, increase precision in AI-based accounting systems.

Compliance With International Standards

As AI-driven technologies keep changing the landscape of accounting, it becomes vital to comply with recognized international standards. The given investigation is aimed at the integration process of AI-based accounting systems with IFRS and preserving the ethical standards prescribed by the International Ethics Standards Board for Accountants (IESBA) to secure uniform financial reporting while using AI tools responsibly.

- **International Financial Reporting Standards (IFRS):** AI-powered accounting systems need to adhere to IFRS practices for consistency and comparability in financial reporting.
- **International Ethics Standards Board for Accountants (IESBA):** Ethical decisions in accounting practices depend on adherence to IESBA's ethical standards, including artificial intelligence.

As AI-driven accounting systems develop, it is important to maintain accountability and transparency to make morally justified decisions. In pursuit of accountability, it is crucial to assign moral responsibility to both accountants and AI engineers for the outcomes generated by artificial intelligence, even as human monitoring continues to be indispensable. Clear outcomes' communication to stakeholders and understandable AI models are crucial for transparency in the decision-making of artificial intelligence. Furthermore, two auditing approaches for AI-based systems that assist in identifying and correcting any biases and data quality problems include algorithmic fairness audits as well as ethical AI audits. Adherence to international standards such as IFRS and the ethical principles from the IESBA further support or show an ethically transparent use of AI in accounting. Accountants can help in the process of negotiating the moral and societal implications by being accountable, transparent, and compliant, so they can assist in creating a credible ethical accounting profession for this age of AI.

SOCIAL IMPLICATIONS OF AI AND DATA ANALYTICS IN ACCOUNTING

In this section, we look at the possible social impacts of data analytics and AI in accounting. Automation, artificial intelligence, and data analytics are dramatically affecting the accounting industry and its employees. Although technology addresses multiple dilemmas, it also has moral concerns regarding resource usage efficiency, skill acquisition processes, and job losses. To properly address such advances, it is imperative to emphasize the issues of moral values and ethical decision-making in addition to the social implications related to AI-driven accounting practices.

Automation and Job Displacement in the Accounting Industry

Data analytics and artificial intelligence (AI) have the potential to change business operations, optimize workflow, and begin conversations about the possible ramifications of replacement jobs in accounting. This part surveys the relationship between automation, ethical dilemmas, and a need for more accounting savvy.

- **Automation of tasks:** This can occur if the accounting work is repetitive and routine, requiring less human interaction through data analytics or AI to automate such tasks.
- **Reskilling and Upskilling:** The accounting profession is also being automated and will continue to be so; therefore, for professionals not to become obsolete, they must change with the times and develop new skills.
- **Ethical Responsibility:** Companies are duty-bound to factor in the ethical ramifications of job loss as a result of automation and help disabled workers.

AI and data analytics would be able to perform even the simplest operations in accounting, meaning that accountants will need to adjust their skills accordingly due to changes happening within this industry. Additionally, employers have an ethical responsibility to help those who may be wrongfully affected by work losses in the future, offering assistance and counsel while weighing the benefits of automation against morality and employees' career growth.

Skill Development in the Age of AI

In the dynamic field of artificial intelligence, skill development has acquired new significance. This section explores the importance of human-centric skills, lifelong learning, and the ethical underpinnings of AI integration.

- **Human-Centric Skills:** While AI automates certain tasks, human-centric skills such as critical thinking, problem-solving, and ethical decision-making become even more valuable in the accounting profession.
- **Lifelong Learning:** Accountants must adopt a mindset of continuous learning to stay updated with emerging technologies and ethical considerations.
- **Ethical AI Development**: AI developers should prioritize creating systems that enhance human capabilities rather than replace them, fostering a collaborative relationship between AI and human accountants.

The value of human-centric traits like ethical reasoning and critical thinking is reinforced by the necessity of skill development in navigating the AI-driven world. Accountants must embrace lifelong learning if they want to stay abreast of evolving technologies and ethical requirements. Designers prioritize technologies that enhance human capabilities and foster cooperation between AI and people, underscoring the importance of moral AI development.

Resource Allocation and Social Impact

The resource distribution capability of AI-driven accounting systems has broad implications for justice, morality, and the welfare of society. Trust and ethical allocation of resources can be enhanced by ensuring accountability and fairness and considering the perspective from an ethnic viewpoint.

- **Equity and Fairness:** Accounting systems, which are driven by artificial intelligence, that allocate resources and financial judgments should be focused on fairness, justice, and equity in the allocation of resources. AI systems should be designed to ensure that outcomes are not biased against any particular group and that resources are fairly distributed. Additionally, AI systems should be regularly monitored to ensure that they remain fair and equitable.
- **Ethical Resource Allocation:** On the other hand, some accountants share resources using AI and should not forget their ethical principles related to determining the count of something a person needs, as people rely on what they have in changing cultures when going from country to country with more individualism than collectivism
- **Transparency and Accountability:** To build trust in AI-based resource allocation, decision-making processes need to be transparent, along with the algorithms' accountability.

The AI-powered accounting systems need to ensure that they address justice and fairness in resource allocation; therefore, accountants have a moral responsibility to consider the larger societal implications. Transparency and accountability are critical because they ensure moral decision-making methods and processes in AI-driven resource allocation.

Ethical Decision-Making in AI-Driven Accounting Procedures

The use of AI and data analytics in accounting emphasizes the need for values that highlight the welfare of society, as well as for AI governance systems that uphold stringent ethical standards. Human-centric skills, continual learning, and ethical audits to control biases, among other things, are crucial for managing job displacement during the transformation. By focusing on ethics and human welfare, the accounting profession may profit from AI's potential for a sustainable and inclusive future.

- **Ethical Frameworks**: Accountants should adopt ethical frameworks that prioritize societal well-being, human rights, and environmental sustainability in AI-driven accounting practices.
- **Responsible AI Governance:** Organizations must establish governance structures that promote ethical decision-making in the development and deployment of AI systems.
- **Ethical Auditing**: Regular ethical audits of AI-driven accounting procedures help identify and address potential biases and ethical dilemmas.

The integration of AI and data analytics in accounting carries significant social implications. As automation transforms the accounting industry, addressing job displacement and skill development becomes crucial for the workforce's well-being. Emphasizing human-centric skills and lifelong learning helps accountants adapt to technological changes responsibly. Resource allocation and its social impact require ethical consideration, ensuring fairness and transparency in AI-driven decisions. Ethical decision-making frameworks and responsible AI governance play a central role in navigating the societal implications of AI-driven accounting procedures. The accounting profession may use the opportunity of AI and data analytics to build a more inclusive, long-lasting, and morally upright future by emphasizing principles of ethics and human welfare.

FUTURE DIRECTIONS AND RECOMMENDATIONS

A better future could be underway for the accounting industry through AI and data analysis. This would encompass taking into account how matters affect people, being principled, and directing thinking towards the ultimate good welfare. Let us focus on the significance of constant research, teamwork, and professional growth, which would enable us to eliminate these problems. We also provide tips on how to use AI and data analysis in a business or leadership role when accounting ethically.

Advancements in AI and Data Analytics

The accounting industry needs to be up-to-date because the areas of AI and data analysis are changing quickly. This needs us to stay updated with the latest technology changes, like big data processing and predicting by analytics, along with analyzing things from machines that can learn on their own, use robots for jobs that repeat tasks automatically, or understand what words mean without being told directly.

- **AI Advancements:** Stay updated on all the latest news in robot tasks, smart learning, and language understanding for numbers.
- **Data Analytics Trends:** See what is new in data analysis, like handling big chunks of information and making predictions. Also, look at ways to show or picture that data helps accountants make better choices.
- **AI in Auditing:** Look into using AI in auditing processes like risk assessment, spotting strange things, and finding fraud. This can make audit work better and more accurate.

Using the newest AI and data analytics technology can make a big change in accounting work. One other way to make better choices is by studying artificial intelligence, learning machines, big data handling, and predictive analytics. When AI is used in checking work, it can help spot danger, find unusual things, and see if any frauds are happening. This makes audits better at finding the truth more quickly than before.

Ethical Considerations in AI-Driven Accounting

As AI keeps evolving the accounting landscape, it is critical to address ethical considerations. Support ethical and open AI development, data governance, and awareness-raising through education that fosters trust and moral behavior.

- **Ethical AI Development:** Promote research and development of AI systems that are transparent, explainable, and aligned with ethical principles to build trust and accountability.
- **Ethical Data Governance:** Implement robust data governance frameworks that prioritize data privacy, consent, and security to ensure ethical data handling practices.

- **Ethical Training and Awareness**: Encourage continuous education and training on ethical considerations in AI and data analytics for accounting professionals and AI developers.

To uphold ethics in AI-driven accounting, several steps must be taken, including the development of moral and open AI systems, robust data governance frameworks to safeguard privacy and security, and the encouragement of ethical awareness through ongoing education for AI developers and accounting professionals. Together, these campaigns aim to lay a foundation for moral accountability as well as consistent performance at work.

Interdisciplinary Collaboration

A multidisciplinary approach is required for problem-solving, since powered by AI accounting has important ethical and societal repercussions. To successfully deal with the issues at hand, this calls for promoting collaboration among legislators, data scientists, ethicists, and accounting specialists.

- **Collaboration Across Disciplines:** Foster collaboration between accounting professionals, data scientists, ethicists, and policymakers to address the complex ethical and social implications of AI-driven accounting.
- **Public-Private Partnerships:** Advocate for public-private partnerships that promote ethical AI practices and facilitate knowledge sharing and ethical guidelines.

Collaboration between disciplines is necessary for the accomplishment of ethical AI-driven accounting. We can manage complex ethical concerns by bringing together accountants, data scientists, ethicists, and policymakers. Encouraging public-private partnerships will also make it easier to share ethical standards and promote information sharing, ultimately creating an ethically sound AI environment in accounting.

Professional Development and Certification

Accountants urgently need to finish the Professional Development and Certification project to employ artificial intelligence (AI) and data analytics in the constantly evolving discipline of modern accounting. To ensure that accountants can use innovative technology while maintaining ethical standards, this comprehensive project includes supporting the development of AI capabilities as well as building ethical credentials.

- **AI Skills Development**: Encourage accountants to upskill in AI-related areas to be better equipped to leverage AI technologies responsibly in their accounting practices.
- **Ethical Certification:** Establish professional certifications focused on ethical AI and data analytics in accounting to uphold ethical standards within the profession.

The primary objective of professional development and certification initiatives is to supply accountants with the knowledge and abilities required to integrate AI into their accounting procedures. By promoting the growth of their AI competence, accountants are encouraged to be knowledgeable and proficient in industries relevant to AI. In order to demonstrate that the accounting profession is committed to sustaining ethical integrity while exploiting cutting-edge technology, the project further promotes the creation of ethical certifications for AI and data analytics.

Ethical AI Adoption by Organizations

The idea of organizations implementing ethical AI is growing in relevance during this period of technological advancement. Businesses must set up strong frameworks for ethical AI and involve stakeholders if they want to ensure the ethical and responsible integration of AI into accounting systems.

- **Ethical AI Frameworks**: Organizations should develop and implement ethical AI frameworks and policies to ensure ethical AI adoption in accounting processes.
- **Stakeholder Engagement:** Involve stakeholders in the decision-making process to ensure their concerns and ethical considerations are adequately addressed.

Ethical AI for businesses and companies implies the requirement of not only technological progress, but also significant attention to be paid to ethics. Lastly, even while considering the broader implications of developing and implementing ethical AI frameworks, businesses may easily embed them in accounting. To provide collaborative effort and create accountability, stakeholders become integrated into the process, where they assure transparency for addressing ethical issues while AI is being integrated in a complex context.

Opportunities and challenges emerge concerning the future of AI, data analytics, and accounting ethics. Accounting and accounting professionals can use new technologies such as AI and data analytics to help them improve their decision-making processes and efficiency issues while at the same time dealing with the issue of ethics because, in running an account, one is also faced with wondering if this motion would prevent some unemployment problems that humans will not take lightly. Collaboration between various disciplines is seen as a link for the sharing of knowledge and the adoption of ethical practice through public-private partnerships. To responsibly implement AI for accountants, continuous professional development and ethical certifications are key. Further, ethical AI frameworks and stakeholder engagement should be a priority for organizations and decision-makers to guarantee the responsible and beneficial implementation of both AI and data analytics in accounting practices. According to Boulianne et al. (2023), big data and artificial intelligence can be useful to accountants in their line of work. They encourage a cooperative approach in which people and technology cooperate rather than compete to develop ideas that are advantageous to both.

CONCLUSION

The main ideas of the chapter will be presented in this section, with an emphasis on the need for ethical awareness and responsible decision-making when integrating AI and data analytics into accounting procedures. It will serve as a wake-up call for all parties engaged in the advancement of organizational management through artificial intelligence and data analytics, encouraging them to give moral issues top priority and lower possible risks. The chapter examined the ethical and social repercussions of AI and data analytics to clarify accounting ethics. Experts, decision-makers, and academics will all receive advice on how to tackle the ethical issues that AI-driven accounting systems supply.

From an accounting ethics standpoint, this chapter explored the ethical and societal consequences of data analytics for organizational management in the age of AI. We have discussed the advantages and challenges that come with their integration while highlighting the transformative effects of AI and data analytics on the accounting profession. A significant subject has persisted throughout our investigation: ethical awareness and responsible decision-making are essential when utilizing AI and data analytics in accounting procedures.

It is crucial to give ethical considerations priority as AI and data analytics continue to transform the accounting field. Only when ethical frameworks are combined with AI can the benefits, such as increased productivity, accuracy, and data handling skills, be completely realized. To minimize risks and unfavorable social effects, organizations and decision-makers must be alert when identifying and resolving the ethical implications of AI-driven accounting methods.

This chapter should serve as a wake-up call for all parties involved in the development of organizational management through AI and data analytics. To make sure that the use of AI technology is consistent with social standards and offers protection from any biases and discriminatory characteristics, every decision must be made with ethics in mind.

Accounting ethics addresses not only the ethical behavior of individual accountants, but also AI in accounting operations and its responsibilities. Therefore, policymakers and educational institutions as well as organizations should embrace the importance of ethical education as well as awareness to assist in the achievement that can offer all accounting professionals an easy way to easily understand the social and ethical implications brought by AI and data analytics uses.

We, as professional accounting experts who include academicians and decision-makers, have an ethical responsibility to address the ethical dilemmas of AI-powered accounting practices. Through fostering cross-cutting collaboration and public-private partnerships, we can collectively tackle these challenges to develop strong ethical frameworks that direct the ethical and responsible use of AI in accounting.

When integrating AI and data analytics into accounting processes, ethical awareness and ethical decision-making are crucial. We can fully harness the potential of these technologies while guarding against unintended repercussions by emphasizing ethical considerations in the deployment of AI. Prioritizing ethical behavior is crucial if we are working towards a future that is more just, transparent, and sustainable. This chapter explains this point and offers advice to all parties involved on how to approach any moral issues posed by AI-driven accounting techniques.

REFERENCES

Al-Haddad, S., & Kotnour, T. (2015). Integrating the organizational change literature: A model for successful change. *Journal of Organizational Change Management*, *28*(2), 234–262. doi:10.1108/JOCM-11-2013-0215

Bansal, G., Zahedi, F. M., & Gefen, D. (2016). Do context and personality matter? Trust and privacy concerns in disclosing private information online. *Information & Management*, *53*(1), 1–21. doi:10.1016/j.im.2015.08.001

Bezboruah, K. C. (2008). Applying the congruence model of organizational change in explaining the change in the Indian economic policies. *Journal of Organisational Transformation & Social Change, 5*(2), 129–140. doi:10.1386/jots.5.2.129_1

Bocean-Vărzaru, A. A. (2022). Assessing the Impact of AI Solutions' Ethical Issues on performance in Managerial Accounting. *Electronics (Basel), 11*(14), 2221. doi:10.3390/electronics11142221

Boulianne, E., Fortin, M., & Leco, A. (2023). Artificial Intelligence and Data Analytics: Ethical Implications for Accounting. In M. Brivot & C. Cho (Eds.), *Research Handbook on Accounting and Ethics* (pp. 168–179)., https://ideas.repec.org/h/elg/eechap/20458_11.html doi:10.4337/9781800881020.00020

Burke, W. W., & Litwin, G. H. (1992). A causal model of organizational performance and change. *Journal of Management, 18*(2), 523–546. doi:10.1177/014920639201800306

Burnes, B. (2011). Introduction: Why does change fail, and what can we do about it? *Journal of Change Management, 11*(4), 445–450. doi:10.1080/14697017.2011.630507

Carnall, C. (2007). *Managing change in organizations* (5th ed.). Prentice Hall: Financial Times.

Costanza-Chock, S. (2020). *Design justice: Community-led practices to build the worlds we need.* The MIT Press. https://direct.mit.edu/books/oa-monograph/4605/Design-JusticeCommunity-Led-Practices-to-Build-the

Cummings, T. G., & Worley, C. G. (2013). *Organization development and change* (10th ed.). South-Western College Publishing. https://www.vitalsource.com/products/organization-development-and-change-thomas-g-cummings-v9781305143036

Cushing, A. L., & Osti, G. (2023). "So how do we balance all of these needs?": How the concept of AI technology impacts digital archival expertise. *The Journal of Documentation, 79*(7), 12–29. doi:10.1108/JD-08-2022-0170

Dattner, B., Chamorro-Premuzic, T., Buchband, R., & Schettler, L. (2019). The legal and ethical implications of using AI in hiring. *Harvard Business Review*. https://hbr.org/2019/04/the-legal-and-ethical-implications-of-using-ai-in-hiring

Deloitte. (2021). 2021 Global Human Capital Trends: The social enterprise in a world disrupted. Delooitte. https://www2.deloitte.com/content/dam/insights/us/articles/6935_2021-HC-Trends/di_human-capital-trends.pdf

Diakopoulos, N. (2016). Accountability in algorithmic decision making. *Communications of the ACM, 59*(2), 56–62. https://cacm.acm.org/magazines/2016/2/197421-accountability-in-algorithmic-decision-making/abstract. doi:10.1145/2844110

Errida, A., & Lotfi, B. (2021). The determinants of organizational change management success: Literature review and case study. *International Journal of Engineering Business Management, 13*, 1–15. doi:10.1177/18479790211016273

Floridi, L., & Taddeo, M. (2016). What is data ethics? *Philosophical Transactions. Series A, Mathematical, Physical, and Engineering Sciences, 374*(2083), 20160360. https://royalsocietypublishing.org/doi/10.1098/rsta.2016.0360. doi:10.1098/rsta.2016.0360 PMID:28336805

Gonzales, R. M. D., & Hargreaves, C. A. (2022). How can we use artificial intelligence for stock recommendation and risk management? A proposed decision support system. *International Journal of Information Management Data Insights, 2*(2), 100130. doi:10.1016/j.jjimei.2022.100130

Hussain, R. (2023). *Organizational Changes And Their Impact On Corporate Productivity,* [Thesis Centria University of Applied Sciences]. https://www.theseus.fi/bitstream/handle/10024/804530/Hussain_Ramzan.pdf?sequence=2&isAllowed=y

Jacobs, G., van Witteloostuijn, A., & Christe-Zeyse, J. (2013). A theoretical framework of organizational change. *Journal of Organizational Change Management, 26*(5), 772–792. doi:10.1108/JOCM-09-2012-0137

Jedynak, M., Czakon, W., Kuźniarska, A., & Mania, K. (2021). Digital transformation of organizations: What do we know and where to go next? *Journal of Organizational Change Management, 34*(3), 629–652. doi:10.1108/JOCM-10-2020-0336

Jiang, L., Pan, Z., Luo, Y., Guo, Z., & Kou, D. (2023). More flexible and more innovative: The impact of flexible work arrangements on the innovation behavior of knowledge employees. *Frontiers in Psychology, 14*, 1053242. doi:10.3389/fpsyg.2023.1053242 PMID:37179861

Kitsios, F., & Kamariotou, M. (2021). Artificial Intelligence and Business Strategy towards Digital Transformation: A Research Agenda. *Sustainability (Basel), 13*(4), 2025. https://www.mdpi.com/2071-1050/13/4/2025. doi:10.3390/su13042025

Kokina, J., & Davenport, T. H. (2017). The emergence of artificial intelligence: How automation is changing auditing. *Journal of Emerging Technologies in Accounting, 14*(1), 115–122. doi:10.2308/jeta-51730

Lee, G., & Xiao, X. (2018). Whistleblowing on accounting-related misconduct: A synthesis of the literature. *Journal of Accounting Literature, 41*(1), 22–46. doi:10.1016/j.acclit.2018.03.003

Lehner, O. M., Ittonen, K., Silvola, H., Ström, E., & Wührleitner, A. (2022). Artificial intelligence-based decision-making in accounting and auditing: Ethical challenges and normative thinking. *Accounting, Auditing & Accountability Journal, 35*(9), 109–135. doi:10.1108/AAAJ-09-2020-4934

Mikalef, P., Conboy, K., Lundström, J. E., & Popovič, A. (2022). Thinking responsibly about responsible AI and 'the dark side' of AI. *European Journal of Information Systems, 31*(3), 257–268. doi:10.1080/0960085X.2022.2026621

Mittelstadt, B. D., Allo, P., Taddeo, M., Wachter, S., & Floridi, L. (2016). The ethics of algorithms: Mapping the debate. *Big Data & Society, 3*(2), 2053951716679679. doi:10.1177/2053951716679679

Mittelstadt, B. D., & Floridi, L. (2015). The ethics of big data: Current and foreseeable issues in biomedical contexts. *Science and Engineering Ethics, 22*(2), 303–341. https://link.springer.com/article/10.1007/s11948-015-9652-2. doi:10.1007/s11948-015-9652-2 PMID:26002496

Moor, J. H. (2005). Why we need better ethics for emerging technologies. *Ethics and Information Technology*, *7*(3), 111–119. doi:10.1007/s10676-006-0008-0

Nadler, D. A., & Tushman, M. L. (1980). A model for diagnosing organizational behavior. *Organizational Dynamics*, *9*(2), 35–51. doi:10.1016/0090-2616(80)90039-X

Nakamura, K. (2023). How the FTC Safeguards Rule may affect your CPA firm, *Jornal of Accountancy*. https://www.journalofaccountancy.com/issues/2023/feb/how-the-ftc-safeguards-rule-may-affect-your-cpa-firm.html

Parry, W., Kirsch, C., Carey, P., & Shaw, D. (2013). Empirical development of a model of performance drivers in organizational change projects. *Journal of Change Management*, *14*(1), 99–125. doi:10.1080/14697017.2012.745894

Rothwell, W., & Sullivan, R. (2005). *Models for change. Practicing organizational development: a guide for consultants* (2nd ed.). Pfeiffer.

Sharma, K. (2020). 4 Types of Organizational Change, Explained. *Whatfix Digital Adoption Blog*. https://whatfix.com/blog/types-of-organizational-change/

Thomas, R. (2005). Business ethics. In R. Mullerat (Ed.), *Corporate Social Responsibility* (pp. 31–36). Kluwer Law International.

Trunk, A., Birkel, H., & Hartmann, E. (2020). On the current state of combining human and artificial intelligence for strategic organizational decision making. *Business Research, 13*, 875–919. https://link.springer.com/article/10.1007/s40685-020-00133-x

van de Wetering, R., Hendrickx, T., Brinkkemper, S., & Kurnia, S. (2021). The impact of EA-Driven Dynamic Capabilities, Innovativeness, and Structure on Organizational Benefits: A Variance and FsQCA Perspective. *Sustainability (Basel)*, *13*(10), 5414. doi:10.3390/su13105414

Varsha, P. S. (2023). How can we manage biases in artificial intelligence systems – A systematic literature review. *International Journal of Information Management Data Insights, 3*(1). https://www.sciencedirect.com/science/article/pii/S2667096823000125

Verhoef, P. C., Broekhuizen, T., Bart, Y., Bhattacharya, A., Dong, J. Q., Fabian, N., & Haenlein, M. (2021). Digital transformation: A multidisciplinary reflection and research agenda. *Journal of Business Research*, *122*, 889–901. doi:10.1016/j.jbusres.2019.09.022

Warren, M. S., & Brandeis, L. D. (1890). The right to privacy. *Harvard Law Review*, *4*(5), 193–220. doi:10.2307/1321160

Wong, P. H. (2020). Democratizing algorithmic fairness. *Philosophy & Technology*, *33*(2), 225–244. https://link.springer.com/article/10.1007/s13347-019-00355-w. doi:10.1007/s13347-019-00355-w

Zhang, C., Zhu, W., Dai, J., Wu, Y., & Chen, X. (2023). Ethical impact of artificial intelligence in managerial accounting. *International Journal of Accounting Information Systems*, *49*, 100619. doi:10.1016/j.accinf.2023.100619

KEY TERMS AND DEFINITIONS

Accountability and Responsibility: Ensuring clear roles and transparency in automated accounting to protect financial integrity.

Automation of tasks: Using AI to automate repetitive accounting duties reduces the need for human involvement.

Collaboration: Joint efforts among stakeholders for ethical AI use in accounting.

Data Breach Risks: Addressing cybersecurity concerns when AI handles financial data.

Data Governance: Establishing ethical data handling practices in AI-driven accounting.

Data Sensitivity: Protecting sensitive financial data from unauthorized access.

Ethical AI Audits: Evaluating AI systems to ensure ethical compliance.

Ethical Awareness: Training accountants on AI ethics.

Ethical Responsibility: Accountants and AI developers take moral ownership of AI decisions.

Ethical Review Boards: Committees ensuring ethical AI use in organizations.

Ethical Training and Awareness: Education on AI Ethics for Accountants and Developers.

Explainability of AI Models: Making AI Decisions Understandable.

External Audits and Certifications: Independent Verification of Ethical AI Practices.

Fairness and Equity in Accounting Practices: Ensuring Fair Financial Decisions.

Financial Data Sensitivity: Protecting sensitive financial information.

Human Oversight: Human Control in AI-Driven Accounting.

Incorporating Ethical Aspects: Integrating Ethics into AI Implementation.

Inclusive and Diverse Leadership: Promoting Diversity in Leadership Roles.

Informed Consent: Obtaining Permission for Financial Data Use.

International Ethics Standards: Adherence to global ethics guidelines.

International Financial Reporting Standards (IFRS): Complying with global financial reporting standards.

Job Displacement: Addressing workforce changes due to AI.

Legal and Regulatory Compliance: Following laws and regulations in AI accounting.

Minimizing Data Collection: Collecting only necessary data.

Over-reliance on Technology: Balancing AI and human control.

Possible Biases in Accounting Algorithms: Detecting and removing bias in AI systems.

Professional Codes of Conduct: Ethical Standards for Accountants.

Remote and Hybrid Workforce Management: Managing Remote Teams Effectively.

Responsible AI Governance: Ethical oversight of AI development.

Sustainable and Responsible Management: Ethical Practices in Organizational Management.

Third-Party Data Sharing: Secure sharing of financial data.

Transparency and Accountability: Open decision-making and accountability mechanisms.

Transparency and Explainability: Making AI processes understandable

Chapter 12
Intelligent Industry 4.0: Artificial Intelligence and Robotic Process Automation as Tendsetters

M. Dileep Kumar
Hensard University, Yenagoa, Nigeria

Alan Cheng Tat Yap
Faculty of Business, Economics and Accounting, Help University, Malaysia

Normala S. Govindarajo
School of Economics and Management, Xiamen University, Malaysia

Alice Tamah
School of Economics and Management, Xiamen University, Malaysia

Vinod Sharma
https://orcid.org/0000-0002-0815-8502
Symbiosis Centre for Management and Human Resource, Symbiosis International University, India

ABSTRACT

Industry 4.0 has witnessed several changes in the way the industries are operating with technology applications and computational intelligence. Industrial automations and decision makings are augmented with artificial intelligence (AI) and robotic process automation (RPA) is reaping several benefits in the form of improvement of operational, organisational and business processes. The objective of current work is to explore the scenario of RPA and AI in varied fields of industry and management and improve the organisational, business and operational functionality with the support of machine learning (ML), deep learning (DL) and network linguistic programs (NLP with the use of algorithms. Deliberations have been made in the paper stating the uses, differentiation, trends, and applications of RPA and AI, in management and industry. The chapter supports the advancement of the body of knowledge detailing the theoretical implications of computational intelligence.

DOI: 10.4018/979-8-3693-1058-8.ch012

INTRODUCTION

The Industrial Revolution, a term historically associated with the profound socio-economic changes of the 18th and 19th centuries, has taken on a new dimension in contemporary discussions. In the present day, the focus is on the advent of Industry 4.0, a paradigm shift in manufacturing and industrial processes that leverages advanced technologies to create smart industries and factories (IBM, 2020).

One of the key pillars of Industry 4.0 is the seamless exchange of information among various components in industrial technologies (B2BNN Newsdesk, 2021). This interconnectedness is facilitated by the Internet of Things (IoT), which enables devices and machines to communicate and share data in real-time. The integration of IoT allows for the creation of intelligent systems that can make informed decisions, leading to enhanced productivity and efficiency (NICE, 2023).

Robotic process automation plays a pivotal role in Industry 4.0 by automating routine tasks and processes (Biscotti, Tornbohm, Villa, Bhullar, & Mehta, 2021). This not only reduces human intervention in mundane activities but also contributes to precision and consistency in manufacturing processes. As a result, industries can achieve higher levels of output and operational excellence (Assistedge, 2023).

Cognitive computing, another cornerstone of Industry 4.0, involves the use of artificial intelligence (AI) and machine learning to simulate human thought processes (SoftwareReviews, 2023). This enables machines to learn from data, adapt to changing circumstances, and make decisions without explicit programming. Cognitive computing enhances the adaptability and responsiveness of industrial systems (Violino, 2016).

Cloud computing provides the necessary infrastructure for the storage, processing, and analysis of vast amounts of data generated by smart industries (Khan, et al., 2023). This cloud-based approach offers scalability, flexibility, and accessibility, empowering organizations to efficiently manage and utilize their data resources (Aceto, Persico, & Pescapé, 2020).

IBM, a prominent player in the tech industry, emphasizes that Industry 4.0 represents the digital transformation of the field, ushering in real-time decision-making capabilities (IBM Cloud Education, 2020). The adoption of Industry 4.0, however, is not uniform across industries. Different sectors face varying degrees of challenges related to absorptive capacity – the ability to assimilate and apply new technologies effectively (IBM, 2020).

For some industries, the journey toward Industry 4.0 may be prolonged due to obstacles such as outdated infrastructure, workforce skill gaps, and concerns regarding data security and privacy (IBM, 2020). Overcoming these challenges requires strategic planning, investments in technology and training, and a collaborative effort from industry stakeholders.

Industry Revolutions 4.0 features are considered by growing automation and the engagement of smart factories well-versed in information to produce commodities more competently and efficiently (Gartner G., 2023). In the manufacturing and service industry, one of the major advantages of RPA is exploring news of work with the automated business process using RPA tools and thereby obtaining real-time data from smart devices (Schroer, 2023). Reducing human involvement and possible errors in the operational process, RPA replaces the traditional repetitive tasks through automated programmes (IBM Cloud Education, 2020) leading sharp reduction in the incurring cost. It is reported that there is a 30% to 50% reduction in operational costs of transactional undertakings with joint services with the application of RPA technologies (Bhatt, 2021). RPA has extended flexible operational processes that support the manufacturers to have mass customization and eventually attain efficiency.

In the age of Industry 4.0, RPA and AI have become integral components in revolutionizing how data is collected, processed, and utilized across various sectors (Biscotti, Tornbohm, Villa, Bhullar, & Mehta, 2021). While their origins were deeply rooted in optimizing manufacturing operations, these technologies have rapidly expanded their influence far beyond the factory floor. Real-time enterprise-wide operational data, which was once confined to manufacturing settings, is now collected and analyzed by RPA and AI, providing valuable insights that empower management to make more informed decisions and exercise better control over their operations (Gartner G., 2023).

The amalgamation of RPA and AI brings forth computational intelligence, allowing managers to navigate through vast volumes of real-time data efficiently. This collective impact has influenced not only manufacturing and traditional Enterprise Resource Planning (ERP) systems but has extended its reach to diverse management functions such as marketing, branding, accounting, and human resources (Anandan, 2015). Within manufacturing, RPA serves as the conduit for real-time data collection from various sensors and machinery, while AI algorithms process this influx of information (Acieta, 2021). This symbiotic relationship assists in optimizing production processes, predicting maintenance needs, and enhancing quality control, ultimately empowering managers to make data-driven decisions promptly, thereby elevating operational efficiency (Atkinson, 2019).

In the context of ERP systems, the integration of RPA and AI has transcended traditional practices. By automating routine tasks such as data entry, analysis, and inventory management, these technologies have significantly improved resource allocation, streamlined workflows, and optimized business processes (Automation Anywhere, 2021). The influence of RPA and AI is also evident in management functions beyond manufacturing. In marketing and branding, AI-driven analytics provide insights into market segmentation and customer behavior, enabling tailored marketing campaigns and strategies. Automating certain marketing tasks through RPA ensures more efficient utilization of resources and a deeper understanding of consumer behavior (Smartbridge, 2023).

In accounting and financial management, RPA automates repetitive financial tasks like invoice processing, while AI aids in fraud detection, risk assessment, and financial forecasting (ElectroNeek, 2020). This combination not only enhances accuracy but also ensures compliance and risk management. Furthermore, in the realm of human resources, RPA and AI are streamlining processes by automating tasks such as resume screening and interview scheduling. AI algorithms assist in identifying talent trends and predicting employee turnover, providing valuable insights for strategic HR planning (Cavero-Baptista, 2021).

The core purpose of this chapter is to explore RPA and AI within the context of Industry 4.0 in both management and manufacturing is to showcase their collective impact on the business as an unabridged. This chapter also highlights how these technologies driven by computational intelligence helps in making informed decisions and significantly enhances business performance across various organizational functions. This chapter through lights on the key challenges faced by organizations while implementing RPA in their system and ways methods to overcome these challenges.

BACKGROUND OF THE STUDY

Application of Computational intelligence where technologies and automation are asserting a major change RPA and AI are covering several benefits in terms of automating administrative and commercial processes. Both these technologies support business managers in the extraction of real-time information, segregating, predicting, and optimizing procedures (Ribeiro, Lima, Eckhardt, & Paiva, 2021).

What is Robotic Process Automation (RPA)?

RPA imitates the acts of human behaviour and facilitates minimizing its activities out of specific software. RPA mitigates repetitive actions in methods whose difference in each repetition is tiny or zero. In fact, RPA is a technology function which configured and regulated by industry rationality and organized responses to aim a computerizing the recurring practice of industry processes on a natural or virtual system. The RPA tools or "robots" are configured to acquire and translate applications for analysis of transactions, handling data, initiating responses, and informing and interacting with other digital techniques (Boulton, 2018).

Several terms are used by research scholars on RPA. However, the common industrial term used is robotics. The objective of robotics technology is to imitate human interfaces, human workers' tasks, gathering information from varied sources, etc. and permits a user to organize one or more scripts (bots) to trigger explicit keystrokes in an automated way (Gartner G., 2023). Such a process integrates the application program interface (API) and user interface (UI) interactions to assimilate and accomplish repetitive activities amongst firms and output applications. During the intervention process, the ordering scripts match with the human practices. RPA equipment completes the independent implementation of several actions and transactions through unconnected software structures (IBM Cloud Education, 2020). As a result, the bots may be applied to imitate or match designated within an inclusive industry or IT course. Such practices comprised manipulating data, transitioning data to and from diverse applications, activating replies, or performing transactions (Gartner G., 2023).

Use of RPA?

Given that Robotic Process Automation (RPA) revolves around the automation and repetition of various business processes, its applicability spans across a multitude of industries, promising significant advantages (NextProcess, 2023). Numerous studies conducted by researchers shed light on the various benefits of incorporating RPA into organizational workflows, with a predominant focus on its software applications:

- **Cost Reduction:** The application of RPA has the potential to substantially reduce operational costs, with estimates suggesting that up to 30% of overall operational expenses can be curtailed (PorV Solutions, 2018). By automating repetitive and time-consuming tasks, organizations can achieve operational efficiency and cost-effectiveness. For instance, in the finance sector, automating data entry processes or reconciling accounts payable and receivable can significantly cut down on manual labor costs. This not only leads to financial savings but also allows human resources to focus on more strategic and value-added tasks.
- **Enhanced Customer Experience:** RPA software plays a pivotal role in elevating the overall customer experience by aligning with their perceived value. The streamlined and automated processes enable organizations to provide quicker, more accurate, and personalized services, leading to heightened customer satisfaction (Albajari, 2021). For instance, a company utilizing RPA in its order fulfilment process can provide real-time updates to customers, reducing delivery times and enhancing overall satisfaction.
- **Lower Operational Risk:** Implementing RPA applications can contribute to a significant reduction in human errors, thereby mitigating operational risks (Blackline Magazine, 2021). The

precision and consistency achieved through automation help maintain a higher level of accuracy, minimizing the potential for costly mistakes (ElectroNeek, 2020). Automating medical billing processes, for example, reduces the chances of billing errors and ensures compliance with regulatory standards. This not only safeguards the organization from financial risks but also enhances the quality of patient care.

- **Improved Internal Processes:** Across various industries, RPA is reported to provide enhanced control over day-to-day governance. This heightened control facilitates quicker execution of core reporting, onboarding procedures, and other internal activities, contributing to improved overall organizational efficiency (NICE, 2023). By leveraging RPA, manufacturers can achieve better control over their internal workflows, resulting in faster production cycles and reduced lead times.
- **Integration without Replacement:** One notable aspect of RPA adoption is its non-invasive nature. Contrary to suggesting the replacement of existing systems, RPA complements and augments current applications and processes seamlessly (Acieta, 2021). This approach ensures a smooth integration that is error-free and enhances operational comfort for businesses (Boulton, 2018; PorV Solutions, 2018). For example, in a software development environment, RPA can be employed to automate testing processes, ensuring the robustness of applications without disrupting the underlying infrastructure (NextProcess, 2023). This enables organizations to leverage automation benefits while preserving their existing IT investments.

In essence, the benefits derived from RPA adoption extend beyond mere operational efficiency and cost reduction. They encompass improvements in customer interactions, risk management, and internal governance, positioning RPA as a versatile and transformative tool applicable across diverse business landscapes.

Trends in RPA

In this evolving digital world, a lot of happening depends on trends. As reported by Gartner, by the end of year 2021 the global revenue of $1.89 billion, is contributed from RPA and could reach more than 20% as compared to the previous year of 2020 (Costello & Rimol, 2020). Why so? One of the reasons is trends. Almost every person in the IT industry knows about RPA services, and these include automating data entry and filling out forms. RPA use cases in almost every industry (Finance, Insurance, Healthcare, logistics, etc.). With this growing trend of automation and benefits, some new innovative approaches are rapidly emerging for example, the smart RPA bots could be the next following trends and might achieve "near-universal adoption" in the coming 5 years as predicted in Deloitte (Bhatt, 2021).

Growth Statistics

The growing statistics of RPA software worldwide from the year 2019 to 2021. The average RPA costs are predicted to decline by 10% to 15% creating a downward pricing pressure in 2021 and 2022 respectively (Costello & Rimol, 2020).

The graph which was predicted by Grand View Research, shows that the market size from 2016 until 2028 of the market growths in RPA is anticipated to evolve with the integration of cognitive technologies and the changing of business processes globally (Grand View Research, 2021).

Figure 1. US RPA market size by type 2016-2028 (USD million)

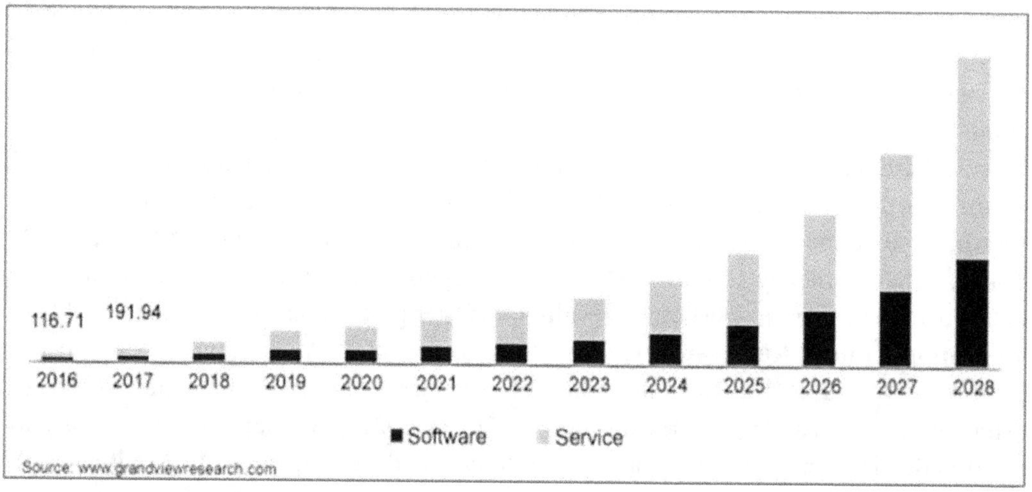

User Statistics

The research reports from various sources clearly indicate that the market share of the global robotic process automation market size is predicted to grow from 9 billion to 10.9 by 2027, growing at a CAGR of 33.6% commencing 2020 to 2027 (Grand View Research, 2021). Another research report on automation clearly indicates that hyper-automation, autonomous things, and AI security are the three top technology applications in the last 5 years duration (Javed, 2020).

The RPA market is increasing day by day and it is anticipated that 72% of the worldwide businesses will be operating with RPA in the coming years (Garner, 2020). As far as technical positions in the job

Figure 2. RPA market

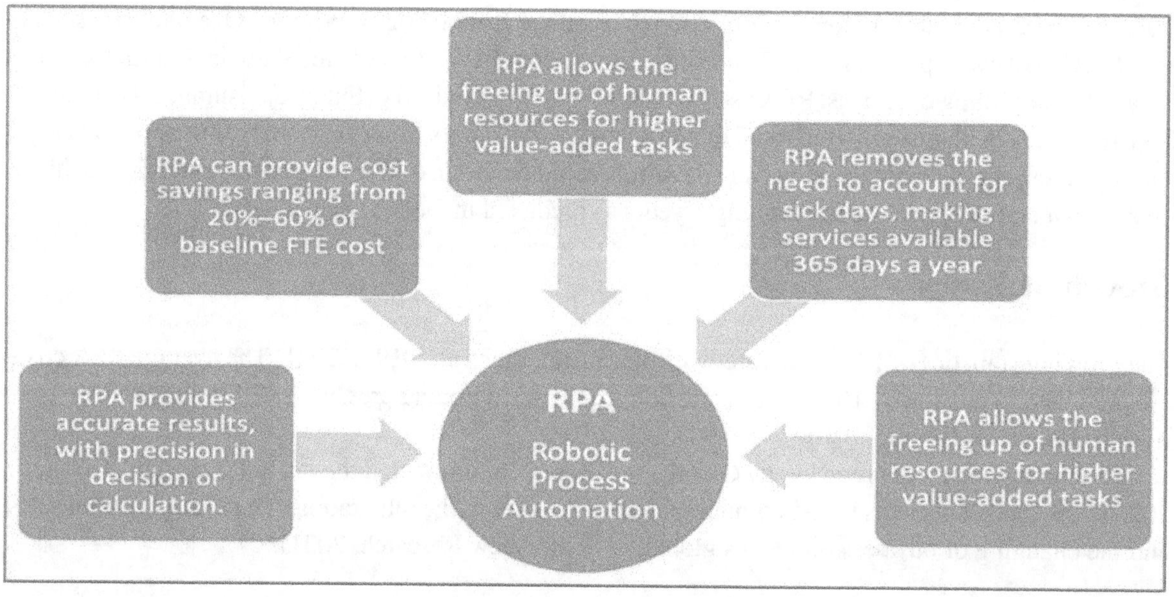

market are concerned almost 70% business functions to be channelised through RPAs, especially the technical applications oriented in finance sector (Casey K., 2019); (Moore, 2019).

Market Share

The latest research analysis provides a compelling outlook for the global RPA market, indicating significant growth and transformative potential in the coming years (NICE, 2023). By 2030, the robotic process automation (RPA) market is expected to have grown to over 13 billion dollars in the United States, a rise of more than 12 billion from 2020 (Lionel, 2023). The anticipated market valuation is poised to be approximately USD 2,659.13 Million in 2022, laying the foundation for a robust expansion (Grand View Research, 2021). Projections paint a dynamic picture, foreseeing the market's revenue soaring to around USD 66,079.34 Million by the year 2032 (Gartner G., 2023).

This remarkable growth trajectory is underpinned by a projected Compound Annual Growth Rate (CAGR) of approximately 37.9% between 2023 and 2032 (Grand View Research, 2021). Such a rapid expansion underscores the increasing recognition and adoption of RPA across various industries (Biscotti, Tornbohm, Villa, Bhullar, & Mehta, 2021). Organizations are evidently recognizing the transformative power of automation in streamlining processes, enhancing efficiency, and unlocking new avenues for innovation.

As businesses continue to navigate an evolving technological landscape, the accelerating adoption of RPA is expected to play a pivotal role in reshaping operational paradigms. The projected market figures signify not only the current momentum but also the widespread anticipation of RPA becoming an integral component of modern business strategies.

Factors contributing to this substantial growth include the pursuit of operational excellence, cost optimization, and the perpetual quest for increased productivity. Industries ranging from finance and healthcare to manufacturing and beyond are acknowledging the instrumental role of RPA in driving digital transformation and staying competitive in a fast-paced global market.

The global market size for robotic process automation reached USD 2.3 billion in 2022 and is anticipated to witness a notable expansion with a Compound Annual Growth Rate (CAGR) of 39.9% from 2023 to 2030 (Lionel, 2023). The surge in demand for robotic process automation can be attributed to the paradigm shift in business practices triggered by the COVID-19 pandemic. Businesses worldwide, in response to the challenges posed by the pandemic, increasingly embraced the automation of business workflows. This proactive approach has, in turn, propelled the growth of robotic process automation throughout the forecast period.

A compelling illustration of this trend is evident in a survey conducted by Blue Prism Limited (Grand View Research, 2021), a prominent RPA solution provider based in the U.K. In their survey report titled "RPA In the APAC Financial Services Sector," published in February 2022, a noteworthy statistic emerged. In the aftermath of the COVID-19 pandemic, 21% of respondents from India's financial services organizations reported the adoption of RPA within their organizations (Shukla, 2023). This underscores the tangible impact of the pandemic on accelerating the integration of robotic process automation, as businesses sought efficient solutions to navigate the evolving landscape brought about by unprecedented global challenges.

ARTIFICIAL INTELLIGENCE (AI)

Computational logic serves as the backbone for the operation of "smart" machineries and computers, where intricate programming dictates the execution of assigned tasks (Ilchenko, 2020). The integration of Machine Learning algorithms further propels Artificial Intelligence (AI) to mimic human brain functionalities, enabling the generation of real-time simulations for efficient decision-making (Schroer, 2023). AI's ability to emulate human-like cognitive processes, coupled with its agility in generating simulations, enhances the speed of decision-making in comparison to the analytical and critical thinking capacities of humans. This heightened efficiency results in superior accuracy, a quality particularly advantageous in the deployment of AI as service robots capable of executing assigned tasks (Schroer, 2023).

The transformative capabilities of AI are manifested in its potential to act as a smart machine, exhibiting a proficiency that goes beyond traditional automated systems. This evolution marks a paradigm shift wherein AI not only performs predefined tasks but also engages in complex decision-making processes akin to human cognition (IBM Cloud Education, 2020).

Within the realm of AI methodologies, four prospective goals can be discerned, delineated along the axes of rationality and thinking versus acting. The human approach encapsulates the development of technology that not only thinks like human beings but also performs tasks with a level of sophistication comparable to human capabilities (Dines, 2023). This aspiration reflects the endeavor to instill AI with a human-like understanding and execution of tasks, blurring the lines between machine and human cognition.

In contrast, the ideal approach centers on developing technology that operates with rationality, emphasizing systems that think and perform in a manner aligned with logical reasoning. This goal underscores the pursuit of AI systems that excel in rational decision-making, devoid of human-like cognitive biases (Ribeiro, Lima, Eckhardt, & Paiva, 2021).

The multidimensional nature of these goals highlights the versatility and potential of AI, showcasing its adaptability to emulate human thought processes or adhere to logical and rational frameworks. As AI continues to advance, the convergence of these approaches promises a future where machines seamlessly integrate into human environments, enhancing efficiency and problem-solving capabilities across diverse domains.

ROBOTIC PROCESS AUTOMATION VS. ARTIFICIAL INTELLIGENCE

According to IEEE, RPA refers to the use of a "preconfigured software instance that uses business rules and predefined activity choreography to complete the autonomous execution of a combination of processes, activities, transactions, and tasks in one or more unrelated software systems to deliver a result or service with human exception management." Where AI is "the combination of cognitive automation, machine learning (ML), reasoning, hypothesis generation and analysis, natural language processing and intentional algorithm mutation producing insights and analytics at or above human capability." In simple it differentiated RPA as a software robot that imitates human activities, while AI is involved with the simulation of human acumen by systems and devices (CFB Bots, 2018).

As evidenced above, the RPA and AI are a few of the major successful technologies for businesses to accomplish the apparently antagonistic goals of improving customer satisfaction and employee self-esteem while lowering operational expenses (NICE, 2023). It is observed that when machine learning gets more acceptance as part of AI applications, that results in better augmentation of imitability and judgment, and behaviour, supplemented with RPA know-how (Casey K., 2019). For example, nowadays it is straightforward for customers to open a bank account with the support of RPA and AI. RPA with AI thus has resulted in better customer satisfaction and efficiency in banking operations (Casey K., 2020) (NICE, 2023).

DIFFERENCE BETWEEN RPA VS. TRADITIONAL PROCESS AUTOMATION

For digital world, automation is not a new thing. Traditional process of automation is different from RPA. As it is understood, the automation solutions are combined with the current software or interact with the system via APIs. Sometimes it requires supplementary changes to the current IT infrastructure. The incorporation of the supplementary changes to the systems can be a difficult task due to boundaries of the several business processes (CFB Bots, 2018). The people who are handling or operating the task could make an instrument to do any activity, or any phase of the functioning process (ElectroNeek, 2020) (Maruti Techlabs, 2023). It demands continuous contribution from IT specialists and software designers, and further controlled by source code, and is not planned for systemic amalgamation (Maruti Techlabs, 2023).

In RPA, technology is particularly prevalent to the front-end of the system and carries out activities in the back-end workplace jobs: sending somebody a bill, data transference, data gathering, examination, customer service act, email, jobs are severely rule-based and usually have detailed orders, invasive and supple enough to mechanise several repetitive tasks (B2BNN Newsdesk, 2021) (ElectroNeek, 2020) (Maruti Techlabs, 2023), works at the speed of the UI by mimicking user actions (ElectroNeek, 2020) (Maruti Techlabs, 2023), and easy-to-program functionality with rapid turnaround times (Maruti Techlabs, 2023).

It is worth pointing out that RPA technology does not replace existing technologies and need not to say, traditional automation is still here to stay. The implementation process of RPA that follow set guidelines to perform repetitive and definite business methods. So, meaning that is some programming algorithm that performs "if, then, else" statements on structured data, typically using a combination of UI interactions or by connecting to APIs to drive client servers, mainframes, or HTML code (Gartner, 2021) (SoftwareReviews, 2023).

Application and Adoption of RPA in Management

Information Technology: RPA depends on technologies and for most organization, the department which will be first to adopt will the Information Technology because of the constant evolving of technologies, which requires expertise in IT skills to help implement and maintain the business digital transformation (Madakam, Holmukhe, & Jaiswal, 2019). RPA constitute software machines that gather and infer existing applications for dealing out communications, manipulating data and communicating with other software systems. RPA applications with the support of IT add efficiencies to enterprise uses such as in financial transactions and control, customer relationship management, Enterprise Resource Planning, supply chain management, logistics and in human resource management (Violino, 2016).

Human Resources: Apart from eliminating the repetitive tasks, it can also reduce errors and human dependence. Additionally, RPA in HR operations also saves many expenses, time, and other key

Figure 3. Benefits of RPA in HR and payroll

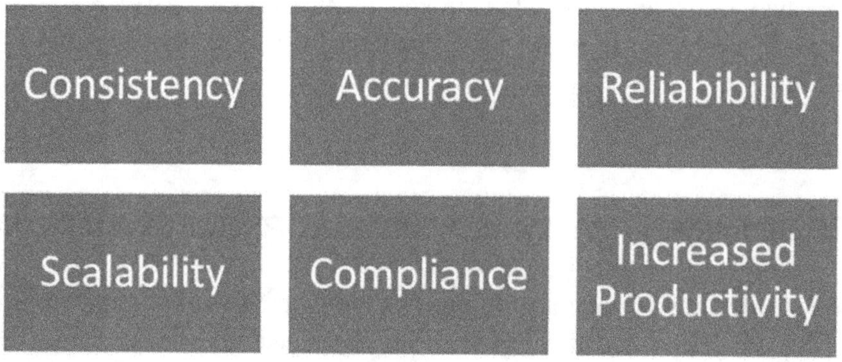

resources of the company that could be used for more productive tasks (Yadav, 2021). RPA adoption is reported by one of the research reports that Human Resources is 8% on complete scale and 17% on applying RPA actively (Technovert, 2023). Given the huge amount of data gathering, checking, updating, validating, form filling, and request processing which means HR managers are shifting their whole focus for admin tasks. Some of the most common tasks that can be fit perfectly in RPA are sourcing and candidate shortlisting, on/offboarding, payroll and benefits, expense and travel management, attendance tracking, and data management and HR analytics (Cavero-Baptista, 2021).

With this implementation, it will streamline the transactional tasks of HR operations, and will helps to improve efficiency and productivity, save time, resources, and enabling them to focus more on strategic tasks (Makadia, 2020). The benefits can be broken down further especially in the payroll systems as show below in Figure 3.

Finance/Accounting: Computational intelligence has facilitated enhancing the financial capability of the several institutions. Industrial leaders started looking into the potentials of technology and digital applications for improving the business and profit (Lyon, 2018). Several minor and major tasks associated with finance and accounting operations like physical certification of account settlements or matching several transactions are now effortlessly taken out with the assistance of robotics process applications (Blackline Magazine, 2021). The leaders in the financial industry have of the opinion that almost 80% financial activities and 89% of accounting operations are highly automatable with the support of RPA. The financial officials must spend more time on data-cleaning prior to they can deploy analytics (Meulen, 2020). The technologist suggests that smart automation, or intelligent automation processes can bring better productivity in financial operations. RPA process can improve the precocity of financial analysis as well as planning the financial processes. By integrating finance robotics with other intelligent automation technologies, the financial and industrial firms can track and assist its monetary benefits (Mixon, 2021).

Sales and Marketing: RPA also contributes to functional marketing in business firms. Upkeep of precise database of consumer's data is crucial for cultivating, developing, and maintaining consumer affairs. As one of the major cross-interactional means, the Customer Relationship Management databases are more susceptible to human errors during business process integration. Therefore, computerizing the CRM system over an RPA amalgamation performs a crucial role, in reducing errors that strained customer relationships (Smartbridge, 2023). Some ways to implement this technology effectively within the department are Storing Existing and New Customer Information, Extracting Marketing and Sales Data from Different Formats, Sales Order and Invoice Processing, Lead Nurturing and Lead Generation,

Pricing and Competition Monitoring, Business Intelligence Reporting, Data Aggregation and Management, Facilitating the Transition from Old to New Solutions, Opportunity Tracking, Quoting process Automation, and Social Media Monitoring (Calisse, 2019); (Karimi, 2020). The benefits of implementing RPA in sales and marketing can automate the transformation on the entire sales value.

Application and Adoption of RPA in Industry

Developing countries have started looking upon the use of robotic applications in manufacturing and service sectors, and has reported improvement in productivity and performance. In manufacturing sector, RPA performs an extensive form of manual jobs more competently and reliably than human being. It is also reported that in addition to manufacturing, the RPA is applied into other sectors such as agriculture, hospitality, and logistics (Atkinson, 2019). All these would be the key contributor to IR5.0 or Society 5.0. Let's investigate some of the popular sectors.

Manufacturing: In manufacturing, the growth in productivity from developments in device sensing, engineering, and machine learning has delivered the chance for the thriving of RPAs which has the competence to pool resources meticulously with human to cross the inconsistencies. The premier of engineering machine starts from the IR1.0, and till at now, the development of next cohort of robotic have spread training and regulation with the non-aggressive contributions such as Non-invasive electroencephalography-based processer crossing point, Wearable indication or microelectronic action devices, Recognition of eye movement, Deciphering of motion capture, and Language recognition (LaRanger, 2020).

With this revolutionizing assembly, robotic have move quickly and accurately, in the growing numbers of products, the standard of vision technology which contribute to the reducing cost of fixturing and tooling (Acieta, 2021). Some of the common industrial robotic applications used such as Arc Fusing, Spot Joining, Materials Treatment, Machine Treatment, Painting, Gathering, Stuffing and Palletizing, Assembly, Machine-driven Cutting, Crushing, Deburring and Refining, Sticking, Adhesive Closing and Spraying Tools, and Additional Procedures - include assessment, waterjet cutting and fusing robots (Shake, 2022); (Joshi, 2019).

Pharmaceutical: RPA function as computerised system that combines a sensor, an intelligent, management algorithm, and an actuator. The mounting need for mechanisation in industrial units, joined with the high charges of novel drug innovation, is considerably growing the call for robotics in scientific trials, drug innovation and laboratories will stimulate progress (Owen-Hill, 2021). The scope associated with the RPA applications in pharmaceutical sector include enhanced manufacturing output and merchandise superiority, increased manufacture suppleness, consumption of less space, no workforce attrition, less operating expenses, improved well-being and security, reduced manufacture idle time and improved waste management (PharmTech, 2009) (Balfour, 2021). The key to finding is a good robot application that focus on those that will give a quick win to the business. Common impacts of robotics on pharmaceutical companies include RPA can improve production output of a particular task, it can complete the task in the same way every time, which improves product consistency, it can run 24 hours a day and does not need to take breaks, the right programming tools of RPA can quickly change the robot's task to respond to changes, and it can help in many pharmaceutical companies to "plan for the unknown" by giving them more responsive R&D.

Many robots could be right for pharmaceutical companies and here are some potential applications that work well in pharmaceutical companies such as Pick and Place, Inspection, Capping bottles, Dispensing, Machine tending, and Packaging (Owen-Hill, 2021).

Information Technology: Robotics will endure to change industrial productions in numerous ways. Nonetheless, there are 6 developments in robotic automation which will play an important part with the IT perspective such as Adoption of Industrial Internet of Things (IIoT) Technology, Engineering Cyber security as a Precedence, Big Data Analysis Come to be a Reasonable Differentiator, Built-up Automation Designs Will Be Applied, Computer-generated Explanations will Occupy Physical Courses, and Combined Robots Will Endure to Produce in Acceptance (Robotics Online Marketing Team, 2018).

Medical/Healthcare: Medical and health care sector is widely using robotic applications for day-to-day treatments and diagnostic applications. Robot-assisted technologies are engaged into operations completed and can be revealed to attain a lesser rate of post-operative difficulties, ensuing in less re-admissions and lesser charges. The facilities have extended to assistive applications for, nurses, caregivers, doctors and patients in clinics and health care facilities (Dolic, Castro, & Moarcas, 2019) (Bieller, 2021). Both robotics and AI ensures a lot of assistances that are shifting each facet of the healthcare network globally (Ilchenko, 2020). The robotics are used in healthcare are supporting physicians and nurses in a variety of purposes which comprises of Spring-cleaning and decontamination, Surgery, Rehabilitation, and Robotic assistance for healthcare workers (Bieller, 2021).

Figure 4. Ten AI applications that could change healthcare

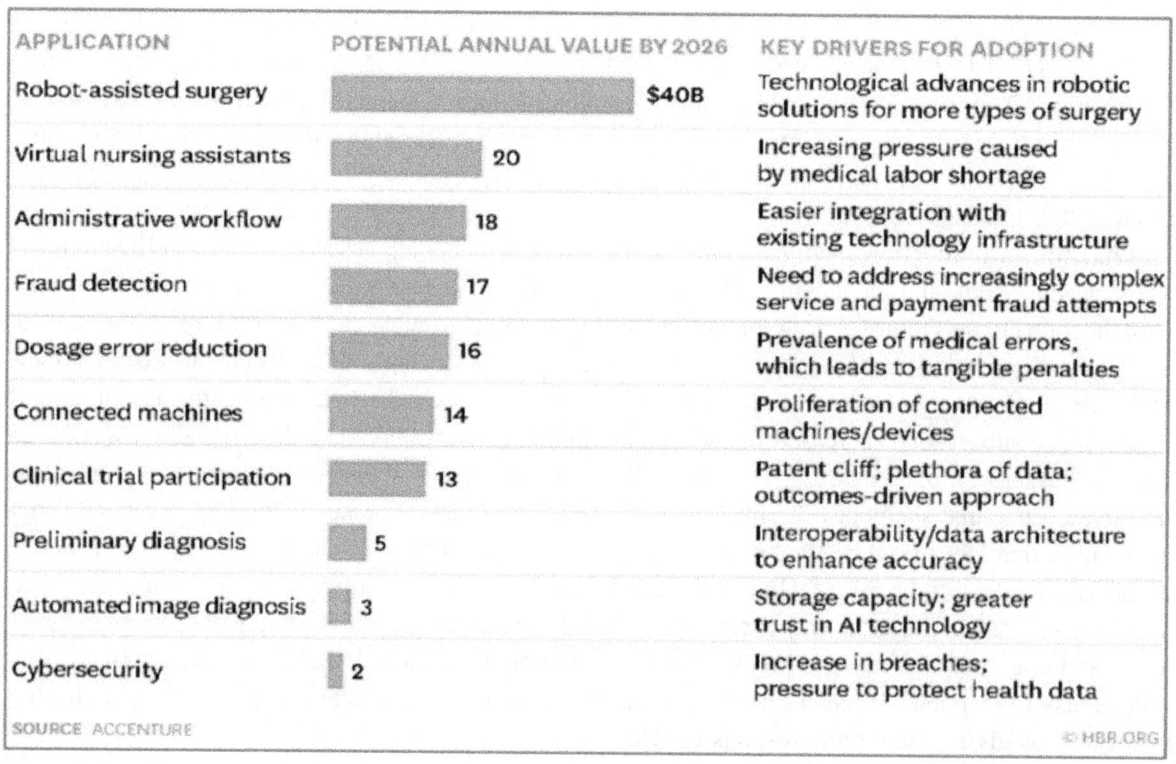

The real magic in this 21st-century "robo-doctor" are commonly connected from AI structures that can study deeply that it will outpace the best physicians by joining all the obtainable information in all therapeutic sources. However impressive the combination of robotics and AI in healthcare, is still a system should be controlled by humans. No matter how experts are these technologies, it is agreed that AI will not replace trained medical staff, but more on assisting in some areas that requires efficient which includes Improving accuracy, Precise diagnosis, Remote treatment, Augmenting human abilities, Supportive psychological health and day-to-day activities, and Auxiliary robots (Marius, 2019).

Supply Chain and Logistics: Supply chain industry is widely influenced by the automated processing of goods and services, with wide range of applications with mobile robots and manipulators. Some of the examples include

E-commerce invoice completion, flexible store rooms, and drone distribution are amongst the paybacks of robots and AI in supply chains. The robots have augmented their level of intellect and elasticity as machine-learning and AI have integrated into the system. A significant level of enhancements to the agility of robots, is observed. In addition to that capacity to associate robots via IoT and improved security actions have also incorporated into the robotic devices (Santagate, 2018).

In facts, logistics industry is the one that is holding and linking this world together, contemporarily. It comprises of an enormous number of diverse procedures like ordering, conveyance, storing, gathering, stuffing, distribution, record, and directing are a few of those courses (Joseph, 2020). With this, business owners and supply-chain professionals are aware of the power of automation. Between 2019 and 2020, a report by MHI shows that the adoption rate for robotics and automation has increased more than any other supply-chain technology (Jaffer, 2021). So, the robotic logistics has been created and the application of robotics are being implemented to one or more processes in the logistics system (Joseph, 2020). Where the application of autonomous robots possibly will determine value by decreasing direct and indirect working costs and growing productivity, and finally the income prospect (Fitzgerald & Quasney, 2017). Robotic palletizing, robotic packaging, robotic picking is some of the major functions performed by the robots in supply chain industry. A few of the innovation system for storehouse robotics in supply chain are Autonomous Mobile Robots (AMR), Aerial Drones, Automated Guided Vehicles, and Automated Storage and Retrieval System (AS and RS) (Joseph, 2020).

RPA AND COVID-19 APPLICATIONS

Traditionally, RPA associated with saving money, business now want automated systems to deliver improved user experience and productivity (Gooding, 2021). So, during the COVID-19 restrictions, most of the countries introduced a contact form to be filled in by people to/from a given country. The goal is to alert passengers in-case there is a positive COVID-19 case detected in the flight. UiPath Robot are being used in this case and will alert all the other passengers who may have contact with that person who has tested positive for COVID-19 (Silva, 2021). Meaning that leverage RPA to speed up response to automate critical COVID-19 processes like testing, diagnosis, screening, updates, etc. (Datamatics, 2021). Similar during the pandemic, huge of inefficiencies of supply chain infrastructure that causes tonnes of issue in inflexibility of delivery. With this, robots are used to improve the speed and accuracy of routine operations, while adding efficiency, safety, and visibility across supply-chain practices, especially the completion of consumers request (Jaffer, 2021). For example Kofax RPA (Ingails, 2020), and Automation Anywhere, has provided solutions to support consumers in steering these unexpected challenges by serving to alleviate commotion during the epidemic and stay connected with groups and systems, continue consumer care, and extend steadiness in times of uncertainty (Shukla, 2023).

Table 1. RPA tools with AI support

Vendors	Support and features
UiPath (Dines, 2023)	UiPath AI scientifically discover automation opportunities and enhance robots with AI Skills. When software robots can reason over data and use AI to make decisions, by unlocking new possibilities that transform RPA and the entire industries. Benefits from this platform: 1. **Discover** - Find more automation opportunities everywhere 2. **Build** - Teach your robots to handle "thinking" tasks 3. **Deploy** - Insert AI into robots easily 4. **Improve** - Leverage learning loop
Kofax (Kofax, 2021)	Intelligent Automation is a platform for Digital Workflow Transformation. It has the power and simplicity of the integrated solutions build in that make it easy to connect systems, applications, and data to streamline any customer, business-critical workflow. The platform includes: 1. Kofax TotalAgility 2. Kofax RPA 3. Kofax Insights 4. Kofax Mobile Capture 5. Kofax SignDoc 6. Kofax Communication Manager 7. Kofax OmniPage 8. Kofax CloudDocs 9. Kofax ControlSuite
Automation Anywhere (Automation Anywhere, 2021)	Automation 360 is the prominent cloud-native endwise intelligent automation boards utilised by the top enterprises to twice over their number of computerised procedures at a segment of legacy RPA systems' structure—with 3X quicker scaling. Such platform enclosed all angles in the virtuous cycle of hyper automation which consist of: 1. Discover 2. Digitize 3. Automate 4. Optimize
WinAutomation (WinAutomation, 2023)	Microsoft Power Automate is an end-to-end intelligent automation featuring expanded RPA technology. It free your team from mundane, time-consuming, repetitive tasks so they can focus on higher-value work with desktop flows.
AssistEdge (Assistedge, 2023)	Automation Singularity denotes to a greatly consumer -oriented and agile leaning state of continuous inventiveness and optimization over an integrated workforce, opening a long-drawn-out prospect of potentials. It reflects a hyper-optimized state which serves as a beacon for enterprises to design, structure and deliver products and services. The core tenets consist of: 1. **Discover** – Create and manage Automation Blueprint 2. **Automate** – Realize and Amplify Value from Automation 3. **Orchestrate** – Accelerate Business specific Process Orchestration
Others (Casey K., 2020)	The Open-source RPA applications: 1. **TagUI** - Maintained by AI Singapore, a command-line interface for RPA that can run on any of the major OSes. 2. **RPA for Python** - Previously dubbed "TagUI for Python," this is a Python package for RPA development. 3. **Robocrop** – is a kind of conjures up some of the darker, Terminator-esque images of RPA – but that's a bit beside the point. This is a relatively new entry into the field, and somewhat unique in that it's a venture-backed start-up promising to deliver cloud-based, open-source RPA tools for developers. 4. **Robot Framework** - is a generic framework for both test automation and RPA. Like others, it emphasizes natural or human-readable language as a means of making it easier to use. 5. **Automagica** – is an open source and free for non-commercial uses, but business uses will require a commercial license. That makes it a potentially good option for individuals looking to learn, experiment, and prototype. 6. **Taskt** - ease-of-use and no- or low-code tools is not the exclusive domain of commercial RPA vendors.

KEY CHALLENGES OF RPA ADOPTION

Based on the above research and finding, adopting any new technologies has its challenges, especially RPA and AI to which is critical to maintaining competitiveness. Robotic Process Automation (RPA) has several challenges that organizations may face when implementing it. However, these challenges can be mitigated with careful planning, strategy, and best practices. Some key challenges of RPA and ways to overcome them include: (Albajari, 2021) (Ward, 2019)

- **Complex Processes:** Challenge: Complex business processes, like financial audits involving multiple regulations, exceptions, and variations, can be difficult to automate seamlessly with RPA. Overcoming strategy: Start by automating simpler, more standardized tasks within the audit process, such as data entry or report generation. Once these are successfully automated, gradually move on to more complex parts. For instance, automating the reconciliation of specific financial data entries before expanding to automate the entire audit process.
- **Legacy System Integration:** Challenge: Integration of RPA with legacy systems that lack modern APIs or compatibility. Overcoming strategy: Consider using middleware solutions that act as a bridge between RPA tools and legacy systems. For example, if a company has an old mainframe system for storing customer data, use middleware to extract and translate the data into a format that RPA tools can understand and work with.
- **Change Management and Resistance:** Challenge: Employees' resistance to RPA due to fear of job displacement or unfamiliarity with new technology. Overcoming strategy: Involve employees in the RPA implementation process. Offer training sessions to familiarize them with RPA tools and emphasize that automation will augment their work, not replace it. For instance, in a customer service department, demonstrate how RPA can handle routine queries, allowing staff to focus on more complex issues, enhancing job satisfaction.
- **Security and Compliance Concerns:** Challenge: RPA handling sensitive data without proper security measures. Overcoming strategy: Implement robust security measures like encryption, role-based access control, and regular security audits. For instance, in a healthcare organization, ensure RPA tools comply with HIPAA regulations and encrypt patient data, restricting access only to authorized personnel.
- **Scalability and Maintenance:** Challenge: Managing and scaling numerous bots across various processes. Overcoming strategy: Establish a dedicated team to manage RPA bots. Implement version control and change management processes. For example, in a supply chain, use a centralized RPA control center to monitor, update, and scale bots, ensuring they adapt to changing demands and conditions.
- **Limited Cognitive Abilities:** Challenge: RPA's inability to handle unstructured data or make decisions. Overcoming strategy: Integrate RPA with AI technologies. For instance, in a document processing scenario, combine RPA with OCR (Optical Character Recognition) and machine learning algorithms to extract and interpret unstructured data, allowing RPA to work with a wider range of information.

By addressing these challenges through strategic planning, training, and a focus on both technological and human aspects, organizations can successfully implement and derive value from Robotic Process Automation.

BRING THE GAP BETWEEN RPA AND THE INDUSTRY NEEDS

It is notable that with RPA introduced and implemented, it does not impact on reducing manpower. In fact, it has created more jobs for most of the industries. Looking on the trend of unemployment, it seems that even with the highest peak of implementation of robotics, yet the un-employment rate is reducing.

Since automation is important, skilled workers continue to be key to all industries success. It is important to keep companies competitive by training skilled workers in the right fields to bridge the gap needed to RPA and AI (RobotWorx, 2018). There are 2 kinds of skill gaps, which are internal or individual and the other is representing or organization to address technological advancement. Some of the coverage for the gap are: (Anandan, 2015) (Kohli, 2017)

- **Rethink community colleges/ Academia-Industry Bridge:** These bridges amongst academia and industry and is crucial in evolving well-rounded automation specialists where instructors and recruiters are combined to train and transfer of skills to the younger generation. Skill set includes automation, material handling, machine tending, assembly, welding applications, quality control, Six Sigma (Green Belt Training), etc.
- **Industrial robotics concentration:** Focus on mechanical, electrical, computer engineering, industrial robots, robotics programming, systems amalgamation, control, kinematics, PLCs, machine-vision, simulation, flow-line examination and optimization, etc.
- **Hands-on, Real-world:** Focus to engage on real-world hands-on training which includes profession-type project covering budgeting, project planning, soft skills, and opportunity to keep up professionally with the industry.
- **Well-Rounded Engineers:** With robust acquaintance with a range of disciplines and automation equipment, soft skills like sturdy team-working, communications, social robotics, etc. can be augmented.
- **Co-op programs:** Co-op program, on the industry side are scoping out cherished ability as well as significant benefits amongst the industry and education. It will deliver noble chance to work with a group and contributes prospect to measure the skills acquires from their advisors.
- **Robotics education carts and curriculum, and options:** is the key-design alterations comprise of a lighter weight, ergonomically-designed cart with even boundaries and an well-lit inner structure. Teaching aids for instructors and beginners come with standard on feedback from the institutes and the training establishments that trained the instructors.
- **Sustainable education funding:** Bringing the industry to the community by proving the sustainable to secure the large educational contributed by the high school students, college scholars, incumbent workforces who needs extra training and engineering maintenance program for grown-up learners.
- **Start young:** Instead of limiting to a sole subject, beginners need to obtain multidisciplinary abilities, right after the start by understanding how hardware and software go together in generating disruptive robotic solutions and the progressed ecosystem. Student must proactively look for chances to work on robotics assignments that solve real-world challenges, by proactively investigating with the given assets and contributing in various robotics competitions, workshops, and conferences.
- **Give back:** Organisations and robotics firms need to initiate partnerships for running labs and projects together, plus recognize learners with the right zeal and provide them with the right ex-

posure through internships. This will not only help firms in recognising and hiring the right talent for the long-term but also organise them for resolving numerous engineering problems over and done with automation (Anandan, 2015); (Kohli, 2017).

THEORETICAL IMPLICATIONS

The current business landscape is increasingly defined by digitalization and the integration of automation technologies like Robotic Process Automation (RPA) and Artificial Intelligence (AI). While their implementation poses certain challenges and cultural shifts, the benefits they bring to organizations are undeniable. These technologies have become pivotal elements in the ongoing digital era, where disruptive technologies and industrial revolutions drive and accelerate their adoption due to the fast-paced nature of modern business and evolving consumer needs.

RPA and AI offer multiple advantages to organizations, streamlining operations, improving efficiency, reducing human error, and enabling better resource allocation. Despite challenges in implementation, limitations in technology, and the necessity for cultural adaptation, their impact in reshaping industries and business processes is substantial.

In the context of this digital transformation, it's crucial to recognize that the term "robotic" in RPA might be misleading. As Sheikh (2021) aptly points out, RPA extends beyond the traditional understanding of robotics. It doesn't solely involve physical robots but encompasses software robots or bots that automate rule-based, repetitive tasks previously performed by humans. These bots simulate human actions within digital systems, working across various applications to execute tasks faster and with higher accuracy.

The ongoing wave of technological disruption and industry revolutions, such as the Fourth Industrial Revolution, is a significant driver in the adoption and integration of RPA and AI. The rapid pace of change and the need for agility in operations are pushing organizations to seek these technologies to stay competitive, improve customer experiences, and enhance operational efficiency.

RPA and AI are not just tools but catalysts for business innovation, augmenting human capabilities and allowing a more strategic allocation of human resources. This automation doesn't replace jobs entirely but rather reallocates human efforts from mundane, repetitive tasks to more complex, creative, and analytical roles. The synergy between human expertise and machine automation is where the true potential of these technologies lies.

Understanding the real essence of RPA, which is not confined to physical robotics, and appreciating its integration within the broader spectrum of digital transformation is vital. The combination of RPA and AI, alongside other disruptive technologies, is driving the ongoing evolution of business practices and industry standards, fostering a more efficient and agile business ecosystem in this era of rapid technological advancement.

THE FUTURE OF RPA

The future of Robotic Process Automation (RPA) is evolving beyond its traditional roots and is poised to integrate with Artificial Intelligence (AI) to give rise to what is termed as Intelligence Process Automation (IPA). This evolution is a response to the changing landscape in which technology is being employed across various sectors, moving beyond manufacturing and robotics.

The current wave of innovation and technological advancement, often associated with the Fourth Industrial Revolution (IR 4.0), is progressing toward the integration of RPA and AI to create IPA. This trend is further enhanced by the concept of Society 5.0, a human-centric society that fuses the physical and digital worlds to improve quality of life. IPA plays a pivotal role in this societal evolution, offering more than just automated processes by introducing intelligence into the equation.

IPA brings a significant shift in how automation is perceived and implemented. It combines the efficiency of RPA with the cognitive capabilities of AI, enabling systems to learn, adapt, and make decisions. Instead of merely following pre-programmed rules, IPA can analyze data, understand patterns, and optimize processes in real-time. This intelligent automation extends beyond performing routine tasks; it encompasses critical thinking, problem-solving, and decision-making abilities.

The application of IPA is not limited to manufacturing or industrial settings. It has the potential to revolutionize various aspects of society, such as:

- **Smart Cities:** Implementing IPA in urban settings can optimize transportation, energy consumption, waste management, and public services. It can improve traffic flow, enhance public safety, and streamline administrative processes.
- **Smart Universities:** IPA can transform educational institutions by automating administrative tasks, personalizing learning experiences, and optimizing resource allocation, thereby improving the overall educational quality.
- **Smart Workforce:** In the professional sphere, IPA can empower workers by handling repetitive tasks, providing data-driven insights, and supporting decision-making processes. This allows human employees to focus on higher-value tasks that require creativity and critical thinking.

The integration of RPA and AI into IPA offers not just automation, but a smarter, more adaptive way of conducting business, governance, education, and various other societal functions. The collective intelligence embedded in systems allows for efficient and informed decision-making, contributing to the growth and betterment of society at large. As this trend continues to develop, we can expect to witness significant advancements in how automation and intelligence converge to shape the future of work, cities, education, and society as a whole.

CONCLUSION

The primary aim of this chapter is to delve into the expansive opportunities presented by robotics applications within the industrial and services sectors, effectively shaping a new paradigm for the world. The integration of Artificial Intelligence (AI) and Robotic Process Automation (RPA) applications emerges as a transformative force capable of significantly enhancing business and manufacturing operations, thereby elevating the overall efficiency of our workplaces. The current study encompasses a comprehensive exploration, incorporating various facets such as emerging trends in computational intelligence, the practical applications of AI and RPA in industries and services, market share trends, the augmentation of skills, and prospective future options.

Despite the continuous evolution and upgrading evident in industrial revolutions, it is crucial to underscore the irreplaceable role of humans in the equation. This paper acknowledges that even with the constant flux and advancements brought about by technology, the fundamental presence of human intelligence, creativity, and decision-making capabilities cannot be substituted by robotics alone. The integration of robotics into industry practices and services is not intended to replace human labor but rather to augment and complement it.

As the future landscape of RPA unfolds, a symbiotic relationship between humanity and robotics is envisioned. The anticipated advancements in the field predict a closer, more interactive human-robotic interface, facilitated by the possibilities offered by computational intelligence. This implies a harmonious collaboration where humans and robots work in tandem, leveraging each other's strengths to achieve unprecedented levels of efficiency and innovation. The paper thus not only delves into the current state of AI and RPA applications but also looks forward to a future where the synergy between humans and robotics results in a harmonized, technologically empowered world.

REFERENCES

Aceto, G., Persico, V., & Pescapé, A. (2020). Industry 4.0 and health: Internet of things, big data, and cloud computing for healthcare 4.0. *Journal of Industrial Information Integration*, *18*, 100129. doi:10.1016/j.jii.2020.100129

Acieta. (2021). *Robotics in Manufacturing*. Acieta. https://www.acieta.com/why-robotic-automation/robotics-manufacturing/

Albajari, M. (2021). *Top 4 RPA Implementation Challenges*. IT Convergence. https://www.itconvergence.com/blog/top-4-rpa-implementation-challenges/

Anandan, T. (2015, April 30). *Closing the Skills Gap in Automation: A Call for Action*. Association for Advancing Automatation - Industry Insights. https://www.automate.org/industry-insights/closing-the-skills-gap-in-automation-a-call-for-action

Assistedge. (2023). *Our NorthStar: Automation Singularity*. Assistedge. https://www.edgeverve.com/assistedge/

Atkinson, R. D. (2019, October 15). *Robotics and the Future of Production and Work*. Information Technology & Information Foundation. https://itif.org/publications/2019/10/15/robotics-and-future-production-and-work

Automation Anywhere. (2021). *Making digital acceleration as easy as point, click, cloud*. Automation Anywhere. https://www.automationanywhere.com/products/automation-360

AutomationEdge. (2020, July 24). *20 Unparalleled Benefits of RPA and AI To Digital Business*. AutomationEdge. https://automationedge.com/blogs/20-unparalleled-benefits-of-rpa-and-ai-to-digital-business/

Balfour, H. (2021, April 23). *Trends to watch out for in the pharmaceutical robot market*. European Pharmaceutical Review. https://www.europeanpharmaceuticalreview.com/news/152077/trends-to-watch-out-for-in-the-pharmaceutical-robot-market/

Bangia, M., Cruiz, G., Huber, I., Landauer, P., & Sunku, V. (2020, May). *Sales automation: The key to boosting revenue and reducing costs.* McKinsey & Company – Marketing & Sales Practice. https://www.mckinsey.com/~/media/McKinsey/Business%20Functions/Marketing%20and%20Sales/Our%20Insights/Sales%20automation%20The%20key%20to%20boosting%20revenue%20and%20reducing%20costs/sales-automation-the-key-to-boosting-revenue.ashx

Bhatt, S. (2021, June 25). *7 Top RPA Trends that you Need to Know in 2021.* Datafloq. https://datafloq.com/read/7-top-rpa-trends-need-know-2021/15784#:~:text=Smart%20Process%20Automation%20is%20the,from%20self%2Dlearning%20AI%20algorithms

Bieller, S. (2021, May 31). *The role of robots in healthcare.* IFR Secretariat Blog: https://ifr.org/post/the-role-of-robots-in-healthcare-part2

Biscotti, F., Tornbohm, C., Villa, A., Bhullar, B., & Mehta, V. (2021, May 25). *Market Share Analysis: Robotic Process Automation, Worldwide, 2020.* Retrieved September 5, 2021, from Gartner Research: https://www.gartner.com/en/documents/4001926/market-share-analysis-robotic-process-automation-worldwi

Blackline Magazine. (2021). *What RPA Really Means for Your Organization.* Blackline Magazine - White Paper. https://www.blackline.com/resources/whitepapers/what-rpa-really-means-for-your-organization/?utm_source=google&utm_medium=cpc&utm_campaign=apac-ase-middle-&utm_term=rpa%20finance&_bt=534428299320&_bk=rpa%20finance&_bm=p&_bn=g&_bg=127908565827&gclid=EAIaIQ

Bots, C. F. B. (2018, April 21). *The Difference between Robotic Process Automation and Artificial Intelligence.* CFB Bots. https://cfb-bots.medium.com/the-difference-between-robotic-process-automation-and-artificial-intelligence-4a71b4834788

Boulton, C. (2018, September 4). *What is RPA? A revolution in business process automation.* CIO – Asean. https://www.cio.com/article/3236451/what-is-rpa-robotic-process-automation-explained.html

Calisse, L. (2019, December 10). *Robotic Process Automation Use Cases in Marketing and Sales.* Momentum Data. https://momentumdata.com/robotic-process-automation-use-cases-in-sales-and-marketing/

Casey, K. (2019, September 18). *Robotic Process Automation (RPA) by the numbers: 14 interesting stats.* The Enterprisers Project. https://enterprisersproject.com/article/2019/9/rpa-robotic-process-automation-14-stats

Casey, K. (2019, August 12). *Robotic Process Automation (RPA) vs. AI, explained.* The Enterprisers Project. https://enterprisersproject.com/article/2019/8/rpa-robotic-process-automation-vs-ai-explained

Casey, K. (2020, July 30). *How to explain Robotic Process Automation (RPA) in plain English.* The Enterprisers Project. https://enterprisersproject.com/article/2019/5/rpa-robotic-process-automation-how-explain

Casey, K. (2020, April 7). *Robotic Process Automation (RPA): 6 open-source tools.* The Enterprisers Project. https://enterprisersproject.com/article/2020/4/rpa-robotic-process-automation-6-open-source-tools

Cavero-Baptista, L. (2021). *How to use RPA in HR.* Leapwork. https://www.leapwork.com/blog/how-to-use-rpa-in-hr-example

Costello, K., & Rimol, M. (2020, September 21). *Gartner Says Worldwide Robotic Process Automation Software Revenue to Reach Nearly $2 Billion in 2021.* Gartner – Newsroom Press Releases. https://www.gartner.com/en/newsroom/press-releases/2020-09-21-gartner-says-worldwide-robotic-process-automation-software-revenue-to-reach-nearly-2-billion-in-2021

Datamatics. (2021). *Speed Up Response to COVID-19 With RPA.* Datamatics - RPA Use Cases. https://www.datamatics.com/intelligent-automation/rpa-trubot/use-cases/covid-19

Dines, D. (2023). *AI and RPA: Transformative on their own, even more powerful together.* UiPath – Automation. https://www.uipath.com/automation/ai-and-rpa

Dolic, Z., Castro, R., & Moarcas, A. (2019). Robots in healthcare: A solution or a problem? In R. Bianchini (Ed.), *Workshop Proceedings Policy Department for Economic, Scientific and Quality of Life Policies Directorate-General for Internal Policies Website.* European Parliament's Committee. https://www.europarl.europa.eu/RegData/etudes/IDAN/2019/638391/IPOL_IDA(2019)638391_EN.pdf

ElectroNeek. (2020, April 3). *RPA 101: Why RPA is better than traditional automation?* ElectroNeek - RPA Technology. https://electroneek.com/blog/rpa/rpa-101-why-rpa-is-better-than-traditional-automation/

Fitzgerald, J., & Quasney, E. (2017). *Using autonomous robots to drive supply chain innovation.* Deloitte. https://www2.deloitte.com/content/dam/Deloitte/us/Documents/manufacturing/us-manufacturing-autonomous-robots-supply-chain-innovation.pdf

Gartner, G. (2023, 07 22). *Robotic Process Automation (RPA).* Gartner – Information Technology. https://www.gartner.com/en/information-technology/glossary/robotic-process-automation-rpa

Gartner. (2021). *Robotic Process Automation Software Reviews and Ratings.* Gartner – Peer Insights. https://www.gartner.com/reviews/market/robotic-process-automation-software

Gooding, M. (2021, February 3). *A robot for every worker: Pent-up demand for automation to drive RPA spree.* Techmonitor – Automation. https://techmonitor.ai/automation/changing-role-of-rpa-covid-19

Grand View Research. (2021, April). *Robotic Process Automation Market Size, Share & Trends Analysis Report By Type, By Service, By Application, By Deployment, By Organization, By Region, And Segment Forecasts, 2021 – 2028* Grand View Research. https://www.grandviewresearch.com/industry-analysis/robotic-process-automation-rpa-market

Granrath, L. (2017, August 29). *Japan's Society 5.0: Going Beyond Industry 4.0.* Japan Industry News. https://www.japanindustrynews.com/2017/08/japans-society-5-0-going-beyond-industry-4-0/

IBM. (2020). *What is Industry 4.0?* IBM. https://www.ibm.com/my-en/topics/industry-4-0

IBM Cloud Education. (2020, Jun 3). *Artificial Intelligence (AI).* IBM Cloud Learn Hub: https://www.ibm.com/my-en/cloud/learn/what-is-artificial-intelligence

IBM Cloud Education. (2020, October 22). *Robotic Process Automation.* IBM Cloud Learn Hub. https://www.ibm.com/cloud/learn/rpa

Ilchenko, V. (2020, September 7). *AI Adoption in Healthcare: 10 Pros and Cons*. Byteant. https://www.byteant.com/blog/ai-adoption-in-healthcare-10-pros-and-cons/

Ingails, A. (2020, October 28). *Reduces Application Processing Time from Nearly Two Hours to Four Minutes, Supporting More than 1,900 Freelance Workers*. Kofax RPA Powers BMconsultants' Solution for BAR Organization to Provide Freelance Workers Rapid Access to COVID-19 Funding. https://www.kofax.com/about/press-releases/2020/kofax-rpa-powers-bmconsultants-solution-to-provide-workers-rapid-access-to-covid-19-funding

Jaffer, Z. (2021, April 9). *The Impact of Robotics on Supply Chain 2.0*. Supply Chain Brain – Think Tank. https://www.supplychainbrain.com/blogs/1-think-tank/post/32909-the-impact-of-robotics-on-supply-chain-20

Javed, A. (2020, July 6). *RPA – Robotics Process Automation Trends and Statistics For 2020*. Xorlogics - Merging Ideas into Technology. https://www.xorlogics.com/2020/07/06/rpa-robotics-process-automation-trends-and-statistics-for-2020/

Joseph, T. (2020, August 4). *How Robotics in Logistics Helps Improve Supply Chain Efficiency*. Fingent Shaping the Future. https://www.fingent.com/blog/how-robotics-in-logistics-helps-improve-supply-chain-efficiency/

Joshi, N. (2019, August 9). 5 Applications Of Collaborative Robots In Manufacturing. *Forbes*. https://www.forbes.com/sites/cognitiveworld/2019/08/09/5-applications-of-collaborative-robots-in-manufacturing/?sh=3972d3dc6507

Karimi, M. (2020, March 30). *8 Use-Cases of RPA In Sales & Marketing*. MyFalcon. https://myfalcon.co.uk/8-use-cases-of-rpa-in-sales-marketing/

Khan, S. I., Kaur, C., Al Ansari, M. S., Muda, I., Borda, R. F., & Bala, B. K. (2023). Implementation of cloud based IoT technology in manufacturing industry for smart control of manufacturing process. *International Journal on Interactive Design and Manufacturing (IJIDeM)*, 1-13.

Kofax. (2021). *Intelligent Automation for Digital Workflow Transformation*. Kofax - Intelligent Automation Platform. https://www.kofax.com/products/intelligent-automation-platform

Kohli, P. (2017, August 16). *Bridging the skill gap in robotics – An imperative for industry today*. People Matters. https://www.peoplematters.in/article/talent-acquisition/bridging-the-skill-gap-in-robotics-an-imperative-for-industry-today-16080

LaRanger, R. (2020, January). *What's driving the adoption of robots in industry*. PreScouter. https://www.prescouter.com/2020/01/whats-driving-the-adoption-of-robots-in-industry/

Lionel, S. V. (2023). *Robotic process automation (RPA) market size worldwide from 2020 to 2030*. Statista. https://www.statista.com/statistics/1259903/robotic-process-automation-market-size-worldwide/

Lyon, J. (2018, September 20). *Embracing robotic automation during the evolution of finance*. ACCA – Think Ahead. https://www.accaglobal.com/lk/en/professional-insights/technology/embracing-robotic-automation-during-the-evolution-of-finance.html

Madakam, S., Holmukhe, R. M., & Jaiswal, D. (2019, November 19). The Future Digital Work Force: Robotic Process Automation (RPA). *JISTEM -. Journal of Information Systems and Technology Management*, *16*, 1–17. doi:10.4301/S1807-1775201916001

Makadia, M. (2020, December 16). *12 Use Cases for Implementing RPA in HR Operations*. Customer Think. https://customerthink.com/12-use-cases-for-implementing-rpa-in-hr-operations/

Marius, E. (2019, May 29). *6 Ways AI and Robotics Are Improving Healthcare*. Retrieved September 6, 2021, from Robotics Business Review: https://www.roboticsbusinessreview.com/health-medical/6-ways-ai-and-robotics-are-improving-healthcare/

Maruti Techlabs. (2023). *Robotic Process Automation vs Traditional Automation*. Maruti Techlabs. https://marutitech.com/robotic-process-automation-vs-traditional-automation/

Meulen, R. (2020, March 26). *Finance Tackles Efficiencies and Costs With RPA*. Gartner – Smarter with Gartner. https://www.gartner.com/smarterwithgartner/finance-tackles-efficiencies-and-costs-with-rpa/

Mixon, J. (2021, 9 5). *The Role of Robotic Process Automation (RPA) in Finance Automation*. Gartner – White Paper. https://www.gartner.com/en/finance/insights/robotics-in-finance

Moore, S. (2019, June 29). *Gartner Says Worldwide Robotic Process Automation Software Market Grew 63% in 2018*. Gartner – Newsroom Press Releases. https://www.gartner.com/en/newsroom/press-releases/2019-06-24-gartner-says-worldwide-robotic-process-automation-sof

Newsdesk, B. N. N. (2021). *Robotic Process Automation vs Traditional Automation*. B2BNN. https://www.b2bnn.com/2019/12/robotic-process-automation-vs-traditional-automation/

NextProcess. (2023). *Top 10 Reasons Why Using Robotic Process Automation for Data Entry Is the Right Choice for Your Business*. NextProcess - Business Process Automation. https://www.nextprocess.com/blog/top-10-reasons-using-robotic-process-automation-data-entry-right-choice-business/

NICE. (2023). *AI and RPA: What's the Difference and which is Best for Your Organization?* NICE - Master Robotic Process Automation. https://www.nice.com/rpa/rpa-guide/rpa-ai-and-rpa-whats-the-difference-and-which-is-best-for-your-organization/

Nividous. (2021, April 7). *Top 8 Benefits of RPA (With Real Examples)*. Nividous. https://nividous.com/blogs/benefits-of-rpa

Owen-Hill, A. (2021, March 23). *6 Robot Applications for Pharmaceutical Companies*. RoboDK. https://robodk.com/blog/6-robot-applications-for-pharmaceutical-companies/

PharmTech. (2009, September 20). Robots: The Next Phase in Pharmaceutical Automation. *Pharmaceutical Technology*, *33*(9). https://www.pharmtech.com/view/robots-next-phase-pharmaceutical-automation-0

Por, V. Solutions. (2018, April 2). *Top-5 Benefits of Robotics Process Automation (RPA) Adoption for Your Company*. PorV Solutions. https://www.provintl.com/blog/top-5-benefits-of-robotics-process-automation-rpa-software

Pritzker, M. D. (2020, May 19). *RPA Drawbacks and Limitations Explained*. IT Central Station. https://www.itcentralstation.com/questions/what-are-the-limitations-of-rpa

Ribeiro, J., Lima, R., Eckhardt, T., & Paiva, S. (2021). Robitic Process Automation and Artificial Intelligence in Industry 4.0 – A Literature Review. *CENTERIS – International Conference on ENTERprise Information Systems/ProjMAN – International Conference on Project MANagement/HCist – International Conference on Health and Social Care Information Systems and Technologies 2020*. Elsevier B.V. https://www.sciencedirect.com/science/article/pii/S1877050921001393

Robotics Online Marketing Team. (2018, December 6). *Top 6 Future Trends in Robotic Automation*. Association for Advancing Automation. https://www.automate.org/blogs/top-6-future-trends-in-robotic-automation

RobotWorx. (2018, April 27). *Bringing Jobs and Bridging the Skills Gap with Automation*. RobotWorx – Robotic Industry News. https://www.robots.com/blogs/staying-competitive-and-bridging-the-skills-gap

Santagate, J. (2018). NextGen Supply Chain: The Robots are Here. *Supply Chain Management Review*. https://www.scmr.com/article/nextgen_supply_chain_the_robots_are_here

Schroer, A. (2023). *Introduction to AI*. Built In. https://builtin.com/artificial-intelligence

Shake, M. (2022). *Ten Popular Industrial Robot Applications*. Jabil. https://www.jabil.com/blog/ten-popular-industrial-robot-applications.html

Sheikh, S. (2021, April 4). *Robotic Process Automation (RPA) - debunked and demystified*. Linkedin. https://www.linkedin.com/pulse/robotic-process-automation-rpa-debunked-demystified-salim/

Shukla, M. (2023). *From continuity to community, our top priority is helping our customers thrive now and beyond*. Automation Anywhere - Automation Solutions COVID-19. https://www.automationanywhere.com/automation-solutions-covid-19

Silva, G. (2021, February 25). *Leveraging UiPath Apps and Data Service: How AIR COVID-19 Manager Works*. UiPath. https://www.uipath.com/community/rpa-community-blog/leveraging-uipath-apps-and-data-service-how-air-covid-19-manager-works

Smartbridge. (2023). *Robotic Process Automation Services for Sales and Marketing*. Retrieved September 5, 2021, from Smartbridge: https://smartbridge.com/automation/explore-rpa/rpa-for-sales-marketing/

SoftwareReviews. (2023). *Best Robotic Process Automation (RPA) Software*. SoftwareReviews - Top Robotic Process Automation Software. https://www.softwarereviews.com/categories/robotic-process-automation

Technovert. (2023). *RPA for HR: Know how HR automation benefits your organization*. Technovert. https://technovert.com/blog/rpa-for-hr/

Vanmali, K., & Paul, A. (2016). *Automation in the CFO World*. Deloitte. https://www2.deloitte.com/content/dam/Deloitte/za/Documents/process-and-operations/za_CFO%20Indaba_Interactive.pdf

Violino, B. (2016, November 18). *Why robotic process automation adoption is on the rise*. ZDNet – Innovation. https://www.zdnet.com/article/rpa-adoption-on-the-rise/

Ward, J. (2019, October 13). *The four key challenges to RPA adoption*. Accountancy Ireland. https://www.charteredaccountants.ie/Accountancy-Ireland/Articles2/News/Latest-News/the-four-key-challenges-to-rpa-adoption

WinAutomation. (2023). *WinAutomation is now part of Microsoft Power Automate*. WinAutomation. https://www.winautomation.com/

Yadav, S. (2021, February 2). *Role of RPA (Robotic Process Automation) in Human Resource (HR) Operations*. Zenesys. https://www.zenesys.com/blog/role-of-rpa-in-hr-operations

Compilation of References

ABES. (2017). *Mercado Brasileiro de Software - Panorama e Tendências*. ABES. https://www.abessoftware.com.br/dados-do-setor/estudo-2017--dados-2016

ACATE. (2021). *Tech Report*. Panorama do setor de tecnologia catarinense.

Aceto, G., Persico, V., & Pescapé, A. (2020). Industry 4.0 and health: Internet of things, big data, and cloud computing for healthcare 4.0. *Journal of Industrial Information Integration*, *18*, 100129. doi:10.1016/j.jii.2020.100129

Acieta. (2021). *Robotics in Manufacturing*. Acieta. https://www.acieta.com/why-robotic-automation/robotics-manufacturing/

Acosta, A. S., Crespo, Á. H., & Agudo, J. C. (2018). Effect of market orientation, network capability and entrepreneurial orientation on international performance of small and medium enterprises (SMEs). *International Business Review*, *27*(6), 1128–1140. doi:10.1016/j.ibusrev.2018.04.004

Adam, M., Wessel, M., & Benlian, A. (2021). AI-based chatbots in customer service and their effects on user compliance. *Electronic Markets*, *31*(2), 427–445. doi:10.1007/s12525-020-00414-7

Adler, P. S., & Clark, K. B. (1991). Behind the learning curve: A sketch of the learning process. *Management Science*, *37*(3), 267–281. doi:10.1287/mnsc.37.3.267

Agostini, L., & Nosella, A. (2017). Interorganizational relationships in marketing: A critical review and research agenda. *International Journal of Management Reviews*, *19*(2), 131–150. doi:10.1111/ijmr.12084

Agostini, L., Nosella, A., & Filippini, R. (2016). Towards an Integrated View of the Ambidextrous Organization: A Second-Order Factor Model. *Creativity and Innovation Management*, *25*(1), 129–141. doi:10.1111/caim.12167

Agrawal, A., Gans, J. S., & Goldfarb, A. (2019). Artificial Intelligence: The Ambiguous Labor Market Impact of Automating Prediction. *The Journal of Economic Perspectives*, *33*(2), 31–50. https://www.jstor.org/stable/26621238. doi:10.1257/jep.33.2.31

AI-based Natural Language Processing (NLP) Systems. (2020). AI-based Natural Language Processing (NLP) Systems. *Journal of Algebraic Statistics*. doi:10.52783/jas.v11i1.1431

Albajari, M. (2021). *Top 4 RPA Implementation Challenges*. IT Convergence. https://www.itconvergence.com/blog/top-4-rpa-implementation-challenges/

Albuquerque, J. C. M. (2011). *Sistemas de informação e comunicação no setor público*. Departamento de Ciências da Administração/UFSC.

Alford, J., & Hughes, O. (2008). Public value pragmatism as the next phase of public management. *American Review of Public Administration*, *38*(2), 130–148. doi:10.1177/0275074008314203

Alghamdi, N. A., & Al-Baity, H. H. (2022). Augmented Analytics Driven by AI: A Digital Transformation beyond Business Intelligence. *Sensors (Basel)*, *22*(20), 8071. doi:10.3390/s22208071 PMID:36298421

Al-Haddad, S., & Kotnour, T. (2015). Integrating the organizational change literature: A model for successful change. *Journal of Organizational Change Management*, *28*(2), 234–262. doi:10.1108/JOCM-11-2013-0215

Alharthi, A., Alhefdi, M., Lipscomb, M. M., & Jololian, L. (2022). Value-Based Modeling of an Addiction Recovery Healthcare System. In *Proceedings SoutheastCon 2022*, IEEE. 10.1109/SoutheastCon48659.2022.9764037

Alhosan, N., & Fayyoumi, A., FARIS, H. (2014). Shaping an Experts Locator System: Recommending the Right Expert. *Journal of Theoretical and Applied Information Technology*, *66*(2).

Allee, V. (1997). The Knowledge Evolution. Expanding Organizational Intelligence. Amsterdam: Butterworth-Heinemann.

Allee, V. (2003). The future of Knowledge. Increasing Prosperity Through Value Networks. Amsterdam: Butterworth-Heinemann.

Allee, V. (2008). Value network analysis and value conversion of tangible and intangible assets. *Journal of Intellectual Capital*, *9*(1), 5–24. doi:10.1108/14691930810845777

Allee, V., Schwabe, O., & Babb, M. K. (2015). *Value Networks and the true nature of collaboration*. Meghan-Kiffer Press.

Almeida, F. (2017). Concept and Dimensions of Web 4.0. *International Journal of Computers and Technology*, *16*(7), 7040–7046. doi:10.24297/ijct.v16i7.6446

Al-Okaily, A., Teoh, A. P., & Al-Okaily, M. (2023). Evaluation of data analytics-oriented business intelligence technology effectiveness: An enterprise-level analysis. *Business Process Management Journal*, *29*(3), 777–800. doi:10.1108/BPMJ-10-2022-0546

Anandan, T. (2015, April 30). *Closing the Skills Gap in Automation: A Call for Action*. Association for Advancing Automatation - Industry Insights. https://www.automate.org/industry-insights/closing-the-skills-gap-in-automation-a-call-for-action

Angelova, M., Vishnu Manasa, D., Boeva, V., Linde, P., & Lavesson, N. (2018). *An Expertise Recommender System-Based on Data from an Institutional Repository (DiVA)*. In 22nd edition of the International Conference on ELectronic PUBlishing-Connecting the Knowledge Commons: From Projects to Sustainable Infrastructure, Toronto.

Ansell, C., & Trofing, J. (2021). Co-creation: The new kid on the block in public governance. *Policy and Politics*, *49*(2), 211–230. doi:10.1332/030557321X16115951196045

Anshari, M., Syafrudin, M., & Fitriyani, N. L. (2022). Fourth industrial revolution between knowledge management and digital humanities. *Information (Basel)*, *13*(6), 292. doi:10.3390/info13060292

Antonescu, D. (2018). Are business leaders prepared to handle the upcoming revolution in business artificial intelligence? *Quality - Access to Success*, *19*, 166.

Anzanello, M. J., & Fogliatto, F. S. (2005). Alocação de modelos de produtos a equipes de trabalhadores baseada em modelos de curvas de aprendizagem. *Production*, *15*(2), 221–234. doi:10.1590/S0103-65132005000200007

Anzanello, M. J., & Fogliatto, F. S. (2007). Curvas de aprendizado: Estado da arte e perspectivas de pesquisa. *Gestão & Produção*, *14*(1), 109–123. doi:10.1590/S0104-530X2007000100010

APQC - American Productivity & Quality Center. (2015). *Knowledge Management Priorities*. APQC. https://www.apqc.org/knowledge-base/download/340305/K05834_2015_KM_Priorities_ExecSum.pdf

Araucária, F. (2023 12 30). *A Fundação Araucária.* FAPPR. https://www.fappr.pr.gov.br/Pagina/Fundacao-Araucaria

Asamoah, D., Agyei-Owusu, B., & Ashun, E. (2020). Social network relationship, supply chain resilience and customer-oriented performance of small and medium enterprises in a developing economy. *Benchmarking, 27*(5), 1793–1813. doi:10.1108/BIJ-08-2019-0374

Asare, A. O., Addo, P. C., Sarpong, E. O., & Kotei, D. (2020). COVID-19: Optimizing business performance through agile business intelligence and data analytics. *Open Journal of Business and Management, 8*(5), 2071–2080. doi:10.4236/ojbm.2020.85126

Asbaş, C., & Erdem Tuzlukaya, Ş. (2023). Siber Uzay Alanını Keşfetmek: Grup İçi ve Gruplar Arası İlişkiler Üzerinde Siber Tehditlerin Etkileri. In M. Kızrak (Ed.), *Örgütlerde Grup İçi ve Gruplar Arası İlişkiler* (pp. 97–109). Siyasal Kitabevi.

Assistedge. (2023). *Our NorthStar: Automation Singularity.* Assistedge. https://www.edgeverve.com/assistedge/

Atkinson, R. D. (2019, October 15). *Robotics and the Future of Production and Work.* Information Technology & Information Foundation. https://itif.org/publications/2019/10/15/robotics-and-future-production-and-work

Audretsch, D. B. & Link, A. N. (2019). Embracing an entrepreneurial ecosystem: an analysis of the governance of research joint ventures. *Small Business Economics, 52*(2), 429–436.

Augl, M., & Stary, C. (2015). Communication-and Value-Based Organizational Development at the University Clinic for Radiotherapy-Radiation Oncology. In *S-BPM in the Wild* (pp. 35–53). Springer International. doi:10.1007/978-3-319-17542-3_3

Augl, M., & Stary, C. (2017). Adjusting Capabilities Rather Than Needs in Computer-Supported Daily Workforce Planning. In *Designing Healthcare that Works* (pp. 175–188). Academic Press/Elsevier.

Automation Anywhere. (2021). *Making digital acceleration as easy as point, click, cloud.* Automation Anywhere. https://www.automationanywhere.com/products/automation-360

AutomationEdge. (2020, July 24). *20 Unparalleled Benefits of RPA and AI To Digital Business.* AutomationEdge. https://automationedge.com/blogs/20-unparalleled-benefits-of-rpa-and-ai-to-digital-business/

Automation, R. P. (RPA) Implementation Drivers: Evidence of Selected Nordic Companies. (2021). *Issues in Information Systems.* doi:10.48009/2_iis_2021_21-40

Awan, U., Kanwal, N., Alawi, S., Huiskonen, J., & Dahanayake, A. (2021). Artificial intelligence for supply chain success in the era of data analytics. *The fourth industrial revolution: Implementation of artificial intelligence for growing business success,* 3-21. doi:10.1007/978-3-030-62796-6_1

Newsdesk, B. N. N. (2021). *Robotic Process Automation vs Traditional Automation.* B2BNN. https://www.b2bnn.com/2019/12/robotic-process-automation-vs-traditional-automation/

Baird, A., & Schuller, B. (2020, September 2). Considerations for a More Ethical Approach to Data in AI: On Data Representation and Infrastructure. *Frontiers in Big Data, 3,* 25. Advance online publication. doi:10.3389/fdata.2020.00025 PMID:33693398

Baiyere, A., Salmela, H., & Tapanainen, T. (2020). Digital transformation and the new logics of business process management. *European Journal of Information Systems, 29*(3), 238–259. doi:10.1080/0960085X.2020.1718007

Baker-Brunnbauer, J. (2020). Management perspective of ethics in artificial intelligence. *AI and Ethics, 1*(2), 173–181. doi:10.1007/s43681-020-00022-3

Balfour, H. (2021, April 23). *Trends to watch out for in the pharmaceutical robot market.* European Pharmaceutical Review. https://www.europeanpharmaceuticalreview.com/news/152077/trends-to-watch-out-for-in-the-pharmaceutical-robot-market/

Ballester, O. (2021). An Artificial Intelligence Definition and Classification Framework for Public Sector Applications. *The 22nd Annual International Conference on Digital Government Research (DG.O'21).* ACM. 10.1145/3463677.3463709

Balog, K. (2012). Expertise Retrieval. Foundations and Trends in Information Retrieval. doi:10.1561/9781601985675

Bangia, M., Cruiz, G., Huber, I., Landauer, P., & Sunku, V. (2020, May). *Sales automation: The key to boosting revenue and reducing costs.* McKinsey & Company – Marketing & Sales Practice. https://www.mckinsey.com/~/media/McKinsey/Business%20Functions/Marketing%20and%20Sales/Our%20Insights/Sales%20automation%20The%20key%20to%20boosting%20revenue%20and%20reducing%20costs/sales-automation-the-key-to-boosting-revenue.ashx

Bansal, G., Zahedi, F. M., & Gefen, D. (2016). Do context and personality matter? Trust and privacy concerns in disclosing private information online. *Information & Management, 53*(1), 1–21. doi:10.1016/j.im.2015.08.001

Bardin, L. (1977). *Análise de conteúdo.* 1. ed. Lisboa, Portugal: Edições 70.

Batra, D. (2020). The impact of the COVID-19 on organizational and information systems agility. *Information Systems Management, 37*(4), 361–365. doi:10.1080/10580530.2020.1821843

Baum, I. A., & Stary, C. (2022). Value exchange exploration supporting project-based learning. In: *Proceedings 17th International Conference on Knowledge Management 'Knowledge. Uncertainty and Risks: From individual to global scale.* ICKM. https://digital.library.unt.edu/ark:/67531/metadc2047067/?q=ickm%202022%20stary

Bean, R. (2018). How Big Data and AI are driving business innovation in 2018. *MIT Sloan Management Review.*

Becerra-Fernandez, I., & Sabherwal, R. (2014). Knowledge Management: Systems and Process (2. Ed). Routeledge.

Becerra-Fernandez, I. (2000). The role of artificial intelligence technologies in the implementation of People-Finder knowledge management systems. *Knowledge-Based Systems, 13*(5), 315–320. doi:10.1016/S0950-7051(00)00091-5

Bencsik, A. (2021). The sixth generation of knowledge management: The headway of artificial intelligence. *Journal of International Students, 14*(2), 84–101. doi:10.14254/2071-8330.2021/14-2/6

Bergeron, B. (2003). Essentials of Knowledge Management. *Studies in Health Technology and Informatics, 160,* 1–208.

Berkes, F. (2010). Adaptive Co-Management and Complexity: Exploring the Many Faces of Co-Management. *Adaptive Co-Management: Collaboration, Learning, and Multi-Level Governance,* 19.

Berliner, H. J. (1974). *Chess as problem solving: the development of a tactics analyzer* [Doctoral dissertation, Carnegie-Mellon University].

Bethune, E., Buhalis, D., & Miles, L. (2022). Real time response (RTR): Conceptualizing a smart systems approach to destination resilience. *Journal of Destination Marketing & Management, 23,* 100687. doi:10.1016/j.jdmm.2021.100687

Bezboruah, K. C. (2008). Applying the congruence model of organizational change in explaining the change in the Indian economic policies. *Journal of Organisational Transformation & Social Change, 5*(2), 129–140. doi:10.1386/jots.5.2.129_1

Bharadiya, J. P. (2023). A Comparative Study of Business Intelligence and Artificial Intelligence with Big Data Analytics. *American Journal of Artificial Intelligence, 7*(1), 24. doi:10.11648/j.ajai.20230701.14

Bhatt, S. (2021, June 25). *7 Top RPA Trends that you Need to Know in 2021*. Datafloq. https://datafloq.com/read/7-top-rpa-trends-need-know-2021/15784#:~:text=Smart%20Process%20Automation%20is%20the,from%20self%2Dlearning%20AI%20algorithms

Bieller, S. (2021, May 31). *The role of robots in healthcare*. IFR Secretariat Blog: https://ifr.org/post/the-role-of-robots-in-healthcare-part2

Binci, D., Belisari, S., & Appolloni, A. (2020). BPM and change management: An ambidextrous perspective. *Business Process Management Journal, 26*(1), 1–23. doi:10.1108/BPMJ-06-2018-0158

Biscotti, F., Tornbohm, C., Villa, A., Bhullar, B., & Mehta, V. (2021, May 25). *Market Share Analysis: Robotic Process Automation, Worldwide, 2020.* Retrieved September 5, 2021, from Gartner Research: https://www.gartner.com/en/documents/4001926/market-share-analysis-robotic-process-automation-worldwi

Blackline Magazine. (2021). *What RPA Really Means for Your Organization.* Blackline Magazine - White Paper. https://www.blackline.com/resources/whitepapers/what-rpa-really-means-for-your-organization/?utm_source=google&utm_medium=cpc&utm_campaign=apac-ase-middle-&utm_term=rpa%20finance&_bt=534428299320&_bk=rpa%20finance&_bm=p&_bn=g&_bg=127908565827&gclid=EAIaIQ

Blumauer, A., & Nagy, H. (2020). *The knowledge graph cookbook: Recipes that work.* Monochrom.

Bocean-Vărzaru, A. A. (2022). Assessing the Impact of AI Solutions' Ethical Issues on performance in Managerial Accounting. *Electronics (Basel), 11*(14), 2221. doi:10.3390/electronics11142221

Boehm, B. (2003). Value-based software engineering: Reinventing. *Software Engineering Notes, 28*(2), 1–11.

Boehm, B., & Huang, L. G. (2003). Value-based software engineering: A case study. *Computer, 36*(3), 33–41. doi:10.1109/MC.2003.1185215

Boes, K., Borde, L., & Egger, R. (2015a). The Acceptance of NFC Smart Posters in Tourism. In I. Tussyadiah & A. Inversini (Eds.), *Information and Communication Technologies in Tourism 2015* (pp. 435–448). Springer. doi:10.1007/978-3-319-14343-9_32

Boes, K., Buhalis, D., & Inversini, A. (2015b). Conceptualising Smart Tourism Destination Dimensions. In I. Tussyadiah & A. Inversini (Eds.), *Information and Communication Technologies in Tourism 2015* (pp. 391–403). Springer. doi:10.1007/978-3-319-14343-9_29

Böhmer, N., & Schinnenburg, H. (2023). Critical exploration of AI-driven HRM to build up organizational capabilities. *Employee Relations: The International Journal.*

Boire, R. (2017). Understanding AI in a world of big data. *Big Data & Information Analytics, 2*(5), 23–43. doi:10.3934/bdia.2018001

Bosilj Vukšić, V., Brkić, L., & Tomičić-Pupek, K. (2018). Understanding the success factors in adopting business process management software: Case studies. *Interdisciplinary Description of Complex Systems: INDECS, 16*(2), 194–215. doi:10.7906/indecs.16.2.1

Botelho, L. L. R., Cunha, C. C. A., & Macedo, M. (2011). O método da revisão integrativa nos estudos organizacionais. *Gestão e Sociedade, Belo Horizonte, 5*(11), 121–136. doi:10.21171/ges.v5i11.1220

Bots, C. F. B. (2018, April 21). *The Difference between Robotic Process Automation and Artificial Intelligence.* CFB Bots. https://cfb-bots.medium.com/the-difference-between-robotic-process-automation-and-artificial-intelligence-4a71b4834788

Boulianne, E., Fortin, M., & Leco, A. (2023). Artificial Intelligence and Data Analytics: Ethical Implications for Accounting. In M. Brivot & C. Cho (Eds.), *Research Handbook on Accounting and Ethics* (pp. 168–179)., https://ideas.repec.org/h/elg/eechap/20458_11.html doi:10.4337/9781800881020.00020

Boulton, C. (2018, September 4). *What is RPA? A revolution in business process automation.* CIO – Asean. https://www.cio.com/article/3236451/what-is-rpa-robotic-process-automation-explained.html

Brachman, R. J., & Levesque, H. J. (2004). *Knowledge representation and reasoning.* Elsevier. doi:10.1016/B978-1-55860-932-7.X5083-3

Brandenburger, A. M., & Nalebuff, B. J. (1996). *Co-opetition.* Currency/Doubleday.

Brandsen, T., Honingh, M. (2015). Distinguishing Different Types of Coproduction: A Conceptual Analysis Based on the Classical Definitions. *Public Administration Review, 76*(3), 427–435.

BRASSCOM - Associação das Empresas de Tecnologia da Informação e Comunicação (TIC) e de Tecnologias Digitais. (2021). *Demanda de Talentos em TIC e Estratégia Σ TCEM.* Brasscom. https://brasscom.org.br/pdfs/demanda-de-talentos-em-tic-e-estrategia-tcem/

Bremer, S. (2019). *Toward a multi-faceted conception of co-production of climate services* (Vol. 13). Climate Services. [s. l.], doi:10.1016/j.cliser.2019.01.003

Brendel, A., Mirbabaie, M., Lembcke, T.-B., & Hofeditz, L. (2021). Ethical Management of Artificial Intelligence. *Sustainability (Basel), 13*(4), 1974. doi:10.3390/su13041974

Brennan, B. S., Koo, C., & Bae, K. M. (2018). Smart Tourism: A Study of Mobile Application Use by Tourists Visiting South Korea. *Asia-pacific Journal of Multimedia Services Convergent with Art, Humanities, and Sociology, 8*(10), 1–9. doi:10.21742/AJMAHS.2018.10.15

BrettM. (2023). Issues to consider relating to Information Governance and Artificial Intelligence Background to AI and Context a practitioner's viewpoint. doi:10.13140/RG.2.2.11285.09442

Broucek, C. E. (2020). eDiscovery for the legal professional. Frederick, MD: Walters Kluwer.

Brown, R. E., & Donald, O. (2020). Hebb and the Organization of Behavior: 17 years in the writing. *Molecular Brain, 13*(1), 55. doi:10.1186/s13041-020-00567-8 PMID:32252813

Bryson, J. M., Crosby, B. C., & Bloomberg, L. (2014). Public value governance: Moving beyond traditional public administration and the new public management. *Public Administration Review, 74*(4), 445–456. doi:10.1111/puar.12238

Buchanan, B. G., & Smith, R. G. (1988). Fundamentals of expert systems. *Annual Review of Computer Science, 3*(1), 23–58. doi:10.1146/annurev.cs.03.060188.000323

Buhalis, D., & Amaranggana, A. (2015). Smart tourism destinations enhancing tourism experience through personalisation of services. In *Information and communication technologies in tourism* (pp. 377–389). Springer.

Bulchand-Gidumal, J. (2022). Impact of artificial intelligence in travel, tourism, and hospitality. In *Handbook of e-Tourism* (pp. 1943–1962). Springer International Publishing. doi:10.1007/978-3-030-48652-5_110

Burke, W. W., & Litwin, G. H. (1992). A causal model of organizational performance and change. *Journal of Management, 18*(2), 523–546. doi:10.1177/014920639201800306

Burnes, B. (2011). Introduction: Why does change fail, and what can we do about it? *Journal of Change Management, 11*(4), 445–450. doi:10.1080/14697017.2011.630507

Burr, C., & Leslie, D. (2022, June 22). Ethical assurance: A practical approach to the responsible design, development, and deployment of data-driven technologies. *AI and Ethics, 3*(1), 73–98. doi:10.1007/s43681-022-00178-0

Cagnin, M. I., & Nakagawa, E. Y. (2021). Towards dynamic processes-of-business processes: A new understanding. *Business Process Management Journal, 27*(5), 1545–1568. doi:10.1108/BPMJ-08-2020-0349

Calisse, L. (2019, December 10). *Robotic Process Automation Use Cases in Marketing and Sales.* Momentum Data. https://momentumdata.com/robotic-process-automation-use-cases-in-sales-and-marketing/

Calle-Lamelas, J. V., García-Hernández, M., & García-Muiña, F. E. (2023). What is a Smart Destination in Practice? The Interpretation of DMO Managers from Spanish World Heritage Cities. *Tourism Planning & Development*, 1–23. doi:10.1080/21568316.2023.2214123

Calza, F. (2023). *Impacto do uso da gestão do conhecimento para a gestão da curva de aprendizagem de uma empresa do setor de TI, da cidade de Florianópolis/SC.* Trabalho de Conclusão de Curso, Universidade Federal de Santa Catarina.

Cantor, M. (Oct 12, 2023). Incredibly smart or incredibly stupid? What we learned from using ChatGPT for a year. *The Guardian.* https://www.theguardian.com/technology/2023/oct/12/chatgpt-uses-writing-recipes-one-year

Carnall, C. (2007). *Managing change in organizations* (5th ed.). Prentice Hall: Financial Times.

Casey, K. (2019, August 12). *Robotic Process Automation (RPA) vs. AI, explained.* The Enterprisers Project. https://enterprisersproject.com/article/2019/8/rpa-robotic-process-automation-vs-ai-explained

Casey, K. (2019, September 18). *Robotic Process Automation (RPA) by the numbers: 14 interesting stats.* The Enterprisers Project. https://enterprisersproject.com/article/2019/9/rpa-robotic-process-automation-14-stats

Casey, K. (2020, April 7). *Robotic Process Automation (RPA): 6 open-source tools.* The Enterprisers Project. https://enterprisersproject.com/article/2020/4/rpa-robotic-process-automation-6-open-source-tools

Casey, K. (2020, July 30). *How to explain Robotic Process Automation (RPA) in plain English.* The Enterprisers Project. https://enterprisersproject.com/article/2019/5/rpa-robotic-process-automation-how-explain

Cavero-Baptista, L. (2021). *How to use RPA in HR.* Leapwork. https://www.leapwork.com/blog/how-to-use-rpa-in-hr-example

Cetindamar, D., Shdifat, B., & Erfani, E. (2022). Understanding big data analytics capability and sustainable supply chains. *Information Systems Management, 39*(1), 19–33. doi:10.1080/10580530.2021.1900464

ChatGPT. (2023). *ChatGPT.* Open AI. https://openai.com/blog/chatgpt-plus on November 1, 2023.

Chen, D. Q., Preston, D. S., & Swink, M. (2015). How the use of big data analytics affects value creation in supply chain management. *Journal of Management Information Systems, 32*(4), 4–39. doi:10.1080/07421222.2015.1138364

Chen, M., Mao, S., & Liu, Y. (2014). Big Data: A Survey. *Mobile Networks and Applications*, 19.

Chintalapati, S., & Pandey, S. K. (2022). Artificial intelligence in marketing: A systematic literature review. *International Journal of Market Research, 64*(1), 38–68. doi:10.1177/14707853211018428

Choe, Y., & Fesenmaier, D. R. (2021). Designing an advanced system for destination management: A case study of Northern Indiana. *Industrial Management & Data Systems, 121*(6), 1167–1190. doi:10.1108/IMDS-02-2020-0063

Clegg, S. R., Pitsis, T. S., Rura-Polley, T., & Marosszeky, M. (2002). Governmentality matters: Designing an alliance culture of inter-organizational collaboration for managing projects. *Organization Studies, 23*(3), 317–337. doi:10.1177/0170840602233001

Cofre-Martel, S., Lopez Droguett, E., & Modarres, M. (2021, October 14). Big Machinery Data Preprocessing Methodology for Data-Driven Models in Prognostics and Health Management. *Sensors (Basel), 21*(20), 6841. doi:10.3390/s21206841 PMID:34696058

Cordova-Moras, L. G., Rodriguez-Elias, O. M., & Serna-Encinas, M. T. (2017). Expert Location Tool for Global Software Development Environments Based on Knowledge Profile Management: A Mobile Application Approach. In *2017 5th International Conference in Software Engineering Research and Innovation* (CONISOFT) (pp. 89-96). IEEE. 10.1109/CONISOFT.2017.00018

Corpakis, D. (2020). Powering Synergies Between Innovation Policy and Regional Development Frameworks: The Case of Smart Specialisation. In: A. Abu-Tair et al. (Eds.*), Proceedings of the II International Triple Helix Summit, Lecture Notes in Civil Engineering.* Springer. 10.1007/978-3-030-23898-8_8

Costanza-Chock, S. (2020). *Design justice: Community-led practices to build the worlds we need.* The MIT Press. https://direct.mit.edu/books/oa-monograph/4605/Design-JusticeCommunity-Led-Practices-to-Build-the

Costello, K., & Rimol, M. (2020, September 21). *Gartner Says Worldwide Robotic Process Automation Software Revenue to Reach Nearly $2 Billion in 2021.* Gartner – Newsroom Press Releases. https://www.gartner.com/en/newsroom/press-releases/2020-09-21-gartner-says-worldwide-robotic-process-automation-software-revenue-to-reach-nearly-2-billion-in-2021

Cranmer, E. E., Dieck, M., & Jung, T. (2018). How can tourist attractions profit from augmented reality? In *Augmented reality and virtual reality* (pp. 21–32). Springer. doi:10.1007/978-3-319-64027-3_2

Crawford, R. (1994). *Na era do capital humano.* Editora Atlas.

Cummings, T. G., & Worley, C. G. (2013). *Organization development and change* (10th ed.). South-Western College Publishing. https://www.vitalsource.com/products/organization-development-and-change-thomas-g-cummings-v9781305143036

Cushing, A. L., & Osti, G. (2023). "So how do we balance all of these needs?": How the concept of AI technology impacts digital archival expertise. *The Journal of Documentation, 79*(7), 12–29. doi:10.1108/JD-08-2022-0170

Da Silva, C. L., Ieis, F., & Farah, M. F. Jr. (2015). As interfaces da Política de Ciência, Tecnologia e Inovação com a Política Industrial: Dilemas na trajetória recente do Brasil. *Desenvolvimento em Questão, 13*(30), 60–100. doi:10.21527/2237-6453.2015.30.60-100

Dalkir, K. (2011). *Knowledge management in theory and practice* (2nd ed.). The MIT Press.

Das, A. K. (2018). European Union's General Data ProtectionRegulation, 2018: A brief overview. [ALIS]. *Annals of Library and Information Studies, 65*(2), 139–140.

Datamatics. (2021). *Speed Up Response to COVID-19 With RPA.* Datamatics - RPA Use Cases. https://www.datamatics.com/intelligent-automation/rpa-trubot/use-cases/covid-19

Dattner, B., Chamorro-Premuzic, T., Buchband, R., & Schettler, L. (2019). The legal and ethical implications of using AI in hiring. *Harvard Business Review.* https://hbr.org/2019/04/the-legal-and-ethical-implications-of-using-ai-in-hiring

Davenport, T. H., & Prusak, L. (1998). *Conhecimento empresarial: como as organizações gerenciam seu capital intelectual.*

Davenport, T., Guha, A., Grewal, D., & Bressgott, T. (2020). How artificial intelligence will change the future of marketing. *Journal of the Academy of Marketing Science, 48*(1), 24–42. doi:10.1007/s11747-019-00696-0

Davis, J., Purves, D., Gilbert, J., & Sturm, S. (2022, January 31). Five ethical challenges facing data-driven policing. *AI and Ethics, 2*(1), 185–198. doi:10.1007/s43681-021-00105-9

Davoudi, S. M. M., Ghiasi, A., & Kowsari, R. (2020). A systematic review of information governance in organizations. *International Journal of Information Management, 54*, 102146.

De Reuver, M., Sørensen, C., & Basole, R. C. (2017). The digital platform: A research agenda. *Journal of Information Technology, 33*(2), 124–135. doi:10.1057/s41265-016-0033-3

De Silva, M., Howells, J., & Meyer, M. (2018). Innovation intermediaries and collaboration: Knowledge-based practices and internal value creation. *Research Policy, 47*(1), 70–87. doi:10.1016/j.respol.2017.09.011

De Spiegeleire, S., Maas, M., & Sweijs, T. (2017). What is Artificial Intelligence? In: Artificial Intelligence and the Future of Defence Strategic Implications or Small and Medium Sized Force Providers (pp. 25–42). Hague Centre for Strategic Studies. http://www.jstor.org/stable/resrep12564.7

Deloitte. (2021). 2021 Global Human Capital Trends: The social enterprise in a world disrupted. Delooitte. https://www2.deloitte.com/content/dam/insights/us/articles/6935_2021-HC-Trends/di_human-capital-trends.pdf

Denhardt, R. B., & Denhardt, J. V. (2003). *The New Public Service: Serving, not Steering*. M. E. Sharpe.

Di Vaio, A., Palladino, R., Hassan, R., & Escobar, O. (2020). Artificial intelligence and business models in the sustainable development goals perspective: A systematic literature review. *Journal of Business Research, 121*, 283–314. doi:10.1016/j.jbusres.2020.08.019

Diakopoulos, N. (2016). Accountability in algorithmic decision making. *Communications of the ACM, 59*(2), 56–62. https://cacm.acm.org/magazines/2016/2/197421-accountability-in-algorithmic-decision-making/abstract. doi:10.1145/2844110

Dines, D. (2023). *AI and RPA: Transformative on their own, even more powerful together*. UiPath – Automation. https://www.uipath.com/automation/ai-and-rpa

Dirican, C. (2015). The Impacts of Robotics, Artificial Intelligence On Business and Economics. *Procedia - Social and Behavioral Sciences, 195*, 564-573. doi:10.1016/j.sbspro.2015.06.134

Djenontin, I. N. S., Meadow, A. M. (2018). The art of co-production of knowledge in environmental sciences and management: lessons from international practice. *Environmental Management*. doi:10.1007/s00267-018-1028-3

Doborjeh, Z., Hemmington, N., Doborjeh, M., & Kasabov, N. (2022). Artificial intelligence: A systematic review of methods and applications in hospitality and tourism. *International Journal of Contemporary Hospitality Management, 34*(3), 1154–1176. doi:10.1108/IJCHM-06-2021-0767

Dolic, Z., Castro, R., & Moarcas, A. (2019). Robots in healthcare: A solution or a problem? In R. Bianchini (Ed.), *Workshop Proceedings Policy Department for Economic, Scientific and Quality of Life Policies Directorate-General for Internal Policies Website*. European Parliament's Committee. https://www.europarl.europa.eu/RegData/etudes/IDAN/2019/638391/IPOL_IDA(2019)638391_EN.pdf

Doloreux, D., & Parto, S. (2005). Regional innovation systems: Current discourse and unresolved issues. *Technology in Society, 27*(2), 133–153. doi:10.1016/j.techsoc.2005.01.002

Dorcic, J., Komsic, J., & Markovic, S. (2019). Mobile technologies and applications towards smart tourism–state of the art. *Tourism Review, 74*(1), 82–103. doi:10.1108/TR-07-2017-0121

Dos Anjos, A. C., Sell, D., Spinosa, L. M., Wahrhaftig, R., Koch, G. L., dos Santos, N., & dos Santos Pacheco, R. C. (2023). Sistemas para Localização de Especialistas: Desafios e oportunidades para o desenvolvimento de ecossistemas de inovação. *Revista Ibérica de Sistemas e Tecnologias de Informação*, (E55), 311–326.

Dwivedi, R., Nerur, S., & Balijepally, V. (2023). Exploring artificial intelligence and big data scholarship in information systems: A citation, bibliographic coupling, and co-word analysis. *International Journal of Information Management Data Insights*, *3*(2), 100185. doi:10.1016/j.jjimei.2023.100185

Ehrlich, K., & Shami, N. S. (2008). Searching for Expertise. CHI 2008, 2008, Florence. *Proceedings of the SIGCHI Conference on Human Factors in Computing Systems*. New York: ACM. 10.1145/1357054.1357224

Eisen, L. S. (2020). *Rules: A guide to drafting respectful policies and directives*. Pixley Press.

Eketu, C. A. (2016). Customer Personality Taxonomy: A Theoretical Analysis of Customer Diversity Management in the Hospitality Industry. *International Journal on Customer Relations*, *4*(1). Advance online publication. doi:10.21863/ijcr/2016.4.1.012

ElectroNeek. (2020, April 3). *RPA 101: Why RPA is better than traditional automation?* ElectroNeek - RPA Technology. https://electroneek.com/blog/rpa/rpa-101-why-rpa-is-better-than-traditional-automation/

El-Najdawi, M. K., & Stylianou, A. C. (1993). Expert support systems: Integrating AI technologies. [-ff.]. *Communications of the ACM*, *36*(12), 55. doi:10.1145/163298.163306

Elo, S., & Kyngäs, H. (2008). The qualitative content analysis process. *Journal of Advanced Nursing*, *62*(1), 107–115. doi:10.1111/j.1365-2648.2007.04569.x PMID:18352969

Endeavor & ENAP. (2021). *Índice de Cidades Empreendedoras*. Brasil. https://repositorio.enap.gov.br/bitstream/1/6097/1/relatorio_ICE_2020.pdf

Errida, A., & Lotfi, B. (2021). The determinants of organizational change management success: Literature review and case study. *International Journal of Engineering Business Management*, *13*, 1–15. doi:10.1177/18479790211016273

Estevao, J., Carneiro, M. J., & Teixeira, L. (2020). Destination management systems' adoption and management model: Proposal of a framework. *Journal of Organizational Computing and Electronic Commerce*, *30*(2), 89–110. doi:10.1080/10919392.2020.1724765

European Commission High-Level Expert Group on Artificial Intelligence. (2018). Definition of AI: Main Capabilities and Scientific Disciplines. Europea. https://ec.europa.eu/futurium/en/system/files/ged/ai_hleg_definition_of_ai_18_december_1.pdf

Fan, H., Wang, F., & Zheng, M. (2016). Research on knowledge fusion connotation and process model. In: China Conference On Knowledge Graph And Semantic Computing (CCKS 2016). Springer. doi:10.1007/978-981-10-3168-7_18

Febriyanti, I. (2023, July 10). Assuring Customer Value, Customer Experience, and Trust to Improve Customer Loyalty. *Jurnal Dinamika Manajemen Dan Bisnis*, *6*(2), 37–51. doi:10.21009/JDMB.06.2.3

Feigenbaum, E. A. (1977). *The art of artificial intelligence*. Stanford University Press.

Femenia-Serra, F., & Ivars-Baidal, J. A. (2021). Do smart tourism destinations really work? The case of Benidorm. *Asia Pacific Journal of Tourism Research*, *26*(4), 365–384. doi:10.1080/10941665.2018.1561478

Ferreira, A. B. H., Anjos, M., & Ferreira, M. B. (1999). *Novo Aurélio, Século XXI: o dicionário da língua portuguesa* (3rd ed.). Nova Fronteira.

Fitsilis, P., Gerogiannis, V., & Anthopoulos, L. (2014). Project team selection based on social networks. *2014 IEEE International Technology Management Conference*. IEEE. 10.1109/ITMC.2014.6918598

Fitsilis, P., Gerogiannis, V., & Anthopoulos, L. (2015). Software Project Team Selection Based on Enterprise Social Networks. In *Gen, M., Kim, K., Huang, X., Hiroshi, Y. (eds.). Industrial Engineering, Management Science and Applications 2015, Lecture Notes in Electrical Engineering*. Springer. doi:10.1007/978-3-662-47200-2_40

Fitzgerald, J., & Quasney, E. (2017). *Using autonomous robots to drive supply chain innovation.* Deloitte. https://www2.deloitte.com/content/dam/Deloitte/us/Documents/manufacturing/us-manufacturing-autonomous-robots-supply-chain-innovation.pdf

Fleischmann, A., Schmidt, W., & Stary, C. (2015). *S-BPM in the wild: Practical value creation.* Springer. doi:10.1007/978-3-319-17542-3

Fleischmann, A., Schmidt, W., Stary, C., Obermeier, S., & Börger, E. (2012). *Subject-oriented business process management.* Springer Nature. doi:10.1007/978-3-642-32392-8

Fleming, Q. W., & Koppelman, J. M. (2016). *Earned value project management.* Project Management Institute. www.pmi.org

Fleury, A., & Fleury, M. T. L. (2007). *Internacionalização e os países emergentes.* Atlas.

Floridi, L., & Taddeo, M. (2016). What is data ethics? *Philosophical Transactions. Series A, Mathematical, Physical, and Engineering Sciences, 374*(2083), 20160360. https://royalsocietypublishing.org/doi/10.1098/rsta.2016.0360. doi:10.1098/rsta.2016.0360 PMID:28336805

Fortino, G., Rovella, A., Russo, W., & Savaglio, C. (2014). On the Classification of Cyberphysical Smart Objects in the Internet of Things. In Ubicitec (pp. 86-94). Springer.

Franks, P. C. (2018). *Records and information management* [2d ed.]. Neal-Schuman.

Freire, P. de S., Alvares, L. M. A. de R., Rizzatti, G., Bresolin, G. G., Martins, G. J. T., Kempner-Moreira, F., & Silva, T. C. (2021). *Glossário: Governança Multinível do Conhecimento e da Aprendizagem e seus mecanismos de Universidade Corporativa em Rede e de Comunicação Dialógica.* CRV.

Frey, P. W. (Ed.). (2012). *Chess skill in man and machine.* Springer Science & Business Media.

Future of Software Testing Using Artificial Intelligence. (2022, December 1). Future of Software Testing Using Artificial Intelligence. *Data Analytics and Artificial Intelligence*, *2*(6), 17–22. doi:10.46632/daai/2/6/4

Fyall, A., & Garrod, B. (2020). Destination management: A perspective article. *Tourism Review*, *75*(1), 165–169. doi:10.1108/TR-07-2019-0311

Gaines, B. R., & Shaw, M. L. G. (1993). Eliciting knowledge and transferring it effectively to a knowledge-based system. *IEEE Transactions on Knowledge and Data Engineering, 5*(1), 4-14. doi:10.1109/69.204087

Garfield, S. (2022). *The five Cs of KM.* Lucidea.

Gartner, G. (2023, 07 22). *Robotic Process Automation (RPA).* Gartner – Information Technology. https://www.gartner.com/en/information-technology/glossary/robotic-process-automation-rpa

Gartner. (2021). *Robotic Process Automation Software Reviews and Ratings.* Gartner – Peer Insights. https://www.gartner.com/reviews/market/robotic-process-automation-software

Geekhunter. (2022). Turnover em TI: como reduzir a rotatividade de desenvolvedores da sua empresa. https://rhtech.geekhunter.com.br/turnover-em-ti-2/#Por_que_ficar_de_olho_no_turnover_em_TI

Geissdoerfer, M., Bocken, N. M., & Hultink, E. J. (2016). Design thinking to enhance the sustainable business modelling process–A workshop based on a value mapping process. *Journal of Cleaner Production, 135*, 1218–1232. doi:10.1016/j.jclepro.2016.07.020

Gelter, J., Lexhagen, M., & Fuchs, M. (2021). A meta-narrative analysis of smart tourism destinations: Implications for tourism destination management. *Current Issues in Tourism, 24*(20), 2860–2874. doi:10.1080/13683500.2020.1849048

Ghosh, G. (2018, August 31). Automation with RPA (Robotic Process Automation). *International Journal on Computer Science and Engineering, 6*(8), 475–477. doi:10.26438/ijcse/v6i8.475477

Ghosh, J. (2016). Big data analytics: A field of opportunities for information systems and technology researchers. *Journal of Global Information Technology Management, 19*(4), 217–222. doi:10.1080/1097198X.2016.1249667

Giermindl, L. M., Strich, F., Christ, O., Leicht-Deobald, U., & Redzepi, A. (2022). The dark sides of people analytics: Reviewing the perils for organisations and employees. *European Journal of Information Systems, 31*(3), 410–435. doi:10.1080/0960085X.2021.1927213

Gil, A. C. (2002). *Como elaborar projetos de pesquisa* (4th ed.). Atlas.

Gil-Garcia, J. R., Zhang, J., & Puron-Cid, G. (2016). Conceptualizing smartness in government: An integrative and multi-dimensional view. *Government Information Quarterly, 33*(3), 524–534. doi:10.1016/j.giq.2016.03.002

Gómez-Pérez, A., Fernandez-Lopez, M., & Corcho, O. (2004). *Ontological engineering with examples from the areas of knowledge management, e-commerce and the semantic web.* Springer-Verlag.

Gonzales, R. M. D., & Hargreaves, C. A. (2022). How can we use artificial intelligence for stock recommendation and risk management? A proposed decision support system. *International Journal of Information Management Data Insights, 2*(2), 100130. doi:10.1016/j.jjimei.2022.100130

Gooding, M. (2021, February 3). *A robot for every worker: Pent-up demand for automation to drive RPA spree.* Tech-monitor – Automation. https://techmonitor.ai/automation/changing-role-of-rpa-covid-19

Gotterbarn, D., & Kreps, D. (2020, November 18). Being a data professional: Give voice to value in a data driven society. *AI and Ethics, 1*(2), 195–203. doi:10.1007/s43681-020-00027-y

Grand View Research. (2021, April). *Robotic Process Automation Market Size, Share & Trends Analysis Report By Type, By Service, By Application, By Deployment, By Organization, By Region, And Segment Forecasts, 2021 – 2028* Grand View Research. https://www.grandviewresearch.com/industry-analysis/robotic-process-automation-rpa-market

Granrath, L. (2017, August 29). *Japan's Society 5.0: Going Beyond Industry 4.0.* Japan Industry News. https://www.japanindustrynews.com/2017/08/japans-society-5-0-going-beyond-industry-4-0/

Gretzel, U. (2022). The Smart DMO: A new step in the digital transformation of destination management organizations. *European Journal of Tourism Research, 30*, 3002–3002. doi:10.54055/ejtr.v30i.2589

Grover, V., Chiang, R. H., Liang, T. P., & Zhang, D. (2018). Creating strategic business value from big data analytics: A research framework. *Journal of Management Information Systems, 35*(2), 388–423. doi:10.1080/07421222.2018.1451951

Guimón, J. (2019). *Policy initiatives to enhance the impact of public research: Promoting excellence, transfer and co-creation, OECD Science, Technology and Industry Policy Papers, No. 81.* OECD Publishing., doi:10.1787/a4c9197a-

Gupta, S., Modgil, S., Lee, C. K., & Sivarajah, U. (2023). The future is yesterday: Use of AI-driven facial recognition to enhance value in the travel and tourism industry. *Information Systems Frontiers, 25*(3), 1179–1195. doi:10.1007/s10796-022-10271-8 PMID:35529102

Gurcaylilar-Yenidogan, T., & Windsperger, J. (2015). Complementarity between formal and relational governance mechanisms in inter-organizational networks: combining resource-based and relational governance perspectives. In *Interfirm Networks* (pp. 229–248). Springer. doi:10.1007/978-3-319-10184-2_12

Guy, I. (2013). Mining Expertise and Interests from Social Media. *International World Wide Web Conference Committee* (IW3C2). ACM. 10.1145/2488388.2488434

Hammer, M. (2015). What is business process management? In *Handbook on business process management 1* (pp. 3–16). Springer. doi:10.1007/978-3-642-45100-3_1

Haney, B. S. (2020). AI Patents: A Data Driven Approach. SSRN *Electronic Journal*. doi:10.2139/ssrn.3527154

Hanum, S., & Salamah, U. (2011). Expert system to predict product lifecycle. *International Conference on Informatics for Development*. Research Gate. https://www.researchgate.net/publication/331829748

Hao, K. (2018). What is AI? We drew you a flowchart to work it out. *City (London, England)*.

Harmaala, M. M. (2015). The sharing city as a platform for a more sustainable city environment? *International Journal of Environment and Health*, *7*(4), 309–328. doi:10.1504/IJENVH.2015.077116

Hartman, S., & Heslinga, J. H. (2022). The Doughnut Destination: applying Kate Raworth's Doughnut Economy perspective to rethink tourism destination management. *Journal of Tourism Futures*.

Hebb, D. O. (1949). The organization of behavior; a neuropsychological theory. NY: Wiley.

Helbin, T., & Van Looy, A. (2021). Is business process management (BPM) ready for ambidexterity? Conceptualization, implementation guidelines and research agenda. *Sustainability (Basel)*, *13*(4), 1906. doi:10.3390/su13041906

Herling, R. W. (2000). Operational definitions of Expertise and Competence. *Advances in Developing Human Resources*, *2*(1), 8–21. doi:10.1177/152342230000200103

Herweijer, C., & Waughray, D. (2018). *Fourth industrial revolution for the Earth harnessing artificial intelligence for the Earth, PWC.* World Economic Forum.

Hess, C., & Ostrom, E. (2005). A Framework for Analyzing the Knowledge Commons: A chapter from Understanding Knowledge as a Commons. *Theory into Practice*.

He, Z., Wu, L., & Li, X. R. (2018). When art meets tech: The role of augmented reality in enhancing museum experiences and purchase intentions. *Tourism Management*, *68*, 127–139. doi:10.1016/j.tourman.2018.03.003

Hilger, J., & Wahl, Z. (2022). *Making knowledge management clickable: Knowledge management systems strategy, design, and implementation.* Springer. doi:10.1007/978-3-030-92385-3

Hoffecker, E. (2019). *Understanding Innovation Ecosystems: A Framework For Joint Analysis And Action.*

Hoffmann, M. G., Sell, D., & da Cunha Lemos, D. (2020). Convergence analysis between federal and state agendas for the promotion of science, technology and innovation (STI): A study focused on ICT sector priorities in the State of Santa Catarina–Brazil. *Base Revista de Administração e Contabilidade da UNISINOS*, *17*(4), 545–572.

Holdren, J. P. & Smith, M. (2016). *Preparing for the future of artificial intelligence.* Executive Office of the President National Science and Technology Council Committee on Technology.

Hotie, F., & Gordijn, J. (2019). Value-based process model design. *Business & Information Systems Engineering*, *61*(2), 163–180. doi:10.1007/s12599-017-0496-y

Houser, K. A., & Voss, W. G. (2018). GDPR: The end of Google and Facebook or a new paradigm in data privacy. *SSRN*, *25*, 1. doi:10.2139/ssrn.3212210

Howells, J. (2005). Innovation and regional economic development: A matter of perspective? *Research Policy*, *34*(8), 1220–1234. doi:10.1016/j.respol.2005.03.014

Hsu, C. C. (2018). Artificial intelligence in smart tourism: A conceptual framework. In *Proceedings of The 18th International Conference on Electronic Business* (pp. 124- 133). ICEB, Guilin, China.

Huang, M. H., & Rust, R. T. (2021). A strategic framework for artificial intelligence in marketing. *Journal of the Academy of Marketing Science*, *49*(1), 30–50. doi:10.1007/s11747-020-00749-9

Hulsen, T. (2023, August 10). Explainable Artificial Intelligence (XAI): Concepts and Challenges in Healthcare. *AI*, *4*(3), 652–666. doi:10.3390/ai4030034

Hussain, R. (2023). *Organizational Changes And Their Impact On Corporate Productivity,* [Thesis Centria University of Applied Sciences]. https://www.theseus.fi/bitstream/handle/10024/804530/Hussain_Ramzan.pdf?sequence=2&isAllowed=y

Hyvarinen, L. P. (1970). *Information theory for systems engineers.* Springer.

IBM Cloud Education. (2020, Jun 3). *Artificial Intelligence (AI).* IBM Cloud Learn Hub: https://www.ibm.com/my-en/cloud/learn/what-is-artificial-intelligence

IBM Cloud Education. (2020, October 22). *Robotic Process Automation.* IBM Cloud Learn Hub. https://www.ibm.com/cloud/learn/rpa

IBM. (2020). *What is Industry 4.0?* IBM. https://www.ibm.com/my-en/topics/industry-4-0

Ihm, J., Shumate, M., Bello-Bravo, J., Atouba, Y., Ba, N. M., Dabire-Binso, C. L., & Pittendrigh, B. R. (2015). How do Service Providers and Clients Perceive Interorganizational Networks? *Voluntas*, *26*(5), 1769–1785. doi:10.1007/s11266-014-9515-5

Ilchenko, V. (2020, September 7). *AI Adoption in Healthcare: 10 Pros and Cons.* Byteant. https://www.byteant.com/blog/ai-adoption-in-healthcare-10-pros-and-cons/

ING. (2013). *ING firms settle email retention case.* Compliance Reporter.

Ingails, A. (2020, October 28). *Reduces Application Processing Time from Nearly Two Hours to Four Minutes, Supporting More than 1,900 Freelance Workers.* Kofax RPA Powers BMconsultants' Solution for BAR Organization to Provide Freelance Workers Rapid Access to COVID-19 Funding. https://www.kofax.com/about/press-releases/2020/kofax-rpa-powers-bmconsultants-solution-to-provide-workers-rapid-access-to-covid-19-funding

Ivars-Baidal, J. A., Celdrán-Bernabeu, M. A., Femenia-Serra, F., Perles-Ribes, J. F., & Giner-Sánchez, D. (2021). Measuring the progress of smart destinations: The use of indicators as a management tool. *Journal of Destination Marketing & Management*, *19*, 100531. doi:10.1016/j.jdmm.2020.100531

Jacobs, G., van Witteloostuijn, A., & Christe-Zeyse, J. (2013). A theoretical framework of organizational change. *Journal of Organizational Change Management*, *26*(5), 772–792. doi:10.1108/JOCM-09-2012-0137

Jaffer, Z. (2021, April 9). *The Impact of Robotics on Supply Chain 2.0.* Supply Chain Brain – Think Tank. https://www.supplychainbrain.com/blogs/1-think-tank/post/32909-the-impact-of-robotics-on-supply-chain-20

Jankowicz, D. (2001). Why does subjectivity make us nervous? Making the tacit explicit. *Journal of Intellectual Capital*, *2*(1), 61–73. doi:10.1108/14691930110380509

Jarrahi, M. H., Askay, D., Eshraghi, A., & Smith, P. (2023). Artificial intelligence and knowledge management: A partnership between human and AI. *Business Horizons, 66*(1), 87-99. doi:10.1016/j.bushor.2022.03.002

Jarrahi, M. H. (2018). Artificial intelligence and the future of work: Human-AI symbiosis in organizational decision making. *Business Horizons*, *61*(4), 577–586. doi:10.1016/j.bushor.2018.03.007

Javed, A. (2020, July 6). *RPA – Robotics Process Automation Trends and Statistics For 2020*. Xorlogics - Merging Ideas into Technology. https://www.xorlogics.com/2020/07/06/rpa-robotics-process-automation-trends-and-statistics-for-2020/

Jayawardena, N. S., Behl, A., Thaichon, P., & Quach, S. (2022). Artificial intelligence (AI)-based market intelligence and customer insights. *Artificial intelligence for marketing management*, 120-141.

Jedynak, M., Czakon, W., Kuźniarska, A., & Mania, K. (2021). Digital transformation of organizations: What do we know and where to go next? *Journal of Organizational Change Management*, *34*(3), 629–652. doi:10.1108/JOCM-10-2020-0336

Jiang, L., Pan, Z., Luo, Y., Guo, Z., & Kou, D. (2023). More flexible and more innovative: The impact of flexible work arrangements on the innovation behavior of knowledge employees. *Frontiers in Psychology*, *14*, 1053242. doi:10.3389/fpsyg.2023.1053242 PMID:37179861

Jin, J., & McKelvey, M. (2019). Building a sectoral innovation system for new energy vehicles in Hangzhou, China: Insights from evolutionary economics and strategic niche management. *Journal of Cleaner Production*, *224*, 1–9. doi:10.1016/j.jclepro.2019.03.118

Jöhnk, J., Weißert, M., & Wyrtki, K. (2021). Ready or not, AI comes—An interview study of organizational AI readiness factors. *Business & Information Systems Engineering*, *63*(1), 5–20. doi:10.1007/s12599-020-00676-7

Joram, M. K., Harrison, B. K., & Joseph, K. N. (2017). A knowledge-based system for life insurance underwriting. *International Journal of Information Technology and Computer Science*, *9*(3), 40–49. doi:10.5815/ijitcs.2017.03.05

Joseph, T. (2020, August 4). *How Robotics in Logistics Helps Improve Supply Chain Efficiency*. Fingent Shaping the Future. https://www.fingent.com/blog/how-robotics-in-logistics-helps-improve-supply-chain-efficiency/

Joseph, C., & Varghese, B. (2023). *Community Resilience and Crisis Management*. Stakeholders Perspective of the Tourism Industry.

Joshi, N. (2019, August 9). 5 Applications Of Collaborative Robots In Manufacturing. *Forbes*. https://www.forbes.com/sites/cognitiveworld/2019/08/09/5-applications-of-collaborative-robots-in-manufacturing/?sh=3972d3dc6507

Kar, A. K., & Kushwaha, A. K. (2021). Facilitators and barriers of artificial intelligence adoption in business–insights from opinions using big data analytics. *Information Systems Frontiers*, 1–24.

Karimi, M. (2020, March 30). *8 Use-Cases of RPA In Sales & Marketing*. MyFalcon. https://myfalcon.co.uk/8-use-cases-of-rpa-in-sales-marketing/

Kashem, M. A., Shamsuddoha, M., Nasir, T., & Chowdhury, A. A. (2022). The role of artificial intelligence and blockchain technologies in sustainable tourism in the Middle East. *Worldwide Hospitality and Tourism Themes*.

Katirai, A. (2023, June 20). Ethical considerations in emotion recognition technologies: A review of the literature. *AI and Ethics*. doi:10.1007/s43681-023-00307-3

Kedziora, D. (2022, October 3). Botsourcing, Roboshoring or Virtual Backoffice? Perspectives on Implementing Robotic Process Automation (RPA) and Artificial intelligence. *Human Technology*, *18*(2), 92–97. doi:10.14254/1795-6889.2022.18-2.1

Keeney, R. L. (2009). *Value-focused thinking: a path to creative decision making*. Harvard University Press.

Kelleher, J. (2019). *Deep Learning*. MIT Press. doi:10.7551/mitpress/11171.001.0001

Kelly, J., Male, S., & Graham, D. (2014). *Value management of construction projects*. John Wiley & Sons. doi:10.1002/9781119007258

Kendal, S., & Creen, M. (2006). *An Introduction to Knowledge Engineering*. Springer.

Khalil, O. E. M. (1993). Artificial Decision-Making and Artificial Ethics: A Management Concern. *Journal of Business Ethics*, *12*(4), 313–321. https://www.jstor.org/stable/25072403. doi:10.1007/BF01666535

Khan, S. I., Kaur, C., Al Ansari, M. S., Muda, I., Borda, R. F., & Bala, B. K. (2023). Implementation of cloud based IoT technology in manufacturing industry for smart control of manufacturing process. *International Journal on Interactive Design and Manufacturing (IJIDeM)*, 1-13.

Khan, M. A., Saleh, A. M., Waseem, M., & Sajjad, I. A. (2023). Artificial Intelligence Enabled Demand Response: Prospects and Challenges in Smart Grid Environment. *IEEE Access : Practical Innovations, Open Solutions*, *11*, 1477–1505. doi:10.1109/ACCESS.2022.3231444

Kitsios, F., & Kamariotou, M. (2021). Artificial Intelligence and Business Strategy towards Digital Transformation: A Research Agenda. *Sustainability (Basel)*, *13*(4), 2021. doi:10.3390/su13042025

Knight, L. (2002). Network learning: Exploring learning by interorganizational networks. *Human Relations*, *55*(4), 427–454. doi:10.1177/0018726702554003

Knuth, D. E., & Moore, R. W. (1975). An analysis of alpha-beta pruning. *Artificial Intelligence*, *6*(4), 293–326. doi:10.1016/0004-3702(75)90019-3

Kofax. (2021). *Intelligent Automation for Digital Workflow Transformation*. Kofax - Intelligent Automation Platform. https://www.kofax.com/products/intelligent-automation-platform

Kohli, P. (2017, August 16). *Bridging the skill gap in robotics – An imperative for industry today*. People Matters. https://www.peoplematters.in/article/talent-acquisition/bridging-the-skill-gap-in-robotics-an-imperative-for-industry-today-16080

Kokina, J., & Davenport, T. H. (2017). The emergence of artificial intelligence: How automation is changing auditing. *Journal of Emerging Technologies in Accounting*, *14*(1), 115–122. doi:10.2308/jeta-51730

Kontogianni, A., Alepis, E., & Patsakis, C. (2022). Smart tourism and artificial intelligence: Paving the way to the post-covid-19 era. *Advances in Artificial Intelligence-based Technologies: Selected Papers in Honour of Professor Nikolaos G. Bourbakis*, *1*, 93–109.

Kooper, M. N. R. (2011). On the governance of information: Introducing a new concept of governance to support the management of information. *International Journal of Information Management*, *31*(3). doi:10.1016/j.ijinfomgt.2010.05.009

Kraatz, M. S. (1998). Learning by association? Interorganizational networks and adaptation to environmental change. *Academy of Management Journal*, *41*(6), 621–643. doi:10.2307/256961

Kranti, N. K. M. M. N. (1997). An approach to value-based modeling of information flows. *The Information Society*, *13*(1), 93–105. doi:10.1080/019722497129304

Kraß, W., & Försterling, U. (2013). Comparison of the results of an authorship-based expert recommender against data from a directory of experts. i-Know '13, Graz, Austria.

Krol, M. (2018). Information governance in a digital world: A general data protection regulation (GDPR) perspective. *Computer Law & Security Review*, *34*(2), 193–204.

Kumar, V., Rajan, B., Venkatesan, R., & Lecinski, J. (2019). Understanding the role of artificial intelligence in personalized engagement marketing. *California Management Review, 61*(4), 135–155. doi:10.1177/0008125619859317

Laguna, M., & Marklund, J. (2018). *Business process modeling, simulation and design.* Chapman and Hall/CRC. doi:10.1201/9781315162119

Lai, L. F. (2007). A knowledge engineering approach to knowledge management. *Information Sciences, 177*(19), 4072–4094. doi:10.1016/j.ins.2007.02.028

Lamsfus, C., Martín, D., Alzua-Sorzabal, A., & Torres-Manzanera, E. (2015). Smart tourism destinations: An extended conception of smart cities focusing on human mobility. In I. Tussyadiah & A. Inversini (Eds.), *Information and Communication Technologies in Tourism* (pp. 363–375). Springer.

Laney, D. B. (2018). *Infonomics: How to monetize, manage, and measure information as an asset for competitive advantage.* Bibliomotion.

LaRanger, R. (2020, January). *What's driving the adoption of robots in industry.* PreScouter. https://www.prescouter.com/2020/01/whats-driving-the-adoption-of-robots-in-industry/

Lee, G., & Xiao, X. (2018). Whistleblowing on accounting-related misconduct: A synthesis of the literature. *Journal of Accounting Literature, 41*(1), 22–46. doi:10.1016/j.acclit.2018.03.003

Lee, H., Chung, N., & Claudia tom Dieck, M. (2018). The effect of hedonic and utilitarian values on satisfaction and loyalty of Airbnb users. *International Journal of Contemporary Hospitality Management, 30*(3), 1621–1645. doi:10.1108/IJCHM-09-2016-0504

Lehner, O. M., Ittonen, K., Silvola, H., Ström, E., & Wührleitner, A. (2022). Artificial intelligence-based decision-making in accounting and auditing: Ethical challenges and normative thinking. *Accounting, Auditing & Accountability Journal, 35*(9), 109–135. doi:10.1108/AAAJ-09-2020-4934

Lexbe. (2023). *eDiscovery platform.* Lexbe. https://lexbe.com/

Leydesdorff, L., & Smith, H. L. (2022). Triple, quadruple, and higher-order helices: Historical phenomena and (neo-) evolutionary models. *Triple Helix (Heidelberg), 9*(1), 6–31. doi:10.1163/21971927-bja10022

Lindsay, R., Buchanan, B., Feigenbaum, E., Lederberg, J. (1993). DENDRAL: a case study of the hypothesis formation. *Artificial Intelligence, 61.* Elsevier.

Lin, S., Hong, W., Wang, D., & Li, T. (2017). A survey on expert finding techniques. *Journal of Intelligent Information Systems, 49*(2), 255–279. doi:10.1007/s10844-016-0440-5

Lionel, S. V. (2023). *Robotic process automation (RPA) market size worldwide from 2020 to 2030.* Statista. https://www.statista.com/statistics/1259903/robotic-process-automation-market-size-worldwide/

Lipscomb, M. M., Mohammad, A., Abdulrahman, A., & Jololian, L. (2022). Value-based modeling for mobile health application development. *mHealth, 8*, 16. doi:10.21037/mhealth-21-32 PMID:35449507

Loebbecke, C. (2019, December 30). Digitization, Big Data Analytics, and Artificial Intelligence Transforming Business, Society, and Research. *Moscow University Economics Bulletin, 2019*(6), 9–11. doi:10.38050/01300105201962

López-Arellano, J. Romero-Rubio, S., Morales-Ávila, M. (2022). La cooperación interacadémica como factor determinante para la productividad académica de la Universidad Autónoma de Sinaloa. *Revista lbérica de Sistemas e Tecnologias de Informação, 47*, 09/2022.

Lyon, J. (2018, September 20). *Embracing robotic automation during the evolution of finance*. ACCA – Think Ahead. https://www.accaglobal.com/lk/en/professional-insights/technology/embracing-robotic-automation-during-the-evolution-of-finance.html

Lyytinen, K., & Damsgaard, J. (2011). Inter-organizational information systems adoption–a configuration analysis approach. *European Journal of Information Systems*, *20*(5), 496–509. doi:10.1057/ejis.2010.71

Macrorie, R., Marvin, S., & While, A. (2021). Robotics and automation in the city: A research agenda. *Urban Geography*, *42*(2), 197–217. doi:10.1080/02723638.2019.1698868

Madakam, S., Holmukhe, R. M., & Jaiswal, D. (2019, November 19). The Future Digital Work Force: Robotic Process Automation (RPA). *JISTEM -. Journal of Information Systems and Technology Management*, *16*, 1–17. doi:10.4301/S1807-1775201916001

Madakam, S., Holmukhe, R. M., & Revulagadda, R. K. (2022). The next generation intelligent automation: Hyperautomation. *Journal of Information Systems and Technology Management*, *19*, e202219009. doi:10.4301/S1807-1775202219009

Makadia, M. (2020, December 16). *12 Use Cases for Implementing RPA in HR Operations*. Customer Think. https://customerthink.com/12-use-cases-for-implementing-rpa-in-hr-operations/

Maleh, Y., Abd El-Latif, A. A., & Zhang, J. (2023). Guest Editorial AI-Driven Decision-Making: Managerial and Organizational Promise and Potential. *IEEE Engineering Management Review*, *51*(1), 11–15. doi:10.1109/EMR.2023.3243071

Mandić, A., & Kennell, J. (2021). Smart governance for heritage tourism destinations: Contextual factors and destination management organization perspectives. *Tourism Management Perspectives*, *39*, 100862. doi:10.1016/j.tmp.2021.100862

Manuti, A., & Monachino, D. (2020). Managing knowledge at the time of artificial intelligence: An explorative study with knowledge workers. *East European Journal of Psycholinguistics*, *7*(2), 179–190. doi:10.29038/eejpl.2020.7.2.man

Ma, R., & Lam, P. T. (2019). Investigating the barriers faced by stakeholders in open data development: A study on Hong Kong as a "smart city". *Cities (London, England)*, *92*, 36–46. doi:10.1016/j.cities.2019.03.009

Mariani, M., Bresciani, S., & Dagnino, G. B. (2021). The competitive productivity (CP) of tourism destinations: An integrative conceptual framework and a reflection on big data and analytics. *International Journal of Contemporary Hospitality Management*, *33*(9), 2970–3002. doi:10.1108/IJCHM-09-2020-1102

Mariano, E. B., & Rebelatto, D. A. do N. (2010). Sistematização do processo de escolha dos modelos e perspectivas da análise envoltória de dados por meio de um sistema especialista. *XXX Encontro Nacional de Engenharia de Produção: Competitividade das Empresas, Condições de Trabalho, Meio Ambiente*. doi:10.13140/2.1.1236.0645

Marius, E. (2019, May 29). *6 Ways AI and Robotics Are Improving Healthcare*. Retrieved September 6, 2021, from Robotics Business Review: https://www.roboticsbusinessreview.com/health-medical/6-ways-ai-and-robotics-are-improving-healthcare/

Marques, M. A. J. (2020). *Framework conceitual do potencial de coprodução de inovação em ecossistemas de inovação* [Thesis, Universidade Federal de Santa Catarina].

Marsland, T. A. (1987). Computer chess methods. Encyclopedia of Artificial Intelligence, 1, 159-171.

Marsland, T. A., & Campbell, M. (1982). Parallel search of strongly ordered game trees. *ACM Computing Surveys*, *14*(4), 533–551. doi:10.1145/356893.356895

Marsland, T. A., & Schaeffer, J. (Eds.). (1990). *Computers, chess, and cognition*. Springer. doi:10.1007/978-1-4613-9080-0

Martin, J. D., & Petty, J. W. (2001). Value based management. *Baylor business review*, *19*(1), 2.

Martins, C. A., Carneiro, M. J. A., & Pacheco, O. R. (2021). Key factors for implementation and success of destination management systems. Empirical evidence from European countries. *Industrial Management & Data Systems, 121*(6), 1287–1324. doi:10.1108/IMDS-11-2019-0598

Maruti Techlabs. (2023). *Robotic Process Automation vs Traditional Automation.* Maruti Techlabs. https://marutitech.com/robotic-process-automation-vs-traditional-automation/

Massingham, P. (2014). An evaluation of knowledge management tools: Part 1–managing knowledge resources. *Journal of Knowledge Management, 18*(6), 10. doi:10.1108/JKM-11-2013-0449

Mauser, W. (2013). Transdisciplinary global change research: The co-creation of knowledge for sustainability. Current Opinion in Environmental Sustainability, 5(4), 420–431. doi:10.1016/j.cosust.2013.07.001

Mayo, S. M. (2023). Restrictions, Challenges and Opportunities for AI and ML. *International Journal of Innovations in Science & Technology, 5*(2), 121–132.

Mazurek, G. (2014). Network value creation through marketing. Management and Business Administration. *Central Europe, 22*(4), 70–77.

McCarthy, J., Minsky, M., Rochester, N., & Shannon, C. (1955). A proposal for the Dartmouth Summer Research Project on Artificial Intelligence; 1955. *Computer History.* https://archive.computerhistory.org/resources/access/text/2023/06/102720392-05-01-acc.pdf

McCulloch, Warren. S., & Pitts, W. (1990). A logical calculus of the ideas immanent in nervous activity, Bulletin of Mathematical Biology, 52(1–2). 1990, pp. 99-115. ISSN 0092-8240, doi:10.1016/S0092-8240(05)80006-0

McElroy, M. W. (2003). *The new knowledge management: Complexity, learning, and sustainable innovation.* Routledge.

McManus, C., & Baeta Neves, A. A. (2021). Funding research in Brazil. *Scientometrics, 126*(1), 801–823. doi:10.1007/s11192-020-03762-5

Menabrea, L. F. (1842). Notions sur la machine analytique de M. Charles Babbage. In: Bibliothèque Universelle de Genève. Nouvelle Série, 41, 352-376.

Meulen, R. (2020, March 26). *Finance Tackles Efficiencies and Costs With RPA.* Gartner – Smarter with Gartner. https://www.gartner.com/smarterwithgartner/finance-tackles-efficiencies-and-costs-with-rpa/

Microsoft. (2023). *Microsoft Copilot.* https://www.microsoft.com/en-us/windows/copilot-ai-features?r=1

Mikalef, P., Conboy, K., Lundström, J. E., & Popovič, A. (2022). Thinking responsibly about responsible AI and 'the dark side' of AI. *European Journal of Information Systems, 31*(3), 257–268. doi:10.1080/0960085X.2022.2026621

Miles, A.; Bechhofer, S. (2009). *SKOS simple knowledge organization system reference.* W3C recommendation.

Miles, L. D. (1961). *Techniques of value analysis and engineering.* McGraw-Hill.

Miller, C. A., & Wyborn, C. (2018). Co-production in global sustainability: Histories and theories. *Environmental Science and Policy.* Elsevier. https://linkinghub.elsevier.com/retrieve/pii/S1462901117306366

Milton, N., & Lambe, P. (2020). *The knowledge manager's handbook: A step-by-step guide to embedding effective knowledge management in your organization* [2d ed.]. Kogen Page.

Minsky, M. L. (1966). Artificial Intelligence. *Scientific American, 215*(3), 246–263. https://www.jstor.org/stable/24931058. doi:10.1038/scientificamerican0966-246

Mittelstadt, B. D., Allo, P., Taddeo, M., Wachter, S., & Floridi, L. (2016). The ethics of algorithms: Mapping the debate. *Big Data & Society*, *3*(2), 2053951716679679. doi:10.1177/2053951716679679

Mittelstadt, B. D., & Floridi, L. (2015). The ethics of big data: Current and foreseeable issues in biomedical contexts. *Science and Engineering Ethics*, *22*(2), 303–341. https://link.springer.com/article/10.1007/s11948-015-9652-2. doi:10.1007/s11948-015-9652-2 PMID:26002496

Mixon, J. (2021, 9 5). *The Role of Robotic Process Automation (RPA) in Finance Automation.* Gartner – White Paper. https://www.gartner.com/en/finance/insights/robotics-in-finance

Moore, S. (2019, June 29). *Gartner Says Worldwide Robotic Process Automation Software Market Grew 63% in 2018.* Gartner – Newsroom Press Releases. https://www.gartner.com/en/newsroom/press-releases/2019-06-24-gartner-says-worldwide-robotic-process-automation-sof

Moor, J. H. (2005). Why we need better ethics for emerging technologies. *Ethics and Information Technology*, *7*(3), 111–119. doi:10.1007/s10676-006-0008-0

Moulaison, S. H. (2018). Ethical information governance: Challenges and opportunities. *Journal of Librarianship and Information Science*, *50*(1), 3–16.

Moynihan, D. P., & Kroll, A. (2016). Information Governance: Compliance, or Competitive Advantage? *Communications of the Association for Information Systems*, *38*(1), 3.

Mrsic, L., Surla, G., & Balkovic, M. (2020). Technology-driven smart support system for tourist destination management organizations. In *International Conference on Innovative Computing and Communications: Proceedings of ICICC 2019,* Volume 1 (pp. 65-76). Singapore: Springer Singapore. 10.1007/978-981-15-1286-5_7

Muniz, E. C. L., Dandolini, G. A., Biz, A. A., & Ribeiro, A. C. (2021). Customer knowledge management and smart tourism destinations: A framework for the smart management of the tourist experience–SMARTUR. *Journal of Knowledge Management*, *25*(5), 1336–1361. doi:10.1108/JKM-07-2020-0529

Murtaza, G., Basit, A., & Ikram, N. (2010). Value elicitation in value based software engineering. In *Proceedings of the 9th WSEAS international conference on Software engineering, parallel and distributed systems,* (pp. 184-189). IEEE.

Nabatchi, T.; Sancino, A.; Sicilia, M. (2017). Varieties of Participation in Public Services: The Who, When, and What of Coproduction. *Public Administration Review*, *77*(5), 766–776.

Nadler, D. A., & Tushman, M. L. (1980). A model for diagnosing organizational behavior. *Organizational Dynamics*, *9*(2), 35–51. doi:10.1016/0090-2616(80)90039-X

Nahm, E. S. (2023, February 28). A Study on Modeling of Activated Sludge Process in Wastewater Treatment System Utilizing XAI(eXplainable AI). *The Transactions of the Korean Institute of Electrical Engineers*, *72*(2), 263–269. doi:10.5370/KIEE.2023.72.2.263

Nakamura, K. (2023). How the FTC Safeguards Rule may affect your CPA firm, *Jornal of Accountancy*. https://www.journalofaccountancy.com/issues/2023/feb/how-the-ftc-safeguards-rule-may-affect-your-cpa-firm.html

Nannelli, M., Capone, F., & Lazzeretti, L. (2023). Artificial intelligence in hospitality and tourism. State of the art and future research avenues. *European Planning Studies*, *31*(7), 1–20. doi:10.1080/09654313.2023.2180321

Neiger, D., Rotaru, K., & Churilov, L. (2009). Supply chain risk identification with value-focused process engineering. *Journal of Operations Management*, *27*(2), 154–168. doi:10.1016/j.jom.2007.11.003

Nesti, G. (2018). *Co-production for innovation: the urban living lab experience experience* (Vol. 4035). Policy and Society. [s. l.], doi:10.1080/14494035.2017.1374692

Neubauer, M., & Stary, C. (2017). *S-BPM in the Production Industry. A stakeholder approach*. Springer. doi:10.1007/978-3-319-48466-2

NextProcess. (2023). *Top 10 Reasons Why Using Robotic Process Automation for Data Entry Is the Right Choice for Your Business*. NextProcess - Business Process Automation. https://www.nextprocess.com/blog/top-10-reasons-using-robotic-process-automation-data-entry-right-choice-business/

Nguyen J. et al. (2014). Defining dimensions in expertise recommender systems for enhancing open collaborative innovation. *Frontiers in Artificial Intelligence and Applications*.

Nguyen, J. (2015). InsERT: the Inspirational Expert Recommender Tool. *2015 IEEE International Conference on Fuzzy Systems* (FUZZ-IEEE), IEEE. 10.1109/FUZZ-IEEE.2015.7337984

Ng, V., & Kim, H. M. (2021). Autonomous vehicles and smart cities: A case study of Singapore. In *Smart cities for technological and social innovation* (pp. 265–287). Academic Press. doi:10.1016/B978-0-12-818886-6.00014-9

NICE. (2023). *AI and RPA: What's the Difference and which is Best for Your Organization?* NICE - Master Robotic Process Automation. https://www.nice.com/rpa/rpa-guide/rpa-ai-and-rpa-whats-the-difference-and-which-is-best-for-your-organization/

Nikiforova, A., Alor Flores, M. A., & Lytras, M. D. (2023). The Role Of Open Data In The Transformation To Society 5.0: A Resource Or A Tool For SDG-Compliant Smart Living? In Smart Cities and Digital Transformation Empowering Communities, Limitless Innovation, Sustainable Development and the Next Generation (pp. 219-252). Emerald Publishing Limited.

Ningsih, A., & Hurnis, D. (2023, June 1). Pengaruh Customer Experience, Customer Expectation Terhadap Customer Satisfaction Dan Customer Loyalty D′ Besto Chicken & Burger. *Jesya*, *6*(2), 2219–2229. doi:10.36778/jesya.v6i2.1240

Nividous. (2021, April 7). *Top 8 Benefits of RPA (With Real Examples)*. Nividous. https://nividous.com/blogs/benefits-of-rpa

Noh, S. M., Kang, H. S., & Jang, S. Y. (2020). The Effects of Smart Tolling for the Improvement of Traffic Flow on the Seoul Tollgate with ARENA. *Journal of Advanced Simulation in Science and Engineering*, *7*(2), 279–290. doi:10.15748/jasse.7.279

Nonaka, I., & Takeuchi, H. (1997). *Criação de conhecimento na empresa. Empresas japonesas geram a dinâmica da inovação* (20th ed.). Elsevier.

Nonaka, I., & Takeuchi, H. (2008). Teoria da criação do conhecimento organizacional. In H. Takeuchi & I. Nonaka (Eds.), *Gestão do conhecimento*. Bookman.

Normann, R. (2001). *Reframing business: when the map changes the landscape*. John Wiley & Sons: Chicester.

Normann, R., & Ramírez, R. (1993). From value chain to value network: designing interactive strategy. *Harvard Business Review*, *71*(4), 65-77.

Novak, J. D., & Cañas, A. J. (2008). The theory underlying concept maps and how to construct and use them. *Technical Report IHMC CmapTools 2006-01 Rev 01-2008*. Florida Institute for Human and Machine Cognition. https://cmap.ihmc.us/Publications/ResearchPapers/TheoryUnderlyingConceptMaps.pdf

Novak, J. D. (1998). *Learning, creating, and using knowledge: Concept Maps as Facilitative Tools in Schools and Corporations*. Lawrence Erlbaum Associates. doi:10.4324/9781410601629

Novak, J. D., & Cañas, A. J. (2006). The origins of the concept mapping tool and the continuing evolution of the tool. *Information Visualization*, *5*(3), 175–184. doi:10.1057/palgrave.ivs.9500126

Noy, N. F. & McGuiness, D. L. (2001). *Ontology Development 101: A Guide to Creating your First Ontology*. Stanford. https://protege.stanford.edu/publications/ontology_development/ontology101.pdf

O'Leary, D. E. (2013). Artificial Intelligence and Big Data. *IEEE Intelligent Systems*, *28*(2), 96–99. doi:10.1109/MIS.2013.39

O'Reilly, T. (2011). Government as a Platform. *Innovations: Technology, Governance, Globalization*, *6*(1), 13–40. doi:10.1162/INOV_a_00056

OECD. (2014). *Industry and Technology Policies in Korea, OECD Reviews of Innovation Policy*. OECD Publishing. doi:10.1787/9789264213227-

OECD. (2017). *OECD Reviews of Innovation Policy: Finland 2017, OECD Reviews of Innovation Policy*. OECD Publishing. doi:10.1787/9789264276369-

Okamuro, H., Nishimura, J., & Kitagawa, F. (2019). Multilevel policy governance and territorial adaptability: Evidence from Japanese SME innovation programmes. *Regional Studies*, *53*(6), 803–814. doi:10.1080/00343404.2018.1500687

Orofino, M. A. R. (2011). *Técnicas de criação do conhecimento no desenvolvimento de modelos de negócio. Dissertação, Programa de Pós-graduação em Engenharia e Gestão do Conhecimento*, Universidade Federal de Santa Catarina.

Ostrom, E. (1990). *Governing the Commons: The Evolution of Institutions for Collective Action* [s.l.]. Cambridge University Press. Cambridge. http://www.cambridge.org doi:10.1017/CBO9780511807763

Ouali, S., Mhiri, M., & Gargouri, F. (2017). Knowledge engineering for business process modeling. *12th International Conference on Evaluation of Novel Approaches to Software Engineering (ENASE 2017)*, (pp. 81-90). ScitePress. 10.5220/0006323200810090

Owen-Hill, A. (2021, March 23). *6 Robot Applications for Pharmaceutical Companies*. RoboDK. https://robodk.com/blog/6-robot-applications-for-pharmaceutical-companies/

Pacheco, C. S. R. (2016). Coprodução em Ciência, Tecnologia e Inovação: fundamentos e visões. *Interdisciplinaridade: Universidade e Inovação Social e Tecnológica*, CRV Editora. https://encurtador.com.br/evERV

Pacheco, R. C. S., Steil, A. V., & Sell, D. (2016). A multi e a interdisciplinaridade na visão de áreas de avaliação da Capes. In: A. Philippi Jr; V. Fernandes, & R. C. S. Pacheco. (eds.). Ensino, Pesquisa e Inovação. Desenvolvendo a Interdisciplinaridade.

Pailai, J., Wunnasri, W., Hayashi, Y., & Hirashima, T. (2018). Correctness-and confidence-based adaptive feedback of kit-build concept map with confidence tagging. In *Int. Conf. on AI in Education*. 395-408, Springer, Cham. 10.1007/978-3-319-93843-1_29

Pallotti, F., Tubaro, P., & Lomi, A. (2015). How far do network effects spill over? Evidence from an empirical study of performance differentials in interorganizational networks. *European Management Review*, *12*(3), 189–208. doi:10.1111/emre.12052

Parker, G. G., Van Alstyne, M. W., & Choudary, S. P. (2016). *Platform revolution: How networked markets are transforming the economy and how to make them work for you*. WW Norton & Company.

Parks, R. B. (1980). *Consumers as coproducers of public services: Some economic and institutional considerations*. Research Gate.

Parolini, C. (1999). *The value net: A tool for competitive strategy*. John Wiley.

Parry, W., Kirsch, C., Carey, P., & Shaw, D. (2013). Empirical development of a model of performance drivers in organizational change projects. *Journal of Change Management*, *14*(1), 99–125. doi:10.1080/14697017.2012.745894

Pasquinelli, C., & Trunfio, M. (2023). Smart and Sustainable Destination Management: An Analytical Framework. *Sustainability-oriented Innovation in Smart Tourism: Challenges and Pitfalls of Technology Deployment for Sustainable Destinations*, 63-110.

Payne, A. F., Storbacka, K., & Frow, P. (2008). Managing the co-creation of value. *Journal of the Academy of Marketing Science*, *36*(1), 83–96. doi:10.1007/s11747-007-0070-0

Payne, A., & Holt, S. (2001). Diagnosing customer value: Integrating the value process and relationship marketing. *British Journal of Management*, *12*(2), 159–182. doi:10.1111/1467-8551.00192

Peeters, M. M., van Diggelen, J., van den Bosch, K., Bronkhorst, A. W., Neerincx, M. A., Schraagen, J. M., & Raaijmakers, S. (2020). Hybrid collective intelligence in a human–AI society. *AI & Society*, *36*(1), 217–238. doi:10.1007/s00146-020-01005-y

Peffers, K., Tuunanen, T., Rothenberger, M. A., & Chatterjee, S. (2007). A design science research methodology for information systems research. *Journal of Management Information Systems*, *24*(3), 45–77. doi:10.2753/MIS0742-1222240302

Pereira, G. V., Parycek, P., Falco, E., & Kleinhans, R. (2018). Smart governance in the context of smart cities: A literature review. *Information Polity*, *23*(2), 143–162. doi:10.3233/IP-170067

Pestoff, V. (2006). Citizens and co-production of welfare services. *Public Management Review*, [s. l.], v. 8, n. 4, p. 503–519.

PharmTech. (2009, September 20). Robots: The Next Phase in Pharmaceutical Automation. *Pharmaceutical Technology*, *33*(9). https://www.pharmtech.com/view/robots-next-phase-pharmaceutical-automation-0

Pillmayer, M., Scherle, N., & Volchek, K. (2021). Destination Management in Times of Crisis-Potentials of Open Innovation Approach in the Context of COVID-19? In *Information and Communication Technologies in Tourism 2021: Proceedings of the ENTER 2021 eTourism Conference,* (pp. 517-529). Springer International Publishing. 10.1007/978-3-030-65785-7_49

Plastino, E., & Purdy, M. (2018). Game changing value from Artificial Intelligence: Eight strategies. *Strategy and Leadership*, *46*(1), 16–22. doi:10.1108/SL-11-2017-0106

Por, V. Solutions. (2018, April 2). *Top-5 Benefits of Robotics Process Automation (RPA) Adoption for Your Company*. PorV Solutions. https://www.provintl.com/blog/top-5-benefits-of-robotics-process-automation-rpa-software

Prasad Agrawal, K. (2023). Towards adoption of Generative AI in organizational settings. *Journal of Computer Information Systems*, 1–16. doi:10.1080/08874417.2023.2240744

Prasad, D., Alizadeh, T., & Dowling, R. (2021). Multiscalar smart city governance in India. *Geoforum*, *121*, 173–180. doi:10.1016/j.geoforum.2021.03.001

Prasertsuk, S., & Busayarat, C. (2022, November 22). 3D Data Visualization and Analysis Tools for AI Ready City: Space Syntax and Social Media Data. *Nakhara : Journal of Environmental Design and Planning*, *21*(2), 214. doi:10.54028/NJ202221214

Pritzker, M. D. (2020, May 19). *RPA Drawbacks and Limitations Explained.* IT Central Station. https://www.itcentralstation.com/questions/what-are-the-limitations-of-rpa

Provan, K. G., Fish, A., & Sydow, J. (2007). Interorganizational networks at the network level: A review of the empirical literature on whole networks. *Journal of Management*, *33*(3), 479–516. doi:10.1177/0149206307302554

Rachmawati, D. G., & Utami, C. W. (2021, March 31). Customer Experience Terhadap Customer Loyalty Dengan Mediasi Customer Engagement Dan Customer Trust Cv. Wahyu Pratama. *Performa, 5*(5), 440–448. doi:10.37715/jp.v5i5.1821

Ragbeer, R. (2021). Texting: Your next big vulnerability. Law Practice Today, Dec (2021). https://www.lawpracticetoday.org/article/texting-your-next-big-vulnerability/

Ramadoss, T. S., Alam, H., & Seeram, R. (2018). Artificial intelligence and Internet of Things enabled circular economy. *The International Journal of Engineering and Science, 7*(9), 55–63.

Ramesh, R., Divya, G., Dorairangaswamy, M. A., Unnikrishnan, K. N., Joseph, A., Vijayakumar, A., & Mani, A. (2019, July). Real-time vehicular traffic analysis using big data processing and IoT based devices for future policy predictions in smart transportation. In *2019 International Conference on Communication and Electronics Systems (ICCES)* (pp. 1482-1488). IEEE. 10.1109/ICCES45898.2019.9002261

Rampisela, T. V. (2020a). Characteristics of Expertise Locator System in Academia: A Systematic Literature Review. *2020 International Seminar on Intelligent Technology and Its Applications* (ISITIA). Springer.

Rampisela, T. V. (2020b). *Expert Locator System for Finding Co-authors Using Snowball Network Method: A Case Study of Fasilkom UI Lecturers. ICEMT.* ACM.

Ranjan, J., & Foropon, C. (2021). Big data analytics in building the competitive intelligence of organizations. *International Journal of Information Management, 56*, 102231. doi:10.1016/j.ijinfomgt.2020.102231

Reim, W., Åström, J., & Eriksson, O. (2020). Implementation of Artificial Intelligence (AI): A Roadmap for Business Model Innovation. *AI, 1*(2), 180–191. MDPI AG. doi:10.3390/ai1020011

Rezende, S. O. (2005). *Sistemas inteligentes: fundamentos e aplicações.* Manole.

Ribeiro Júnior, D. I. (2010). *Modelo de sistema baseado em conhecimento para apoiar processos de tomada de decisão em ciência e tecnologia.* [Tese]. Programa de Pós-graduação em Engenharia e Gestão do Conhecimento, Universidade Federal de Santa Catarina (UFSC), Florianópolis. https://repositorio.ufsc.br/bitstream/handle/123456789/94123/297613.pdf?sequence=1&isAllowed=y

Ribeiro, J., Lima, R., Eckhardt, T., & Paiva, S. (2021). Robitic Process Automation and Artificial Intelligence in Industry 4.0 – A Literature Review. *CENTERIS – International Conference on ENTERprise Information Systems/ProjMAN – International Conference on Project MANagement/HCist – International Conference on Health and Social Care Information Systems and Technologies 2020.* Elsevier B.V. https://www.sciencedirect.com/science/article/pii/S1877050921001393

Ribes, J. & Baidal, J. (2019). Smart sustainability: A new perspective in the sustainable tourism debate. *Investigaciones Regionales., 42*, 151–170.

Rice, S. (2021, March 23). Ethical Considerations: Applying Natural Systems to AI for Better Situational Understanding. *A Common Place.* doi:10.21428/6ffd8432.d47f1790

Robotics Online Marketing Team. (2018, December 6). *Top 6 Future Trends in Robotic Automation.* Association for Advancing Automation. https://www.automate.org/blogs/top-6-future-trends-in-robotic-automation

RobotWorx. (2018, April 27). *Bringing Jobs and Bridging the Skills Gap with Automation.* RobotWorx – Robotic Industry News. https://www.robots.com/blogs/staying-competitive-and-bridging-the-skills-gap

Rochet, J. C., & Tirole, J. (2003). Platform competition in two-sided markets. *Journal of the European Economic Association, 1*(4), 990–1029. doi:10.1162/154247603322493212

Rossatto, M. A. (2003). *Gestão do Conhecimento: a busca da humanização, transparência, socialização e valorização do intangível.* Interciência.

Rothwell, W., & Sullivan, R. (2005). *Models for change. Practicing organizational development: a guide for consultants* (2nd ed.). Pfeiffer.

Russell, S. J. (2010). *Artificial intelligence a modern approach.* Pearson Education, Inc.

Russel, S., & Norvig, P. (2009). *Artificial Intelligence: A Modern Approach. Prentice Hall PressOne.* NJ ISBN.

Rustad, M. L., & Koenig, T. H. (2019). Towards a global data privacy standard. *Florida Law Review, 71*, 365.

Sabrina, N. N., Ginting, P., & Silalahi, A. S. (2023, May 4). The Effect Of Customer Value, Customer Experience And Customer Trust On Customer Satisfaction (Ace Hardware Medan Customer). *Warta Dharmawangsa, 17*(2), 718–732. doi:10.46576/wdw.v17i2.3183

Saldanha, T. (2019). *Why digital transformations fail: The surprising disciplines of how to take off and stay ahead.* Barrett-Koehler Publishers, Inc.

Samoili, S., López Cobo, M., Gómez, E., De Prato, G., Martínez-Plumed, F., & Delipetrev, B. (2020). Defining Artificial Intelligence. Towards an operational definition and taxonomy of artificial intelligence. EUR 30117 EN. Publications Office of the European Union, Luxembourg. doi:10.2760/382730

Samuel, A. L. (2000). Some studies in machine learning using the game of checkers. *IBM Journal of research and development, 44*(1.2), 206-226.

Santagate, J. (2018). NextGen Supply Chain: The Robots are Here. *Supply Chain Management Review.* https://www.scmr.com/article/nextgen_supply_chain_the_robots_are_here

Santana, M., & Díaz-Fernández, M. (2023). Competencies for the artificial intelligence age: Visualisation of the state of the art and future perspectives. *Review of Managerial Science, 17*(6), 1971–2004. doi:10.1007/s11846-022-00613-w

Schildt, H. (2017). Big data and organizational design–the brave new world of algorithmic management and computer augmented transparency. *Innovation (North Sydney, N.S.W.), 19*(1), 23–30. doi:10.1080/14479338.2016.1252043

Schmiedel, T., Recker, J., & vom Brocke, J. (2020). The relation between BPM culture, BPM methods, and process performance: Evidence from quantitative field studies. *Information & Management, 57*(2), 103175. doi:10.1016/j.im.2019.103175

Schreiber, G., Akkermans, H., Anjewierden, A., Hoog, R., Shadbolt, N., Velde, W., & Wielinga, B. (2002). *Knowledge engineering and management: the commonKADS methodology.* MIT Press.

Schroer, A. (2023). *Introduction to AI.* Built In. https://builtin.com/artificial-intelligence

Scott, T., & Thomas, C. (2015). Do collaborative groups enhance interorganizational networks? *Public Performance & Management Review, 38*(4), 654–683. doi:10.1080/15309576.2015.1031008

Seiner, R. S. (2014). *Non-invasive data governance: The path of least resistance and greatest success.* Technics Publications.

Sen, E., Yilmaz, O., & Mert, G. (2020). *Data, Information and Knowledge Management.* Nobel Bilimsel Eserler.

Shake, M. (2022). *Ten Popular Industrial Robot Applications.* Jabil. https://www.jabil.com/blog/ten-popular-industrial-robot-applications.html

Shaoyu Liu, S. L. (2022, December). Robotic Process Automation (RPA) in Auditing: A Commentary. *International Journal of Computer Auditing, 4*(1), 022–027. doi:10.53106/256299802022120401003

Sharda, R., Delen, D., & Turban, E. (2015). *Decision support and expert system: Business intelligence and analytics systems for decision support. 10.* Pearson.

Sharma, K. (2020). 4 Types of Organizational Change, Explained. *Whatfix Digital Adoption Blog.* https://whatfix.com/blog/types-of-organizational-change/

Sharma, S. (2019). *Data privacy and GDPR handbook.* John Wiley & Sons. doi:10.1002/9781119594307

Shearmur, R., Carrincazeaux, C., & Doloreux, D. (Eds.). (2016). *Handbook on the Geographies of Innovation.* Edward Elgar Publishing. doi:10.4337/9781784710774

Shedroff, N. (2000). 11 Information Interaction Design: A Unified Field Theory of Design. *Information design, 267.*

Sheikh, S. (2021, April 4). *Robotic Process Automation (RPA) - debunked and demystified.* Linkedin. https://www.linkedin.com/pulse/robotic-process-automation-rpa-debunked-demystified-salim/

Shukla, M. (2023). *From continuity to community, our top priority is helping our customers thrive now and beyond.* Automation Anywhere - Automation Solutions COVID-19. https://www.automationanywhere.com/automation-solutions-covid-19

Silva, G. (2021, February 25). *Leveraging UiPath Apps and Data Service: How AIR COVID-19 Manager Works.* UiPath. https://www.uipath.com/community/rpa-community-blog/leveraging-uipath-apps-and-data-service-how-air-covid-19-manager-works

Silva, T. C. (2019). *Framework Ponte TAP: Gestão da curva de aprendizagem para a efetivação da transferência de aprendizagem para a prática do trabalho* [Dissertação, Universidade Federal de Santa Catarina].

Singh, V. (2022, July 31). Automation of Business Process Using RPA (Robotic Process Automation). *International Journal for Research in Applied Science and Engineering Technology, 10*(7), 68–71. doi:10.22214/ijraset.2022.45111

Sivill, T. (2019, August 16). Ethical and Statistical Considerations in Models of Moral Judgments. *Frontiers in Robotics and AI, 6*, 39. doi:10.3389/frobt.2019.00039 PMID:33501055

Slomiany, M., Galli, J., Harris, B., & Kuehn, M. (2018, October). Prm140 - Utilizing Advanced Data Analysis And Visualization, Powered By Artificial Intelligence, To Analyze Price Migration Data For Oncology Products. *Value in Health, 21*, S380. doi:10.1016/j.jval.2018.09.2260

Smallwood, R. F. (2014). *Information governance: Concepts, strategies, and best practices.* Wiley.

Smartbridge. (2023). *Robotic Process Automation Services for Sales and Marketing.* Retrieved September 5, 2021, from Smartbridge: https://smartbridge.com/automation/explore-rpa/rpa-for-sales-marketing/

Smuts, H., & Van der Merwe, A. (2022). A knowledge management in Society 5.0: Sustainability perspective. *Sustainability (Basel), 14*(11), 6878. doi:10.3390/su14116878

Snoeck, M., & Wautelet, Y. (2022). Agile MERODE: A model-driven software engineering method for user-centric and value-based development. *Software & Systems Modeling, 21*(4), 1–26. doi:10.1007/s10270-022-01015-y

Soares, J. C., Domareski Ruiz, T. C., & Ivars Baidal, J. A. (2022). Smart destinations: A new planning and management approach? *Current Issues in Tourism, 25*(17), 2717–2732. doi:10.1080/13683500.2021.1991897

SoftwareReviews. (2023). *Best Robotic Process Automation (RPA) Software.* SoftwareReviews - Top Robotic Process Automation Software. https://www.softwarereviews.com/categories/robotic-process-automation

Solazzo, G., Maruccia, Y., Lorenzo, G., Ndou, V., Del Vecchio, P., & Elia, G. (2022). Extracting insights from big social data for smarter tourism destination management. *Measuring Business Excellence, 26*(1), 122–140. doi:10.1108/MBE-11-2020-0156

Solti, E. (2016). Os conhecimentos declarativo e processual de John Anderson no ensino a distância de guitarra elétrica e violão popular. *Simpósio Internacional de Educação a Distância (SIED) e Encontro de Pesquisadores em Educação a Distância (EnPED).* UniCamp. www.bibliotecadigital.unicamp.br/document/?code=000951159

Song, R., Vanthienen, J., Cui, W., Wang, Y., & Huang, L. (2019). Towards a comprehensive understanding of the context concepts in context-aware business processes. In *Proceedings of the 11th International Conference on Subject-Oriented Business Process Management* (pp. 1-10). ACM. 10.1145/3329007.3329020

Sorokina, E., Wang, Y., Fyall, A., Lugosi, P., Torres, E., & Jung, T. (2022). Constructing a smart destination framework: A destination marketing organization perspective. *Journal of Destination Marketing & Management, 23*, 100688. doi:10.1016/j.jdmm.2021.100688

Sousa, W. G. d., Melo, E. R. P. d., Bermejo, P. H. D. S., Farias, R. A. S. & Gomes, A. O. How and where is artificial intelligence in the public sector going? A literature review and research agenda. *Government Information Quarterly, 36*(4).

Stair, R. M., & Reynolds, G. W. (2002). *Princípios de Sistemas de Informação: uma abordagem gerencial.* Livros Técnicos e Científicos.

Stamper, M., Phillips, J., Goodman, D., & Bonney, B. (2022). *Data privacy program guide: How to build a privacy program that inspires trust.* CISO DRG Publishing.

Stary, C. (2014). Non-disruptive knowledge and business processing in knowledge life cycles–aligning value network analysis to process management. *Journal of Knowledge Management, 18*(4), 651–686. doi:10.1108/JKM-10-2013-0377

Stary, C. (2020). The Internet-of-Behavior as organizational transformation space with choreographic intelligence. In *International Conference on Subject-Oriented Business Process Management.* Springer, Cham. 10.1007/978-3-030-64351-5_8

Stary, C., Elstermann, M., Fleischmann, A., & Schmidt, W. (2022). Behavior-Centered Digital-Twin Design for Dynamic Cyber-Physical System Development. *Complex Systems Informatics and Modeling Quarterly*, (30), 31–52. doi:10.7250/csimq.2022-30.02

Stollenwerk, M. F. (2001). *Gestão do Conhecimento, inteligência competitiva e estratégia empresarial: em busca de uma abordagem integrada.* Anais do Workshop Brasileiro de Inteligência Competitiva.

Sun, J., Ma, J., Cheng, X., Liu, Z., & Cao, X. (2013). *Finding an expert: A model recommendation system.* Research Gate.

Sun, W., Nan, Y., Yang, T. Z., Hu, X. Y., & Jiang, Y. (2021). Integration Innovation of Competitive Intelligence, AI and Big Data Analysis. In *Advances in Artificial Intelligence and Security: 7th International Conference, ICAIS 2021*, (pp. 347-357). Springer International Publishing. 10.1007/978-3-030-78621-2_28

Sun, Z., Sun, L., & Strang, K. (2018). Big data analytics services for enhancing business intelligence. *Journal of Computer Information Systems, 58*(2), 162–169. doi:10.1080/08874417.2016.1220239

Taherdoost, H., & Madanchian, M. (2023). Artificial intelligence and knowledge management: Impacts, benefits, and implementation. *Computers, 12*(4), 1-18.

Tallon, P., Ramirez, R., & Short, J. (2013). The Information Artifact in IT Governance: Toward a Theory of Information Governance. *Journal of Management Information Systems, 30*(3), 141–178. doi:10.2753/MIS0742-1222300306

Tamang, M. D., Shukla, V. K., Anwar, S., & Punhani, R. (2021, April). Improving business intelligence through machine learning algorithms. In *2021 2nd International Conference on Intelligent Engineering and Management (ICIEM)* (pp. 63-68). IEEE. 10.1109/ICIEM51511.2021.9445344

Technovert. (2023). *RPA for HR: Know how HR automation benefits your organization.* Technovert. https://technovert.com/blog/rpa-for-hr/

Terra, J. C. C. (2000). *Gestão do conhecimento: o grande desafio empresarial.* Editora.

Thomas, H. R., Mathews, C. T., & Ward, J. G. (1986). Learning curve models of construction productivity. *Journal of Construction Engineering and Management, 112*(2), 245–258. doi:10.1061/(ASCE)0733-9364(1986)112:2(245)

Thomas, R. (2005). Business ethics. In R. Mullerat (Ed.), *Corporate Social Responsibility* (pp. 31–36). Kluwer Law International.

Traoré, M. K., Zacharewicz, G., Duboz, R., & Zeigler, B. (2019). Modeling and simulation framework for value-based healthcare systems. *Simulation, 95*(6), 481–497. doi:10.1177/0037549718776765

Treem, J. W., & Leonardi, P. M. (2017). Recognizing Expertise: Factors Promoting Congruity Between Individuals' Perceptions of Their Own Expertise and the Perceptions of Their Coworkers. *Communication Research, 44*(2), 198–224. doi:10.1177/0093650215605154

Trocin, C., Mikalef, P., Papamitsiou, Z., & Conboy, K. (2021). Responsible AI for digital health: A synthesis and a research agenda. *Information Systems Frontiers*, 1–19.

Trunk, A., Birkel, H., & Hartmann, E. (2020). On the current state of combining human and artificial intelligence for strategic organizational decision making. *Business Research, 13*, 875–919. https://link.springer.com/article/10.1007/s40685-020-00133-x

Tsolkas, D., Giannopoulou, K. (2023). *Technoeconomic Analysis and Stakeholders Engaging (Intermediate Report), Horizon 2020.* European Union, Deliverable 6.2, evolved5G-Project.

Tulcanaza-Prieto, A. B., Cortez-Ordoñez, A., & Lee, C. W. (2023, August 16). Influence of Customer Perception Factors on AI-Enabled Customer Experience in the Ecuadorian Banking Environment. *Sustainability (Basel), 15*(16), 12441. doi:10.3390/su151612441

Turing, A. M. (1950). Computing Machinery and Intelligence. *Mind, LIX*(236), 433–460. doi:10.1093/mind/LIX.236.433

Turnhout, E., Metze, T., Wyborn, C., Klenk, N., & Louder, E. (2020). The politics of co-production: Participation, power, and transformation. *Current Opinion in Environmental Sustainability, 42*, 15–21. doi:10.1016/j.cosust.2019.11.009

Ubaid, A. M., & Dweiri, F. T. (2020). Business process management (BPM): Terminologies and Methodologies Unified. *International Journal of System Assurance Engineering and Management, 11*(6), 1046–1064. doi:10.1007/s13198-020-00959-y

van de Wetering, R., Hendrickx, T., Brinkkemper, S., & Kurnia, S. (2021). The impact of EA-Driven Dynamic Capabilities, Innovativeness, and Structure on Organizational Benefits: A Variance and FsQCA Perspective. *Sustainability (Basel), 13*(10), 5414. doi:10.3390/su13105414

Van Kerkhoff, L. E.; Lebel, L. (2015). Coproductive capacities: Rethinking science-governance relations in a diverse world. *Ecology and Society, 20*(1).

Vanmali, K., & Paul, A. (2016). *Automation in the CFO World.* Deloitte. https://www2.deloitte.com/content/dam/Deloitte/za/Documents/process-and-operations/za_CFO%20Indaba_Interactive.pdf

Vargo, S. L., Maglio, P. P., & Akaka, M. A. (2008). On value and value co-creation: A service systems and service logic perspective. *European Management Journal, 26*(3), 145–152. doi:10.1016/j.emj.2008.04.003

Varsha, P. S. (2023). How can we manage biases in artificial intelligence systems – A systematic literature review. *International Journal of Information Management Data Insights, 3*(1). https://www.sciencedirect.com/science/article/pii/S2667096823000125

Vashishth, T. K., Sharma, V., Chaudhary, S., Panwar, R., Sharma, S., & Kumar, P. (2023). Advanced Technologies and AI-Enabled IoT Applications in High-Tech Agriculture. In Handbook of Research on AI-Equipped IoT Applications in High-Tech Agriculture (pp. 155-166). IGI Global.

Vashishth, T. K., Kumar, B., Sharma, V., Chaudhary, S., Kumar, S., & Sharma, K. K. (2023). The Evolution of AI and Its Transformative Effects on Computing: A Comparative Analysis. In *Intelligent Engineering Applications and Applied Sciences for Sustainability* (pp. 425–442). IGI Global. doi:10.4018/979-8-3693-0044-2.ch022

Vergne, M., & Susi, A. (2015). Breaking the Recursivity: Towards a Model to Analyse Expert Finders. *Lecture Notes in Computer Science, 9381*, 539–547. doi:10.1007/978-3-319-25264-3_40

Verhoef, P. C., Broekhuizen, T., Bart, Y., Bhattacharya, A., Dong, J. Q., Fabian, N., & Haenlein, M. (2021). Digital transformation: A multidisciplinary reflection and research agenda. *Journal of Business Research, 122*, 889–901. doi:10.1016/j.jbusres.2019.09.022

Vial, G. (2021). Understanding digital transformation: A review and a research agenda. *Managing Digital Transformation*, 13-66.

Violino, B. (2016, November 18). *Why robotic process automation adoption is on the rise*. ZDNet – Innovation. https://www.zdnet.com/article/rpa-adoption-on-the-rise/

Wang, D., Li, X. R., & Li, Y. (2013). China's "smart tourism destination" initiative: A taste of the service-dominant logic. *Journal of Destination Marketing & Management, 2*(2), 59–61. doi:10.1016/j.jdmm.2013.05.004

Wang, X. (2020). KM 3.0: Knowledge Management Computing Under Digital Economy. In *Matos, F. (ed.) Knowledge, People, and Digital Transformation. Contributions to Management Science*. Springer. doi:10.1007/978-3-030-40390-4_13

Ward, J. (2019, October 13). *The four key challenges to RPA adoption*. Accountancy Ireland. https://www.charteredaccountants.ie/Accountancy-Ireland/Articles2/News/Latest-News/the-four-key-challenges-to-rpa-adoption

Warren, M. S., & Brandeis, L. D. (1890). The right to privacy. *Harvard Law Review, 4*(5), 193–220. doi:10.2307/1321160

Weber, M., Engert, M., Schaffer, N., Weking, J., & Krcmar, H. (2023). Organizational capabilities for ai implementation—Coping with inscrutability and data dependency in ai. *Information Systems Frontiers, 25*(4), 1549–1569. doi:10.1007/s10796-022-10297-y

Weigand, H., Johannesson, P., Andersson, B., & Bergholtz, M. (2009, June). Value-based service modeling and design: Toward a unified view of services. In *International Conference on Advanced Information Systems Engineering* (pp. 410-424). Springer, Berlin, Heidelberg. 10.1007/978-3-642-02144-2_33

Wheeler, S. F. (2010). The HAL (Heuristic Associative Linear-algorithm) Chess Program. *Chess Programming Wiki*. https://www.chessprogramming.org/HAL

Wheeler, S. F. (1987). A Performance Benchmark of the Alpha-Beta Procedure on Randomly Ordered Non-Uniform Depth-First Game-Trees Generated by a Chess Program. *ICGA Journal, 10*(1), 43–43. doi:10.3233/ICG-1987-10108

Whittemore, R., & Knafl, K. (2005). The integrative review: Updated methodology. *Journal of Advanced Nursing, 52*(5), 546–553. doi:10.1111/j.1365-2648.2005.03621.x PMID:16268861

Widder, D. G., West, S., & Whittaker, M. (2023). Open (For Business): Big Tech, Concentrated Power, and the Political Economy of Open AI. SSRN *Electronic Journal*. doi:10.2139/ssrn.4543807

WinAutomation. (2023). *WinAutomation is now part of Microsoft Power Automate*. WinAutomation. https://www.winautomation.com/

Wong, P. H. (2020). Democratizing algorithmic fairness. *Philosophy & Technology, 33*(2), 225–244. https://link.springer.com/article/10.1007/s13347-019-00355-w. doi:10.1007/s13347-019-00355-w

Woodruff, R. B. (1997). Customer value: The next source for competitive advantage. *Journal of the Academy of Marketing Science, 25*(2), 139–153. doi:10.1007/BF02894350

Wright, T. P. (1936). Factors Affecting the Cost of Airplanes. *Journal of the Aeronautical Sciences, 3*(4), 122–128. doi:10.2514/8.155

Wu, Q., Yan, D., & Umair, M. (2023). Assessing the role of competitive intelligence and practices of dynamic capabilities in business accommodation of SMEs. *Economic Analysis and Policy, 77*, 1103–1114. doi:10.1016/j.eap.2022.11.024

Wyborn, C. (2015). Co-productive governance: A relational framework for adaptive governance. *Global Environmental Change, 30*, 56–67. doi:10.1016/j.gloenvcha.2014.10.009

Xie, Y., & Lin, S. Y. (2016). Tagclouds and group cognition: Effect of tagging support on students' reflective learning in team blogs. *British Journal of Educational Technology, 47*(6), 1135–1150. doi:10.1111/bjet.12293

Yablonsky, S. A. (2020). AI-driven digital platform innovation. *Technology Innovation Management Review, 10*(10), 4–15. doi:10.22215/timreview/1392

Yadav, S. (2021, February 2). *Role of RPA (Robotic Process Automation) in Human Resource (HR) Operations*. Zenesys. https://www.zenesys.com/blog/role-of-rpa-in-hr-operations

Yarosh. (2013). I Need Someone to Help! A Taxonomy of Helper-Finding Activities in the Enterprise. CSCW, 13, San Antonio.

Yates-Mercer, P., & Bawden, D. (2002). Managing the paradox: The valuation of knowledge and knowledge management. *Journal of Information Science, 28*(1), 19–29. doi:10.1177/016555150202800103

Yigitcanlar, T., Kankanamge, N., & Vella, K. (2021). How are smart city concepts and technologies perceived and utilized? A systematic geo-Twitter analysis of smart cities in Australia. *Journal of Urban Technology, 28*(1-2), 135–154. doi:10.1080/10630732.2020.1753483

Young, R. (2020). *Asian Productivity Organization (org.). APO Knowledge Management: tools and techniques manual*. Omega Communications. doi:10.61145/COEE1851

Zainal-Abidin, H., Scarles, C., & Lundberg, C. (2023). The antecedents of digital collaboration through an enhanced digital platform for destination management: A micro-DMO perspective. *Tourism Management, 96*, 104691. doi:10.1016/j.tourman.2022.104691

Zhang, B., Lin, J., Du, L., & Zhang, L. (2023, May 8). Harnessing Data Augmentation and Normalization Preprocessing to Improve the Performance of Chemical Reaction Predictions of Data-Driven Model. *Polymers, 15*(9), 2224. doi:10.3390/polym15092224 PMID:37177370

Zhang, C., Zhu, W., Dai, J., Wu, Y., & Chen, X. (2023). Ethical impact of artificial intelligence in managerial accounting. *International Journal of Accounting Information Systems*, *49*, 100619. doi:10.1016/j.accinf.2023.100619

Zhang, K., Wang, J., Feng, L., & Cheng, Y. (2019). The evolution mechanism of latecomer firms value network in disruptive innovation context: A case study of Haier Group. *Technology Analysis and Strategic Management*, *31*(12), 1488–1500. doi:10.1080/09537325.2019.1628939

Zittrain, J. L. (2006). The generative internet. *Harvard Law Review*, *119*(7), 1975–2040.

Zohuri, B., & Moghaddam, M. (2020). *From business intelligence to artificial intelligence. Journal of Material Sciences & Manufacturing Research.* SRC/JMSMR.

About the Contributors

Tereza Raquel Merlo is a researcher, professor, practitioner, and consultant working for the University of North Texas, where she teaches courses in Knowledge Management Tools and Technologies. She is CEO of Merlo Management Consulting, providing solutions to businesses around the globe. She is an avid investigator focused on Knowledge Management Systems and their impact on organizational operations and strategies. Her professional interests include business strategies and process improvement, sales strategies, knowledge management, business intelligence, machine learning, artificial intelligence, and leadership. She received her Ph.D in Organizational Management with a minor in Information Technologies, and holds two Master degrees in Information Sciences from the Federal University of Bahia (UFBa) and University of North Texas. Dr. Merlo has been the recipient of multiple awards for leadership, data and project management, information literacy, diversity and inclusion, and business development. She was also the recipient of multiple scholarships, including Coordenacão de Aperfeiçoamento de Pessoal de Nível Superior (CAPES) for her Master research and Fundação de Amparo à pesquisa do estado da Bahia (Fapesb) for research focusing on digital repositories in a post graduate program at UNIFACS University in Salvador, Bahia, Brazil. Dr. Merlo is part of scientific committees for Knowledge and Performance Management, Knowledge-Based System, and the Journal of Information and Knowledge Management journals, among others. Dr. Merlo serves on the international advisory board for the International Conference on Knowledge Management (ICKM), having served as co-chair, organizing the 15th, 18th, and 19th annual ICKM Conferences. Dr. Merlo was the Keynote Speaker for the 15th and 18th ICKM Conferences at the University of Santa Catarina, Brazil in 2019, and 2023. In addition, she has a background as a consultant and professional in the field of library management and has built several information units, including libraries and archives. She worked for the City of Austin, Texas for a decade, where she managed multiple projects within Information Sciences, chaired the Culture and Diversity Committee for several years and had an active role serving as chair for the Texas Library Association. Dr. Merlo was the recipient of the Junior Guild Award in 2015 for best project and leadership on diversity and inclusion in public libraries in the state of Texas. Dr. Merlo's research interests include Knowledge Management Systems (tools, technologies, governance, and processes), information systems, artificial intelligence and machine learning, business intelligence, data analytics and governance, leadership, and cloud computing. Her professional experience in the private sector includes work at multiple Fortune 100 companies. She is the editor and author of the book Understanding, Implementing, and Evaluating Knowledge Management in Business Settings by IGI-Global.

***

Ana Claudia Abreu holds a Bachelor's degree in Business Administration from Candido Mendes University (1992), a Master's degree in Business Administration from the Federal University of Santa Catarina (1997), and a Ph.D. in Engineering and Knowledge Management from the Federal University of Santa Catarina (2016). She has previously held positions as a Professor at UFSC, UNIVALI, ESTÁCIO, and FESAG. At these universities, she taught courses such as General Theory of Administration, Decision-Making Process, People Management, and Knowledge Management. She also served as the Secretary of International Relations of Florianópolis. In addition, she worked as a Parliamentary Advisor in the Chamber of Deputies, where she was involved in management roles, particularly in the areas of innovation ecosystems, smart cities, digital education, entrepreneurship, science and technology, and political gender-based violence.

Lillian Alvares is Professor at the Faculty of Information Science at the University of Brasília (UnB), since 2006. Permanent Professor of the Postgraduate Program in Information Science at the Brazilian Institute of Information in Science and Technology (IBICT) in broad association with the School of Communication (ECO) from the Federal University of Rio de Janeiro (UFRJ). Post-doctorate at the Escola Superior de Tecnologia i Ciències Experimentals at Universitat Jaume I, Spain (2017) and at the Department of Knowledge Engineering at the Federal University of Santa Catarina (2021). Deputy leader of the Organizational and Competitive Intelligence research group (IOC/UnB) and member of the Open Science and Open Access to Scientific Information (IBICT/MCTI) research group. PhD in Information Science from the University of Brasília and in Information and Communication Sciences from the Université de Toulon (on a co-tutel basis) in 2010. Specialist in Competitive Intelligence from the Brazilian Institute of Information in Science and Technology (Ibict) in partnership with the National Institute of Technology (INT) and Federal University of Rio de Janeiro (UFRJ) in 2001. Master in Library Science from the University of Brasília (1997) and Graduate in Mechanical Engineering (1990) from the same university. The main research areas are Information Management, Knowledge Management and Organizational and Competitive Intelligence.

Iniga Antonia Baum is a researcher at the Institute for Business Informatics/Communications Engineering, Johannes Kepler University, Linz, Austria with focus on facilitator development in project-based Learning in digitized learning environments. She brings 14 years of professional experience in the field of tertiary education, working as docent for Scientific Work and Knowledge Management with focus on innovative seminary design, as didactical and methodological coach for professors and students, as assessor and advisor of chair at Cooperative State Universities in Southern and Northern Germany and Upper Austria. Before her academic career she held several positions with lead in Project Consulting, Business Development and Human Resources. Mrs. Baum has a Master of Arts in General Management and a Master of Arts in Theater Science, Communication and Media Science and Cultural Sciences.

Filipe Calza is a specialist in web application development using languages such as Python, PHP, Smarty, JavaScript, jQuery, Bootstrap, MySQL. Development of microservices in Python. Automation of processes with Python, Selenium, and Scrapy. Cloud integration using Amazon (AWS) services such as Lambda, SNS, SQS, Step Functions, S3, DynamoDB. Proficient in agile methodologies like Scrum and Kanban. Experienced in developing applications and solutions for the consigned credit market. Strong competencies in SOLID principles, cloud infrastructure, agile and waterfall methodologies, and SQL.

Sachin Chaudhary completed his Graduation from MJPRU, and Post Graduation from AKTU, Moradabad, U.P. Currently Pursuing his Ph.D. in Computer Science and Engineering from Govt. Recognized University. Presently, he is working as an Assistant Professor in the Department of Computer Science and Applications, IIMT University, Meerut, U.P, India. He has been awarded as Excellence in teaching award 2019. He is the reviewer member of some reputed journals. He has published several book chapters and research papers of national and international reputed journals.

Patricia de sá Freire is a professor at the Federal University of Santa Catarina (UFSC), affiliated with the Department of Knowledge Engineering (dEGC). She is a faculty member of the PPGEGC (Graduate Program in Engineering, Management, and Knowledge Media), focusing on the Knowledge Management concentration. She holds a Ph.D. in Engineering and Knowledge Management (UFSC). She has a degree in Education, specializing in Educational Technologies, from PUC/RJ (1986). She is also a specialist in Marketing (ESPM/RJ) and in Psychopedagogy (UCB/RJ). She is the leader of ENGIN Laboratory for Engineering of Multilevel Integration and Governance of Knowledge and Organizational Learning, and a member of the IGTI (Nucleus of Intelligence, Management, and Technology for Innovation/UFSC), KLOM (Interdisciplinary in Knowledge, Learning, and Organizational Memory/UFSC), and the Digital Commons Research Group. For two consecutive years, 2011 and 2012, she was chosen as one of the top five executives in Knowledge Management excellence in Brazil by the MAKE Award Brazil. She serves as the Editor of the International Journal of Knowledge and Management (IJKEM). Her involvement in projects has focused on research, teaching, and extension related to the Networked Corporate University Model; Multilevel Governance of Knowledge and Organizational Learning; Integration Engineering of knowledge assets; Implementation of Knowledge Management in Organizational Networks and People.

Alfredo Cesar dos Anjos received a Master in Engineering and Knowledge Management at the Federal University of Santa Catarina - UFSC and bachelor in Information Systems at the University of Southern Santa Catarina - UNISUL. He is currently a doctoral student in Engineering and Knowledge Management at the Federal University of Santa Catarina-UFSC, researcher and senior systems programmer at Instituto Stela. The research focuses on artificial intelligence, engineering and knowledge management, knowledge services, expert location, ontologies and the semantic web.

Neri dos Santos holds a PhD in Engineering Ergonomics; from the Conservatoire National des Arts et Metiers (1985) - France and a Post-doctorate in Cognitive Engineering from the École Polytechnique de Montréal- Canada. Former President of ABEPRO, Management 92/93 and 94/95. Former Dean of the Polytechnic School of the Pontifical Catholic University of Paraná – PUCPR 2015/2018. He is currently CEO of the STELA Institute and Senior Professor of the Graduate Program in Engineering and Knowledge Management at the Federal University of Santa Catarina (EGC/UFSC)

Manisha Semwal is an Assistant Professor at KL University, Vaddeswaram, Andhra Pradesh. She has 6 years of experience in academics. Articles published in several high impact journals. Her research interests are employee engagement, employee satisfaction, international human resource management, HR analytics. Being an academician she has devoted her life teaching and learning.

Sandhya H. is pursuing PhD in Tourism Management from Christ University Bangalore. She successfully completed her Mphil and Masters in Tourism Administration (MTA) from Christ University Bangalore by securing the first rank. She has industry experience of one year having worked with one of the leading multinational tour operations companies, Kuoni SOTC, Bangalore and teaching experience of over 6 years having associated with some of the prestigious academic institutions and colleges in Kerala. She has worked as Research Associate of the Major Research Project on the lines of Destination Management Organisations. She is a very passionate and keen researcher and her research interests include Destination Management, Destination Branding and Smart Tourism. She is currently working as Academic Auditor and Deputy Academic Coordinator at Kairos Institute, Cochin, Kerala.

Kris S. Helge serves as Deputy Director of Information Management at Colorado Judicial. He is creating and sustaining an information governance program at Judicial. He also adjunct teaches at Rutgers University and Texas A&M University School of Law. Kris publishes books, book chapters, and peer reviewed articles; and offers information governance presentations at international and national conferences.

Laksitha M. Herath earned her Master of Science in Accounting degree at New York University's Stern School of Business and works at Pricewaterhouse Coopers (PwC). Prior to her current endeavor, she gained valuable experience as a program accountant at Enstar Group Limited, a well-known global insurance company, and at Deloitte, a Big Four accounting firm, in Atlanta and New York. Laksitha holds a Bachelor of Arts degree in Accounting from Clark Atlanta University, where she held executive positions in its Toastmasters Club and she and a team of selected classmates won the Deloitte Regional Case Study Competition. She also published two book chapters and an article in a reputable journal. In her leisure time, she enjoys photography, cooking, and quality time with her family and friends.

Siriyama Kanthi Herath is an Associate Professor of Accounting at Clark Atlanta University's School of Business (CAU) and was a Renwick Faculty Fellow at New York University's Stern School of Business in 2022. She earned a Bachelor of Commerce Honors and an MBA from the University of Colombo in Sri Lanka, as well as a Ph.D. and a Master of Commerce Honors in Accounting from the University of Wollongong in Australia. She worked at the University of Lynchburg, Georgia State University and Georgia Institute of Technology before joining CAU. Prior to relocating to the United States, Dr. Herath worked in Australia at the University of Wollongong and Western Sydney University and in Sri Lanka at the University of Ruhuna and the University of Colombo. She holds positions on the editorial boards of multiple academic journals and has contributed over 70 publications to a diverse range of journals. Her research areas include Accounting Education, Management Control and Outsourcing, Cost Management, Corporate Governance, Data Analytics, and Sustainability Accounting. She is a Distinguished Toastmaster and served as the President and Treasurer of the Georgia Institute of Technology Toastmasters International Club from 2019 to 2020, the Treasurer of the Emory University Toastmasters International Club from 2019 to 2020, and as an Area Director from 2020 to 2021 in Georgia, United States. Additionally, she possesses the TESOL Professional Certificate from Arizona State University and the Professional Certificate in Google Data Analytics. In her leisure time, she enjoys traveling and gardening.

Gérson Luiz Koch holds a master's degree in Management Sciences and a PhD in Project Management from the University of Science and Technology of Lille, France. Career employee of the State Secretariat of Administration and Welfare of the State of Paraná, he was administrative director of Paraná Tecnologia (1999-2002), general director of the State Secretariat of Science, Technology and Higher Education-Seti (2002); coordinator of the Management Unit of the Paraná-UGF Fund of Seti (2011-2012). He also held the position of director of the School of Public Management of the Court of Auditors of the State of Paraná (in the periods of 2007-2010 and 2013-2014). Since 2019 he has held the position of Director of Administration and Finance of the Araucária Foundation

Bhupendra Kumar completed his Graduation and Post Graduation from Chaudhary Charan Singh University, Meerut, U.P. and Ph.D. in Computer Science and Engineering from Mewar University, Hapur. Presently, he is working as a Professor in the Department of Computer Science and Applications, IIMT University, Meerut, U.P. He has been a huge teaching experience of 19 years. He is the reviewer member of some reputed journals. He has published several book chapters and research papers of national and international reputed journals.

Dileep Kumar M. holds the positions of Deputy Vice Chancellor and Full Professor of Business Management. His research interests include strategic management, consumer behavior, entrepreneurship, SME development, tourism development, human resource management, and organizational behavior. He holds a dual doctorate in behavioral sciences and business administration. He also enjoys reading, and writing. He has published 180 peer-reviewed articles in international and national journals, 80 brief case studies in business management, and more than 76 papers at worldwide and national conferences. He has two patents, four patent publications, six copyrights, and nine books on business management, and three monographs, to go along with his academic credentials. He serves as an editor and editorial board member for several high-impact international publications. He has trained academics, researchers, and business leaders from more than 25 nations, and for more than 18 years. He has worked as a consultant and in research and development at both the national and international levels. He has dedicated his life to academia, research, corporate development, and institution building, making significant contributions to both the corporate and academic sectors.

Maria Angélica Jung Marques holds a PhD in Engineering and Knowledge Management from the Federal University of Santa Catarina (2020). He is currently a member of the Research Group on Knowledge Management, Innovation, Interdisciplinarity - KMi2 of PUCRS, and a collaborating member of the research group on Knowledge Engineering applied to Information Management and Organizational Knowledge of the Stela Institute and of the research group on Co-production of Digital Commons, of the Federal University of Santa Catarina (UFSC). She is currently a Technology and Innovation consultant at World Transforming Technologies (WTT Brasil)

Roberto Carlos dos Santos Pacheco holds a PhD in Production Engineering (UFSC, 1996) and is a professor at the Department of Knowledge Engineering at UFSC. Participated in the creation and coordinates the Graduate Program in Engineering and Knowledge Management (EGC / UFSC). He was the founding researcher of the Stela Institute. Its academic and technological production results from the co-production with more than 600 collaborators and includes more than 200 publications, as well as software and technical activities of advisory and technical-scientific collaboration. He is currently the leader of the Digital Commons Co-production Research Group

Rajneesh Panwar Graduated and Post Graduated in Mathematics and Computer Application from Ch. Charan Singh University, Meerut (U.P.) and received his M. Tech. in Computer Science from Shobhit University, Meerut. Presently, he is working as an Assistant Professor in the School of Computer Science and Application IIMT University, Meerut, U.P. He qualifies GATE 2021 and UGC-NET June 2020 and December 2020. He has published several book chapters and research papers of national and international repute.

Denilson Sell is professor of Knowledge Engineering and Management at the Federal University of Santa Catarina and at the State University of Santa Catarina (Brazil). He is also a director at Instituto Stela. He has led several research and development projects with public and private organizations. His most recent work focuses on Knowledge Management, Analytics, Resilience, Digital Platforms and Digital Transformation.

Kewal Krishan Sharma is a professor in computer sc. in IIMT University, Meerut, U.P, India. He did his Ph.D. in computer network with this he has MCA, MBA and Law degree also. He did variously certification courses also. He has an overall experience of around 33 year in academic, business and industry. He wrote a number of research papers and books.

Vikas Sharma completed his Graduation and Post Graduation from Chaudhary Charan Singh University, Meerut, U.P. Currently Pursuing his Ph.D. in Computer Science and Engineering from Govt. Recognized University. Presently, he is working as an Assistant Professor in the Department of Computer Science and Applications, IIMT University, Meerut, U.P. He has been awarded as Excellence in teaching award 2019. He is the reviewer member of some reputed journals. He has published several book chapters and research papers of national and international reputed journals.

Vinod Sharma has around 22 years of experience including both academia and industry, at different levels of management, prepare him to be an effective researcher and instructor. He is specialized in Marketing Strategy, Marketing Research & Analytics, and Consumer Behaviour. He has authored over 85 papers in national and international journals and completed in 3 International projects with Yale University, USA on Climate Change and Business Strategy. He has been involved in various consultation research projects, conducted various research workshops and also conducted training program in association with MSME and FIEO on various subjects of management. He is MBA from University of Wales, UK and PhD in Management from University of Indore, India.

Talita Silva earned her Ph.D. from the Graduate Program in Engineering and Knowledge Management (EGC) at the Federal University of Santa Catarina (UFSC). She holds a master's degree (2016) in Psychology from the same university, with a focus on Organizational and Work Psychology and a research line in Professional Formation, Career Development, and Work Insertion. Additionally, she is a specialist in Strategic People Management from Faculdade Estácio de Sá (2016). She completed her Bachelor's and Teaching degree in Psychology from UFSC (2013). She is a member of the research group ENGIN - Center for Knowledge Integration and Governance for Innovation. Currently, she has been dedicated to the following topics: Knowledge Management; Corporate Education; Networked Corporate University; Knowledge Governance; Career guidance and development; Stricto sensu postgraduate programs; People management and Training, Development & Education. She is the author of the book "Framework Ponte TAP: 4 layers for accelerating the learning curve using canvases."

Luiz Márcio Spinosa holds a Postdoctoral Degree in Innovation from the University of California at Berkeley (USA), a PhD and a Master's Degree (DEA) in Informatics and Productions from the University of Aix-Marseille (FR). Currently a professor and researcher in the area of innovation ecosystems and knowledge engineering, coordinator of the Research Group National Models and Systems of Innovation of the Triple-Helix Association originating from Stanford University (USA), visiting researcher at the University of California at Berkeley (USA) and Academic and Scientific Director of LabCHIS (Unilivre/UFSC). Since 2019 he has held the position of director of ST&I of the Araucária Foundation.

Christian Stary holds a PhD in usability engineering from the Vienna University of Technology. He is currently a full professor in Business Information Systems at the JKU Department of Business Informatics-Communications Engineering. He also chairs the JKU Knowledge Management Competence Center aside his duties as Department Head and Study Admission Chair. Christian Stary is the Chair of ICKM (International Council of Knowledge Management) and Austrian representative of the S-BPM steering committee. He is past president of SOL Austria (2012-2016). His research interests are knowledge elicitation ,modelling of socio-technical systems, learning support, and organizational development. These topics are also researched in international R&D projects he is responsible for. The results are regularly published in leading scientific juornals and presented at international conferences.

Alice Tamah is a distinguished Senior Lecturer at Xiamen University Malaysia, located in Sepang, Malaysia. She holds expertise in Teaching International Business and Commercial Law, contributing significantly to the academic community through her dynamic and engaging approach to legal education. Her research interests are diverse and encompass areas such as Company Law, Contract Law, Consumer Behaviour, and Artificial Intelligence (AI). Dr. Tamah actively explores the intersections between legal frameworks, business practices, and emerging technologies, contributing valuable insights to the evolving landscape of commercial law. In addition to her role as a Senior Lecturer, Dr. Tamah actively engages in scholarly activities, presenting her research at national and international conferences. Her work contributes to the ongoing discourse in legal academia, particularly in areas critical to contemporary business environments.

Marta Valentim is a Full Professor at Sao Paulo State University (Unesp), 2018. Post-Doctorate from the University of Salamanca (USAL), Spain, 2012. Associete Professor in Information, Knowledge and Organizational Intelligence at Unesp, 2009. PhD in Communication Sciences at Sao Paulo University (USP), 2001. Master's degree from the Pontifical Catholic University of Campinas (PUC-Campinas), 1995. Teaching undergraduate and graduate courses at Unesp, Marilia campus. Research Productivity Scholarship (PQ-1D) of the National Council for Scientific and Technological Development (CNPq) in the area of organizational intelligence, information management, knowledge management and information culture since 2002. Leader of the Research Group Information, Knowledge and Organizational Intelligence. Coordinates the research project Organizational intelligence and social intelligence in the context of the big data: data analysis for the generation of competitive differentials. Coordinator of the

Graduate Program in Information Science (PPGCI), Unesp, management 2017-2021. Organizing of several books in the Information Science area. President of the Brazilian Association of Education in Information Science (ABECIN), management 2016-2019. Vice President of the Association of Education and Research in Information Science of Latin America and the Caribbean (EDICIC), management 2009-2011. Coordinating the Working Group 'Information Management and Knowledge in Organizations' (GT-4), the National Association for Research and Graduate Studies in Information Science (ANCIB), management 2009-2010. President of the Association of Education in Information Science (ABECIN), management 2001-2004.

Bindi Varghese has a Doctorate in Commerce, with 19 years of Academic experience;Currently, affiliated with Christ University, as an Associate Professor and is the Research Coordinator at School of Business and Management. Served as a national and international expert, and is working with Indian Tourism Congress (ITC) and is the honorary director at Kerala Development Society (KDS), New Delhi. The active researches undertaken include Impact Assessment Studies, Medical Tourism, Destination Management Organization and Ecological Studies. Dr. Bindi completed a major research project on the title "Strategic Intervention of Destination Management Organizations to Enhance Competitiveness of Tourism Destinations– A Model for Karnataka" funded by Christ University. Along with her academic expertise, she is also an Section editor for 'ATNA- Journal of Tourism Studies', published by Christ University, Bengaluru. She has authored one book; on Medical Tourism in India: and has edited a book on "Evolving Paradigms in Tourism and Hospitality in Developing Countries: A Case Study of India". The book is published by CRC Press, Taylor and Francis group - international publisher in US and released in 2018.

Tarun Kumar Vashishth is an active academician and researcher in the field of computer science with 21 years of experience. He earned Ph.D. Mathematics degree specialized in Operations Research; served several academic positions such as HoD, Dy. Director, Academic Coordinator, Member Secretary of Department Research Committee, Assistant Center superintendent and Head Examiner in university examinations. He is involved in academic development and scholarly activities. He is member of International Association of Engineers, The Society of Digital Information and Wireless Communications, Global Professors Welfare Association, International Association of Academic plus Corporate (IAAC), Computer Science Teachers Association and Internet Society. His research interest includes Cloud Computing, Artificial Intelligence, Machine Learning and Operations Research; published more than 20 research articles with 1 book and 10 book chapters in edited books. He is contributing as member of editorial and reviewers boards in conferences and various computer journals published by CRC Press, Taylor and Francis, Springer, IGI global and other universities.

Ramiro Wahrhaftig is a Civil Engineer graduated from UFPR, with a master's degree in Energy Planning from UFRJ and a PhD in Technology and Innovation at the University of Technology of Compiègne – UTC, France. He interrupted his studies in 1995 to assume the portfolio of Secretary of State for Education of Paraná. He has also been a visiting researcher at Twente University of Technology, the Netherlands, McGill University, Canada, and the University of Texas at Austin, USA. Since 2019 he has held the position of president of the Araucaria Foundation

Stephen F. Wheeler was nominated and selected by Marquis Who's Who for Who's Who in America, 2022 – 2023. The following year, 2023, He was nominated and selected for Who's Who in the World, 2023 – 2024. Dr. Wheeler have been a Principal Consultant for several of the largest computer consulting companies, including Cap Gemini America, Decision Consultants, Inc., and Wipro, Ltd. Early in my career he served as Senior Systems Engineer for Compaq Computer Corporation in Houston, Texas. Prior to joining the UNT faculty he was a senior AI research scientist and consulting partner with Wipro, Ltd. My most recent contract was as a Data Scientist on the Lockheed Martin Aeronautics advanced analytics team performing advanced analytics on the F-35 JSF (Joint Strike Fighter), the most advanced military jet fighter aircraft in the world. Prior to joining the UNT faculty, he has served as Senior Professor of Information Systems for Keller Graduate School of DeVry University, Dallas, Texas, a position he held from 2002 to 2017. He has also held a faculty appointment at LeTourneau University. His undergraduate (BSc.) degree is in Computer Science from Texas A&M University - Commerce, where he also received my Graduate (MSc.) degree in Computer Science with thesis research in Artificial Intelligence. Dr. Wheeler holds a Postgraduate (Ph.D.) degree in Artificial Intelligence from Walden University. His research domain was linear symbolic problem-solving systems utilizing Aspiration Search modeled on the Iterative-Deepening Alpha-Beta search procedure known as Negamax Fail-Soft Alpha-Beta. His Doctoral research also involved Natural Language Processing (NLP), and his dissertation is titled "A Performance Analysis of the Iterative-Deepening Alpha-Beta Search Procedure Under Variations of the Ordering Interval within a Chess Program." He is presently conducting unfunded postdoctoral research in intelligent problem-solving systems, and quantum computing. He is an FAA Licensed Commercial Pilot with an Instrument Rating and serve as a Transport Mission Pilot with Texas Wing, Group III of the United States Air Force Auxiliary with the rank of Captain (active). He has successfully completed the Squadron Leadership School, and He is the Aerospace Education Officer of his Squadron. He has achieved the Chuck Yeager Aerospace Education Excellence Award. Dr. Wheller also been trained in Emergency Services, and has successfully completed the ICS-300 and ICS-400 Incident Command System certification. He has also been a NASA Field Research Astronaut serving as Mission Commander of NASA / MDRS Crew 88 at the Mars Desert Research Station in Utah, January 2010. His research and that of his crew of aerospace scientists was reported to the Johnson Space Center (JSC) in Houston, Texas, the NASA Jet Propulsion Laboratory (JPL), and NASA Ames Research Center to provide research data in support of the planned 2033 manned Mars mission.

Yuqing Yao has a Bachelor of Science in Psychology, Neuroscience (University of British Columbia | 2016). In the area, she worked as an assistant in the Medical Office, performing MoCa cognitive tests independently. As an assistant in the Laboratory of Evolutionary Social Cognition at UBC, she worked with analyzes of individual differences in parental care activation and motivational systems. As an entrepreneur, she has launched and manages an international e-commerce venture and retail establishment. The interest in studies and research is focused on the areas of psychology and education, mainly on people, counseling, care and development of human skills for life and work.

Alan Yap's combination of academic qualifications, extensive professional experience, and dedication to research positions him as a dynamic and influential figure in the field of ICT, contributing significantly to both education and industry advancements. With an extensive career spanning over 25 years, Alan has made significant contributions to various areas of IT, including Infrastructure, Communications, Technology, and Information Security. His practical experience and strategic acumen have positioned him as a thought leader in the dynamic field of ICT. Alan's intellectual pursuits are centered around ICT Management and Artificial Intelligence (AI). His research interests underscore his dedication to exploring the strategic and operational aspects of managing information and communication technologies, as well as delving into the transformative potential of AI in contemporary business landscapes. As a faculty member at Help University, Malaysia, Alan imparts his wealth of knowledge to students in courses such as Business Analytics for Decision Making, E-Business, Information Technology for Business, and Decision Support Systems. His teaching philosophy integrates theoretical concepts with practical insights, offering students a holistic understanding of the intersection between business and technology.

Ayşe Aslı Yilmaz is Assist.Prof. Civil Aviation School, Atilim University. She received her Ph.D in Business Administration (English prg.) with dissertation titled "The Value Added by Digital Transformation Criteria to Intellectual Capital Components: Network Analysis on Esenboğa Airport " in Social Sciences Institute at Atılım University in 2022. In 2011 she was assigned as the course director and instructor on Peace Support Operations (PSO), Cultural awareness in Multinational Environments, Strategic Communication, Civil Military Cooperation and Gender Awareness in PSOs in Partnership for Peace Training Centre as well as different UN and NATO affiliated agencies and training centres. Her research focuses on social networks, intellectual capital, and digital transformation. Her major publications include writings of book chapters and articles in management and organization fields. She teaches classes in management, Airport Management, Airport Master Planning, International Aviation Law and Air Traffic Rules and Regulations.

Index

R

S

T

V

www.ingramcontent.com/pod-product-compliance
Lightning Source LLC
LaVergne TN
LVHW062140300926
849161LV00010B/2580